lon

D0401984

Mongolia

Northern
Mongolia
p129

Western
Mongolia
p206

Ulaanbaatar
⭐ p56

Eastern
Mongolia
p160

Central
Mongolia
p98

The Gobi
p179

THIS EDITION WRITTEN AND RESEARCHED BY
Michael Kohn,
Anna Kaminski, Daniel McCrohan

Contents

COSTUMED PERFORMER
AT NAADAM (P50)

BRUNO MORANDI/GETTY IMAGES ©

WALL OF ERDENE ZUU
KHIID (P114)

PETER DEMARCO/GETTY IMAGES ©

Mongolia's
Top 14

0 / 500 km
0 / 300 miles

Amarbayasgalant Khiid
Mongolia's best-preserved
monastery (p136)

**Gorkhi-Terelj
National Park**
Biking, hiking and horse-
riding opportunities (p105)

Ulaanbaatar
Cosmopolitan capital with
nightlife and museums (p56)

Dadal
On the trail of
Chinggis Khaan (p166)

*Lake Baikal
(Baygal Nuur)*

Irkutsk

Chita

Ulan Ude

Zaudinsky

RUSSIA

Border
Crossing
Altanbulag
Sükhbaatar
Amarbayasgalant
Khiid
Darkhan

**Mongol Daguur
Strictly Protected
Areas**

Chuluunkhoroot

Mǎnzhōulǐ

Hǎilā'ěr

Bayandun

**Onon-Balj
National
Park**
Dadal

Bayan Uul

Bayangol

Batshireet

SELENGE
**Gorkhi-Terelj
National Park**
Batsumber
ULAANBAATAR
Lun
Nalaikh
Zuunmod

Binder

Bayan-
Ovoo

Choibalsan

Bulgan

Khalkhiin
Gol

**Nömrög Strictly
Protected Area**

KHENTII

**Chinggis Khot
(Öndörkhaan)**

Kherlen Gol

Mönkh
Khaan

Matad

DORNOD

**Dornod Mongol
Strictly Protected
Area**

TÖV

Buren

Bayantsagaan

Choir

Uulbayan

Baruun-Urt

Erdenetsagaan

Shiliin
Bogd Uul

Erdenedalai

Mandalgov

Airag
Öndöshil

Delgerekh

SÜKHBAATAR

Ongon

Dariganga

DUNDGOV

Khuld

Delgerkhaan

Altanshiree

Sainshand

Mandakh

DORNOGOV

Erdene

Manlai

Border
Crossing
Zamyn-
Üüd
Èrlián
(Ereen)

Dalanzadgad

Tavan
Tolgoi
Khanbogd

Khatanbúlag

Bayan-
Ovoo
Oyu
Tolgoi

**Small Gobi B
Strictly Protected
Area**

Sonid
Yoqui

**Khustain National
Park**
Protected area for the
endangerd *takhi* horse (p110)

**Small Gobi A
Strictly Protected
Area**

Chéngdé

Jíníng

Zhāngjiākǒu

Hohhot

Běijīng

CHINA

Dàtóng

Wūhǎi

Tiānjīn

Mongolia

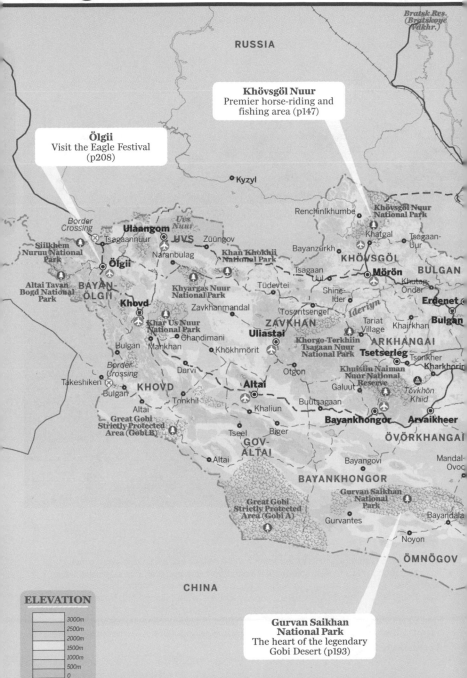

RUSSIA

Bratsk Res.
(Bratskoye
Vdkhr.)

Khövsgöl Nuur
Premier horse-riding and
fishing area (p147)

Ölgii
Visit the Eagle Festival
(p208)

Kyzyl

Renchinlkhumbe •   Khövsgöl Nuur
National Park

Border
Crossing   Ulaangom   *Uvs Nuur*   Khatgal   Tsagaan-Üür

Tsagaannuur   Züüngov   Bayanzürkh

Siilkhem
Nuruu National
Park   Naranbulag   Khan Khokhii
National Park   KHÖVSGÖL   BULGAN

Ölgii   Tsagaan
Üül   Mörön

Altai Tavan
Bogd National
Park   BAYAN-
ÖLGII   Khyargas Nuur
National Park   Tüdevtei   Shine-
Ider   Khutag-
Öndör   Erdenet

Khovd   Zavkhanmandal   Tosontsengel   *Ideriyn*   Bulgan

Khar Us Nuur
National Park   ZAVKHAN   Tariat
Village   Khairkhan   ARKHANGAI

Bulgan   Mankhan   Chandmani   Uliastai   Khorgo-Terkhiin
Tsagaan Nuur
National Park   Tsetserleg

Khökhmörit   Tsenkher   Kharkhorin

Border
Crossing   Darvi   Otgon   Khuisiin Naiman
Nuur National
Reserve   Tövkhön
Khiid

Takeshiken   KHOVD   Altai   Galuut

Bulgan   Tonkhil   Khaliun   Buutsagaan   Bayankhongor   Arvaikheer

Altai   Tseel   Biger

Great Gobi
Strictly Protected
Area (Gobi B)   GOV-
ALTAI   ÖVÖRKHANGAI

Altai   Bayangovi   Mandal-
Ovoo

BAYANKHONGOR

Gurvan Saikhan
National Park

Great Gobi
Strictly Protected
Area (Gobi A)   Gurvantes   Bayandala

Noyon

ÖMNÖGOV

CHINA

**Gurvan Saikhan
National Park**
The heart of the legendary
Gobi Desert (p193)

ELEVATION

3000m
2500m
2000m
1500m
1000m
500m
0

Why I Love Mongolia

By Daniel McCrohan, Author

If you love the outdoors, you'll fall head over heels for Mongolia. I did. What's not to love about a country that's so vast, so remote, so beautiful? How can you fail to adore the hiking, the horse trekking, the camping? You can't. But it's more than just that raw, physical attraction. Centuries of nomadic living have given Mongolians a natural bond with travellers. Break down in the countryside, and the next driver to pass will stop to help. Stuck for a room, and a family can often find you a bed. And break at a herdsman's ger for directions and you'll end up with tea, snacks and a fascinating glimpse into the daily routines of a remarkable culture.

For more about our authors, see p312

Above: Mongolian boy carrying a lamb

Welcome to Mongolia

Rugged Mongolia is an adventure destination where travellers can see the traditions of the past still practised today by hardy nomads dwelling on the country's vast steppes and deserts.

An Open Country

For most of the 20th century, Mongolia was sealed off from the world; seemingly so distant that the very name of the country became a byword for remoteness and isolation. The 21st century promises the polar opposite. As Mongolia has opened up to the world, its citizens are travelling the globe and outsiders are arriving by the planeload for business and travel opportunities. Visas are relatively easy to acquire; a handful of nationals won't even require one. Authorities see tourism as a key growth sector of the Mongolian economy and an important revenue earner for local communities. Despite the warm welcome you will receive, Mongolia is not a pleasure cruise. This is still a developing country with rudimentary infrastructure and mostly basic facilities outside the capital.

Mongolian Wilderness

Mongolians are fully aware of the unique beauty of their country. Ask locals and they will probably start gushing about the spectacular countryside, vast steppes, rugged mountains, clear lakes and abundant wildlife and livestock. It's this true wilderness experience that many people find so appealing.

Nomad Hospitality

Mongolia's nomadic culture is famous – visitors can sleep in a traditional ger (yurt), help round up the sheep, ride horses and simply 'get back to nature'. The legacy of Chinggis Khaan and resurgent nationalist pride sharpens the experience. A culture of tremendous hospitality makes locals more accessible. In a world beset by locks and gates, it's refreshing to meet people willing to open their doors to strangers.

Not Just Grass & Horses

There are few countries in the world with such a stark difference between the rural and urban populations. While nomadic Mongols live the simple life, their cousins in Ulaanbaatar are lurching headlong into the future. The capital is changing at a dizzying pace and many Mongolians have bought wholeheartedly into the global economy, capitalism and consumerism. Urban hipster or nomadic shepherd, however, both share a love of democracy. The country is often held up as a model emerging democratic state, despite being surrounded by democracy-challenged countries. Mongolia is eager to be part of the global community; by visiting you are contributing to the remarkable developments in this extraordinary land.

Contents

CAMEL RIDING, GOBI
DESERT (P179)

Naadam Festival

1 Mongolians love their naadam (p50). With two or three days of serious wrestling action, awesome horse racing and dazzling archery, who wouldn't? While 'naadam' literally means games, the celebration is much more than that. It's all about fun, getting together with friends and relatives, eating a lot of *khuushuur* (mutton pancakes) and emptying a bottle or two of vodka. The most traditional festivals happen in small towns such as Khatgal in northern Mongolia (p151), where every member of the community is somehow involved. These village naadams are also ultra-photogenic – the burly wrestlers, sharp-eyed archers and tough jockeys make for quite a spectacle.

Staying in a Ger

2 Of all the experiences you are likely to have in Mongolia, the most memorable will be your visits to gers (traditional felt yurts; see p250). From the outside, gers look like simple tents, but step inside and you'll be surprised by the amount of furnishings and modern appliances a nomadic family can have – not just beds and tables but also surprises like TV and radio and a smartphone or two. Visitors are always welcome inside a ger and you don't even need to knock (Mongolians never do). Instead, when approaching a ger, call out *'Nokhoi khor'*, which means 'Hold the dog'.

THOMAS L KELLY/GETTY IMAGES ©

NICK LEDGER/GETTY IMAGES ©

Horse Riding

3 Mongolians have been traversing their country on horseback for thousands of years. You should do the same. Short day rides are possible right around Ulaanbaatar – but the best areas are Gorkhi-Terelj National Park (p105) and Bogdkhan Uul Strictly Protected Area (p102). Multiday horse treks can be made at Khövsgöl Nuur (p147), the Darkhad Depression, Khan Khentii Strictly Protected Area (p106) and Naiman Nuur (p118). It can take some getting used to the half-wild Mongolian horses and their short and stocky build. Fortunately, local guides know their animals well – pay attention and follow their lead.

Gobi Desert

4 The idea of going to the Gobi for a vacation would probably have Marco Polo turning in his grave. The Venetian traveller, and others like him, dreaded crossing this harsh landscape. Thankfully, travel facilities have improved in the past 800 years, and it's now possible to make a reasonably comfortable visit. There are two-humped camels to ride and dinosaur boneyards to explore. The real highlight is the scenic Khongoryn Els in Gurvan Saikhan National Park (p193) – towering sand dunes that whistle when raked by high winds.

Khongoryn Els (p195)

Mongolian Hospitality

5 It may sound clichéd, but the truth is that you won't find a more hospitable people than the Mongols. Stop for directions at a ger and soon bowls of sweets appear, then cups of tea, then possibly lunch and even a bed if you're in need of a nap. Camp by a group of nomads and chances are you'll get a visit from children bearing fresh milk and cheese. It's all part of a time-honoured tradition, allowing for the mutual survival of Mongolians themselves as they travel across their vast nation. The further from the city the more welcoming the reception, so try far-flung Ölgii (p208).

Wildlife Watching

6 Mongolia provides an ideal landscape for watching wildlife. In the east you'll spot hundreds (sometimes thousands) of gazelle streaking across the plains at supersonic speeds. In mountainous areas, especially in the Gobi, you stand a good chance of seeing argali sheep and ibexes, and in the taiga north of the Darkhad Depression (p155) you can see majestic reindeer. The easiest place to watch wildlife is at Khustain National Park (p110), home to *takhi* (wild horses). And no matter where you travel, there are huge eagles, falcons and vultures circling overhead.

Hiking

7 With its mountains, river valleys and fields of wildflowers, the Mongolian backcountry is begging to be explored on foot. Hiking is a new activity in Mongolia, but with some improvisation, it's possible at places such as Gorkhi-Terelj National Park (p105). Although there are no warming huts and few marked trails, you'll find shelter in gers and encounter locals who are more than willing to show you the way. There are no sherpas, but a packhorse will do nicely. Good maps, a sturdy tent and a sense of adventure will help see you through.

Ulaanbaatar

8 Mongolia is said to be the least-densely populated country on the planet. You would have a hard time believing that if you only visit its capital (p56). The crush of people, cars and development in Ulaanbaatar can be overwhelming and exciting all at once. Beyond the heady nightlife, chic cafes and Hummers, the city has a peaceful side, too. Turn a prayer wheel at Gandan Khiid, saunter across Chinggis Khaan (Sükhbaatar) Sq and climb up Zaisan Hill to take a break from this bewildering and ever-changing city. Gandan Khiid (p67)

Khövsgöl Nuur

9 The natural highlight of Mongolia is Khövsgöl Nuur (p147), a 136km-long lake set on the southernmost fringe of Siberia. For Mongolians the lake is a deeply spiritual place, home to powerful *nagas* (water spirits) and a source of inspiration for shamans who live there. For foreigners Khövsgöl is a place for adventure, with horse riding, fishing, kayaking, trekking and mountain biking a few of the possibilities. Hard-core adventurers can even embark on a 15-day trek around its glorious shoreline.

On the Trail of Chinggis Khaan

10 Amateur historians shouldn't miss the chance to track down Chinggis Khaan. Pack a copy of *The Secret History of the Mongols*, climb into your jeep and head east. Start at the place where Chinggis found his famous golden whip, Tsonjin Boldog (p104), which is now a hill topped with a huge statue of the great conqueror. Continue on to Khökh Nuur (p165), the site of his coronation before 100,000 soldiers. The trail gets wilder the further you go, until finally reaching Dadal (p166), the great conqueror's alleged birthplace.

Statue (p104) at Tsonjin Boldog, designed by architect J Enkhjargal and sculptor D Erdenebileg

TIMOTHY ALLEN/GETTY IMAGES ©

Mongolian Food & Drink

11 When it comes to cuisine, Mongolians make the most of limited ingredients (see p256). Meat (especially mutton), flour and milk products feature prominently in traditional dishes. The best meals tend to be at a ger in the countryside, where a family feast includes meat, animal organs, intestines and even the head. There are other dishes too, such as *buuz* (dumplings) and *tsuivan* (fried noodles), which you can find in every city. Drinking *airag* (fermented mare's milk) is a uniquely Central Asian experience, one your belly won't soon forget.

Fossils

12 Time travellers setting their destination to 70 million years in the past would find the Gobi Desert to be lusher and wetter than it is today. The wildlife would be different too – instead of wild ass and gazelle, the landscape would be alive with lumbering Protoceratops, hissing Velociraptors and the fearsome Tyrannosaurus Bataar. While these creatures no longer walk the earth, their bones can be found buried in the sands of the Gobi (p193). In Ulaanbaatar, the best examples are to be housed in a new Museum of Dinosaurs (p66).
Bayanzag (p197)

Eagle Hunters

13 For centuries, using eagles to catch prey has been a traditional sport among Central Asian nomads. Even Marco Polo mentioned the great raptors kept by Kublai Khaan. The sport is alive and well today, but you'll only find it in a small corner of Mongolia. Travel to Bayan-Ölgii and link up with the Kazakh hunters who capture and train these magnificent birds. The best time to visit is in early October, when you can attend the colourful Eagle Festival (p210) in Ölgii city.

Monasteries

14 The Buddhist monasteries *(khiid)* that dot the landscape are the most immediate window on Mongolia's spiritual roots. Lamas sit quietly in the pews, carrying on the legacy of a religion brought here from Tibet centuries ago. The laypeople who visit the monasteries pay homage with the spin of a prayer wheel and whispered mantras. As well as a place of pilgrimage, the monasteries are also slices of tangible history, filled with Buddhist icons, Sutras and delicate paintings. Amarbayasgalant Khiid (p136) is dedicated to the sculptor Zanabazar. Erdene Zuu Khiid (p114)

14

TIM MAKINS/GETTY IMAGES ©

Need to Know

For more information, see Survival Guide (p265)

Currency
Tögrög (T), also spelled tugrik

Language
Mongolian and Kazakh

Visas
Most nationalities can purchase a 30-day visa at a Mongolian consulate or embassy. Certain nationalities can visit visa-free.

Money
ATMs are widely available in Ulaanbaatar (UB) and regional capitals. Most businesses only accept cash, although you can use credit cards at some businesses in UB.

Mobile Phones
Mongolia has four carriers (two GSM and two CDMA). With an unlocked phone, buy a local SIM card and top up with units.

Time
Ulaanbaatar and most of the country is GMT/UTC plus eight hours. The three western aimags (provinces) are GMT/UTC plus seven hours.

When to Go

Khövsgöl Nuur
National Park
GO Jun–Aug

Altai Tavan Bogd
National Park
GO Jun–Sep

Ulaanbaatar
GO Jun–Aug

Dornod
GO May–Sep

Ömnögov
GO May, Aug–Oct

Warm to hot summers, cold winters
Mild summers, cold winters
Dry climate
Desert, dry climate

High Season
(Jun–Aug)

➡ Expect warm and mostly dry weather in June and July, with some thunderstorms.

➡ Late August sees cooler temperatures and more rain.

➡ Book flights and accommodation in advance, especially around Naadam.

Shoulder
(May & Sep)

➡ Some ger (traditional yurt) camps may be closed.

➡ Weather can be changeable so plan for a cold snap.

➡ Fewer tourists means more available train and plane tickets.

Low Season
(Oct–Apr)

➡ Most ger camps and some guesthouses close; discounts available.

➡ Frigid in December/January, air pollution in Ulaanbaatar. Winds and dust storms March/April.

➡ Activities like dog sledding, ice skating and skiing.

Websites

➡ **News.mn** (www.news.mn) Mongolia's leading news portal.

➡ **Info Mongolia** (www. infomongolia.com) Another good site for news and information.

➡ **Mongolia National Tourism Centre** (www.mongoliatourism. gov.mn) Events, sights and trip planning.

➡ **To Mongolia** (www. tomongolia.blogspot.com) Reams of up-to-date info on Naadam, events and transport.

➡ **Lonely Planet** (www. lonelyplanet.com/mongolia) Destination info, hotel bookings, traveller forum and more.

➡ **Mongolia Expat** (www. mongoliaexpat.com) Slew of articles on living in Mongolia.

Important Numbers

Country code	☎976
Directory assistance	☎109
Ambulance	☎103
Police	☎102
Immigration office	☎1882

Exchange Rates

Australia	A$1	T1573
Canada	C$1	T1576
China	Y1	T286
Euro zone	€1	T2404
Japan	¥100	T1708
New Zealand	NZ$1	T1451
Russia	R1	T49
USA	US$1	T1750
UK	US£1	T2912

For current exchange rates, see www.xe.com. See also p271 for details on the fluctuating exchange rate.

Daily Costs

Budget:
Less than US$50

➡ Dorm bed: US$7–15

➡ Double room at a guesthouse: $20–45

➡ Countryside camping: free

➡ Meal at a simple restaurant: US$4–7

➡ A 650km bus ride: around US$22

Midrange:
US$50–140

➡ Double room at a standard hotel: US$75

➡ Ger camp with room and board: average US$40

➡ Meal at a restaurant in Ulaanbaatar: US$8–14

Top End:
More than US$140

➡ Top-end hotel or ger camp (only found in a few areas): from US$150

➡ Meal at a fancy restaurant: US$25–40

➡ Horse trek with professional outfitter per day: US$200–400

➡ Land Cruiser with driver per day: from US$150

Opening Hours

Operating hours in Ulaanbaatar are generally consistent, but are only loosely followed in the countryside.

Banks 9am–6pm Monday to Friday. Main branches remain open on weekends.

Restaurants 10am–8pm (to 10pm in UB) Monday to Saturday. Some remain open on Sunday.

Shops 9am–6pm (to 10pm in UB) Monday to Saturday. Large markets remain open on Sunday.

Arriving in Mongolia

Chinggis Khaan airport (Ulaanbaatar; p95) In July an airport bus service connects the terminal with downtown, with a stop by the National Library. Private taxis are risky (some may overcharge). It's best to organise a pick-up from the airport through your guesthouse or hotel. A taxi should cost US$18–25.

Ulaanbaatar train station (p95) The station is close to the city centre – from here you can catch a public bus or walk. Like the airport, it's best to organise a pick-up. A taxi should cost US$3–6 to most downtown areas.

Getting Around

Public transport is slow and destinations are limited. Most visitors hire a guide and driver for countryside tours. Jumping on a tour at the last minute is very difficult so streamline your trip by booking a tour several weeks prior to arrival.

Bus The provincial capitals are accessible by bus and services run daily to most cities. Connections to the western aimags are less regular.

Car The main way to get around the countryside. Hiring a car and driver is actually cheaper than hiring a car without a driver. Drive on the right. A 4WD is essential for most destinations outside the capital.

Train Useful for getting in and out of the country but unnecessary for domestic travel. The lone exception is for a side trip to Sainshand (for Khamaryn Monastery). Best for trips to Zamyn-Üüd for travellers heading to the Chinese border.

For much more on **getting around**, see p286.

If You Like...

Spotting Wildlife

Ikh Nartiin Chuluu Nature Reserve One of the best places in the country to spot wildlife in their natural habitat, including argali sheep and ibexes. (p189)

Dornod Mongol Strictly Protected Area Tens of thousands of gazelles inhabit this park in an incredibly remote corner of the country. (p175)

Nömrög Strictly Protected Area This geographically distinct region is home to some stunning flora and fauna; possible sightings include otters, bears and moose. (p173)

Mongol Daguur B Strictly Protected Area Excellent place for ornithologists hoping to spot a white-napped crane. (p173)

Khustain National Park Easily accessible from Ulaanbaatar, this is the place to visit for sightings of the *takhi* (Przewalski's) horse. (p110)

Hiking

Renchinlkhumbe Trail One of the best multiday hikes in the country goes from the gorgeous shores of Lake Khövsgöl over the mountains to the quaint village of Renchinlkhumbe. (p150)

Bogdkhan Uul For a long day hike or an overnight walk, start at Mandshir Khiid and walk over the mountain to Ulaanbaatar. (p102)

Gorkhi-Terelj National Park The main valley in the park is crowded with ger camps but hike over a mountain or two and you'll be in total isolation. (p105)

Burkhan Khalduun Foreigners are not allowed to climb up the actual peak, but a new 'observation route' will take you up a nearby mountain. (p168)

Otgon Tenger Uul Strictly Protected Area The locals don't want you climbing this mountain (it's sacred) but it's perfectly OK to hike around its base. (p231)

Altai Tavan Bogd National Park The park has a lot of varied terrain to tackle. You can hike along the side of the glacier at Tavan Bogd, or go down to the lake area for a trek around Khoton Nuur. (p214)

Monasteries

Gandan Khiid The cultural and religious highlight of Ulaanbaatar. The incredible Migjid Janraisig statue looms 26m over the pious visitors below. (p67)

Amarbayasgalant Khiid Set in a wide valley, this magnificent complex has whiled away the centuries in almost complete obscurity. Camp by its walls and you'll have it almost to yourself. (p136)

Baldan Baraivun Khiid Lost in the wilderness of Khentii aimag, this remote, ruined monastery was once one of the largest in the country. (p165)

Khamaryn Khiid The home monastery of Danzan Ravjaa, a poet-monk who established Mongolia's first theatre here in the mid-19th century. (p189)

Tövkhön Khiid Recently revived, this former workshop of Zanabazar receives crowds of visitors who march uphill to discover this spiritual nook. (p119)

IF YOU LIKE... CLUBBING

Ulaanbaatar has booming nightclubs and a thriving hip-hop scene with local DJs, rappers and folk-rock fusion bands (p82).

The Obscure

A lot of strange stuff happens in Mongolia. One day you're strumming a guitar in the shadow of John Lennon, the next day you're feasting on sheep-head stew. Keep your itinerary loose and expect the unexpected.

Techie nomads From the outside, the simple gers in far-flung corners of the steppe may appear oh-so-12th-century, but inside the 21st century is all too apparent, as weather-beaten nomads text, tweet, surf and maybe fling an angry bird or two on their mobile devices.

Camel beauty pageants How the judges determine a winner, we don't know. These happen as part of camel festivals held in late winter near Ulaanbaatar (p20) and the Gobi (p197).

Pyongyang Down some vodka shots and toast the Kim Dynasty at this North Korean restaurant in UB. (p78)

Khar Temis Dig your toes in the sand and listen to the seagulls caw at this oddball beach located 2000km from any ocean. (p228)

Barefoot Paul McCartney The bewildering monument to the Fab Four in Ulaanbaatar is just a few years old but has already become a local landmark. Paul's bare feet are a tribute to the cover of *Abbey Road*. (p67)

Sheep-head stew The Mongolian experience isn't complete without trying the local delicacy – boiled sheep offal and eyeball. Try it at Mongolians (p82) or Nomad Legends Mongols Club (p81) in UB, or at a countryside ger. When in Mongolia...

Top: Bactrian camels (p185)
Bottom: Amarbayasgalant Khiid (p136)

Month by Month

January

Cold. Damn cold. Frozen-toes-and-eyelashes cold. Ulaanbaatar can suffer severe levels of air pollution and is best avoided. If properly prepared, this is a good time for short winter walks in Terelj.

February

Icy temperatures across the country (typically -15°C during the day and -25°C at night), although skies are usually clear. Deep snows can block roads but driving over lakes and rivers is possible. Pollution still lingers in Ulaanbaatar.

🎆 Tsagaan Sar

The Lunar New Year. This is a good time to meet Mongolians and, if you're lucky, get invited to a family celebration. Note: this may occur in late January or early March.

🎆 Bulgan Camel Festival

Over Tsagaan Sar you'll see camel polo, camel racing and other camel games. (p197)

🎆 Khatgal Ice Festival

A celebration that includes ice skating, horse-sledding races, ice fishing and thickly dressed locals. It'll be bitterly cold but skies are usually clear. (p151)

🎆 Ice Anklebone Shooting Competition

Staged on the frozen Tuul River in Ulaanbaatar. The competition is similar to curling, except with anklebones (of goats or sheep) replacing the blocks of Scottish granite. (p72)

🏃 Winter Sports

Long-distance ice skating and dog sledding are possible at Lake Khövsgöl (check with tour companies; p147), or try downhill skiing at Sky Resort (p71).

March

March sees strong winds, sub-zero temperatures, snow and dust storms. You may get all four seasons in one day and the inclement weather often cancels flights. Melting snows will reveal a brown, harsh landscape. The long winter and lack of fodder will make livestock thin – a bad time for horse riding.

🎆 Bactrian Camel Polo Tournament

Camel polo teams assemble for a two-day tournament, camel race and traditional performances. Typically held in the second weekend of March at the Chinggis Khaan statue near Nalaikh, but dates and place could change.

🎆 Navrus

The Kazakh spring festival begins in Bayan-Ölgii on 22 March. Visit a family feast and watch traditional games and contests. (p211)

April

April sees frequent dust storms and cold snaps, but warmer weather later in the month. If the winter has been severe, livestock will die off rapidly at this time. Melting snow can cause flooding and vehicles are prone to falling through ice. Air pollution in Ulaanbaatar is mostly gone.

May

The weather will be warming up this month and the tourist season will start tepidly as some ger camps open. Snowfalls may still occur, especially in the north. Central areas will see a rainstorm or two.

✾ Ikh Duichin

Buddha's birthday is marked with a lantern-lighting ceremony at UB's Naadam Stadium. Thousands gather to release the floating lanterns into the sky. It's held in the third or fourth week of May according to the lunar calendar.

June

Temperatures will reach the mid- to high 20s (Celsius). The weather tends to be dry this month but an occasional rainstorm will bring relief to the parched grasslands.

☆ Roaring Hooves

Often held at a remote location in the Gobi Desert, this international music festival can be staged anywhere in the country. See www.roaringhooves.com for details.

🏃 Fishing Season Starts

Fishing season kicks off on 15 July in Mongolia.

July

This is peak travel season. Weather is good although a heatwave usually hits around this time; temperatures in the Gobi can reach 35°C.

Top: Naadam costume parade, Ulaanbaatar (p72)
Bottom: Man with eagle, Altai Eagle Festival, Sagsai (p213)

🎪 Naadam

Mongolia's premier summer sports festival erupts in July. The date is fixed in Ulaanbaatar (11–12 July) but will change from year to year in other cities and towns. Good village naadams can be found at Dadal (p166) or Khatgal (p151).

🎪 Altai Horse Games

This festival on the third weekend in July in Altai Tavan Bogd National Park features traditional Kazakh horse games. (p215)

🏃 Sunrise to Sunset Ultramarathon

A 100km race (there's also a 42km segment for wimps) is held on the shores of Lake Khövsgöl. Check www.ultra mongolia.org. (p147)

August

In terms of weather, this tends to be the best month in Mongolia. Temperatures are pleasant and there is enough rainfall to keep the dust down and turn the grasslands an electric green. However, heavy rains can turn jeep tracks into mud pits, causing vehicles to get bogged.

🎪 Gongoriin Bombani Hural

Religious festival held at Amarbayasgalant Monastery. Bring your tent and camp in the fields with other festival-goers. (p137)

🏃 Mongolia Bike Challenge

Event that brings together serious mountain bikers for a cycling rally.

🎪 Khongoryn Els Naadam

A naadam is held nearby these iconic sand dunes, usually on 15 August. (p195)

🎪 Khatgal Naadam

A late-summer naadam (usually 11 August) taking place at Khatgal. (p151)

☆ Playtime

Two-day alternative music fest in Gachuurt. A great chance to meet young Mongol music fans. Sometimes held late July. (p72)

September

As summer ends, expect changeable weather. Temperatures will be fair but you should bring a fleece layer and light jacket. A cold snap may occur and you might even see a brief snowstorm.

🏃 Gobi Marathon

Go for a 42km run in one of the world's most inhospitable deserts. See www.gobimarathon.org for information.

🎪 Altai Eagle Festival

One of several eagle festivals held in Bayan-Ölgii. This one is held in Sagsai in late September. (p213)

🏃 Fishing

September is a great time for fishing. The weather is good and rivers are calm after the August rains.

October

October is cool and sees snow flurries up north but is still fine for travel, especially in the Gobi. By now most ger camps are closed, except for a few around Terelj.

🎪 Eagle Festival

The Eagle Festival in Ölgii is an annual highlight. (p210)

🎪 Swan Migration

Visit Ganga Nuur in Sükhbaatar aimag to watch thousands of migrating swans. (p176)

November

The mercury dips below zero and will continue to plummet. Despite the cold there are still a few visitors around – some take trips down to the Gobi where it's a touch warmer.

🎪 Chinggis Khaan's Birthday

Birthday celebrations for CK are held on the first day of the first winter month, usually early November but the date changes each year. It's an official bank holiday.

🎪 Eagle Hunting

This is a good time to visit Bayan-Ölgii and watch eagle hunters in action. (p213)

December

Brace yourself, the Mongolian winter is upon you. Sky Resort near Ulaanbaatar opens. The air pollution in Ulaanbaatar can be unbearable.

🎪 New Year's Eve

Mongolians celebrate New Year's Eve enthusiastically, usually with lots of beer, vodka and fireworks.

Itineraries

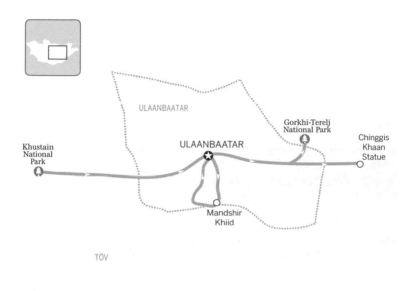

 ## Around Ulaanbaatar

Short trips from Ulaanbaatar can offer a taste of the countryside without having to invest too much time travelling along endless country roads.

From UB, head to **Khustain National Park** for the night to watch the wild *takhi* horses. Back in Ulaanbaatar, catch a ride to **Mandshir Khiid** in Töv aimag, from where you can hike back over the mountain to Ulaanbaatar. This can be done either as a full day trip or as an overnight hike.

Next, head east to **Gorkhi-Terelj National Park**. There are a number of activity options here, including mountain biking, horse riding, rock climbing, hiking and river rafting. You can even learn the art of cheese-making from Bert, the Dutch cheesemaker.

If you have your own vehicle, push on a little further east to see the enormous **Chinggis Khaan Statue** at Tsonjin Boldog.

Back in **Ulaanbaatar**, leave one day for visiting the National Museum of Mongolia, Gandan Khiid and the Winter Palace of the Bogd Khan.

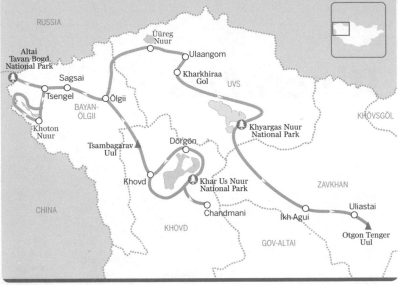

4 WEEKS Western Mongolia

The western aimags offer adventurous travel and exploration. Adrenalin junkies can break out the mountain bike, kayak or mountaineering gear. Start with a flight to **Khovd**, from where you can hire a jeep and driver for a birdwatching and wildlife expedition to **Khar Us Nuur National Park**. At nearby **Chandmani,** visit the renowned throat singers. Stop by **Dörgön** *sum* (district) for the chance to meet Megjin, a bona fide Green Tara (enlightened Buddha).

Looping back through Khovd, continue northwest to the beautiful pastures and valley around **Tsambagarav Uul**. You could easily spend a couple of days here before moving on to **Ölgii**, a great place to recharge your batteries.

Heading west from Ölgii, spend three to four days around **Altai Tavan Bogd National Park**. With proper equipment and permits it's even possible to scale Mongolia's highest peak, the 4374m Tavan Bogd, though a visit to the base camp and glacier is more feasible. With more time, consider doing a horse trek around **Khoton Nuur**.

On the way to or from Tavan Bogd, stop in **Tsengel** or **Sagsai**, authentic Kazakh villages that offer a taste of life in the Wild West. A few families here keep eagles and it may be possible to meet them. From Sagsai it's even possible to go rafting back to Ölgii. The best time to make this journey is in late September or early October, which gives you the chance to watch the spectacular Eagle Festival in Ölgii or Sagsai.

From Ölgii, the main road winds northeast, passing **Üüreg Nuur**, another gorgeous camping spot, en route to **Ulaangom**. Allow a week for trekking around **Kharkhiraa Gol**. An experienced driver can get you from Ulaangom to Uliastai, visiting **Khyargas Nuur National Park** and **Ikh Agui** cave en route. If you arrive at Khyargas Nuur before mid-September, you'll have a chance to see hundreds of squawking cormorants at Khetsuu Khad.

From **Uliastai** you can take a horse-riding or hiking trip to **Otgon Tenger Uul**. Catch a flight back to Ulaanbaatar from Uliastai, or spend a few more days and go overland.

Top: Camel herding, Bayanzag (p197)

Right: Winter Palace of the Bogd Khan (p69), Ulaanbaatar

JANE SWEENEY/GETTY IMAGES ©

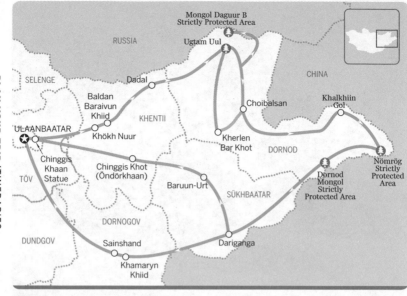

3 WEEKS Eastern Mongolia

Eastern Mongolia offers a delightful romp through grasslands, forest and some unique historical sights. Best of all, it's almost completely devoid of tourists.

In a hired jeep, head east from UB and pass the new **Chinggis Khaan Statue** on the way to **Khökh Nuur**, a pretty alpine lake that saw the coronation of the great khaan. Continue northeast, visiting the restored monastery of **Baldan Baraivun Khiid** and nearby sights as you travel through Khentii's scenic countryside. There are ger camps all along this route where you can stop for horse-riding trips in the mountains. Take a break in **Dadal,** a handsome village with horse-trekking options and an excellent naadam.

Following the Ulz Gol further east, you'll pass pretty Buriat villages and nature reserves including **Ugtam Uul**. If you're interested in meeting a shaman you may be fortunate enough to get the opportunity by asking around in this area. It's possible to continue northeast towards Chuluunkhoroot to visit **Mongol Daguur B Strictly Protected Area**, a protected area for wader birds. From northern Dornod, sweep south towards **Choibalsan**; some routes go via the ancient ruins at **Kherlen Bar Khot**.

The adventurous can push further east across the empty steppes to **Khalkhiin Gol**, a remote landscape of lakes, rivers, wildlife and historical sights. Highlights include a giant Buddha statue carved into a hillside and numerous WWII memorials.

You'll need another couple of days to visit the lush **Nömrög Strictly Protected Area**. From Nömrög, tackle the rough terrain in **Dornod Mongol Strictly Protected Area** to spot some truly massive herds of gazelle.

The **Dariganga** region, with its sand dunes, cinder cones and scattered stone statues, requires two or three days. Horse trekking is possible here. If you're in the area in early October, you'll catch the large migration of swans at Ganga Nuur.

Return to Ulaanbaatar via **Baruun-Urt** and **Chinggis Khot** (Öndörkhaan), or travel via **Sainshand** for a taste of the Gobi and a visit to **Khamaryn Khiid** monastery.

2 WEEKS The Big Loop

From **Ulaanbaatar**, head south to the eerie rock formations of **Baga Gazryn Chuluu** and the ruined castle at **Süm Khökh Burd**, stopping at **Eej Khad**, the Mother Rock, en route.

At least three days are needed to explore Ömnögov: check out the spectacular ice canyon at **Yolyn Am**, the massive sand dunes at **Khongoryn Els** and the dinosaur quarry at **Bayanzag**. From here, go north to the ruined desert monastery of **Ongiin Khiid**, a perfect place to organise a camel trek.

Leaving the Gobi, your first stop is **Erdene Zuu Khiid**, the country's oldest monastery. Head west up the Orkhon valley, to **Tövkhön Khiid**, a monastery in pine forest, and then on to the **Orkhon Khürkhree**. The waterfall is the perfect place to unwind after a long trip to the Gobi, so spend a couple of nights here (and wash away the Gobi dust in the falls).

On your way back to Ulaanbaatar, spend a night at **Khustain National Park**. This route can be combined with the Northern Mongolia itinerary.

4 WEEKS Northern Mongolia

Start week one of this trip by flying from **Ulaanbaatar** to **Mörön**. Hire a vehicle in Mörön and drive to **Tsagaannuur**. Drop into the TCVC here and hire a guide and horses to get you out to the taiga and **Tsaatan camps**. Plan for a week of travel in the area.

To start week two, get a lift to **Renchinlkhumbe** and trek your way over to the shores of **Khövsgöl Nuur**. Then walk down the lakeshore until you reach Jankhai. Spend a few days relaxing at Nature's Door Guesthouse and then continue on to **Khatgal**.

From Khatgal, the adventurous will make their way all the way up to **Khankh** on the northern shore of the lake. Alternatively, there are some gorgeous areas east of the lake in the **Chandman-Öndör** area. You'll need another week to explore this region.

The trip back to Ulaanbaatar goes through a remote part of Bulgan aimag to the pleasant aimag capital of **Bulgan**. Further east, after passing through **Erdenet**, make a short detour to visit the magnificent **Amarbayasgalant Khiid**.

Plan Your Trip

Outdoor Activities

Mongolia is a gigantic outdoor park. With scattered settlements, few roads and immense areas of steppe, mountain and forest, the entire country beckons the outdoor enthusiast. There are excellent opportunities for hiking, fishing and long-distance cycling and any journey in Mongolia always includes a bit of horse riding.

Top Activities

Most Popular Activity

Mongolians practically invented horse riding, making this one of the most iconic activities you can do here. Extended horse treks are best made in Arkhangai, Khövsgöl and Khentii, while Terelj is good for day trips.

Best Off-Season Activity

Visit Mongolia in winter and you can try your hand at dog sledding. French tour guide Joel Rauzy (p37) harnesses up teams of strong huskies to pull your sled through the Mongolian wilderness.

Best Area for Adventure

The varied terrain of Khövsgöl is ideal for horse riding or mountain biking. This is also one of the premier areas for fishing. For mountaineering try Uvs or Bayan-Ölgii.

Best Adventure near Ulaanbaatar

A nice option is a float down the Tuul Gol on an inflatable kayak or canoe. Several tour operators can facilitate this. Hiking is possible on Bogdkhan Uul.

Planning Your Trip

Almost anywhere you go in Mongolia involves some form of off-road adventure. However, only a few areas (for example, Khövsgöl Nuur, Terkhiin Tsagaan Nuur and Gorkhi-Terelj National Park) are set up to handle independent travellers. Signing up with a tour group, on the other hand, gives you instant logistical help. Tour agencies can act like mobile support centres, using vans, trucks and helicopters to shuttle clients and their gear around; see p35 for more details. Independent travellers hoping to explore remote areas of the country will need to be completely self-sufficient.

When to Go

Summer offers the best weather for horse riding, hiking and mountain biking but winter sports are also possible – think ice fishing, dog sledding and long-distance ice skating. Independent travellers arriving in summer will have a good chance to link up with others to share costs.

Best Times

July and August Weather is fair across the country and summer rains bring life back to the pasturelands. This is an especially good time for horse trekking.

September This is perhaps the best month for fishing. It's also a great time for trekking in northern Mongolia.

February If you are considering a winter sport like cross-country skiing, February is a good time. There will be a decent amount of snow cover by now and temperatures will be warming slightly by the day.

Times to Avoid

March and April Spring weather is plagued by strong winds and dust storms. This is not a good time for horse trekking as animals will be weak after the long winter. The landscape – bare, brown earth – is at its least photogenic.

December and January These are the coldest months of the year and you'll get the least amount of daylight. Temperatures can plummet to -35°C at this time.

Hiking

The number of marked hiking trails in Mongolia is almost zero. So hikers need to plan their own routes and have good navigational skills (plus maps, GPS and a compass). Pay any fees and procure any permits required by local authorities. Be aware of local laws, regulations and etiquette about wildlife and the environment.

Mosquitoes and midges are a curse. The situation is at its worst during spring and early summer, with the marshy lakes and canyons in the western deserts the most troublesome areas.

Western Mongolia Prime hiking areas include Altai Tavan Bogd National Park, around Khoton Nuur or between the lakes and Tavan Bogd. In Uvs aimag try the Kharkhiraa and Türgen Uuls, which are good for three to seven days of backcountry hiking.

Northern Mongolia There is great hiking in the Khövsgöl Nuur area.

Central Mongolia Try the Naiman Nuur area. Nomadic Journeys (p36) runs trips here using yaks as pack animals.

Near Ulaanbaatar You can explore the valleys north of Terelj or hike over Bogdkhan Uul.

Camping

With 1.5 million sq km of unfenced and unowned land, spectacular scenery and freshwater lakes and rivers, campers are spoilt for choice.

Security Local people may come to investigate your camping spot, but you are very unlikely to encounter any hostility. However, be mindful of your security. If drunks spot your tent, you could have a problem.

Towns If you are hitching, it is not hard to find somewhere to pitch a tent within walking distance of most aimag capitals and towns.

Washing To wash yourself, you'll probably need to use the local town's bathhouse. Be aware, though, that the bathhouses aren't like what you'd find in Turkey, for example; in Mongolia they are simply for getting a hose-down.

MONGOLIA'S HIGHEST PEAKS

Tavan Bogd (4374m; p214) In Bayan-Ölgii, on the border of Mongolia, China and Russia. This mountain cluster is full of permanent and crevassed glaciers.

Mönkh Khairkhan Uul (4362m; p222) On the border of Bayan-Ölgii and Khovd aimags. You will need crampons, an ice axe and ropes.

Tsambagarav Uul (4208m; p217) In Khovd; it is relatively easy to climb with crampons and an ice axe.

Tsast Uul (4193m; p217) On the border of Bayan-Ölgii and Khovd aimags. It's accessible and the camping here is great.

Sutai Uul (4090m; p203) On the border of Gov-Altai and Khovd aimags.

Kharkhiraa Uul (4037m; p226) In Uvs; a great hiking area.

Türgen Uul (3965m; p226) One of the most easily climbed with spectacular views; in Uvs.

Otgon Tenger Uul (3905m; p231) Mongolia's holiest mountain, located in Zavkhan aimag. Its sanctity means that climbing is strictly prohibited.

Gers If the owners (and their dog) give you permission, camping near a ger is a good idea for extra security; otherwise camp at least 300m from other gers.

Supplies You can often get boiled water and dairy products from nearby gers in exchange for other goods or money. Always leave something and don't rely on nomads, who may have limited supplies of food, water and fuel. It is also best to bring a portable petrol stove rather than use open fires, which use precious wood. Store your food carefully to protect it from creatures of the night.

Mosquitoes Burn dried dung if you are being eaten alive by mosquitoes and bring strong repellent with as much DEET as possible. Other measures include wearing light-coloured clothing, avoiding perfumes or aftershave, impregnating clothes and mosquito nets with permethrin (nontoxic insect repellent), making sure your tent has an insect screen and camping away from still water or marshes.

Weather Make sure your tent is waterproof before you leave home and always pitch it in anticipation of strong winds and rain.

Gear Ensure your gear is warm enough for sub-zero temperatures. Cheap and flimsy Chinese-made tents and sleeping bags bought in UB won't cut it, especially for camping in the mountains.

Bring the best stuff you can get your hands on for an enjoyable trip.

Pitches Don't pitch your tent under trees (because of lightning) or on or near riverbeds (flash floods are not uncommon).

Horse & Camel Trekking

Horse treks range from easy day trips with guides to multiweek solo adventures. Inexperienced riders should begin with the former, organising your first ride through a ger camp or tour operator.

Cost The prettiest, most accessible places to try are the camps at Terelj and Khövsgöl Nuur, where you can normally hire a horse for around T25,000 a day. Per-hour costs are around T7000. Note that you will also have to cover the cost of your guide, if you have one. Horse hire in a less-touristy area will run T10,000 to T20,000 per day.

Equipment If you need to buy a saddle or other equipment, the best place is the Naran Tuul Market (p87) in UB.

Lessons Even the most experienced riders will benefit from a lesson on how to deal with a

ZEN & THE ART OF HORSE MAINTENANCE

➡ Mongolians swap horses readily, so there's no need to be stuck with a horse you don't like, or which doesn't like you, except perhaps in April and May, when all animals are weak after the long winter and before fresh spring plants have made their way through the melting snows. The best time for riding is in the summer (June to September).

➡ Mount a horse (or camel) only from the left. They have been trained to accept human approach from that side, and may rear if approached the wrong way.

➡ The Mongolians use the phrase 'chu!' to make their horses go. Worryingly, there is no word for 'stop'.

➡ If you are considering a multiday horse trip, remember that horses attract all kinds of flies.

➡ A saddle, bridle, halter and hobble can all be bought at the Naran Tuul Market in Ulaanbaatar (p87). An English hybrid saddle can be bought for T75,000 to T95,000, packsaddles for half that. Riders with long legs might consider bringing narrow stirrup leathers from home.

➡ Buying a horse is best done with the help of a Mongolian friend. A decent-quality horse will cost between T500,000 and T1 million. Herders will be reluctant to sell their best (ie quiet and calm) horses and may try to sell you a nag. Buyer beware. Test-ride any horse you are considering and try loading up potential packhorses to make sure they don't crumple under the weight.

➡ The most important thing to consider when planning a trip is where to get water. Following a river is a good idea, or you can ask around for a well, though these can be dry. As a rule of thumb, where there are animals and people, there is water.

Top: Horse riding,
Khovsgol Nuur (p147)

Bottom: Tourist camp,
Arkhangai (p122)

SHENZHEN HARBOUR/GETTY IMAGES ©

Mongolian horse. The local breed is short, stocky and half-wild; Mongolian horsemen can provide instruction on saddling, hobbling and caring for your horse. You'll also get tips on the best places in which to ride and where to purchase saddles and other equipment. Try Stepperiders (p103) in Töv aimag.

Trekking Areas

Of the dozens of possible horse treks, several are popular and not difficult to arrange.

➡ The most popular horse-trekking area is Khövsgöl Nuur, largely because there is such a good network of guides and available horses. Some travellers have horse-trekked from Terkhiin Tsagaan Nuur to Khövsgöl Nuur. By land (following the twisting river valleys) it's around 295km and takes at least two weeks by horse.

➡ Tsetserleg to Bayankhongor is a rugged wilderness trip that crosses a series of alpine passes.

➡ In the east, try the Binder area of Khentii aimag, which can include a ride to Dadal near the Siberian border.

➡ Closer to Ulaanbaatar, the areas of Terelj and Bogdkhan are both excellent if you don't have a lot of time.

➡ In western Mongolia there is great horse trekking around Otgon Tenger Uul; it can take six days to circle the mountain.

➡ In Altai Tavan Bogd National Park, try a horse trek around Khoton Nuur. There is also horse trekking around Tsast Uul and Tsambagarav Uul. Tour operators in Ölgii can help set something up, or just turn up in any nearby village and ask around for horses.

➡ Some of the ger camps at Ongiin Khiid can arrange one-hour camel rides. Multiday camel treks can be arranged at Bayanzag and Khongoryn Els for T25,000 to T30,000 per camel per day. A trip between the two places takes about five days.

Cycle Touring

On the plus side for cyclists, there are few fences, lots of open spaces and sparse traffic. On the downside, the conditions will shake the bolts loose from your bike. Roads mainly consist of jeep trails so the going can be slow, usually 40km to 50km per day. Cycle tourists need to be totally self-sufficient in terms of tools and spare parts. Other factors include washed-out bridges, fierce dogs, trails that disappear into rivers or marshland and, in late summer, heavy rain and mud. Locals will be pleasantly intrigued by your bike and you'll have lots of inquiries to test it out, but don't forget to show them how to use the brakes! Specialist tour operators include Bike Mongolia (www.bikemongolia. com) and Mongolia Expeditions (p36).

Routes

The following trips require several days. They can be made solo provided you are equipped with a tent, sleeping bag, food and spare parts. Another option is to use vehicle support: hire a jeep and driver to take you out to the best biking areas and keep all your gear in the vehicle while you ride

---

SAFE CYCLING TIPS

➡ Dogs can be ferocious and will chase you away from gers. If you stop and hold your ground they will back off; it helps to pick up a rock. The faster you cycle away, the more they want to chase you.

➡ Cyclists usually follow river valleys. However, in Mongolia it's often better to go over the mountains. Roads along rivers are usually sandy or consist of loose stones that make riding difficult.

➡ Most cyclists consider the best trip to be a cross-country adventure but in Mongolia (where there are vast areas of nothingness) consider focusing on one small area and doing a loop. There are great routes to explore in Khövsgöl and Bayan-Ölgii aimags.

➡ Bring all the spare parts you may need, including brake pads, cables and inner tubes. Spare parts are hard to find in Mongolia, but you could try the Seven Summits (p88) or Attila bike shop (p88), both in Ulaanbaatar.

unhindered. Gobi areas, due to their lack of water and facilities, are places to avoid.

Chinggis Khaan Trail This trail in northern Khentii offers plenty of cultural heritage and nice riding terrain. Get a ride from Ulaanbaatar to Tsenkhermandal in Khentii aimag, then cycle north to Khökh Nuur, in the Khentii Mountains. Continue northwest to Khangil Nuur, Balden Bereeven monastery, Öglögchiin Kherem, Batshireet, Binder and, finally, Dadal. This trip takes four to six days.

Khövsgöl aimag A nice route leads south from Mörön to Tariat in Arkhangai, via the towns of Shine-Ider, Galt and Jargalant. The more popular route is from Mörön up to Khatgal and then along either side of Khövsgöl Nuur. The slightly more adventurous could cycle in the spectacular Chandman-Öndör area.

Ölgii to Ulaanbaatar This mammoth 1450km expedition will take three or four weeks. In summer, the prevailing winds in Mongolia travel from west to east, which means that you'll enjoy tailwinds if you start in Ölgii and end in Ulaanbaatar. The northern route, via either Mörön or Tosontsengel, is more interesting than the southern Gobi route.

Fishing

With Mongolia's large number of lakes *(nuur)* and rivers *(gol)*, and a sparse population that generally prefers red meat, the fish are just waiting to be caught. Several shops in Ulaanbaatar sell fishing equipment, the best is Ayanchin Outfitters (p88).

Lake Fishing

The season is mid-June to late September. For the truly intrepid, visit either lake in winter for some hard-core ice fishing. The best places to dangle your lines:

Khövsgöl Nuur (p147) For grayling and lenok.

Terkhiin Tsagaan Nuur (p126) Has a lot of pike.

River Fishing

Serious anglers will want to try out Mongolia's rivers. The major target is taimen, an enormous salmonoid that spends its leisure time hunting down unfortunate rodents that fall in the rivers. These monsters can reach 1.5m in length, weigh 50kg and live for 50 years. Taimen are a sensitive species and the authorities have taken care to protect them from habitat degrada-

tion and poaching. To avoid any problems, you must fish for taimen with a reputable outfitter. Catch and release is mandatory, using only single barbless hooks (never use treble hooks). Outfitters run fishing trips on the Ider, Chuluut, Selenge, Orkhon, Onon and Delgermörön rivers. For more information, check www.taimen.mn.

Fly-Fishing Operators

The per-person cost for a 10-day package trip runs at least US$5000, more if you take a Cessna flight direct to the camps from UB. Three responsible fly-fishing tour operators:

Fish Mongolia (www.fishmongolia.com)

Mongolia River Outfitters (www.mongoliarivers.com)

Sweetwater Travel (www.sweetwatertravel.com)

Permits

For national parks, you can get a fishing permit from the park office. Permits are valid for two days or 10 fish, whichever comes first. While it's relatively easy to get a fishing permit in a national park, buying one for other areas is much more difficult. Anglers must have a special permit authorised by the **Ministry of Nature & Green Development** (051-266 286; www.mne.mn; Negdsen Undestnii Gudamj 5/2, Government Bldg II, Ulaanbaatar), which costs US$330 a week. As a tourist you cannot get one on your own – you must get one through a tour operator (and only a few operators qualify to receive them). Before signing up, make sure your outfitter has the necessary permits; some take the risk of fishing illegally, which can get you in big trouble if you're caught.

Kayaking, Canoeing & Rafting

Mongolia's numerous lakes and rivers are often ideal for kayaking and rafting. There is little white water but, during the summer rains, rivers can flow at up to 9km/h. The best time for kayaking or rafting is July to September, after some decent rain. There is nothing stopping you from heading out on your own. Seven Summits (p88) rents inflatable kayaks and Mongolia Canoeing rents canoes.

➡ One of the most popular river trips is down the Tuul Gol, from the bridge at the entrance to Terelj and back to Ulaanbaatar.

➡ There are more adventurous options that begin in Khövsgöl aimag. Boat or kayak trips on the Eg Gol can start at Khatgal.

➡ In Bayan-Ölgii it's possible to raft down the Khovd Gol from Khurgan Nuur, past Ölgii city and onto Myangad in Khovd aimag.

Operators

Avoid cowboy outfitters that may not be qualified to run boating trips. Rafting and kayaking is organised along the Tuul Gol and Khovd Gol by agencies based in Ulaanbaatar, including Goyo Travel (p36) and Nomadic Journeys (p36). MS Guesthouse, Garage 24 and Bond Lake, all in Khatgal (p151), rent kayaks and may have rafts. Specialist companies that run boating trips include:

Mongolia Canoeing (☎9982 6883, 11-685 503; www.mongoliacanoeing.com) Runs trips on the Chuluut, Eg, Orkhon and Yeroo rivers. It also rents canoes if you want to mount your own expedition.

Mongolia River Adventures (MRA; ☎9950 1685; www.mongoliariveradventures.com) Run by experienced American river guides, MRA has trips in western and central Mongolia, using both rafts and kayaks. Contact Pat Phillips.

Birdwatching

Mongolia is rich in birdlife and the Ministry of Tourism has identified this activity as a priority for development. Start your online research with the **Mongolia Ornithological Society** (www.mos.mn). These are the best places to get out your binoculars and telephoto lens:

Ganga Nuur (p176) Migratory swan.

Khar Us Nuur and Khar Nuur (p220) Goose, woodgrouse and relict gull, and migratory pelican.

Khyargas Nuur and Airag Nuur Migratory cormorant and pelican.

Mongol Daguur B Strictly Protected Area (p173) White-naped crane and other waterfowl.

Sangiin Dalai Nuur (p184) Mongolian lark, eagle, goose and swan.

Uvs Nuur (p225) Spoonbill, crane and gull.

Winter Sports

Ice skating In winter you won't have to worry about falling through the ice, as many lakes and rivers freeze right down to the bottom. Many Mongolians are keen ice skaters – at least those who live near water, or in big cities with rinks. The National Amusement Park (p66) in Ulaanbaatar has ice skating and skate hire.

Long-distance skating With proper planning, long-distance skating is possible on Lake Khövsgöl (the tour operator will need to dig the toilet holes in August). Nomadic Journeys (p36) is most qualified to run this trip.

Skiing The only downhill ski resort in Mongolia is Sky Resort (p71), which will only be of interest to beginners. There is much potential for cross-country skiing, although there are no developed trails and hiring equipment is difficult. If you have your own equipment, the best places to try are Nairamadal, about 20km west of Ulaanbaatar city centre, Khandgait or Terelj. The best months for skiing are January and February – but be warned: the average temperature during these months hovers around a very chilly -25°C.

Dog sledding Trips, organised by Wind of Mongolia (p37), are offered in Terelj (December to February) for US$60 to US$80 per day, and in Khövsgöl Nuur (March to April); cross-lake trips take eight days (all-inclusive US$2600).

Mountaineering

Mongolia offers spectacular opportunities for mountain climbing. In the western aimags there are dozens of glaciers, and 30 to 40 permanently snow-capped mountains. You must have the necessary experience, be fully equipped and hire local guides. The best time to climb is July and August. Karakorum Expeditions (p36) is a leader in this area. There is good potential for rock climbing in Mongolia, though you'll need to bring your own equipment. For more info see this blog on climbing: http://climbonmongolia.com/wordpress.

Plan Your Trip

Organised Tours

Mongolia's limited public-transport network makes independent travel challenging, because the best sights can only be reached by private vehicle. Most travellers wisely opt for a tour in order to see more of the country in a limited period of time. Guided trips range from budget camping tours to high-end hot-air balloon trips.

In Mongolia

There are dozens of travel agencies in Ulaanbaatar (UB) although many are little more that cowboy outfits, happy to take your money and drive you around the countryside for a few days, but with little knowledge of quality customer service or sustainable tourism. The agencies included in this chapter are recommended for their reputation and experience.

Cost Per-day costs start at around US$100 (for two people), including food, accommodation, tickets to sights, a guide (who will double as a cook), driver and jeep. These costs can go up or down depending on several factors (eg whether you're staying in tents or a ger camp).

Guesthouse tours The tours run by guesthouses get mixed reactions from travellers, but they are recommended for day trips in and around UB and Töv aimag as prices are usually much lower than what the bigger companies offer.

Outside UB Note that nearly all tour operators are based in Ulaanbaatar. The exception is Bayan-Ölgii, where you can find a handful of independent tour companies, the best of which is Kazakh Tour (p210).

Professional Tour Operators

Active Adventure Tours Mongolia (Map p70; ☑11-354 662; www.tourmongolia.com; Erkhuugiin Gudamj) Good for bike and horse trips, this eco-conscious Mongolian-run outfit also runs traditional homestays (per night, full board

Best Tours

Best Horse Treks

Everyone and their uncle runs horse treks but if you are a serious rider consider going with a specialist company. Leading outfitters include Stepperiders (p37), Stone Horse (p37) and Horseback Mongolia (p36).

Best for Budget Travel

Most budget travellers will sign up for a tour with their guesthouse but it's a good idea to compare prices with bona fide travel companies with proven track records for service and sustainability, including Rinky Dink Travel Mongolia (p37) and Tseren Tours (p37).

Best for Adrenalin Junkies

A few companies specialise in serious adventures on bike trails, mountains and rivers. Try Active Mongolia (p36), Wind of Mongolia (p37), Mongolia Expeditions (p36) and Karakorum Expeditions (p36).

Best Way to Enhance Your Tour

Set aside time for some independent travel. Take advantage of bus routes to popular destinations like Terelj, Khövsgöl and Kharkhorin to get a feel for what it's like to travel like a local.

$15) and employs sustainable tourism practices by hiring local guides rather than shipping them out from Ulaanbaatar.

Active Mongolia (Map p60; ✆11-329 456; www.activemongolia.com; Seven Summits) This reliable Scottish-German operation specialises in rugged hiking, rafting and horseback trips, plus mountain biking. Most of the trips are to Khövsgöl, Arkhangai and Khentii aimags. Co-owner Pete Weinig runs many of the tours. It's based at Seven Summits, opposite the central post office.

Black Ibex (Map p60; ✆7012 0011; www. discovermongolia.mn; Sükhbaatar Gudamj, Metro Business Centre, Room 1101) Mostly generic countrywide tours. Good for logistics such as vehicle hire and train tickets.

Drive Mongolia (Map p60; ✆9911 8257; www.drivemongolia.com; Sükhbaatar District, Bldg 33, Entrance V) This unique company specialises in driving tours of the countryside – as in, you drive the car. You can head off by yourself or bring along a guide. Motorbike tours are also available.

Goyo Travel (Map p60; ✆9959 8468, 11-313 050; www.goyotravel.com; Peace Ave, Golomt Town, Tower A, Door 1A) An experienced and reliable British-Mongolian outfit, Goyo has a variety of countryside trips and some unique tours that can include hot-air ballooning and kayaking on the Tuul Gol. Particularly good with film and media groups or high-end travel. Well-regarded for personal service and tailored trips.

Horseback Mongolia (Map p60; ✆9411 0314; www.horseback-mongolia.com; Baruun Selbe Gudamj) French-managed company that offers horse trips around the country. Quality saddles, horse tack and equipment are available. Very competitive rates. The office is behind the State Department Store but you need to call to make an appointment as there is often no one there.

Hovsgol Travel Company (Map p70; ✆9911 5771, 11-460 368; www.hovsgoltravel.com; PO Box 2003, Namyanjugiin Gudamj) Runs countrywide tours but specialises in boat and horse trips around Khövsgöl. Operates the popular Camp Toilogt at Khövsgöl Nuur. Works with the Taimen Conservation Fund as a responsible fishing outfitter. Also sponsors the annual 100km ultramarathon at Khövsgöl.

Juulchin (Map p60; ✆11-328 425, 11-328 428; www.juulchin.com; Olympiin Örgön Chölöö) Mongolia's oldest tour operator, Juulchin has been in business since the 1950s. It offers 15-day group tours departing on six different dates each summer. Well-regarded for its experienced staff and good-quality vehicles. The office is east of the Japanese Embassy, in the same building the KIA dealership.

Karakorum Expeditions (Map p60; ✆11-315 655, 11-320 182; www.gomongolia.com; PO Box 542) A leader in bike, hiking and mountaineering tours in western Mongolia, this is a good outfit if you want to climb Tavan Bogd. Runs a unique trip with snow leopard researchers. Owner Graham Taylor is an experienced mountaineer and runs some of the trips.

Khövsgöl Lodge Company (Map p60; ✆9911 5929; www.boojum.com; Sükhbaatar District, Bldg 33, Room 16) This experienced outfit is part of the US-based Boojum Expeditions and has been running trips in Mongolia since 1994. It offers countrywide tours but is particularly experienced in the Darkhad valley and Khövsgöl region. Good for horse treks in northern Mongolia. The office is in an apartment block behind the Drama Theatre, but you are better off calling first to get someone to meet you.

Mongolia Expeditions (Map p60; ✆9909 6911, 11-329 279; www.mongolia-expeditions. com; Jamyn Gunii Gudamj 5-2) Specialises in adventure travel, including cycle touring, mountaineering, caving and rafting trips, as well as less vigorous options such as birdwatching tours. This is a good option if you are planning a climbing trip to Tavan Bogd or if you want to do a tour by bike. Sponsors the Mongolia Bike Challenge.

Nomadic Expeditions (Map p60; ✆11-313 396; www.threecamellodge.com; Peace Ave 76) This is the Mongolian office of the US-based travel company. Runs countrywide tours but is especially good for the Gobi, where it runs the excellent Three Camel Lodge. A leader in environmental conservation and work with Mongolian scientists to protect plant and animal species in the Gobi.

Nomadic Journeys (Map p60; ✆11-328 737; www.nomadicjourneys.com; Sükhbaataryn Gudamj 1) A joint Swedish-Mongolian venture, this business concentrates on low-impact tourism, environmental protection and community development. It runs fixed-departure yak, camel and horse treks and can also arrange rafting trips on the Tuul Gol. Its trip in Terelj is unique – you walk while yaks haul your own portable ger on a cart. Also good for taimen fishing trips. If you are looking for a standard jeep tour this operator may not suit your needs as it caters to travellers seeking unique experiences.

Nomads (✆7011 9370; www.nomadstours.com; Khan Uul District, PO Box 1008) In business since

1992, this is a well-established company known for its horse-trekking tours. It offers a wide range of fixed-departure trips, including popular horse treks in Khentii and through Terelj, visiting Günjiin Süm. Also good for hiking and trekking in western Mongolia. The office is located in Khan Uul District, 600m south of the train station. Has English- and German-speaking guides.

Rinky Dink Travel Mongolia (☑9965 2371, 9672 0227; www.rinkydinktravel.com; PO Box 1927) A shoestring outfit that has homestays in ger districts and takes you out of Ulaanbaatar to meet nomad families. It is involved in social development programs in poor neighbourhoods and invites tourists to volunteer for its projects. There is no actual office – you just contact the company and someone will pick you up.

Stepperiders (☑9911 4245; www.stepperiders.mn) A leader in horse-riding trips near Ulaanbaatar. Runs its own camp with horses near Bogd Khan Uul.

Stone Horse (☑9592 1167; www.stonehorse-mongolia.com) Offers horse treks in the Khan Khentii Mountains (trips start from just one hour out of Ulaanbaatar). Professional outfit with quality horses and eco-conscious policies. Also offers reasonably priced homestay opportunities with herders near Ulaanbaatar.

Tseren Tours (Map p60; ☑11-327 083, 9911 1832; www.tserentours.com; Café Amsterdam,

Peace Ave) Dutch- and Mongolian-run outfit that does countrywide tours, biking trips and stays with nomad families. Specialises in family-friendly tours. Good for budget travellers.

Tsolman Travel (Map p60; ☑9911 4913, 11-322 870; www.tsolmantravel.com; btwn Peace Ave & Seoul St) Established in 1993, this is one of the oldest private tour operators in Mongolia. It runs a wide variety of trips at competitive rates and operates two ger camps, one in Terelj and a second at Khögnö Khan Uul Nature Reserve.

Wind of Mongolia (☑9909 0593, 7602 6699; www.windofmongolia.mn; Bayangol District, Bldg 10A, 11th fl, Apt 103) This French-run tour operator, located on the east side of UB Palace, offers creative and offbeat trips, including rock climbing, kayaking and tours that focus on Buddhism, archaeology and botany. Owner Joel Rauzy is perhaps best known for his winter dog-sledding trips in Terelj and Khövsgöl. Call ahead before turning up as there is not always someone there.

Start-Up Tours

Some of the more entrepreneurial guides, fed up with working for tour operators and guesthouses, have set up their own mini-companies – some official, some not.

Finding a start-up Guides advertise their services using word-of-mouth, a website, social media, ads at cafes and business cards passed out at the

---

GUIDES

Few people in the countryside speak anything other than Mongolian and Russian, so a guide-cum-translator is very handy, and almost mandatory. A guide will explain local traditions, help with any hassles with the police, find accommodation, explain captions in museums and act as a linguistic and cultural interpreter.

Finding a guide In Ulaanbaatar you can find guides through travel agencies and guesthouses. In the countryside, there is nothing to do but ask – try the hotels and schools. Guides are easier to find between 15 June and 1 August, when schools and universities are on summer break. The pickings are slimmer at other times of the year.

Pre-trip meeting It's a good idea to meet your guide before setting off on a two-week trip to the Gobi. Try to spend a little time with him/her to gauge if the match will be a good one – we have heard plenty of horror stories from travellers sent into the countryside with well-meaning guides who can barely speak English.

Cost For getting around Ulaanbaatar, a nonprofessional guide or a student will cost a negotiable US$15 to US$25 per day. To take one around the countryside from the capital you will have to include expenses for travel, food and accommodation. In an aimag capital, a guide (if you can find one) costs about US$10 per day, plus any expenses. For a professional guide who is knowledgeable in a specific area, such as birdwatching, and fluent in your language, the bidding starts at US$40 to US$60 per day.

train station to new arrivals. Some recommendations appear on Lonely Planet's Thorn Tree.

Negotiating Many of these guides offer top-notch service at low costs by cutting out the middleman. However, there are obvious risks in dealing with a transitory company, so don't hand over all your money up front; ask to pay a little before the trip and the rest at the end of the tour (if all goes well). They usually ask for a 50% deposit.

Research Do some homework first by asking for references or search online to see what past travellers have posted. Also check that they have a 4WD vehicle and proper camping and cooking equipment.

Guesthouse Tour Operators

Almost every guesthouse in Ulaanbaatar also runs tours, grouping together solo travellers and couples that wash upon their doorsteps. The guesthouses offer bargain-basement prices and run no-frills jeep tours of the countryside.

Rivalry Competition is stiff between guesthouses and some will be none too pleased if you stay at their guesthouse and then take a tour with a rival outfit. We have even heard of people getting thrown out of their guesthouse after booking a tour with another company.

Cost For the most basic driving tour, prices start at around US$50 per day per person, provided you have four or more people.

Inclusions Some budget tours don't include food or accommodation; however, they usually include stoves for cooking your own food and tents for camping out. The guesthouses rarely offer special activities such as biking, kayaking or horse expeditions – for that it's better to try an actual tour operator.

Guides Guides employed by the guesthouses are often students on a summer break, who may have limited knowledge of Mongolian history or off-the-beaten-path destinations. If you think you might need a guide who can offer some in-depth knowledge about the country, the best place to look, again, are the professional tour operators.

Fishing If you want to fish, note that some low-end companies take tourists fishing without a permit – if you are concerned, check with the operator before signing up for the trip or steer clear of the cheaper options. As a general rule of thumb, sustainable tourism is not a high priority of the guesthouse tours.

Recommended tours It's difficult to recommend one guesthouse tour over another because the drivers and guides change frequently and the tours are often almost identical (following the same standard itinerary of the Mongolian highlights, ie the Gobi, Kharkhorin, Great White Lake and Khövsgöl). What sets the tours apart is their levels of organisational skill and the ease of doing business with the guesthouses themselves. The guesthouses that tend to get the most consistently good feedback include: UB Guesthouse (p73), Khongor Guesthouse (p75), LG Guesthouse (p77) and Idre's Guest House (p77). Check two or three and compare prices and itineraries, meet the guide/driver and carefully scrutinise their payment and refund policies.

Outside Mongolia

Reliable agencies outside Mongolia can help with the logistics of travel in Mongolia, including visas, excursions or the whole shebang, including tickets, individual itineraries or group packages. These include travel agencies, adventure-tour operators and homestay agencies.

These companies are particularly good at handling multination trips, for example if you plan to combine Mongolia with a trip to China or other countries in the region. They are also useful for door-to-door service: you can meet the guides in your home country before setting off.

Asia

Monkey Business Shrine (☎8610-6591 6519; www.monkeyshrine.com; 27 Beisanlitun, bldg 2, room 202, Běijīng, China) Specialises in Trans-Siberia Railway trips. Based in Běijīng, 50m west of Yashow Market.

Moonsky Star Ltd (☎852-2723 1376; www.monkeyshrine.com; Flat D, 11th fl, Liberty Mansion, 26E Jordan Rd, Yau Ma Tei, Kowloon, Hong Kong) Monkey Business Shrine's Hong Kong office.

Australia

Intrepid Travel (☎03-9473 2626; www.intrepidtravel.com.au)

Peregrine Adventures (☎03-8601 4444; www.peregrine.net.au)

UK & Continental Europe

Equitour (☑061-303 3105; www.equitour.com) Switzerland-based company that specialises in horse-riding tours.

In the Saddle (☑01299-272 997; www. inthesaddle.com) UK-based company that runs horse-riding tours, mainly in Khentii aimag.

KE Adventure (☑017687-73966; www.kead-venture.com) UK-based outfitter that runs trekking tours and guided ascents of Tavan Bogd Uul.

Mongolei Reisen GmbH (☑030-4660-4924; www.mongolei-reise.de) Germany-based outfit specialising in Mongolia. Offers countrywide trekking, horse riding and jeep tours.

Off the Map Tours (☑0116-2402625; www. mongolia.co.uk) A Mongolia specialist with a broad range of adventure tours, including mountaineering on Kharkhiraa Uul (Uvs aimag) and group motorbike trips in the Gobi. Horse riding, hiking and mountain biking are other options. It has offices in the UK, Germany and Ulaanbaatar.

Panoramic Journeys (☑1608 676821; www. panoramicjourneys.com) UK-based specialist in Mongolia trips, with highly regarded tailor-made tours to off-the-beaten-path destinations as well as standard tours. Excellent sustainable development philosophy. Especially recommended for trips to visit the Tsaatan.

Steppes Travel (☑01285-880 980; www. steppestravel.co.uk) UK-based operator with 15-day jeep tours.

USA & Canada

Boojum Expeditions (☑406-587-0125, 1-800-287-0125; www.boojum.com) Offers horse-riding, mountain-biking, fishing and trekking trips. In Ulaanbaatar, Boojum's local office is called Khövsgöl Lodge Company (p36).

Geographic Expeditions (☑1-888-570-7108; www.geoex.com) Horse-riding trips to Khentii and jeep trips combining western Mongolia and Tuva in western Siberia.

Hidden Trails (☑604-323-1141; www.hid-dentrails.com) Horse-riding tours to Terelj and Darkhad Depression, in conjunction with Equitour.

Mir Corporation (☑1-800-424-7289; www. mircorp.com) Specialists in Russia, Central Asia and Mongolia. Good for multination tours and the Trans-Siberia Railway.

Nomadic Expeditions (☑609-860-9008, 1-800-998-6634; www.nomadicexpeditions.com) One of the best Mongolia specialists, offering everything from palaeontology trips to eagle hunting and camel trekking. Well-regarded for its sustainable practices, especially around the Gobi where it runs the Three Camel Lodge. It also has an office in Ulaanbaatar (p36).

PLAN YOUR TRIP ORGANISED TOURS

Plan Your Trip

Road Trip

Travelling around Mongolia with your own car or motorcycle has the makings of the adventure of a lifetime. The open prairies and deserts are begging to be explored by travellers willing to take on the world's most sparsely populated country with their own wheels. For details on bringing a car across Mongolian borders, see p285.

Behind the Wheel

Best Driving Routes

Off-road adventures can be had almost anywhere. Do a loop around eastern Mongolia, down to the Gobi or through Arkhangai to Khövsgöl Nuur. Most Mongol Rally cars make the cross-country trip from Bayan-Ölgii to Ulaanbaatar (UB).

Best Mongolian Phrases for Drivers

The tyres need air (duguindaa hii nemuulie); fill the tank to the top (durgei); I am lost (bi tuurson); we're out of petrol (benzin duussan); may I park here? (int mashin tavij boloh uu?); where is a petrol station? (benzin colonk khaana baina ve?)

Best Ways to Pass the Time

Diversions to pass the time across long stretches of nothingness might include listening to traditional Mongolian music CDs or car games like yak counting.

Guides

Guides can communicate with locals for directions and road conditions, and give advice on destinations. Consider a guide with vehicle experience as it's handy to have another body around in case of a breakdown. See p37 for more details.

Road Conditions

What look like main roads on the map are often little more than tyre tracks in the dirt, sand or mud, and there is hardly a signpost in the whole country. In Mongolia, roads connect nomads, most of whom by their nature keep moving, so even the roads are seminomadic, shifting like restless rivers.

Remote tracks quickly turn into eight-lane dirt highways devoid of any traffic, making navigation tricky. Expect to get lost.

While conditions are rough in most parts of the country, the government has been busy paving roads from Ulaanbaatar to the provincial capitals. The entire 1000km between the northern border at Altanbulag to the southern border at Zamyn-Üüd has been paved. Other paved roads from Ulaanbaatar now reach Tariat (Arkhangai), Bayankhongor, Bulgan/Erdenet and Öndörkhaan. By the time you read this the roads to Choibalsan, Mandalgov, Dalanzadgad and Mörön should be paved. The road from Mörön to Khatgal is also paved.

Shortages of petrol and spare parts are uncommon, except in remote regions. Accidents are not uncommon. Try to avoid travelling at night, when unseen potholes, drunk drivers and wildlife can wreak havoc. Driving in the dark is also a great way to get completely lost.

Vehicle Hire & Purchase

Self-drive If you want to hire a car (and drive it yourself), contact Drive Mongolia (p36), a tour operator that rents out Land Cruisers and other suitably rugged vehicles. You can contact them through Chuka Guesthouse (p74). Another company that offers self-drive trips is **Happy Camel** (☑9911 2075; www.happycamel.com), with rates somewhat higher than Drive Mongolia. A third option is Sixt (p96), which has a range of vehicles including compacts for driving in UB or off-road vehicles for the countryside.

Car and driver In Ulaanbaatar, the best place to organise such an arrangement is at the various guesthouses. These guesthouses will take a commission, but you'll get a driver and/or guide who should know tourist routes and can locate hard-to-find attractions such as caves, deer stones and ruined monasteries.

Vehicles The type of car you hire will depend on the size of your group. Four or more passengers (plus driver and guide) usually fit in a van. Smaller numbers can take a Russian jeep. The downside of a jeep (aside from being terribly uncomfortable) is the lack of windows in the back seat.

Cutting costs You can save money by using public transport to major regional gateways – that is Mörön for Khövsgöl Nuur, Khovd for the west, Dalanzadgad for the south Gobi and Choibalsan for the far east. Then, from these places rent a jeep and driver from the market, though drivers outside Ulaanbaatar will have little experience of dealing with tourists. You will likely need an interpreter to help communicate your plans to the driver and negotiate costs. Finding an English-speaking guide in the countryside is difficult so bring one from Ulaanbaatar (see p37).

Village hire Villages are less likely to have vehicles for hire, as they may not be available or running.

Return fare Note that when hiring a vehicle in the countryside to take you to another rural city, you will have to pay for the return fare because the driver has to go back with an empty van. This does not apply when travelling to Ulaanbaatar as the driver can find passengers there. The upshot is that it will cost almost the same to hire a driver to take you from, for example, Ulaangom to Mörön as it would from Ulaangom to Ulaanbaatar.

Purchase If you want to buy a vehicle, you will have to ask around (guesthouse owners may have ideas on where to shop), or check out the tsaiz zakh (car market) in the northeastern part of Ulaanbaatar. An old Russian 4x4 could go for around US$3500. A good-condition, used Ij Planeta – the Russian-made motorcycle you see all over the countryside – sells for around US$1000. These tend to break down often but people in the countryside can help with repairs. A Japanese motorcycle will be more reliable. In markets the sign *zarna* (Зарна) on a jeep means 'for sale'.

Costs

On a long-distance trip, tour operators will have a per-day charge (US$80 to US$150 depending on the vehicle). This may be more if they throw in camping and cooking gear. For this price, petrol is usually not included. Some tour operators will build the cost of petrol into the price.

Russian vehicles that you hire on your own (from a market) usually charge US$60 per day without petrol. Russian jeeps have terrible fuel economy: you'll need 20L to travel around 100km. Petrol was around T1650 per litre at the time of research.

Some drivers may want to charge a per-kilometre rate; in the countryside this is around T700 to T800. Vehicle hire is more expensive the further you get from Ulaanbaatar.

Agreeing on Terms

It is vital that you and the driver agree to the terms and conditions – and the odometer reading – before you start.

Ask about all possible 'extras' such as waiting time, food and accommodation. There are several private bridges and tolls around the countryside (each costing about T500), which are normally paid for

---

SELF-DRIVE OR HIRE A DRIVER?

A self-drive tour is hard work and potentially hazardous. You have to deal with breaking down, getting bogged and getting hopelessly lost.

Most travellers hire a car *and* a driver. In terms of price, it can often work out to be the same or even cheaper than renting without a driver.

by you. If you arrange for a jeep to pick you up, or drop you off, agree on a reduced price for the empty vehicle travelling back one way.

Trip Preparation

Supplies

Food Drivers from tourist agencies will assume that you will feed them along the way. On a longer trip it's easiest for everyone to cook, eat and wash up together. If you don't want to do this, you will have to agree on a fee for the driver's food or supply the food yourself. This shouldn't cost more than T15,000 per day.

Cooking gear Experienced drivers will have their own Soviet-era petrol stove, though it's a good idea to bring your own stove as a backup, and to boil water for tea while the other stove is cooking dinner. If you are cooking for a group you'll need a big cooking pot and a ladle. Everyone should bring their own penknife, cutlery, bowl and torch. Avoid drinking from the same water bottles as this spreads viruses around the group.

Camping gear Breakdowns may force you to sleep by your car, so be sure to have camping equipment.

Other gear For long expeditions, also equip your vehicle with the following items. Most of these items can be purchased from the Naran Tuul Market (p87) in Ulaanbaatar.

➡ jerrycans, for extra petrol

➡ water drum

➡ wide-mouthed plastic drum (useful for storing food, as boxes will rapidly disintegrate)

➡ resealable bags (useful for opened bags of sugar, pasta etc)

➡ water- and dust-proof bag (your backpacks will get filthy so it's a good idea to put them in one)

➡ bungee cords/luggage straps (handy for storing gear in a luggage rack)

➡ jack and lug wrench

➡ torch (flashlight)

➡ jumper cables

➡ standard toolkit

➡ steel wire rope with hook ends (handy for hauling a jeep out of the mud)

➡ fire extinguisher

Fuel Up

Three types of Russian fuel, and one Mongolian fuel, are available. Petrol stations are marked by the initials 'ШТС', which is Mongolian for station.

'95' This is the best and the type used by Japanese jeeps, but it's only generally available in Ulaanbaatar.

'92' Slightly lower quality and cheaper but acceptable for most vehicles.

'76' All Russian-made vehicles use this type, which is often the only fuel available in remote areas.

'Mongol 93' This the newest fuel, made from Mongolian crude oil (but actually refined in China).

Repair & Maintenance

Flat tyres These are a time-honoured tradition in Mongolia and it's essential that you know how to deal with one. The best solution, of course, is to have a good-quality spare tyre in your car. In fact, taking two spare tyres is not a bad idea as it's quite possible you could incur two flats before finding a repair shop. Test the jack before setting off.

Tyre repair Just about every town in the country has a tyre-repair shop and these are even available at small villages along main routes.

UB repairs In Ulaanbaatar, a good place to start with repairs is the Oasis Café & Guesthouse (p74), which has a big yard for parking and caters to overlanders.

Breakdowns

Serious mechanical breakdowns are a definite possibility. Should your vehicle break down irreparably in a rural area, you'll be faced with the task of trying to get back to civilisation either on foot (not recommended), by hitching, or by whatever means is available.

The safest solution is to travel with a small group using two jeeps. Make sure your driver has tools and at least one spare tyre.

A warning: Russian jeeps easily overheat. There is no easy solution, but it helps to travel during the early-morning or late-afternoon hours when temperatures are relatively low.

ROAD DISTANCES (KM)

	Altai (Gov-Altai aimag)	Arvaikheer	Baruun-Urt	Bayankhongor	Bulgan	Choibalsan	Dalanzadgad	Darkhan	Khovd	Mandalgov	Mörön (Khövsgöl aimag)	Ölgii	Öndörkhaan (Chinggis Khot)	Sainshand	Sükhbaatar	Tsetserleg	Ulaanbaatar	Ulaangom
Arvaikheer	571																	
Baruun-Urt	1561	990																
Bayankhongor	371	200	1190															
Bulgan	874	373	878	503														
Choibalsan	1656	1085	191	1285	973													
Dalanzadgad	948	377	856	577	725	1074												
Darkhan	1122	596	779	751	248	874	772											
Khovd	424	995	1985	795	1180	2080	1372	1519										
Mandalgov	879	308	613	508	578	741	293	479	1303									
Mörön (Khövsgöl aimag)	583	679	1231	627	353	1326	1056	601	853	913								
Ölgii	635	1206	2196	1006	1344	2291	1583	1582	211	1314	991							
Öndörkhaan (Chinggis Khot)	1332	761	229	961	649	324	710	550	1756	417	1002	1967						
Sainshand	1234	663	340	863	781	531	516	682	1658	355	1134	1869	302					
Sükhbaatar	1214	688	871	830	340	966	864	92	1612	571	693	1823	642	774				
Tsetserleg	502	266	1013	218	289	1108	643	537	438	500	413	1220	784	855	629			
Ulaanbaatar	1001	430	560	630	326	655	553	219	1425	260	671	1636	331	463	311	430		
Ulaangom	662	1188	1896	988	1033	991	1585	1281	238	1383	680	311	1667	1738	1373	883	1336	
Uliastai	218	659	1544	497	807	1639	1074	989	465	967	388	676	1315	1355	1147	531	984	529

Getting Bogged

Most of Mongolia is grassland, desert and mountains. You might think that mountain driving would pose the worst problems, but forests cause the most trouble of all. This is because the ground is often a springy alpine bog, holding huge amounts of water in the decaying grasses, which are instantly compacted under tyres, reducing a wildflower meadow to slush.

Mongolian drivers have one of two reactions when they get bogged. Some will sit on their haunches, have a smoke and then send word to the nearest town for a tractor to come and tow the vehicle out. Other drivers will get out a shovel and start digging; you can help by gathering flat stones to place under the wheels (drivers usually try to jack the tyres out of the mud).

Navigation

Telephone lines Some of the best navigation tools are the telephone lines strung across the steppes, as these (almost) always lead to the next town.

Local advice Mongolian drivers like to stop and ask for directions and road conditions from families along the way, partly to stay on the right track and partly to have a rest and chat with the locals.

GPS Of course, the best way to navigate is with a GPS device. For ease of use, bring along a dashboard mount to keep the unit secured. A GPS is not foolproof as it won't be able to tell you there's a muddy bog or flooded riverbed ahead, so you'll need to constantly correct; see p287.

Maps Good maps are essential and readily available in Ulaanbaatar; see p270 and p91.

THE MONGOL RALLY & MONGOLIA CHARITY RALLY

In an age when getting from point A to point B has been simplified to the point of blandness, the Mongol Rally attempts to put a bit of spark back into the journey to Mongolia. According to rally rules, the London-to-Mongolia trip must be made in a vehicle that has an engine capacity of 1L or less. In other words, you have to travel 16,000km (10,000 miles) across some of the world's most hostile terrain in an old clunker barely capable of making it over the A83 to Campbeltown.

The wacky idea of driving from London to Mongolia in a clapped-out banger was dreamt up in 2001 by Englishman Thomas Morgan, whose own attempt to accomplish the feat failed miserably somewhere east of Tabriz. Morgan had more success on a second trip in 2004 and the Mongol Rally became an annual event.

The journey begins by selecting a vehicle. Gutless wonders such as old Fiat Pandas and Citroëns are suitable (so long as it's a 1.0ish-litre engine). Next, assemble your team – you can have as many people as you can squeeze into the darn thing. For the truly insane, there is the option of riding a moped.

Next, pay your dues: it's £630 to enter and then you must raise another £1000, which will go to a charity in Mongolia or another country en route (the Mongol Rally has raised more than £2 million in charity money so far). Moped riders pay just £350. Finally, zoom out of London with 500 other like-minded drivers in July.

The organisers give absolutely no advice on how to actually get to Mongolia; that you've got to figure out on your own. Teams have travelled as far north as the Arctic Circle and as far south as Afghanistan on their way across the Asian landmass. This is by no means a race – whether you arrive first or last, your only reward is a round of free beers at the finish line. Some teams make the trip in around five weeks, while others have taken as long as three months, stopping off at places en route.

The rally is organised by the grandly titled **League of Adventurists International** (www.theadventurists.com). If you want to sign up, contact the organisers early as spots can fill up a year in advance.

In addition to the Mongol Rally, a second rally, the **Mongolia Charity Rally** (http://mongolia.charityrallies.org), has also formed. The cost to join is £149 and participants must raise £1000 for charity.

Road Rules

Drive on the right Where there are paved roads, Mongolians will drive on the right side.

Right-hand-drive vehicles More than half the cars on the road have right-hand-drive configuration (due to the preference for Japanese imports). As Mongolians drive on the right, this can make passing cars on the highway somewhat hazardous. (Officials are trying to ban the import of right-hand-drive cars from 2015.)

Traffic infringements In Ulaanbaatar, traffic police can pull you over for any number of traffic violations (although most locals flaunt the rules regularly). If you are pulled over, be prepared to show a driving licence, car registration and insurance.

Fines Reckless driving and illegal manoeuvres are standard protocol on the streets of Ulaanbaatar. Fines are typically T5000 to T15,000.

Accidents If you are involved in an accident, don't move your car. The traffic police will eventually arrive on the scene and make a report based on the position of the vehicles.

Legal Requirements

A licence from your home country can be used within 30 days of your arrival. If you plan to spend more time driving in Mongolia, it's best to carry an international driving licence (IDP), which you can get in your home country for a nominal fee.

Expat residents need to apply for a local licence. If you buy a vehicle, inquire about registration with the traffic police. Insurance is also mandatory and travellers can purchase an insurance plan at the border.

On the Road

➡ Shop as a group when you reach a city or town. If you are travelling with strangers, it's a good idea to keep everyone happy by rotating seats so that everyone (including the guide) has a go in the front seat.

➡ Don't push the driver or guide too hard; allow them (and the vehicle) to stop and rest. However, regular and lengthy stops for a chat and a smoke can add time to the journey.

➡ Lastly, if you are on a long trip, you'll find morale boosted by a trip to a bathhouse (hot water!) in an aimag capital. Another morale booster is the occasional meal in a decent *guanz* (canteen). If you are camping a lot then add in at least one night in a decent hotel to clean up and sort out your stuff.

Shortcuts

The quickest distance between two points is a straight line, and the only thing that could put off a Mongolian jeep driver from taking a shortcut is a huge mountain range or raging river. If renting a jeep by the kilometre, you will welcome a shortcut, especially to shorten an uncomfortable trip.

If you have an experienced driver, allow him to take shortcuts when he feels it is worthwhile, but don't insist – he is the expert. The downside of shortcuts is the possibility of breaking down on more-isolated roads.

Plan Your Trip

Trans-Mongolian Railway

The Trans-Mongolian Railway is part of the vast network of track that links Běijīng and Moscow, a crucial piece of the world's longest continuous rail route. For rail enthusiasts, a journey on the Trans-Siberian is the railroad equivalent of climbing Mt Everest. This section offers a broad planning overview; for details on the schedule and ticket prices, see p285.

Trip Prep

Best Pre-Trip Movie

Transsiberian (2008) is a Hollywood thriller staring Woody Harrelson and Ben Kingsley. The film even includes a cameo by a Lonely Planet guidebook.

Best Ways to Meet the Locals

Pack Chinese-, Mongolian- and Russian-language phrasebooks to meet and greet the locals. Card or chess games can pass the time, or break out a stash of food and booze to share with new-found friends. Head to shop.lonelyplanet.com to purchase a downloadable PDF of Lonely Planet's Chinese or Russian phrasebooks.

Best Online Tool

Google has uploaded the entire Moscow-to-Vladivostok rail journey online. It even comes with a soundtrack of Russian books and music. Go to www.google.ru/intl/ru/landing/transsib/en.html.

By the Numbers

The gauge of the Mongolian railroad is 5ft wide, as it is in Russia. This is slightly wider than the 4ft 8.5in used in most other parts of the world. Mongolia has 1810km of railway track (ranking it 76th in the world).

Trans-Siberia Primer

The idea of building a rail route from Moscow to the Pacific Ocean was hatched in the mid-19th century. This was the age of imperialism, when the powers of Europe were expanding across continents in a race to gobble up as much land and as many resources as possible. In 1916, after some 25 years of planning and building, the final link along the Moscow–Vladivostok route was complete. The section across Mongolia, on the other hand, was only completed in 1956.

Line Names

The names of the rail lines can be a bit confusing. The Trans-Mongolian Railway goes from Běijīng through Ulaanbaatar (UB) and on to a junction called Zaudinsky, near Ulan Ude in Russia, where it meets the Trans-Siberian line and continues on to Moscow. The Trans-Siberian Railway runs between Moscow and the eastern Siberian port of Vladivostok – this route does not go through either China or Mongolia. The Trans-Manchurian Railway crosses the Russia–China border at Zabaikalsk-Mǎnzhōulǐ, also completely bypassing Mongolia.

Practicalities

Station vendors At the stations in Mongolia and Russia, there may be someone on the platform selling basic food (dumplings, soft drinks). Vendors in China offer a better variety of foods, including fruit and a range of snacks and drinks.

Restaurant cars The restaurant cars on the Russian and Chinese trains have decent food and drinks on offer for around US$3 to US$5.

Toilets Remember that toilets are normally locked whenever the train is pulled into a station and for five minutes before and after.

Showers Showers are only available in the deluxe carriages. In 2nd and 1st class, there is a washroom and toilet at the end of each carriage – which gets filthier as the trip progresses.

Charging devices Keeping your electronic devices charged can be a challenge, as outlets are limited. The attendant's cabin usually has a decent outlet and you can ask to use it.

Security The trains are reasonably safe but it's still a good idea to watch your bags closely. For added safety, lock your cabin from the inside and also make use of the security clip on the upper left-hand part of the door. The clip can be flipped open from the outside with a knife, but not if you stuff the hole with paper.

Non-Ulaanbaatar stops If you want to get off or on the Trans-Mongolian at Sükhbaatar, Darkhan or Sainshand, you'll still have to pay the full Ulaanbaatar fare. If you're not actually getting *on* the train in Ulaanbaatar, you should arrange for someone (your guesthouse manager, guide or a friend) to let the attendant know that you'll be boarding the train at a later stop. This is to ensure that your seat is not taken.

Arrive early Tickets list the train's departure times. Get to the station at least 20 minutes before *arrival* to allow enough time to find the platform and struggle on board, as the train only stops in Ulaanbaatar for about 30 minutes.

Timetable A timetable of stops hangs inside the carriage but times can shift so it's wise to double-check departure times with the *provodnista* (on-board attendant) if you get off at a station.

Bringing a bike In Běijīng, you need to take the bike to the train station one day prior to departure. No box is needed, they just wheel it onto a cargo car. If you are in Ulaanbaatar, bring your bike to the train station two days prior to departure with the bike packed in a box. A cargo fee of around T3000 is usually charged.

Smoking Lighting up is not allowed in any of the cabins but many travellers will smoke at the ends of the train cars.

What to Bring

Currency It is handy to have some US dollars in small denominations to buy meals and drinks on the train, and to exchange for the local currency so you can buy things at the train stations. It's also a good idea to buy some Russian roubles or Chinese yuan at a bank or licensed moneychanger in UB before you leave Mongolia.

Food Stock up on bread, cheese, salami, pickles and fruit before you depart, and bring some bottled water and juice. A small samovar at the end of each carriage provides constant boiling water, a godsend for making tea and coffee, as well as instant meals of packet noodles or soup.

Sleeping-bag liner Train cars are heated in winter and sheets and blankets are provided so a sleeping bag is not necessary. However, it's a good idea to bring along a sleeping-bag liner, which offers a little added comfort and warmth.

Other essential items Thongs (flip-flops) or slippers, torch (flashlight), toiletries, a mug or coffee tumbler, toilet paper, a jumper, a washcloth (or towel), some plastic cutlery, reading material, a deck of cards and comfortable long pants. Tracksuits are a must for blending in with the locals.

Baggage allowance On Chinese international trains it's 35kg (20kg on domestic trains). On all Russian trains it's 36kg. You can store your luggage inside the base of a bottom bunk (you can lift up the bunk) or in the space above the door.

Classes

With a few exceptions, all international trains have two or three classes. The names and standards of the classes depend

---

WANT MORE?

For full coverage of the Trans-Mongolian, Trans-Siberian and Trans-Manchurian routes, head to shop.lonelyplanet.com to purchase a downloadable PDF of Lonely Planet's *Trans-Siberian Railway* guide.

Trans-Mongolian Railway

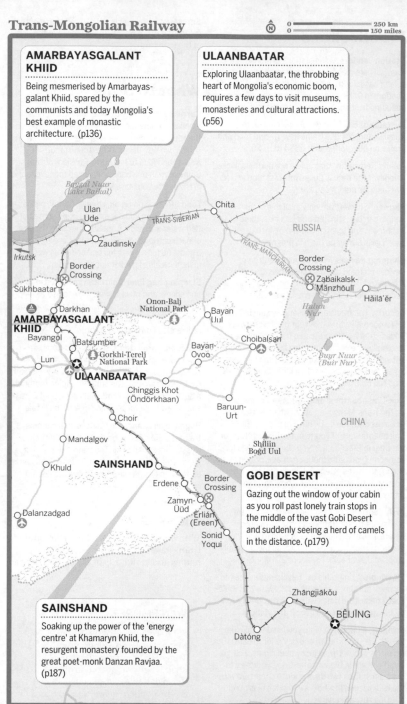

N

| 0 | 250 km |
| 0 | 150 miles |

AMARBAYASGALANT KHIID

Being mesmerised by Amarbayasgalant Khiid, spared by the communists and today Mongolia's best example of monastic architecture. (p136)

ULAANBAATAR

Exploring Ulaanbaatar, the throbbing heart of Mongolia's economic boom, requires a few days to visit museums, monasteries and cultural attractions. (p56)

GOBI DESERT

Gazing out the window of your cabin as you roll past lonely train stops in the middle of the vast Gobi Desert and suddenly seeing a herd of camels in the distance. (p179)

SAINSHAND

Soaking up the power of the 'energy centre' at Khamaryn Khiid, the resurgent monastery founded by the great poet-monk Danzan Ravjaa. (p187)

Baygal Nuur
(Lake Baikal)

Ulan Ude

Chita

RUSSIA

TRANS-SIBERIAN

TRANS-MANCHURIAN

Zaudinsky

Irkutsk

Border Crossing

Border Crossing

Zabaikalsk-Mănzhōulǐ

Sükhbaatar

Halun Nur

Hǎilā'ěr

Darkhan

Onon-Balj National Park

Bayan Uul

AMARBAYASGALANT KHIID

Bayangol

Batsumber

Bayan-Ovoo

Choibalsan

Buyr Nuur
(Buir Nur)

Lun

Gorkhi-Terelj National Park

ULAANBAATAR

Chinggis Khot (Öndörkhaan)

Baruun-Urt

CHINA

Choir

Mandalgov

Shiliin Bogd Uul

Khuld

SAINSHAND

Erdene

Border Crossing

Dalanzadgad

Zamyn-Üüd

Érlián (Ereen)

Sonid Yoqui

Zhāngjiākǒu

Dàtóng

BĚIJĪNG

on whether it's a Mongolian, Russian or Chinese train.

Second class On the Russian (and Mongolian) trains, most travellers travel in 2nd class – printed on tickets and timetables as '1/4' and known as 'hard sleeper', 'coupé' or *kupeynyy* in Russian. These are small, but perfectly comfortable, four-person compartments with bunk-style beds.

First class Sometimes called a 'soft sleeper' or *myagkiy* in Russian, this is printed as '2/4'. It has softer beds but hardly any more space than a Russian 2nd-class compartment and is not worth the considerably higher fare charged.

Deluxe class The real luxury (and expense) comes with Chinese deluxe class (printed as '1/2'): it involves roomy, two-berth compartments with a sofa, and a shower cubicle shared with the adjacent compartment. The deluxe class on Russian trains (slightly cheaper than the Chinese deluxe) has two bunks but is not much different in size from 2nd class and has no showers.

Customs & Immigration

There are delays of three to six hours at the China–Mongolia and Russia–Mongolia borders, usually at night. The whole process is not difficult or a hassle, just annoying because they keep interrupting your sleep. Your passport will be taken for inspection and stamping. When it is returned, inspect it closely – sometimes they make errors such as cancelling your return visa for China. Foreigners generally sail through customs without having their bags opened, which is one reason people on the train may approach you and ask if you'll carry some of their luggage across the border – *this is not a good idea*. During stops, you can alight and wander around the station, which is just as well because the toilets on the train are locked during the inspection procedure.

Tickets

For info on prices and schedules, see p285.

Breaking the journey The only practical way to break a journey is to buy separate tickets. If you're travelling Moscow–Běijīng and want to stop in Irkutsk and Ulaanbaatar, it's best to take a Russian domestic train to Irkutsk and then pick up the twice-weekly K23/24 between Ulaanbaatar and Běijīng.

Book early The international trains, especially the Trans-Mongolian Railway, are popular, so it's often

BOGIES

Don't be concerned if you get off at Èr-lián (on the Chinese side of the border) and the train disappears from the platform. About an hour is spent changing the bogies (wheel assemblies), because the Russians (and, therefore, the Mongolians) and the Chinese use different railway gauges. Train buffs may want to see the bogie-changing operation. Stay on the train after it disgorges passengers in Èrlián. The train then pulls into a large shed about 1km from the station. You can watch from the window of your train car.

hard to book this trip except during winter. Try to plan ahead and book as early as possible.

Leaving from UB If you are in Ulaanbaatar and want to go to Irkutsk, Běijīng or Moscow, avoid going on the Běijīng–Moscow or Moscow–Běijīng trains; use trains which *originate* in UB. In UB, you cannot buy tickets in advance for the Běijīng–Moscow or Moscow–Běijīng trains, because staff won't know how many people are already on the train. For these trains, you can only buy a ticket the day before departure. Get to the ticket office early and join the Mongolian scramble for tickets.

Booking Agents

Overseas branches of China International Travel Service (p283) or **China Travel Service** (CTS; www.chinatravelservice.com) can often book train tickets from Běijīng to Ulaanbaatar. However, the best company to deal with Trans-Siberia rail tickets is Běijīng-based Monkey Business Shrine (p284). Or try the following places:

Gateway Travel (☏02-9745 3333; www.russian-gateway.com.au; Australia)

Intourist (☏020-7538 8600; www.intourist. com; UK)

Lernidee Reisen (☏030-786 0000; www.lernidee-reisen.de; Germany)

Mir Corporation (☏206-624 7289; www.mircorp.com; USA)

Regent Holidays (☏0845-277 3317; www.regent-holidays.co.uk; UK)

The Russia Experience Ltd (☏020-8566 8846; www.trans-siberian.co.uk; UK)

Trek Escapes (☏866-338 8735; www.trek escapes.com; Canada)

Plan Your Trip
Naadam

Mongolia's penchant for war games comes to a head each summer on the vast grasslands, where competitors show off their skills in wrestling, archery and horse racing. The annual Naadam Festival is the much-anticipated culmination of these events, and it's a colourful spectacle enjoyed by locals and tourists alike.

Need to Know

Best Places to See a Naadam

While most tourists see Naadam in Ulaanbaatar (p72), the most authentic festivals are in the countryside. Khatgal, near Lake Khövsgöl, has naadams on 11–12 July and a second 'mini naadam' on 11 August (p151).

Best Party During Naadam

Around 9pm on 11 July, half of Ulaanbaatar piles into Chinggis Khaan Sq for the biggest party of the year. Light shows, fireworks, music and family fun.

Traditional Food at Naadam

The favourite treat at naadam is *khuushuur* (mutton pancakes) and everyone lines up at food stalls to get a stack. Expect to pay T700 to T1000 per *khuushuur*. As for beverages, don't miss trying some fresh *airag* (fermented mare's milk).

Going Online

Dan Golan's excellent blog (tomongolia.blogspot. co.il) is a great resource with dates for countryside naadams and a schedule of events for the Ulaanbaatar Naadam.

The Events

The Horse Races

Mongolians hold a special place in their hearts for horse racing, and naadam is the best time of year to watch this sport.

Jockeys – traditionally children between the ages of seven and 12 years – race their horses over open countryside rather than around a track. Distances range between 15km and 28km and are both exhausting and dangerous – every year jockeys tumble from their mounts and horses collapse and die from exhaustion at the finish line.

Winning horses are called *tümnii ekh*, or 'leader of 10,000'. Riders and spectators rush to comb the sweat off the best horses with a scraper traditionally made from a pelican's beak. Pelicans being quite rare these days, most people use a wooden curry-comb called a *khusuur*.

The five winning riders must drink some special *airag* (fermented mare's milk), which is then often sprinkled on the riders' heads and the horses' backsides. During the naadam festival, a song of empathy is also sung to the two-year-old horse that comes in last.

To get a good feel for it all, consider camping out at the horse-race area on 11 July, which will give you more time to explore the area in the evening and morning when the crowds are smaller. Most people visit on 12 July to see the popular five-year-old horse race, which finishes between 10am and 10.30am.

The Wrestling

Mongolian-style wrestling *(bokh)* has no weight divisions, so the biggest wrestlers (and they are big!) are often the best.

Out on the steppes, matches can go on for hours, but matches for the national Naadam have a time limit – after 30 minutes the match goes into 'overtime' (the referees give the leading wrestler a better position from the get-go). The match ends only when the first wrestler falls, or when anything other than the soles of the feet or open palms touches the ground.

The unique uniform *(jodag shuudag)* worn by the wrestlers needs some explaining. A Mongolian legend recounts that one Amazonian female entered a wrestling competition and thrashed her male competitors. In order to prevent such an embarrassing episode from happening again, the wrestling jacket was redesigned with an open chest, 'exposing' any would-be female contenders.

The Archery

After the horse races and wrestling, the third sport of naadam is archery, which is performed by both men and women. Archers use a bent composite bow made of layered horn, bark and wood. Usually arrows are made from willow and the feathers are from vultures and other birds of prey. Targets are small leather cylinders placed 4m across and 50cm high. After each shot judges, who stand near the target, emit a short cry called *uukhai*, and raise their hands in the air to indicate the quality of the shot. The first archer to knock down all his cylinders is the winner of that round.

The website www.atarn.org has a number of informative articles on Mongolian archery.

The Ankle-Bone Shooting

A new Naadam game, added in the 1990s, is ankle-bone shooting. This entails flicking a square-shaped projectile made of reindeer horn at a small target (about 3m away) made from ankle bones. It's a sort of Mongolian version of darts. The competition is held in the Ankle-Bone Shooting Hall near the archery stadium.

FOREVER TITAN BAT-ERDENE

The greatest naadam champion of all time was B Bat-Erdene, who won 11 straight naadams from 1988 to 1999. In 2000 he did not lose the naadam but rather stepped aside in order to give younger wrestlers a chance at the championship. His title, 'Dayar Dursagdah, Dalai Dayan, Tumniig Bayasuulagch, Darkhan Avarga Bat-Erdene', translates loosely as 'Renowned by All, Oceanic, Joy-Giving, Forever Titan Bat-Erdene'. Following his career in wrestling Bat-Erdene entered politics and currently serves as a member of parliament representing his native Khentii aimag. In 2013 he ran for president, losing to President Elbegdorj.

Ulaanbaatar Naadam

Countryside naadams are easy: just turn up and enjoy. In Ulaanbaatar, the Naadam needs a little more preparation.

Dates While Naadam officially kicks off on 11 July, other events get underway several days before. Uriankhai- and Buriat-style archery is held on 7 and 8 July while a children's archery tournament is held on 9 July. On 10 July, two horse races are held, the archery tournament officially begins, as does the ankle-bone shooting competition.

Banner march The festival officially begins at 9.30am on 11 July at Chinggis Khaan (Sükhbaatar) Sq when an honour guard marches the nine horse-tail banners to the stadium.

Opening ceremony The opening ceremony, which starts at 11am at the Naadam Stadium, includes a speech from the president and a 40-minute show featuring traditional music, dancing and colourful costumes.

Wrestling The wrestling starts in the stadium about 20 minutes after the ceremony and continues all day.

Horse races The horse racing is held about 40km west of the city on an open plain called Hui Doloon Khutag. Buses and minivans go there from the road north of the Naadam Stadium for around T1000. The races can be disappointing from a spectator's point of view because although the race lasts about two hours you can only see the finish. Traffic to and from the racecourse can also

COUNTRY OR CITY NAADAM?

Every village and city has a naadam; some (including the one in Ulaanbaatar) are held on 11 and 12 July, coinciding with Independence Day. Other rural naadams are held a few days before or after this date, so some planning is required if you want to see one. Once you find one, hunker down, as shops and restaurants close and transport grinds to a halt.

If you must choose between a city naadam or a country one, choose the latter. Country naadams are friendlier, more photogenic and actually easier from a logistical point of view (you won't have to deal with big crowds or traffic). These smaller festivals also feel more authentic and traditional although they too are showing signs of modernising.

Naadam in Ulaanbaatar has all the trappings of a big sporting event, with jostling crowds, souvenir salesmen, traffic and screeching loudspeakers. Most locals will simply watch the events at home on TV. Although it's less intimate than small naadams, it is nice to see Ulaanbaatar in a more relaxed mood with plenty of associated concerts and theatre events.

be horrendous. What is nice about the event is not so much the race itself but the generally festive atmosphere around the horse-race grounds.

Other events Most people file out of the stadium after the opening ceremony to catch a little archery or ankle-bone shooting. Around the stadium are carnival games and rides for kids, as well as food tents. On the night of 11 July, a concert and fireworks display are held on Chinggis Khaan Sq.

Closing ceremony In comparison with the opening ceremony, almost nothing happens at the closing ceremony. The winning wrestler is awarded, the ceremonial horse banners are marched away, and everyone goes home. It is held at about 8pm on 12 July, but the exact time depends on when the wrestling finishes.

Post-Naadam events Quite a few events now happen on 13 July at the horse-race area. A mini-naadam is held for the benefit of trainers; you'll see cultural performances and wrestling. You could even ride your own horse to the racing grounds. Stepperiders (p103) does four-day trips from its base near Bogd Khan Uul.

Program To find out what is going on during the festival, look for the events program in the two English-language newspapers.

Information The website http://naadam.viahistoria. com has pictures and historical information on naadam and the associated sporting events.

Naadam Tickets

Admission to the stadium (except for the two ceremonies) and to the archery and horse racing is free, but you'll definitely need a ticket for the opening ceremony and possibly the last round or two of the wrestling and closing ceremony.

Cost Ticket costs vary per section; the north side of the stadium (which is protected from the sun and rain by a roof) is more expensive, with tickets going for US$40 or more. The cheapest ones are around US$12.

Buying tickets Tickets are sold at the Naadam Stadium and at the Cultural Palace (p59). They usually go on sale on 6 July but can be nearly impossible to get on your own, as locals stand in line for hours to scoop them all up. The guesthouses and hotels always manage to get a few for their guests and this is the best way to get one. You can try to buy one from a scalper outside the stadium before the opening ceremony, but the going price is around T50,000.

Regions at a Glance

Most first-time travellers to Mongolia spend a day or two in the capital Ulaanbaatar before setting off for the countryside. The most popular destination is the iconic Gobi; a trip here usually loops in part of central Mongolia as it's fairly easy to combine the two regions. Northern Mongolia, specifically Lake Khövsgöl, is the second most popular destination. All three of these areas have built up a solid tourist infrastructure, with lots of ger camps along established routes.

Western Mongolia sees fewer visitors, largely because of its great distance from Ulaanbaatar and the cost of getting a flight there. However, the west does offer some spectacular scenery and is a great place for the adventurous. The east is Mongolia's least-known and least-visited region (only 3% of tourists head this way), a blessing for explorers wanting an off-the-beaten-path experience.

Ulaanbaatar

Shopping
Museums
Entertainment

Art & Clothing

Ulaanbaatar is the best place for shopping. Pick up cashmere jumpers, artwork, crafts, antiques, traditional clothing, CDs and souvenirs. Visit galleries and buy directly from the artists.

Mongolia's Best Museums

Mongolia's best museums are a must for a deeper understanding of the country. Some are neglected; others recently renovated and modernised. The National Museum is a must-see.

Culture & Nightlife

Options include Mongolian culture shows, operas, dramas, concerts and fashion shows, especially during the summer tourist season. Bars and nightclubs cater to both foreigners and locals.

p56

Central Mongolia

Historic Sites
Nature
Horse Riding

Ancient Art

Arkhangai aimag has deer stones and ancient Turkic monuments carved with runic script. Some ancient monasteries survived Stalin's purge; the best is Erdene Zuu, with walls built from the ruins of Karakorum.

Lakes & Mountains

There's marvellous scenery in the Khan Khentii Strictly Protected Area. Or head west to the Khangai Mountains to explore the Orkhon waterfall, the Great White Lake and the remote Naiman Nuur.

Lakeside Rides

The Orkhon valley is great for horse trekking, especially from the Orkhon waterfall to Naiman Nuur. Terkhiin Tsagaan Nuur is also good, or closer to UB, try the forests north of Terelj.

p98

Northern Mongolia

Fishing
Culture
Hiking

Fishing Holes

Fishing holes in northern Mongolia are world class. The big prize here is taimen, the world's largest salmonoid. Help protect this endangered species and go with an experienced guide.

Tsaatan People

Khövsgöl is a culturally distinct part of Mongolia. The aimag features the unique Tsaatan, a tribe of reindeer herders, and if you're lucky you can visit a shaman ceremony while in the north.

Backcountry Trips

There is wonderful backcountry in Khövsgöl aimag. Hikes can last from one day to more than a week. One of the most popular is along the west shore of Khövsgöl Nuur and through the mountains to Renchinlkhumbe.

p129

Eastern Mongolia

Wildlife
Historic Sites
Horse Riding

Gazelle Spotting

Spotting gazelles on the eastern steppe rivals any wildlife experience you can have in Asia. Nömrög, in the country's far east, is another place to see wildlife, including moose, otters and bears.

Chinggis Khaan

In Khentii take a trip along the Chinggis Khaan Trail, visiting sites associated with his life. The adventurous can head to Khalkhiin Gol to see the enormous Janraisag Buddha and WWII battlefields.

Mountain Rides

The horse trekking through the mountains of Khentii, especially around Dadal, is among Mongolia's best. Follow rivers, camp amid gorgeous scenery and learn horse-handling skills from local Buriats.

p160

The Gobi

Camel Riding
Off-The-Beaten-Track
Palaeontology

Sand-Dune Camel Treks

Trekking across sand dunes on a camel is the iconic Gobi experience. Pack camping gear and plenty of water – you can trek at Khongoryn Els and Ongiin Khiid.

Gobi Desert

The Gobi Desert is the most sparsely populated region of Mongolia and there are huge areas where the number of yearly tourists can be counted on one hand. Head for Khermen Tsav or southern Gov-Altai.

Dinosaur Bones

The palaeontological record in the Gobi is astounding – a little digging and you might find a cache of fossilised bones or dinosaur eggs. Try Bayanzag, where Roy Chapman Andrews uncovered hundreds of dinosaur skeletons in the 1920s.

p179

Western Mongolia

Historic Sites
Hiking
Eagle Hunting

Bronze Age Art

The Altai Mountains are rich in Bronze Age sites, many unmarked and undocumented. Altai Tavan Bogd National Park has petroglyphs, massive burial mounds and ancient stone statues of warriors. The rock-art gallery at Tsagaan Sala is one of the most impressive in Central Asia.

Tough Treks

Western Mongolia is ripe for experienced hikers in search of a challenge. Try the lakes in Altai Tavan Bogd National Park or in the Kharkhiraa Uul region of Uvs.

Kazakh Eagles

Visit Bayan-Ölgii from November to March and you may see Kazakh eagle hunters in search of prey. A stunning experience, it requires time, patience, a good guide and luck.

p206

On the Road

Ulaanbaatar
Улаанбаатар

☑ 011, 021, 051, 7035 / POP 1,287,100 / AREA 1368 SQ KM

Best Places to Eat

➡ Millie's Café (p80)

➡ Namaste (p81)

➡ Mongolians (p82)

➡ Rosewood Kitchen + Enoteca (p79)

Best Places to Stay

➡ Lotus Guesthouse (p73)

➡ Zaya's Hostel (p75)

➡ Hotel Örgöö (p74)

➡ Best Western Tuushin Hotel (p75)

Why Go?

If Mongolia's yin is its pristine countryside, then Ulaanbaatar (UB) conforms nicely to its yang. An enormous city of pulsating commerce, wild traffic, sinful nightlife and bohemian counter-culture, the Mongolian capital elicits as much shock as it does excitement. The contrasts within the city can be exasperating too: Armani-suited businessmen rub shoulders with mohawked punks and *del*-clad nomads fresh off the steppes. One minute you're dodging the path of a Hummer H2 and the next you're mystified by groaning Buddhist monks at Gandan Khiid. It's a wild place that bursts into life after slumbering through a long winter. This chaotic capital is not the easiest city to navigate, but with a little patience, travellers can take care of all their logistical needs, watch traditional theatre, sample international cuisine and party till three in the morning. This ever-changing city may be the biggest surprise of your Mongolian adventure.

When to Go
Ulaanbaatar

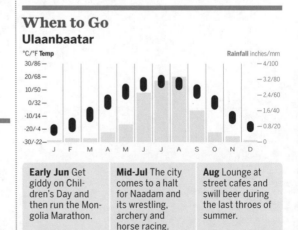

Early Jun Get giddy on Children's Day and then run the Mongolia Marathon.

Mid-Jul The city comes to a halt for Naadam and its wrestling, archery and horse racing.

Aug Lounge at street cafes and swill beer during the last throes of summer.

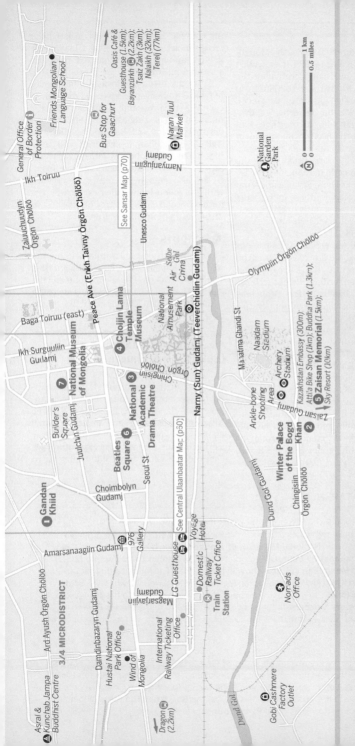

Ulaanbaatar Highlights

1 Walk the prayer circuit around **Gandan Khiid** (p67), the country's largest monastery.

2 Wonder at the eccentric collection of curios and artefacts at the **Winter Palace of the Bogd Khan** (p69).

3 Take in a performance of traditional dance and music at the **National Academic Drama Theatre** (p84).

4 Step back in time with a tour of the **Choijin Lama Temple Museum** (p55), an ancient relic surrounded by modern downtown.

5 Amble up the steps at **Zaisan Memorial** (p70) for sweeping views of the city.

6 Chill out on **Beatles Square** (p67), the summertime haunt of fashionable youth, skaters and travellers.

7 Weave through Mongolia's ancient past at the **National Museum of Mongolia** (p59).

History

The first recorded capital city of the Mongolian empire was created in 1639. It was called Örgöö and was originally located at the monastery of Da Khuree, some 420km from Ulaanbaatar in Arkhangai aimag (province). The monastery was the residence of five-year-old Zanabazar who, at the time, had been proclaimed the head of Buddhism in Mongolia. Because it consisted of felt tents, the 'city' was easily transported when the grass went dry. Some 25 movements were recorded along the Orkhon, Selenge and Tuul Gols (rivers). Throughout these movements the city was given some fairly unexciting official and unofficial names, including Khuree (Camp) in 1706.

In 1778 Khuree was erected at its present location and called the City of Felt. Later the city became known as Ikh Khuree (Great Camp) and was under the rule of the Bogd Gegeen (Living Buddha). The Manchus, however, used Uliastai as the administrative capital of Outer Mongolia.

In 1911 when Mongolia first proclaimed its independence from China, the city became the capital of Outer Mongolia and was renamed Niislel Khuree (Capital Camp). In 1918 it was invaded by the Chinese and three years later by the Russians.

Finally, in 1924 the city was renamed Ulaanbaatar (Red Hero), in honour of the communist triumph, and declared the official capital of an 'independent' Mongolia (independent from China, not from the Soviet Union). The *khangard* (garuda), symbolising courage and honesty, was declared the city's official symbol. In 1933 Ulaanbaatar gained autonomy and separated from the surrounding Töv aimag.

From the 1940s the Soviets built the city in typical Russian style: lots of large, brightly coloured theatres and cavernous government buildings. Tragically, the Soviets also destroyed many old Russian buildings as well as Mongolian monasteries and temples. Today the city heaves with construction projects fueled by Mongolia's mining boom. It has also enjoyed a cultural resurgence with lots of museums, galleries, theatre performances and clubs bringing out the best in 21st-century Mongolian culture.

◉ Sights

Most sights are located within a 15-minute walk of Chinggis Khaan (Sükhbaatar) Sq. The Winter Palace of the Bogd Khan and the Zaisan Memorial are a short bus ride south of the city. Gandan Khiid is about 2km to the west.

◉ Chinggis Khaan (Sükhbaatar) Square

In July 1921 in the centre of Ulaanbaatar, the 'hero of the revolution', Damdin Sükhbaatar, declared Mongolia's final independence from the Chinese. The **square** (Чингис Хааны (Сүхбаатарын) Таллбай; Map p60) now features a bronze **statue of Sükhbaatar** astride his horse. In 2013 the city authorities changed the name from Sükhbaatar Sq to

---

ULAANBAATAR IN...

Two Days

Ulaanbaatar's main sights can be seen in a couple of days. On your first morning in town pay a visit to the **National Museum of Mongolia** then take a turn around **Chinggis Khaan (Sükhbaatar) Square**. After lunch visit the **Choijin Lama Temple Museum**. Watch a **Mongolian cultural show** in the evening. The following day get up early to visit **Gandan Khiid** in time to catch the monks chanting. Head down to the **State Department Store** to shop for souvenirs and then make your way to the **Mongolian Statehood History Museum**. Later in the day, head south to the **Winter Palace of the Bogd Khan**. Finally, climb the steps to **Zaisan Memorial** to watch the sun set over the city.

Four Days

On day three visit the **Zanabazar Museum of Fine Arts** and then head over to **Naran Tuul Market**. In the evening down a pint or two on the deck of the **Grand Khaan Irish Pub** and then hit **iLoft** nightclub after midnight. On day four take a day trip out of town to mountain bike to the **Observatory** or hike over the **Bogdkhan Uul**. Have dinner at **Namaste** then listen to live music at **River Sounds**.

Chinggis Khaan Sq, although many citizens still refer to it by the old name.

Peaceful anti-communism protests were held here in 1990, which eventually ushered in the era of democracy. Today, the square (talbai) is occasionally used for rallies, ceremonies and rock concerts and festivals, but is generally a relaxed place where kiddies drive toy cars and teens whiz around on bikes. An ice-skating rink is set up on the square in winter. Near the centre of the square, look for the large **plaque** that lists the former names of the city – Örgöö, Nomiin Khuree, Ikh Khuree and Niislel Khuree. The large **warehouse** on the square houses temporary exhibits. Poke your head inside to see what's on.

To the east of the square is the 1970s Soviet-style **Cultural Palace** (Map p60; ☑ 11-321 444), a useful landmark containing the Mongolian National Modern Art Gallery (p66) and several other cultural institutions. At the southeast corner of the square, the salmon-pinkish building is the State Opera & Ballet Theatre (p85). Just south of the Opera House is the symbol of the country's new wealth, **Central Tower** (Map p60), which houses luxury shops including Louis Vuitton and Armani.

The bullet-grey building to the southwest is the **Mongolian Stock Exchange** (Map p60), which was opened in 1992 in the former Children's Cinema.

Chinggis Khaan Statue   MONUMENT
(Map p60; Chinggis Khaan Sq) The enormous marble construction at the north end of UB's main square was completed in 2006 in time for the 800th anniversary of Chinggis Khaan's coronation. At its centre is a seated bronze Chinggis Khaan statue, lording it over his nation. He is flanked by Ögedei (on the west) and Kublai (east). Two famed Mongol soldiers (Boruchu and Mukhlai) guard the entrance to the monument.

Parliament House   GOVERNMENT BUILDING
(Засгын Газрын Ордон, Government House; Map p60; Chinggis Khaan Sq) Behind the Chinggis Khaan Statue stands Parliament House, which is commonly known as Government House. An inner courtyard of the building holds a large ceremonial ger used for hosting visiting dignitaries.

Mongolian Statehood History Museum   MUSEUM
(Монголын Төрийн Түүхийн Музей; Map p60; Chinggis Khaan Sq; ◎10am-1pm & 2-5pm Tue-Sun)

ℹ REGISTRATION
The Office of Immigration, Naturalisation & Foreign Citizens, which registers passports, is located about 2km from the airport. If you need to register your passport or need to apply for a visa extension, you should visit this office when you land (if that's during working hours). This will save you having to make a second trip out to the airport for registration. To get there from the airport, walk out to the main road, turn right and walk 900m, then turn right again and walk 350m. The large round building (a sports arena) is a nearby landmark. For more on registration and visa extensions, see p277.

FREE Located inside Government House, this free museum showcases Mongolia's diplomatic relations stretching back to the time of the great khaans.

The highlight is the upstairs hall where visiting heads of state gather in front of the nine horsetail banners (the same ones on display in the stadium during Naadam). On the main level you can see seals used by Mongolian royalty and gifts given by foreign leaders to Mongolia's presidents.

The museum also has an interesting gift shop where you can buy government-sanctioned souvenirs, such as commemorative coins and Chinggis Khaan replica statues.

Statue of S Zorig   MONUMENT
(Map p60; Chinggis Khaan Sq) Across from the Central Post Office (CPO) is a statue of S Zorig, who at the age of 27 helped to lead the protests that brought down communism in 1990 (and was assassinated in 1998).

◉ West of Chinggis Khaan Square

★National Museum of Mongolia   MUSEUM
(Монголын Үндэсний Музей; Map p60; ☑ 7011 0913; cnr Juulchin Gudamj & Sükhbaataryn Gudamj; adult/student T5000/2500; ◎9.30am-5.30pm, closed Sun & Mon mid-Sep–mid-May) Mongolia's National Museum sweeps visitors from the Neolithic era right to the present day.

The 1st floor has some interesting exhibits on Stone Age sites in Mongolia, as well as petroglyphs, deer stones (stone sculptures of reindeer and other animals) and burial sites from the Hun and Uighur eras. Look

Central Ulaanbaatar

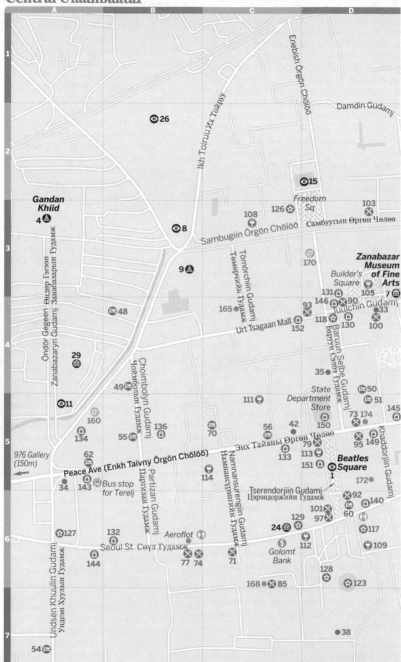

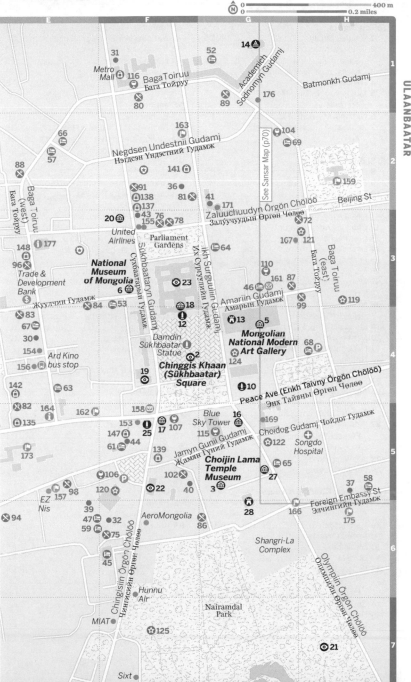

0   400 m
0   0.2 miles

31
Metro
Mall
116   BagaToiruu
Бага Тойруу
80
52
14
Academich
Sodnomyn Gudamj
Batmonkh Gudamj
89
176
163
104
69
66
57
Negdsen Undestnii Gudamj
Нэгдсэн Үндэсний Гудамж
88
159
Baga Toiruu
(west)
Бага Тойруу
141
36
91
81
41
171
Zaluuchuudyn Örgön Chölöö
Залуучуудын Өргөн Чөлөө
Beijing St
138
137
43   76
155   78
72
20
United
Airlines
Sükhbaataryn Gudamj
Сүхбаатарын Гудамж
Parliament
Gardens
64
148   177
96
Trade &
Development
Bank
National
Museum
of Mongolia
6
Ikh Surguuliin Gudamj
Их Сургуулийн Гудамж
167   121
Baga Toiruu
(east)
Бага Тойруу
110
161   87
46
99
119
Жуулчин Гудамж
84   53
23
Amariin Gudamj
Амарын Гудамж
83
67
30
154
156
Ard Kino
bus stop
18
12
Damdin
Sükhbaatar
Statue
13
5
Mongolian
National Modern
Art Gallery
68
124
19
2
Chinggis Khaan
(Sükhbaatar)
Square
10
Peace Ave (Enkh Taïvny Örgön Chölöö)
Энх Тайвны Өргөн Чөлөө
142
82
164
162   158
135
153   25
147   17   107
Blue
Sky Tower
16
115
169
Choidog Gudamj Чойдог Гудамж
122
Songdo
Hospital
61   44
173
139
Jamyn Gunii Gudamj
Жамян Гүний Гудамж
Choijin Lama
Temple
Museum
3
65
27
106
120
98
157
EZ
Nis
39
47   32
59   75
102
22
40
28
166
175
58
37
Foreign Embassy St
Элчингийн Гудамж
94
AeroMongolia
86
45
Shangri-La
Complex
Chingisiin Örgön Chölöö
Чингисийн Өргөн Чөлөө
Hunnu
Air
MIAT
125
Nairamdal
Park
Olympiin Örgön Chölöö
Олимпиин Өргөн Чөлөө
21
Sixt

ULAANBAATAR

Central Ulaanbaatar

THE BIG ASHTRAY

Ulaanbaatar means 'Red Hero'. However, in winter a more apropos name would be 'Kharbaatar', the 'Black Hero', as the city is often cloaked in a thick cloud of noxious smoke that can linger for days until a strong wind blows it away.

By 2011 the air pollution had reached such epic levels that the World Health Organization (WHO) rated Ulaanbaatar the world's second most polluted city, after Ahvaz in western Iran.

But unlike Ahvaz, which is polluted year-round, Ulaanbaatar's pollution is packed into the winter months, from November to March, when families in the ger districts furiously burn coal to fend off the extreme cold. Around 92% of the smoke in UB comes from stoves in the ger districts.

In the worst-affected areas of the city, the levels of PM2.5 (particulate matter that is 2.5 micrometres or less) can exceed an appalling 2500. According to WHO, 300 or above is considered 'hazardous'. Levels in the city centre aren't quite so horrific but can still regularly exceed 1000 in winter.

To help cut pollution the government has sold around 120,000 subsidised Turkish-built stoves to families in ger areas. The stoves are more fuel-efficient and cleaner burning than the traditional Mongolian stove, however they still emit some smoke so the project is considered just a temporary fix.

The longer-term solution is to bring central heat and apartments to the gers areas. But with a short building season and 180,000 families needing modern housing, the project could be years, if not decades, in the making.

To see the latest PM2.5 measurements in Ulaanbaatar, search for the 'UB Air Quality Info' page on Facebook.

---

for the remarkable **gold treasure** (including a golden tiara), found in 2001 by archaeologists digging near the Kul-Teginii Monument in Övörkhangai.

The 2nd floor houses an outstanding collection of costumes, hats and jewellery, representing most of Mongolia's ethnic groups. Take a gander at some of the elaborate silverwork of the Dariganga minority or the outrageous headgear worn by Khalkh Mongols. Some of the outfits contain 20kg to 25kg of silver ornamentation!

The 3rd floor is a must-see for fans of the Mongol horde. The collection includes real examples of 12th-century Mongol armour, and correspondence between Pope Innocent IV and Guyuk Khaan. Written in Latin and Persian and dated 13 November 1246, it bears the seal of the khaan. There is also a display of traditional Mongolian culture with, among other things, a furnished ger, traditional herding and domestic implements, saddles and musical instruments. In the 20th-century-history section, look out for D Sükhbaatar's famous hollow horsewhip, inside which he hid a secret letter written in 1920 by the Bogd Khan enlisting the aid of the Russian Red Army.

The final hall contains a self-congratulatory display of Mongolia's recent history and the 1990 democratic revolution, with no mention of the breadlines of the early 1990s or other hardships of the transition from communism to democracy.

Museum of Natural History   MUSEUM
(Байгалийн Түүхийн Музей; Map p60; cnr Sükhbaataryn Gudamj & Sambugiin Örgön Chölöö) Built in the 1950s, this antique building served as a repository of natural exhibits for many decades. It contained displays of Mongolia's geology, flora, fauna and fossils. However, at the time of research the building was closed due to structural damage.

★ Zanabazar Museum of Fine Arts   MUSEUM
(Занабазарын Уран Зургийн Музей; Map p60; ☑11-326 060; Juulchin Gudamj; adult/student T5000/2000; ☉9am-5.30pm) This fine-arts museum has a superb collection of paintings, carvings and sculptures, including many by the revered sculptor and artist Zanabazar (see p138). It also contains other rare, and sometimes old, religious exhibits such as scroll *thangka* (paintings) and Buddhist statues, representing the best display of its kind in Mongolia. A bonus is that most of the exhibit captions in the museum are in English.

The second room contains some fine examples of the sculptor's work, including five Dhyani, or Contemplation, Buddhas (cast in 1683) and Tara in her 21 manifestations.

Also worth checking out are the wonderful *tsam* masks (worn by monks during religious ceremonies) and the intricate paintings, *One Day in Mongolia* and the *Airag Feast*, by the renowned artist B Sharav. These paintings depict almost every aspect of nomadic life.

As you enter the building, on the left a room displays ancient art, including deer stones that date to the Bronze Age. To the right is a shop selling souvenirs and contemporary art.

The building itself carries some historical value. It was built in 1905, making it one of the oldest Manchu-era commercial buildings in the city. It was first used as a Chinese Bank, Soviet troops stayed here in the 1920s and it later served as Ulaanbaatar's first State Department Store. It has been an art museum since 1966.

South of Chinggis Khaan Square

★ **Choijin Lama Temple Museum** MUSEUM
(Чойжин Ламын Хийд-Музей; Map p60; ☑11-324 788; off Jamyn Gunii Gudamj; adult/student/child T5000/2500/500; audio guide T5000; ⊙9am-7.30pm daily Jun-Sep, 10am-4.30pm Tue-Sat Oct-May) This temple museum is a hidden gem of architecture and history, smack in the middle of downtown Ulaanbaatar. It was the home of Luvsan Haidav Choijin Lama ('Choijin' is an honorary title given to some monks), the state oracle and brother of the Bogd Khan. Construction of the monastery commenced in 1904 and was completed four years later. It was closed in 1938 and probably would have been demolished had it not been saved in 1942 to serve as a museum demonstrating the 'feudal' ways of the past. Although religious freedom in Mongolia recommenced in 1990, this monastery is no longer an active place of worship.

There are five temples within the grounds. As you enter, the first temple you see is the **Maharaja Süm**. The **main temple** features statues of Sakyamuni (the historical Buddha), Choijin Lama and Baltung Choimba (the teacher of the Bogd Khan), whose mummified remains are inside the statue. There are also some fine *thangka*s and some of the best *tsam* masks in the country. The

gongkhang (protector chapel) behind the main hall contains the oracle's throne and a magnificent statue of *yab-yum* (mystic sexual union).

The other temples are **Zuu Süm**, dedicated to Sakyamuni; **Yadam Süm**, which contains wooden and bronze statues of various gods, some created by the famous Mongolian sculptor Zanabazar; and **Amgalan Süm**, containing a self-portrait of Zanabazar himself and a small stupa apparently brought to Ulaanbaatar by Zanabazar from Tibet.

The complex is located off Jamyn Gunii Gudamj, with the entrance on the south side.

Mongol Costumes Centre GALLERY
(Map p60; ☑11-328 840; Olympiin Örgön Chölöö; adult/child T3000/1000; ⊙10am-6pm Mon-Sat, 11am-5.30pm Sun) This place designs and manufactures many of the fabulous *dels* (traditional coats) that are worn during the Naadam opening ceremony and other state events. You can see the different varieties of *del* and even dress up in traditional Mongolian gear for a professional photo shoot.

The highlight of the centre is a small **museum**, which features traditional Mongolian garments, as well as ethnographic artefacts, old chess sets, jewellery and replica 13th-century battle gear. The museum is in an adjacent room that is sometimes locked so you may have to ask for it to be opened up.

Victims of Political Persecution Memorial Museum MUSEUM
(Улс Төрийн Хилс Хэрэгт Хэлмэгдэгсдийн Дурсгалын Музей; Map p60; ☑7011 0915; cnr Gendeniin Gudamj & Olympiin Örgön Chölöö; adult/child T3000/1000; ⊙10am-5pm, closed Sat & Sun Nov-Feb) This little-known museum houses a series of haunting displays that chronicle the communist purges of the 1930s – an aggressive campaign to eliminate 'counter-revolutionaries'. During the campaign, intellectuals were arrested and put on trial, sent to Siberian labour camps or shot. Mongolia lost its top writers, scientists and thinkers.

The neglected building that houses the museum is one of the oldest in Ulaanbaatar. It was once the home of former prime minister P Genden, who was executed in Moscow by the KGB in 1937 for refusing Stalin's orders to carry out the purge. Stalin found a more willing puppet in Marshall Choibalsan, whose purge ended in the deaths of more than 27,000 Mongolians, mostly lamas. On the ground floor of the museum is a

DON'T MISS

MUSEUM OF DINOSAURS

One of Mongolia's biggest attractions is its rich collection of dinosaur fossils and dinosaur eggs, found mainly at spots throughout the Gobi such as the famous 'Flaming Cliffs'.

At the time of writing, the Ministry of Tourism, Sport and Culture was planning to open a brand-new **Museum of Dinosaurs** in Ulaanbaatar to show off the finest specimens. A final location has not been determined although it might be housed in the **Former Lenin Centre** (Map p60; Freedom Sq). Check with the Ulaanbaatar Information Centre (p92) for news on the museum location and details. For more on Mongolia's fossil record see p198.

replica of Genden's office, with his desk and other personal effects.

The descriptions are only in Mongolian so it's a good idea to bring a guide who can make sense of it all. The guard who keeps the key to the place sometimes disappears for several days so you may find it closed during normal hours.

Wedding Palace   PALACE

(Map p60; Khurimiin Ordon) The large, white square building located just southwest of the Victims of Political Persecution Memorial Museum is called the Wedding Palace. Built in 1976 by the Russians, it has since been used for tens of thousands of wedding ceremonies, including the marital vows of a few foreigners.

Mongolian Artists' Exhibition Hall   ART GALLERY

(Монголын Зураачдын Үзэсгэлэнгийн Танхим; Map p60; ✆11-327 474; cnr Peace Ave & Chingisiin Örgön Chölöö; ⊙9am-6pm) **FREE** If you want to see Mongolian art, and maybe buy some, head into the Mongolian Artists' Exhibition Hall, on the 2nd floor of the white-marble building diagonally opposite the CPO. This is a rotating collection of modern and often dramatic paintings, carvings, tapestries and sculptures, and a good souvenir shop.

National Amusement Park   AMUSEMENT PARK

(Үндэсний Соёл Амралтын Хүрээлэн, Children's Park; Map p60; adult/student T1000/700; 👶) Known to almost everyone as the 'Children's Park', this small amusement park features rides, games and paddleboats. The target audience is the 12-and-under set, so it's perfect if you are travelling with small kids. The park entrance is on the southeast corner. For the rides you buy individual tickets, around T3000 to T5000 a pop. It's open year-round; in winter there's ice skating for T2000 per 90 minutes.

◉ East of Chinggis Khaan Square

★Mongolian National Modern Art Gallery   ART GALLERY

(Монголын Уран Зургийн Үзэсгэлэн; Map p60; ✆11-331 687; www.art-gallery.mn; admission T2000; ⊙10am-6pm May-Sep, 9am-5pm Oct-Apr) Sometimes called the Fine Art Gallery, this place contains a large and impressive display of modern and uniquely Mongolian paintings and sculptures, with nomadic life, people and landscapes all depicted in styles ranging from impressionistic to nationalistic. The Soviet romantic paintings depicted in *thangka* style are especially interesting, but the most famous work is Ochir Tsevegjav's 1958 *The Fight of the Stallions*.

The entrance is in the courtyard of the Cultural Palace. The main gallery is on the 3rd floor and there are temporary exhibits on the 2nd floor.

Theatre Museum   MUSEUM

(Map p60; Amariin Gudamj; admission T1500; ⊙9am-5pm Mon-Fri) The history of film and theatre in Mongolia is told through photographs and models at this small museum located on the 3rd floor of the Cultural Palace. The collection includes old costumes, cameras and musical instruments used by actors, producers and musicians that have worked in Mongolia's entertainment industry. One room is dedicated to the saint Danzan Ravjaa, the 18th-century poet and playwright who directed theatre in the Gobi Desert (see p186). Displays include costumes and masks used in his opera, the *Life Story of the Moon Cuckoo*. The entrance is on the north side of the Cultural Palace, opposite XacBank.

North of Chinggis Khaan Square

Dashchoilon Khiid BUDDHIST MONASTERY
(Дашчойлон Хийд; Map p60; ☑11-350 047; Academich Sodnomyn Gudamj) FREE Originally built in 1890 and destroyed in the late 1930s, this monastery was partially rebuilt and is now located in three huge concrete gers that once formed part of the State Circus. There are plans afoot to expand the monastery to include a six-storey building which will house a 17m-high statue of Maidar. So far, the only part of the statue to exist is the 108-bead rosary, donated by monks from Japan (each bead weighs 45.5kg, making it the largest rosary in the world). You can get to Dashchoilon from a lane running off Baga Toiruu – look out for the orange-and-brown roof.

State Department Store Area

★ Beatles Square SQUARE
(Tserendorjiin Gudamj; Map p60) The plaza located between the State Department Store and the Circus has an unofficial name: Beatles Square, named after a new monument to the Fab Four located close to its northern end. The monument features bronze images of John, Paul, George and Ringo on one side, and on the other a sculpture of a young man sitting in a stairwell strumming a guitar. The sculpture recalls the 1970s era in Ulaanbaatar when groups of teenagers would gather in apartment stairwells and sing Beatles songs, which they learned from contraband records smuggled here from Eastern Europe. The plaza – surrounded by cafes, restaurants and cashmere shops – is a popular meeting place and hub of activity in summer when locals relax by the fountains.

Red Ger Art Gallery GALLERY
(Map p60; Seoul St, ground fl, Khan Bank Bldg; ◔9am-6pm Mon-Sat) The Red Ger Art Gallery showcases modern artwork by Mongolia's top contemporary painters. The artwork is for sale and 30% of the proceeds go to supporting the Arts Council of Mongolia. The gallery is located inside the Khan Bank building on Seoul St. Check their Facebook page for events and info.

Gandan Monastery Area

★ Gandan Khiid BUDDHIST MONASTERY
(Гандан Хийд, Gandantegchinlen Khiid; Map p60; Öndör Gegeen Zanabazaryn Gudamj; admission T3500; ◔8.30am-7pm) Around the start of the 19th century, more than 100 *süm* (temples) and *khiid* (monasteries) served a population of about 50,000 in Urga (the former name of Ulaanbaatar). Only a handful of these buildings survived the religious purges of 1937. It wasn't until the early 1990s that the people of Mongolia started to openly practise Buddhism again. This monastery is one of Mongolia's most important, and also one of its biggest tourist attractions. The full name, Gandantegchinlen, translates roughly as 'the great place of complete joy'.

Building was started in 1838 by the fourth Bogd Gegeen, but as with most monasteries in Mongolia, the purges of 1937 fell heavily

ULAANBAATAR'S HIDDEN TREASURE OF BUDDHIST TEXTS

The **National Library of Mongolia** (Map p60; ☑11-322 396; Chingisiin Örgön Chöloo; ◔9am-5pm Mon-Fri Jun-Sep, 9am-8pm Mon-Fri, 9am-5pm Sat & Sun Oct-May), an unassuming neoclassical building in downtown Ulaanbaatar, houses a secret. Deep in its bowels is the world's largest collection of Buddhist texts.

Most of the collection was built from the mid-1960s to the 1980s, several decades after the Buddhist purge destroyed nearly every monastery in the country. Researchers started collecting the Sutras (Buddhist texts) from families that had hidden them during the purge. More than one million texts have so far been identified, including verses by Nagajuna, a 2nd-century Indian philosopher, inscribed on birch bark.

Tibetan, Mongolian and Sanskrit manuscripts have been found. A project to catalogue them all using a digital archive began in 1999 with assistance from New York–based nonprofit Asia Classic Input Project (ACIP). Work is expected to continue until at least 2016.

Unfortunately, the National Library is closed to casual visitors. If you are particularly interested in the collection, an Ulaanbaatar-based tour operator might be able to set up a visit.

THE WORLD'S BIGGEST PARK?

A new park, still under construction in the southern part of Ulaanbaatar, has been named the 'National Garden Park' but most locals simply call it the 'Big Park'.

The park contains a circular bike path and bike rentals (T2000 for one ride around), sport courts, a fountain and a replica Korean garden (Seoul Park). The park is still a bit raw and forlorn but as the trees grow it should improve over the years.

There are plans to expand the park, eventually creating what local officials say will be the world's largest city park. Such a concept could be decades in the making, but given the lack of parks in the city centre such a development is highly anticipated.

At the time of writing the park was not on any city bus route but would make a nice destination if you are biking around the city. Travel south along Olympiin Örgön Chölöö, go over the train tracks and take the second left.

on Gandan. When the US vice president Henry Wallace asked to see a monastery during his visit to Mongolia in 1944, Prime Minister Choibalsan guiltily scrambled to open this one to cover up the fact that he had recently laid waste to Mongolia's religious heritage. Gandan remained a 'show monastery' for other foreign visitors until 1990, when full religious ceremonies recommenced. Today more than 600 monks belong to the monastery.

As you enter the main entrance from the south, a path leads towards the right to a courtyard containing two temples. The northeast building is **Ochidara Temple** (sometimes called Gandan Süm), where the most significant ceremonies are held. As you follow the *kora* (pilgrim) path clockwise around this building, you see a large statue behind glass of Tsongkhapa, the founder of the Gelugpa sect. The two-storey **Didan-Lavran Temple** in the courtyard was home to the 13th Dalai Lama during his stay here in 1904 (when he fled Lhasa ahead of a British invasion of Tibet).

At the end of the main path as you enter is the magnificent white **Migjid Janraisig Süm**, the monastery's main attraction. Lining the walls of the temple are hundreds of images of Ayush, the Buddha of Longevity, which stare through the gloom to the magnificent Migjid Janraisig statue.

The original statue was commissioned by the eighth Bogd Khan in 1911, in hopes that it might restore his eyesight – syphilis had blinded him; however, it was carted away by Russia in 1937 (it was allegedly melted down to make bullets). The new statue was dedicated in 1996 and built with donations from Japan and Nepal. It is 26m high and made of copper with a gilt gold covering. The hollow statue contains 27 tonnes of medicinal

herbs, 334 Sutras, two million bundles of mantras, plus an entire ger with furniture!

To the east of the temple are four **colleges of Buddhist philosophy**, including the yellow building dedicated to Kalachakra, a wrathful Buddhist deity.

To the west of the temple is the **Öndör Gegeen Zanabazar Buddhist University**, which was established in 1970. It is usually closed to foreigners.

You can take photos (camera T5000, video T10,000) around the monastery and in Migjid Janraisig Süm, but not inside the other temples. Try to be there for the captivating ceremonies – they generally start at around 9am, though you may be lucky and see one at another time. Most chapels are closed in the afternoon.

976 Gallery
ART GALLERY

(Map p57; www.976gallery.com; Max Mall, 5th fl, Peace Ave; ☺10am-8pm) Ulaanbaatar's best contemporary art gallery, featuring the most established and emerging Mongolian artists. It's located in the open atrium of the Max Mall on the 5th floor. It's run by Ms Gantuya, a passionate advocate for local art, who is present at special exhibit openings.

Centre of Shaman Eternal Heavenly Sophistication
SHAMAN CENTRE

(Мөнх Тэнгэрийн Шид Бөө Шүтээний Төв; Map p60; ☏ 9929 8909; Öndör Gegeen Zanabazaryn Gudamj; ☺10am-6pm Sun-Fri May-Sep) FREE Ulaanbaatar's official Shaman Centre is a ramshackle collection of squalid gers teetering on the slope that leads to Gandan Khiid. While not particularly mystifying at first sight, this is the real deal, with a bona fide shaman at its helm, holding daily court. The resident shaman, Zorigtbaatar, is known for his fiery orations that whip up the faithful into a frenzy. The main ger contains a smattering of icons, from a stuffed owl to bottles of vodka. If there is a ceremony going on, and you want your fortune told, you'll need to make a small donation. If you want to see a ceremony, call ahead to confirm times.

If you find the centre closed (which happens when Zorigtbaatar is out of town) you can also see shamans in the open grass areas south of the Tuul Gol. This area is about 3km east of the Zaisan Memorial (you will spot the silk scarves tied to the poles on the right side of the road).

Wildlife Museum   MUSEUM
(Map p60; Öndör Gegeen Zanabazaryn Gudamj; admission T2500; ☺10am-6pm) The Wildlife Museum (formerly known as the Hunting Museum) is on the 2nd floor of the Baigal Ordon (Nature Palace) on the street leading to Gandan Khiid. The museum shows off centuries-old trapping and hunting techniques that are used by both nomads and urban cowboys. It's usually locked, so ask for the key from the watchman downstairs.

Badma Ega Datsan   TEMPLE
(Gesar Süm; Map p60; ☑11-313 148; cnr Sambugiin Örgon Choloo & Ikh Toiruu west; ☺9am-8pm) FREE Belonging to Gandan Khiid, Badma Ega is a small, ramshackle place on a busy intersection. While Badma Ega is the original name for the temple, many know it by the alternative name Gesar Süm (Gesar was a mythical Tibetan king). It is a popular place for locals to request, and pay for, *puja* (a blessing ceremony). Allegedly, the temple was placed here to stop the movement of the hill behind it, which was slowly creeping towards the centre of the city. It's easy to visit the temple as it lies between Gandan and the city centre.

Tasgany Ovoo (Map p60), about 300m north of Gesar Süm, is worth a look if you haven't yet seen an *ovoo*, a sacred pyramid-shaped collection of stones.

Bakula Rinpoche Süm   BUDDHIST MONASTERY
(Pethub Stangey Choskhor Ling Khiid; Map p60; ☑11-322 366; ☺9am-6pm) FREE The Bakula Rinpoche Süm was founded in 1999 by the late Indian ambassador, himself a reincarnated lama from Ladakh. The Rinpoche's ashes were interred inside a golden stupa inside the temple in 2004. The monastery, used mainly as a centre for Buddhist teaching, also has a **Centre for Buddhist Medicine** (Map p60; ☑9199 7894; ☺9am-5pm Mon-Fri, 9am-noon Sat). The monastery is not a must-see unless you are interested in learning about traditional medicine. The complex is located where Ikh Toiruu meets Sambugiin Örgön Chölöö, behind a high white wall.

⊙ Khan Uul District & Zaisan

★**Winter Palace of the Bogd Khan**   MUSEUM
(Богд Хааны Өвлийн Ордон; Map p57; ☑11-342 195; Chingisiin Örgön Chölöö; adult/student T5000/2000; ☺9am-5.30pm mid-May–mid-Sep, 9.30am-4.30pm Fri-Tue mid-Sep–mid-May) Built between 1893 and 1903, this palace is where Mongolia's eighth Living Buddha, and last king, Jebtzun Damba Hutagt VIII (often called the Bogd Khan), lived for 20 years. For reasons that are unclear, the palace was spared destruction by the Russians and turned into a museum. The summer palace, on the banks of Tuul Gol, was completely destroyed.

There are six temples in the grounds; each now contains Buddhist artwork, including sculpture and *thangka*. The white building to the right as you enter is the Winter Palace itself. It contains a collection of gifts received from foreign dignitaries, such as a pair of golden boots from a Russian tsar, a robe made from 80 unfortunate foxes, and a ger lined with the skins of 150 snow leopards. Mongolia's Declaration of Independence (from China in 1911) is among the exhibits.

The Bogd Khan's penchant for unusual wildlife explains the extraordinary array of stuffed animals in the palace. Some of it had been part of his personal zoo – look out for the photo of the Bogd's elephant, purchased from Russia for 22,000 roubles.

MOUNTAIN BIKING NEAR ULAANBAATAR

The best short bike ride from Ulaanbaatar goes from Zaisan to the Observatory. From the city centre, travel south to the Zaisan Memorial (p70). From Zaisan, continue in an easterly direction. The road – under construction at the time of research – follows the southern bank of the Tuul Gol for 11km until you reach the ski hill, Sky Resort (p71). The Observatory is a little bit further along; follow the switchbacks uphill until you reach it. It's a two- to three-hour return trip.

ULAANBAATAR SIGHTS

The Winter Palace is a few kilometres south of Chinggis Khaan Sq. It is a bit too far to walk, so take a taxi or catch bus 7 or 19. There a fee of T50,000/70,000 to use a camera/video.

★ Zaisan Memorial   MONUMENT

(Зайсан Толгой; Zaisan Hill) The tall, thin landmark on top of the hill south of the city is the Zaisan Memorial. Built by the Russians to commemorate 'unknown soldiers and heroes' from various wars, it offers the best views of Ulaanbaatar and the surrounding hills. The enormous tank at the bottom of the hill – part of the Mongolia People's Tank Brigade – saw action against the Nazis during WWII. At the time of research an enormous property development was underway on the hill itself. According to the company building it, the site will include theatres, restaurants and cultural activities. Take bus 7 from the Bayangol Hotel or Baga Toiruu.

Buddha Park   PARK

FREE This peaceful park features an 18m-tall standing Sakyamuni image. When it was erected in 2007, five tons of juniper were placed inside. Below the statue is a small room containing *thangkas*, Sutras and images of the Buddha and his disciples. You can combine a visit with the Zaisan Memorial, right next door. To get there, catch bus 7 to the memorial. This bus departs from the Bayangol Hotel or Baga Toiruu near Ard Kino.

⊙ Sansar

★ International Intellectual Museum   MUSEUM

(Оюун Ухааны Олон Улсын Музей, Mongolian Toy Museum; Map p70; ☑11-461 470; www.iqmuseum.mn; Peace Ave 10; admission T3000; ⊙10am-6pm Mon-Sat; 🚹) This museum has a collection of puzzles and games made by local artists. One puzzle requires 56,831 move-

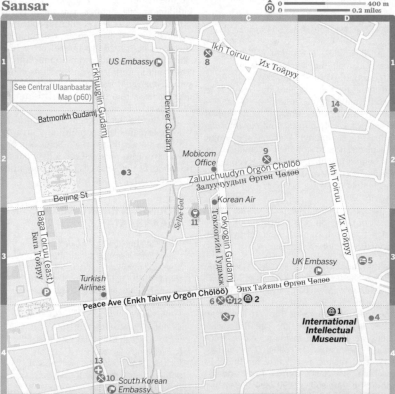

Sansar

ments to complete, says curator Zandraa Tumen-Ulzii. There are dozens of handmade chess sets and traditional Mongolian puzzles that are distant cousins to Rubik's cube. An enthusiastic guide will show you how the puzzles operate and will even perform magic tricks. It's a fascinating place for both kids and adults. The museum is located in eastern UB, in a hard-to-spot building hidden behind an abandoned circular building which appears to have suffered a fire at some point.

Ulaanbaatar City Museum MUSEUM
(Map p70; ☑11-450 960; Peace Ave; admission T1500; ☉9am-6pm) The Ulaanbaatar City Museum offers a brief but insightful view of Ulaanbaatar's history through old maps and photos. The most interesting item is a huge painting of the capital as it looked in 1912, in which you can clearly make out major landmarks such as Gandan Khiid and the Winter Palace of the Bogd Khan. A portion of the museum is dedicated to special photo exhibits that change frequently.

🏃 Activities

Sky Resort SKIING
(☑9100 7847; www.skyresort.mn; ☉11am-9pm Mon-Fri, 9am-10pm Sat & Sun; ☸) This small ski resort includes a couple of beginner runs, two chairlifts and full ski services (equipment rental, lessons, cafeteria) and even night skiing! A half-day lift ticket including ski rental costs T34,000 on a weekend or T28,000 on a weekday. A golf course operates here in summer. To get here, go to Zaisan and take the road east for about 10km. On weekends in winter, a bus (T1000) departs hourly from the parking lot opposite the Bayangol Hotel. Skiing is possible between mid-November and March.

M Bowling Centre BOWLING
(Map p60; ☑11-319 866; Baruun Selbe Gudamj; 1 frame before 7pm T5000, after 7pm T7000; ☉11am-midnight Tue-Sun) Located in Mobicom (Tedy Centre).

🎓 Courses

A number of language schools in Ulaanbaatar offer short- and long-term courses with flexible schedules. You might be able to organise a 'language exchange' with a Mongolian student through one of the universities. The English-language department of any school would be the obvious place to begin your search.

Friends Mongolian Language School LANGUAGE
(Map p57; ☑9978 9321; apt 64/2 Bayanzürkh District, 5th Microdistrict) Short-term survival Mongolian classes are available here. A 90-minute lesson at the school costs T14,000 or staff can meet you in a central location for T19,000. The location is northeast of the Jukov monument. Ask for Uranchimeg. More details are available on their Facebook page.

Institute of International Studies LANGUAGE
(Map p60; ☑11-328 681, 9911 4269; dashpurev@ magicnet.mn) Located opposite the university. Offers flexible group and private Mongolian-language lessons. It usually charges T20,000 per 90-minute session, with classes three times a week.

Federation for the Preservation of Mahayana Tradition BUDDHISM
(FPMT; Map p60; ☑11-321 580; www.fpmtmongolia. org; Builder's Sq, Juulchin Gudamj) The centre is involved in the regeneration of Buddhist

ASRAL & KUNCHAB JAMPA LING BUDDHIST CENTRE

Located in the northwest corner of the city, **Asral** (Map p57; ☑ 11-304 838, 9810 7378, 9595 2272; www.asralmongolia.org) is an NGO and a Buddhist social centre that supports impoverished families. Its main aim is to stop disadvantaged youths from becoming street children. It also provides skills and jobs for unemployed women; an on-site felt-making cooperative turns out some lovely products.

The Buddhist arm of the organisation has classes on Buddhism and meditation, although for now these are only offered in Mongolian. In summer, a high Tibetan lama, Panchen Otrul Rinpoche, visits the centre and provides religious teachings.

Asral encourages travellers to visit the centre. You can meet the felt-makers and buy their products or even volunteer your time. The centre is always looking for English teachers or gardeners to work on a small farm in Gachuurt (in summer). The centre is in the 3/4 district opposite the Gobi Sauna, slightly off the main road. It's best to call before you visit: ask for Davaa, the English-speaking director. Take bus 10 or 43 from Tengis cinema to the last stop and continue walking for 300m. Asral is a two-storey cream-coloured building on your right.

culture in Mongolia and offers free lectures and courses on various aspects of Buddhist tradition and meditation. Lectures are given in English (at the time of writing, Wednesday at 6pm); look for the pink-tiled building with a stupa in front.

Ananda Meditation Centre   YOGA, MEDITATION
(Map p60; ☑ 9913 2100; Baga Toiruu, bldg 23, apt 4) Offers yoga courses nightly at 6.30pm (Hatha yoga with chanting and meditation) in a building near UB Guesthouse. It's best to call ahead to reserve a space. Note that it's in a private apartment, accessed through the back of the building.

National University of Mongolia   LANGUAGE, CULTURE
(NUM; Map p60; ☑ 7730 7730; www.num.edu.mn; Ikh Surguuliin Gudamj 1, PO Box 46a/523, 210646) Northeast of Chinggis Khaan Sq, the school offers specialised classes on Mongolian culture and language, and has a foreign-student department. The office is in the main building, room 213. If your primary goal is to learn Mongolian, the private language schools do a better job.

American Center for Mongolian Studies   LANGUAGE, CULTURE
(Map p60; ☑ 7011 0486; www.mongoliacenter.org; Natsagdorj Library, east entrance, Seoul St) Has a good website listing courses and can recommend study options.

★ Festivals & Events

Around Naadam and other public holidays, special cultural events and shows are organised. It is worth reading the local English-language newspapers and asking a Mongolian friend, guide or hotel staff member to find out what may be on.

Naadam   CULTURAL
(⊙ 11 & 12 Jul) The biggest event in Ulaanbaatar is undoubtedly the Naadam (Festival). Some visitors may not find the festival itself terribly exciting, but the associated activities during the Naadam week and the general festive mood make it a great time to visit.

Tsam-Mask Dancing   CULTURAL
(⊙ late Jul) On a date set by the lunar calendar you can see *tsam*-mask dancing at Dashchoilon Khiid.

City's Birthday   CULTURAL
(⊙ late Oct) The last week in October sees the city's birthday – it was founded in 1639. Events and concerts are usually put on at this time at the Cultural Palace or State Opera & Ballet Theatre.

Ice Ankle-Bone Shooting Competition   SPORT
(⊙ early Feb) The city hosts an Ice Ankle-bone Shooting Competition, which is something like bowling on ice (but with a ball made of cowhide). It's held on the Tuul Gol.

Playtime   MUSIC
(⊙ Aug) The annual two-day music festival Playtime features the country's top rock bands and hip-hop artists. It's held at a venue outside the city, usually in August. Check the Hi-Fi CD Shop (p88), or any CD shop, for location and tickets.

Chinggis Khaan's Birthday CULTURAL
(☉ early Nov) The birthday of the Great Khaan is celebrated on the first day of the first winter month, according to the lunar calendar, so it has no fixed date but is usually early November. Celebrations are held on Chinggis Khaan Sq.

🛏 Sleeping

There is a wide range of places to stay in the capital city, with some of the best deals at the bottom and top ends. During the week surrounding Naadam, accommodation may be in short supply and prices are often higher.

If you are planning to stay in Ulaanbaatar for an extended period or you are travelling in a small group, it's worth looking around for an apartment to rent. A reasonable, furnished, one-bedroom apartment with a kitchen in an old Russian building in the city centre costs around US$400 to US$800 per month (discounts are available in winter). Check the classified sections of the local English-language newspapers. **Mongolian Properties** (Map p60; ☏ 11-324 545; www.mongolia-properties.com; Seoul St 48/13) has apartments for rent on a long-term basis. You could also ask at the guesthouses, which sometimes rent out apartments for around US$20 to US$30 per night for short-term stays.

🛏 West of Chinggis Khaan Square

⭐**Lotus Guesthouse** GUESTHOUSE $
(Map p60; ☏ 11-325 967, 9909 4943; www.lotuschild.org; Baga Toiruu West; dm US$8-15, r US$30; @ 🛜) This homey place feels more like a boutique hotel than a guesthouse. Rooms are individually styled, some with traditional Mongolian furniture. It has a cosy atmosphere but some parts can be a little dim. Location is central and quiet. It's run by the Lotus Children's Centre, an NGO that helps orphaned children, and it employs young Mongolians who used to live in the orphanage. An annex, in an apartment away from the centre, takes overflow if the main block is full.

Sunpath Guesthouse GUESTHOUSE $
(Map p60; ☏ 11-326 323, 9914 3722; www.sunpathmongolia.com; Baga Toiruu West, bldg 37, door 56; dm/d US$6/20; @ 🛜) This bright, family-run guesthouse offers spacious dorms and private rooms across a couple of stairwells. The facilities are very clean and well maintained and it occupies a cute downtown location.

There's the usual guesthouse services including wi-fi, a jam-and-toast breakfast and countryside tours. On the downside, there is just one bathroom, which means waiting in line in the morning. Travellers also report pressure to book a tour through the guesthouse.

UB Guesthouse GUESTHOUSE $
(Map p60; ☏ 9119 9859, 11-311 037; www.ubguest.com; Baga Toiruu, bldg 41, entrance 2, door 21; dm/s/tw/d US$8/20/22/25; @ 🛜) This well-established and central guesthouse has several rooms stretching around a Soviet-era apartment block. It's clean and there are plenty of bathrooms but the common room is a bit small and the place does get very busy in summer. Owner Bobbi has plenty of experience in helping backpackers with logistics and trip planning. Midnight curfew and 10am check-out are minuses, free early morning pick-up from the train station a plus. Skip the meagre breakfast and try one of the nearby cafes. Enter from the back of the building, behind Golomt Bank.

Nassan's Guesthouse GUESTHOUSE $
(Map p60; ☏ 11-321 078; www.nassantour.com; Baga Toiruu West; dm/s/d/tr US$10/32/38/45; @ 🛜) Nassan has been in the guesthouse business for 20 years and runs a clean and centrally located hostel. Spacious rooms are bright and have functional bathrooms and kitchen facilities. However, there is not much colour or personality to the place so the experience is somewhat underwhelming. Travellers report mixed results when dealing with the management. The guesthouse overlooks Baga Toiruu but to find the entrance you need to walk through the alley behind the bus stop (east side of the road), look for the gate into the small courtyard. It's the middle entrance.

ℹ **UB BUNK RATES**

Hotel rates in Ulaanbaatar are, on the whole, significantly higher than in the countryside, especially in the mid-to-high price range. In UB we define prices as follows (for a double room), based on US$1=T1600:

$ Less than US$70 (T112,000)

$$ US$70 to US$120 (T112,000 to T192,000)

$$$ More than US$120 (T192,000)

★ Hotel Örgöö   BOUTIQUE HOTEL **$$$**
(Map p60; ☑ 7011 6044; www.urgoohotel.com; M100 bldg, Juulchin Gudamj; d/ste with breakfast T185,000/225,000; ❈ ☎) This boutique hotel has just 10 rooms, each one decked out in brown and beige furnishings, with flat-panel TVs and modern, but small, bathrooms. The prime selling point here is the location, overlooking a little park near the National Museum. The breakfast is a bit disappointing for the price. Note that the air-con units in the back can be noisy at night and service is generally spotty. Overall it's a nice place to stay if you are looking for something quaint but keep expectations in check.

South of Chinggis Khaan Square

★ Chuka Guesthouse   GUESTHOUSE **$**
(Map p60; ☑ 9856 1999, 9999 5672; chuka927@gmail.com; bldg 33, entrance V; dm/r US$15/25; ☎) This new guesthouse enjoys a central location in a quiet courtyard set behind the National Academy Drama Theatre. It's a pricier than some of its competitors but the quality of the rooms stands out. It's well kept, furnishings are modern and the bunk beds are soft and warm. It has a fully equipped kitchen and a cosy lounge. Look for the red awning over the outside windows.

Mongolia Steppe Vision   GUESTHOUSE **$**
(Map p60; ☑ 9910 6880, 11-322 369; info@mongolia-visiontours.com; bldg 33 door 67; dm/r US$7/25; ☎) This four-room apartment has small rooms in a boxy building behind the National Academic Drama Theater. The English-speaking staff are friendly and keep the place tidy. There's a kitchen for self-catering and a simple breakfast.

Mongolian Steppe   GUESTHOUSE **$**
(Map p60; ☑ 9919 4331; steppeinmongolia@yahoo.com; Peace Ave 61, entrance I, door 5; dm US$8, d US$30-40; ☎) English-speaking owner Natsaga has established a guesthouse in this rambling apartment right across the street from the Central Post Office. One double room has a tiny en suite bathroom. There is a second room with shared bath and a large dorm room. Another apartment in a different entrance handles overflow. Laundry service is available for US$5. The door is in the courtyard of the building, which is accessed through a narrow gap just west of Air Market. Look for entrance 1.

Mika Hotel   HOTEL **$$**
(Map p60; ☑ 11-310 903; www.mika.mn; Elchingiin Gudamj; s/d US$50/87; ℗ ☎) The Mika is a nondescript midrange place that offers reasonably comfortable rooms at good rates in a fairly central location. Rooms are a bit bland and dated (think gold and green drapery) and the hot water is not always there when you need it. The wi-fi is reliable and some of the staff are quite helpful.

Bayangol Hotel   HOTEL **$$$**
(Map p60; ☑ 11-328 869; www.bayangolhotel.mn; Chingisiin Örgön Chölöö 5; s/d T182,000/224,000; ℗ @ ☎) One of Ulaanbaatar's biggest and most reliable hotels, the Bayangol consists of two 12-storey towers a five-minute walk south of Chinggis Khan Sq (along a very busy road). It was built in 1964 to accommodate overseas tour groups and the structures are now dated, with small elevators and shabby decor. The standard rooms are badly in need of renovation but the business rooms have been tastefully updated. Only basic English is spoken. Prices include breakfast.

East of Chinggis Khaan Square

Oasis Café & Guesthouse   GUESTHOUSE **$**
(☑ 9928 4702, 11-463 693; www.intergam-oasis.com; Nalaikh Gudamj; dm with breakfast T22,000, d without bathroom T64,000; ℗ @ ☎) European-run place with beautiful accommodation in dorms, gers and private rooms with attached bathroom. It has a large yard and a brightly painted cafe, which serves excellent Austrian meals and pastries. A simple breakfast is included. Because it has secure parking, it's popular among overlanders with their own motorbike or car. Motorcycles may be available for hire for US$100 to US$150 a day. The main downside is the isolated location: it's 5km east of Chinggis Khaan Sq (in the Amgalan district), on the edge of a ger district and just off a busy boulevard. The nearest landmark is the large, round Catholic Church; the guesthouse is 300m past the church.

Zaluuchuud Hotel   HOTEL **$$**
(Map p60; ☑ 11-324 594; www.zh.mn; Baga Toiruu 43; s/d/ste with breakfast US$50/75/90; @) One of Ulaanbaatar's oldest hotels, the Zaluuchuud (Young People) has seen marginal upgrades since the Soviet era. Although bland and dated, it does have a quiet location in the University area. Just don't expect much

in the way of service. Most disappointing are the uncomfortable beds. Well, that and the noise from the nearby karaoke bar. Not all the rooms are the same size, so you might try asking for an en-suite standard, which includes a bedroom and a living room with TV. Room No 300 is a good choice.

⭐ **Best Western Tuushin Hotel** HOTEL $$$
(Map p60; ☑11-323 162; www.bestwesternmongolia. mn; Amaryn Gudamj 15; s US$165-185, d US$215-235; 🅿️🛜📶) Opened in 2013, this is the newest upscale hotel in Ulaanbaatar, with a prime location steps away from Chinggis Khaan Sq with easy access to downtown museums and theatres. Facilities include a spa, fitness centre, a couple of restaurants, and a lounge on the 25th floor with epic city views. The 200 guestrooms are tastefully decorated and come with wi-fi and a work desk. The included breakfast is very good but avoid the mediocre grill restaurant on the 3rd floor.

Springs Hotel HOTEL $$$
(Map p60; ☑11-320 738; www.springshotel.mn; Olympiin Örgön Chölöö 2a; s/d with breakfast US$120/145; 📶🛜) This hotel feels squeezed between other buildings and it's a bit ugly from the outside but there are good views from the upper floors. Its best features are its helpful staff, good-quality wi-fi connection, and central location just a short walk from Chinggis Khaan Sq. Price includes use of the fitness room. It's a popular place for business travellers and has an in-house Korean restaurant.

Puma Imperial HOTEL $$$
(Map p60; ☑11-313 043; www.pumaimperialhotel.mn; Ikh Surguuliin Gudamj; s/d with breakfast T170,000/210,000; 🅿️📶🛜) Popular with visiting journalists and diplomats wanting to be close to the square, so you are paying more for the location than the quality of the rooms. Rooms that face the road can be a tad noisy but side-facing rooms have no view, so pick your poison. On the plus side, it has courteous and accommodating staff and a pretty good in-house Indian restaurant.

Ulaanbaatar Hotel HOTEL $$$
(Map p60; ☑11-320 620; www.ubhotel.mn; Baga Toiruu; s T150,000-180,000, d T240,000, lux T280,000; 🅿️🛜📶🛜) The Ulaanbaatar Hotel is the grand old dame of Mongolia. Opened in 1961, this was where Soviet dignitaries stayed during their visits to the 'Red Hero'. It still carries an air of the Khrushchev era with its high ceilings, chandeliers, marble staircase and lavish ballroom. Rooms are well appointed but some are a bit small. Despite being considered a top-end hotel you might experience some imperfections here: fickle air-con, poor service, spotty hot water, unreliable wi-fi, and other minor inconveniences. Consider it part of the adventure. The hotel also contains two restaurants, a coffee shop, a travel agency, business centre and sauna.

🛏 North of Chinggis Khaan Square

Guide Hotel HOTEL $
(Map p60; ☑11-353 582; www.guide-hotel.mn; Baga Toiruu North; d/ste with breakfast US$60/70; 🛜) Between Dashchoilon Khiid and Baga Toiruu, this hidden hotel offers clean and comfortable rooms. Its best feature is its large and modern bathrooms, plus the free breakfast. The surrounding courtyard is pretty scruffy but the hotel itself is fine. You can get here by walking through the arch on Baga Toiruu across the street from Namaste restaurant.

🛏 State Department Store Area

⭐ **Khongor Guest House** GUESTHOUSE $
(Map p60; ☑9925 2599, 11-316 415; www.khongor-expedition.com; Peace Ave 15, apt 6; dm/s/d US$8/15/18; 📶🛜) This popular guesthouse is run by a friendly couple, Toroo and Degi, who work hard to help guests with logistical matters, tours, visa issues and airport or train-station runs. Their countryside tours get positive reports from travellers and business is casual – tours are usually paid for when you get back. The guesthouse is a simple affair with small private rooms and slightly larger dorms. There's a cosy lounge with three computers and a kitchen. The entrance of the guesthouse is around the back of the third building west of the State Department Store. Credit cards are accepted.

⭐ **Zaya's Hostel** GUESTHOUSE $
(Map p60; ☑9918 5013, 11-331 575; www.zayahostel.com; Peace Ave; s US$30-35, d US$40, tr US$45; 📶🛜) While most guesthouses in town are located in crumbling old Russian flats, this one is in a modern building with hardwood floors, sparkling bathrooms, a comfortable lounge, fresh paint and new furnishings. Owner Zaya speaks English, enjoys a good conversation and is happy to help travellers looking for volunteer opportunities. A simple

breakfast is included. Zaya is not too keen on groups of noisy backpackers, however, so if you are looking for a party guesthouse, skip this one. The hostel is on the 3rd floor of an orange building, about 100m north of Peace Ave (behind the glass-fronted Peace Tower, and then a bit past the Seoul Hotel).

Green Steppe Guesthouse
GUESTHOUSE $
(Map p60; ☎ 7010 5588, 8803 3080; www.green-steppemongolia.com; dm US$7; @ 🛜) This popular cheapie has a couple of scruffy dorms, a kitchen and a large outdoor courtyard where you can chill in the summer months and swap travel info. Lots of DVDs and books to borrow. The staff are friendly and don't pressure guests to take their tours, but are not always there when you need them. The main problem is that the hostel has just one (often musty) bathroom so when the place is busy it's in high demand. Location is very central, in a courtyard 100m east of the State Department Store.

Golden Gobi
GUESTHOUSE $
(Map p60; ☎ 9665 4496, 11-322 632; www.gold-engobi.com; dm US$7, d with/without bathroom US$23/19; @ 🛜) This family-run place has a fun, youthful vibe, with colourful walls, two lounges and lots of soft sofas. Dorms and private rooms are clean and comfortable and the bathrooms are kept tidy. On the downside, it can get very crowded in summer and just trying to get some face time with the manager could require getting in a long line. This has led to some mixed reviews by guests. It's inside a courtyard about 100m east of the State Department Store.

Genex Hotel
HOTEL $
(Map p60; ☎ 11-319 326; www.generalimpex.mn; Choimbolyn Gudamj 10; s/d US$35/60; @) Genex Hotel is one of the cheapest hotels in the city centre and gives you a room for under US$70. But you get what you pay for – the pseudo-European atmosphere is tacky and the lux rooms are odd-looking, with two queen-size beds pushed into a triangular-shaped alcove. Standard rooms are poky and not well maintained so expect wonky plumbing, toilets and light fixtures. The dim-lit karaoke bar in the basement is another red flag.

Kharaa Hotel
HOTEL $$
(Map p60; ☎ 11-313 717; www.kharaahotel.com; Choimbolyn Gudamj 6; d US$75, half-lux US$85, lux US$120; P @) The Kharaa has a decent location, a polished overall look and a filling breakfast that makes it fine for a short stay. But typical of midrange hotels in this town, there a number of shortcomings. The walls are too thin and bathrooms are tiny. Beds can be lumpy and the fittings in the bathroom are coming loose. Internet connection is also not reliable. Finally, no elevator means you may have to lug your bags up four flights of stairs. Staff are friendly and speak basic English. Pricier rooms offer a little more comfort so consider an upgrade.

Narantuul Hotel
HOTEL $$$
(Map p60; ☎ 11-330 565; www.narantuulhotel.com; Baruun 4 Zam; s/d/tr T159,000/229,000/259,000; @ 🛜) This friendly hotel has modern and large rooms that are clean and well maintained. A hot breakfast is included and the rooms have wi-fi. While the staff is friendly, very little English is spoken. Rooms facing the street and those on the 11th floor (under the lounge) can be a bit noisy. Another problem is that some rooms can get hot in summer and there is no air-con, just a fan. The location is reasonably central and easy

---

GER DISTRICT DIGS

As Ulaanbaatar's centre booms with high-rise construction sites and multimillion-dollar property developments, its ger (yurt) districts remain trapped in time. By staying in one you'll get a real sense of traditional Mongolian family life, and at the same time gain an appreciation of the difficulties that ger residents must endure in these unplanned areas with bare-bones infrastructure. Several tour companies offer walks through ger districts, but to achieve the full living experience contact Rinky Dink Travel Mongolia (p37), which can set you up with a homestay in a ger district and place you as a volunteer in its social development projects. A typical stay might include digging a pit toilet, repairing a fence, doing art projects with street kids or teaching English. You'll live like the locals (pit toilets, no running water, difficult transport) but you'll also encounter some of the friendliest people anywhere, and gain a rare perspective on the city. Visits can last from three days to several weeks.

to spot but this little stretch of Peace Ave is busy and grubby. A business centre, sauna and a beauty salon are also on-site.

Sun Bridge (Narny Guur) Area

Idre's Guest House GUESTHOUSE **$**
(Map p60; ☑ 7011 0846; www.idretour.com; Undsen Khuulin Gudamj; dm US$7, r with/without bathroom US$28/24; @ 🛜) This single-floor guesthouse has several dorms and small private rooms. It has a central lounge, a small kitchen and a book exchange. Bathrooms are small and slightly decrepit. The hostel is on a busy road near the new bridge over Narny Zam, not the flashest neighbourhood in town. It's about a 20-minute walk from the hostel to the centre of the city.

LG Guesthouse GUESTHOUSE **$**
(Map p57; ☑ 7011 8243, 9985 8419; www.lghostel. com; Narny Gudamj; dm US$8, s/d US$25/30; @ 🛜) With 34 rooms, this is the largest guesthouse in the city. It has dorms and private rooms with attached bathroom, a common area, a kitchen where you can cook your own meals and a restaurant on the ground floor with dishes for T5000 to T8500. Bathrooms are clean and have hot-water boilers – important in summer when other places only have cold water. It's a little out of the centre, on the road towards the train station. It also has a small annex close to the State Department Store.

Voyage Hotel HOTEL **$**
(Map p57; ☑ 11-327 213; www.voyagehotel.mn; Narny Gudamj; s/d/lux T150,000/105,000/ 140,000; @ 🛜) Representing good value, the 30-room Voyage has attentive staff and pleasant rooms. Facilities include two restaurants (European and Korean), free internet and sauna. The low price is a reflection of its less-than-perfect location, on the busy road to the train station.

Gandan Monastery Area

Gana's Guest House HOSTEL **$**
(Map p60; ☑ 9911 6960; www.ganasger.mn; Gandan Khiid ger district, house No 22; dm/s/d/tr US$7/20/25/30; ⊙ closed winter; @ 🛜) If you fancy staying in a ger, drop by this longtime backpacker hangout. Owner Gana has accommodation in private rooms inside a main block, or you could stay in a ger on the roof. The attractions are the quirky nature of the place and the cheap prices, but

overall it's a pretty ramshackle place with a lot of parts simply held together with tape. It's easiest to spot from the western end of Juulchin Gudamj – the two-storey brick building is well signed and looms above the neighbouring houses.

Sansar

Kempinski Hotel Khan Palace HOTEL **$$$**
(Map p70; ☑ 11-463 463; www.kempinski.com/ en/ulaanbaatar; East Cross Rd; s/d T310,000/ 360,000; P ❄ @ 🛜) This Kempinski-managed, Japanese-invested venture on the east end of Peace Ave is one of the best-run places in town. Rooms are plush, with a tasteful design and little niceties such as humidifier, robes and slippers. The hotel also has free internet, a fitness centre and sauna, but no swimming pool. The European-American buffet breakfast (T35,000 for nonguests) is one of the best in town.

🍴 Eating

The sheer number and range of restaurants in Ulaanbaatar boggle the mind. There's Mexican, Japanese, Italian, Indian, French and even a North Korean restaurant, to name a few, catering to both foreigners and locals. There's also a few hundred budget places, which tend to serve a Mongolian-Russian food fusion. 'Restaurant Row' is Seoul St, where you'll find a number of upscale places.

Note that most pubs and bars also serve food (some of it quite good) so places to consider also include those in our Drinking & Nightlife section on p82.

🍴 West of Chinggis Khaan Square

Luna Blanca VEGAN **$**
(Map p60; M-100 Bldg, Juulchiin Gudamj; dishes T5000-8500; ⊙ 10am-9pm; 🚼 🖶 👪) 🥬 Famous for being the first vegan restaurant in Mongolia, this place remains very popular for its consistently tasty and healthy food. The kitchen whips up classic Mongolian dishes such as the Flour Power (*tsuivan* – fried noodles), and Mongol Combo Plate (with *buuz* and *khuushuur*), as well as European fare like spaghetti and goulash. We're particularly fond of the 'Power Lunch', with soy meat, mashed potatoes and gravy. The atmosphere is refreshingly clean, alcohol-free, kid-friendly and (best of all) it's great value for money. There is also some excellent local

DINING GUANZ-STYLE

There are dozens of Mongolian budget restaurants (guanz) and they can be found on every block in the city. Some are chain restaurants and you'll start to recognise prominent eateries, including Zochin Buuz (Зочин Бууз), Khaan Buuz (Хаан Бууз) and Zochin Cafe (Зочин Кафэ). They serve up buuz (steamed mutton dumplings), tsuivan (fried noodles) plus soups and bifshteks ondogtei (beefsteak with egg). They are often quite dire – think globs of mashed potatoes, chunks of fatty mutton, and rice topped with ketchup – so keep your expectations at ground zero. Some of the chains operate 24 hours. Meals cost T4500 to T8000.

Look for them at these locations:

Khaan Buuz (Map p60; Peace Ave) Opposite the State Department Store. One of the most popular of the bunch, owing to its landmark location on Peace Ave. English-language and picture menu available.

Zochin Cafe (Map p60; Sambuugiin Örgön Chölöö) This place is 80m east of the fire station. One of the better of the cheapies.

art on the walls created by the well-known painter Tugs-Oyun.

Mongol National Khuushuur & Buuz
MONGOLIAN $

(Map p60; Ankara Gudamj; meals T4000-6000; ⊙11am-8pm Mon-Sat; 🍴) This cute, better-than-the-average guanz is decked out with ger-style furniture and old black-and-white photos of steppe life on the walls. Menu items include freshly made buuz (T700) and khuushuur (T1200), plus guriltei shuul (noodle soup) made in a hotpot (T6000). It's a friendly place with quality food, although the overall scene is a bit scruffier than it needs to be. You can't miss the fantastic signboard outside, designed like a Mongolian table.

✖ Juulchin (Tourist) Gudamj

Stupa Café
VEGETARIAN $

(Map p60; ☎11-319 953; Builder's Sq, Juulchin Gudamj; meals T4500-7000; ⊙10am-8pm Mon-Fri, 10am-7pm Sat & Sun; 🍴🚭🍴) 🌱 This charming cafe serves light vegetarian meals and sweet snacks. Good for pastas, sandwiches and soups. It also has a shelf full of English-language books and magazines, which you can read while enjoying a sandwich, coffee or tea. It's part of the FPMT Buddhist Centre (p71) and profits go towards supporting the restoration of Buddhism in Mongolia.

Loving Hut
VEGAN $

(Map p60; Juulchin Gudamj; meals T4000-5500; ⊙11am-8.30pm Mon-Sat; 🚭🍴) With a run-down facade and a bare-bones interior, this

cafe may not be the most cosy place in town, but the all-vegan menu does offer a good variety of healthy and tasty dishes. Try the mogul, a veggie stir-fry served on a sizzling platter, one of the half-dozen soups, or veggie buuz. Ask to see the 'special menu' featuring fruit shakes and herbal teas.

Narya Café
COFFEE, AMERICAN $$

(Map p60; ☎11-317 098; Builder's Sq, Juulchin Gudamj; dishes T6000-10,000; ⊙8.30am-8pm Mon-Fri, 9am-7pm Sat & Sun; 🌐🍴) The Latin music playing in the background, ochre-painted walls and contemporary artwork make for a pleasant welcome when entering this laid-back cafe. It's popular with students and travellers looking for some cheap eats and wi-fi. The menu offers reasonably priced sandwiches, soups and home-baked muffins. The food is so-so in terms of taste, but it's usually pretty filling and fairly priced. There is also a shop downstairs where you can get imported goods and bakery items.

Pyongyang
NORTH KOREAN $$

(Map p60; ☎9134 0333; Urt Tsagaan; T9000-12,000; ⊙noon-9pm; 🍴) How often do you say, 'Hey, let's go for some North Korean tonight!' It's possible in UB, at this authentic restaurant where specialities include Pyongyang cold buckwheat noodles and crispy cabbage kimchi, and kimchi pancakes. Staff sometimes put on rousing North Korean videos during the meals. It's the sixth door on the right as you walk east on Urt Tsagaan pedestrian mall. The sign can be really hard to spot among the clutter of boards on this building.

✕ Seoul Street

Shilla
KOREAN $$

(Map p60; ✍ 9667 2231; Seoul St; ◷ 10am-10pm; 🖼) The well-established Shilla is a good spot for a hot *bibimbap* (T8000) a filling meal loaded with rice, egg and veggies in a sizzling claypot (add meat for another T2000). A portion of *samgyebsal* (raw pork fried on your table) costs T28,000 and is enough for two people.

★ Rosewood Kitchen + Enoteca
ITALIAN $$$

(Map p60; Seoul St, Mandal bldg; mains T9500-38,000; ◷ 7.30am-9.30pm Mon-Sat; 🛜✍🖼) Run by a jovial Bostonian named Cliffe, this new place serves gourmet pastas, pizzas, sandwiches and salads. It's all made with high-quality local and imported ingredients and many items are made in-house, including the tasty breads. The grilled asparagus is a favourite appetiser. There's also a bakery and deli with delicious muffins, bagels, cookies and salads that make for good snacks. The atmosphere is smart and businesslike. It's tucked off the street in the ground floor of a five-storey grey building next to a large ger. A **second location** (Map p70; ✍ 7731 0561; Elchingiin Gudamj; ◷ 7.30am-9pm Mon-Sat) is just north of the Korean embassy.

★ Bull
HOT POT $$$

(Map p60; Seoul St; meal per person T15,000; ◷ 11.30am-midnight; ✍🖼) A local favourite, this hot-pot place gets a steady stream of patrons at its three locations – two on Seoul St and another **branch** (Map p60; Blue Mon bldg, Baga Toiruu East; ◷ 11.30am-10pm) diagonally opposite the Chinese embassy. Order an array of raw vegetables, sauces and thinly sliced meats, which are brought to your table on platters, then cook the ingredients in your personal cauldron of boiling broth. It's a great alternative to the meat-heavy menus you'll experience at most other restaurants in town and service is top-notch.

California
ECLECTIC $$$

(Map p60; ✍ 11-319 031; Seoul St; mains T12,000-30,000; ◷ 8am-midnight; 🛜✍🖼) One of Ulaanbaatar's most popular restaurants, this place has a 24-page menu with everything from burgers and pasta to sushi and traditional Mongolian dishes. There are big salads, including Thai steak and Caesar, and Latino fare including chicken tacos. The US-style breakfasts are some of the best around. Sit in the airy atrium for maximum sunlight and try to catch the attention of the waiters as they zip around serving mountainous portions to the hungry masses.

SELF-CATERING

For self-caterers, there are many shops around the city that sell food imported from China, Korea, the US and Europe. Fresh fruit and veggies are also available; some items are home-grown in Mongolia, although most of what you'll find is imported from China. Some tasty local products include yoghurt, cheese, apples, berries, tomatoes and cream. Most markets are open from about 10am to 8pm daily.

Bread is available everywhere but the best is found at small bakeries like the French-run Le Boulange (p81) bakery and the State Department Store. The German-run **Sachers Café** (Map p60; ✍ 11-324 734; Baga Toiruu west; snacks T800-2500, light meals T8000-10,000; ◷ 9am-9pm; 🛜🖼) has nice bread loaves, and pretzels that are best when purchased early in the day when they are still warm out of the oven.

Merkuri Market (Мэркури; Map p60; ◷ 10am-7pm Mon-Sat, 10am-6pm Sun) At Merkuri food market private vendors sell imported goods, meat, cheese, fruit and vegetables – easily the best selection of fresh food products in the country. The door is small and there is no sign but you can find it by walking to the right side of the large 'Minii Delguur' supermarket (or just follow the crowds and ask for 'Merkuri'). The complex itself is hidden behind apartment buildings about about 200m west of the State Circus.

State Department Store (Map p60; ✍ 11-319 292; Peace Ave 44) A supermarket is on the ground floor of the State Department Store.

Good Price (Map p60; Seoul St) This shop sells imported food products from the US, including sauces, canned vegetables and dried fruit. Has a good (but pricey) fruit and veggie section, plus readymade sandwiches and salads.

South of Chinggis Khaan Square

★ Millie's Café
AMERICAN $$

(Map p60; ☎ 11-330 338; Marco Polo bldg; mains T10,000-18,000; ⊗ 8am-8pm Mon-Sat; 🛜🖨📶) Since it first opened its doors in 1998, Millie's has been a favourite among expats seeking Western comfort food. The owners – Daniel and Densmaa – warmly greet patrons to their sun-lit restaurant, and promptly serve up tasty burgers, sandwiches and soups. Special treats include smoothies, lemon pie and a delicious chocolate cake (which sells out early). Don't miss Daniel's famous Cuban sandwich, only available on Tuesdays.

★ Veranda
WESTERN $$$

(Map p60; ☎ 11-330 818; Jamyn Gunii Gudamj 5/1; mains T12,400-23,000; ⊗ 7am-midnight Mon-Fri, noon-midnight Sat & Sun; 📶📷) While it's not particularly old, this fine-dining restaurant has an almost colonial air to it, with couch seating inside and a big porch overlooking the Choijin Lama Temple Museum. The food is surprisingly good, with starters that include smoked-salmon rolls and spinach salad with feta, and an array of delectable main dishes that fuse Italian and French recipes, such as lamb ratatouille, grilled duck and peppercorn steak. Breakfast is available on weekdays.

Silk Road
INTERNATIONAL $$$

(Map p60; ☎ 9191 0211, 11-318 864; Jamyn Gunii Gudamj 5/1; mains T10,000-23,000; ⊗ 12.30pm-midnight; 📷) A long-time Ulaanbaatar eatery, Silk Road is so named for its bas-relief scenes of the ancient route from China to Europe. The menu also carries a trans-Eurasian theme, with sprinklings of Indian, Central Asian and Mediterranean treats, including shish kebabs, chicken tikka and pork *gyros* (pitta with meat and vegetables). It's in the same building as Veranda.

East of Chinggis Khaan Square

Shilmel Buuz
MONGOLIAN $

(Map p60; ☎ 8881 0518; Amaryn Gudamj; buuz T600, salads T1500; ⊗ 10am-6pm Mon-Fri) This small *guanz*, with plastic tablecloths and bare walls, may not have much atmosphere but it's well known for serving some of the best *buuz* in the city (nearly home-made quality). Unlike most other cafes, the dumplings here are not overly fatty and come piping hot from a special steamer. Try a few with *suutei tsai* (Mongolian milk tea). It's the westernmost in a string of five, small restaurants. Look for the picture of the two kids gorging on a big plate of *buuz*.

Modern Nomads 2
MONGOLIAN $$

(Map p60; ☎ 7012 0808; Amaryn Gudamj; meals T7500-22,000; ⊗ 10am-midnight Mon-Fri, 11am-11pm Sat & Sun; 📷) The menu is actually mostly European but there are a few classic Mongolian dishes, so this is a decent place to try *khuushuur*, *buuz*, a Mongolian soup or even sheep head. It's part of a chain of restaurants but this branch seems to get slightly better reviews than the others. A picture menu makes ordering easy.

GOURMET MONGOLIAN FOOD IN UB

When Mongolians look for fine-dining options in Ulaanbaatar, the restaurants of choice tend to be international (why go out for Mongolian food when you can cook it at home?). As a result, finding a top-notch Mongolian-food restaurant is more difficult than you might expect.

Tour operators usually bring their groups to one of the Modern Nomads (p80) restaurants (there are five branches in UB), although the food is often underwhelming. A better option for both atmosphere and food quality is Mongolians (p82) – the downside here is the somewhat inconvenient location.

Several of the top-end hotels in Ulaanbaatar have restaurants that serve excellent Mongolian food. The most popular is the **Chairman restaurant** (Map p60; Corporate Hotel, 2nd fl Chinggisiin Örgon Chölöö; ⊗ 11am-11pm) on the 2nd floor of the Corporate Hotel. Also recommended is the **Karakorum restaurant** (Map p70; Kempinski Hotel Khan Palace; ⊗ 11am-11pm) in the Kempinski Hotel.

Of course, the best option for Mongolian food is home-cooking. **EcoVoyage Mongolie** (☎ 9556 0270; www.ecovoyagemongolie.com) has occasional visits to Terelj to eat traditional foods with local families.

North of Chinggis Khaan Square

Coffee Kid
COFFEE, SANDWICHES $

(Map p60; light meals T4500-6000; ⊘ 7.30am-8pm Mon-Fri, 10am-8pm Sat & Sun; 🛜 🖰) This cafe behind behind Government House is easily spotted from the outside, thanks to its unique plywood facade and paintings of smiling Mongolian children. It's a lively little places that serves a tasty tuna sandwich and other light meals, plus good coffee and teas. A great place for a quick pick-me-up as you wander the city.

Hashi
JAPANESE $$

(Map p60; ✎ 9519 9163; udon T9000; 🛜 🖰) This small Japanese restaurant offers tasty, high-quality food at reasonable prices. Try the udon soup served in a small metal pot or add a side of tempura and sushi for T4000 extra. Has a handy location just behind Government House.

Nomad Legends Mongols Club
MONGOLIAN $$

(Map p60; ✎ 11-326 631; Sükhbaataryn Gudamj 1; meals T6000-12,000; ⊘ noon-midnight; 🖰) This tiny restaurant is a good place to try some Mongolian food in a somewhat upscale atmosphere. Try a Mongolian milk tea or plate of *khuushuur* (fried meat pancake). Sheep head is also available for the culinarily adventurous.

★ Namaste
INDIAN $$$

(Map p60; ✎ 9927 0957; Baga Toiruu North; dishes T12,000-18,000; ⊘ 11.30am-10pm; 🛜 ✎ 🖰) Treat your taste buds to some gourmet Indian cuisine prepared by three chefs from Uttaranchal. Try the delicious *saag gosht* (beef in spinach sauce) or *murg makhni* (butter chicken) – both will melt in your mouth. Order a side of garlic naan and rice and if you are still hungry there are kebabs and juicy chicken meatballs. Vegetarian options are available, as well as classic street food like *gol-gappa* (pastry with chickpeas). The main branch is on the northeast bend of Baga Toiruu, 270m north of the Zaluuchuud Hotel, and there is another restaurant in the Flower Hotel (Map p70).

Le Bistro Français
FRENCH $$$

(Map p60; ✎ 11-320 022; Ikh Surguuliin Gudamj 2; meals T15,000-35,000; ⊘ 9am-10pm Mon-Fri, 10am-10pm Sat & Sun; 🛜 🖰) The soft lighting, cream-coloured walls and French art give this bistro a peaceful, romantic ambience. Try the foie gras for a starter, followed by a lamb goulash or beef fillet, washed down with a French red wine. Classic French delicacies like frogs legs and escargot are sometimes available. It's popular with expats and Mongolian corporate big shots looking for some Rive Gauche ambiance.

State Department Store Area

★ Shashlik Stands
SHASHLIK $

(Map p60; State Department Store; ⊘ noon-11pm Jun-Aug) In summer you can get shashlik (meat kebab), usually served with onions and cucumber, prepared by Uzbek and Mongolian street vendors and served in tents outside the State Department Store. A true taste of Central Asia not to be missed!

★ Le Boulange
FRENCH BAKERY $

(Map p60; ✎ 9916 9970; ⊘ 8am-7pm; 🛜 🖰) A popular haunt among Ulaanbaatar expats and travellers alike, this bakery and coffee shop serves an array of reasonably priced treats, including apple turnovers and chocolate croissants. Come in the morning when these items are straight out of the oven. You can also enjoy freshly made sandwiches and paninis while listening to a great music playlist. It's an excellent place to load up on snacks before heading off on an expedition. It's located on a narrow lane behind the Cashmere House.

★ Sakura Bakery
JAPANESE $

(Map p60; Tserendorjiin Gudamj; mains T4500-8000; ⊘ 9am-8pm Tue-Sat, 9am-4pm Sun; 🖰) This authentic Japanese cafe has a dedicated following, who come for the simple curry lunches, fried chicken, ramen noodles, excellent cakes (try their famous cheesecake and cream puffs!) and friendly atmosphere. Manga fans will appreciate the collection of comic books. Note this place is usually closed in July.

★ Sugiya Ramen
RAMEN $$

(Map p60; ✎ 9810 0077; Beatles Sq; dishes T9200-14,000; ⊘ 11.30am-9pm) Run by a Mongolian woman who lived in Fukuoka, this place has an authentic Japanese blue-collar feel to it, with a mostly bar-stool seating arrangement. Several types of ramen are available: we liked the *tonkotsu ajitama* (tonkotsu broth with a marinated egg). The soups also contain delectable sliced meat, chopped onions and noodles. Among the side dishes, the *chatamadon* (egg and rice) is highly

---

ⓘ LIGHTS OUT

A strict ban on smoking was passed by parliament in 2013 so don't even think about sparking up in any public places, including bars, restaurants and hotel lobbies. Smokers seen in public places have been shouted at by local vigilantes.

---

recommended. Make sure to ask for garlic *(sermis)* and they will bring you a raw clove and garlic crusher – a nice touch.

Round Table Pizza   PIZZA $$
(Map p60; ☑ 9710 7711, 7710 7711; Peace Ave; large pizza from T28,000; ☺ 10.30am-midnight; 👶) One of the best places for pizza. Has a family-friendly branch on Peace Ave and delivery is available.

Café Amsterdam   COFFEE, SANDWICHES $$
(Map p60; ☑ 11-321 979; Peace Ave; items T6000-9000; ☺ 7am-10pm; 📶◎👶) A pit stop for independent travellers, road-weary folk can be found here fuelling up with soups, salads and sandwiches before heading out to the streets for more city explorations. While the food gets mixed reviews it's hard to beat the English breakfast eaten on the sunny porch in summer. There's a handy noticeboard for posting messages, and outside the summer season the cafe hosts a movie night every Wednesday.

Oriental Treasure   TAIWANESE $$
(Map p60; ☑ 7013 5055; Beatles Sq; mains T10,000-16,000; ☺ 11.30am-10pm) Among the numerous Chinese-style restaurants in Ulaanbaatar, this is one of the cleanest and most welcoming. The speciality here is steamed dumplings stuffed with chicken, pork, veggies or shrimp – all are delicious and fresh. Glass windows allow you to peek into the kitchen to watch how the dumplings are expertly prepared. On the downside, prices are a tad high considering the small portions.

✕ Sansar

★Mongolians   MONGOLIAN $$
(Map p70; ☑ 9909 7716; Ikh Toiruu 93, Barilga Mega Store; mains T7000-12,000; ☺ 11am-midnight; ◎👶) Part museum, part restaurant, this place sports great atmosphere, with walls lined with Mongolian antiques and old photos. The menu is contemporary Mongolian, with stir-fried meats, dumplings and boiled mutton with some Russian and European influence. If you want to go all out, order the *khorkhog* (meat chunks cooked in a metal steamer with scalding-hot rocks added to the pot to aid cooking), enough for six to eight people (you must call and order six hours in advance). Two nights a week a traditional Mongolian band plays here at 8pm (usually Monday and Tuesday). Mongolians is 600m east of the US embassy.

Hazara   INDIAN $$$
(Map p70; ☑ 9919 5007, 11-480 214; Peace Ave 16; dishes T12,000-16,000; ☺ noon-2.30pm & 6-10pm; 🍴◎) Tucked into a squat building behind the Wrestling Palace, this North Indian restaurant has consistently been one of the best restaurants in Ulaanbaatar for over 15 years. Each table is covered by a colourful *samiyan* (Rajasthani tent), where you sit back and enjoy tandoori baked delights. Try the chicken *tikka* (grilled with a marinade), *aloo gobi* (potato and cauliflower) or the *raan-e-hazara* (lamb marinated in rum). The *saag paneer* (cheese with pureed spinach) should also find a spot on your table.

🍷 Drinking & Nightlife

There are many good, clean and safe bars and pubs in Ulaanbaatar; most of them are located downtown, around the Drama Theatre or on Seoul St. There are an equal number of dark and dingy nightspots, usually out in the suburbs, the 3/4 District and Ikh Toiruu (north of the Kempinski Hotel).

Bars and pubs come in all shapes and sizes. There seems to be an over-abundance of Irish-themed pubs, and while few serve Guinness on tap, good imported ales are easy to find. A better idea would be to try something more Mongolian, like a cup of *airag* (*koumiss*; fermented mare's milk), available at sidewalk gers in summer.

One fine option is the open-air beer and shashlik stands (p81) that open in summer near the State Department Store. For something really swanky, try VLVT (p84).

Places go out of fashion pretty quickly, so you'll need to ask the locals about what is popular. Note that alcohol sales are banned on the first of the month so bars and clubs are closed.

★Hanzo Lounge & Night Club   CLUB
(Map p60; ☑ 11-310 019; Sambuugiin Örögon Chölöö; Fri & Sat from T5000; ☺ 6pm-midnight Sun-Wed, 6pm-3am Thu-Sat; 📶) Hanzo attracts Ulaanbaatar's alternative crowd; in the dimly

lit corners of the scruffy bar-club, revellers gather over cheap beers or dance to an eclectic music set. Hanzo is also known as Ulaanbaatar's only gay bar and nightclub. It's hidden in a courtyard with several other small clubs and karaoke bars, about 200m west of the Tengis cinema. Use Sunset Karaoke or Amrita Club as nearby landmarks

★ iLoft   CLUB
(Map p60; 📱9909 0528; Amaryn Gudamj; admission T20,000; drinks from T5000; ⊘10am-3am; 🛜) This multi-use venue operates as a restaurant and cafe during the day and transforms into a pulsing nightclub after dark. There's leather seating, a large dance floor, techno beats and a mature crowd. iLoft hosts salsa dancing on Thursdays (starting at 8pm) and an exciting line-up of DJs or themed parties on other days. It's located behind the Best Western Hotel.

Greenland   BEER GARDEN
(Map p60; Peace Ave; ⊘noon-midnight Jun-Aug) Oktoberfest-style biergarten, opposite Chinggis Khaan Sq. Beers cost around T2500.

Dundgol Art Cafe   LOUNGE
(Map p60; 📱8827 8017; Seoul St; ⊘2pm-midnight; 🛜) This funky underground space is a hybrid cafe the morphs into a mini club after dark. There are DJ-mixing turntables, a bar that serves coffee, beer and snacks, and comfortable couch seating. It's located under the Hi-Fi CD Shop. Check the Facebook page for events.

Rock Sugar   PUB
(Map p60; 📱7611 7777; Namnansurengiin Gudamj; beer & cocktails T3500-9000; ⊘11am-midnight; 🛜) It's standing room only on weekends at this popular cocktail bar where local 20-somethings mix and mingle. Food is also served and the steaks are not half bad.

Izakaya Yorimichi   PUB
(Map p60; ⊘noon-midnight) Authentic *izakaya* (Japanese pub) run by the affable Kobe-native Satoru Kimuru. Cheap beers from Japan and tasty authentic udon soup (mains T8500 to T9500). It's the northernmost door in building 12 (just in front of the Mandukhai Hotel). You need an eagle's eye to spot the sign on the door.

Revolution   PUB
(Map p60; Beatles Sq; beer T3000-7000; ⊘8am-midnight Mon-Fri, noon-midnight Sat & Sun; 🛜) Revolution is like your neighborhood pub

back home, everyone seems to know each other. A friendly and welcoming place for a beer or cocktail. Tasty Western-style meals (mains T7000 to T13,000) available too.

Mojito Cocktail House   COCKTAILS
(Map p60; 📱7710 0808; Seoul St; cocktails T8000-12,000; ⊘4pm-midnight Sun-Fri, 4pm-2am Sat) Hip spot for drinking and meeting Ulaanbaatar's young urbanites. Unsurprisingly, mojitos are the house speciality. The swanky interior, soothing playlists and sophisticated drinks make this a must-visit if you are painting the town red.

Grand Khaan Irish Pub   PUB
(Map p60; 📱11-336 666; Seoul St; ⊘11am-midnight; 🛜) In summertime it seems like half of Ulaanbaatar is crowded onto the deck of this old stand-by. Order a pint and join them. The pub-grub menu (meal with beer T18,000 to T45,000) includes an array of salads.

Ikh Mongol   BEER HALL
(Map p60; 📱11-305 014; Seoul St; draught beer from T3500; ⊘noon-midnight) Jugs o' beer to fill your gut, daily live music (10pm) and a large beer patio built on two levels. It's located on the east side of the State Circus.

Brix Nightclub   CLUB
(Map p60; Baga Toiruu East, admission T10,000-20,000; ⊘10-3pm) One of the top clubs in town, Brix is always busy and caters to a mostly 20s crowd of young professionals

---

BARS WITH A VIEW
....

If you are looking for a bar with a great view, you've got a few good options in UB. The **View Lounge Club** (Map p60; ⊘5pm-midnight), on the top floor of the Corporate Hotel; the **Sky Lounge** (Map p60; ⊘noon-midnight), on the 17th floor of the Central Tower; and the **Blue Sky Lounge** (Map p60; 📱7010 9779; Blue Sky Tower, 23rd Fl, Peace Ave 17; ⊘noon-midnight) on the 23rd floor of the Blue Sky Tower are all worth checking out. They serve pricey drinks (beers T5000, cocktails T7000 to T12,000) and have a dimly lit, Manhattan-style atmosphere, with big windows overlooking the city below. If you're in party mode, try the Sky Lounge on Thursday or Friday (admission T5000 to T10,000) when the tables are cleared and DJs spin the latest Mongolian electronica.

letting their hair down. Professional DJs spin club music and top-40 dance music while bartenders serve up potent, and sometimes flammable drinks. There are theme parties a couple of times a month, frequent dance acts on stage and unexpected surprises – confetti, CO_2, foam or other non-lethal objects may be shot in your direction.

Dorgio
CLUB

(Map p60; Builders Sq; men/women Fri & Sat T10,000/5000; ☺9pm-midnight Sun-Tue, 9pm-3am Wed-Sat) Buried under Builder's Sq, this popular pick-up club has two circular-shaped bars and tables suggestively illuminated with red lamps. Cramped and seedy, it attracts a young, working-class crowd that comes to party hard. The admission fee is lower than most places and it's just stumbling distance from most guesthouses, making this a good option for the backpacker set.

Metropolis
CLUB

(Map p70; ☎9973 0569; Sky Shopping Centre; admission T10,000; ☺10pm-4am) Metropolis (mispronounced 'Metro Police' by most locals) has a large dance floor and a VIP voyeur terrace. The DJ plays an eclectic mix of disco, salsa, pop, rock and techno. Drinks go for T4000 to T6000. It's set inside a large vault next to the entrance to the Sky Shopping Mall. Although once the most popular place in town, it now has a reputation for attracting mostly a college-age (and younger) clientele.

Vegas
CLUB

(Map p60; ☎7010 9889; Peace Ave 17, Blue Sky Tower; admission T10,000-20,000; ☺10pm-4am) Located in the basement of the landmark Blue Sky Tower, this bunker-like nightclub runs a variety of events through the week, such as nights for R&B, electro and salsa. The band Shanz 3 (a female trio who play the *shanz* while wearing slinky outfits) often plays here. Music is loud to a point and there is often a good mix of foreigners and locals.

VLVT
CLUB

(Map p60; ☎7711 0031; www.vlvt.mn; Baga Toiruu North, Metro Mall; before 10pm free, after 10pm T40,000; ☺noon-midnight Mon-Thu, noon-3am Fri & Sat; ☏) In this dimly lit den of luxury, Ulaanbaatar's young entrepreneurs cut business deals over pricey cocktails and platters of sushi while sitting at a translucent bar made from marble. In a separate room, revellers dressed to the nines dance to the latest hip-hop and dance mixes. While the

standard drinks menu has cocktails starting at around T10,000, rock stars should ask for the VIP menu featuring bottles of champage for a cool T35 million. Dress code is smart casual.

☆ Entertainment

Both the *UB Post* and the *Mongol Messenger* English-language newspapers contain weekly events listings. The **Arts Council of Mongolia** (Map p60; ☎11-319 015; www.artscouncil.mn) produces a monthly cultural-events calendar, which covers most theatres, galleries and museums. You can pick up a brochure in hotel lobbies and many restaurants. Theatres and galleries sometimes post English ads outside or you could just buy a ticket and hope for the best.

Theatre

Apart from traditional song and dance, you can also watch opera, drama and orchestral performances.

★Mongolian National Song & Dance Ensemble
MUSIC, DANCE

(Map p60; ☎11-323 954; admission T7000) The Mongolian National Song & Dance Ensemble puts on performances for tourists throughout the summer in the National Academic Drama Theatre. Shows are less frequently staged at the Cultural Palace (p59) on the northeast corner of Chinggis Khaan Sq.

You can also see traditional song and dance at the Choijin Lama Temple Museum (p65) in summer at 5pm.

★National Academic Drama Theatre
DRAMA

(Map p60; ☎7012 8999, 7011 8187; cnr Seoul St & Chingisiin Örgön Chölöö; admission T15,000-30,000; ☺ticket sales 10am-7pm) During most of the year, this large, red-hued theatre shows one of a dozen or so Mongolian-language productions by various playwrights from Mongolia, Russia and beyond. *Don Quixote* was playing when we last visited. Schedules are sporadic. You can buy tickets in advance at the booking office, which is inside the small concrete guardhouse on the right-hand side of the theatre.

On the left-hand side of the theatre, as you approach it from the road, is a door that leads to a **puppet theatre** (☎11-321 669; admission T1500-2500; ☺noon, 2pm, 4pm Sat & Sun; ☖), which is great if you are travelling with children.

State Youth & Children's Theatre
MUSIC, DANCE

(Map p60; 9665 0711; www.tumen-ekh.mn; Nairamdal Park; admission T15,000; ⊙6pm May-Oct; ⊕) The Tumen Ekh Song & Dance Ensemble at the State Youth & Children's Theatre is the most popular cultural show in town, featuring traditional singers, dancers and contortionists. It's a great chance to hear *khöömii* (throat singing) and see some fabulous costumes. You can buy folkmusic CDs (T22,000) or a DVD (T30,000) of the show. There is a cafe and gallery in the traditional-style hall. Enter the western gate of the National Amusement Park (Children's Park; p66) and make the first left.

Tsuki House
MUSIC, DANCE

(Map p60; 11-318 802; admission US$7; ⊙7pm May-Sep) The Moonstone Song & Dance Ensemble at Tsuki House puts on a Mongolian cabaret. You get the lot: contortionists, throat singers, musicians, *tsam* mask dancers and an electrifying shaman dance done in contemporary fashion. Snacks and drinks are available at an additional cost. Tsuki House is the squat, two-storey building about 100m northwest of the State Circus.

State Opera & Ballet Theatre
OPERA, BALLET

(Map p60; 7011 0389; admission T8000-15,000; ⊙closed Aug, box office 10am-1pm & 2-6pm Wed-Sun) Built by the Russians in 1932, the State Opera & Ballet Theatre is the salmon-pinkish building on the southeast corner of Chinggis Khaan Sq. On Saturday and Sunday evenings throughout the year, and sometimes also on weekend afternoons in the summer, the theatre holds stirring opera (in Mongolian) and ballet shows.

Mongolian original operas include *Three Fateful Hills* by famous playwright D Natsagdorj, and the more recent *Chinggis Khaan*, by B Sharav. Other productions include an exhilarating (but long) rendition of *Carmen*, plus plenty of Puccini and Tchaikovsky.

A board outside the theatre lists the shows for the current month in English. Advance purchase is worthwhile for popular shows because tickets are numbered, so it's possible to score a good seat if you book early.

Live Music

★Altain Orgil
FOLK MUSIC

Well-known folklore ensemble that plays traditional Mongolian music, including long songs and throat singing. Their stage outfits

TRADITIONAL SONG & DANCE

The groaning chants of a throat singer ringing through your ears and the high-flying acrobatics of a traditional dancer soaring before your eyes are cultural experiences not be be missed in Ulaanbaatar.

At small theatres you are pretty much guaranteed to hear *khöömii* (throat singing) and Mongolia's unique horse-head fiddle, the *morin khuur*.

The best places to get your fill of Mongolian traditional theatre include Tsuki House and the State Youth & Children's Theatre. You can buy performance CDs and DVDs at the shows or look for them at souvenir shops around town.

are influenced by the robes worn by shaman. In summer they play 30-minute concerts every night in one of the restaurants owned by the Modern Nomads chain, usually either **City Nomads** (Map p70; 11-454 484; Peace Ave; ⊕) or **Khaan Ger Grill & Bar** (Map p60; 7711 5544; www.modernnomads.mn; mains T9000-24,000; ⊙11am-midnight). The concert, which begins at 7.30pm, is free to watch if you order something from the restaurant. You'll need to call ahead to these restaurants to find where the band will be playing.

River Sounds
LIVE MUSIC

(Map p60; 11-320 444; Olympiin Örgön Chölöö; admission T20,000; ⊙6pm-3am) This is one of the best places to hear music as it's a dedicated live-music venue with jazz bands and the occasional indie rock band. It's located behind the Foreign Ministry.

UB Jazz Club
JAZZ

(Map p60; 9969 8146; Seoul St; admission free; ⊙10am-midnight) FREE As the name suggests, this is a dedicated jazz club, the only one in Ulaanbaatar.

Cinemas

Örgöö 2 Cinema
CINEMA

(Map p60; 7011 7711; www.urgoo.mn; Baga Toiruu East; regular T4000, VIP seat T10,000) This comfortable theatre has air-conditioned halls and a modern projection system.

Tengis
CINEMA

(Map p60; 11-313 105; www.tengis.mn; Liberty Sq; regular T6000, 3D film T7000)

MODERN MONGOLIAN MUSIC MASH-UPS

There is a thriving contemporary music scene in Ulaanbaatar. While you are in town, make sure to pick up some CDs of the newest artists. Even better, try to catch a live performance. You can hear live music at many downtown bars like River Sounds (p85) or Grand Khaan Irish Pub (p83). Popular music genres include pop, rap and hip-hop, as well as a totally Mongolian brand of folklore-rock fusion music that includes drums and guitars along with traditional instruments.

For folklore-rock, Altan Urag (www.altanurag.mn) is regarded as one of the best. Their mash-ups of Western percussion and Mongolian string instruments will have you entranced. Their website has a full range of videos (we like 'Raakh II' and 'Abroad'). We are also huge fans of the Boerte Ensemble, which fuses all sorts of instruments into a mellow sound good for long road trips. Their videos are available on YouTube. Another band enjoying some success is Khusugtun (www.khusugtun.com); they were recently recorded by the BBC's *Human Planet* series.

If you are into hip-hop, look out for upcoming artists Opozit, Quiza, Tatar and Tsetse. The emulation of American inner-city gangsta rap speaks volumes about Mongolia's eagerness to embrace Western culture; however, if you can get someone to translate the lyrics you'll hear a distinct Mongolian flavour as popular topics include lost loves, mothers, wild nature and blue skies.

Rock groups include the Lemons, Pips and Nisvanis. For mellow R&B, the best are BX, Maraljingoo and Bold. Nominjin (www.nominjin.com) is an up-and-coming R&B voice on the international scene; she sings in both English and Mongolian. You can hear most of these artists on YouTube.

The recent breakout in Mongolian rap has not gone unnoticed. Australian filmmaker Benj Binks has documented the phenomena in the film *Mongolian Bling* (www.mongolianbling.com). Not to be outdone, American Lauren Knapp created *Live From UB* (www.livefromub.com), a documentary exploring Mongolian rock music.

Gay & Lesbian Venues

The only dedicated gay bar in UB is Hanzo (p82), a friendly bar-nightclub that is pretty tame most of the week but lets loose on Friday and Saturday nights. One-off drag queen shows are sometimes held at different locations around the city but you'll need to tap into the community to find out when and where these take place.

Circus

State Circus   CIRCUS

(Map p60; ☑11-325 522; admission T10,000-15,000; 🖝) In the recognisable round building with the orange roof south of the State Department Store. Circus performances only happen a few times a year when an international circus is in town. Concerts are sometimes held here in summer. Shows are advertised in the *UB Post* or at tourist information centres.

Sport

The annual Naadam (p72) features wrestling, horse racing and archery. In the lead-up to Naadam, you should be able to catch some informal, but still competitive, wrestling and archery at the Naadam Stadium.

Wrestling Palace   WRESTLING

(Map p70; ☑11-456 978; www.undesniibukh.mn; Peace Ave; admission T5000-10,000) For wrestling outside of Naadam, check out the schedule at the Wrestling Palace, which is the ger-shaped building south of the Chinggis Khaan Hotel.

Central Sports Palace   SPORTS

(Map p60; Baga Toiruu) Wrestling, basketball and boxing are held at the Central Sports Palace during the year. A more modern sports complex has opened near the airport.

Fashion Shows

Torgo Fashion Salon   FASHION SHOW

(Map p60; ☑ 9191 9050, 11-324 957; www.torgo.mn; Baruun 4 Zam; admission T13,000) Mongolian models strut their stuff on the catwalk at the Torgo Fashion Salon nightly at 6pm from 1 June to 25 September. The designs, by local designers, usually blend traditional Mongolian outfits into contemporary fashions. You can buy products here or just kick back, watch the show and listen to the accompanying music.

Lectures

American Center for Mongolian Studies CULTURAL CENTRE
(Америкийн Монгол Судлалын Төв; Map p60; ☑ 7711 0486; www.mongoliacenter.org; Natsagdorj Library, east entrance, Seoul St; ⊙ 10am-6pm Mon-Fri) Has a small library of books on Mongolia. Hosts occasional lectures by Western and Mongolian academics, authors and other people of interest (check the website for events).

🔒 Shopping

Just about everything you can think of is available in UB, from ancient Buddhist antiques to the latest generation iPhone. Some higher-end places accept credit cards but cash is still king at most shops.

The antique trade is booming in Mongolia, but you need to be careful about what you buy, as some of it is illegal to export. Make sure the seller can produce a certificate of authenticity. Some dealers will suggest shipping the antiques in the mail to avoid customs at the airport – if you get caught, you may end up in prison.

The numerous souvenir shops in town sell landscape paintings, wool slippers, Mongolian jackets, felt dolls and Chinggis Khaan T-shirts. On Chinggis Khaan (Sükhbaatar) Sq and in the Central Post Office (CPO) you will undoubtedly encounter amateur artists selling watercolours for US$1 to US$5. Contemporary Mongolian artwork can be purchased at a small number of galleries around town. The biggest souvenir outlet is on the 6th floor of the State Department Store.

Traditional musical instruments make perfect gifts for friends who are musically inclined. The *morin khuur* (horse-head fiddle) is particularly nice as a piece of decorative art (and Mongolians consider it good luck to have one in the home).

Cashmere also makes good gifts. The major cashmere and wool factories are Goyo, Gobi Cashmere and Altai. The State Department Store has cashmere on the 2nd and 6th floors. Some shops around Beatles Sq also deal in cashmere.

Be aware that Western-quality camping gear is not cheap in Mongolia, so you may want to bring stuff from home. Cheap Chinese-made products are available if you're desperate, though most of it breaks down before you even leave the city. There is a decent camping section on the 3rd floor of the State Department Store. For second-hand stuff, check the noticeboards at the guesthouses and at Café Amsterdam (p82).

For a country with such a rich tradition in horse riding there is a surprising lack of shops selling saddles and tack. The best selection is still at the Naran Tuul Market. You may also be able to pick up a secondhand saddle from another traveller (check guesthouse noticeboards).

English-language bookshops are small and limited. You could try poking around the newspaper kiosk in the CPO or the bookshop on the 6th floor of the State Department Store.

★ Naran Tuul Market MARKET
(Наран Туул Зах; Map p57; ⊙ 9am-7pm Wed-Mon) **FREE** East of the centre, this is also known as the Black Market (Khar Zakh), but it's not the sort of place where you go to change money illegally and smuggle goods – though this certainly happens.

A covered area has a decent selection of clothes and accessories, such as bags, jeans and fake North Face jackets. This is also one of the cheapest places to get traditional Mongolian clothes such as a simple *del* (starting from around T80,000) and *huruum* (Mongolian jacket, for around T50,000). Carpet sellers are also in the covered area. Just to the west of this section are stalls for the hat and boot sellers, where furry winter hats start from T20,000 and traditional boots start at around T50,000. All these make great gifts.

Towards the back of the market you'll find saddles (T90,000 for a soft Russian saddle or T120,000 for a simple Mongolian saddle), riding tack, Mongolian furniture and all the parts needed to build your own ger. The back area is also where you'll find antique and coin dealers, but they don't issue any official documentation (unlike the antique shops in town), making it illegal to export their stock. New items, such as the snuff bottles (made in China anyway), can be purchased without worry. You can also buy authentic shaman drums starting from around T120,000.

In 2013 a fire destroyed the food section of the market, but other parts of the market survived.

The market is notorious for pickpockets and bag-slashers, so don't bring anything you can't afford to lose. Don't carry anything on your back, and strap your money belt to your body. Naran Tuul is definitely worth a visit – just be careful.

A taxi to the market should cost about T5000 from the centre of town. To walk from Chinggis Khaan Sq will take about 40 minutes. Try to avoid the area on weekends, when the crowds (and traffic) can be horrendous.

★ Mary & Martha Mongolia   SOUVENIRS
(Map p60; www.mmmongolia.com) 🍃 Fair-trade shop selling handicrafts, felt products and modern Kazakh wall hangings. Has some innovative little products like computer bags and mobile-phone cases made with traditional designs. It's a couple of doors past Le Boulange bakery (p81).

State Department Store   SHOPPING CENTRE
(Их Дэлгүүр; Map p60; ☎11-313 232; www.nomin. mn; Peace Ave 44) Known as *ikh delguur* (big shop), this is virtually a tourist attraction in itself, with the best products from around the city squeezed into one building.

The 1st floor has a foreign-exchange counter and a supermarket. The 2nd and 3rd floors have outlets for clothing, cashmere and leather goods. The 4th floor has a children's section. The 5th floor has electronics. The 6th floor has a food court, bookstore and a large room containing souvenirs, traditional clothing, maps and books about Mongolia.

Seven Summits   OUTDOOR GEAR
(Map p60; ☎11-329 456; www.activemongolia.com/ seven_summits; btwn Peace Ave & Seoul St) Stocks German-made Vaude gear, GPS units, maps, stoves and gas, travel books and accessories. It also hires out gear, including tents, sleeping bags, gas stoves, mountain bikes and inflatable kayaks. It's opposite the CPO.

Ayanchin Outfitters   OUTDOOR GEAR
(Map p60; ☎11-319 211; www.ayanchin.mn; Seoul St 21) This place sells camping, fishing and hunting equipment, plus GPS units, mainly imported from the US.

Attila Bike Shop   BICYCLES
(☎9929 8921; 79-8 Uildver Gudamj, Khan-Uul District) The best bike bike shop in UB is located in a difficult-to-find apartment area in the south of the city. Turn right 430m south of the Bogd Khan Winter Palace and take this road 850m until you find the shop on your right. Note that there are two separate bike shops here, the one in the back is Attila.

Amarbayasgalant Antique   ANTIQUES
(Map p60; ☎11-310 000; Juulchin Gudamj 37/31) A quality shop for the serious buyer, it sells enormous Sutras, traditional headdress, Buddhist statues and other rare items. Some of the items are creations of Zanabazar and not for sale. Great for browsing.

Books in English   BOOKS
(Map p60; ☎9920 3360; Peace Ave) Sells used books, including guidebooks. It's tough to spot, located in the basement of an apartment block. Keep your eyes peeled for the yellow-and-blue sign.

Librairie Papillon   BOOKS
(Map p60; ☎11-331 859; Ikh Surguuliin Gudamj) Ulaanbaatar's classiest bookshop. Has plenty of classic books in English, but the collection of French books is by far the most interesting.

Egshiglen Magnai National Musical Instrument Shop   MUSICAL INSTRUMENTS
(Map p60; ☎11-328 419; Sükhbaataryn Gudamj) At this shop on the east side of the Museum of Natural History, *morin khuur* range from T200,000 to T950,000. There are also *yattag* (zithers) and two-stringed Chinese fiddles.

Hi-Fi CD Shop   MUSIC
(Map p60; Seoul St) Mongolian music CDs make great gifts for friends back home and this place has one of the best collections. Also check the State Department Store.

Cashmere House   CASHMERE
(Map p60; Peace Ave; ☺11am-7pm Mon-Sat) Excellent cashmere garments can be purchased here. It's opposite the Russian embassy.

Gobi Cashmere Shop   CASHMERE
(Map p60; Chingisiin Örgön Chölöö; ☺11am-7pm Mon-Sat) This downtown outlet of the iconic brand shows off the latest fashions in cashmere and wool.

Gobi Cashmere Factory Outlet   CASHMERE
(Map p57; Industrial St, Khan-Uul District; ☺11am-7pm) Has slightly lower prices than the cashmere shops in the city centre, although much of it is last year's stock. It's in the industrial suburbs and hard to find on your own. If you take a taxi, have your hotel write down the address for the driver.

Computerland   ELECTRONICS
(Map p60; Peace Ave; ☺10am-7pm Mon-Sat) This three-storey building is crammed with dozens of private dealers selling everything from

flashdrives to the latest laptops. It is located behind the Canon Showroom, which also has a computer shop.

Shilmel Torgo TRADITIONAL CLOTHING
(Map p60; 📋 11-325 968; Baga Toiruu 14; ⊘ 10am-6pm Mon-Sat) This shop produces custom-made *dels* and other traditional Mongolian outfits. A custom-made silk *del* will cost around T280,000.

Nomads Culture Antique Shop ANTIQUES
(Map p60; 📋 11-333 939; Juulchin Gudamj 35) Good for silver cups, *thangkas*, Buddhist art, brasswork and jewellery.

Mongolian Quilting Shop SOUVENIRS
(Map p60; 📋 9909 9930; www.mongolianquilts.com; Seoul St; ⊘ 9am-7pm Mon-Fri) 🖋 Sells handmade quilts produced by low-income families. The money earned here goes to the New Life NGO, which directly supports the women who produce the quilts.

Möngön Zaviya SILVER PRODUCTS
(Map p60; Peace Ave; ⊘ 10.30am-8.30pm Mon-Fri, 11am-7.30pm Sat & Sun) An enormous, non-touristy showroom of silver cups, belt buckles and jewellery. The basement has some of the best traditional silverwork.

Souvenir House SOUVENIRS
(Map p60; 📋 11-320 398; cnr Peace Ave & Khaddor-jiin Gudamj) One of the largest souvenir shops in town.

Art House Centre ANTIQUES
(Map p60; 📋 11-328 948; Juulchin Gudamj 44) Several small antique shops are located on the 2nd floor of this building, hidden behind Narya Café.

Eternal Antique & Art Gallery ANTIQUES
(Map p60; Sükhbaataryn Gudamj) One of the best antique shops in the city, this place has a good selection of brass tea jugs and ger furniture. Worth a browse even if some items are too big to take home.

Tsagaan Alt Wool Shop FELT PRODUCTS
(Map p60; 📋 11-318 591; www.mongolianwoolcraft.com; Tserendorjiin Gudamj) 🖋 This non-profit store, which sends money directly back to the craftspeople, has all manner of wool products, including toys, clothes and artwork.

Urt Tsagaan PEDESTRIAN MALL
(Long White; Map p60; Juuchin Gudamj) This pedestrianised shopping mall is a leftover from the communist era and badly in need

of renovation but it's still worth wandering down here. In summer, a yellow outdoor tent serves fresh *airag*. In the building itself there are small shops for cobblers, silversmiths, barbers, tailors, eye-glass repair shops and more. In the easternmost door is a seamstress who sells low-price *dels*. In the middle of the mall is a sign indicating the North Korean restaurant Pyongyang (p78), which serves fairly mediocre meals.

Mon Nip Camera Shop PHOTOGRAPHY
(Map p60; 📋 9912 2338; Baruun 4 Zam) Sells a range of cameras, tripods and other photographic equipment.

Cartography Co Map Shop MAPS
(Map p60; 📋 9115 6023; Ikh Toiruu; ⊘ 9am-6pm Mon-Fri, 10am-4pm Sat year-round, 10am-4pm Sun May-Sep) For maps, try this shop near the Elba Electronics shop, although the stock is starting to age.

ℹ Orientation

Most of the city spreads from east to west along the main road, Enkh Taivny Örgön Chölöö, also known as Peace Ave. Confusingly, locals refer to this road as Töv Zam (Central Road).

At the centre is Chinggis Khaan Sq, aka Sükhbaatar Sq, often simply known as 'the Square' *(talbai)*, which is just north of Peace Ave. Sprawling suburbia is limited by the four mountains that surround the city: Bayanzürkh, Chingeltei, Songino Khairkhan and Bogdkhan.

The city is divided into six major districts, but there's a multitude of subdistricts and micro-districts. Mongolians rarely use street names and numbers (because of their nomadic roots, they prefer to use landmarks), so tracking down an address can be difficult. Another problem is that many buildings are not on any road at all, instead located behind another building (sometimes behind a number of buildings).

A typical address might be something like: Microdistrict 14, Building 3, Flat 27. However, you are unlikely to know which microdistrict it refers to, building numbers can be hard to spot and most street signs are in Mongolian Cyrillic. As a result, most locals will give you an unofficial description, such as 'door 67, building 33, last door of a white-and-red building, behind the Drama Theatre'. Because of the confusing state of affairs, business cards usually have small maps on the back.

If you think your destination might be hard to find, call ahead. The staff will send someone out to meet you at a nearby landmark. Most places you are likely to call (tour operators, hotels, etc) will probably have an English speaker.

ⓘ Information

Head to **Lonely Planet** (lonelyplanet.com/mongolia/ulaanbaatar) for planning advice, author recommendations, traveller reviews and insider tips.

DANGERS & ANNOYANCES

Ulaanbaatar is a fairly carefree and easygoing city but there are a few concerns to keep in mind.

Theft

Pickpockets and bag-slashers are still a problem, though the situation is not as dire as it was a few years ago. When it happens, robbery is seldom violent against foreigners, just opportunistic.

Be particularly vigilant on Peace Ave between the Central Post Office and the State Department Store, or other main streets where tourists wander. Pickpockets also target public buses and the Naran Tuul Market. Keep an eye on your bag when sitting in cafes. Be very careful around the stadium during Naadam.

➔ Pickpockets often work in teams. One perpetrator may distract you while his friend picks your pocket.

➔ Leave passports, credit cards, large amounts of cash and valuables locked up in your hotel (preferably in a safe). Just carry the cash you need for food, admission fees and incidentals. Carry this small cash in a shirt pocket rather than a trouser pocket.

➔ If carrying a backpack, clip the zippers together with a luggage lock or caribiner.

➔ Money belts are handy but not fail-safe (thieves might slice the belt with a razor).

➔ If you are a robbed, you may need to file a report with the police to satisfy your insurance company. Immediately report the incident to the Department of Pickpockets, a division of the police, located in the police office on the block west of the Russian embassy.

Violent Crime

Reports of violence against foreigners have increased in recent years. The problem often occurs in or near a bar and alcohol often contributes to the problem. When moving about at night, stick to well-lit streets and do so with a group of friends – there is safety in numbers. Sexual assault against foreign women is rare and local women walk around at night, often alone, though it's not a great idea because of pickpockets.

Some foreigners have reported being assaulted and robbed in a taxi. Use an official taxi – as opposed to a private vehicle – late at night.

Alcoholism

Alcoholism is a problem in Ulaanbaatar, especially among out-of-work middle-aged and older Mongolian men. It's worse around Naadam time, but drunks are usually more annoying than dangerous.

Traffic

Probably the most dangerous thing you can do in Ulaanbaatar is cross the street. Pedestrians are given no special treatment so expect that you could get run over at any given moment. The zebra crossings are not safe either because at some intersections the right-turn arrow and the pedestrian arrow turn green simultaneously, so as you step into the crosswalk a car will come around the corner into your path. Look out!

Other Annoyances

➔ Some stairwells aren't lit, so a small torch (flashlight) is handy. Blackouts and hot-water shortages are common throughout the year.

➔ Police often mean well but language barriers and cultural differences can make dealing with them a challenge.

➔ Garbage collection is a serious problem in Ulaanbaatar and you'll spot mounds of trash everywhere, especially in courtyards and back alleys.

➔ The number of street children and beggars in Ulaanbaatar has noticeably decreased but there are still a few around. One way of helping out is to make a donation to a local orphanage. In terms of offering something to a street kid, handing out fruit or other fresh food is better than money (as money collected is often taken from them by older boys or gangs).

EMERGENCY

It might take a few minutes to get hold of an English speaker for these numbers.

Emergency Aid/Ambulance (☏103)

Fire (☏101)

Police Emergency (Map p60; ☏102)

Department of Pickpockets (Map p60; ☏7012 0137) This police department is the place to go if you have been robbed. It's located in a courtyard just west of the Russian embassy.

INTERNET ACCESS

Widespread use of wi-fi has killed off most of the internet cafes (Интэрнэт Кафэ) in Ulaanbaatar but there are still a few around; just look for the

---

ⓘ WI-FI ACCESS

Ulaanbaatar is awash with wi-fi hotspots. Most likely your hotel or guesthouse will offer it – we've indicated which ones with the 🛜 symbol. Nearly all cafes and restaurant in UB offer free wi-fi. There are several public wi-fi hotspots, mainly in public squares and parks, you just need to search for the name 'Kewiko_Free' then click the link when it appears on your screen. Wi-fi is available in some places at the airport.

signs, which are usually in English. Hourly rates are reasonable at about T600 to T800, but double that price at hotel business centres. Connections are generally good.

Internet Cafe (Map p60; ☑ 7010 2486; Peace Ave; per 10min T100; ⊗ 9am-8pm Mon-Fri, 11am-5pm Sat & Sun) Located inside the Central Post Office.

LAUNDRY

Almost all of the hotels in Ulaanbaatar offer a laundry service for between T2000 and T3000 per kilogram, but they may not advertise it – so just ask. If you can be bothered, it's not difficult to do some laundry yourself – the markets and shops sell small packets of detergent and bleach.

Metro Express (Map p60; ☑ 9919 4234, 11-470 789) Has 10 branches scattered across the city, including one next to the Minii Delguur supermarket. It also has a kiosk on the ground floor of the State Department Store. A load of laundry costs T8500 and turnaround time is about four hours.

LEFT LUGGAGE

Most hotels and guesthouses can store luggage while you are off getting lost in the Gobi. There is usually no fee if you've stayed a few nights.

MAPS

Several maps of Ulaanbaatar are available; a good one is the 1:10,000 *Ulaanbaatar City Map*. The most extensive selection of maps is at Seven Summits (p88). The Cartography Co Map Shop (p89) is another place to check.

MEDIA

Ulaanbaatar's two English-language newspapers, *Mongol Messenger* (weekly) and *UB Post* (thrice weekly), are well worth picking up for local news and entertainment information. *That's Ulaanbaatar*, a free magazine packed with updated tourist information, is available at hotels and tourist offices. You can listen to the BBC World Service on 103.1PM.

MEDICAL SERVICES

The best place for most of your health-care needs is the SOS Medica Mongolia Clinic, but life-or-death emergencies are sent to Seoul or Běijīng. Pharmacies (*aptek;* Аптек) are common in Ulaanbaatar, stocking Mongolian, Russian, Chinese and Korean medicine. Check expiry dates carefully. The US embassy website (p269) has an extensive list of medical services.

City Optic (Map p60; ☑ 7011 4567) An optometrist, located on the 1st floor of the Metro Mall.

Degfim Dentist (Map p70; ☑ 11-331 313; www. degfim.com; D Natsagdorj St) A modern, recommended dentist office with some English-speaking staff.

Songdo Hospital (Map p60; ☑ 7011 1163; Choidog Gudamj; ⊗ 8.30am-5pm Mon-Fri, 8am-noon Sat) Modern Korean-run hospital with examinations starting at T20,000.

SOS Dental Clinic (Map p70; ☑ 11-464 330; 4a bldg, Big Ring Rd) The best place for dental work. In the same building as SOS Medica Mongolia Clinic.

SOS Medica Mongolia Clinic (Map p70; ☑ 11-464 325; 4a bldg, Big Ring Rd; ⊗ 9am-6pm Mon-Fri) This clinic has a staff of Western doctors on call 24 hours (after hours call ☑ 9911 0335). Its services don't come cheap (examinations start from around US$195), but it's the best place to go in an emergency.

MONEY

Banks, ATMs and moneychangers are widespread. Banks with the best services include Golomt, Khan Bank and Trade & Development Bank. ATMs (you'll find them in department stores, mini markets and hotel lobbies) dispense tögrög; you can get dollars or euros from a bank teller, with your debit card and passport (expect a fee of around 1% to 3% from your home bank). The moneychanger on the ground floor of the State Department Store is handy but rates here are not the best. The moneychangers at Ard Kino and Ikh Naiman Sharga have the best rates.

Both Golomt and Trade & Development Bank will allow you to receive money wired from abroad. It will cost the sender about US$40 to wire any amount of money; there is no charge for receiving cash.

Ard Kino Money Changers (Map p60; Baga Toiruu West; ⊗ 9am-7pm) There are several exchange offices on this square, on Baga Toiruu.

Ikh Naiman Sharga (Map p60; Tömörchiin Gudamj; ⊗ 9am-7pm) This building contains several moneychangers on the ground floor. The exchange rates here are the best in UB. The sign on the building says: Их 8 Шарга.

Trade & Development Bank (T&D Bank; Map p60; ☑ 11-327 095; ⊗ 9am-4pm Mon-Fri) Will change travellers cheques into tögrög for a 1% fee or into US dollars for a 2% fee. Will also replace lost Amex travellers cheques.

PERMITS

If you are travelling to border areas such as Altai Tavan Bogd National Park in Bayan-Ölgii, the **General Office of Border Protection** (Map p57; ☑ 11-454 142; Border Defence Bldg; ⊗ 10am-12.30pm & 2-5pm Mon-Fri), in the east of the city, is the place to go for permits. Permits are free but you must send a Mongolian on your behalf to apply. The office requires a passport photocopy and a map showing your route. The office is in a grey building just west of the Mongolian Military Museum.

POLICE

The **police** (Map p60; ⏼102, 11-311 002; www.ubpolice.mn) are located on Sambugiin Örgön Chölöö and on Negdsen Undestnii Gudamj. A separate police office (p90) near the State Department Store is the place to go if you have been the victim of a pickpocket.

POST

Central Post Office (CPO, Töv Shuudangiin Salbar; Map p60; ⏼11-313 421; cnr Peace Ave & Sükhbaataryn Gudamj; ☺7.30am-9pm Mon-Fri, 9am-8pm Sat & Sun) Located near the southwest corner of Chinggis Khaan Sq. The Postal Counter Hall is the place to post mail, packages and check poste restante (counter No 9; you'll need to show your passport). EMS express (priority) mail can also be sent from here. There is also a good range of postcards, small booklets about Mongolia in English, and local newspapers for sale. On Sunday, although it's open, most services are nonexistent. Express services such as FedEx are more reliable if sending important documents.

FedEx (Map p60; ⏼11-320 591; fedex@tuushin.mn; Amaryn Gudamj 2; ☺9am-6pm Mon-Fri) Located next to the Best Western Tuushin Hotel. A 500g letter to most Western countries costs around $45.

TELEPHONE & FAX

For local calls, you can use the phone at your hotel, often for free. Other hotels, including those with business centres, charge T400 for a call to a landline (six digits) or a mobile number (eight digits). You can also make local calls from the CPO. Where available, internet cafes are equipped with headsets and webcams for Skype calls.

International phone calls from the CPO require purhasing prepaid cards starting from T2000.

Most midrange to top-end hotels have a fax that can be used by guests for about T1500 to T2000 per page. Hotels charge around T500 to receive a fax on your behalf.

For info on area codes, see p274.

TOILETS

There are a handful of public toilets in UB, including in front of the Ulaanbaatar Hotel.

TOURIST INFORMATION

Guide Tourist Information Centre (Map p60; ⏼7010-1011; cnr Baga Toiruu West & Peace Ave; ☺9am-9pm May-Sep, 10am-7pm Oct-Apr) This privately run info centre is located in the Erel Bank Building. Friendly and helpful service.

Ulaanbaatar Information Centre (Map p60; ⏼7010-8687; www.tourism.ub.gov.mn; Baga Toiruu 15; ☺9am-6pm) Located in the Ulaanbaatar Bank building (door is on the north side). This office (run by the city) has a rack of brochures but the staff here seem pretty indifferent to visitors.

TRAVEL AGENCIES

Staff at backpacker guesthouses can help with visa registration and train tickets. All the guesthouses mentioned in this book offer reliable help. For a small fee, some guesthouses even help visitors staying at other hotels.

The following agencies are good for organising air tickets.

Air Market (Map p60; ⏼11-305 050; www.air-market.mn; cnr Peace Ave & Chingisiin Örgön Chölöö; ☺9am-8pm)

Air Network (Map p60; ⏼11-322 222; airnetwork@magicnet.mn; Baga Toiruu West; ☺9am-7pm Mon-Fri, 10am-3pm Sat & Sun)

Air Trans (Map p60; ⏼11-313 131; airtrans@magicnet.mn; cnr Sükhbaataryn Gudamj & Sambugiin Örgön Chölöö; ☺9am-7pm Mon-Fri, 10am-3pm Sat)

Silk Road Network (Map p60; ⏼11-320 405; silkroad@mongolnet.mn; Peace Ave; ☺10am-8pm) Located on the east side of State Department Store.

ⓘ Getting There & Away

AIR

For details on prices and routes for international flights, see p279.

Chinggis Khaan International Airport (⏼11-983 005, 198; www.airport.mn; ☎) is 18km southwest of the city. The airport has ATMs and banking services, a post office, and internet access for T50 per minute. A tourist booth operates inside the baggage hall when planes arrive.

Mongolia has three domestic carriers: Hunnu Airlines, AeroMongolia and EZ Nis. On domestic routes with Hunnu Air and AeroMongolia you are allowed 15kg of baggage (combined carry-on and check-in). EZ Nis allows 20kg. You'll pay around T3000 per kilogram over the limit. Flight days always change, so check updated schedules. The airlines accept credit cards for international and domestic flights.

Aeroflot (Map p60; ⏼11-320 720; www.aeroflot.ru; Seoul St 15; ☺9am-6pm Mon-Fri, 10am-3pm Sat)

AeroMongolia (Map p60; ⏼11-330 373; www.aeromongolia.mn; Monnis Bldg, ground fl)

Air China (Map p57; ⏼7575 8800; www.airchina.com; Narny Gudamj 87; ☺9am-1pm & 2-5pm Mon-Fri, 10am-4pm Sat, 9am-noon Sun) Located on Narny Gudamj in the southeast of town.

EZ Nis (Map p60; ⏼7575 3232; www.eznis.com; 8 Zovkhis Bldg, Seoul St)

Hunnu Air (Map p60; 7000 2222; www.hunnuair.com; 10-1 Chingisiin Örgon Chölöö) 9am-6pm Mon-Sat, 9am-3pm Sun) It only offers international flights.

Korean Air (Map p70; 11-317 100; www.koreanair.com; 2nd fl, Chinggis Khaan Hotel; 9am-6pm Mon-Fri)

MIAT (Mongolian Airlines; Map p60; 11-333 999; www.miat.com; Chinggisiin Örgön Chölöö;

Turkish Airlines (Map p70; 7585 9999; www.turkishairlines.com; Sonor Plaza, Peace Ave)

United Airlines (Map p60; 11-323 232; www.united.com; Air Trans office, Sükhbaataryn Gudamj 1; 9am-6pm Mon-Fri, 10am-4pm Sat)

ULAANBAATAR BUS TIMETABLES

From Bayanzürkh Avto Vaksal

DESTINATION	PRICE (T)	DURATION (HR)	FREQUENCY (DAILY)	DEPARTURES
Baganuur (Багануур)	4000	2	2	11am, 5pm
Baruun-Urt (Баруун-Урт)	26,500	11	2	8am, 4pm
Chinggis Khot (Чингис Хот)	13,200	5	2	8am, 4pm
Choibalsan (Чойбалсан)	31,000	14	2	8am, 4pm
Dalanzadgad (Даланзадгад)	27,500	13	2	8am, 4pm

From Dragon Avto Vaksal

DESTINATION	PRICE (T)	DURATION (HR)	FREQUENCY	DEPARTURES
Altai (Алтай)	46,000	25	Tue, Wed, Fri, Sun	11am
Arvaikheer (Арвайхээр)	20,000	8	3 daily	8am, 2pm, 8pm
Bayankhongor (Баянхонгор)	27,000	15	2 daily	8am, 2pm
Bayan-Ölgii (Баян-Өлгий)	80,000	46	Mon, Wed, Fri, Sun	3pm
Bulgan (Булган)	16,500	8	Tue, Thu, Sat, Sun	noon
Darkhan (Дархан)	10,000	3½	hourly	9am-8pm
Erdenet (Эрдэнэт)	15,000	7	6 daily	10am, 1pm, 1.30pm, 2.30pm, 4pm, 5.30pm
Kharkhorin (Хархорин)	17,000	8	daily	11am
Khovd (Ховд)	65,000	36	daily	1pm
Mandalgov (Мандалговь)	13,000	5	2 daily	8am, 2pm
Mörön (Мөрөн)	32,000	18-22	2 daily	2pm, 5pm
Tsetserleg (Цэцэрлэг)	23,000	12	2 daily	8am, 2pm
Ulaangom (Улаангом)	63,000	46	daily, except Tue	3pm
Uliastai (Улиастай)	48,000	20	Mon, Wed, Thur, Fri, Sun	9am
Zuunmod (Зуунмод)	2000	1	hourly	8am-8pm

United does not fly to Mongolia but this office can help book flights out of Seoul and Běijīng.

BUS

Two stations handle most bus traffic. The eastern depot, **Bayanzürkh Avto Vaksal** (Баянзүрх Авто Вокзал; ☎ 7015 3386), is 6km east of Chinggis Khaan (Sükhbaatar) Sq. The western bus station, called the **Dragon Avto Vaksal** (Dragon Bus Stand; ☎ 7017 4902), is on Peace Ave, 7km west of Chinggis Khaan Sq.

In addition to the buses listed on p93, minivans run daily to many of the same destinations (at a similar price), departing when full. It's best to have a Mongolian friend call the bus station to inquire about the minivans as schedules change frequently. An online schedule can be found at www.transdep.mn – click the box on the left side of the front page that shows a Greyhound bus drawing.

Buses are always full so buy your ticket as early as possible. Tickets can be bought one day in advance from the station.

HITCHING

Given the size of Ulaanbaatar, hitching your way out of city is no easy feat. The easier way to hitch a ride would involve first travelling by bus to a city en route to your final destination and then trying to hitch from there. Many drivers will expect you to pay your way before hopping in.

MINIVAN & JEEP

The national bus network is now fairly comprehensive but if you are unable to get a ticket the fallback option is to take a privately operated jeep or minivan.

Vehicles heading for destinations in the north and west (but not east) leave from the Dragon Avto Vaksal, the same place as the main bus departures. For eastern destinations, use the Bayanzürkh Avto Vaksal. Minivans are also available from the Naran Tuul Market (p87) but it's a fairly chaotic place and far less user-friendly compared to the bus stations. Note that there are no vehicles at Naran Tuul on Tuesdays, when the market is closed. Shared cars to Darkhan can sometimes be found across the street from the train station.

Minivans are privately run, so drivers will try to stuff as many people and as much luggage as they possibly can into their vehicle. There is no set schedule; never expect to leave straight away, even if the van is full. Some might not be leaving for another day. If you can find out when it will leave, you could ask the driver to save your seat, and return later. For destinations reachable by paved road you might find a Korean compact car.

Van destinations are posted on the dashboard (in Cyrillic). Prices are usually about 10% to 15% higher than the bus trip (eg to Chinggis Khot, bus T13,000, minivan around T15,000). Most travellers prefer buses, as they tend to leave on time and are considered safer and more reliable.

TAXI

At the time of writing, the cost of hiring a taxi to places near Ulaanbaatar started at T700 per kilometre, although by the time you read this it will likely be higher. The taxi drivers may want more for waiting if you are, for example, visiting

DOMESTIC TRAIN TIMETABLE

Departure times are approximate as they shift from year to year. Trains 34 and 22 are international trains which continue on to Hohhot in China.

DESTINATION	TRAIN NO	FREQUENCY	DEPARTURE	DURATION (HR)	FARE (SEAT/HARD SLEEPER/SOFT SLEEPER)
Darkhan	271	daily	10.30am	7	T5000/10,000/15,300
Erdenet	273	daily	8.20pm	11	T6800/12,300/20,300
Sainshand	286	daily	9.35am	10	T7400/13,200/21,500
Sükhbaatar	263	daily	9.10pm	7¾	T6300/11,800/19,900
Sükhbaatar	271	daily	10.30am	7¾	T6300/11,800/19,900
Zamyn-Üüd	22 (fast)	Thu, Sun	8pm	12	T-/22,100/39,200 (sleeper only)
Zamyn-Üüd	34 (fast)	Mon, Fri	8pm	12	T-/22,100/39,200 (sleeper only)
Zamyn-Üüd	44 (fast)	Sat*	8pm	12	T-/22,100/39,200 (sleeper only)
Zamyn-Üüd	276	daily	4.30pm	15½	T9600/16,300/27,300

*Day of departure can shift to Tuesday or Wednesday.

Mandshir Khiid, or because they may be returning with an empty vehicle if dropping you off somewhere remote. This is not unreasonable, but it *is* negotiable.

To avoid any argument about the final charge, make sure that you and the driver have firstly agreed on the cost per kilometre, and have discussed any extra charges. Then write down the number shown on the odometer/speedometer before you start.

TRAIN

The train station has a left-luggage office, some small kiosks and a restaurant.

From Ulaanbaatar, daily trains travel to northern Mongolia and on to Russia, via Darkhan and Sükhbaatar, and southeast to China, via Choir, Sainshand and Zamyn-Üüd. There are also lines between Ulaanbaatar and the coal-mining towns of Erdenet and Baganuur.

To buy a ticket you must show identification; a passport or driving licence will do (student ID won't work).

Domestic

The **domestic railway ticket office** (Map p57; ☑ 21-24137, Mongolian enquiries number 21-24194; ⊙ 8am-12.30pm & 2.30-9pm) is located in the modern-looking building on the east side of the train station. Boards inside the office show departure times (in Cyrillic) and ticket prices. There's also a full timetable at the information desk on the station platform. Times and schedules are available at ubtz.mn (in Mongolian).

Tickets can be booked for a seat *(niitin obshe)*, hard sleeper *(untlagiin obshe)* or a soft sleeper *(tasalgat)*. Advanced booking is possible, see p291 for details.

International

The yellow **International Railway Ticketing Office** (Map p57; Narny Gudamj) is about 200m northwest of the train station. Inside the office, specific rooms sell tickets to Irkutsk and Moscow in Russia, and to Běijīng, Èrlián and Hohhot in China. The easiest place to book a ticket is in the **foreigners booking office** (☑ 21-24133, enquiries 21-243 848; room 212; ⊙ 8am-8pm Mon-Fri). It's upstairs and staff here speak some English. On weekends you can use the downstairs booking desk.

For more on international train travel, see p285.

🛈 Getting Around

TO/FROM THE AIRPORT

If it's your first visit to Mongolia, the best way to get into the city is to organise a pick-up from your hotel/guesthouse (just email them with your flight details). This may be free (usually if you book three nights' accommodation) or cost around US$15 to US$20. Taxi drivers will find you

in the airport terminal but will almost certainly try to overcharge first-time visitors. After agreeing a price, some might demand more (up to US$50) when you reach your destination; drivers also might hold your luggage hostage until you pay their price; to avoid this, keep your luggage with you in the car, rather than in the boot.

During the month of July the city runs an airport bus to and from the Bayangol Hotel bus stop. The bus runs every 30 minutes and the fare is T2000. However, the service was new in 2013 and it's not clear if it will continue.

If you don't mind walking a little, you can use either bus 11 or 22 (T500). These connect the city centre and the district of Nisekh, close to the airport. At the airport, go out of the terminal and across the parking lot to the main road (a 500m walk). At the main road turn right and walk about 400m, until you reach the bus turn-out (there is no sign but you'll see others waiting). Only do this during daylight (for safety reasons). A bus comes by every 15 minutes or so until 9pm. Once in the city you can get off at the bus stop near the main library (opposite the Drama Theatre).

To the airport, bus 11 or 22 will stop at Ard Kino on Baga Toiruu, and also near the Bayangol Hotel, but it won't drop you at the terminal. You still have to haul your luggage 500m from the bus stop on the highway.

TO/FROM THE TRAIN STATION

It's a 25-minute walk from the train station to the State Department Store. International trains arrive early in the morning while the city is still quiet, so with a backpack it's easy to walk into town. Guesthouses and hotels may pick you up if contacted ahead of time (some hostel owners will be at the station anyway, trawling for guests).

The nearest bus stop is across the street from the station. Bus 20 will get you to the State Department Store and Chinggis Khaan (Sükhbaatar) Sq. To the train station, bus 20 takes Seoul St so you won't see it if waiting near the State Department Store. In this direction you should take trolleybus No 4.

ULAANBAATAR'S MAIN BUS ROUTES

The following destinations can be reached by bus from downtown Ulaanbaatar. The same buses go in the reverse direction. A map of bus routes (in Cyrillic) can be found on www.gogo.mn.

Bayanzürkh Avto Vaksal (Eastern Bus Station) Take bus 27 or 41, or trolleybus 4 from anywhere on Peace Ave, heading east.

Chinggis Khaan Airport Take bus 11 or 22 from either Ard Kino or Bayangol Hotel.

Dragon Avto Vaksal (Western Bus Station) Take bus 23, 26 and 27 from anywhere on Peace Ave, heading west.

East Cross Road For Intellectual Museum and Kempinski Hotel; take trolleybus 4 east running on Peace Ave, or bus 1 or 27.

Naadam Stadium Bus 33 and 43 from Ard Kino or Bayangol Hotel.

Naran Tuul Market Bus 23 goes here from anywhere on Peace Ave.

Three/Four District Take bus 13 from Peace Ave, 43 from Tengis cinema, or 45 from Bayangol Hotel or Mongon Zaviya; bus 10 from the Chinese Embassy or Tengis cinema; trolleybus 5 (heading east) comes here from Peace Ave.

Train Station Bus 20 goes here from Bagshiin Deed (near Ulaanbaatar Hotel), via Seoul St; trolleybus 4 comes here from Peace Ave.

Winter Palace and Zaisan Take bus 33 and 43 from either Ard Kino or Bayangol Hotel; bus 12 goes here from Peace Ave.

Some taxi drivers at the train station, like those at the airport, may agree on one price and then charge more once you reach the hotel. If this happens, stay calm and be patient and polite. Don't give in to their demands. Eventually they will get bored with trying to rip you off and will just accept a reasonable price. Keep your luggage in their car so they can't hold it hostage in the boot. If you must use a taxi, head out of the station and up the road to escape the sharks, then flag down a taxi and pay the standard rate of T800 per kilometre.

BICYCLE

Mongolian drivers are downright dangerous so riding a bike around town can be hazardous to your health. There are no bike lanes and you should never expect to have right of way. Seven Summits (p88) rents mountain bikes for US$35 per day (or US$25 per day for five or more days). Mongolia Expeditions (p36) rents bikes for a more reasonable T20,000 per day. If you want to buy a mountain bike, try Seven Summits, the State Department Store (p88) or the Naran Tuul Market (p87); the market sells new and used bikes.

BUS

Local public transport is reliable and departures are frequent, but buses can get crowded. Conductors collect fares (at the time of writing, T500 for a bus or T300 for a trolleybus for any trip around Ulaanbaatar, including to the airport) and usually have change. Pickpockets and bag-slashers occasionally ply their trade on crowded routes. Seal up all pockets, hold your bag on your chest and be careful when boarding.

The route number is next to the (Cyrillic) destination sign on the front of the trolleybus or bus. The route is often marked on the side of the bus. For short trips it's just as cheap to take a taxi, especially for two or more passengers.

Overcrowded green minivans connect the ger suburbs to the fringe of downtown but are of little use to travellers.

CAR

Drive Mongolia (p36) offers driving tours of Mongolia, allowing you to drive the car with a backup support vehicle. **Sixt** (Map p60; ☎ 7575 0002; www.sixt.mn; Narny Gudamj) is another company that has vehicles for hire in the city.

TAXI

In Ulaanbaatar, there are official and unofficial taxis. The official ones are noticeably labelled on the exterior and inside may or may not have a meter. The unofficial taxis are simply locals trawling for passengers.

All charge a standard T800 per kilometre (check the current rate, as it increases regularly). Don't agree to a set daily price because it will always be more than the standard rate per kilometre.

Most drivers will happily rip off UB newcomers. The more confident you appear, the better chance you have of getting a fair deal. Before you get in the cab, have some idea of the route and the price. Always have the driver reset the odometer to zero and agree on a per-kilometre rate before setting off.

To find a taxi, just stand by the side of a main street and hold your arm out with your fingers down. After dark, avoid using a private car, stick to an official taxi.

Help Taxi (☑9965 2371; www.helptaxi3.com) Has an English-speaking dispatcher and reputation for being reliable, safe and honest. Its main clients are expats and the prices are slightly higher than other companies. Flagfall is T5000 for the first 5km and then T800 per kilometre. A ride to/from the airport to the city centre is T30,000. You can also hire a car for a city tour for T50,000.

Noyon Zuuch Taxi Company (☑1950) Reliable service with English-speaking dispatchers.

ULAANBAATAR GETTING AROUND

Central Mongolia

POP 274,100 / AREA 199,000 SQ KM

Best for Hiking

➡ Terelj (p106)
➡ Naiman Nuur (p118)
➡ Tariat (p126)
➡ Khögnö Khan Uul Nature Reserve (p121)
➡ Bogdkhan Uul Strictly Protected Area (p102)

Best for Staying with Herdsmen

➡ Orkhon Khürkhree (p120)
➡ Khustain National Park (p110)
➡ Khögnö Khan Uul Nature Reserve (p121)
➡ Terelj (p107)

Why Go?

Roll out of Ulaanbaatar (UB) in a Russian jeep, or even just on a public bus, and you'll only need to put a hill or two between yourself and the city before the vast steppes of central Mongolia begin to unfold before your eyes.

Verdant swaths of empty landscapes are sprinkled with tiny gers (traditional yurts) stretching to the horizon while magical light plays across the valleys. This is the Mongolian heartland, loaded with both historical sites and natural beauty, with plenty of scope to horse trek in forested mountains, camp by pretty lakes or soak in hot springs.

Because the region is relatively close to Ulaanbaatar (and many sights are right beside the city), infrastructure is a little better than in other areas, with many places reachable by public transport. The most scenic sub-region is the Khangai Mountains, but you'll find beautiful scenery even if you only venture as far as Terelj.

When to Go
Tsetserleg

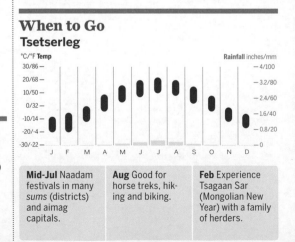

Mid-Jul Naadam festivals in many *sums* (districts) and aimag capitals.

Aug Good for horse treks, hiking and biking.

Feb Experience Tsagaan Sar (Mongolian New Year) with a family of herders.

History

The many deer and 'animal-art' steles found in the valleys of Arkhangai aimag are evidence of tribal existence here around 1300 BC, but the region really came into its own in the 3rd century BC, when the nomadic Xiongnu set up a power base in the Orkhon valley. Various 'empires' rose and fell in the Xiongnu's wake, including the Ruan-Ruan, the Tujue and the Uighurs, who built their capital at Khar Balgas in AD 715. These Turkic-speaking peoples held sway over vast portions of inner Asia and harassed the Chinese (whose attempts to defend the Great Wall were never really successful). They had their own alphabet and left several carved steles that describe their heroes and exploits. The most famous is the Kul-Teginii Monument, located relatively close to Kharkhorin.

Chinggis Khaan and his merry men were only the latest in a string of political and military powers to use the Orkhon valley as a base. Chinggis never spent much time here, using it mainly as a supply centre for his armies, but his son Ögedei built the walls around Karakorum (near present-day Kharkhorin) in 1235, and invited emissaries from around the empire to visit his court.

Centuries after the fall of the Mongol empire it was religion, rather than warriors, that put the spotlight back on central Mongolia. Erdene Zuu Khiid (Buddhist monastery) was built from the remains of Karakorum and, with Manchu and Tibetan influence, Buddhism pushed the native shaman faith to the fringe of society.

ⓘ Getting There & Away

At the time of research, paved highways heading west and southwest from Ulaanbaatar had reached just beyond both Tsetserleg and Arvaikheer.

If you're travelling from western Mongolia to Ulaanbaatar, the route through Arkhangai is more interesting than the journey via Bayankhongor.

If you are travelling in the Gobi and heading towards northern Mongolia, go to Bayankhongor and pick up the scenic 210km road over the mountains to Tsetserleg. Local vehicles are rare on this route so it's best to have your own vehicle.

ⓘ Getting Around

Töv aimag has a network of good unpaved and paved roads, so you can easily use public transport to make day or overnight trips from the capital.

Further afield, you can also reach places such as Kharkhorin, Tsetserleg and Tariat by public bus.

Off the main paved roads, though, traffic is light. In Övörkhangai, for example, you'll need your own transport to visit Tövkhön Khiid or Orkhon Khürkhree falls, and horse is the best way to reach Naiman Nuur.

Hitchhiking is relatively easy all along the main road from UB to Tariat, a route which takes in a number of worthwhile sights.

TÖV ТӨВ

AREA 81,000 SQ KM / POP 88,889

The 'Central' province surrounds Ulaanbaatar, and its forested mountains offer a welcome escape from the city. Popular but picturesque Gorkhi-Terelj National Park is great for horse-trekking, hiking and camping, and it's only an hour or so away by bus! Further afield, you can spot *takhi* (wild horses) at Khustain National Park. For something a little surreal, check out the 40m-tall, silver statue of Chinggis Khaan outside Nalaikh.

Zuunmod Зуунмод

☏ 01272, 7045 / POP 86,800 / ELEV 1529M

In great contrast to the big city on the other side of the mountain, Zuunmod is a peanut-sized place, even smaller than most Mongolian provincial capitals. There is little reason to linger in the capital of Töv but you'll probably pass through on the way to Mandshir Khiid in the Bogdkhan Uul Strictly Protected Area.

The main sight in town is the **Aimag Museum** (admission T1000; ⓧ 9am-1pm & 2-6pm), about 200m beyond the bus stand, and opposite the southeast corner of the park – look for the sign in English. There are exhibits on local history and a section of stuffed animals including an enormous moose. It also has some interesting black-and-white photos of Mandshir Khiid, including the once-regular *tsam* (lama dances, performed by monks wearing masks during religious ceremonies).

A minibus runs on a paved road to Zuunmod (T2000, one hour, hourly, 8am and 8pm) from Ulaanbaatar's Dragon Avto Vaksal (p94). From the bus stand in Zuunmod, keep walking straight and the museum will be on your right. Mandshir Khiid is a pleasant 6km hike northeast of here (beyond the town and up to your left).

Central Mongolia Highlights

1 Saddle up for a horse trek to the beautiful, remote **Khuisiin Naiman Nuur Nature Reserve** (p118).

2 Camp, hike and swim your way around **Terkhiin Tsagaan Nuur** (p126), the volcanic lake by the village of Tariat.

3 Stay with herdsmen in the meadows surrounding **Orkhon Khürkhree** (p120), Mongolia's tallest waterfall.

4 Take a break from UB, and head to the nearby hills and valleys of **Terelj** (p105).

5 Visit history-laden Kharkhorin for the ancient temples and ruined remains

SELENGE

Bulgan

Khan Khentii
Strictly Protected Area

Jargalant

Bornuur

▲ Asralt Khairkhan
(2800m)

Tseel

▲ Altan Olgii
Uul

Ugataaltaidam

Zaamar

Terelj

Günjiin ▲ 4 ▲ Jalman Uul
Süm (2051m)

ULAANBAATAR

Hui Doloon
Khutag

ULAANBAATAR

Terelj
Village

Lun

Khustain
National Park 6

Chinggis Khaan
Airport

Nalaikh

Bogdkhan Uul Strictly
Protected Area

Baganuur

Khögnö Khan Uul
Nature Reserve

Altanbulag

Zuunmod

Mongol
Els 8

TÖV

Stepperiders
Camp

Steppe
Nomads

Övgön
Khiid

Rashaant

Öndörshireet

Stone
Monuments

Sergelen

Bayan

Erdenesant

Eej Khad

Batkhaan Uul
Nature Reserve

Burd

Buren

Rayan
Önjuul

Bayantsagaan

Esönzüil

Bayan-
Öndör

Delgerkhaan

Sant

Bayangol

Mandalgov

DUNDGOV

N   0   50 km
           0   25 miles

of **Erdene Zuu Khiid** (p114), Mongolia's first Buddhist monastery.

6 Search for the rare *takhi* (wild horse) at **Khustain National Park** (p110).

7 Rent a mountain bike in Tsetserleg and cycle over the hills to the **Tsenkher hot springs** (p125).

8 Explore the boulder-strewn landscape of **Khögnö**

Khan Uul Nature Reserve (p121), before hopping on a camel at the nearby sand dunes of Mongol Els.

A chartered taxi from Ulaanbaatar will cost at least US$20 one way. Taxis can be hired in Zuunmod from the taxi stand on the east side of the park (past the museum then left). The fare to Mandshir Khiid is around T15,000 plus waiting time.

Bogdkhan Uul Strictly Protected Area Богдхан Уул

The Bogdkhan Uul (2122m) is said to be the world's oldest nature reserve. Established in 1778, the **park** (admission T3000) was guarded by 2000 club-wielding lamas. Animal poachers were hauled away in chains, beaten within an inch of their lives, and locked inside coffin-like jail cells.

These days it's perfectly safe and legal to walk on the mountain and you can enjoy some terrific hiking and horse-riding trails. Wildlife is more difficult to spot than it used to be, but you still stand a chance of seeing red deer.

◉ Sights

Mandshir Khiid   BUDDHIST MONASTERY
(Мандшир Хийд; GPS: N 47°45.520', E 106°59.675'; admission T5000; ☺9am-sunset) For the 350 monks who once called this place home, the gorgeous setting around this monastery (elevation 1645m) must have been a daily inspiration. Like most monasteries in Mongolia, Mandshir Khiid was destroyed in 1937 by Stalin's thugs, but was partially restored in the 1990s. Just 6km northeast of Zuunmod and 46km by road from Ulaanbaatar, the monastery is a perfect half-day trip from the capital, or can be used as a starting point for hikes into the Strictly Protected Area. One possibility is to take the bus here from Ulaanbaatar early in the morning, then hike back over the hills.

The main temple has been restored and converted into a museum, but the other buildings remain in ruins. The monastery and museum are not as impressive as those in Ulaanbaatar – it is the beautiful forest setting that makes a visit worthwhile.

As you enter from the main track from Zuunmod you'll be required to pay an admission fee of T5000 per person, which covers the T2000 museum entrance fee and the T3000 national park fee. You'll have to buy both tickets even if you don't plan on entering the museum.

From the gate it's a couple of kilometres to the main area, where there is a car park, a shop, a lacklustre **nature museum** a restaurant (that isn't always open) and several gers offering accommodation. Look for the huge two-tonne **bronze cauldron**, which dates from 1726 and was designed to boil up 10 sheep at a time.

The remains of the monastery (and monastery museum) are about 800m uphill from the car park. The **monastery museum** has *tsam* masks, exhibits on the layout of Mandshir and some photos that show what it looked like before Stalin's followers turned it into rubble. Look out for the controversial **Ganlin Horn**, made from human thigh bones.

If you have time, it's worth climbing up the rocks behind the main temple, where there are some 18th-century Buddhist **rock paintings**. The views from the top are even more beautiful, and you'll find yourself in the midst of a lovely pine forest.

🏃 Activities

Hiking
Bogdkhan Uul has a broad and flat summit, so many routes cross it. Most hikers get dropped off on one side and hike to the other on a day or overnight hike. The summit, known as **Tsetseegün Uul** (GPS: N 47°48.506', E 107°00.165') is 2256m and a popular destination, but including this part of the mountain requires a bit more time.

Don't underestimate the weather up here. Even in summer strong thunderstorms can tear across the mountain without much warning. In June 2010, an American hiker died of hypothermia after getting stranded on the mountain during a major thunderstorm. Even if you are just doing it as a day hike, bring warm, waterproof clothing, a compass, food and water. Yellow paint on the trees marks the trail, but it can be hard to spot.

Some scrambling over fields of granite boulders is necessary, and the chance of slipping and injuring yourself should not be taken lightly. It would be wise to inform a friend or guesthouse owner in Ulaanbaatar of your itinerary and the time of your expected return.

Mandshir Khiid to Ulaanbaatar   HIKE
This approach to Tsetseegün from the south side is the easiest route by far. As you face the monastery, cut over to your right (east) until you get to the stream. Just follow the stream until it nearly disappears and then head north. About three hours' walking should

bring you out over a ridge into a broad boggy meadow, which you'll have to cross. If you've walked straight to the north, the twin rocky outcrops of the summit should be right in front of you. When you start to see Ulaanbaatar in the distance, you're on the highest ridge and close to the two large *ovoo* (a shamanistic pyramid-shaped collection of stones as an offering to the gods) on the summit From the *ovoo* you can return to Mandshir or descend to Ulaanbaatar.

A second route from the monastery begins from the left (west) side of the temples, passing a stupa on the way up to the ridge. This route, marked with yellow tags, is faster but you'll miss the *ovoo* on Tsetseegün.

Coming down from Tsetseegün the quickest way is to head due north, towards the **Observatory** ('Khureltogoot' in Mongolian), and descend to the valley where you'll cross the train tracks. You can catch a taxi from here to town for around T10,000. A new route from the Observatory goes downhill and then west one valley to the Sky Resort, where its possible to hike or hitch on a new road to UB along the southern bank of the Tuul River.

Another route takes you to the Zaisan Memorial (p70), on the southern fringe of the city. Be careful not to drop down too soon or you'll end up at **Ikh Tenger**, one valley short of Zaisan. Ikh Tenger is where the president lives with machine-gun-wielding guards, who will be none too pleased if you drop by unannounced. If you see a barbed-wire fence you are in Ikh Tenger; to get out, just continue west along the fence and over the next ridge.

From Mandshir Khiid straight to Zaisan, plan on walking about six to seven hours. From Mandshir Khiid to the Observatory, figure on six hours.

Horse Riding

In summer, some of the ger camps around Mandshir Khiid rent out horses.

Stepperiders Camp HORSE RIDING
(☑9665 9596, 9911 4245; www.stepperiders.mn; GPS: N 47°43.649', E 106°47.418'; rides per day from US$45) Horses are available from Stepperiders Camp, just off the main Ulaanbaatar–Zuunmod road. Stepperiders is run by Minde, a recommended local horse guide who can give lessons, instructions and support to independent travellers planning their own expedition. This is a perfect place to test ride a Mongolian horse before a longer trip. Rides include pick-up, drop-off, guides, horses, food and even entry fees to the national park.

As this camp is something of a hang-out for dedicated riders, you may be able to find partners for a trip. Horse-loving volunteers are also welcome. Check the website for details.

🛏 Sleeping

The area around the monastery is one of the best camping spots near Ulaanbaatar. You should get permission from the caretaker at the monastery (p102) if you are camping nearby, or just hike off into the woods.

Ovooni Enger Ger Camp TOURIST GER CAMP **$$**
(☑7027 2011, per ger T80,000-100,000, mains T5000-7000) Larger, better equipped and open later in the year than neighbouring Mandshir Ger Camp, Ovooni has a modern shower block with sit-down flush toilets, a comfortable restaurant ger with terrace seating and even areas where you can play volleyball and basketball. The meadow setting affords pleasant views, but isn't as pretty as Mandshir's forest location. To get here, turn right just after entering the park gate.

Mandshir Ger Camp TOURIST GER CAMP **$$**
(☑01272-22535; 4-bed ger T40,000) In a lovely spot amid trees about 200m up to the right of the monastery's car park, this fairly basic ger camp has hot showers but Mongolian-style toilets. The restaurant isn't always open, so bring some emergency food supplies if

NATIONAL PARKS OF TÖV

Bogdkhan Uul Strictly Protected Area (41,700 hectares; p102) Protects red deer, foxes, wolves and contains the ruined Mandshir Khiid monastery.

Gorkhi-Terelj National Park (293,200 hectares; p105) A playground for Ulaanbaatarites. The park contains numerous ger (traditional circular felt yurt) camps and two golf courses. It's more pristine north of the Terelj Gol.

Khustain National Park (50,620 hectares; p110) Important rehabilitation site for *takhi* (wild horses). Also contains gazelle, marmot and wolves, among other creatures.

LOCAL KNOWLEDGE

TRAIL RIDE DAY TRIPS NEAR ULAANBAATAR

A number of tour operators can organise horse-riding day trips near Ulaanbaatar. They are usually in Terelj National Park, which can get crowded on summer weekends. A handful of companies offer specialised day trips on horseback in the backcountry, away from the ger camps. These are some of the best:

➡ Stepperiders (p103) in Bogdkhan Uul

➡ Xanadu (p109) near Gachuurt and Terelj

➡ Stone Horse (p109) near Gachuurt to Terelj route

possible. Horse riding is sometimes available. Note, the camp tends to close down by mid-September.

ⓘ Getting There & Away

The most accessible entrances to the park are reached from the ger camp at the southern end of Zaisan valley, the Observatory and Mandshir.

The monastery is easy enough to visit in a day trip from Ulaanbaatar, via Zuunmod (from where it's a 7km drive). If you are walking from the north of Zuunmod it's 6km; you can either walk along the main northern road, or save some time by walking directly north from Zuunmod, eventually joining up with the main track which heads up the valley to your left.

At Mandshir, wranglers from the nearby ger camps rent horses for around US$5 to US$10 per hour.

Nalaikh   Налайх

This town, 35km southeast of the capital, is part of the Ulaanbaatar autonomous municipality because it once supplied the capital city with its coal. The state mine shut down years ago but small-scale private excavations (legal and illegal) continue in the mines.

A community of Kazakhs settled here in the 1950s to work at the mines and they still represent a quarter of the population. To find Nalaikh's **mosque**, face the bright-blue town hall, turn 180 degrees and walk about 25 minutes over a small hill. It's very basic and has a greenish tin roof. About 200m past the mosque is the family home of Ibrahim (also known as Erakhun), a Kazakh who operates a small **ger museum** in his yard. The museum only opens in summer but Ibrahim is happy to have you visit his home at other times of the year. Visiting his home is a great chance to experience small-town life without going too far from UB.

Buses for Nailakh (T800, one hour, 7.30am to 7pm) run along Peace Ave every 10 minutes or so. From Nailakh, shared minivans shuttle to Terelj (T1300) roughly every hour.

Around Nalaikh

Around 19km southeast of Nalaikh is an 8th-century Turkic **stele of Tonyuok** (GPS: N 47°41.661', E 107°28.586'). The stele is covered in runic script and there are *balbals* (stone figures believed to be Turkic grave markers) and grave slabs nearby. To get to the stele you'll need to have your own transport. From Nalaikh, take the main highway towards Baganuur and travel for 16km until you see a sign that says 'Tonyuok'. Turn right onto this track and travel another 11km to reach the stele. Just past the site, a huge hangar contains a few **relics** found around the site; you could ask the local watchman to let you inside, though there is little to see.

One of Mongolia's newest landmarks is a 40m-high silver **Chinggis Khaan statue** (GPS: N 47°48.494', E 107°31.860'; admission T7000; ☉ 9am-sunset) located just off the main road between Nalaikh and Erdene, at a place called Tsonjin Boldog. The dramatic statue, built with private funds, has a lift (elevator) rising up its tail, from where there are steps to the horse's head. It was built here, so the legend goes, because this was the spot where Chinggis Khaan found a golden whip. The complex includes a **museum** (with Hunnu artefacts and items from the Mongol empire), cafe and souvenir shop. A six-minute **film** describes how the monument was built. For an extra T1000 you can don Chinggis Khaan armour for a photo shoot in front of an enormous Mongolian boot. A round trip in a taxi from Ulaanbaatar will set you back about T80,000.

About one hour's drive east of the Chinggis Khaan statue is **Steppe Nomad** (☑9134 3498, 7018 3498; www.mongoliagercamp.com; GPS:

N 47°36.27', E 108°23.17'; per person including breakfast US$42-52, lunch/dinner US$15/12), a well-run, high-end ger camp that offers horse riding, kayaking and mountain biking.

Terelj Area   Тэрэлж

Terelj *sum* (district), about 55km northeast of Ulaanbaatar, is a playground for urban-weary Ulaanbaatarites. At 1600m, the area is cool and the alpine scenery magnificent, and there are great opportunities for hiking, rock climbing, swimming (in icy-cold water), rafting, horse riding and, for hard-core extreme-sports fanatics, skiing in the depths of winter.

Terelj was first developed for tourism in 1964 and 30 years later it became part of **Gorkhi-Terelj National Park** (per person T3000). It's a bit crowded with ger camps these days but you can easily get away from the hustle and bustle. Be prepared for mosquitoes, especially in late summer.

Pay the admission fee at the park entrance. Note, passengers on the public bus from Ulaanbaatar rarely have to pay this as the bus usually drives past the entrance without stopping.

Terelj village (GPS: N 47°59.193', E 107°27.834') is located about 27km from the park entrance, at the end of a paved road. It's in a nice spot near the river and has a few shops, a handful of ger camps and a couple of hotels.

◉ Sights

Günjiin Süm   TEMPLE
(Гүнжийн Сүм; GPS: N 48°11.010', E 107°33.377')
Surrounded by magnificent forests and not far from a lovely river, the Baruun Bayan Gol, this Buddhist temple (elevation 1713m) was built in 1740 by Efu Dondovdorj to commemorate the death of his Manchurian wife, Amarlangui. Once part of a huge monastery containing about 70 sq metres of blue walls, five other temples and a tower, Günjiin Süm is one of very few Manchurian-influenced temples in Mongolia to survive over the centuries. Only a couple of buildings and walls remain.

Unlike most other monasteries in Mongolia, Günjiin Süm was not destroyed during the Stalinist purges, but simply fell into ruin from neglect, vandalism and theft.

The temple is not a must – there are many better and more accessible temples and monasteries in Ulaanbaatar and Töv – but more of an excuse for a great **overnight trek**, on horse or foot, or as part of a longer trip in the national park.

CENTRAL MONGOLIA TERELJ AREA

Terelj Area

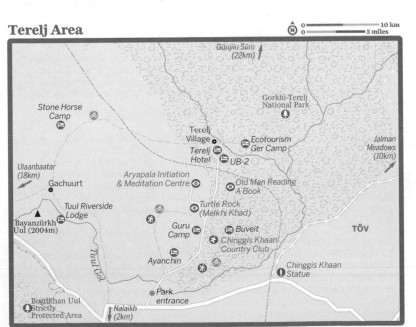

Günjiin is about 25km by foot (or horse) from the UB-2 hotel (p108), heading in a northwest direction. The jeep trail is longer (about 40km in total), as you need to skirt around the mountains, but easier if you don't want to walk the hills. You can do the trip on your own with a good map and compass (or GPS) but it's best to take a local guide.

Khan Khentii Strictly Protected Area   PROTECTED AREA

(Khentii Nuruu; admission T3000) To the northeast, Gorkhi-Terelj National Park joins the Khan Khentii Strictly Protected Area, comprising more than 1.2 million hectares of the Töv, Selenge and Khentii aimags. The Khan Khentii park is almost completely uninhabited by humans, but it is home to endangered species of moose, brown bear and weasel to name but a few, and to more than 250 species of birds. If you come from Terelj, the fee at the gate there covers this protected area as well.

🏃 Activities

Hiking

If you have good maps, a compass and some experience (or a proper guide), hiking in the Terelj area is superb in summer, but be prepared for mosquitoes and unpredictable weather.

For more sedate walks in the Terelj ger camp area, follow the main road and pick a side valley to stroll along at your leisure. From the main road, look out for two interesting rock formations: **Turtle Rock** (Melkhi Khad; GPS: N 47°54.509', E 107°25.428') in a side valley to the south of Terelj, which really looks like one at a certain angle; and the less dramatic **Old Man Reading a Book**, which can be spotted on the left side of the road when travelling south from Terelj village. Head north 3km from Turtle Rock to reach the **Aryapala Initiation & Meditation Centre** (GPS: N 47°56.121', E 107°25.643; admission T2000) set on a spectacular rocky hillside. The **temple** at the top of the hill is a new creation. If you are lucky, you might arrive during a prayer session, when you can sit and hear monks chanting.

Some suggested easier hikes are to Günjiin Süm or along the Terelj or Tuul Gols towards Khan Khentii. This is a great area for wildflowers, particularly rhododendron and edelweiss.

Places of interest on more difficult, longer treks in Khan Khentii include **Altan-Ölgii Uul** (2656m), the source of the Akhain Gol; **Khagiin Khar Nuur**, a 20m-deep glacial lake, about 80km up Tuul Gol from the ger camps at Terelj; and **Yestii Hot Water Springs**, which reach up to 35°C, and are

---

MOUNTAIN BIKING AROUND TERELJ

Note, you'll need to rent a bike from Ulaanbaatar (see p96) as, at the time of research, there weren't any places in Terelj that rented bikes. Depending on your fitness levels, Terelj is about half a day's cycle from the capital. The road is paved the whole way, but mostly uphill.

Terelj to Gachuurt (Central)

This rugged route takes in two passes along the way. Get a ride all the way to the town of Terelj and then start riding on the road that heads west; it's about 2km to the next small settlement of gers. The trail continues west and starts heading into the wilderness, up a valley with a forest to your left. The ridge tops out at 1859m and descends to another valley. The trail climbs again, slightly to the right, to another 1859m ridge, from where you begin a long descent towards Gachuurt. At the end of the valley (it's about 15km) you'll reach Tuul Gol, which you follow to Gachuurt town. All up it's a 30km ride and should take around five hours.

Turtle Rock Loop

This convenient route begins and ends at Turtle Rock (p106) in the Gorkhi valley. From Turtle Rock ride west down the slope until the road goes right into a ger camp (the camp was built over the trail). Go around the camp and then it's a 30-minute climb to the top of the hill. From the top you get some great views of the rock formations in the next valley. The trail continues south past several ger camps and eventually leads back to the main road and back to Turtle Rock. This loop is 15km.

fed by the Yeroo and Yestii Gols. Yestii is about 18km north of Khagiin Khar Nuur.

Horse Riding

Travelling on a horse is the perfect way to see a lot of the park, including Günjiin Süm and the side valleys of Tuul Gol. To travel long distances, you will need to have experience, or a guide, and bring most of your own gear. Horses can be hired through any of the ger camps, but you'll pay high tourist prices (around US$35 to US$40 a day). A mob of horse boys hang around Turtle Rock (p106) offering horse riding at US$5 per hour, or somewhere between US$12 and US$20 for the day. Alternatively, approach one of the Mongolian families who live around the park and hire one of their horses, though they may not be much cheaper. Bert the Dutch cheese maker, who owns Ecotourism Ger Camp (p108), can help you hire horses from nearby herdsmen for around €5 per hour. Horse-rental guys sometimes hang out in front of Terelj Hotel (p108), offering horse rides for T5000 to T10,000 per person per hour.

Rafting

Tuul Gol, which starts in the park and flows to Ulaanbaatar and beyond, is one of the best places in the country for rafting. The best section of the river starts a few kilometres north of Terelj village, and wraps around the park until it reaches Gachuurt, near Ulaanbaatar. Nomadic Journeys (p36) runs rafting trips here for around US$45 per day (minimum four people). You can also get a raft from Seven Summits (p88), a good-quality camping shop in UB, and Goyo Travel (p36).

Golf

Chinggis Khaan Country Club   GOLF
(☑ 0400 1235, 8050 3322) If you want to play golf, the Chinggis Khaan Country Club is just off the road in Gorkhi valley, and has a par-72 course with artificial greens. Green fees are T95,000, club rental T30,000 and caddies T20,000. Golf shoes (T8000) and hand carts (T5000) are also available. There's also a par-three course at the UB-2 hotel (p108).

☞ Tours

Most foreign and local tour companies include a night or two in a tourist ger at Terelj in their tours. Local agencies based in Ulaanbaatar, such as Nomadic Journeys (p36) and Nomads (p36), run some of the more interesting trips around Terelj.

⌂ Sleeping & Eating

Unless you hike out into the hills it's best to get permission for camping, either from the nearest ger or, for a fee, a ger camp. Pitch your tent away from the main road, don't use wood fires and take all of your rubbish out.

During the peak season of July and August (and also at the more popular camps), it's not a bad idea to book ahead. Outside the normal tourist season (July to September), it's also a good idea to ring ahead to make sure the camp is open and serves food. A few places stay open in winter.

Apart from ger camps, many individual families rent out a spare ger and/or hire horses, normally at cheaper rates than the ger camps. You'll have to ask around as none advertise. Expect to pay around T10,000 per person per bed. Meals usually cost around T5000.

⌂ Road to Terelj Village

Otgoo Family Ger   GUEST GER $
(☑ 8915 6391; per person with meals US$20) There are a few family gers as you approach the Buveit camp, where you may be able to find cheap, basic accommodation. One is Otgoo Family Ger, which also rents out horses.

Guru Camp   TOURIST GER CAMP $$
(☑ 9909 6714; per person with meals US$45) Located 14km along the main road from the Gorkhi-Terelj National Park entrance, Guru has clean showers, a comfortable restaurant-bar and sweeping views. There's also a small art shop and a foot-massage centre. Boya, the manager, speaks some English. Closes by October.

Buveit   TOURIST GER CAMP $$
(☑ 9911 4913; per person with/without meals US$45/20) About 13km along the main road from the Gorkhi-Terelj National Park entrance, Buveit is in a beautiful secluded valley 3km east of the main road (walk past Chinggis Khaan Country Club then turn right and bear left).

Ayanchin   TOURIST GER CAMP $$$
(☑ 9909 4539; www.ayanchinlodge.mn; ger bed T120,000, wood cabin d T150,000, f T250,000; ⊛) This luxury, American-built camp has a Western-style lodge, modern shower and toilet block, a children's play area and a top-notch restaurant (mains T19,000–T32,000) serving dishes such as cheeseburgers, steak,

pasta and grilled salmon. It's about 10km from the main Gorkhi-Terelj National Park entrance, marked with a big billboard. Open year-round.

Terelj Village Area

★**Ecotourism Ger Camp** TOURIST GER CAMP $$
(☑ 9973 4710; bergroo@hotmail.com; GPS: N 47°58.722', E 107°28.907'; per person with meals €35) For an offbeat experience, cross Terelj Gol and hike to a simple but pleasant ger camp run by an eccentric Dutchman named Bert. Bert and his Mongolian wife make Dutch cheese at the camp, and if you want to get your hands dirty, get up at the crack of dawn and help them milk the cows. The meadow location here is gorgeous, and there's great hiking opportunities in the surrounding hills. Bert also organises horse trips up to Günjiin Süm, or can just help you arrange a quick ride on a neighbour's horse (per hour €5).

To find the place on your own, go to the UB-2 hotel and walk around the right side of the building. Cross the iron bridge over the river, follow the path to a second river, cross the wooden bridge here, and then walk east (right). Follow the electric poles, crossing streams on fallen tree trunks a number of times, until you get to pole 35; from here you will see the gers off to your right. It's 2.5km from the UB-2 (a 40-minute walk). If that sounds complicated, call Bert and he will meet you at the UB-2, possibly on one of his neighbours' ox-carts.

Terelj Hotel HOTEL $$$
(☑ 9900 7206; www.tereljhotel.com; s/d from T360,000/440,000; @🛜❄🐾) Mongolia's first luxury hotel and spa is an incongruous neoclassical building set on the edge of tiny Tererlj village. Opened in 2008, the hotel is a self-contained complex with a gourmet French restaurant (mains T20,000 to T40,000), professional spa, indoor swimming pool, library and children's play centre. Rooms are immaculate, and it's a nice place to come if you want to splurge on a fancy meal, even if you're staying elsewhere. Rates include use of pool, sauna and gym. The spa costs extra.

UB-2 HOTEL $$$
(☑ 9977 4125; www.ub2hotel.mn; ger bed T35,000; s/d from T70,000/100,000) This place – a branch of the Ulaanbaatar Hotel – is not bad on its own but looks a little sad compared to

the swanky Terelj Hotel next door. The food at the restaurant (served 8am to 9pm; mains T7000 to T10,000) is disappointing, but the rooms are fine. Facilities here include a golf driving range and par-three golf course (green fees T60,000, club hire T15,000).

Northern Terelj

Jalman Meadows TOURIST GER CAMP $$$
(☑ 11-328 737; www.nomadicjourneys.com; per person with meals US$85-95) Nomadic Journeys (p36) runs this remote and low-impact ger camp in the upper Tuul valley, which makes a nice base if you are headed to Khagiin Khar Nuur, which is an eight-hour horse ride away. The camp has a library of books on Mongolia and a number of great activities, including horse riding ($35 per day), mountain biking, yak carting, river boating and even portable saunas! You'll need to book well in advance for these trips. The price includes transfers to and from Ulaanbaatar (around three hours, one way). Free transfers are on Wednesday and Saturdays only, though. On other days you will have to pay for a private transfer.

❶ Getting There & Away

BICYCLE
A mountain bike is an excellent way of getting around some of the Terelj area. Seven Summits (p88) is one of a number of places in Ulaanbaatar that rents bikes.

BUS
The road from Ulaanbaatar to Terelj Village, which goes through part of the national park, is in pretty good nick. A bus (T2500, 90 minutes) departs at noon and 4pm in summer, or 3pm in winter (1 October to 15 May), from Peace Ave, opposite the Narantuul Hotel. It then stops at every bus stop heading east along Peace Ave. Get there with 15 minutes to spare as they sometimes depart early.

Going the other way, it leaves Terelj at 8am and 7pm; catch it near the UB-2 hotel, on the road. You may have to pay an extra T2500 for a bike or heavy luggage. For additional information, ask a Mongolian speaker to contact the bus conductor, **Ms Nara** (☑ 9665 4818). She doesn't speak English.

Another option is to take one of the frequent buses between Ulaanbaatar and Nalaikh (T800, every 10 minutes), and then to hook up with one of the shared minibuses which shuttles between Nalaikh and Terelj Village (T1300 per person, roughly every hour).

HITCHING

Hitching *out* of Ulaanbaatar can be difficult because vehicles going to Terelj could leave from anywhere. The cheapest way to hitch to Terelj is to take a minivan for Baganuur or Nalaikh and get off at the turn-off to Terelj, where you are far more likely to get a lift.

Hitching *back* to Ulaanbaatar from along the main road through Terelj is not difficult, as almost every vehicle is returning to the capital.

TAXI

A taxi from Ulaanbaatar (T70,000 one way) is easy to organise; jeeps aren't necessary because the road is paved all the way. The driver may understandably want more than the one-way fare because his taxi may be empty for part of the return journey. You can also arrange with your taxi to pick you up later.

When there's enough demand, shared taxis to Terelj sometimes leave from Naran Tuul market jeep station in Ulaanbaatar. This is more likely on summer Sundays when locals make a day trip to the area.

Gachuurt Гачуурт

Around 20km east of Ulaanbaatar, the town of Gachuurt offers the chance to quickly trade city traffic and bustle for riverside walks, horse riding, camping, fishing and rafting. The town is a rapidly growing suburb of the capital, popular with wealthy Mongolians who build gated villas on the hills surrounding the town. Despite the increased development, it remains a pleasant-enough setting and an easy half-day trip from Ulaanbaatar.

Activities

Xanadu ADVENTURE
(9975 6964; www.mongolienomade.mn) Frenchman Côme Doerflinger runs adventure trips through his outfit based in Gachuurt. He mainly runs horse trips (T30,000 per day), including all-inclusive multiday trips, and has French, Russian and English saddles. Côme also has kayaks and canoes (US$30 per person, minimum four people) that you can use to float down Tuul Gol, and mountain bikes which are great for excursions up Gachuurt's side valleys towards Terelj. Côme also offers accommodation at his camp (T25,000 per person, meals T6000 to T10,000).

Stone Horse Expeditions HORSE RIDING
(9938 1128, 9592 1167; www.stonehorsemongolia.com) Another Western-run company, Stone Horse is located 16km north of Gachuurt and offers a variety of trips, such as

BORNUUR

A small *sum* (district) located 5km off the Ulaanbaatar–Darkhan road, Bornuur (Борнуур) contains an interesting **museum** (admission T1000; ☺10am-5pm) of local artefacts and Buddhist relics. Some exhibits are a bit gruesome, including a stack of human skulls pulled out of a mass grave. They are the skulls of local lamas who were executed by communist forces in 1937. G Purevbat, a lama and master of Buddhist sculpture and painting, created the museum using artefacts from his personal collection.

one-day horse rides (T130,000) that include a pre-ride snack, riding introduction and a gourmet lunch. Longer trips (up to 14 days) include lodging at the staging area and camping equipment when on the trail. They use comfortable saddles and have quality horses. All trips are organised ahead of time so don't just turn up at the camp, phone first.

Sleeping

Gachuurt offers reasonable camping opportunities. About 2km before the town centre, near Tuul Gol, there are spots to pitch your tent. Just try to avoid the clusters of ger camps.

Tuul Riverside Lodge TOURIST GER CAMP $$$
(7011 9370; www.tuulriverside.com; s/d/tr ger US$84/148/180, lunch/dinner US$17/24;) This upmarket, family-friendly option has ensuite gers that include bath and shower. It's good for a short break from Ulaanbaatar (total driving time is one hour) or family holiday. It's about 10km past Gachuurt, at the foot of Bayanzurkh mountain, on the backroads to Terelj. Pick up from Ulaanbaater costs US$20 per person.

Hotel Mongolia HOTEL $$$
(9909 2819, 11-315 513; s/d ger T85,000/115,000, s/d T115,000/175,000, ste T250,000/350,000) Kitsch-tastic Hotel Mongolia is an unmissable walled palace of a hotel resembling ancient Karakorum. It's 2km short of Gachuurt, on the right side of the road. Luxurious rooms have private bath and shower, and the price includes breakfast. Even if you don't stay here, it's worth visiting for the kitsch

TAKHI – THE REINTRODUCTION OF A SPECIES

The year was 1969 and a herder in western Mongolia spotted a rare *takhi* (wild horse) in the distance. It was an extraordinary find as so few *takhi* were left in the wild. Alas, it was also the final sighting; with no new reports thereafter, scientists had to declare the species extinct in the wild – the result of poaching, overgrazing by livestock and human encroachment on their breeding grounds.

All was not lost for the *takhi*, however, as a dozen individual horses were known to exist in zoos outside Mongolia – their ancestors had been captured by game hunters in the early 20th century. A small group of conservationists dedicated themselves to breeding the animals with the hope that one day they could be reintroduced to Mongolia.

The conservationists did not fare so well with Mongolia's suspicious communist government, but when democracy arrived in the early 1990s they were welcomed with open arms. By that time the worldwide population was around 1500, scattered around zoos in Australia, Germany, Switzerland and the Netherlands.

Between 1992 and 2004, *takhi* were reintroduced into Mongolia at Khustain National Park, Takhiin Tal in Gov-Altai, and Khomyn Tal in Zavkhan. Today there are more than 300 *takhi* in Khustain, 80 in Takhiin Tal and 12 in Khomyn Tal. Given the political and logistical challenges to the project, their reintroduction is nothing short of miraculous, making it one of the most successful conservation stories of our times. In 2013, 40 new foals were born in Khustain alone.

The *takhi*, also known as Przewalski's horse (named after the Polish explorer who first 'discovered' the horse in 1878), are now descended from the bloodline of three stallions, so computerised records have been introduced to avoid inbreeding. They are the last remaining wild horse worldwide, the forerunner of the domestic horse, as depicted in cave paintings in France. They are not simply horses that have become feral or wild, as found in the USA or Australia, but a genetically different species, boasting two extra chromosomes in their DNA make-up.

Within the parks, the laws of nature are allowed to run their course; an average of five foals are killed by wolves every year in Khustain. The park gets locals onside by hiring herders as rangers, offering cheap loans to others and offering employment at a cheese-making factory on the outskirts of the park.

For more info, including volunteering possibilities, check out www.treemail.nl/takh.

ambience and excellent Asian-style restaurant (meals T8000 to T20,000), which serves a mixture of Mongolian and other Asian dishes and has an English menu and terrace seating. On hot summer days you can lounge on the 'beach' by the river, where there are simple, bathroomless 'beach cottages' for rent (twin/triple T40,000/50,000 per night).

ℹ Getting There & Away

Buses pick up passengers every hour or so from the east end of Peace Ave in Ulaanbaatar, near the Jukov statue, a couple of kilometres east of the city centre, bound for Gachuurt (T600, 45 minutes). You can also get a taxi from UB (T8000).

Khustain National Park
Хустайн Нуруу

This **park** (Khustain Nuruu, Birch Mountain Range; ☑ 21-245 087; www.hustai.mn; admission T10,000, Mongolians free) was established in 1993 and is about 100km southwest of Ulaanbaatar. The 50,620-hectare reserve protects Mongolia's wild horse, the *takhi*, and the reserve's steppe and forest-steppe environment. In addition to the *takhi*, there are populations of *maral* (Asiatic red deer), steppe gazelle, deer, boar, manul (small wild cat), wolves and lynx. A visit to the park has become a popular overnight excursion from Ulaanbaatar in recent years.

It's worth spending at least one night in the park, as you are most likely to see *takhi* and other wildlife at dusk or dawn.

The park is run by the now self-financed Hustai National Park Trust (p111). The **information centre** (☑ 9323 0169) at the entrance to the park has a ger with displays on the park and the *takhi*, a small souvenir shop and videos that include a documentary on Mongolian horses. There's a large ger camp here with a restaurant and shower block, plus volunteer accommodation. Ten kilometres south into the park's core area is the former park headquarters. Another 13km or so west of that is Moilt camp.

◎ Sights & Activities

Horse riding (per hour/day T7000/42,000), hiking, mountain biking (per hour/day T4000/16,000) and jeep excursions (per kilometre T1400) are all on offer. There's a good hike that takes you from the visitors centre to Moilt camp (22km) in about five hours.

A fun horseback trek heads to Turkic **stone monuments** (Хүн Чулуу; GPS: N 47°33.201', E 105°50.991') southwest of the park, and then on to Tuul Gol.

With your own jeep you can drive to Moilt camp. Park regulations require you to take a park guide (free within the park) and stick only to existing tracks. Wildlife watching is best at dusk and at dawn. The *takhi* could be in any number of places, and park guides can direct your driver to the best spots.

The park runs a **volunteer program** (www.ccovolunteer.org) where you can help with research, which includes monitoring *takhi*. Ideally you need to commit to at least two weeks.

🛏 Sleeping

A community-based tourism project at Khustain allows visitors to stay with nomad families just outside the park by the Tuul River. You can ride horses, learn felt-making and experience daily life in the countryside. The per-day cost is US$25 per person including meals. You need to arrange things at the park entrance, but you pay the families directly.

Independent camping is not allowed inside the park so you have to camp outside the park boundary. The best place to go is the south side of the park by Tuul Gol.

To book accommodation in the park, contact the **Hustai National Park Trust** (☎ 21-245 087; www.hustai.mn; Hustai Bldg, 2nd khoroo, Bayangol District) in Ulaanbaatar. The office is about 2km west of the State Department Store (p88), off Peace Ave. Turn north off Peace Ave directly opposite Decor Hotel then, following the small signs for 'Hustai Trust', turn right, left, right, left and right again, and you'll see the office in front of you. This is also where the twice-weekly minibus to the park leaves from.

Hustain Tourist Camp   TOURIST GER CAMP **$$**
(per person with 3 meals T82,500, with breakfast only T32,000) There is a large ger camp at the entrance to the park (the payment for accommodation includes the park entrance). The rather average restaurant here charges T17,500 for dinner, T23,000 for lunch.

Moilt Camp   CABIN **$$**
(per person with 3 meals T82,500, with breakfast only T32,000) Basic wooden cabins plus two gers clustered in a pretty valley. Prices are the same as at Hustain Tourist Camp, although facilities aren't as good. The location, though, is far nicer.

❶ Getting There & Away

To get to the park, travel 100km west from Ulaanbaatar, along the road to Kharkhorin, where there is a signpost pointing you 13km south to the park entrance. A minivan (one way US$15) travels from the park to Ulaanbaatar and back twice a week, departing the park at about noon on Friday and Sunday, and returning from Ulaanbaatar at 6pm on the same days (5pm in winter). The van only has 10 seats, and is really for workers and volunteers, so you need to make an advanced booking. In UB it leaves from the **Hustai National Park Trust office** (☎ 21-245 087; off Peace Ave).

ÖVÖRKHANGAI
ӨВӨРХАНГАЙ

POP 102,100 / AREA 63,000 SQ KM

Övörkhangai contains one of Mongolia's top attractions, the Erdene Zuu monastery in Kharkhorin. This is Mongolia's oldest monastery and it has become a regular stop on most tour circuits. But while travellers flock to this site and then rush off to points further west, many miss some of the best parts of Övörkhangai, including the stunning Naiman Nuur area, the impressive Orkhon Khürkhree Falls and the mountain-top monastery, Tövkhön Khiid. The southern part of the aimag, past Arvaikheer, is less interesting desert steppe.

Arvaikheer   Арвайхээр

☑ 01322, 7032 / POP 25,622 / ELEV 1913M

A nondescript but friendly aimag capital, Arvaikheer is mainly used by travellers as a place to eat and rest, refuel the jeep or arrange onward public transport.

Note, there is no need to go to Arvaikheer if you only want to visit Kharkhorin and northern Övörkhangai, as a paved road runs to Kharkhorin from Ulaanbaatar.

Arvaikheer

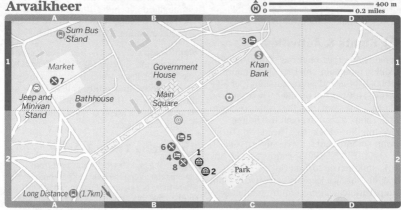

Arvaikheer

◉ Sights
1 Aimag Museum.....................................B2
2 Zanabazar Memorial Museum............C2

🛏 Sleeping
3 Arvaikheer Palace Hotel C1
4 Kharaa Hotel.......................................B2
5 Zalaa Hotel..B2

✦ Eating
6 Altan Holbo...B2
  Arvaikheer Palace Hotel
    Restaurant................................(see 3)
7 Container Market.................................A1
8 Jargalan..B2

◉ Sights

Gandan
Muntsaglan Khiid　　BUDDHIST MONASTERY
(Гандан Мунцаглан Хийд) This comparatively large monastery contains a fine collection of *thangka* (scroll paintings), including
one depicting the original monastery, which
was destroyed in 1937. The current monastery was opened in 1991, and now has about
60 monks in residence. It is located 900m
northwest of the town square, through the
ger districts.

Aimag Museum　　MUSEUM
(☏01322-22 075; admission T2000; ⊙9am-1pm
& 2-6pm Mon-Fri, 10am-5pm Sat & Sun) Since
Övörkhangai lies partly in the forested
Khangai region and the Gobi Desert, the
Aimag Museum boasts a better-than-average
selection of stuffed mountain and desert animals. There are also some fossils and arrows,

local artwork and leftovers from Karakorum.
If you wish to take photos, you'll have to
pay between T1000 and T8000 depending
on which exhibits you wish to photograph.
Entrance to next-door Zanabazar Memorial
Museum is included in the admission price.

Zanabazar Memorial Museum　　MUSEUM
(admission free with Aimag Museum ticket) Has
a small collection of religious artwork connected to the master sculptor (see p138). Ask
at the Aimag Museum for the key.

🛏 Sleeping

Kharaa Hotel　　HOTEL $
(☏7032 3655; tw & tr per bed T10,000, half-lux tw
per bed T20,000, lux d T35,000; 🛜) A good-value
option, Kharaa was recently renovated and
has bright rooms with clean bathrooms,
wi-fi and a restaurant. Almost all rooms
have their own hot showers.

Zalaa Hotel　　HOTEL $
(☏9904 2832; tw & tr per bed T12,000, lux tw/
tr T30,000/45,000) A clumsy building with
wobbly halls and a mishmash of furniture.
Rooms are basic but clean. It's well worth
paying slightly more for the 'lux' rooms as
the standard ones have no showers and
there's no shower in the common bathrooms. The restaurant isn't always open and
the wi-fi wasn't working when we stayed,
but the showers were hot.

Arvaikheer Palace Hotel　　HOTEL $$$
(☏7032 6598; arvaikheerpalace_hotel@yahoo.
com; tw T60,000-80,000, half-lux T100,000, lux
T140,000) If you want to swank it up, look
no further than this new six-storey hotel.

Rooms are enormous, in immaculate condition and are well equipped without being luxurious. There's internet access through a cable, although no wi-fi, and en-suite bathrooms are modern.

✖ Eating

There are *guanz* (canteens) around town, several of them in the container market.

Jargalan MONGOLIAN **$**
(mains T2000-4000; ☺7am-8pm) A warm, friendly canteen that opens earlier than most for breakfast. It serves *buuz* (T500 per dumpling), goulash (T3000), various soups (from T2000) and warming mugs of *suutei tsai* (salty milk tea; T200). No English sign or menu.

★Arvaikheer Palace Hotel Restaurant ASIAN **$$**
(mains T5000-10,000; ☺8am-10pm; 🗐) The town's smartest restaurant is on the ground floor of Arvaikheer's top hotel and has a fabulous range of Mongolian and pan-Asian dishes, including soups, salads, kebabs, chicken dishes and plenty of vegetarian options. It's excellent value, spotlessly clean and the menu has English translations and photos.

Altan Holbo MONGOLIAN **$$**
(mains T4500-10,000; ☺10am-8pm Mon-Sat) A simple but bright and clean restaurant serving hearty Mongolian meals, with a wood-panelled pub out the back. Beer from T2000.

ℹ Information

The police station is southeast of the town square.
Bathhouse (shower/sauna T2000/5000; ☺9am-10pm Tue-Sun) Look for a small sign over the door saying 'bath-place saun'.
Internet Cafe (per hr T600; ☺8am-11pm) In the Telecom office, along with the post office.
Khan Bank (☺9am-6pm Mon-Fri) The town's largest bank. Has money-changing facilities and an ATM.

ℹ Getting There & Away

You can travel quickly along the 430km paved road between Ulaanbaatar and Arvaikheer. And the paved road continues for more than 100km west of Arvaikheer, towards the next aimag capital of Bayankhongor. With a jeep, an experienced driver and lots of time you could venture south to Dalanzadgad, 377km away in Ömnögov aimag,

either via Saikhan-Ovoo or (more adventurously) via Guchin Us, Khovd and Khongoryn Els.

BUS

Two daily buses travel from Arvaikheer to Ulaanbaatar (T20,300, eight hours), departing at 8am and 2pm. The bus station is southwest of the centre, near the highway, in a two-storey brown-brick building.

The local bus stand, or sum bus stand, has minivans that ply set routes to other *sums* within the aimag, including Kharkhorin (T10,000 per person). Prices here tend to be cheaper than those at the jeep stand by the market.

HITCHING

The Ulaanbaatar–Arvaikheer route is pretty busy so hitching a ride should be fairly easy. Going further west along the main road to Bayankhongor won't be as easy, but it is possible (although it's less scenic than the route through Arkhangai).

TAXIS, JEEPS & MINIVANS

Minivans, jeeps and taxis run along the paved road between Arvaikheer and Ulaanbaatar daily (T22,000 per person, seven hours). Look for them on the west side of the market. Shared vehicles travel to Khujirt (T7000, two hours), Kharkhorin (T10,000, three hours) and Bayankhongor (T15,000).

MOTORBIKE TAXIS

Motorbike taxis charge T1000 per person to take you between the town centre and the bus station.

Kharkhorin (Karakorum)
Хархорин (Каракорум)

📞01322, 7032 / POP 8977 / ELEV 1913M
In the mid-13th century, Karakorum was a happening place. Chinggis Khaan established a supply base here and his son Ögedei ordered the construction of a proper capital, a decree that attracted traders, dignitaries and skilled workers from across Asia and even Europe.

The good times lasted around 40 years until Kublai moved the capital to Khanbalik (later called Běijīng), a decision that still incites resentment among some Mongolians. Following the move to Běijīng and the subsequent collapse of the Mongol empire, Karakorum was abandoned and then destroyed by vengeful Manchurian soldiers in 1388.

Whatever was left of Karakorum was used to help build, in the 16th century, the enormous monastery, Erdene Zuu Khiid,

Kharkhorin

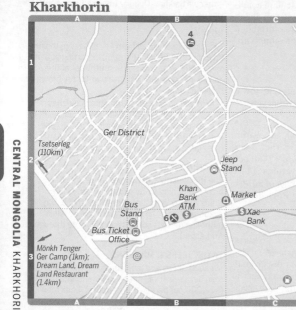

Kharkhorin

which itself was badly damaged during the Stalinist purges.

The rather nondescript Soviet-built town of Kharkhorin was built a couple of kilometres away from Erdene Zuu Khiid, and there is little of interest in the town itself (don't come expecting the glories of the Middle Ages!). But the remains of the monastery and a very impressive new museum – both walking distance from town – pull in punters by the busload, while the town's

strong selection of ger camps and guest-ger accommodation, plus some decent horse-trekking outfits, ensure plenty of people linger for a while.

Kharkhorin is also within easy striking distance of a number of worthwhile sights – the stunning lakes of Naiman Nuur, Orkhon Khürkhree waterfall, the secluded hilltop monastery, Tövkhön Khiid, the sand dunes known as Mongol Els, and the magnificently stark rocky nature reserve, Khögnö Khan Uul – making this the best place to base yourself for a tour of Övörkhangai aimag.

◎ Sights

★**Erdene Zuu Khiid**   BUDDHIST MONASTERY
(Эрдэнэ Зуу Хийд; ☎ 9926 8286, ticket desk 01322-82 285; grounds/temples free/T3500; ◷ 9am-6pm May-Sep, 10am-5pm Oct-Apr) Founded in 1586 by Altai Khaan, Erdene Zuu (Hundred Treasures) was the first Buddhist monastery in Mongolia. It had between 60 and 100 temples, about 300 gers inside the walls and, at its peak, up to 1000 monks in residence.

The monastery went through periods of neglect and prosperity until finally the Stalinist purges of 1937 put it completely out of business. All but three of the temples in Erdene Zuu were destroyed and an unknown number of monks were either killed or sent to Siberian gulags.

However, a surprising number of statues, *tsam* masks and *thangkas* were saved – possibly with the help of a few sympathetic military officers. The items were buried in nearby mountains, or stored in local homes (at great risk to the residents).

The monastery remained closed until 1965, when it was permitted to reopen as a museum, but not as a place of worship. It was only with the collapse of communism in 1990 that religious freedom was restored and the monastery became active again. Today Erdene Zuu Khiid is considered by many to be the most important monastery in the country, though no doubt it's a shadow of what it once was.

Entrance to the walled monastery grounds is free. If you want to see inside the temples, however, you'll have to go to the ticket desk and souvenir shop on your left as you enter the grounds from the south and buy a ticket, which includes a guided tour of the site with an English-speaking guide.

The main temples date from the 16th century. Most of the artefacts you'll see – wall paintings, *thangkas*, masks etc – are 18th century. Many are in excellent condition. The monastery is an easy 2km walk from the centre of Kharkhorin.

➡ Temples

The monastery is enclosed in an immense walled compound. Spaced evenly along each wall, about every 15m, are 108 **stupas** (108 is a sacred number to Buddhists). The three temples in the compound – Baruun Zuu, Zuu of Buddha and Zuun Zuu – which were not destroyed in the 1930s, are dedicated to the three stages of Buddha's life: childhood, adolescence and adulthood.

Dalai Lama Süm was built in 1675 to commemorate the visit by Abtai Khaan's son, Altan, to the Dalai Lama in Tibet. The room is bare save for a statue of Zanabazar and some fine 17th-century *thangkas* depicting the Dalai Lamas and various protector deities.

Inside the courtyard, **Baruun Zuu**, the temple to the west, built by Abtai Khaan and his son, is dedicated to the adult Buddha. Inside, on either side of Sakyamuni (the historical Buddha), are statues of Sanjaa ('Dipamkara' in Sanskrit), the Past Buddha, to the left; and Maidar ('Maitreya' in Sanskrit), the Future Buddha, to the right. Other items on display include some golden

'wheels of eternity', *naimin takhel* (the eight auspicious symbols), figurines from the 17th and 18th centuries, and *balin* (wheat dough cakes, decorated with coloured medallions of goat or mutton fat), made in 1965 and still well preserved. Look out for the inner circumambulation path leading off to the left, just by the entrance.

The main and central temple is called the **Zuu of Buddha**. The entrance is flanked by the gods Gonggor on the left and Bandal Lham (Palden Lhamo in Sanskrit) on the right. Inside, to the right of the statues of the child Buddha, is Otoch Manal (the Medicine Buddha), while to the left is Holy Abida (the god of justice). The temple also contains statues of Niam and Dabaa, the sun and moon gods respectively, a few of the *tsam* masks that survived the purges, some carved, aggressive-looking guards from the 16th and 17th centuries, and some displays of the work of the revered sculptor and Buddhist, Zanabazar.

In the temple to the east, **Zuun Zuu**, there's a statue depicting the adolescent Buddha. The statue on the right is Tsongkhapa, who founded the Yellow Hat sect of Buddhism in Tibet. The figure on the left is Janraisig (Chenresig in Tibetan, Avalokitesvara in Sanskrit), the Bodhisattva of Compassion.

As you walk north you will pass the **Golden Prayer Stupa**, built in 1799. The small locked temple next to it, with a blue-tiled roof, is thought to pre-date the monastery itself by around 200 years.

The large white temple at the far end is the Tibetan-style **Lavrin Süm**, where ceremonies are held every morning, usually starting at around 11am; the times vary so ask at the office. Visitors are welcome, but photographs during ceremonies are not. This temple is the most active and atmospheric part of the whole complex.

➡ Other Sights

Apart from the main temples, there are several other interesting things to see. The **gravestones** of Abtai Khaan (1554–88) and his grandson Tüshet Khaan Gombodorj (the father of Zanabazar) stand in front of the Dalai Lama Süm and are inscribed in Mongol, Tibetan and Arabic scripts. In the northeast of the monastery are the base stones of a gigantic ger, now called the **Square of Happiness and Prosperity**, set up in 1639 to commemorate Zanabazar's birthday. The ger was reported to be 15m high and 45m in

THE ANCIENT CAPITAL

Mongolia's ancient capital may be gone, but Karakorum is certainly not forgotten. By piecing together the accounts of the city written by visiting missionaries, ambassadors and travellers, we have some idea of what the imperial capital once looked like.

The missionary William of Rubruck (1215–95) dismissed the city as being no bigger than the suburb of Saint Denis in Paris. Giovanni de Piano Carpine (1180–1252), an envoy sent to the Mongols in 1245 by Pope Innocent IV, described the city vaguely as 'at the distance of a year's walk' from Rome.

The city never had much time to expand; it was only active for 40 years before Kublai moved the capital to Khanbalik (Běijīng). Interestingly, few Mongols lived there, most preferring to stay in their gers several kilometres away on the steppe. It was mainly inhabited by artisans, scholars, religious leaders and others captured by the Mongols during their foreign raids.

Its main feature was a brick wall with four gates that encircled the city. Each gate had its own market, selling grain in the east, goats in the west, oxen and wagons in the south and horses in the north.

The Mongol khaans were famed for their religious tolerance and split their time equally between all the religions, hence the 12 different religions that coexisted within the town. Mosques, Buddhist monasteries and Nestorian Christian churches competed for the Mongols' souls. Even powerful figures such as Ögedei's wife and Kublai's mother were Nestorian Christians.

The centrepiece of the city was the Tumen Amgalan (Palace of Worldly Peace) in the southwest corner of the city. This 2500-sq-metre complex, built in 1235, was the palace of Ögedei Khaan. The two-storey palace had a vast reception hall for receiving ambassadors, and its 64 pillars resembled the nave of a church. The walls were painted, the green-tiled floor had underfloor heating, and the Chinese-style roof was covered in green and red tiles.

A team of German archaeologists recently uncovered the foundations of the palace, close to one of the stone turtles. You can see a model of the palace in the National Museum of Mongolia in Ulaanbaatar, while inside the new Karakorum Museum (p116), in Kharkhorin itself, there is a model of the whole ancient city.

Arguably, the most memorable aspect of the city was a fountain designed in 1253 by the French jeweller and sculptor Guillaume Bouchier (or Bouchee) of Paris, who had been captured by the Mongols in Hungary and brought back to embellish Karakorum. The fountain was in the shape of a huge silver tree, which simultaneously dispensed mare's milk from silver lion heads, and wine, rice wine, bal (mead) and airag (fermented mare's milk) from four golden spouts shaped like snakes' heads. On top of the tree was an angel. On order, a servant blew a pipe like a bugle that extended from the angel's mouth, giving the order for other servants to pump drinks out of the tree.

diameter, with 35 concertina-style walls, and could seat 300 during the annual assemblies of the local khaans.

★**Karakorum Museum**   MUSEUM
(admission T5000; ☺ Apr-Sep 9am-8pm, Oct-Mar 9am-5pm Mon-Fri; ☎) Kharkhorin's new museum is small, but highly impressive – probably the country's best museum outside Ulaanbaatar. Everything is beautifully designed and well displayed. The building is fully air-conditioned, there are English-speaking guides available, English captions throughout and there's even free wi-fi in the small cafe (although the cafe itself is

disappointing). The camera/video fee is T10,000/15,000 extra.

The exhibits include dozens of artefacts dating from the 13th and 14th centuries which were recovered from the immediate area, plus others that were found from archaeological sites in other parts of the aimag, including prehistoric stone tools. You'll see pottery, bronzes, coins, religious statues and stone inscriptions. There's also a half-excavated kiln sunk into the museum floor. Perhaps most interesting is the scale model of ancient Karakorum, which aims to represent the city as it may have looked in the 1250s, and is based on descriptions written by the missionary William of Rubruck.

Stone Turtles   HISTORIC SITE
(Turtle Rocks) Outside the monastery walls are two stone turtles. Four of these sculptures once marked the boundaries of ancient Karakorum, acting as protectors of the city (turtles are considered symbols of eternity). The turtles originally had an inscribed stone stele mounted vertically on their back.

One is easy to find: just walk out of the northern gate of the monastery and follow the path northwest for about 300m. Often, an impromptu **souvenir market** is set up here, lining the path. You'll need a guide to find the other remaining turtle, which is on the hill south of the monastery.

Ancient Karakorum   RUINS
Just beyond the closest stone turtle, stretching for about 1km east, is the site of ancient Karakorum. The foundations of Karakorum's buildings are all underground and little has been excavated, so you need lots of imagination when contemplating the grandness of it all, or visit the Karakorum Museum to see the model. The plain was littered with bricks, ruined walls and pillars until the mid-16th century, when everything was picked up and used to build the walls and temples of nearby Erdene Zuu. Next to the stone turtle you can see an area of raised earth surrounded by a wire fence. It is thought this was the site of Ögedei Khaan's palace.

☞ Tours
Most of the ger camps can help to arrange horse trips around Kharkhorin. Family Guesthouse, located in the ger district at the north end of town, also organises horse treks and jeep tours to surrounding sights in the region.

Morin Jim   HORSE RIDING
(☑ 9924 2980, 9605 2980; www.horsetrails. mn) The best tour operator is Morin Jim, a French-run operation based at Morin Jim Café. Horse trips cost T20,000 per day per horse, plus the same again for your guide.

🛏 Sleeping
Head out towards the main cluster of ger camps in the lovely valley southwest of town, and you'll be able to find somewhere nice to pitch a tent beside the river, Orkhon Gol.

★ Family Guesthouse   GUEST GER $
(☑ 9645 8188, 9931 2735; www.horsetripganaa. com; GPS: N 47°12.496', E 102°49.151'; per person with breakfast & dinner US$12; P @) This friendly family home has a couple of six-bed guest gers in its compound, offering excellent-value budget accommodation. Ganbaatar and his wife Suvd both speak good English and, as well as looking after their four kids, treat guests to a cheerful welcome, provide breakfast and dinner, a hot shower and internet access from a computer terminal in the kitchen ger, which is also free for guests to use. The toilet is in an outhouse, but is clean and of the sit-down variety. Ganbaatar and Suvd can help you buy bus tickets to onward destinations. They also organise multiday jeep tours and horse treks in the surrounding region.

Morin Jim   GUEST GER $
(☑ 9924 2980; www.horsetrails.mn; ger T8000) The French owner of the excellent Morin Jim Café has placed a handful of gers behind his restaurant. It was still pretty basic when we visited, but there was a new two-storey shower block in the making which should include some extra rooms once finished. Management speak English. Horse treks arranged here are professionally run and come highly recommended.

OFF THE BEATEN TRACK

SHANKH KHIID   ШАНХ ХИЙД

Shankh Khiid (GPS: N 47°03.079', E 102°57.236'; admission T1000), once known as the West Monastery, and Erdene Zuu are the only monasteries in the region to have survived the 1937 purge. Shankh was founded by the great Zanabazar in 1648 and is said to have once housed Chinggis Khaan's black military banner. At one time the monastery was home to more than 1500 monks. As elsewhere, the monastery was closed in 1937, temples were burnt and many monks were shipped off to Siberia. Some of those that survived helped to reopen the place in the early 1990s.

The monastery is about 26km south of Kharkhorin. You'll see it on the right side of the road as you approach the village of Shankh.

Mönkh Tenger Tourist Ger Camp
TOURIST GER CAMP $$
(☑9915 9890; www.munkh-tenger.com; GPS: N 47°11.500', E 102°47.720'; per person T25,000; P@) This is the first ger camp you see in the middle of the valley as you walk southwest from town. It's relatively new so still in good condition compared to some of the others in the valley. It has about 20 gers, a restaurant, hot showers and laundry facilities. Free internet access is a plus. Some staff speak English.

Mukhlai Hotel
HOTEL $$
(tw T45,000-60,000; P🛜) This new hotel offers an OK alternative if you're desperate to sleep in something other than a ger. Rooms are large, clean and bright and come with wall-mounted TV and attached bathroom. There's no English spoken, but staff are welcoming. Wi-fi wasn't working when we were here.

Dream Land
TOURIST GER CAMP $$$
(☑9908 8605, 9191 1931; www.asa-travel.com; GPS: N 47°11.586', E 102°47.374'; ger s/d US$36/64, lux ger s/d US$60/84; P✳@) A stone's throw away from Mönkh Tenger, but secreted away from the grassy valley behind an oasis of trees, Dream Land, owned by a famous Mongolian suma champion, is Kharkhorin's top luxury ger-camp option. The standard gers are similar to those at any decent ger camp, but the luxury gers come with a king-sized bed, upholstered furniture, a fridge, air-conditioning and even cable TV! There are also nine, good-quality rooms (twins are US$90 to US$130) within the main building which houses reception. A beautiful Japanese-style sauna and bathhouse completes the picture. English is spoken.

✖ Eating

All the accommodation options reviewed serve meals, too.

★ Morin Jim Café
MONGOLIAN $
(☑9924 2980; mains T3500-6500; ⊙8am-10pm; 🅳) This French-run restaurant has a simple, but excellent-value menu containing mostly Mongolian dishes, but also salads, fried chicken and vegetarian stew. There's roadside terrace seating out front, and they serve French wine and fresh coffee as well as beer.

Dream Land Restaurant
WESTERN $$$
(☑9908 8605, 9191 1931; www.asa-travel.com; dishes T10,000-15,000; ⊙9am-11pm; 🅳) Housed at Dream Land ger camp, 20 minutes walk southwest of town, this branch of Ulaanbaatar's California restaurant serves Western meals, including pizza and burgers, plus Mongolian classics, and offers some of the best food in Kharkhorin.

❶ Information

Internet Cafe (per hr T1000; ⊙9am-10pm Mon-Fri, 11am-5pm Sat & Sun) Located in the Telecom office, which also houses the post office.

Khan Bank ATM Foreign-card friendly.

XacBank (⊙9am-5.30pm Mon-Fri) Changes money and gives cash advances on MasterCard.

❶ Getting There & Away

BUS

A daily bus goes to Ulaanbaatar at 10am (T17,000, eight hours). You can buy tickets from the **ticket office** (⊙9am-2pm & 3-8pm) at the bus stand two days in advance, and it's wise to do so if possible, though UB-bound minivans

---

WORTH A TRIP

NAIMAN NUUR
НАЙМАН НУУР

The area of Naiman Nuur (Eight Lakes), which was created by volcanic eruptions centuries ago, is now part of the 11,500-hectare **Khuisiin Naiman Nuur Nature Reserve** (GPS: N 46°31.232', E 101°50.705'). Despite the name, there are actually nine, not eight, lakes. The lakes are about 35km southwest of Orkhon Khürkhree (waterfall), but the roads are often virtually impassable. Locals around the waterfall can hire horses for the two-day trip to the lakes (around T15,000 per horse per day, plus the same again for your horse guide). Family Guesthouse (p117) in Kharkhorin also organises horse treks here (US$60 per day, plus US$60 each way for the jeep transfer to the waterfall).

This area is environmentally fragile; vehicles that attempt to make the trip end up tearing new tracks through the grasslands, so local communities are working on ways to prevent cars from coming here. If your driver says he can make it all the way to the lakes by car, insist on going by horse.

Ulaanbaatar-based companies such as Nomads, Nomadic Journeys and Nomadic Expeditions (p36) also run tours here, including horse-riding trips.

wait to sweep up ticket-less passengers, so you won't get stranded.

It's sometimes possible to snag a seat on the daily Ulaanbaatar to Tsetserleg bus if you wait on the main road at around 1pm to 2pm and flag it down as it passes. Otherwise, try to find a shared minivan heading west. You may have to charter your own vehicle, though (about T60,000 plus petrol).

HITCHING

Hitching along the main road between Ulaanbaatar and Kharkhorin is fairly easy, but remember that a lot of vehicles will be carrying tourists, so they may not want to pick up a hitchhiker. Getting a lift between Arvaikheer and Kharkhorin is less likely, but if you're patient something will come along.

MINIVANS & JEEPS

Minivans run daily to Ulaanbaatar (T17,000 to T20,000, seven hours), either from the bus stand or the jeep stand by the market. The road is sealed the whole way. There are far fewer vehicles going to Khujirt (T3000) and Arvaikheer (T6000) – maybe once a day if at all.

For Tsetserleg (T20,000), you may need to flag down a shared minivan from the main road as it passes by from Ulaanbaatar. Again, the road is paved all the way.

Coming here, minivans from Ulaanbaatar to Kharkhorin leave when full from the Dragon Avto Vaksal (p94) bus station.

West of Kharkhorin

Khar Balgas   Хар Балгас

The ruined citadel of **Khar Balgas** (Kara Balgasun in Turkic; GPS: N 47°25.782; E 102°39.490') is in Khotont *sum* on the banks of the Orkhon Gol. The city was founded in AD 751 as the capital of the Uighur Khaganate, which ruled Mongolia from 744 to 840.

There's not much to see except the outer walls (with gates in the north and south), a **Buddhist stupa** and the ruler's **kagan** (castle), in the southwest corner. From the walls you can see the rows of stupas on either side and the remains of irrigated fields in the surrounding countryside. The city had an elaborate plumbing system, which brought water into the city from the nearby river.

The ruins are in Arkhangai aimag, but are only 33km northwest of Kharkhorin, so are best accessed from there. Take the road from Kharkhorin towards Tsetserleg for 20km, then follow rough dirt tracks another 13km to the site.

Tövkhön Khiid   Төвхөн Хийд

Hidden deep in a pine forest in the Khangai mountains, this scenic **monastery** (GPS: N47° 00.772; E102° 15.362'; admission T3000) has become a major pilgrimage centre for Mongolians. Zanabazar founded the site in 1653 and lived, worked and meditated here for 30 years. The monastery was destroyed in 1937 but rebuilt with public funds in the early 1990s.

The monastery is situated at the top of Shireet Ulaan Uul, and Zanabazar apparently liked the unusual formation of the peak; the rocky outcrop looks like an enormous throne. It was here that Zanabazar (see p138) created many of his best artistic endeavours, some of which can be found now in the Zanabazar Museum of Fine Arts (p64) in Ulaanbaatar.

Six or seven monks live here year-round, although sometimes more are here. Several **pilgrimage sites** have grown up around the temple and hermits' caves, including one that is said to be Zanabazar's boot imprint. Local monks will likely instruct you to squeeze through the narrow **rebirth cave**, representative of a woman's uterus, although this is not recommended if you have a fear of heights, are susceptible to claustrophobia or have the frame of a sumo wrestler.

The temple is in **Khangai Nuruu National Park** (admission T3000) and best reached with your own vehicle. A good 4WD can drive the steep road up to the monastery in 20 minutes, but old Russian jeeps and vans can't make the trip so you'll have to walk (one hour) up the hill through the forest. From the car park it's 2.5km. The route is obvious and in summer locals offer horse rides (T10,000 return) to the top and back. It's a pleasant hike to the top, although swarms of flies can plague your ascent in summer; wrap a T-shirt, bandana or towel around your head to keep them away. A small shop at the top sells bottled water and snacks.

It's not possible to camp at the monastery, but there are a couple of **family-run ger camps** at the bottom, by the entrance to the national park. Expect to pay around T20,000 per person including meals. Don't expect showers.

The monastery is around 60km from Kharkhorin. Just follow the Orkhon Gol southwest for around 50km and turn north, up a side valley. This brings you to the ger camps and the trailhead up the eastern side of the mountain. Note that if you are coming from Orkhon Khürkhree, you will arrive at the western slope of the mountain and will end up taking a different trail to the top. From this side you'll also find basic ger camps and herdsmen offering horse rides to the monastery.

Orkhon
Khürkhree   Орхон Хүрхрээ

After a strong rain the magnificent seasonal **Orkhon Khürkhree** (Ulaan Tsutgalan, Улаан Цутгалан; GPS: N 46°47.234', E 101°57.694'), is one of the best sights in central Mongolia. About 250m downstream from the waterfall you can climb down to the bottom of the **gorge**; it's 22m deep and dotted with pine trees.

Ask your tour operator about the status of the falls. The water doesn't run all year and will only start to flow after the first good summer rain. Late July and August are the best times to see it, although it's still a very attractive spot in autumn. If you arrive when the waterfall is not in flow, take solace in the fact that the region is still gorgeous, and a fine area for **camping** and **horse riding**.

There are a few different ways to approach the waterfall; all of them involve rough travel in parts, on very rocky roads. Coming directly from Ulaanbaatar, most traffic will go on the road via Khujirt (around 35km from the falls). You'll pass a lovely **view-point** (GPS: N 46°53.465' E 102°22.762') on this track, as the river skirts a cliff face it helped carve into the steppe. One or two kilometres further along you'll pass a remarkable collection of large, Bronze-Age **square graves** (GPS: N 46°52.899' E 102°20.687') on your left. The road from Kharkhorin is longer but by taking this route you can stop at Tövkhön Khiid (p119) on the way. From Arvaikheer, it's possible to take a remote backcountry road via Züünbayan-Ulaan and Bat-Ölzii; but you'll need an experienced driver and a very sturdy 4WD to attempt it.

In summer, a number of nomad families open up **guest gers**, charging around T10,000 per person. One such place, less than 1km back from the falls, is run by a herdsman known as **Shar** (☑ 8832 7388). He charges T8000 per bed, T2500 for breakfast and T4500 for lunch or dinner. Like most of the families here, he also rents horses (T7000/15,000 per hour/day, plus the same again for the guide). The three- or four-day round trip to Naiman Nuur (p118) is popular from here.

Nearby **Orkhon Tushee** (☑ 9588 7175; GPS: N 46°46.537' E 101°57.575'; per person incl meals US$35) has hot showers, and is the nearest tourist ger camp to the falls, although there are a number of others further downstream.

If you have a rod and reel, you could try catching your dinner. Good spots for catching lenok trout can be found downstream from the waterfall.

OFF THE BEATEN TRACK

KUL-TEGINII MONUMENT

When Chinggis Khaan decided to move his capital to Karakorum, he was well aware that the region had already been the capital of successive nomad empires. About 20km northeast of Khar Balgas lies the remainder of yet another of these, the Turkic *khaganate* (pre-Mongol empire). All that's left of the *khaganate* is the 3m-high inscribed monument of Kul-Tegin (AD 684–731), the *khagan* (ruler) of the ancient empire.

The **monument** (Кул-Тэгиний Хөшөө; GPS: N 47°33.837', E 102°49.931') was raised in 732 and is inscribed in Runic and Chinese script. You can see a copy of the stele in the entrance of the National Museum of Mongolia in Ulaanbaatar.

Just over 1km away is another **monument to Bilge Khagan** (683–734), older brother of Kul-Tegin. Ten years after the death of Bilge, the Turkic *khaganate* was overrun by the Uighurs.

A Turkish-funded archaeological expedition has built a **museum** at the site. In fact, the outdoor monuments are replicas and the originals have been moved inside the museum. If the museum is locked, the watchman at the ger next door should be able to let you inside.

The museum and monuments are 45km north of Kharkhorin, on a paved road. About 3km before the museum (if coming from Kharkhorin) is **Tsaidam Ger Camp** (☑ 9923 6888; per person US$10), which has comfortable gers and hot showers.

East of Kharkhorin

There are several interesting places between Kharkhorin and Khustain National Park en route to/from Ulaanbaatar.

Khögnö Khan Uul Nature Reserve   Хөгнө Хан Уул

Located just off the main Ulaanbaatar–Kharkhorin highway, this 46,900-hectare nature reserve centres on a large, boulder-strewn rocky mountain which rises up surreally from its semidesert surrounds. The arid terrain is good for short hikes (there's plenty of rock clambering to be done), and there are old temples to explore, both ruined and active. We saw some majestic red deer when we were here last. You might also spot ibexes, various varieties of hawk, and even wolves.

The mountain is in Bulgan aimag but most easily accessed from the Ulaanbaatar–Kharkhorin highway.

○ Sights

Erdiin Khambiin Khiid   RUINS
(GPS: N 47°25.561', E 103°41.686'; admission T2000) At the southern foot of the mountain are these ruins, with a couple of new temples and the remains of one older temple. About five monks reside here in the summer months. The head lama is a charming woman who professes soothsaying abilities.

Övgön Khiid   RUINS
(Өвгөн Хийд; GPS: N 47°26.267', E 103°42.527') These ruins are a lovely 45-minute (2km) walk along a well-defined path up the valley to the right of Erdiin Khambiin Khiid. The monastery was built in 1660 and destroyed (and the monks massacred) by the armies of Zungar Galdan Bochigtu, a rival of Zanabazar's, in 1640.

🛏 Sleeping

Camping is excellent in the valley, though the only water comes from a hard-to-find well at its lower end.

Ider-Tsogt's Family Ger   GUEST GER $
(☑ 9579 0048; GPS: N 47°22.553' E 103°40.961'; per person T5000, meals T4000-5000) Ider-Tsogt is one of a number of herdsmen who rent out guest gers to travellers visiting the national park. He doesn't speak English, but is warm and friendly. His gers are between

the main mountain and the sand dunes known as Mongol Els. Turn up to your left as you approach the mountain from the main road. He also rents horses (per hour/day T7000/15,000, plus the same again for your horse guide) for treks in and around the mountain range. It takes three days to complete a circuit of the mountain by horse or by foot.

Övgön Erdene Tour Camp TOURIST GER CAMP $$
(Monastery Ger Camp; ☑ 9927 2873; per person with/without meals US$50/25) This well-built ger camp and wood lodge is just beside the entrance to the Erdiin Khambiin Khiid temple. It's a bit rough around the edges compared to Khögnö Khan ger camp, but it has hot showers and a restaurant. It's run by the monks at the temple.

Khögnö Khan   TOURIST GER CAMP $$
(☑ 9910 2885; www.naturetours.mn; GPS: N 47°24.430', E 103°40.364'; with/without meals T62,000/24,000) Located 4km southwest of Övgön Khiid in an attractive setting at the foot of the mountain, this comfortable camp has a large restaurant ger, a clean and spacious shower block and great rock-clambering opportunities all around it.

ℹ Getting There & Away

To get to Khögnö Khan Uul from Kharkhorin by jeep, turn north off the main road, 80km east of Kharkhorin, just past the huge sand dunes known as Mongol Els. From the turn-off, the track passes several herdman's gers (Ider-Tsogt's Family Ger is up to your left from here) until, after 8km, you reach Khögnö Khan ger camp, where you turn right for the remaining 4km or so to the monastery ruins. There is a shortcut if you are coming from Ulaanbaatar (the turn-off is marked by a sign that says 'Ar Mongol', 1.2km after the Bichigt Khad ger camp).

There is no public transport to the monastery but you can take a Kharkhorin-, Khujirt- or Arvaikheer-bound minivan from Ulaanbaatar, get off at the turn-off on the main road and then hitch (or more likely walk) the remaining 12km.

Mongol Els   Монгол Элс

As you approach Khögnö Khan Uul Nature Reserve, on the road from Kharkhorin to Ulaanbaatar, one surprising sight that livens up a fairly boring stretch of road is the sand dunes of **Elsen-Tasarkhai** (GPS: N 47°19.819' E 103°41.618). Better known in Ulaanbaatar's tourist industry as Mongol Els, these large dunes stretch for some 70km, and are worth stopping off at if you're not planning to visit the much more spectacular Khongoryn Els in the Gobi Desert. At the turn-off to the sand dunes there is a group of camel herders who hang around and sell camel rides. Expect to pay T5000 to have your photo taken on a camel, or T10,000 for a one-hour ride across the dunes.

ARKHANGAI   АРХАНГАЙ

POP 85,200 / AREA 55,000 SQ KM

Arkhangai is something of an oasis in the centre of Mongolia's harsh climatic zones; to the south lies the hot Gobi Desert and to the north lies the frigid Siberian taiga. Arkhangai is right in the middle, a mixed landscape of rugged mountains, peaceful forests, rushing streams and rolling steppe. All this wild nature and mixed topography makes for some interesting independent travel options: horse riding, mountain biking, fishing and trekking are all possible here.

The Khangai Mountains in the southern part of the aimag rise to a height of 3300m. The mountains are by no means impenetrable and it's possible to travel through the passes on horse and jeep trails to Bayankhongor aimag. In winter, nomads use the passes on traditional *otors* (treks) to find grazing land for their animals.

NATIONAL PARKS OF ARKHANGAI

....

Khorgo-Terkhiin Tsagaan Nuur National Park (77,267 hectares; p126) Protected area for migratory birds as well as fish. The park includes lakes, cinder cones and volcanic flows.

Most travellers make stops at the Tsenkher hot springs and Tsetserleg before heading off to Tariat for Terkhiin Tsagaan Nuur (Great White Lake). From the White Lake there are trails north to Khövsgöl aimag. With a few extra days up your sleeve you could dangle a fishing line at Ögii Nuur and check out the historic Turkic-era stone monuments of Kul-Tegin.

Tsetserleg   Цэцэрлэг

📞 01332, 7033 / POP 16,300 / ELEV 1691M

Nestled comfortably between rugged mountains, and with a charming temple overlooking the town, Tsetserleg is one of the country's more appealing aimag capitals.

It's a perfect place to break up your journey between Kharkhorin and Tariat, especially if you manage to snag a bed at the standout Fairfield Guesthouse. Nature lovers will appreciate the hiking opportunities and good camping spots in the surrounding area.

◉ Sights

★ **Museum of Arkhangai Aimag**   MUSEUM
(📞 01332-22 281; admission T5000; ⊙9am-6pm)
This is one of the best aimag museums in the country, not least because it is housed in the charming courtyard-temple complex of **Zayain Gegeenii Süm**, which was first built in 1586 but expanded in 1679, when it housed five temples and up to 1000 monks. Miraculously, the monastery escaped the Stalinist purges because it was made into a museum.

The main hall concentrates on traditional Mongolian lifestyle, with exhibits of costumes, traditional tools, a ger, musical instruments, weaponry and saddles. The displays have some useful English captions. The second hall concentrates on religious icons. The other two rooms of the former main prayer hall are empty, while the last hall focuses on local artwork. Look out for the traditional Mongolian board games and playing cards.

Galdan Zuu Temple   TEMPLE
Up the hill from the aimag museum, this temple has been renovated with donations from locals. It stands behind an impressive 7m statue of the Buddha. Behind the temple is a large, near-vertical, rocky hill called Bulgan Uul, where there are some **Buddhist inscriptions**.

LOCAL KNOWLEDGE

JAMSRANJAV BAYARSAIKHAN: ARCHAEOLOGIST

Jamsranjav Bayarsaikhan is a seasoned archaeologist based at the National Museum of Mongolia in Ulaanbaatar. He spoke with us about his excavations in Arkhangai. To contact the National Museum about joining an archaeological dig, visit www.national-museum.mn.

Khannui Valley

One of the most interesting places to visit in central Mongolia is the Khannui Valley. Very few people get there because it's off the main tourist route, but for me this in one of the most beautiful valleys in the country.

Archaeological Remains

Khannui is also a historically significant region with a huge ritual complex, the remains of a 14th-century settlement and around 30 deer stones. This is one of the largest concentrations of deer stones in Central Asia. Around the deer stones there are about 1700 horse mounds. These mounds contain horse skulls, which were buried according to local custom. Even today nomadic people honour these horse skulls – you can see them placed on *ovoos*.

Tips for Visitors

If travellers come here, I recommend they bring a Polaroid camera. It would please herders very much to receive an instant picture of their family. I also recommend that foreigners join an archaeological dig in Mongolia – it's a great way to see Mongolia and gain an appreciation of its history.

Buyandelgerüülekh Khiid MONASTERY
(Буяндэлгэрүүлэх Хийд) Tsetserleg's small monastery (next to the museum) has a handful of monks who hold services at 11am in summer and 10am in winter. The **main statue** here is Sakyamuni; you'll also see a picture of the last Zayan Gegeen (to the left of the throne), who was the traditional head of the monastery in Tsetserleg.

Gangin Gol VALLEY
In the north of town a trail leads to the pretty Gangin Gol, which offers great hiking potential. At the mouth of the valley is a ger camp and a pitiful nature museum of stuffed animals, which isn't worth the T1000 the caretaker will demand. From the camp you can hike up the mountain to the left, and walk along the ridge until you reach the peak of Bulgan Uul (1953m), the mountain that overlooks Tsetserleg.

🛏 Sleeping

Gangin Gol has some great camping spots, though someone may come and collect a dubious 'fee' for camping in a 'nature reserve' (it's not). A few hundred metres past a ger camp is a grassy enclosure that's perfect for camping. There are also some nice spots a few kilometres south of town on the banks of the river.

★**Fairfield Guesthouse** GUESTHOUSE $$
(☑ 7033 3036; www.fairfield.mn; per person with breakfast T32,500; 🛜) Attached to the excellent cafe-restaurant of the same name, this nine-room guesthouse, run by an Australian guy called Murray, his young family and their team of friendly local staff, is a hugely popular choice and one of the only hotels in the countryside where you need a reservation in summer. Rooms are simple, but clean and cosy and there is an excellent Western breakfast included in the price. The shared showers are spotless, and always hot, and clean towels are provided for all guests. Staff can also arrange horse-trekking trips (guides T35,000 per day, horses T16,000 per day), and they have a fleet of good-quality Trek mountain bikes for rent (T25,000). Laundry costs T5000, and the free wi-fi extends into some of the rooms. If rooms are full, ask about their large eight-bed spill-over ger (per person T15,000), which is within walking distance of the guesthouse.

Zamchin Hotel HOTEL $$
(☑ 9933 9819; r from T35,000; @) A reliable place, Zamchin has a restaurant, sauna and hot shower. Rooms are spacious but it's away from the centre, on the western road out of town.

Tsetserleg

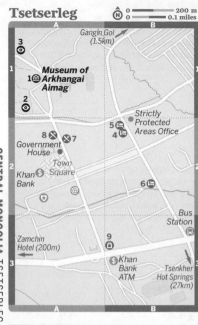

0 — 200 m
0 — 0.1 miles

Tsetserleg

Naran Hotel   HOTEL $$
(☎ 9949 6679; tw T20,000-60,000) Next to Fairfield Guesthouse, this place is OK as a last resort, although only the more expensive rooms have attached bathrooms. No English spoken.

OD Hotel   HOTEL $$$
(☎ 8811 9004; r T85,000-100,000) This reasonably new hotel has smart rooms with attached bathrooms, but is seriously overpriced. English sign, but no English spoken.

🍴 Eating

Orgil Pub   MONGOLIAN $
(mains T4000-6000; ⊘ 10am-9pm) No English menu, but there's a handy photo menu stuck to one wall so you can point and choose. All the usual Mongolian favourites are here, and it's a decent place to come to for a beer in the evening. They keep serving drinks until at least 10pm.

U-Tsakhiur   MONGOLIAN $
(mains T4000-6500; ⊘ 10am-10pm) A little fancier than other places in town, this 2nd-floor restaurant serves local favourites such as *buuz*, goulash and *puntutste khuurag* (glass noodles). Also does roast chicken *(takhia-ny makh)* and various rice dishes. No English menu.

★ Fairfield Cafe & Bakery   CAFE $$
(☎ 7033 3036; mains T5000-10,000; ⊘ summer 7am-9pm, winter 9am-6pm, closed Sun; 🛜🐾🖥) This Australian-run cafe-restaurant is one of the highlights of Tsetserleg and should not be missed even if you aren't staying at the guesthouse it's attached to. A full English breakfast (T14,400) consists of bacon, sausage, eggs, toast and pancakes and will fill up even the hungriest of overland travellers. Lunch and dinner options include lasagne, chilli con carne, beef in beer sauce, Indian curries, a monstrous Aussie burger and some vegetarian dishes to boot. Pastries, cakes and cookies are served all day long, as is a selection of takeaway sandwiches (T4500 to T5000). And there's proper, fresh, espresso-machine coffee (T2000 to T3800) – wahoo! The cafe is also a good place to ask about travel conditions and look for a ride if you are hitching around the country. Note that it's closed on Sundays (although guests staying at the guesthouse will still get their complimentary breakfast). Also worth noting: no alcohol.

🔒 Shopping

There's a **gift shop** in a ger by the entrance to Fairfield Guesthouse, while the equally small **Nooslog Wool Shop** is next door.

The daily **market** (Khunsnii Zakh) has a supermarket next door.

ℹ Information

Internet Cafe (☎01332-21 110; per hr T600; ⊗8am-10pm) In the Telecom office, along with the post office.

Khan Bank (⊗9am-6pm Mon-Fri, to 4pm Sat) Overlooking the town square. Changes cash and has an ATM. There's another Khan Bank ATM opposite the market.

Strictly Protected Areas Office (☎01332-21 179; khangainuruu@yahoo.com; ⊗9am-6pm) Has information on Arkhangai's national parks and can give advice on tourist sites, fishing licences and park fees.

ℹ Getting There & Away

BUS

A daily bus departs Tsetserleg at 8am and 2pm for Ulaanbaatar (T23,000, 12 hours). Purchase the ticket at least one day ahead. Fairfield Cafe & Bakery will get your ticket for a T500 commission. The driver may impose a 15kg limit and charge you T3000 for an extra bag.

HITCHING

All types of vehicles go to/from Tsetserleg and, generally, along the main road through Arkhangai. Wait on the main road into and out of town (heading east or west), and something will eventually stop.

MINIVAN & JEEP

Microbuses and minivans run between Tsetserleg and Ulaanbaatar (T25,000, 10 hours). In Tsetserleg, minivans will wait by the bus stand. Expect to pay around T20,000 for Kharkhorin (three hours, 115km).

Minivans and Jeeps to other places will wait at a car park near the market. You can probably find a vehicle going to Tariat (T20,000).

There are two routes between Tsetserleg and Ulaanbaatar – northeast via Ögii Nuur (453km) or along the longer but better road via Kharkhorin (493km).

Tsetserleg to Tosontsengel is 350km to the northwest, but the paved road only stretches around halfway towards Tariat.

Tsenkher Hot Springs
Цэнхэрийн Халуун Рашаан

Set between forested hills, these **hot springs** (GPS: N 47°19.241′, E 101°39.411′) are becoming an increasingly popular detour from the main road. Four ger camps have been built around the springs; each pumps water into splash pools that, for nonguests, cost around US$10 to enter. If you are already in Tsetserleg, it's possible to head south on a jeep trail 27km to get here. It's around T45,000 return in a taxi from Tsetserleg. You could also consider cycling.

If you are coming from Ulaanbaatar, the turn-off is at Tsenkher *sum*. From the *sum* centre it's 24km to the hot springs.

🛏 Sleeping

Shiveet Mankhan   TOURIST GER CAMP **$$**
(☎9918 7847; shiveetmankhan@yahoo.com; per ger T40,000-50,000; ✉) One of a clutch of midrange tourist ger camps with similar facilities – comfortable gers, OK restaurant, open-air hot spring – but not in the same league as Duut Resort. The hot spring here costs US$10 for nonguests.

Duut Resort   TOURIST GER CAMP, LODGE **$$$**
(☎9898 1499; duutresort@yahoo.com; ger per person US$35, lodge tr T120,000-140,000) The most luxurious place to stay at the hot springs, and one of the better ger camps in

---

CYCLING TO TSENKHER HOT SPRINGS

Route: Tsetserleg to Tsenkher Hot Springs

Distance: 27km

Duration: 2½ hours one way

This rewarding countryside ride includes three tough climbs over passes at 1768m, 1820m and 1943m respectively (Tsetserleg, by comparison, lies at 1691m). The rural scenery is lovely, though, and the promise of a soak in a hot spring helps spur you on. Bike rental from Fairfield Guesthouse costs T25,000.

Ask Murray at Fairfield Guesthouse (p123) for detailed directions, but basically; turn right out of the guesthouse, and keep cycling straight out of town until the road bears right at the river. Follow the river for a couple of hundred metres, then cross it over the wooden bridge. Continue across the grassland, cycling south (roughly straight on) as you follow the main tracks up and down the three passes before bearing very slightly right as you descend to the springs.

the country. The lodge, made entirely from local timber, is beautifully constructed and furnished. It includes a cosy restaurant that serves Western and Mongolian dishes (T9000 to T13,000). The two hot springs pools are located out back and a communal shower block is located in the lodge. Non-guest use of the pool is T30,000.

Tsetserleg to Tariat

Cutting straight through Arkhangai aimag, this 180km stretch of road is one of the most scenic in Mongolia. It's rough in patches but road crews continue the slow process of paving it.

The first place worth stopping is **Taikhar Chuluu** (Тайхар Чулуу) rock formation, just 22km east of Tsetserleg. The rock is the subject of many local legends, the most common one being that a great *baatar* (hero) crushed a huge serpent here by hurling the rock on top of it. Locals claim there are some ancient Tibetan inscriptions on the rock, though you'll be lucky to spot them through 30 years of modern graffiti. There is even an *ovoo* at the top. You could camp anywhere along the Khoid Tamir Gol. **Taikhar Ger Camp** (☑ 9911 4060; per person with/without meals T56,000/18,000) next to the rock, has hot-water showers and flush toilets. Taikhar Chuluu is about 2km north of

---

OFF THE BEATEN TRACK

ÖGII NUUR   ӨГИЙ НУУР

On the road between Ulaanbaatar and Tsetserleg, near the border with Bulgan aimag, this **lake** (GPS: N 47°47.344', E 102°45.828') is a wonderful place for birdlife. Cranes and ducks, among other species, migrate to the area around late April. A **visitors centre** (GPS: N 47°45.023', E 102°46.314') located on the southern shore of the lake helps travellers get acquainted with the wildlife. The lake is also popular for **fishing**.

Ögii Nuur can only be reached from the direct road linking Tsetserleg with Ulaanbaatar. The lake makes a nice overnight stop with plenty of camping spots. There are also four ger camps by the lake, the best being **Khatan Ögii** (GPS: N 47°45.114', E 102°47.489'; ger from T30,000) which has accommodation in gers and *orts* (tepees).

Ikh Tamir along the river – you can see it from the main road.

The next landmark is **Chuluut Gur** (GPS: N 48°05.666', E 100°19.025') the bridge over the Chuluut River (*gur* means bridge). Near the bridge are a few tyre-repair shops and several *guanz* selling basic meals. About 2km past the bridge (on the south side of the road) is the **Chuluut Ger Camp** (☑ 9911 8066; ger T25,000), the best place to stay in the area.

About 30km east of Tariat is the dramatic **Chuluut gorge**, which makes a pleasant picnic stop.

Tariat   Тариат

The dusty village of Tariat is the jumping off point for Khorgo-Terkhiin Tsagaan Nuur National Park, which includes the region's standout natural sight, Terkhiin Tsagaan Nuur, or the Great White Lake. This large, freshwater lake glistens against a dramatic backdrop of volcanic craters and pine-clad lava fields and is a wonderful place for walking, swimming, camping and horse riding.

⊙ Sights

★**Terkhiin Tsagaan Nuur**   LAKE (Great White Lake) The freshwater Terkhiin Tsagaan Nuur is not as forested or as large as Khövsgöl Nuur, but it is closer to Ulaanbaatar, relatively undeveloped and just about perfect for camping (though there are a few flies in summer). The lake, birdlife and mountains are now protected within the 77,267-hectare **Khorgo-Terkhiin Tsagaan Nuur National Park** (admission T3000).

According to legend, the lake was formed when an elderly couple forgot to cap a well after fetching water. The valley was flooded until a local hero shot a nearby mountain top with his arrow; the shorn top covered the well and became an island in the lake (Noriin Dund Tolgoi). Another theory is that it was formed by lava flows from a volcanic eruption many millennia ago.

The lake is around 16km long, east to west, and around 4km to 6km wide, north to south. It takes around two hours to walk from Tariat to the northeast corner of the lake (6km). Here you'll find the largest concentration of ger camps, plus some shops selling drinks, snacks, cooking provisions and even gas cannisters for camping stoves. Most of the rest of the ger camps and the best camping spots are then strung out along the northern lakeshore.

Around Tariat

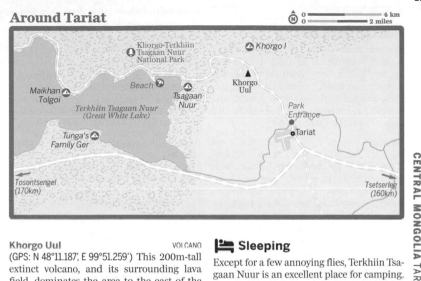

Khorgo Uul
VOLCANO

(GPS: N 48°11.187', E 99°51.259') This 200m-tall extinct volcano, and its surrounding lava field, dominates the area to the east of the lake. You walk around it on your way to the lake from Tariat, but you can also climb up to the rim of the crater for some fabulous views. There are steps up to the crater from the west side. Those with more energy, and a good sense of balance, could try climbing the slippery scree slope on the volcano's eastern side. You can then walk around the rim of the crater (anticlockwise is easiest) and climb down the steps. Sliding back down the scree sounds fun, but is pretty dangerous.

🏃 Activities

Terkhiin Tsagaan Nuur is excellent for swimming (if a little cold). Hidden along the shore are stretches of sandy beach, perfect for lounging with a book or fishing line. One nice spot is the beach on the sandy spit which juts out from the northern shore at the northeast corner of the lake.

The fishing is great, though you should get a permit for around T3000 per day. There are several park rangers who sell permits, or try asking at the park entrance by the **bridge** (GPS: N 48°09.777' E 99°53.312') that crosses the river as you exit Tariat.

There is also the option of exploring the lake by boat. Khorgo I and Maikhan Toilgoi ger camps both have rowboats for rent (T20,000 per hour). It's also a pretty place to go horse riding, or to just hike around. Most of the ger camps in the area rent horses, as does Tunga Guesthouse in Tariat itself.

🛏 Sleeping

Except for a few annoying flies, Terkhiin Tsagaan Nuur is an excellent place for camping. There is good fishing, endless fresh water, and flat ground for pitching a tent. And there are very few mosquitoes, even in summer. The western end of the lake, where it joins the Khoid Terkhiin Gol, is muddy. The best place to camp is the northern shore. The area can be cold at night, year-round, and is often windy, so a good sleeping bag is important.

Several ger camps are built up along the shore of the lake (mostly the northern and northeastern shores), but they are all fairly spread out so it's not too crowded. In Tariat itself, head for Tunga Guesthouse.

🛏 Tariat Village

Tunga Guesthouse
GUESTHOUSE **$**

(📞 9928 5710; www.tungaguesthouse.com; per person with breakfast US$15, with 3 meals US$35, dinner T4500) Backpacker Central in Tariat, this family guesthouse is pretty basic (there's no shower, and the toilet is a long-drop in the yard), but is run by the welcoming Tunga, who speaks good English. Rooms are clean and comfortable and she'll let you camp in the yard if they are full. She organises horse riding (per day per horse US$15, plus US$10 per guide), can help with onward transport, and has a **family ger** (GPS: N 48°09.318' E 99°45.206'; per person T10,000) on the quiet south side of the lake, where travellers can stay. The guesthouse is at the far eastern end of the main strip in Tariat, just a short walk from the bridge into the park.

Khorgo-Terkhiin Tsagaan Nuur National Park

Tsagaan Nuur   TOURIST GER CAMP **$**
(☑9981 7465; GPS: N 48°10.621', E 99°48.691';
per bed T30,000, meals T5000) Off to your left
as you come down the hill to the lake, this
camp is simple but clean, with showers and
a concrete restaurant ger with great lake
views. Not much English spoken.

Khorgo I   TOURIST GER CAMP **$$**
(☑11-322 870, 8869 2847; GPS: N 48°12.246',
E 99°50.834'; per person with/without meals
T56,000/20,000) In a lovely grassland loca-
tion in the Zurkh Gol Khundii (Heart River
valley), around one-hour's walk from the
lake, Khorgo I is an immaculate ger camp.
There are hot showers, a cosy restaurant ger
with a bar, staff who speak good English and
excellent hiking nearby.

Maikhan Tolgoi   TOURIST GER CAMP **$$**
(☑9911 9730; GPS: N 48°10.821', E 99°45.725'; per
person with/without meals T50,000/20,000) Set
on a pretty headland on the northern shore
of the lake, this is perhaps the most attractive camp on the lake. It has flush toilets, hot
showers and a cosy restaurant-bar (mains
T5000 to T10,000). There's also a private
beach for guests.

✖ Eating

All the camps around the lake provide
reasonably priced meals, as does Tunga
Guesthouse. Self-caterers can stock up on
supplies in either Tariat (there's a supermarket near Khan Bank), or at the shops
by the lake.

ⓘ Information

At the time of research there was no internet in
Tariat, but locals claim it's on the way.

Khan Bank (☉9am-1pm & 2-5pm Mon-Fri) In
Tariat village, at the western end of the main
strip. Changes US dollars and euros, and can
give cash advances on some credit cards
(MasterCard seems to work). There is no ATM,
though.

Tariat Bathhouse (shower T3000; ☉8am-
8pm) Turn north at the basketball court in
the centre of Tariat's main strip, and it's in
front of you in a small white building with a
blue roof.

ⓘ Getting There & Away

The bus stand is by the yak statue, just beyond
Khan Bank on the main drag. A bus leaves twice
a week for Ulaanbaatar (T32,000, 12 hours), via
Tsetserleg (T15,000). The days of travel are not
fixed, so ask at Tunga Guesthouse for the latest.

Minivans run the same route daily, if demand
warrants it. They tend to charge T40,000
and T20,000 for Ulaanbaatar and Tsetserleg
respectively. You'll also find them at the bus
stand.

Heading north or west will probably require
chartering your own vehicle (about T80,000 per
day plus petrol). The road west of Tariat is unpaved and in poor condition. Heading east, the
road becomes paved after a couple of hours, and
is good from there to Ulaanbaatar.

Northern Mongolia

POP 466,300 / AREA 194,620 SQ KM

Includes ➡

Why Go?

Log cabins? Pine forests? Mountains? Whatever happened to the steppes and the herds of camels? If it weren't for the gers and motorbike riders in traditional Mongolian dress, you could confuse this lush and rugged land with Switzerland.

Selenge, Bulgan and Khövsgöl aimags actually have more in common with Siberia than the rest of Mongolia, with long, cold winters and wildflower-dotted summers. This is the adventure playground of Mongolia, with superb opportunities for horse riding, hiking, mountain biking, kayaking and boating along the glorious shores of Lake Khövsgöl.

The inhospitable border area between Russia and Mongolia is home to the Tsaatan reindeer herders doing their best to preserve their traditional lifestyle. And if you're interested in spiritual practices, shamanism is once again alive and well in northern Mongolia after decades of suppression under communism, as is Buddhism in the splendid Amarbayasgalant monastery.

Best Off-the-Beaten-Track

➡ Bow-making workshop (p133)

➡ Uushigiin Uver (p146)

➡ Bulnai Hot Springs (p154)

➡ Zuun Nuur (p158)

Best Places to Stay

➡ Windhorse Ger Camp (p152)

➡ Nature's Door (p153)

➡ Toilogt (p153)

➡ Ashihai (p152)

When to Go

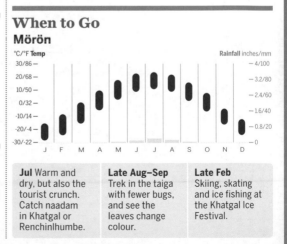

Mörön

Jul Warm and dry, but also the tourist crunch. Catch naadam in Khatgal or Renchinlhumbe.

Late Aug–Sep Trek in the taiga with fewer bugs, and see the leaves change colour.

Late Feb Skiing, skating and ice fishing at the Khatgal Ice Festival.

Northern Mongolia Highlights

❶ Drop a fishing line into **Khövsgöl Nuur** (p147), and while away an afternoon by Mongolia's loveliest alpine lake.

❷ Visit Tsaatan reindeer herders from the remote **Darkhad Depression** (p155).

❸ Wander the grounds of **Amarbayasgalant Khiid** (p136), the architectural highlight of the country.

❹ Visit the bow-and-arrow-making workshop in **Dulaankhaan** (p133), one of the last in Mongolia.

❺ Journey to **Chandman-Öndör** (p154), a little-visited region of fish-filled streams, hot springs and sacred caves.

❻ Study the curious deer-stone carvings at **Uushigiin**

Uver (p146), one of the best examples of ancient rock art in Mongolia.

❼ Enjoy the excellent dining in **Erdenet** (p138) or peer into the depths of the city's copper mine.

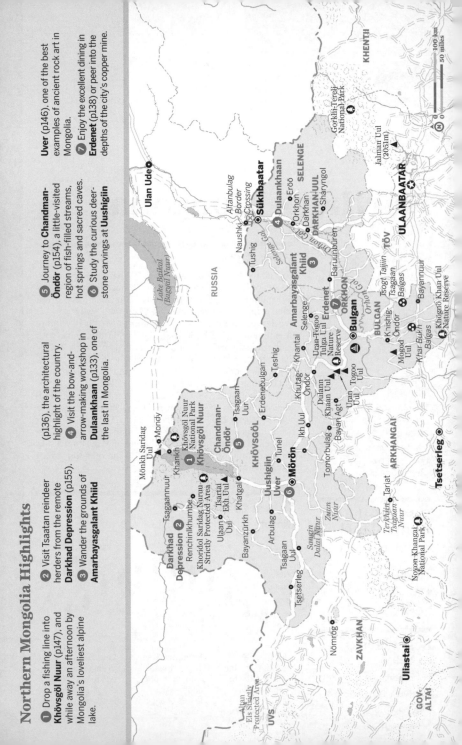

History

For thousands of years northern Mongolia was the borderland between the Turkic-speaking tribes of Siberia and the great steppe confederations of the Huns, Uighurs and Mongols. Some of the Siberian tribes still survive in Mongolia, notably the Tsaatan people of northern Khövsgöl. Evidence of the steppe nomads is also found in Khövsgöl in the form of numerous burial mounds and deer stones.

Settled history really began in the 18th century under Manchu rule when thousands of monks poured into the area from Tibet and China to assist in the construction of monasteries. As the nomads were converted to Buddhism, local shamans were harassed into giving up traditional practices. The largest centre of religion, Amarbayasgalant Khiid, had more than 2000 lamas.

During communism, religious persecution boiled over into a 1932 rebellion that left thousands of monks and Mongolian soldiers dead. Meanwhile, an attempt by the monks to form an insurrectionist government ended in failure. Later, the Russians improved their standing with the locals by developing a variety of industries. Darkhan and Selenge became important centres of agriculture, Bulgan became home to the Erdenet copper mine, and Khövsgöl developed a thriving industry of timber mills, fisheries and wool processing, the lake serving as an important gateway for Russia–Mongolia trade until the collapse of the Soviet Union.

ⓘ Getting There & Away

A good paved road runs from Ulaanbaatar (UB) all the way to the Russian border and also west from Darkhan to Bulgan City and beyond. Darkhan, Sükhbaatar and Erdenet can all be reached by rail from Ulaanbaatar. The quickest way to Khövsgöl Nuur is a flight from Ulaanbaatar to Mörön. The road from Bulgan to Mörön has been paved for the first 100km or so and should be completely paved within the lifetime of this book. To travel between Selenge aimag and the east, you'll have to come back through Ulaanbaatar first, or go by horse.

ⓘ Getting Around

Frequent buses, minibuses and shared taxis whiz along the paved roads between Darkhan, Sükhbaatar, Erdenet and Bulgan. The fun starts as you travel further west, with the usual dirt roads, rocky terrain and bridges that come and go with the floods. In the Khövsgöl area, there are frequent minibuses between Mörön

and Khatgal, with less frequent minibuses doing arduous overnight trips to Tsagaannuur, Renchinlkhumbe, and some destinations west and south. For everything else you'll need a jeep, though if you're travelling light, you may well be able to persuade locals with motorbikes to give you lifts. To visit the reindeer herders, you will need a horse, and some tour companies offer mountain-biking trips in the region.

In the region around Khövsgöl aimag, the terrain is mainly taiga (subarctic coniferous forest) of Siberian larch and pine trees, where there's plenty of rain (often 600mm a year). Snowfall can exceed 2m in some regions during winter. After winter the lakes and rivers remain frozen until May; travel can be hazardous at this time, as trucks and jeeps can fall through the thin ice. Travelling in winter means faster drive times, as vehicles won't get bogged in the mud.

SELENGE   СЭЛЭНГЭ

POP 201,400 (INCL DARKHAN-UUL) / AREA 44,480 SQ KM

Mongolia's breadbasket, Selenge is a fertile landscape of rolling wheat fields, apple orchards and meandering rivers. Wide-scale agriculture has settled many nomads and nowadays wood cabins and trucks far outnumber gers (traditional yurts) and camel caravans. For travellers, the main reason to visit is the majestic, remote monastery, Amarbayasgalant Khiid.

This region is quite heavily populated and industrialised (for Mongolia), with Darkhan, Sükhbaatar, and Erdenet the main population centres. In the southeast, the open-pit coal mine at Sharyngol produces approximately two million tonnes of coal each year to provide electricity for the Erdenet mine in Bulgan aimag, and the mine itself is an offbeat attraction for visitors who've never seen one.

The mighty Selenge Gol starts in the mountains of western Mongolia and flows into Lake Baikal in Siberia, meeting the other great river, the Orkhon Gol, near Sükhbaatar.

NATONAL PARKS OF SELENGE

Gorkhi-Terelj National Park Just over an hour's drive from Ulaanbaatar, this popular national park comprises alpine scenery and strange rock formations and is home to numerous bird species. Part of the park is in Töv (p105).

Sükhbaatar Сухбаатар

🖉 7036, 01362 / POP 19,700 / ELEV 626M

With its unfinished, rubble-strewn look typical of urban Mongolia, Sükhbaatar nevertheless features an attractive leafy park by the main square with its namesake general as its centrepiece. The town makes for an uneventful stopover for travellers heading into or out of Russia the slow way, but is not worth a detour.

◎ Sights

Khutagt Ekh Datsan　　BUDDHIST MONASTERY
(Хутагт Эх Дацан; Tsagaan Eregiin Gudamj) This small temple near the town square has a woman for a head lama, unusual for a Mongolian monastery.

Eej Mod　　LANDMARK
(Mother Tree, Ээж Мод) Locals frequently come to this sacred tree 10km south of Sükhbaatar to pray to the spirits that inhabit the trees; a rite that predates Buddhism. According to shamanic beliefs, the spirits have the power to grant wishes (on the condition that the devotee visits three times). Look for the blue 'Ээж Мод' sign on the right-hand side as you head south on the main road; from the sign it's another 1.7km to the tree.

🛏 Sleeping & Eating

The daily **market**, behind the Khutagt Ekh Datsan, is lively and friendly and, as a border town, well stocked.

Station Hotel　　HOTEL **$**
(📞 02362-40371; per hr T3000, s/d T7000/12,000) No-frills rooms with shared facilities in a building attached to the train station; travellers can take a room and pay per hour.

Hotel Nine　　HOTEL **$$$**
(📞 7036 3433; www.hotelnine.mn; d/lux US$60/90; 🅿 🛜) This new lime-green hotel is the swishest stay in town. Rooms are decorated in soothing pastel shades, there's on-site pampering in the form of sauna, Jacuzzi and massage. Little English spoken.

Khairkhan　　MONGOLIAN **$**
(Хайрхан; meals T4000-9000; ⊙ 9am-10pm) Popular restaurant near the town square gets packed at lunchtime with locals. The extensive picture menu features hearty soups, good dumplings and meat-and-rice dishes.

Modern Nomads　　MONGOLIAN **$$**
(Hotel Nine; mains T6000-12,000; 🖉 📱) This branch of the popular Modern Nomads chain restaurant is a breath of fresh air in a town where, frankly, good eateries are thin on the ground. If you can get the nervous staff to serve you, you can choose from meat dishes, soups, dumplings and vegetarian-friendly salads.

ℹ Information

Private moneychangers appear at the station whenever a train arrives. If you are leaving Mongolia, try to get rid of all your tögrög – they are worthless outside Mongolia.

Khan Bank (Хаан Банк; ⊙ 9am-7pm Mon-Fri, 10am-3pm Sat) Changes money and has an ATM.
Telecom Office (Tsagaan Eregiin Gudamj; ⊙ 8am-10pm) The post office is also located here.

ℹ Getting There & Away

MINIVAN & TAXI

The road to Ulaanbaatar (311km) through Darkhan (92km) is well paved. Shared vehicles to Ulaanbaatar (T25,000, six hours), Darkhan (T10,000, two hours) and Altanbulag (T3500, 20 minutes) depart from outside the train station.

Sükhbaatar

DOWN ON THE RANCH

Anak Ranch (📞 9909 9762, 9983 8205; www.anakranch.com; per person US$49) is a working ranch where guests can get their hands dirty doing farm work. You can milk cows, herd the sheep, make cheese and lasso a half-wild horse or two. There is also plenty of time to relax, enjoy a barbecue, hike and fish. The price includes everything: food, accommodation, horse riding etc. The ranch is close to the town of Orkhon, which is 11km off the main Darkhan–Sükhbaatar road. Taking a bus to Darkhan and then a taxi to Orkhon (T25,000) is a nicer option than taking a direct 9.10pm train from Ulaanbaatar and arriving at 4.20am. Contact the ranch ahead of time so that someone meets you with horses.

TRAIN

International trains going to/from Moscow, Irkutsk or Běijīng stop at Sükhbaatar for two or more hours (usually in the evening) while customs and immigration are completed. See p284 for more details.

Direct, local trains travel between Ulaanbaatar and Sükhbaatar (hard seat/hard sleeper/soft sleeper T6300/11,800/19,900, about 10 hours), with a stop at Darkhan (hard seat/hard sleeper/soft sleeper T2300/4200/6200, about four hours). Train 272 departs for Ulaanbaatar at 6.25am; train 264 departs Sükhbaatar at 9.05pm.

The **train station** (📞 02362-40124) sells local tickets and also tickets for Ulan Ude (T63,630), Irkutsk (T96,180) and Moscow (T259,910), to purchase them you'll need a Russian visa. The ticket office opens up an hour or two before the train leaves.

Altanbulag Алтанбулаг

Just 24km northeast of Sükhbaatar is Altanbulag, a small, peaceful border town opposite the Russian city of Khyakhta with an immediately noticeable golden-domed church. Both Khyakhta and Altanbulag are of some historical importance to Mongolians. In 1915 representatives from Russia, China and Mongolia met in Khyakhta to sign a treaty granting Mongolia limited autonomy. At a meeting in Khyakhta in March 1921, the Mongolian People's Party was formed by Mongolian revolutionaries in exile, and the revolutionary hero Sükhbaatar was named minister of war.

The surprisingly entertaining **aimag museum** (Аймгийн Музей; admission T3000; ⏰9am-2pm & 3-5pm Mon-Fri), in a curious building topped with giant drinking glasses behind the Altan Plaza hotel, features exhibits dating back to Mongolia's independence movement of 1921. Standout relics include heroic Soviet-style mosaics of Sükhbaatar, a life-size golden statue of the man meeting Lenin and some of Sükhbaatar's personal effects – his boots, gun and even his desk. Sükhbaatar's office was allegedly in the small red building outside the museum.

Minivans (T3500) run between Sükhbaatar and Altanbulag at various times during the day, or you could charter a taxi (T10,000).

The **border** (⏰8am-5pm) is located right at the edge of Altanbulag. If you're heading into Russia, you cannot cross it on foot. The border guards can pair you up with any private car that has room, and after you go through the border formalities, you can then catch a bus from Kyakhta to Ulan-Ude.

Dulaankhaan Дулаанхаан

Forty-seven kilometres south of Sükhbaatar, this tiny village is worth a stop if you have your own vehicle. Dulaankhaan is home to a **bow-making workshop** (📞9913 1491; bayarmoa1129@yahoo.com), one of only three in Mongolia. In a large, dusty room, exquisite bows and arrows are made from ibex and reindeer horn, bamboo and even fish guts. Only around 100 sets are crafted every year and each bow takes about four months to complete. A set sells for about T400,000 (bow plus four arrows). If there are no finished bows available, ask where they might be sold in Ulaanbaatar. It is far easier to ship your acquisition home from the capital.

To find the workshop, cross the railroad tracks to enter the village then look for the long, decrepit-looking warehouse with the 'Hornbow factory' sign pointing to it behind the railway-station building.

The village is 6km west of the Sükhbaatar–Darkhan Hwy along a newly paved road. Expect to pay at least T20,000 for a taxi from Sükhbaatar.

Darkhan Дархан

7037, 01372 / POP 74,738

This minor city on the Trans-Mongolian Railway looks a bit like a mini-Ulaanbaatar, albeit with less traffic and with fewer new buildings going up, making Darkhan an appealing short stop en route to Amarbayasgalant Monastery or the Russian border.

Darkhan was created by the Soviets in the 1960s as an industrial base for the north. During communism it worked as a model urban cooperative of factory workers, tractor drivers, coal miners and government officials. The economy took a nosedive in the early 1990s but is slowly picking up again, thanks to grain production and coal mining. The city is part of an autonomous municipality, Darkhan-Uul, that sits in the centre of the Selenge aimag.

Darkhan is divided into an 'old town' near the train station and a 'new town' to the south, with most hotels, restaurant and amenities located in the latter. If you're approaching the city from the south, you'll pass a statue made of wires of a man wearing a hard hat.

Sights

Museum of Darkhan-Uul MUSEUM

(admission T2500; 9am-1pm & 2-6pm Mon-Fri) This appealing little museum contains a well-laid-out collection of archaeological finds, traditional clothing, religious artefacts and taxidermied examples of aimag wildlife. You may spot a wind instrument made of a human femur and a jade chess set, but the museum's most valued piece is the original painting of Lenin meeting Sükhbaatar, a classic work of myth-making, painted by B Tsultem in 1953.

Kharaagiin Khiid BUDDHIST MONASTERY

(Хараагийн Хийд; 8am-6pm) A little difficult to find but worth seeking out is this attractive little monastery. Housed in a pretty log cabin in the old town, it has a host of protector deities and a tree encased in blue *khatag* (silk scarves).

> **MOVING ON?**
>
> If you're travelling on to Russia, head to lonelyplanet.com to purchase a downloadable PDF of Lonely Planet's *Russia* guide.

Morin Khuur Statue & Seated Buddha MONUMENTS

These two monuments, linked by a pedestrian bridge across a busy road, are near the roundabout between the new and old towns. Locals come here to socialise at sunset.

Sleeping

Kharaa Hotel HOTEL $$

(01372-26019; tw/half-lux/lux with breakfast T25,000/35,000/55,000; @ wi-fi) The ground floor bar adds a bit of spice to this compact hotel, so unless you're a night owl, ask for a room upstairs. The renovated rooms are clean and feature new furnishings but the service is a little harried. It's set back behind the Urtuchin and Comfort hotels.

Darkhan Hotel HOTEL $$

(7037 6001, 7037 3785; d/half-lux T25,000/45,000, lux with breakfast T65,000-135,000; P @) This Soviet throwback offers refurbished en-suite rooms with tall ceilings and good showers, a restaurant with chintzy decor, a sauna (T5000 per hour) and a fitness room. For a real blowout, go for the three-room deluxe lux, with rather old-fashioned furnishings but oodles of space.

★ **Comfort Hotel** HOTEL $$$

(7037 9090; www.comforthoteldarkhan.com; Naadamchid Gudamj; s/d/half-lux/lux from US$40/50/60/90; wi-fi) Darkhan's best hotel has spotless, well-maintained, yet largely unmemorable rooms decorated in pastel shades. There's a decent restaurant, a fitness centre to help burn off the calories, a sauna to steam in and friendly staff who speak some English. Wi-fi is temperamental. Book ahead.

Eating & Drinking

Sondor Bakery & Cafe CAFE $

(meals T1500-4000; 10am-midnight; menu) This cute cafe and bakery serves up pizzas and pastas and has recently expanded to serve up even more cakes and provide more seating for hungry customers.

Nomin Supermarket SUPERMARKET $

Southeast of the central park in the new town, this is the best place for self-caterers.

★ **Bulgogi Family** KOREAN $$

(meals T6000-12,000; 10am-midnight; wi-fi) Bright, friendly, genuine Korean restaurant featuring *bulgogi* (grilled meat), spicy

Darkhan

soups, tasty *bibimbap* (rice topped with meat, vegetables and an egg, choice of hot or cold) and noodle dishes, all mains are accompanied by an array of obligatory little side dishes. Alternatively, cook your own meal on the teppanyaki grill in the middle of your table. Picture menu and some English spoken.

Texas Pub　　　　　　　　AMERICAN **$$**
(meals T6500-12,000; ⊙11am-midnight; 🛜 🗐)
Though Texans are about as common in Darkhan as Mongolians who can't ride a horse, the menu at this dark wood, modern bar features enough burgers, fries, steaks and sandwiches to put a smile on the face of any Lone Star State resident (and a visiting traveller or two). Wednesday is cocktail night and there's live music Monday and Saturday.

Darkhan

Empire
PUB

(☺noon-late) One of the hottest spots in town, this friendly pub is a great place to drink with both expats and locals.

ℹ Information

Golomt Bank (Голомт Банк; ☺9am-6pm Mon-Fri, 10am-3pm Sat) This bank is 200m west of the taxi stand. There are also ATMs at the train station and the bus station.

Internet Cafe (per hr T600; ☺8am-10pm) At the same location as the Telecom Office.

Telecom Office (☺24hr) ATM and post office are also located here.

ℹ Getting There & Away

BUS

From the main **bus station** (Авто Вокзал), buses depart hourly between 9am and 8pm for Ulaanbaatar (T10,000, 3½ hours). Two buses a day leave for Erdenet (T10,000, three hours) at 11am and 5pm. For Khövsgöl (T33,500, 13 hours) buses depart several times weekly.

MINIVAN, TAXI & JEEP

Plenty of shared taxis (T15,000) do the three-hour run to Ulaanbaatar, departing from the bus station in the new town. The station also has share taxis to Erdenet (T15,000, 2½ hours).

For Sükhbaatar (T6000, two hours), vans leave from outside the market in the new town; there are signs for different destinations (in Mongolian). For Amarbayasgalant Khiid hire your own jeep near the market or a taxi from the taxi stand; a round trip should cost about T130,000 but you'll need to bargain.

TRAIN

Darkhan is the only train junction in Mongolia: all northern trains to/from Ulaanbaatar, and all trains to/from Erdenet stop here.

Travelling to Ulaanbaatar (hard seat/hard sleeper/soft sleeper T5000/10,000/15,300), a daytime train (272) leaves Darkhan at 8.48am, arriving in Ulaanbaatar at 4.20pm. An overnighter (264) departs Darkhan at 11.40pm, arriving at 6.10am. Other trains leave in the middle of the night.

The daily five-hour trip between Darkhan and Erdenet (hard seat/soft seat/soft sleeper T2900/6200/9800, five hours) leaves Darkhan at an ungodly 3am.

The daily Ulaanbaatar–Sükhbaatar train (271) leaves Darkhan for Sükhbaatar at 5.55pm (hard seat/hard sleeper/soft sleeper T2300/4200/6200, about three hours).

ℹ Getting Around

Darkhan is spread out, so you will probably have to take a taxi to get between the new and old towns.

Amarbayasgalant Khiid
Амарбаясгалант Хийд

Far in the wilds of Selenge aimag, this **monastery** (www.amarbayasgalant.org; GPS: N 49°28.672', E 105°05.121') FREE is considered to be one of the top three Buddhist institutions in Mongolia (along with Erdene Zuu in Kharkhorin and Gandan in Ulaanbaatar) and the country's most attractive and intact architectural complex. It is well worth visiting on the way to/from Khövsgöl Nuur, or other areas in northern or western Mongolia. As it's about six hours away from Ulaanbaatar on mostly decent roads, it can also be done as an overnight trip from the capital, either solo or with the aid of one of several tour companies.

Amarbayasgalant Khiid was built between 1727 and 1737 by the Manchu emperor Yongzheng, and dedicated to the great Mongolian Buddhist and sculptor Zanabazar (see p138), whose mummified body was moved here in 1779. It is in the Manchu style, down to the inscriptions, symmetrical layout, imperial colour scheme and roof guardians on every roof corner.

In spite of extensive restoration by UNESCO, there's a sense of genteel decay and gradual takeover by nature, from the faded wooden beams, thickly coated in bird droppings, and riotous greenery blocking some entrances, to the scurrying marmots and cawing jackdaws that seem to rule the place.

The monastery was largely spared during the 1937 purge, possibly because of sympathetic and procrastinating local military commanders. These days about 30 monks live in the monastery, compared with more than 2000 in 1936.

Most of the temples in the monastery are normally closed, so if you want to see any statues or *thangkas* (scroll paintings), you'll have to find the monks with the keys

---

ℹ OPEN FOR BUSINESS?

Opening times (for museums, monasteries etc) are never exact. Places open and close at the whim of the manager (or keeper of the keys) so be flexible when visiting these sites of interest.

Amarbayasgalant Khiid

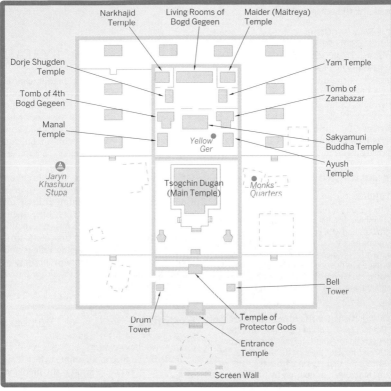

Narkhajid Temple
Living Rooms of Bogd Gegeen
Maider (Maitreya) Temple
Dorje Shugden Temple
Yam Temple
Tomb of 4th Bogd Gegeen
Tomb of Zanabazar
Manal Temple
Sakyamuni Buddha Temple
Yellow Ger
Ayush Temple
Jaryn Khashuur Stupa
Tsogchin Dugan (Main Temple)
Monks' Quarters
Bell Tower
Drum Tower
Temple of Protector Gods
Entrance Temple
Screen Wall

in the monks' quarters, the yellow concrete buildings on the right side (east) of the monastery.

The richly decorated main temple, **Tsogchin Dugan**, has a disturbingly lifelike, life-size statue of Rinpoche Gurdava, who was a lama from Inner Mongolia who lived in Tibet and Nepal before returning to Mongolia in 1992 and raising much of the money for the temple's restoration. Photography inside the temple seems to be allowed, but unlike some less-than-respectful local tourists, do not turn your back to the deities.

Ceremonies are usually held at 10am, so arrive early or stay overnight to see them.

A couple of new monuments – a golden Buddhist statue and a stupa – are situated on the hills behind the monastery. You could continue hiking up the mountains for even better views of the valley.

🎊 Festivals & Events

Gongoriin Bombani Hural PRAYER CEREMONY
(⊙ 14-15 Aug) The most interesting time to visit Amarbayasgalant Khiid is when the Gongoriin Bombani Hural is held. As part of the rituals, the locals hike up to the eight white stupas in the hills around the monastery. Festival-goers usually camp in the fields near the monastery – like a Buddhist version of Woodstock, only minus the illegal substances.

🛏 Sleeping

There are excellent camping spots all around Amarbayasgalant Khiid.

Stupa Ger Camp TOURIST GER CAMP **$**
(per 2-person ger T30,000) Located 300m west of the monastery, with four stupas just to the south of it, this camp has flush toilets, hot showers and a restaurant. It is operated by the monks of Amarbayasgalant so any money

you spend here goes towards the continued preservation of the temples. It's particularly popular with homegrown tourists.

★ IF Tour Ger Camp TOURIST GER CAMP $$
(☑ 9119 0808, 9918 9981; iftour@yahoo.com; ger/r/cabin T40,000/50,000/60,000; ⊘ May-Oct) This camp, furthest west from the temple complex, is the one with the best facilities. Choose between a cosy ger with electricity, individual cabin or a bright room inside the lodge. It's clean, comfortable, offers hot showers and flushing toilets and serves hearty meals (dinner around T13,500). Some English and German spoken.

ℹ Getting There & Away

HITCHING
The monastery is reachable by a pitted dirt road that branches off the paved main A1101 that connects Darkhan with Erdenet. A couple of cars a day come here in summer so you may be able to hitch a lift. The cheapest way from Ulaanbaatar is to get a bus or share car to Erdenet, and ask the driver to let you off at the turn-off to Amarbayasgalant, and then hitch from there.

JEEP
From Ulaanbaatar, travel north to the T-intersection for Erdenet (just short of Darkhan). Take the Erdenet road for 90km and then turn right onto a dirt road; look for the sign (GPS: N 49°12.814', E 104°59.131') that says 'Amarbayasgalant 35km'. Altogether, the journey to/from Ulaanbaatar takes around five or six hours. If you don't

have your own car you could charter one from Darkhan for about T130,000 (but you'll need to negotiate).

BULGAN БУЛГАН

POP 147,300 (INCL ORKHON) / AREA 49,540 SQ KM

Most visitors to northern Mongolia charge through Bulgan aimag en route to more popular sights such as Khövsgöl Nuur and Amarbayasgalant Khiid, but travellers with a bit of time on their hands can find some interesting, rarely visited sights in Bulgan, as well as some beautiful scenery that makes for nice cycle touring.

A small mountain range, the Bürengiin Nuruu, bisects the aimag and, though it only reaches a maximum altitude of 2058m, it provides plenty of lush habitat for wild animals and livestock. In the south of the aimag are two unique historical sights, Tsogt Taijiin Tsagaan Balgas and Khar Bukh Balgas, which are both geographically more in line with sights found in central Mongolia.

Erdenet Эрдэнэт
☑ 7035, 7039, 01352, 01392 / POP 83,379

Erdenet is a busy working city that revolves around the large copper mine, which employs about 8000 people and is the lifeblood of the city.

ZANABAZAR: THE MICHELANGELO OF THE STEPPES

Zanabazar, an artist, statesman and Living Buddha, is today considered one of the greatest Renaissance artists in all of Asia. He was born in 1635 and at the tender age of three was deemed to be a possible *gegeen* (saint), so when he turned 14 he was sent to Tibet to study Buddhism under the Dalai Lama. Known in Mongolia as Öndör Gegeen, he was also proclaimed the reincarnation of the Jonangpa line of Tibetan Buddhism and became the first Bogd Gegeen (reincarnated Buddhist leader of Mongolia).

When he returned from his studies in Tibet, the artist-lama kick-started a Mongolian artistic renaissance. Besides sculpting and painting he also invented the *soyombo*, the national symbol of Mongolia, and reformed the Mongolian script. A political figure, Zanabazar's struggle with the Zungar leader Galdan led to Mongolia's submission to the Manchus in 1691.

Zanabazar died in Běijīng in 1723 and his body was later entombed in a stupa in Amarbayasgalant Khiid. You will see many of Zanabazar's creations in monasteries and museums in Mongolia, and there is a fine collection of his art in the Zanabazar Museum of Fine Arts in Ulaanbaatar (p64). You can recognise images of Zanabazar by his bald, round head, the *dorje* (thunderbolt symbol) he holds in his right hand and the bell in his left hand.

For more on Zanabazar, look for the *Guidebook to Locales Connected with the Life of Zanabazar*, by Don Croner.

Erdenet

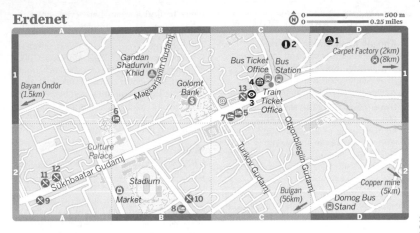

Up to one-third of the population of Erdenet was Russian during communist times, though now only about 1000 Russians still work as technical advisers at the mine. You'll hear plenty of Russian on the streets and will find restaurant menus featuring *pirozhki* (meat-filled fried pastries) rather than *buuz* (steamed mutton dumplings).

Erdenet is a good place to enjoy the above-average crop of hotels and restaurants before heading to wilder parts of the region. Technically the city is within the tiny municipality of Orkhon, on the eastern edge of Bulgan.

Sights

Copper Mine   MINE
(www.erdnetmc.mn) The open-cut mine, easily seen to the southeast of the city centre, was one of the biggest infrastructure projects developed in Mongolia during the communist era. Copper and molybdenum concentrate are still central to Erdenet's economy, though production has been dwarfed by that of the Oyu Tolgoi mine in the southern Gobi.

Still, the mine is worth a visit if you've never seen one like this before and is popular with international visitors. You need an invitation to visit the mine, which is easily arranged through your hotel, and on arrival you'll need to show your passport to the guard at the gate. While peering down into its subterranean vastness holds its own appeal, the mine is particularly entertaining during explosion days. A taxi to the mine and back from the town centre costs about T10,000, including waiting time.

Erdenet

Sights
1 Buddha statue D1
2 Friendship Monument C1
3 Marx Mural C1
4 Museum of Orkhon Aimag C1

Sleeping
5 Erdenet Inn C1
6 Molor Erdene B1
7 Selenge Hotel C1
8 Tamir Hotel B2

Eating
9 Eternal Springs A2
10 Marco's Pizza B2
11 Modern Nomads A2
12 Nomin Supermarket A2
13 Traktir C1

Museum of Orkhon Aimag   MUSEUM
(Орхон Аймгийн Музей; admission T1500; ⊙9am-5pm) Hidden in a concrete complex on the right side of the Marx mural, this small museum showcases a mix of subjects – from Khalkha, Kazakh and Buriad national costume, traditional musical instruments and snuff bottles made of semi-precious stones to a model of the copper mine (you can see it in 'day' or 'night') and a model of a modern ger with a TV inside. Look out for the two-headed calf, and the positively demented expressions on the faces of the taxidermied wildlife.

Friendship Monument   MONUMENT
This communist monument, about 200m northeast of the Selenge Hotel, is worth a quick look. On the way from the town centre

---

NATIONAL PARKS OF BULGAN

Khögnö Khan Nature Reserve A 46,900-hectare reserve off the main Ulaanbaatar–Kharkhorin highway, its rocky semi-desert terrain is home to wolves, ibexes and various birds of prey.

Uran-Togoo Tulga Uul Nature Reserve A protected area of 5800 hectares of undulating hills and grass-land, encompassing three extinct volcanoes.

---

you pass a fine **Marx mural** and the ever-recognisable Lenin's profile bolted to the wall. Head north of the Friendship Monument into the hills above town for good views of the city. Around 400m east of the monument you'll find Erdenet's shiny new **Buddha statue**.

Bayan Öndör　　　　　　　　MOUNTAIN
(Баян Өндөр) Rising above Erdenet, to the northwest of the city centre, the summit of Bayan Öndör mountain offers a splendid view of the surrounding area, including the copper mine. The road to the top is rough and muddy, but you can take a taxi (T10,000). Other hills surrounding Erdenet also provide good hiking in summer, but none have claim to Bayan Öndör's view.

🛏 Sleeping

Erdenet has a reasonable selection of hotels but no guesthouse or ger camp. Camping is much better around Amarbayasgalant Khiid.

Molor Erdene　　　　　　　　HOTEL $$
(Молор Эрдэнэ; ☎ 01352-20309; d/half-lux/lux with breakfast T30,000/50,000/60,000; P@⌨) Rooms at the Molor Erdene are large and comfortable, with an internet cable for laptop users (although the connection is slow). There's a decent breakfast of eggs, toast and sausage and an excellent hot-pot restaurant on-site.

Selenge Hotel　　　　　　　　HOTEL $$
(Сэлэнгэ Зочид Буудал; ☎ 7035 8882; d/semi-lux/lux T30,000/35,000/50,000; P⌨) Occupying the quietest part of a three-in-one hotel building, Selenge doesn't have terribly memorable decor, but the rooms are spacious and clean (if a little musty) and you're more likely to find a room here even when the other two wings are completely booked up.

Tamir Hotel　　　　　　　　HOTEL $$
(Тамир Төв; ☎ 7035 8600; s/d/lux T30,000/40,000/60,000; P⌨) One of several new hotels in town, reasonably central Tamir, just south of the stadium, is all mid-sized beige rooms, intermittent wi-fi and a couple of billiards tables for entertainment. Popular with a Mongolian business clientele.

★**Erdenet Inn**　　　　　　　　HOTEL $$$
(☎ 01352-30715; tw/half-lux/lux T60,000/100,000/120,000; P@⌨) The renovated east wing of this monolithic Soviet-style hotel, that now combines three hotels in one, is the nicest place to lay your head in Erdenet. Expect crisp white bed linen, modern bathrooms with heated towel racks and reliable wi-fi throughout. There is a good cafe right by the entrance, too.

🍴 Eating

★**Eternal Springs**　　　　　　　BAKERY $
(Мөнхийн Булаг; meals T3200-5000; ⊙9am-6pm; ☑) Vegetarians rejoice, as this tiny, cute-as-a-button Swedish-American bakery not only does a daily selection of vegetable soups (pumpkin, broccoli), but also meatless pizzas, great baked goodies and an extensive loose-leaf tea selection. The daily soup, sandwich and drink special is a steal at T5000.

Nomin Supermarket　　　　　SUPERMARKET $
(⊙9am-8pm) A good place to buy food or pick up supplies.

Traktir　　　　　　　　RUSSIAN $$
(Трактор; Sükhbaatar Gudamj; mains T5000-13,000; ⊙noon-11pm) A magnet for visiting Russians, Traktir serves you the likes of *pelmeni* (boiled meat dumplings), chicken cutlets and grilled meats with mushroom sauce, with welcome helpings of vegetables on the side. Eat in the cosy dining room, decked out with photos of ye olde Russia, or sip a beer on the shaded summer terrace.

Marco's Pizza　　　　　　　ITALIAN $$
(☎ 9955 1974; pizzas T6000-15,200; ⊙noon-11pm daily; ⊡⌨) Thin and crispy pizzas are served by Erdenet's resident Italian in this homey little cafe across the street from the football pitch. Toppings range from veggie to meat lover's (bacon, beef, chicken) and delectable melt-in-your-mouth homemade fettucine is also on the menu. Finish off with a chocolate pizza or ice cream with espresso.

Modern Nomads
MONGOLIAN $$

(Sükhbaatar Gudamj; mains T6000-12,000; 🍴)
A branch of this ever-popular restaurant has finally made its way to Erdenet, bringing you large portions of Mongolian dishes, salads and soups selected from a traveller-friendly picture menu. The adjoining Aurora bar shares a kitchen with Modern Nomads and serves American-style steaks and burgers alongside regular live music and beer.

🛍 Shopping

Carpet Factory
CARPETS

(☺9am-7pm Mon-Fri, 10am-7pm Sat & Sun) The city's carpet factory is open year-round but production is low in summer (June to August) when supplies of wool are scarce. Prices at the shop and the attached new outlet are similar to those at the Naran Tuul Market in Ulaanbaatar, but the selection here is much better and a carpet makes a fine souvenir. Floor carpets measuring 2m by 3m start from around T180,000 and the factory has now branched out into cashmere products. It's just off the main road to the train station, about 2km from the Friendship Monument.

ℹ Information

Golomt Bank (Голомт Банк; ☺8am-7.30pm Mon-Fri, 9am-5.30pm Sat & Sun) Changes US dollars and euros.

Internet Cafe (Sükhbaatar Gudamj; per hr T600; ☺9am-7pm) Internet access at the Telecom office.

Telecom Office (cnr Sükhbaatar Gudamj & Natsagorjiin Gudamj; ☺24hr) Golomt Bank ATM and post office are also located here.

ℹ Getting There & Away

Erdenet makes a good stopover en route between Ulaanbaatar and Mörön. You can take the sleeper train from Ulaanbaatar to Erdenet and catch a shared vehicle to Mörön. Erdenet-to-Mörön vehicles are typically jam-packed with as many people as they can hold. It's easier to get a lift from Erdenet than from Bulgan.

BUS, MINIVAN & JEEP
Erdenet's **bus station** (Авто Вокзал) is a car park at the foot of the Friendship Monument from which daily buses depart to Ulaanbaatar's Dragon Avto Vaksal bus stand (T15,000, six hours, 412km) at 10am, 11.30am, 1pm, 2.30pm, 4pm and 5.30pm. Private vans (T15,000) and shared taxis (T25,000) also depart for Ulaanbaatar when full, and there are also buses to Darkhan (T10,000, 2½ hours) leaving at 8am and 2pm, as well as vans (T13,000) and shared taxis (T15,000).

Shared minibuses to Mörön (Хөвсгөл; T25,000, 10 to 15 hours, several weekly around 4pm), Bulgan (Булган; T5000, one hour, two or three times per day) and Tsetserleg (Цэцэрлэг; T25,000, seven hours, three times per week) leave from the **Domog bus stand** (Домог Вокзал) in front of the Боса Hypermarket in the southeast part of town.

TRAIN
The train to Ulaanbaatar (via Darkhan) leaves Erdenet at 7.40pm, arriving in UB at 7.05am (hard seat/hard sleeper/soft sleeper T6800/12,300/20,300).

To Darkhan, train 273 (hard seat/soft seat/soft sleeper T4100/7700/12,000, five hours) arrives at 11.55pm. For Sükhbaatar, change trains in Darkhan.

It's better to queue on the day of, or before, departure at the **train ticket office** (☺8am-1pm & 2-7pm) in the northeast end of town.

The train station is located around 9km east of the centre. Minibuses (T1000) meet arriving trains or you can take a taxi (T10,000). Buses to the train station leave from the car park opposite the train ticket office.

Bulgan City
Булган

📞 7034, 01342 / POP 11,320 / ELEV 1208M

Imagine a compact grid of poorly lit streets, a hotel sign in neon flickering eerily on and off and no signs of life. That's Bulgan at night, its vibe of ample appeal to Hitchcock and Stephen King fans. During the day, it's a laidback little place with a grassy pine-clad park in the middle of town and a lazy main street where you are just as likely to see a horseman as you are a passing vehicle. Bulgan's dilapidated charm makes it an offbeat stopover if you are travelling between Mörön and Ulaanbaatar.

👁 Sights

Bulgan Aimag Museum
MUSEUM

(Булган Аймгийн Музей; admission T5000; ☺9am-6pm) This museum on the main street has some information on obscure sights in the aimag; a display on J Gurragchaa, Mongolia's first man in space; war photos, and a few musical instruments, including the ol' human-femur-cum-wind-instrument. The ethnography section features a red-eyed wolf and a demented-looking lynx; elsewhere there are a few period surgical instruments that make you glad you live in the 21st century, some *airag* (fermented mare's milk) churners and saddles.

NORTHERN MONGOLIA BULGAN CITY

Bulgan City

Bulgan City

Dashchoinkhorlon Khiid BUDDHIST MONASTERY
(Дашчойнхорлон Хийд; GPS: N 48°47.821', E 103°30.687) Like most monasteries in Mongolia, this one (built in 1992) replaced the original monastery, Bangiin Khuree, which was destroyed in 1937. About 1000 monks lived and worshipped at Bangiin Khuree before they were arrested and, presumably, executed. The remains of several stupas from the old monastery complex can be seen nearby.

The modern monastery contains statues of Tsongkhapa and Sakyamuni, and features a painting of the old monastery layout. A couple dozen monks now reside here. It's about 2.5km southwest of Bulgan City, hidden behind some hills. The pavilion next to the temple was built in 1876.

Khatanbaatar Magsarjav Mausoleum MAUSOLEUM
(Хатанбаатар Магсаржавын Бунхан) Located 1km southwest of the Bulgan Hotel, across the stream and at the top of a hill, this curious silver building resembling a concrete ger is actually a mausoleum in the shape of a hat. It allegedly contains the remains of Khatanbaatar Magsarjav, a key figure in the 1911 Revolution, who helped to liberate the city of Khovd from Chinese rule. There are some murals of battle scenes inside, but to see them you'll need to get the keys from the caretaker. Ask at the Aimag Museum.

Museum of the West Road Military Unit MUSEUM
(Баруун Замын Тусгай Ангийн Штаб; admission T1500; ⊙9am-5pm) The West Road Military Unit was a key force in freeing Mongolia from White Russian rule in 1921. Its history is described in this small museum, 2.5km south of Bulgan. Choibalsan and Khatanbaatar Magsarjav both stayed here during Mongolia's military campaigns of the early 20th century. The museum contains, among other things, Choibalsan's saddle and sword. If the museum is closed, find the caretaker at the ger next door.

🛏 Sleeping & Eating

There are a few hole-in-the-wall *guanz* (canteens) on the main street serving standard plates of goulash and *buuz*.

★**Khantai Hotel** GUESTHOUSE $
(✍01342-22964; per person T15,000; ℗) This small B&B offers six spotless double rooms, one with a gorgeous balcony overlooking the park. The bathroom and shower are both downstairs and there is 24-hour hot water. The friendly owner sometimes offers breakfast (eggs, bread and rice milk) for an extra cost. An extension was being built during the time of our visit.

Bulgan Hotel HOTEL $
(✍01342-22811; tw/lux T10,000/30,000) This charmingly rundown Soviet hotel is in a peaceful location overlooking the park. With its moose on the wall, and (defunct) Russian slot machines in the lobby, it has character, if little else. It's worth splashing out on a lux room with cable TV and hot-water shower. Not to be confused with the other Bulgan Hotel on the main street.

ℹ Information

Internet Cafe (per hr T700; ⊙9am-9pm) In the same building as Telecom.

Telecom Office (⊙9am-9pm) In the middle of the main drag, about 150m southeast of the jeep stand. The post office is also located here.

XacBank (Хас Банк; Chin Van Khandorj Gudamj; ⊙9am-5pm Mon-Fri) Exchanges US dollars.

ℹ Getting There & Away

BUS, MINIVAN & JEEP

A bus departs Bulgan for Ulaanbaatar (T17,500, seven hours) on Tuesday, Thursday, Saturday and Monday at 8am. Minivans and jeeps go between Bulgan and Ulaanbaatar (T25,000, six hours) on demand, but most people take a minivan to Erdenet (T5000, one hour, 55km) and then take the bus or overnight train. Shared taxis (T5000) run to Erdenet on demand several times a day; if you're in a hurry, just pay the fare for the entire taxi (T20,000).

To go to Mörön (or anywhere else), go to Erdenet, as vehicles tend to leave from there.

There are two routes between Ulaanbaatar and Bulgan City: the rougher but more direct southern route (318km) via Dashinchilen, or the paved northern route (434km) via Darkhan and Erdenet. To visit Amarbayasgalant Khiid, the northern route is the way to go.

HITCHING

Bulgan is on the main road from Erdenet to Mörön. Since most cars leaving Erdenet are already packed to the gills, it's best to make your way to Erdenet first.

KHÖVSGÖL   ХӨВСГӨЛ

POP 117,600 / AREA 100,600 SQ KM

If Switzerland and Montana were to have a love child, Khövsgöl would be it. It is a land of thick forests, rushing rivers, sparkling lakes, rugged mountains. and endless taiga. It does rain a lot during summer, but this only adds to the scenery: rainbows hang over meadows dotted with white gers, grazing horses and yaks.

While the Khalkh dominate the south, there are also pockets of minority ethnic groups, including Uriankhai, Khotgoid and Darkhad people. The Tsaatan, who live in the taiga in the far north of the aimag, herd reindeer and live in tepees resembling those of Native Americans.

The jewel in Khövsgöl's crown, the region's most dramatic geographical feature and visitor magnet is the enormous Khövsgöl Nuur. While most travellers stay close to the lake, the rest of the aimag has much to offer. The Darkhad valley, Chandman-Öndör and Jargalant all make fine destinations, with many opportunities for fishing, hiking and cycle touring.

Mörön   Мөрөн

☑ 7038, 01382 / POP 35,789 / ELEV 1283M

Imagine a loose, spread-out grid of streets surrounded by green hills, with a wrestling stadium here, a large, leafy park there, a couple of multistorey hotels, a busy, labyrinthine market, a few gers and a temple complex on the outskirts. That's Mörön (pronounced mu-roon, not moron) – a transport hub in northern Mongolia that's also the centre of civilisation in this part of the country (think internet, actual tourist office, as well as a couple of half-decent restaurants).

The town comes alive in summer when tourists pass through on their way to Khövsgöl Nuur, and if you're exploring the area, you'll probably find yourself lingering here a day or two. Unless your tour operator whisks you straight from the airport to the big blue yonder up north, that is. If travelling solo, this is your last chance to stock up on supplies.

NORTHERN MONGOLIA MÖRÖN

WORTH A TRIP

DASHINCHILEN   ДАШИНЧИЛЭН

There are a couple of unique ruins in Dashinchilen *sum* (district), in the south of the aimag, which are worth seeking out if you are travelling between Ulaanbaatar and Tsetserleg, via Ögii Nuur.

On the western side of the Tuul Gol, about 35km northeast of Dashinchilen, are the impressive ruins of **Tsogt Taijiin Tsagaan Balgas** (GPS: N 48°01.422', E 104°21.091'), a 17th-century fort that was the home of the mother of Prince Tsogt, a 17th-century poet who fought against Chinese rule. There is a **stone stele** nearby.

About 12km west of the *sum* capital, the ruined **Khar Bukh Balgas** (Khar Bakhin Fortress; GPS: N 47°53.198', E 103°53.513') is worth exploring and is easy to reach as it's just a few kilometres north of the main road. The fortress, inhabited by the Kitan from 917 to 1120, is sometimes known as Kitan Balgas. A small **museum** nearby is unlocked by a caretaker when visitors arrive.

Mörön

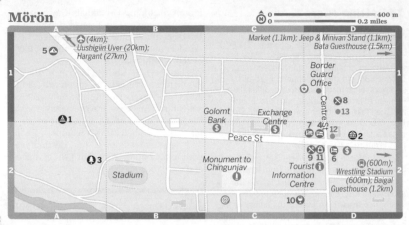

Mörön

◉ Sights
1 Danzandarjaa Khiid A1
2 Khövsgöl Aimag Museum D2
3 Khövsgöl Park A2

🛏 Sleeping
4 50° 100° Hotel D2
5 Altan Ulias A1
6 Chinggis Hotel D2
7 Gan Oyu Guesthouse D2

✗ Eating
50° 100° Hotel .... (see 4)
8 And Restaurant D1
9 Shine Ögööj Supermarket D2

🍷 Drinking & Nightlife
10 Neg Ye Pub C2

🛍 Shopping
11 Antique Souvenir House D2
Handicraft Shop .... (see 4)

ⓘ Transport
12 AeroMongolia D2
EZ Nis .... (see 4)
13 Hunnu Air D1

◉ Sights

Khövsgöl Aimag Museum   MUSEUM
(Хөвсгөл Аймгийн Музей; Peace St; admission T3000; ⏰10am-2pm & 3-6.30pm) Given the variety of wildlife in the aimag, stuffed animals such as the ibex and the lynx are, not surprisingly, the main feature of the museum, as well as a large tusk from a woolly mammoth dating back at least 40,000 years. Highlights of the ethnographic display include a beribboned shaman outfit and Jew's harp (*amiin khuur*, or mouth fiddle), a wooden Tsaatan saddle and furry skis, a Choijin robe with a skull-bedecked headpiece and a grain bag made of antelope skin.

Danzandarjaa Khiid   BUDDHIST MONASTERY
(Данзандаржаа Хийд) The original (Möröngi-in Khuree) was built around 1890 and was home to 2000 monks. It was rebuilt and reopened in June 1990 and now has around three dozen monks of all ages. The concrete ger contains a great collection of *thangkas* (Buddhist scroll paintings).

Khövsgöl Park   PARK
This appealing park consists of a giant map of Khövsgöl aimag with each *sum* (district) represented, showing off all the highlights of the aimag. A large **Buddha statue**, which was donated by South Koreans, is located nearby.

Monument to Chingunjav   MONUMENT
With a fierce expression on his face, the statue of mounted Chingunjav looks set to trample you under its hooves. One of the two major leaders of the 1755–1756 rebellion in Outer Mongolia, he ultimately failed, but today he is nevertheless recognised as a fighter for Mongolia's independence from the Manchu when Mongolia was under the rule of the Qing Dynasty.

☞ Tours

Most guesthouses can help with arranging transport out of Mörön.

Saraa GUIDE
(☎9938 5577; saraa_m3@yahoo.com) Local English-speaking guide Saraa can help with logistics and travel in the area.

Tugsuu GUIDE
(☎8855 8399; Tugsuu_0220@yahoo.com) An English teacher and guide, who also runs a small tourist center called **Best Idea** (Noyon Building, 4-4-1).

🛏 Sleeping

If you have a tent there are good camping spots by the river, the Delgermörön Gol.

Bata Guesthouse GUESTHOUSE $
(☎9138 7080, 9809 7080; bata_guesthouse@yahoo.com; GPS: N 49°39.053', E 100°10.018'; per person with breakfast T10,000; @) This *hashaa* (enclosed) guesthouse is a 20-minute walk from the centre, 400m past the market. Turn right at the water pump house and walk for another 150m; it's on the left, marked 'Bata Guesthouse'. Friendly English-speaking owner, Bata, can help arrange transport and homestays with nomad families. There's a ger cafe on-site and guests can make international phone calls. Laundry services and showers cost T2000.

Gan Oyu Guesthouse GUESTHOUSE $
(☎9938 9438, 8869 3838; ganoyu_n@yahoo.com; Peace St; dm/tw with breakfast T10,000/15,000; @☎) This good-value guesthouse has spotless dorm rooms and a hot-water shower. It is on the 2nd floor of an apartment block next to the 50° 100° Hotel. The friendly proprietress speaks a few words of English and is eager to please.

Baigal Guesthouse GUESTHOUSE $
(☎9938 8408; baigal.gh@gmail.com; per person with breakfast T10,000; GPS: N 49°38.176', E 100°10.798') Around 600m east of the wrestling stadium you spot a bright purple gate inscribed with the words 'guest house'. Inside there are three neat guest gers and friendly English-speaking Baigal feeds you breakfast with eggs fresh from under her own chickens. She can also assist with travel logistics. Hot showers are T2000.

Altan Ulias TOURIST GER CAMP $
(☎8829 3686; GPS: N 49°38.483', E 100°08.618'; per person US$25) This ger camp, owned by the 50° 100° Hotel, has clean and simple rooms in the lodge or comfortable gers. The toilets and showers are also clean.

Chinggis Hotel HOTEL $$
(Чингис Төв; ☎9938 5447, 9997 7961; s/d/lux T45,000/50,000/80,000; @☎) Bright orange-and-yellow Chinggis Hotel aspires to be the top hotel and the reliable internet connection in its rooms (if you have your own laptop) works in its favour. However, most of the beds are hard, the sheets are too small, a peculiar smell reigns in some rooms, and you have to ask for pillows and towels.

★50° 100° Hotel HOTEL $$$
(☎7038 2200; d/half-lux/lux US$40/50/60; P☎) This is still the best hotel in town. Rooms are spotless and comfortable with modern bathrooms, reliable hot water and cable TV. Wi-fi comes and goes like a stray cat. Friendly staff will help with your luggage and some English is spoken. It's named after a particular geographical phenomenon in Khövsgöl, where the 50° north latitude meets 100° east longitude.

🍴 Eating & Drinking

And Restaurant MONGOLIAN $
(mains T3000-5000) The prissy bows on the comfy white-leather seats suggest aspirations beyond small-town horizons. The menu consists mostly of solid Mongolian standards, but exotica in the form of a few

---

DEER STONES

Found across Mongolia, deer stones are ancient markers that date from the Bronze Age and there are several theories for their existence. The ancient steppe tribes believed that after death a soul departed this world and ascended to the sky on the backs of deer. The deer carved onto the stones seem to be representational of this act. However, since human remains have never been found near deer stones, they do not appear to be gravestones, but rather serve some sort of religious or spiritual purpose. Many deer stones are also carved with a belt, from which hang various tools including axes and spears. These accessories would be required for successfully navigating the afterlife. Of the 700 deer stones known to exist worldwide, 500 are located in Mongolia. The best collection of deer stones is at Uushigiin Uver (p146).

salads, excellent *kimchi* soup and even 'shpagetti' and 'mousaka' also make an appearance.

Shine Ögööj Supermarket
SUPERMARKET $

(Шинэ Өгөөж Супермаркет) The largest and best-stocked supermarket in town.

★50° 100° Hotel
MONGOLIAN $$

(mains T7000-15,000; ⊙9am-midnight; 🖊 🔟) Located in the hotel of the same name, the 50° 100° serves the best food in town. There is a range of salads, imaginative meat dishes such as beef in plum sauce and huge portions of Korean dishes, such as *bibimbap*, though Korean food is not always available. Vegetarian soups and veggie salads are sometimes missing key ingredients, such as olives.

Neg Ye Pub
PUB

(Нэг Ye Pub; ⊙10am-7pm) This local watering hole features two giant barrels outside its entrance. The local drink of choice is *kvas*, a brew made from fermented rye bread. The alcohol content is so low (1%) that you'd need to drink a few gallons of the stuff to feel any of its effects. Mongolian dishes also available (meals T2500 to T5500).

🛍 Shopping

Antique Souvenir House
SOUVENIRS

(⊙9am-9pm) Sells books, antiques, useful maps of the region and a modest selection of locally produced handicrafts. It's located inside the drycleaners just east of the large supermarket.

Handicraft Shop
HANDICRAFTS

(⊙9am-6pm) Sells high-quality handicrafts produced in Khövsgöl Aimag. It's inside the 50° 100° Hotel.

Market
MARKET

(Зах; ⊙9am-7pm, from 11am Sun) If you have forgotten any expedition gear, check out the market; you'll find torches (flashlights), tents, stoves, fishing equipment, bags and bike parts. Quality and variety won't be great but it will do in a pinch. Close to the market is a strip of vehicle repair shops that can help out if you need to fix a flat or pick up spare car parts.

ℹ Information

Border Guard Office (📞01382-24136, 01382-24662; ⊙9am-noon & 2-6pm Mon-Fri) Can issue permits for border towns such as Tsagaannuur, but only if you have a Mongolian-speaking local with you posing as your guide. Otherwise, get your pass in Ulaanbaatar (p92).

Golomt Bank (Голомт Банк; ⊙9am-5pm Mon-Fri) Changes cash. There's also a Golomt Bank ATM inside the Shin Ogooj supermarket.

Internet Cafe (per hr T700; ⊙9am-9pm Mon-Fri, 10am-5pm Sat & Sun) Attached to the Telecom office.

Telecom Office (⊙24hr) Opposite the town square. The post office is also located here.

Tourist Information Centre (📞9938 2050, 9938 6070; www.huvsgul.wix.com/info; Centre St; ⊙10am-6pm Mon-Fri) Very helpful office run by foreign and local volunteers. Can put you in touch with local guides, provide maps of town, and help organise accommodation and onward travel. Also maintains a noncommercial website dedicated to providing accurate infor-

---

DON'T MISS

UUSHIGIIN UVER
УУШИГИЙН ӨВӨР

A Bronze Age site, **Uushigiin Uver** (GPS: N 49°39.334', E 99°55.701') contains 14 upright carved deer stones, some with splendid white design against an ochre-coloured background, plus sacrificial altars *(keregsuur)*. This remarkable collection is located 20km west of Mörön, and about 1km north of the Delgermörön Gol. The area is enclosed by a fence and small placards describe the stones. The most unique, **stone 14**, is topped with the head of a woman; there are only a handful of such deer stones in Mongolia. The carved stones are 2500 to 4000 years old, and the nearby mountain range contains about 1400 burial tombs. When we visited, the whole area was alive with Russian archaeologists digging for possible burial remains.

Perched on a ridge over the Delgermörön valley, the attractive **Khargant** (Харгант; 📞9538 3796; GPS: N 49°38.485', E 99°50.028'; 2-/3-person ger T30,000/50,000) ger camp has hot showers and tasty meals. It's run by a helpful English-speaking local named Bat who can assist with tours of the area. Even if you're not staying, it's a nice place for lunch after visiting the deer stones at Uushigiin Uver. It is 7km past Uushigiin Uver.

mation on the region. It's around 200m south of the 50° 100° Hotel.

ⓘ Getting There & Away

Be wary of people at the airport or bus station in Mörön who claim to be affiliated with one guesthouse or another. In fact, they are freelancers looking to sweep you off to their own ger camp or hostel.

AIR

Tickets for **AeroMongolia** (☑ 9997 7705, 8990 8111; khuvsgul@aeromongolia.mn) flights to Ulaanbaatar start from T99,900 one way. Its office is across the street from the 50° 100° Hotel. **EZ Nis** (☑ 01382-21199, 9904 9930) prices start from T180,400 return; its office is in the 50° 100° Hotel. **Hunnu Air** (www.hunnuair.com) offers similar prices; between these three airlines there should be at least two flights a day in summer. Winter schedules are cut back.

Moron airport is about 5km from the centre of town. A taxi will cost T5000.

BUS & MINIVAN

Two daily direct buses depart Mörön for Ulaanbaatar (T32,000, 18 to 20 hours), officially at 1.30pm and 4.30pm, but often later if there aren't enough passengers. Get your ticket well in advance in late summer when the buses fill up with students headed for the capital. Direct buses to the capital travel on the rough road via Ikh Uul, Khairkhan and Ölziit, but this looks set to change as the northern route via Bulgan was under construction at the time of research and should be paved within the lifetime of this book.

Minivans run between Mörön and Ulaanbaatar daily (T50,000, 17 hours, 671km), departing at around 1pm. Minivans also run to Erdenet (T25,000, 12 hours) and Darkhan (T30,000, 15 hours); there's usually one daily, departing at around 4.30pm; it can drop passengers off in Bulgan (same price as Erdenet) on request. Buses and minibuses leave from the car park next to the concrete **bus station** (Авто вокзал) building, diagonally across from the wrestling stadium.

From Mörön it is 273km to Tosontsengel in Zavkhan aimag and 353km to Bulgan City.

HITCHING

The Ulaanbaatar–Erdenet–Mörön road is fairly busy, so hitching a ride shouldn't be a problem. But be warned: the trip by truck between Ulaanbaatar and Mörön is a tough 27 or more nonstop hours and can cost as much as the faster bus. Some travellers do it one way for the 'experience', and then gratefully fly back. It's best to fly here from Ulaanbaatar, as it's easier to get a seat. It's also easier to hitch *to* UB rather than *from* it, as all traffic funnels back to the capital.

NATIONAL PARKS OF KHÖVSGÖL

Khövsgöl Nuur National Park With Mongolia's deepest and second-largest lake at its heart, this national park features craggy mountains, grass plains and thermal springs.

Khoridol Saridag Nuruu Strictly Protected Area This park consists of 188,634 hectares of mountains and plains, sandwiched between Lake Khövsgöl and the Darkhad Depression.

MINIVAN & JEEP

The local jeep and minivan stand to *sums* around Khövsgöl is a small lot about 250m north of the market, hidden behind a building. Vehicles to Tsagaannuur (T30,000) and Renchinlkhumbe (T30,000) leave two or three times a week, as do vehicles south to Jargalant (T25,000), depending on demand. Vehicles leave most afternoons to Khatgal (T20,000, one hour), either from the north of the market or from a separate parking area just off the main road opposite the clothing stalls.

When there is demand, Bata Guesthouse (p145) organises shared jeep trips to Ulaanbaatar via Terkhiin Tsagaan Nuur.

Khövsgöl Nuur National Park Хөвсгөл Нуур

The **Khövsgöl Nuur** (Blue Pearl of Mongolia) is an extraordinary lake that stretches 136km deep into the Siberian taiga. As with its larger sibling across the border, Siberia's Lake Baikal, superlatives don't really do this immense, mountain-fringed lake justice. Its moody blue waters, ranging from midnight blue to tropical aquamarine, form the basis for this popular **national park** (admission T3000) and attract thousands of Mongolian and international tourists every year.

In surface area, this is the second-largest lake (2760 sq km) in Mongolia, surpassed in size only by Uvs Nuur, a shallow, salty lake in the western part of the country. Khövsgöl Nuur (sometimes transliterated as Hövsgöl or Hovsgol) is Mongolia's deepest lake (up to 262m deep) as well as the world's 14th-largest source of fresh water – it contains between 1% and 2% of the world's fresh water (that's 380,700 billion litres!). Geologically speaking, Khövsgöl is the younger sibling (by 23 million years) of Siberia's Lake Baikal,

195km to the northeast, and was formed by the same tectonic forces.

The lake is full of fish, such as lenok and sturgeon, and the area is home to argali sheep, ibexes, bears, sables, moose and a few near-sighted wolverines. It also has more than 200 species of bird, including the Baikal teal, bar-headed goose (*kheeriin galuu* in Mongolian), black stork and Altai snowcock.

The region hosts three separate, unique peoples: Darkhad, Buriat and Tsaatan (aka Dukha). Shamanism, rather than Buddhism, is the religion of choice in these parts.

⊙ Sights

⊙ Khatgal   Хатгал

Bisected by a brand-new paved road, cheerful Khatgal is a scattering of colourful roofs, dirt alleyways and wooden houses, spread out beneath the foothills and along

Khövsgöl Nuur National Park

the narrow arm of Khövsgöl Nuur that funnels into the Egiin Gol. The southern gateway to the lake, Khatgal is the largest town in the area, with some of the best budget accommodation in Mongolia. It is a good launchpad for multiday adventures in the area as well as hiking, biking, kayaking and horse riding.

For a good **view** of the lake, just climb the hill immediately north of Nature's Door camp (p153). You can also check out the **Mogoi Mod** (Snake Tree; GPS: N 50°27.080', E 100°07.274'), 4km from town, past the defunct airport, towards Jankhai Davaa (Jankhai Pass). This tree, which curves into a unique spiral, is honoured with hadak (ritual scarves).

⊙ Western Shore

From Khatgal, a good, packed-gravel road first heads southwest before swinging northeast across several dry riverbeds and over the pass, **Jankhai Davaa**, 17km from Khatgal, where you'll come across a few minor **ovoos** (GPS: N 50°34.023', E 100°07.797') and a cluster of reindeer herders selling handicrafts. These few Tsaatan, sometimes accompanied by a so-called shamaness, have been lured down to the lake by the promise of tourist tögrög and their token reindeer are adversely affected by the lowland climate.

Over the pass, the road, lined with ger camps, continues past the gorgeous headlands of **Jankhai** and the Toilogt eco-camp (p153) to a **military post** (you're supposed to get permission to travel up the west side of the lake). The road then deteriorates into a swampy mess. It's only really possible to travel here by vehicle when the ground freezes, though you can carry on up the coast on horseback.

About 30km north of Toilogt is **Khar Us** (GPS: N 50°56.132', E 100°14.835'), a series of springs surrounded by meadows of beautiful wildflowers. In June locals flock here to eat the bailius fish for its medicinal properties (these fish are smoked and served with wild green onions, or sometimes boiled).

Almost exactly halfway up the western shore lies **Jiglegiin Am** (GPS: N 51°00.406', E 100°16.003'), from where a decent westbound road runs to Renchinlkhumbe, on the way to Tsagaannuur.

To get a ride up the western shore, you have to pay for a taxi from Khatgal (around T50,000). Alternatively, if you're travelling solo and travelling light, ask at your guesthouse whether anyone can give you a ride on the back of a motorbike.

The western shore makes a good trekking route; see p150.

Eastern Shore

The eastern shore is less mountainous than the west, but offers spectacular views across Khövsgöl Nuur. It gets far fewer visitors than the western shore, making it a great destination for travellers seeking an off-the-beaten-path experience. The main drawback to this side of the lake is the appalling road that heads up to Khankh. Expect mud, rocks, roots and the odd collapsed bridge.

From Khatgal, head for the bridge over the Egiin Gol. The trail meanders over some hills and continues past a prominent *ovoo* at the **Ikh Santlln Davaa** (Их Сантын Даваа; GPS: N 50°52.622', E 100°41.185') pass to a gorgeous spot called **Borsog** (Борсог; GPS: N 50°59.677', E 100°42.983'), six hours by jeep and 103km from Khatgal.

If your spine hasn't suffered permanent damage, you could carry on further to a couple of gers known as **Sevsuul**. The road actually improves a little here, then hugs the lake and is usually passable all the way to Khankh.

From Khatgal, allow at least 11 hours by jeep (less by motorcycle) to travel about 200km to **Khankh**, a former depot for oil tankers headed to and from Siberia. From here, trucks used to cross the lake in winter, carrying oil to Khatgal before the collapse of the Soviet Union. Khankh is more Buriat and Russian than Mongolian because most visitors are Russian holidaymakers from Irkutsk.

Remember that if you reach Khankh, you will have to come *all* the way back along the same bone-crunching eastern road: there is no way any vehicle can get from Khankh down the western shore. At the moment going all the way around the lake is only possible by boat or horse. The nearby border crossing with Russia is closed to third-country nationals.

Activities
Fishing
If your idea of heaven is sitting utterly still for hours on end and contemplating the bobbing of your rod in the water, well, welcome to Eden! If you don't have fishing gear

already, Buren Khaan shop in Khatgal has the best selection.

Around a dozen species of fish inhabit the lake, including grayling, omol, Siberian roach, perch and lenok. A fishing permit costs T15,000 and is valid for three days or 10 fish, whichever comes first. You can get them from Khatgal's Government House (ask for directions at your accommodation). Fishing is not allowed between 15 April and 15 June. The fine for fishing illegally depends on what it is you've caught; it's worked out using the value of the fish multiplied by 10, with a US$40 fine on top of that.

Hiking
One of the best ways to see the lake and the mountains surrounding it is on your own two feet. You will need to be self-sufficient, although there are a few gers in the area from which to buy some meat or dairy products. The trails around the lake are easy to follow.

Of the mountains in the southwestern region, the most accessible is **Tsartai Ekh Uul** (2515m), immediately west of Jankhai, where the hiking is excellent. Also try the numerous other mountains in the mountain range of Khoridol Saridag Nuruu, such as **Khuren Uul** (3020m), not far north of the trail to Renchinlkhumbe; **Ikh Uul** (2961m), a little northwest of Toilogt; and the extinct volcano of **Uran Dösh Uul** (2792m).

TREKKING FROM KHÖVSGÖL TO DARKHAD

One of the most adventurous treks in Mongolia, done by either horse or foot, begins in Khatgal, goes up the western shore of the lake and over the Jiglegiin Davaa (Jiglegiin Pass) to Renchinlkhumbe.

From Khatgal to Jiglegiin Am, about halfway up the western shore of Khövsgöl Nuur, will take five days (four hours' riding each day). You start to feel the isolation after the military checkpoint (the end of the jeep road), from where it's a 10-hour journey to Khar Us (p148). There are endless camping spots along this route.

From Khar Us it's just three hours to Jiglegiin Am (p148), where you can find accommodation in a cabin (T10,000) and get a cooked meal (T5000) – it's best to have exact change. The jeep trail that heads up to Jiglegiin Davaa (2500m) is very muddy even after a long dry spell – this is where a pair of Russian NBC overboots will come in handy. Expect to get to the pass in around three hours.

From the pass it's a gentle walk down to the Arsayn Gol, which you'll need to cross at least twice. There are also some side streams to cross. These crossings are usually OK, but if it's been raining hard you can be stuck for hours or even days. In dry spells the river can disappear completely so you need to fill up with water whenever possible.

After a seven-hour walk from the pass you should be at Ooliin Gol (25km west of Jiglegiin Am), where there are some camping spots. It's then another seven hours to Renchinlkhumbe. When you reach the broad expanse of the Darkhad, make a beeline south for the town.

The final three hours of the trek are often marred by horrific swarms of flies and mosquitoes – a sanity-saving measure is to wrap your head with a towel or T-shirt, or to invest in a mosquito head net in advance.

From Renchinlkhumbe it's another two-day trek to Tsagaannuur, from where you can organise a trip to the Tsaatan camps. Alternatively, return to Khatgal via the old Russian logging route that runs through the mountains that's currently being used only by the hardiest of vehicles. If you don't intend to go to Tsagaannuur, you could skip Renchinlkhumbe and take a shortcut back to Khatgal. This involves following the Arsayn Gol around 35km upstream, eventually picking up the logging route.

This route involves moderate trekking in good weather. However, the area is prone to heavy rain and flash flooding that can stop you in your tracks. Hikers and horse riders are frequently forced to wait on river banks (sometimes for several days) until water levels drop low enough for them to cross. Bring wet-weather gear, warm clothes and preferably a guide to get you across. If you don't have a guide, at least bring a good map, such as the *Lake Khövsgöl National Park Satellite Map* from Conservation Ink (p271). Contact MS Guesthouse in Khatgal (p151) for further details.

Longer treks are possible around the Ikh Sayani Nuruu range, which has many peaks over 3000m. It is right on the border of Russia, so be careful not to accidentally cross it or you may be shot at by border guards. A popular hike is up the western shore of the lake from Khatgal to Renchinlkhumbe via Jinglegiin Am; it takes roughly about a week.

Horse Riding

The only place to organise a horse trek around the lake is in Khatgal. The guesthouses here can arrange everything within 24 hours. Prices are negotiable but reasonable at about T20,000 to T25,000 per horse per day, and about the same per day for a guide. Ger camps along the lake can organise horse hire for day trips.

A guide is recommended for horse-riding trips in the region and, in fact, park regulations stipulate that foreigners should have one local guide for every four tourists. Even if you have great equestrian skills, there are concerns that tourists riding solo may get lost or have their horses stolen. Guides will expect you to provide food while on the trail.

A complete circuit of the lake on horseback will take from 15 to 21 days. A return trip by horse from Khatgal to Tsagaannuur, and a visit to the Tsaatan, will take 14 to 20 days, most of which will be spent in the saddle, giving you only a day or two with the Tsaatan themselves.

An interesting two-week trip could take you east of the lake to Chandman-Öndör and Dayan Derkhiin Agui, a sacred cave. A trip to the Bulnai hot springs would take eight to nine days.

Shorter trips include one to Toilogt, through the mountainous Khoridol Saridag Nuruu Strictly Protected Area, or up to Khar Us and back in five or six days.

Kayaking & Boating

The lake is full of glorious coves, perfect for kayaking. Nomadic Expeditions in Ulaanbaatar (p36) runs kayaking trips in the region. Garage 24 (p152) and MS Guesthouse rent kayaks for about T50,000 per day, and MS Guesthouse also offers the fun option of sending you downriver along Egiin Gol and agreeing on where to fish you out; you can kayak for up to 100km – and come back by jeep (T100,000).

Almost exactly in the middle of the lake lies **Modon Huys**, a picturesque little island surrounded by turquoise, tropical-looking waters. Several guesthouses, including MS Guesthouse and Garage 24, own motor boats; the latter can run travellers up to its camp and beyond to the island and the northern reaches of the lake. Other boat owners are happy to whisk three to four passengers up to a smaller island near Khatgal (around two hours return). For something a bit longer, ask about the two-day boat trip to Jiglegiin Am (T600,000 for up to five people, including meals).

In summer (July to mid-August) the **Sükhbaatar** (Сухбаатар Усан Онгоц; adult/child T15,000/5000; ☉12pm & 3pm) passenger ferry does daily 90-minute scenic/party boat trips, to the loud accompaniment of Mongolian pop and with plenty of passenger 'fuel' in the form of beer.

✰ Festivals & Events

Khatgal Ice Festival　　ICE FESTIVAL
(☉28 Feb) Ice fishing, cross-country skiing, ice skating and horse-sledding competitions.

Naadam　　TRADITIONAL
(☉11 July) Khatgal's naadam (traditional sports festival) is held in July. A second naadam on 11 August is sponsored by MS Guesthouse; profits from the event go towards ecoprojects in the area.

Mongolia Sunrise to Sunset　　MARATHON
(www.ms2s.org) In mid-summer the Mongolia Sunrise to Sunset ultra-marathon is held further up the lakeshore, with Mongolian and international runners competing in 42km or 100km divisions.

🛏 Sleeping

🛏 Khatgal

If you have a tent you can camp along the shores of the Egiin Gol.

At the beginning of the season the main ger camps in town set a standard price which tends to be the same across the board. At the time of research the price was T15,000 per person for a ger and T4000 for camping.

Beware of small-scale family operations that undercut official ger camps by running small, unofficial 'ger camps' that are not environmentally friendly. The same problem exists along the western shore of the lake.

At the time of writing, a new law had been passed that all ger camps must be located at least 200m away from the lake's water line; it remains to be seen whether the law will be enforced.

★ **MS Guesthouse**　　TOURIST GER CAMP $
(☑9979 6030; lake_hovsgol@yahoo.com; per son T15,000; camping T4000; @☎) This year-round camp, in the extreme south of town, is perhaps the most congenial of lodgings around Khatgal. English-speaking owner Ganbaa makes visitors feel at home, with communal meals in the lodge (T1500) and plenty of advice on hiking and horse-trekking in the area. There are hot showers, clean pit toilets and another lodge being built to provide guest rooms.

Bond Lake　　TOURIST GER CAMP $
(☑8986 3994, 9860 7649; mongoliantrips@yahoo. com; per person with shower T15,000) This long-time Khatgal camp is located on the main road heading north, just past the shops. Though the main building is crying out for a coat of paint, it's a friendly place, with four-bed gers and one ger with a double bed. The hot showers work well and the English-speaking owner (Bayaraa) has kayaks for rent. Dinner costs T4500.

Blue Sky　　TOURIST GER CAMP $
(☑9898 5597; 3-person ger T30,000; ☎) Compact ger camp in a fenced yard not far from the petrol station. English not spoken, but it's run by a friendly family (ask for Ulzinyam), there is hot water to be had and even

slow, intermittent wi-fi for travellers wielding wi-fi-enabled devices.

★ **Garage 24**   LODGE $$
(☑ 9908 0416, 9838 9750; www.naturesdoor.mn; per person T50,000; camping with shower access T25,000) ✎ North of town, at the base of the hill, not far from the petrol station, this environmentally conscious backpacker hang-out is built from a reclaimed Soviet-era truck garage. Choose between staying in a ger or a dorm with comfy bunks in the fireplace-warmed lodge, and take some of the best food in Mongolia out onto the veranda. Kayaks, horses and camping gear are available for hire and English is spoken.

🛏 Modot Bulan

This area extends due north of Khatgal, up the Egiin Gol mouth for about 6km. The road up the coast bypasses this section, so take the road that curves right around the hill to get here. If you're exploring the lake by foot, you can walk here and continue up the shore, which is blissfully ger-camp-free for another 7km. The road is short but very rough.

Huvsgul Dalai   TOURIST GER CAMP $$
(☑ 9811 4408, 11-7011 0045; with breakfast/full board US$30/50) On a raised bit of land just up from the lake shore, this few-frills ger camp offers regimental rows of two- and three-person gers, a sauna and a dining hall serving solid Mongolian standards.

★ **Ashihai**   TOURIST GER CAMP $$$
(☑ 9968 5185, 11-7015 1459; www.ashihai.mn; per person with/without meals T98,000/75,000) This camp nearly qualifies as a work of art. Elevated onto wood platforms, the hand-carved, beautifully decorated gers are embroidered with traditional patterns and the interior contains exquisitely carved furniture. Each is in a tranquil spot offering lake views. Meals are served in the airy dining room of the appealing wooden lodge, and you can partake in massages and steamy sauna sessions in between motor-boating, horse riding and yak riding.

Sant Ger Camp   TOURIST GER CAMP $$$
(☑ 9931 1913, 9915 5145; www.khuvsgul-sant. mn; 2-person ger US$160, mini-house per person US$100) Just over the small hill beyond Khatgal, luxurious Sant is a study in how to enjoy the great outdoors without foregoing any creature comforts. It's all hand-carved gers with traditional beds, and cute-as-a-button mini-houses with fireplaces and compact bedrooms in which to canoodle with your sweetie. Delicious meals are served in the large restaurant ger and all manner of outdoor adventures are on offer.

🛏 Western & Eastern Shores

Secluded camping spots are surprisingly difficult to come by along the stretch of western lake shore lined with ger camps. With the exception of the Jankhai headland, you can pretty much pitch your tent anywhere you want, though try to stay 100m from the gers. The best camping spots on the western shoreline are anywhere between Jankhai and Ongolog Nuur, 10km north of Toilogt. If you have your own jeep, the best spot to camp on the eastern shoreline is at Borsog (p149).

There are numerous ger camps in stunning locations on the western shore (but only a couple on the east). Most have electricity, running water, flush toilets and showers, and offer a lower price if you bring

---

WINDHORSE – PORTABLE GER CAMP

The unique **Windhorse Ger Camp** (mongolwindhorse@gmail.com; per person with 3 meals from US$100) ✎ is an upscale bush camp located in the Darkhad valley. The fact that it's portable (like a traditional Mongolian *ail*) means that there's no concrete or permanent structures that can scar the landscape, making this camp about as eco-friendly as you can find.

Although basic in concept, the camp offers first-rate services; it includes a dining ger, a shower ger and a bathroom tent with chemical toilets. Solar panels provide a limited energy source. Gourmet cuisine and quality wine can be ordered. Horses with Western saddles are available to ride and the camp can organise pack trips into the taiga to visit the Tsaatan or across the Saridag mountains to Lake Khövsgöl.

The location of the camp changes from year to year depending on the whims of its owner. To confirm where it is and to reserve a place, email them way in advance.

and cook your own food. The majority open in mid-June and close around the end of August or early September. If you're looking for eco-sustainability, both Nature's Door and Toilogt score highly.

The main group of camps start where the road meets the lake, after descending from the Jankhai Davaa pass.

Jigleg Camp
LODGE $

(☑ 9914 0965; dm T10,000) Basic lodge that serves as a handy pit stop for trekkers on their way to Renchinlkhumbe (it's right at the Jigleg trail head). The camp is 90km north of Khatgal. Book through Boojum in Ulaanbaatar (p39) or contact Mishig (in Mongolian or Russian) in advance.

★ Toilogt
TOURIST GER CAMP $$

(☑ 11-460 368; www.hovsgoltravel.com; per person with/without meals US$45/25; ⊕) ✔ This eco-conscious camp is in a splendid location on its own little peninsula north of the other ger camps. Accommodation is a mix of tee-pees, gers and adorable wooden cabins, English is spoken, and the dining room is a hive of activity in the evenings. The camp offers bikes, boats and horses for hire, and boat transfers from Khatgal can be organised in advance at the Ulaanbaatar office.

★ Nature's Door
TOURIST GER CAMP $$$

(☑ 9838 0004, 9908 0416; www.naturesdoor.mn; per person with/without meals US$50/40, camping US$5) This popular backpacker hang-out has plush cabins, a lodge, English-speaking staff and welcome pizza and pasta on the menu, not to mention the best hot (solar-powered) showers in northern Mongolia. Even if you're staying in one of the gers or camping (the price includes hot showers), you get access to the lounge with games. As an eco-conscious camp, Nature's Door gets high marks for composting and recycling. Nature's Door is associated with Garage 24 in Khatgal; it's about 5km northeast of Jankhai Davaa.

Khuvsgol Sor
TOURIST GER CAMP $$$

(☑ 9905 0046, 9905 4601, 9919 0330; khuvs-gul_travel@yahoo.com; per person with/without meals T75,000/60,000) The first camp after the pass, Khuvsgul Sor consists of gers and basic cabins playing hide and seek among the trees on the gentle, wooded slope down to the lake. The camp has proper flushing loos, hot showers and a restaurant on-site. A friendly cocker spaniel scampers about the property.

🛏 Khankh

Northern Gate
Ger Guesthouse
GUESTHOUSE $

(☑ 9979 6030; per person T20,000) Operated by the people from MS Guesthouse in Khatgal (p151). It's just outside the town (within walking distance) but can be hard to find. Call for directions.

Last Frontier
TOURIST GER CAMP $$$

(Саян Радиан; ☑ 8808 9141; www.sayan-radian.ru; GPS N 51°30.566', E 100°39.296'; ger per person with 3 meals T66,000, r from T87,000) A cluster of gers surrounding an appealing wooden lodge on the lake shore. Most of the wood-panelled rooms have own bathrooms and activities on offer range from horse riding to fishing and hunting. Caters to a predominantly Russian clientele.

🍴 Eating

There are several basic shops in Khatgal (mostly clustered near the Telecom office). If possible, stock up in Mörön or Ulaanbaatar. The following places are all in Khatgal.

MS Guesthouse
MONGOLIAN $

(meals around T5000; 🖬) MS is a nice place to eat and will occasionally prepare *khorkhog* (a mutton dish cooked using hot stones) and authentic Mongolian barbecue for guests and visitors.

Rose Cafe
MONGOLIAN $

(Сарнай Кафе; meals T5000) Centrally located joint popular with locals for its heaped portions of Mongolian classics.

★ Garage 24
WESTERN $$

(meals T6500-10,000; 🖬) Garage 24 has a Western-oriented menu that will come as a welcome break after a few days of roughing it in the wilderness. The English breakfast includes bacon, toast, beans and sausage. Lunch and dinner menu items include surprisingly good shepherd's pie and pizza. Give some advance warning as preparations take around an hour.

ℹ Information

On the main road, 12km south of Khatgal, you'll be required to pay the park entrance fee at a gate to the national park. If there's no one there you can buy permits at the information centre or from the ranger, who patrols the lakeside on horseback. With your permit you should receive a visitors' pamphlet explaining how to limit your impact on the lake. Hang onto the ticket as you may be asked to show it.

Information Centre (◎9am-8pm) Located near the MS Guesthouse in Khatgal with a large 'tourist information' sign, this centre has limited practical info, though this may change. During the lifetime of this book the building may also house an office of the **Mongol Ecology Center** (www.mongolec.org) who are currently working with the park administration and ger camp owners to ensure the sustainability of the national park.

Khan Bank (Хаан Банк; ◎9am-1pm & 2-5pm Mon-Fri) Changes cash. The closest guaranteed ATM is in Mörön.

Telecom Office (◎8am-11pm) The post office is also located here.

❶ Getting There & Away

HITCHING

For lifts from Mörön, hang around the market or the petrol station – and keep asking. In Khatgal, most trucks will stop in front of the post office.

From Khatgal, hitching a ride to Jankhai or Toilogt shouldn't be difficult in the summer, but you'll probably end up paying a fair bit. Ask the guests at the camps for a lift.

Hitching around the eastern shore is much more difficult; you could wait for days for a lift.

JEEP

Minivans and jeeps regularly make the trip between Mörön and Khatgal (one hour) for T20,000 per person or T100,000 for the jeep. Enquire at the stand at the northern end and eastern side of the market in Mörön and around the post office in Khatgal.

Transport also meets the Ulaanbaatar flight at Mörön airport to take passengers directly to Khatgal. Some jeep owners try to charge foreigners up to US$80 for the run; local drivers with the 'ХӨ' at the beginning of their licence plate are likely to be fairer. Contact Bata Guesthouse in Mörön (p145) for transport to Khatgal.

A chartered jeep should cost around T500 per kilometre. There are plenty of jeeps in Mörön but few in Khatgal, where it is best to ask at the guesthouses. Khatgal is 101km from Mörön via a newly paved road, though at the time of writing, a section of it had already been damaged by floods.

MOTORCYCLE

Since everyone and their grandmother owns a motorcycle, if you're travelling light and on your own, it's worth asking around if you can catch a ride up either lake shore on the back of a motorbike. Some travellers have been known to motorbike on their own from Ulaanbaatar to Khatgal, but unless you have ample experience of off-road driving and fixing your own bike, the roads around the lake can be really challenging.

Chandman-Öndör
Чандмань-Өндөр

Nestled between pine-clad mountains and consisting almost entirely of log cabins, the village of Chandman-Öndör sits in one of the most picturesque locations in the country. The surrounding area is ideal horse-riding country, with clear streams, alpine forests and wildflowers.

Around 11km south of town is a red **statue of Alan Goa** (Алун Гуа; GPS: N 50°24.987', E 100°58.564'), looking like a Roman legionary planted incongruously in the middle of an alpine meadow. Alan is, in fact, a woman, 'goa' meaning 'the beauty'. In Chandman-Öndör itself, you'll find the **Alan Goa Museum** (admission T1000), housed inside the ger-shaped log cabin. Alan Goa was an ancestor of Chinggis Khaan, mentioned in *The Secret History* and preceding him by 10 generations, and is revered locally.

Every three years (the next is August 2015) a large **naadam** is held here to honour Alan Goa. It attracts Mongols from Inner Mongolia, Kalmyks, Tuvans and Buriats as well as a host of Khalkh Mongols. The only place to stay in town is a small **hotel** around the corner from the Alan Goa Museum.

Shared jeeps going to Chandman-Öndör (T15,000) occasionally leave from the northern side of the market in Mörön; if you have your own wheels, a good road winds its way to Chandman-Öndör via the village of Tunel, around green hills and lush meadows. From Khatgal there are two roads to Chandman-Öndör; the one that approaches it from the south is particularly rough, muddy, boggy and can take up to five hours; don't attempt it after heavy rain. The slightly shorter road that branches off the main lakeside road to the north of Khatgal is easier to drive, and there's a turnoff for the Bulnai hot springs halfway along.

In the rainy season, the best way to Chandman-Öndör is by horse; the trek from Khatgal takes four to five days. The route is spectacular, but marred by swarms of flies.

Around Chandman-Öndör

Chandman-Öndör is the jumping-off point for several sites, including the **Bulnai hot springs** (Булнайн Рашаан; per person T15,000), about 60km northwest of town. This Soviet-era resort has wood cabins over the springs, some of which reach 48°C. Besides the

Bulnai Tour Camp (per person T25,000) near the springs with its log cabins, there's a new ger camp right next to the springs with hot showers; MS Guesthouse in Khatgal (p151) arranges trips here.

Heading east of Chandman-Öndör, the road follows the Arig Gol. After 41km you'll pass a row of 13 **shamanic tepees** (GPS: N 50°30.727', E 101°17.478') made from sticks. These represent the 12 years according to the Asian calendar, plus one central *ovoo*. After another 18km you'll reach the town of **Tsagaan-Uur**, with basic shops and *guanz*. The bridge east of town was present at the time of writing but is occasionally washed away. The road to Tsagaan-Uur is notoriously rough and can take up to six hours from Chandman-Öndör.

Around 38km past Tsagaan-Uur (and 97km past Chandman-Öndör) is the **Dayan Derkh Monastery** (Даян Дэрх Хийд; GPS: N 50°26.804', E 101°53.328'), set on a beautiful bend of the Uur Gol. The log-cabin temple, rebuilt in 2006 over the remains of an older monastery, is home to a half-dozen lamas. Another 15km east of the temple is the **Dayan Derkhiin Agui** (Даян Дэрхийн Агуй), a cave considered holy by local Buddhists and shamanists. According to legend, the monastery was founded after the famed shaman Dayan Derkh turned to stone rather than be captured by Chinggis Khaan, whose wife the shaman had stolen. In winter you could reach the cave by vehicle, in summer the only way is by horse (a six-hour return journey). It is only possible to get halfway to the monastery by vehicle; the rest has to be by horse. Herders in the area may be able to rent you a horse for T10,000. In theory you need a border permit for Tsagaan-Uur and Dayan Derkhiin Agui.

About 26km downstream from the monastery is the confluence of the Eg and Uur Gols. Head west at the Eg and after about 35km you'll reach the town of **Erdenebulgan**, from where it's possible to double back to Mörön. The road from Dayan Derkh Monastery to Erdenebulgan has been made easier by the building of bridges across the two river crossings, but we can't vouch for their state of repair.

Darkhad Depression
Дархадын Хотгор

About 50km west of Khövsgöl Nuur, behind a wall of mountains, sits a harsh, mystical landscape of prairie, forest and 300-odd lakes scattered over a wide plain called the Darkhad Depression. The depression is roughly the same size as Khövsgöl Nuur and was also originally formed as a glacial lake.

The difficulty in reaching the region ensures the unique Tsaatan people, who are among the inhabitants of the valleys, are still able to continue their traditional lifestyle.

THE REINDEER HERDERS

Not far from Khövsgöl Nuur live the Tsaatan (literally 'Reindeer People'). Their entire existence is based on their herds of reindeer, which provide milk for making cheese, antlers for carving and medicine, transport (the males can carry up to 90kg of weight) and, very occasionally, meat.

The Tsaatan are part of the Tuvan ethnic group, which inhabits the Tuvan Republic of Russia, and they speak both Tuvan and Mongolian. There are only about 400 to 500 Tsaatan in total (around 250 live in taiga), spread over 100,000 sq km of northern Mongolian taiga landscape. They are truly nomadic, often moving their small encampments (*ail*) in search of the special types of grass and lichen loved by the reindeer (of which there are less than 1000). The Tsaatan do not use gers, but prefer *orts*, similar to Native American tepees, traditionally made from birch bark but now from store-bought canvas. Shamanism plays an important part in Tsaatan; the shaman also acts as a healer, providing traditional remedies for ailments.

When the president of Mongolia visited the Tsaatan in winter of 2012, he decreed that elders and families with many children will receive a stipend from the government. Before communism and forced collectivisation the Tsaatan were completely self-sufficient, with enough reindeer per family to feed themselves. These days, in autumn, the Tsaatan gather berries, pine nuts and wild potato, and fish and hunt when possible as further means of subsistence. January to March is the hungriest time of all.

For information on visiting the Tsaatan, see p158.

BLUE VALLEY AWARDS FESTIVAL

Taking place mid-June annually in the Darkhad Depression, this cultural festival features traditional horse games and singing competitions. The venue moves between the four towns of Renchin-lkhumbe, Ulaan Uul, Arbulag and Bayanzürkh; check the location in advance at the tourist office in Mörön (p146).

The area is also one of Mongolia's strongest centres of shamanism – the genuine kind, not the let's-pose-for-the-tourists kind.

This is one of the best-watered regions in Mongolia and the lakes are full of white carp and trout. Salmon and huge taimen can also be found here.

One drawback to visiting the region are the insects that invade the area in summer. If you don't fancy being a moveable feast for the little bloodsuckers, come fully prepared with mosquito nets and repellent.

The entrance to the region is most dramatic, marked with a **gate** (GPS: N 50°34.645', E 099°08.567') and a number of large *ovoos* sprinkled with food offerings, and a few kilometres beyond you have to pay the national park fee of T5000.

Renchinlkhumbe   Рэнчинлхүмбэ

Mountain-fringed Renchinlkhumbe is 42km west of the Jiglegiin Am trailhead on Khövsgöl Nuur, an adventurous two-day journey on foot or horseback or else reachable by a fairly rough road via Ulaan-Uul. Most travellers heading further into the taiga will rest here for at least one night.

Renchinlkhumbe hosts an excellent local **naadam** (11 July) complete with 'barrel racing' (horse racing around barrels) and mounted archery events, along with the usual wrestling, horse racing and standing archery.

The local ger camp, **Saridag Inn** (☑ 9914 0965; GPS: N 51°06.852', E 099°40.135'; camping/r/ ger per person T5000/10,000/15,000) is run by Khövsgöl Lodge Company and consists of homey gers and musty rooms inside the main lodge building, with stupas on its property. Its hot-water showers and sit-down toilets are legendary. Contact Mishig.

Tsagaannuur   Цагааннуур

About 40km beyond Renchinlkhumbe is Tsagaannuur, the last stop before the Tsaatan encampments in the taiga. Besides the picturesque lakeside location, there's little here besides a few small grocery stores and a couple of guesthouses.

🛏 Sleeping & Eating

Food and cooking fuel is scarce in the taiga; proper preparation includes bringing everything you need from Tsagaannuur or (even better) Mörön. A **bathhouse** (per person T2000) is located 100m west of the school.

★TCVC Guesthouse Accommodation   GUESTHOUSE $
(☑ 9525 8500; dm T10,000) The Tsaatan Community & Visitors Center offers guesthouse accommodation in the form of two rooms upstairs from the main visitor centre and a guest kitchen. The visitor centre is staffed by a Tsaatan caretaker who lives next door; the money you spend here will go directly back to the community.

Erdene's Guesthouse   GUESTHOUSE $
(☑ 9950 8657) A friendly option consisting of a basic bed and breakfast deal. The owner's wife speaks English.

☞ Tours

Travellers can visit the Tsaatan year-round. The winter camp is reachable by jeep, whereas the rest of the year, you must come on horseback.

The TCVC can provide guides (but not interpreters), rent horses and offer information about the location of the Tsaatan camps. The centre is fully owned and operated by the Tsaatan and works to both help travellers and give the Tsaatan a chance to control tourism to their community. Arrangements can also be made with the assistance of **Zaya** (zaya_004@yahoo.com), the English-speaking member of the community. She checks her email weekly, though the community has no phone reception between mid-June and mid-August.

Once you've left Tsagaannuur, figure on spending around US$50 to US$55 a day for horses, guides, accommodation and meals. People typically stay for a couple of days, but you can stay longer if you're really interested in the Tsaatan way of life.

The Tsaatan live in two groups, known as the east (*zuun*) and west (*baruun*) taiga (this is a little confusing as the west taiga is actually southwest of the east taiga). Most visitors head for east taiga; the communities communicate via two-way radio. From Tsagaannuur, it can take four to 12 hours to reach either the west or east taiga by horse (the camps move but are usually closer in the early summer or late autumn). The east taiga is 20km north of the Shishged Gol, with a bridge over it.

Getting to the Tsaatan involves a wonderfully picturesque horse trek through pristine forest and mountains. If you don't want to come by horseback all the way from Tsagaannuur, it's possible to arrange for horses to meet you at the **exchange point** (GPS: N 51°29.930', E 099°28.803'), north of Renchinlkhumbe and only five hours' ride from the camp. If you are intent on making the trip, check up about permits with the General Office of Border Protection in UB (p92), as you'll need one to travel to this border area.

Tsaatan Community & Visitors Center

COMMUNITY TOURS

(TCVC; ☎ 9977 0480, 9525 8500; www.visittaiga. org) Provides background info on the Tsaatan, important tips on travel in the area and logistical support.

ℹ Information

Permission from Ulaanbaatar (p92) is required to visit Tsagaannuur and you have to register at the local **checkpoint** (Хилийн 0258 Дугаар Тусгай Салбар). It's best to bring a guide and interpreter who can help smooth out any permit issues. It may be possible to obtain a permit from the border guards in Mörön (p146), but as this requires the assistance of your guide, or a local posing as your guide, it's best to get permits in Ulaanbaatar. You must also register in Mörön.

Border permits are free and are processed in one to three working days. You'll need a map of where you intend to travel and passport copies. In a pinch, guesthouses can arrange the permit in Khatgal through their Mörön contacts. This involves handing over your passport for a few days (which many travellers are unwilling to do). Check the TCVC website for possible updates.

ℹ Getting There & Away

HITCHING

Since all traffic to Tsagaannuur and Renchinlkhumbe starts from Mörön your best bet is to hang around in Mörön and ask around for a ride from there.

HORSE

There is really only one way to get to the taiga in the warmer months: by horse. Horses can be hired in Tsagaannuur and this is best done through the TCVC in accordance with the Tsaatan wishes. Some travellers make the journey all the way from Khatgal – a return trip from Khatgal to Tsagaannuur, with a day's visit to the Tsaatan, will take from 14 to 20 days, which means a lot of time in the saddle. You could go from Khatgal to Tsagaannuur on an easy trail in about five days (bypassing Jiglegiin Am and Khövsgöl Nuur). If you do come from Khatgal, switch to fresh horses and a Tsaatan guide through the TCVC in Tsagaannuur. Horse hire in Tsagaannuur starts from T15,000 per day.

JEEP & MINIVAN

By chartered jeep you can get to Tsagaannuur from Mörön (but rarely from Khatgal) in a bone-crunching 10 to 12 hours, depending on the state of the road. You'll have to pay for all the petrol and pay the driver about US$70 a day. Contact the guesthouses in Mörön and ask if they can set you up with a vehicle, or arrange one through a UB tour operator.

With your own wheels, you can either take the picturesque but rough (and often muddy) road that runs from just south of Khatgal, via the rest stop of **Toom** (Тоом; GPS: N 50°23.139', E 099°18.804') and the town of Ulaan-Uul, before reaching the **fork** (GPS: N 50°50.453', E 099°18.407') which branches towards Renchinkhumbe and Tsagaannuur. If you have a particularly sturdy vehicle, you can try the old logging road that cuts through the mountains pretty much directly to Renchinlkhumbe from around the Jankhai pass (we witnessed three van-loads of shamans braving that road). From Mörön, there's a good but rather long road up north that runs through Bayanzürkh.

Two or three times a week Russian minivans run between Tsagaannuur and Mörön and Renchinlkhumbe and Mörön – a seat to either destination will cost around T30,000 to T50,000. Ask at the jeep stand in Mörön.

ℹ TOP UP ON PETROL!

As the towns in the Darkhad Depression in particular are subject to frequent power cuts, top up on petrol whenever you get the opportunity when travelling in the region. Sometimes there's no electricity for days, petrol pumps do not function and you can be stuck in some one-horse town for an interminable period of time.

Mörön to Terkhiin Tsagaan Nuur

A popular route out of Khövsgöl is south to Terkhiin Tsagaan Nuur in Arkhangai aimag. This is also an excellent road for cyclists. About 97km southwest of the aimag capital is **Zuun Nuur** (Зүүн Нуур; GPS: N 49°03.727', E 99°31.096'), a large lake and the scenic highlight of the region. There is good camping here or you can stay at the **Dalai Vam 2 ger camp** (☑ 8829 3524; GPS: N 49°02.870',

E 99°29.359'; per person US$40), on the southern side of the lake (meals T4000 to T7000). The lake is 13km north of Shine-Ider village.

Around 30km south of Shine-Ider, right on the main road, is an area of **standing stones and graves** (GPS: N 48°45.808', E 99°23.084'). A further 8km brings you to a scenic pass and the historic **Gelenkhuugiin Suvraga** (Гэлэнхүүгийн Суврага; GPS: N 48°41.182', E 99°22.650'), an old stupa built in 1890 by local hero Khainzan Gelenkhuu (1870–1937), who leapt off a 200m cliff with

VISITING THE TSAATAN

A visit to the Tsaatan community of reindeer herders is a fascinating experience. It's a rare chance to learn about a unique traditional way of life and a highlight of any trip to northern Mongolia (see p155). You can stay with the community and have the opportunity to volunteer for activities such as reindeer milking and churning milk to be made into cheese. You'll come away with a great appreciation for the remoteness and self-sufficiency of this tiny community.

However, irresponsible tourism, research and evangelical activities have put the Tsaatan culture and their reindeer at risk, and a trip must be approached with sensitivity. If you are planning a trip to the taiga, the Tsaatan prefer it if you organise it via the Tsaatan Community & Visitors Center (p157). The concept of the TCVC began in the mid-2000s after years of unregulated tourism to the Tsaatan camps. While tour operators were financially benefiting from running trips to the taiga, the Tsaatan themselves were often left empty-handed, despite being the main attraction to the area. Unfortunately, that is once more the case; the only tour company that works directly with the Tsaatan is Panoramic Journeys (p39).

The Tsaatan are happy to receive visitors who are genuinely interested in learning about their way of life. They'd rather not have visitors who are not interested in talking with them and are only keen to take photos, which makes them feel like zoo exhibits, or those who wash their clothes and dishes in the Tsaatan's drinking water and drop trash. Tour companies are often at fault as well: discouraging clients from bringing spending money, encouraging them to bring tents when there are guest teepees available, and bringing horses that are not used to reindeer.

Visiting the Tsaatan is difficult and exhausting. The climate is exceedingly harsh, the area is prone to insects, the terrain is rough and mountainous, and it's easy to get lost without a good local guide. Do not underestimate how sore you'll feel after five or more hours in the saddle.

If you do wish to visit, behave like a responsible guest. Give the community advance warning of your arrival. Bring your hosts a useful gift (toothpaste, good batteries, soap, colouring books for children, makeup for women, small torches, blocks of crystal salt for the reindeer, mementoes from your home country, etc). Do not bring sweets as there's no dentist here. Also make sure you rent horses via the TCVC. There have been incidents when horses from Khatgal and elsewhere, who were not used to reindeer, have freaked out and crippled some of the Tsaatan reindeer – the livelihood of the herders.

Be self-sufficient and carry more than enough food for yourself; the Tsaatan have horror stories to tell about visitors who turn up without food and deplete their already meagre supplies. Bring a tent (just in case), camping supplies and 100% DEET to keep the bugs at bay. Contribute a little to the community by staying a guest teepee (T10,000 per person). Bring small-denomination tögrög (not dollars!) in case you wish to purchase some handicrafts. Show willingness to engage in everyday activities; they'll be happy to put you to work! Bring your own interpreter, as even though one member of the community speaks English, she is not employed to work as your guide.

a set of sheepskin wings and flew as if he were some kind of Icarus-incarnate. From the pass it's an easy 19km to Jargalant.

Jargalant is a pretty town near the confluence of the Ider and Khonjil Gols. The *sum* is perhaps most famous for being the homeland of a herder named Öndöör Gongor (Tall Gongor, 1879–1931), who was 2.57m tall. The one attraction in town is **Jargalantiin Dugan** (Жаргалантын Дуган; also called Dashbijeliin Süm), an old, boarded-up monastery that dates back to 1890.

The best place to stay in Jargalant is the **Jargal Jiguur** (Жаргал Жигүүр; ☎ 11-450 093; admin@ajnew tour.mn; GPS: N 48°33.615', E 99°22.061'; per person US$20, meals US$8, shower US$2), a ger camp 3km south of town. The highlight of the camp is a **mineral spring pool** (you can see the natural pool across the river; just follow the pipes).

A cheaper option is **Wild Nature Guest Ger** (☎ 9550 5617; GPS: N 48°33.989', E 99°21.984'; per ger T20,000, shower US$3), between Jargal Jiguur and the town. The guest ger is run by a friendly local lady named Batchimeg; she may bring you delicious fresh cream and berries in the morning.

From Jargalant it's another 80km to **Terkhiin Tsagaan Nuur**. About 6km south of town are several **burial mounds**, including one with a tree growing from it. Some 26km south of Jargalant there is a small **ger hotel** and, on the hill behind it, a **Buddhist temple** constructed in 2001 to replace an older temple on the same spot. About 46km from Jargalant is **Orokhiin Davaa** (Орохийн Даваа; GPS: N 48°17.484', E 99°23.130'), the final pass on the way to Terkhiin Tsagaan Nuur. There is a delicious cold water **spring** by the road on the north side of the pass.

Eastern Mongolia

POP 191,400 / AREA 286,200 SQ KM

Why Go?

Eastern Mongolia is where heaven and earth fuse into one – a boundless blue sky colliding with an equally limitless sea of green. The occasional shack or ger reminds you that humans do inhabit this landscape, but for the most part it's an un- spoilt amphitheatre of bounding gazelle, scurrying marmots and jeep tracks that squiggle endlessly into the distance. This is one of the world's last great unharmed grassland ecosys- tems, and you can imagine yourself galloping along it on horseback. The new oil fields are bringing change, however, so get here before the prairie disappears. The other major feature of the region is the Khan Khentii Mountains. This was the homeland of Temujin, the embattled boy who grew up to become Chinggis Khaan. Travelling by horseback or jeep, you can visit places associated with the world's greatest conqueror. The final frontier, this is by far the most remote part of Mongolia, and a venture into its depths is a challenge even for the most experienced of travellers.

Best Chinggis Khaan Sights

➡ Burkhan Khalduun (p168)

➡ Deluun Boldog (p166)

➡ Chinggis Khaan obelisk (p167)

➡ Khajuu Bulag (p167)

Best Off-the-Beaten-Track

➡ Buir Nuur (p172)

➡ Ikh Burkhant (p173)

➡ Shiliin Bogd Uul (p177)

➡ Ganga Nuur (p176)

When to Go
Choibalsan

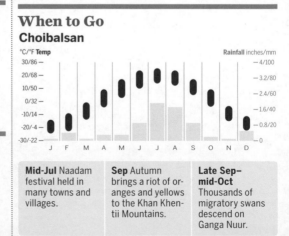

Mid-Jul Naadam festival held in many towns and villages.

Sep Autumn brings a riot of or- anges and yellows to the Khan Khen- tii Mountains.

Late Sep– mid-Oct Thousands of migratory swans descend on Ganga Nuur.

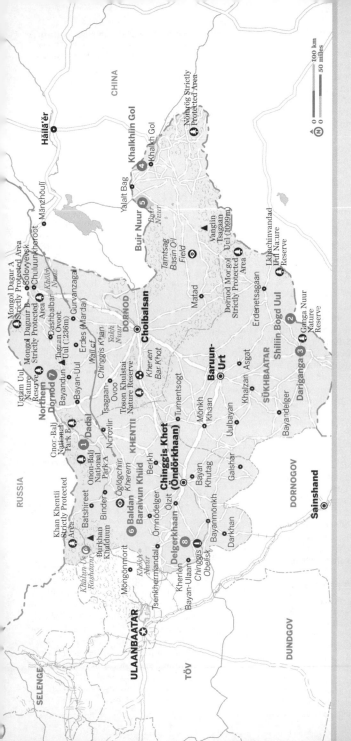

Eastern Mongolia Highlights

1 Spend a few days around **Dadal** (p166), a pretty village of log cabins and Chinggis Khaan legends.

2 Pay your respects to the local deities with an ascent of sacred **Shiliin Bogd Uul** (p177).

3 Tour the area around **Dariganga** (p176), rich in cultural relics and eerie volcanic landscapes.

4 Contemplate the war memorials and impressive stone statues around **Khalkhiin Gol** (p172).

5 Travel across the steppe to watch the sun rise and set over the immense **Buir Nuur** (p172).

6 Seek out the restored **Baldan Baraivun Khiid** (p165) and get blessed by a local lama.

7 Go in search of mysterious temple ruins and shamans in **Northern Dornod** (p173).

8 Restore your health with medicinal spring and lake waters around **Delgerkhaan** (p167).

History

The Tamtsagbulag Neolithic site in Dornod, active more than 4000 years ago, is proof that agriculture predated nomadic pastoralism on the eastern steppes. But it was the Kitan, a Manchurian tribal confederation, who made the first big impression on the region, building forts and farming communities in the 10th century, including Kherlen Bar Khot in Dornod.

Another Manchu tribe, the Jurchen, deposed the Kitan in the early 12th century, renamed itself the Jin, and returned eastern Mongolia to its warring ways. It wasn't until Chinggis Khaan united the fractured clans in 1206 that peace took over.

It was from Avarga (modern Delgerkhaan) that Chinggis launched expeditions south towards China. When the capital was moved to Karakorum in 1220, the region withdrew into obscurity. It wasn't until 1939 that eastern Mongolia was again in the headlines, this time as a battlefield between Japanese and joint Soviet–Mongolian forces. Heavy losses forced the Japanese military machine south, a crucial turning point in WWII.

The discovery of zinc and oil in the region in the 1990s brought the promise of development, with change hot on its heels. These natural resources have altered the local landscape, with oil wells and other mining infrastructure now a permanent fixture of the Dornod landscape.

Climate

Eastern Mongolia's climate and landscape have more in common with northeastern China than with Central Asia. Temperature extremes are less severe and winds less violent than in the west. While the Khan Khentii Mountains get a lot of rain in the summer, annual precipitation on the steppes is about 250mm. Winter daytime temperatures fall to -20°C but skies are usually blue.

ℹ Getting There & Away

A paved road connects Ulaanbaatar and Chinggis Khot and work is ongoing to take it to Baruun-Urt. The road to Choibalsan is also under construction. Both should be finished within the lifetime of this book. Other towns and attractions are connected by decent dirt or dirt and gravel roads, often boggy after heavy rains.

Buses for Chinggis Khot, Baruun-Urt and Choibalsan depart from Ulaanbaatar's Bayanzürkh Avto Vaksal bus station (p94). Private vehicles wait at the Naran Tuul (p87) jeep station. Another route into the region is through northern Khentii – daily minivans from Naran Tuul travel to Dadal via Ömnödelger and Binder (these are not well advertised so you may need a local to help you contact the drivers).

ℹ Getting Around

Public transport can get you to most towns in the region provided you're armed with the patience of an angel. But if you want to see what the region really has to offer you'll need your own transport.

KHENTII   ХЭНТИЙ

POP 67,500 / AREA 80,300 SQ KM

Khentii is Chinggis Khaan territory. The great man grew up here, established his empire on its grasslands and, from Delgerkhaan, launched his mighty horde at the heart of Asia. Few physical traces remain of the nomad empire, but armed with a copy of *The Secret History of the Mongols* and a GPS unit you could launch your own expedition to scour the land for the 50 or so historical sites relating to Chinggis Khaan's life.

Appropriately enough for the region that spawned a horseback warlord, parts of this lush land are best explored on the back of a horse. It's named for the Khentii Nuruu (Khentii Mountain Range) that's part of the giant 1.2-million-hectare Khan Khentii Strictly Protected Area, which is mostly in Töv aimag (p106).

Chinggis Khot (Öndörkhaan)
Чингис Хот (Өндөрхаан)

🖉 7056. 01562 / POP 19,000 / ELEV 1027M

A centre of relative sophistication in the middle of barren plains, the aimag capital of Chinggis Khot (Chinggis City), previously known as Öndörkhaan (Supreme Emperor), was renamed in 2013 in honour of Chinggis Khan. It is a welcome sight, with its tree-lined streets, scattered Chinggis Khaan monuments and a small collection of well-preserved 18th-century buildings. It sits on the northern bank of the Kherlen Gol, which provides a fishing hole for locals and riverside camping spots for travellers, though during Naadam these get way too busy. Chinggis Khot celebrates Naadam in late July rather than on 11 July.

◉ Sights

★ **Ethnography Museum**   MUSEUM
(☑01562-22187; admission T2000; ◷9am-1pm & 2-6pm Tue-Sat) This excellent museum is inside the 18th-century home of the Tsetseg Khan, who governed most of eastern Mongolia during the Manchu reign. Standout exhibits include ethnic costumes and Khalkha silver jewellery, a shaman outfit complete with skull and feathers, a portrait of the last Tsetseg Khan, painted in 1923, handmade chess sets, and wooden spiral puzzles. The corner building houses 13th-century weaponry including arrowheads and daggers. Also, look out for the ceremonial ger with delicately carved wood furnishing and ornaments.

Shadavdarjaliin Khiid   BUDDHIST MONASTERY
(Шадавдаржаалийн Хийд) Shadavdarjaliin Khiid, in the western part of town near the Sports Palace, is a freshly painted, walled temple complex with some *ovoo* (shamanistic offering) trees and a dozen monks. The original monastery in this area was built in 1660 and housed the first Buddhist philosophy school in Mongolia and at its peak, before the Stalinist purges of 1938, the monastery was home to more than 1000 monks.

Aimag Museum   MUSEUM
(Аймгийн Музей; admission T2000; ◷9am-1pm & 2-6pm Tue-Sat) The small Aimag Museum features a mastodon tusk, a Protoceratops skull, some Chinggis Khaan–era armour and an array of stuffed aimag wildlife, including a saluting bear. In the central park, across the road, you'll find **statues of famous wrestlers** from this aimag – a popular photo stop for locals.

Balbal   MONUMENT
(GPS: N 47°16.722', E 110°36.096') A well-preserved Turkic-era *balbal* (stone grave marker) is 7km west of Chinggis Khot, past the airport.

The squat-figured statue, covered in blue silk *hadak* (ritual scarves), has a disproportionately large head with pronounced eyebrows and deep-set eyes. His long hair is curled behind his ears, an unusual feature for this type of statue.

🛏 Sleeping

If you want to camp, head south past the wrestling stadium, and walk along the Kherlen Gol to the west until you've found a quiet spot.

Negdelchin Hotel   HOTEL $
(Нэгдэлчин Төв; ☑01562-22333; d T15,000-30,000, lux T50,000) The Negdelchin sports some of the best rooms in town, though still with ubiquitous box-spring beds. The

Chinggis Khot (Öndörkhaan)

EASTERN MONGOLIA CHINGGIS KHOT (ÖNDÖRKHAAN)

cheapest doubles share facilities and have enough room to swing only the smallest of cats. Try a lux room for a little more space. There is a decent Chinese restaurant downstairs.

Jonon Hotel　　　　　　　　HOTEL $
(Жонон Төв; ☑ 01562-23845, 9956 2222; r per person T10,000, half-lux/lux T30,000/50,000; ℗) About 350m north of Government House, this hotel looks better from the outside than the inside, but it's the one place where you can find room even during Naadam. If you're really pinching your pennies, you can opt for a spartan four-person room. Only the lux rooms have private showers.

★Khanburged Hotel　　　　　HOTEL $$
(☑ 8924 7337, 9890 6867; d/half-lux/lux T55,000/70,000/85,000; ℗ 🛜) Easily the city's swishest hotel, this professionally run new place comes with all the bells and whistles: marble-floored lobby, helpful receptionists and stylish rooms decked out in creams and browns. There's reliable hot water in the modern bathrooms and it's in a great central location.

✖ Eating & Drinking

Oasis　　　　　　　　INTERNATIONAL $
(Temujiidiin Gudamj; meals T4000-6000; ⊙ 10.30am-8.30pm; 🔟) Adding a little diversity to the restaurant scene in Chinggis Khot, this small cafe serves tacos, pizzas, pastas, shakes and burgers, plus some Korean dishes. It's on the 2nd floor, next to the Modern Bar.

Negdelchin　　　　　　　CHINESE $$
(Temujiidiin Gudamj; mains T6500-12,000; ⊙ 8.30am-10.30pm) In the hotel of the same name, this place serves large portions of tasty Chinese dishes; expect such exotica as black fungus and ribs.

ℹ Information

Internet Cafe (per hr T600; ⊙ 8am-9pm Mon-Fri, 10am-5pm Sat & Sun) In the Telecom office.
Telecom Office (⊙ 24hr) On the eastern end of the main road; the post office is also located here.
XacBank (Хас Банк; ⊙ 9am-5pm Mon-Fri) Changes dollars and offers cash advances on Visa.

ℹ DIY EASTERN MONGOLIA

For independent travellers, eastern Mongolia is both a godsend and a logistical nightmare. You're certainly not likely to be tripping over ger-loads of Gobi-lovers here, but making your solitary way across this region requires a considerable amount of patience, effort and forward planning.

You can't just wing it, as the region's biggest highlights lie in the border area and even non-local Mongolians require permission to travel here. You must have a set itinerary if you wish to travel beyond the major cities, and you must obtain permission in advance from the Border Protection Office in Ulaanbaatar (p92). Make the itinerary as detailed as possible and specify the order in which you wish to visit the proposed locations. Easy enough? On the road, you will have to register at police stations or military bases in Batshireet, Dadal, Choibalsan, Khalkh Gol and other areas. As rules change from time to time, find out in Ulaanbaatar exactly where you have to register – and register you must, since if you fail to register at one of your set itinerary points, when you then try to register at your next destination, the police could, in theory, send you back to your previous destination to register before you can proceed further. If you don't speak Mongolian, registering can be tricky, as can renting a horse and anything else that requires language skills.

Always carry your passport, as there are several military checkpoints, particularly in the easternmost part of the region, and a photocopy just won't do.

All the highlights require you to have your own wheels...or hooves. It's possible to rent jeeps with drivers in several towns, though it's easiest in Ulaanbaatar. As northern Khentii tends to suffer from muddy roads bad enough to sink a jeep, the best way to explore the region is on horseback; both Batshireet and Dadal are good places to launch an expedition. A GPS is essential for finding more remote sites. Unless you're supremely confident of your equestrian abilities and have a GPS, it's not advisable to go off without a guide. That's about it. Not put off yet? Then you qualify for our 'most intrepid traveller' award.

❶ Getting There & Away

BUS, MINIVAN & JEEP

Two daily buses head to Ulaanbaatar (T13,200) at 8am and 4pm. Daily buses to Choibalsan and Baruun-Urt both originate in Ulaanbaatar so they tend to be full by the time they arrive. Both pass through between 1pm and 2pm, to check availability, wait at the **Hangard petrol station** (Хангард).

Daily taxis and minivans go between Ulaanbaatar and Chinggis Khot (taxis T20,000, vans T13,000, five hours, 331km). To go further east your best bet is to wait for the bus.

Early morning postal trucks run to Dadal (T15,200) on weekdays, to Binder (T10,100) on Tuesday and Thursday, and to Batshireet (T11,300) on Monday and Thursday. It's best to hire your own jeep and driver from Ulaanbaatar.

HITCHING

Chinggis Khot is the gateway for eastern Mongolia, so all vehicles heading to Dornod and Sükhbaatar aimags come through here. Getting a lift to Ulaanbaatar, Choibalsan and Baruun-Urt is comparatively easy.

Khökh Nuur   Хөх Нуур

According to *The Secret History of the Mongols*, it was at **Khökh Nuur** (Blue Lake, Хөх Нуур; GPS: N 48°01.150', E 108°56.450') that Temüjin first proclaimed himself a khaan (emperor) of the Mongol tribe. It's a great place for a coronation site; the imaginatively-named Blue Lake nestles at the foot of what is called **Heart-Shaped Mountain**.

The lake is about 35km northwest of Tsenkhermandal, off the Ulaanbaatar–Chinggis Khot road. Roads can be muddy and you'll need your own transport and a driver who knows where it is. If you're approaching from the west, a small 'Хөх Нуур' sign several kilometres west of the Tsenkhermandal turnoff indicates a shortcut.

You can camp in the woods on the southwest side of the lake, or, alternatively, rent one of the two-storey log cabins at **Khar Zurkhnii Khukh Nuur** (Хар Зурхний Хөх Нуур; ☑9917 1675; GPS: N 48°01.042', E 108°57.029'; 3-/6-person cabin with meals US$40/80). It's popular with locals, so can get rowdy on weekends.

Baldan Baraivun Khiid
Балдан Барайвун Хийд

This **monastery** (GPS: N 48°11.819', E 109°29.402'; admission T5000) in Ömnödelger *sum* was first built in 1700. At its peak it was one

NATIONAL PARKS OF KHENTII

Khan Khentii Strictly Protected Area
(1.2 million hectares; p162) Mostly in Töv aimag, the strictly protected area includes the northwest corner of Khentii, protecting taiga, steppe and the sacred mountain Burkhan Khalduun (p168).

Onon-Balj National Park (415,752 hectares; p166) Protects taiga and steppe along the Mongolia–Russia border. It's divided into two parts; part A is west of Dadal and part B covers the area to the northeast.

of the three largest monasteries in Mongolia and home to 5000 lamas. Communist forces destroyed it in the 1930s. It has now been mostly restored, the main temple with splendid dragon motifs on the ceiling was renovated in 2010. Around 10 lamas are back and if you're lucky, one of them will chant a blessing over you and anoint you with water. By the main gate there's a map showing a circular walk that takes in the temple buildings, the ruins, a mountain viewpoint and **Eej (Mother) Cave**, which acts as a purifying place for anyone who passes through it.

The road to the monastery heads north from Khangil Nuur and goes straight over the hills; it is about 9km. A flatter but more circuitous route goes northeast from Khangil Nuur. You can camp nearby, stay at the small **ger camp** (☑9866 5324; GPS: N 48°11.618', E 109°29.403'; ger per person T10,000) around the corner or proceed to the **Bayangol Ger Camp** (☑9912 5293, 11-451 016; GPS: N 46°09.621', E 105°45.590'; per person with/without food US$45/25), 15km to the west.

About 17km past the monastery, on the way to Binder, are two **deer stones** (GPS: N 48°11.920', E 109°35.714'), which may have served as burial markers during the Bronze and Iron Ages.

Öglögchiin Kherem
Өглөгчийн Хэрэм

Literally 'Almsgivers Wall', but also known as 'Chinggis Khaan's Castle', this 3.2km-long **stone wall** (GPS: N 48°24.443', E 110°11.812'), believed to date from the 8th century, stretches around a rocky slope in Batshireet *sum*. It was once thought to be a defensive work or a game preserve, but recent archaeological digs by a Mongolian–American research team have identified at least 60 ancient graves within the walls, indicating that it may have been a royal cemetery. Chinggis would be hard pressed to live in his 'castle' as all that's left is the crumbling fortification several feet high. The site is 8km west of the road from Chinggis Khot to Batshireet.

Close to the turn-off to Öglögchiin Kherem is the most important **ovoo** (GPS: N48 °22.757′, E 110°17.439′) in the area, as well as **Rashaan Khad** (GPS: N 48°22.763′, E 110°17.950′), a huge rock with 20 different types of (barely discernible) script carved upon it.

Binder   Биндэр

At the confluence of the Khurkh and Onon Gols, the village of Binder is a good place to rustle up some horses for an expedition to Burkhan Khalduun or to dine at one of the *tsainii gazar* (teahouses) on your way to or from Dadal. An excellent place to stay is the luxurious **Ichon Khurkh Urguu ger camp** (☑7733 5588; GPS: N 48°34.891′, E 110°41.545′; 4-person ger T40,000), 7km from the village. Each comfortable bed has its own mosquito net, there are hot showers, and hot meals are served on request. You'll need to summon up your nerve and plunge your vehicle into the shallow part of the river (follow the other jeep tracks).

OFF THE BEATEN TRACK

BATSHIREET   БАТШИРЭЭТ

Remote Batshireet, 45km northwest of Binder, with its wide dirt streets, is worth a detour for some excellent trekking, camping and fishing opportunities. From this small Buriat community of around 3000 people you can follow the Eg Gol to the Onon and trek back to Binder. More challenging trails lead west towards the Khan Khentii Strictly Protected Area (p106) and Burkhan Khalduun; come armed with a good map and GPS.

The town itself is pretty charmless; the only place to stay is **Anu Hotel** (Ану Төв; per person T10,000) located near the Telecom office; its spartan rooms containing saggy beds. It can arrange horses for T10,000 per day and fishing trips, but no English is spoken.

If you are travelling onto Dadal you'll need to cross the Onon Gol. A hilly road behind the ger camp leads down to the **pontoon** (GPS: N 48°35.835′, E 110°43.419′; T10,000; ☺8am-6pm) dock. Passengers pull the small car ferry across the river using a cable. Alternatively, there's a **bridge** across the river a few kilometres south of Binder.

Dadal   Дадал

He united the many nomadic tribes of northeast Asia, subjugated huge chunks of Central Asia, Rus, Europe, the Middle East and China, and created the Mongol empire which became the largest contiguous empire in history. Yet the fearsome Chinggis Khaan's origins are surprisingly humble. As written in *The Secret History of the Mongols*, it is now generally accepted that he was born at the junction of the Onon and Balj Gols in Dadal *sum*, near the town of the same name (though his date of birth is still subject to great conjecture).

Dadal is a gorgeous area of lakes, rivers, forests and log huts. Besides the few sights associated with the Great Khaan there's good hiking to be had around Dadal, and the village itself is a cheerful place of wide dirt streets, cute log cabins and a few *tsainii gazar*.

If you approach Dadal from the south, via Norovin, a gleaming white **gate** (GPS: N 48°59.557′, E 111°36.688′), flanked with steles and statues of Mongol warriors, welcomes you in.

The 415,752-hectare **Onon-Balj National Park** (entrance T3000), extending north from the village towards Russia, offers enticing **camping spots**, **fishing holes** and chances for spotting **wildlife**. Buy your national park ticket (T3000) at the WWF office (p169).

◉ Sights

★**Deluun Boldog**   MONUMENT
(Дэлүүн Болдог) About 3.5km north of Dadal village is a collection of hills known as Deluun Boldog. On top of one of the hills is a **stone marker** (GPS: N 49°03.155′, E 111°38.590′), erected in 1990 to commemorate the 750th anniversary of the writing of *The Secret History of the Mongols*. The inscription says that Chinggis Khaan was born here in 1162. Behind it is a large *ovoo* emitting a pungent smell thanks to all the food offerings.

DELGERKHAAN   ДЭЛГЭРХААН

Locals, and some historians, claim that Avarga, not Karakorum, was the first capital of the Mongol empire. The ancient tent-city was located in the modern-day Delgerkhan *sum* (district), on a 20km-wide plain, Khödöö Aral (Countryside Island), so named because it is encircled by the Kherlen and Tsenkheriin Gols.

As in days of old, the town is a huge ger encampment bisected by several streets, with a few incongruous-looking wooden houses sticking up here and there.

The main sight is the **Avarga Toson Nuur** (Аварга-Тосон Нyyp; GPS: N 47°10.978', E 109°08.696'), the lake that flanks Delgerkhaan, fenced off to keep out livestock and campers. Its water and mud are reputed to have medicinal properties, and it's the one place in eastern Mongolia where you'll find locals bathing, strolling and jogging around the lake. On one bank stands an impressive *ovoo;* on the other, a shrine.

Thirteen kilometres south of Delgerkhaan village stands the **Chinggis obelisk** (GPS: N 47°06.155', E 109°09.363'), featuring the visage of the khaan on one side. It was erected in 1990 to commemorate the 750th anniversary of the writing of *The Secret History of the Mongols*. The symbols on the side of the obelisk are the brands used by about 300 different clans in the area for marking livestock.

One kilometre east of the statue is the **Avarga Toson Mineral Spring** (GPS: N 47°05.662', E 109°10.114'; T100), from which Ögedei Khaan drank and was cured of a serious stomach ailment. You can fill your water bottles with the delicious, naturally slightly salty and carbonated spring water at a pump house near the site for T100 a bottle.

Take the paved road between Ulaanbaatar and Chinggis Khot to Jargaltkhaan, then travel 42km southwest on a decent dirt road to Delgerkhaan.

Hunting Museum   MUSEUM
(admission T2000) For an offbeat adventure, drop by the home of Zundoi-Davag, a 96-year-old hunter who will be happy to show you his contribution to the demise of endangered species, such as the snow leopard and the wolverine, sitting cheek by jowl in the large barn. He may also regale you with hunting stories and show off his impressive collection of antique guns. His **summer camp** (ger) is about 5km northwest of Dadal, literally over the hill and through the woods. A local should be able to take you there on horseback, motorbike (T5000) or jeep (T10,000).

Chinggis Khaan Obelisk   MONUMENT
This enormous, wedge-shaped white rock was placed in the middle of the Gurvan Nuur holiday camp in 1962 to commemorate the 800th anniversary of Chinggis' birth. This was at the height of the communist era, though somehow the monument itself was allowed to stand.

★ Khajuu Bulag   SPRING
(GPS: N 49°02.787', E 111°36.867') This trickle of a mineral water spring, where Chinggis Khaan once allegedly drank, is about 2.2km west of Deluun Boldog and is easily spotted by the beribboned tree next to it. Fill your bottles, but watch out for the leeches!

Dadal Museum   MUSEUM
(admission T5000) The entertaining village museum consists of a wooden ger, with a statue of young Temuujin out front, and paintings of the grown-up Khaan and his descendants inside, along with black stallion tail-hair pennants (the most prestigious kind!), a map depicting Mongol empire conquest and a model of a massive ger, pulled by scores of oxen. Standout exhibits inside the second building include a particularly creepy artistic depiction of Chinggis Khaan, Buriat swan-head fiddles and an intricately carved horse-sweat scraper. The caretaker tends to be around the Government House next door.

Stupa Memorial   MONUMENT
(GPS: N 49°01.085', E 111°36.761') This memorial, comprising three stupas, was built to honour the 607 people from Dadal who died in the political repression of the 1930s. The list of names is printed on the main prayer wheel. The Buriats were treated much more harshly than Khalkh Mongols during the purge era, largely due to rumours that some Buriats were in league with the Japanese.

🏃 Activities
There are several **hiking** and **horse-riding** routes out of Dadal. Locals recommend the 30km hike to the junction of the Onon and

BURKHAN KHALDUUN

Remote **Burkhan Khalduun** (Бурхан Халдуун; GPS: N 48°45.728′, E 109°00.629′), elevation 2350m, is one of the sites mooted as the burial place of Chinggis Khaan, and also Mongolia's holiest mountain. Whether or not Chinggis was buried at God's Hill, *The Secret History of the Mongols* does describe how the khaan hid here as a young man and later returned to give praise to the mountain and give thanks for his successes.

Because of its auspicious connections, Mongolians climb the mountain, topped with many **ovoos** (GPS: N 48°45.430′, E 109°00.300′), to gain strength and good luck. To get to this remote location you'll need to head to Möngönmorit in Töv, and then travel north along the Kherlen Gol. Foreigners may only travel as far as the foot of the mountain as they are not allowed to climb it and there are plans to create an observation route to make their visit worthwhile.

Around 22km due north of Burkhan Khalduun (as the falcon flies) is **Khalun Us Rashant** (Hot Water Springs; GPS: N 48°57.206′, E 109°00.217′). The site has more than a dozen hot springs, a collection of log bathhouses and a small **Buddhist temple** (built in honour of Zanabazar, who frequented the site).

In warmer months, coming on horseback from Batshireet is your best bet. (It's also possible to drive there in winter when the ground freezes.)

Balj Gols, or the 45km trek further along the Onon Gol to the gorge at the confluence of the Onon and Agats Gols. You'll need to inform the border patrol of your itinerary and it would be wise to take a local guide; ask at the ger camps or track down Dorjsuren, who runs the eponymous homestay.

There is good **fishing** in the area. Get a permit at the Government House (T10,000, good for five days), next to the Dadal Museum, or with the help of a licensed tour operator.

🎊 Festivals

Dadal is a great place to be for **Naadam** (11 and 12 July). You can get up close and personal with the archers and jockeys, and perhaps make up the numbers in the wrestling tourney!

🛌 Sleeping & Eating

This is perfect camping country, so just find a secluded spot away from the village. There are also two brand new ger camps near the Chinggis Khaan obelisk. Dadal has a few *guanz* (canteens/restaurants) of comparable quality that serve up hot soup and goulash.

Dorjsuren's Homestay   HOMESTAY $
(📞9822 4720, 9997 7534; dorjsurengalsan2009@yahoo.com; GPS: N 49°01.280′, E 111°38.562′; per person about T10,000; @) Dorjsuren, a friendly retired Buriat, has a small log cabin for guests next to his home, consisting of a rather cramped but tidy dorm and a hot-water shower block (T2000). There's a cast-iron stove for cooking and Dorjsuren can provide a breakfast of tea, homemade bread and clotted cream (and wild strawberry jam in summer!) for T3000. It is a 10-minute walk southeast of the centre, across the river, but there is no sign, so ask for directions from the Telecom office. Dorjsuren can arrange horse riding, ice-fishing in winter and other activities.

Chingisiin Deluun Nuur   TOURIST GER CAMP $
(Чингисийн Дэлүүн Нуур; 📞9820 4132, 9861 2494; GPS: N 49°02.233′, E 111°39.646′; per person with/without meals T40,000/20,000) Choose between a room in a log cabin with your own porch or a bed in a four-person ger at this attractive new ger camp in a lakeside meadow. The cabins have intermittent electricity and mosquito nets. Meals available on request.

★Altargara   TOURIST GER CAMP $$
(Алтаргана; 📞9972 3629, 9833 1384; gombogerel@yahoo.com; per person with/without breakfast US$22/19) Sitting in a beautiful clearing, this cheerful collection of two-storey log cabins and gers is the best tourist camp in the area. English is spoken, there are reliable hot showers, a chill-out picnic area with tables, and hot meals can be ordered in advance from the dining room. Our one quibble is the strange locking system in the cabins.

ℹ️ Information

Dadal is in a sensitive border area so it's best to register with the police – if you can find them, as the two police officers are often away. If you are heading any further out of town, it's also a good idea to register with the border guards, on the western side of Dadal.

The closest thing Dadal has to a tourist information centre is the **WWF office** (GPS: N 49°01.771', E 111°38.410') located between the village and Chinggisiin Gurvan Nuur ger camp. Staff here sell tickets to the Onon-Balj National Park; if you're planning to stay at any of the three ger camps, the T3000 national park fee is compulsory.

ℹ Getting There & Away

One minivan or jeep a day runs to Ulaanbaatar (T30,000, 515km, 12 to 22 hours), and there's a bus on Wednesday, Friday and Sunday (T25,000).

A postal truck travels from Chinggis Khot (T15,000) every Monday and Thursday morning at around 7am, returning to Chinggis Khot on the same day.

Ask around the shops for the few vehicles for hire. Expect to pay at least T60,000 per day, depending on your route, plus petrol.

For travel from Dadal to Chinggis Khot or Dornod (but not Binder), you'll need to cross the Onon Gol at a lone bridge crossing (GPS: N 48°50.403', E 111°38.746').

DORNOD   ДОРНОД

POP 71,300 / AREA 123,600 SQ KM

Enough to sate anyone's love of wide open spaces, Dornod is pure steppe, with pancake-flat grassland in all directions for days on end. It's an inhospitable land for humans, with few water sources beyond the splendid Buir Nuur, and equally few places to ask for directions. An especially remote region in a country where the word 'remote' can so easily be overused, Dornod presents a challenge even to the most experienced of travellers. Conversely, it's an important ecological zone and habitat for white-tailed gazelle, which can outrun even the best jeep driver.

In a land that most historians forgot, fierce battles were fought by joint Soviet–Mongolian forces against the Japanese at Khalkhiin Gol in 1939. Their traces remain, as does a mysterious stone giant from a bygone era. Natural attractions include Khökh Nuur, the lowest point in the country; and some nature reserves – the last bastion of highly endangered wildlife.

The northern *sums* of Bayan-Uul, Bayandun and Dashbalbar are home to the Buriats, who still practise traditional shamanism; if you are lucky, you may be able to meet a shaman or stumble upon a shamanist ceremony.

Choibalsan   Чойбалсан

🖉 7058, 01582 / POP 38,537 / ELEV 747M

Lying on the banks of the Kherlen Gol, 324km downstream from Chinggis Khot, is Choibalsan, Mongolia's easternmost capital and a most welcome sight if you're craving a hot shower, a decent bed, and an opportunity to dine out that doesn't involve camping food after days in the steppe. It's in two parts: a half-abandoned district to the west where there was widespread looting following the Russian departure in 1990, and a more functional eastern section. Russia is not quite out of the picture; Choibalsan is twinned with Chita, poor thing.

Centuries ago, the city was a trading centre and part of a caravan route across northeast Asia. In 1941 it was named after the Stalinist stooge Khorloogiin Choibalsan, an honour bequeathed while the dictator was still in power.

Although the city is spread out along a 5km-long main street, most accommodation options, restaurants and facilities are clustered around the Kherlen Hotel.

◉ Sights

★ **Aimag Museum & Gallery**   MUSEUM
(admission incl Natural History Museum T7000; ⊙10am-5pm Mon-Fri, to 3pm Sat & Sun) In the former Government House, the thorough collections here stampede through the aimag's history, from Stone Age and Bronze Age finds to the communist years and beyond. Standout exhibits include a painting of Nine Punishments, one of which involves a man wearing female underwear, fascinating war photos, some Choibalsan memorabilia including his desk and short-wave radio (a real antique gem) and fine examples of national costume, including a shaman's outfit and an elaborate headdress weighing 6kg.

Natural History Museum   MUSEUM
(admission incl Aimag Museum T7000; ⊙10am-5pm Mon-Fri, to 3pm Sat & Sun) Here you'll find a collection of stuffed wildlife from around the aimag, wearing bemused expressions as an unintended effect of the inexpert taxidermy, plus mildly interesting exhibits on local geology and flora. Entry is free if you've already paid for the Aimag Museum.

Choibalsan

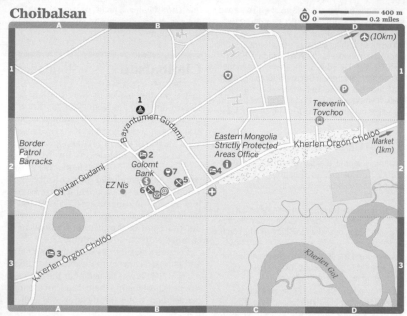

Mongolian Heroes' Memorial　MONUMENT
This large arch with a soldier on horseback flying through it towards the enemy is one of the more dramatic pieces of Stalinist architecture in Mongolia. Mosaics depicts cavalry stampeding into battle behind it. A small Soviet tank next to the monument saw action during the 1939 Khalkhiin Gol war.

Danrig Danjaalin Khiid　BUDDHIST MONASTERY
(Данриг Данжаалин Хийд) This monastery was built around 1840 and was once very active. It contained three northern temples and four southern temples, but less than half the 800 monks could be accommodated at one time, so most had to pray outside. It was closed in 1937. The monastery reopened in 1990 and has two small temples where about a dozen monks worship. It's located about 400m behind the Kherlen Hotel.

🛏 Sleeping

A new upmarket hotel, the Royal Palace, was due to open imminently when we visited; it's 100m east of To Van Hotel.

Chadanguud　HOTEL $$
(Чадангууд; ☏ 9957 7427, 01582-22355; half-lux/lux T40,000/43,000; ▣ 🛜) Spacious, renovated rooms? Check. Powerful hot showers? Check. Wi-fi in all the rooms, in spite of the thick walls? You betcha. The exterior of Soviet throwback Chadanguud may not inspire confidence, but inside it's one pleasant surprise after another. There's delicious rice porridge for breakfast, too.

★ To Van Hotel　HOTEL $$$
(To Van Зочид Буудал; ☏ 9958 7438, 7058 4025; Kherlen Örgön Chölöö; s/d/tr with breakfast from T80,000/100,000/60,000; ▣ 🛜) When Mongolia's president visits Choibalsan, he stays here. Probably because he appreciates a proper, comfortable mattress rather than the ubiquitous box-spring ones available

elsewhere. Expect stylish, well-lit rooms with flat plasma-screen TVs and wi-fi that functions. Even the 'economy' triple is a great bet.

East Palace Hotel HOTEL $$$
(East Palace Зочид Буудал; ☑01582-22277, 9906 6777; Kherlen Örgön Chölöö; s/tw with breakfast from T50,000/90,000; ☎) East Palace has comfortable, modern rooms with bright colours and lots of sunlight, as well as a sauna and fitness room. They may not have a presidential suite, but you can stay in 'parliament' (T150,000). It's about 600m west of the centre.

✗ Eating & Drinking

Both the To Van and the East Palace hotels have decent restaurants.

Khishig Supermarket SUPERMARKET $
(Хишиг; ⊙9am-10pm Mon-Sat, noon-7pm Sun) Next to the post office.

★Azu Restaurant CHINESE $$
(Азу Ресторан; Kherlen Örgön Chölöö; mains T8000-12,000) Delicious smells lure you into this pink restaurant, sit you down at one of the dark-wood tables and make sure you order one of the sizzling platters of spicy pork with vegetables, or a noodle dish, or, or...it doesn't matter, it's all glorious. This great restaurant is perpetually packed with locals who come for its Chinese-style offerings.

Winners Pub PUB
(⊙noon-11pm Mon-Sat) The first theme pub in Choibalsan sports English Premier League paraphernalia on the walls, comfy red-leather sofas and a variety of Western and Mongolian dishes. The limited beer menu (Heineken? Really??) doesn't score too highly with us, though.

🔒 Shopping

Market MARKET
(Зах; ⊙9am-7pm) Choibalsan's proximity to China means that its market is well stocked. Purchase anything from fresh produce, dried dairy products and a local relish made of spring onion and garlic (great for livening up that mutton!) to saddles, Mongolian hats and boots.

ℹ Information

Eastern Mongolia Strictly Protected Areas Office (☑9901 9697, 7058 3373; dornodmongol_mon@yahoo.com; ⊙8am-5pm Mon-Fri) Pro-

vides information on visiting protected areas in both Dornod and Sükhbaatar aimags. Arranges permits and sells tickets to protected areas and nature reserves. If you stop by to enquire about visiting protected areas, they will make you pay the T5000 protected area fee, just in case.

Golomt Bank (Голомт Банк; Kherlen Örgön Chölöö) Next to Khishig Supermarket.

Internet Centre (per hr T600; ⊙8am-10pm) Inside the Telecom office.

Post Office (Kherlen Örgön Chölöö) Next door to the Telecom office.

Telecom Office (Kherlen Örgön Chölöö; ⊙6am-6pm)

ℹ Getting There & Away

AIR

EZ Nis (☑7058 4477; www.eznisairways.com; 2nd floor, Galttai Invest Building) flies to/from Ulaanbaatar on Thursday and Sunday (one way/return US$76/152). The office is near the Trade & Development Bank. The airport is about 10km east of the centre; around T14,000 by taxi.

BUS, MINIVAN & JEEP

Buses depart for the Bayanzürkh Avto Vaksal (p94) bus station in Ulaanbaatar (T31,000, 13 hours, 655km) daily at 8am and 4pm from **Teevriin Tovchoo** (Тээврийн Товчоо; ☑7058 4845) at the eastern end of town. From the same station it's also possible to get a seat in a minivan for T36,000 to Ulaanbaatar or T16,000 to Chinggis Khot, which doesn't have a specific departure time but generally leaves when full.

Private minivans and jeeps run between Ulaanbaatar and Choibalsan daily (T36,000), departing from Ulaanbaatar's Naran Tuul jeep station (p87). Minivans from Choibalsan market depart when full. Private vans and jeeps (also from the market) go to Chinggis Khot (T15,000, 324km), Baruun-Urt (T20,000, 191km) and, less frequently, nearby sums such as Bayandun (T20,000).

Local drivers charge around T80,000 per day plus petrol. A postal minivan to Khalkhiin Gol (T17,000, 10 hours) leaves on Wednesday at 8am.

HITCHING

Choibalsan is a large city by Mongolian standards, so hitching a ride on a truck or any other vehicle in or out of the city should not be difficult. Ask around the market.

Kherlen Bar Khot
Хэрлэн Бар Хот

These small-scale **ruins** (GPS: N 48°03.287', E 113°21.865') consisting of the remains of four temples and eroded pedestals of statues, as well as a poorly preserved 10m-high brick

NATIONAL PARKS OF DORNOD

Dornod aimag is the focus of numerous environmental projects that protect one of the world's last undisturbed grasslands.

Mongol Daguur Strictly Protected Area (103,016 hectares) This is divided into northern 'A' and southern 'B' sections. Mongol Daguur A is hill steppe and wetland bordering Russia's Tari Nuur and Daurski Reserve, protecting endemic species such as the Daurian hedgehog; Mongol Daguur B, along the Ulz Gol, protects the *tsen togoruu* (white-naped crane) and other endangered birds. The area is part of a 1-million-hectare international reserve, linking the Siberian taiga with the inner-Asian steppe.

Nömrög Strictly Protected Area (311,205 hectares) An unpopulated area, which contains rare species of moose, crane, otter and bear. Ecologically distinct from the rest of Mongolia, the area takes in the transition zone from the eastern Mongolian steppe to the mountains and forest of Manchuria. Access is restricted to all but research biologists.

Toson Khulstai Nature Reserve (469,928 hectares) The nature reserve protects large herds of white-tailed gazelle; it's an easy detour if travelling between Khentii and Dornod.

Ugtam Uul Nature Reserve (46,100 hectares) Forested area that contains wildlife and the ruins of an old temple.

tower is all that remains of a 12th-century fortress town that was once part of the ancient state of Qidan.

Kherlen Bar Khot is about 90km west of Choibalsan, on the main road between Choibalsan and Chinggis Khot. It is worth a look only if you have your own vehicle and are heading that way.

Buir Nuur   Буйр Нуур

This vast 40km lake on Mongolia's eastern thumb is well known for its large stocks of fish and its bird life, particularly in the northeast area around the Khalkhiin Gol delta. Given that the northern shore is in China, most of the fish end up on the plates of Chinese restaurants – a source of much bitterness on the Mongolian side.

The area around the lake is Mongolia's equivalent of Arabia's Empty Quarter – it's seriously remote, and the only way to get there is by jeep from Choibalsan, 285km away over an interminable flat dirt road that runs through mostly featureless grassland (allow at least nine hours). The road passes through a military checkpoint (make sure your paperwork is in order) and skirts an oil field before following the eastern shore of the lake.

There's the deserted **Buir Nuur ger camp** (GPS: N 47°51.652', E 117°53.231'), with flimsy locks, towards its northern end, but the best place to pitch a tent is by the lake shore, near the small **Buddha shrine** (GPS:

N 47°51.687', E 117°53.494'), where you can watch the spectacular crimson-and-gold show called sunset. The mosquitoes love the view too, so come prepared.

Khalkhiin Gol   Халхын Гол

In 1939, the Khalkhiin Gol (Khalkhiin River) in the far eastern part of Dornod ran red with blood as Japan tried to realise its ambition of adding Siberia to its territory. Unfortunately for Japan, Mongolia got in the way, and it's on these river banks that the decisive battles between the Japanese and the joint Soviet and Mongolia forces took place.

⊙ Sights

War Memorials   MONUMENTS
Numerous war memorials, built to honour the Soviet and Mongolian dead, are scattered about the area, most of them on the road to Khalkh Gol (town). Near the river bank there's a modest memorial marking the **unknown heroes' grave** (GPS: N 47°51.809', E 118°28.243'), where 90 nameless Mongolian men are seeing out eternity. Others are real socialist masterpieces, the most impressive being the **Yakovlev Chuudiin Tank Khoshuu** (Яковлевчуудын Чуудийн Танк Хөшөө, Monument for Yakovlev Tank Brigade; GPS: N 47°48.813', E 118°32.856'), a Soviet tank on a pedestal 23km northwest of the town, and the 10m-high **Yalaltiin Khoshuu** (Ялалтын Хошуу, Victory Monument; GPS: N 47°38.091', E 118°35.944'), just outside Khalkh Gol, a

stylised Mongolian maiden on one side and grim-faced Soviet and Mongolian soldiers side by side on the reverse.

Museum   MUSEUM

(admission T3000; ☺10am-5pm Mon-Fri, to 3pm Sat) You can play with the anti-aircraft guns in the courtyard outside the history museum in Khalkh Gol, and peek out of the recreated dugout. Inside, a caretaker shows you the diorama of the area, the battle maps, the photos of the soldiers and the tools of war scattered throughout, accompanied by sombre music over the loudspeakers. The museum is supposed to get a facelift by 2019 to celebrate the 80th victory anniversary.

★Ikh Burkhant   MONUMENT

(Их Бурхант; GPS: N47° 52.402', E118° 27.175') At Ikh Burkhant, a huge image of Janraisag ('Avalokitesvara' in Sanskrit) is carved into the hillside, its legs splayed out. The carving was commissioned in 1864 by local regent Bat Ochiriin Togtokhtooriin, or Tovan (van means 'lord') and was renovated in the mid-1990s. There are fearsome deities guarding the prayer wheels and eerie shattered stone faces scattered about. If you walk up to its head, you'll see a couple entwined in an eternal stone embrace. Ikh Burkhant is right on the roadside, about 32km northwest of Khalkh Gol; there's a military checkpoint here.

🛏 Sleeping & Eating

The only place to stay in the town of Khalkh Gol is inside the **museum** (per person T10,000), of course! Several clean but spartan rooms share bathroom facilities. In the centre of town, a cafe offers 'hangover soup' and Chinese-y takes on Mongolian dishes.

ℹ Information

Khalkhiin Gol is near the Chinese border and a military base, and there is one military checkpoint en route from Choibalsan along the main road to Buir Nuur. Besides a border permit you also have to register at the military base in Khalkh Gol.

If you stop at the new **Nömrög Strictly Protected Area** office in Khalkh Gol town (near the museum), you'll have to pay T5000 just for being in the area, even though you can't get permits to visit Nömrög. The head Nömrög

EASTERN MONGOLIA KHALKHIIN GOL

WORTH A TRIP

NORTHERN DORNOD

A loop around northern Dornod makes for a good, offbeat, three- or four-day jeep trip. From Choibalsan, what looks like a main road on the map is in fact a dirt track that loosely parallels the railway line that runs to the Russian border.

Around two thirds along the way, near the village of Gurvangazal, keep an eye out for the **Wall of Chinggis Khaan** (Чингисийн Хэрэм). Despite the name, it was probably built during the Liao dynasty to prevent rampaging Mongol hordes from heading east. Locals know it as the Chingissiin Zam, or Chinggis' Rd, which gives some indication of just how worn down the wall has become, so it's not quite as impressive as that other, more famous wall built by the Chinese.

The road continues northeast to **Khökh Nuur**, a medium-sized freshwater lake at an altitude of 560m (the lowest point in Mongolia). There's a desolate beauty to this home of waders and shore birds.

From Khökh Nuur you could head northwest to **Mongol Daguur B Strictly Protected Area**; if you're lucky, you may come across a roaming herd of gazelle. The nearest town is Chuluunkhoroot, near the border crossing with Russia – an unappealing mess of ramshackle concrete buildings, gers and junkyards.

A good dirt road leads west from Chuluunkhoroot through the village of Dashbalbar and the mountainous **Ugtam Uul Nature Reserve**, the home of deer, situated along the Ulz Gol. If you take the **turnoff** (GPS: N 49°26.686', E 113°48.120') from the main road into the hills, you'll soon come across some mysterious **monastery ruins** (GPS: N 49°17.175', E 113°46.196'). It's not known exactly when the monastery was built but some effort has been made to stop it from disintegrating completely.

Jeep tracks lead further west along the main road to Bayandun and Bayan-Uul, both fine areas for camping and horse riding. There is a good road from Bayan-Uul back to Choibalsan (187km, 3½ hours) or you could take the rough road further west to Dadal via Norovlin (140km, four hours).

THE BATTLE OF KHALKHIIN GOL

After occupying Manchuria in 1931, which borders Mongolia's eastern Dornod province as well as Siberia, Japan turned its attention to the west. It seems that Japan's intention was to integrate Siberia into its territory and overrun Mongolia, creating a buffer zone between itself and the Soviet Union. Skirmishes were fought on both sides of the Khalkhiin Gol throughout the summer of 1939, until the numerically superior Japanese forces were destroyed by a joint Soviet–Mongolian effort led by Marshal Zhukov at the end of August, with Japan losing up to 45,000 men. A nonaggression pact was subsequently signed by Japan and the Soviet Union, leaving Stalin free to forge the temporary alliance with Nazi Germany and invade Poland. Had Mongolia joined forces with Japan, the outcome of WWII may have been markedly different.

ranger, **Mr Batbold** (☑8855 7082), is one of three rangers staffing the office.

ℹ Getting There & Away

Khalkh Gol is about 325km from Choibalsan, at least a nine-hour drive. It's best to hire your own vehicle in Choibalsan, as shared vans (T20,000) to Khalkh Gol are infrequuent and there's no other way to get to the sights.

SÜKHBAATAR
СУХБААТАР

POP 52,600 / AREA 82,300 SQ KM

Pancake-flat Sükhbaatar is wedged between the Gobi Desert and the pure steppes of Dornod. It contains elements of both – shifting sand dunes and barren rock feature prominently in the southwest, while the knee-high grass in the east provides important habitat for huge herds of gazelle.

The southern *sum* of Dariganga contains some 20 extinct volcanoes. This is a legendary region of horse thieves, holy mountains and ancient stone statues. A highlight is watching a glorious sunrise or getting caught in the holy rain on top of sacred Shiliin Bogd Uul.

Baruun-Urt   Баруун-Урт

☑ 7051, 01512 / POP 16,130 / ELEV 981M

Sükhbaatar's compact capital is located smack in the middle of eastern Mongolia's vast plains. It's a fairly desolate location, with no river or lake nearby, ferocious winters and scorching summers. However, the revenue from the nearby Chinese-funded zinc mine makes a welcome appearance in the form of paved streets, funky street lights (though only half of them seem to work), and a clean bus station.

The devil would feel right at home here due to the high levels of sulphur in the soil; the rest of us are better off buying bottled water.

⊙ Sights

★ **Ethnography Museum**   MUSEUM
(admission T3000; ⊘ 9am-5pm Mon-Fri) Baruun-Urt's museum has a fine collection of costumes representing the three ethnic groups that inhabit the region: the Khalkh (the majority), the Dariganga (around 30,000 live in the south of Sükhbaatar aimag) and the Uzemchin (about 2000 live in Dornod aimag and Sükhbaatar aimag). Look out for the brass-studded Uzemchin wrestling jacket.

There are also beautiful examples of products from Dariganga's renowned silversmiths and blacksmiths, some stuffed gazelle, and two rooms dedicated to the famed poet, author and politician Ochirbatyn Dashbalbar (1957–99), including his electric razor and record collection.

The museum is located just past the drama theatre, 400m south and then right of the square.

Erdenemandal Khiid   BUDDHIST MONASTERY
(Эрдэнэмандал Хийд) This monastery was originally built in 1830, about 20km from the present site. At the height of its splendour, there were seven temples and 1000 monks in residence, but the Stalinist purges of 1938 put a rather abrupt end to that. The new monastery, surrounded by a wall topped with 108 stupas and with strings of prayer flags aflutter, is about 400m west of the square. If you wander into the courtyard, during the warmer months, you may catch groups of crimson-robed monks chanting outside.

🛏 Sleeping & Eating

There are a couple of hole-in-the wall joints by the bus station selling *buuz* and Korean food.

Tansag Hotel
HOTEL $$

(📞 01512-22444; half-lux s/d T30,000/35,000, lux T50,000/55,000; 📶) Easily the best in town, the bright yellow Tansag has six rooms in a newish building on the east side of the main square. The lux rooms are somewhat bigger than the compact half-lux; both have fancy showers with fairly reliable hot water but only half the nozzles working. Wi-fi is erratic. There will be few surprises with the mutton-heavy menu, but they also do a decent kimchi soup and there's even porridge for breakfast.

Solo Hotel
HOTEL $$

(📞 9572 7627, 01512-21499; d/tr T35,000/34,000) This topsy-turvy, mint-green hotel is all wobbly floorboards and lopsided hallways, but the revamped en-suite doubles and triples that share facilities are comfortable enough for a night's stay. The downstairs restaurant does its best to bring you Chinese-style dishes and the staff practise their karaoke numbers between serving.

🍷 Drinking & Nightlife

On summer evenings, locals like to hang out on the main square, graced by a mounted Sükhbaatar statue. There's some drinking and karaoke going on on weekends, but the rest of the time the scene is dead as Heaven on a Saturday night.

Smile Pub
BAR

(Смайл Зоогийн Газар; ⏰ 9am midnight) The youngsters patronise this place, off the street that runs west from the northwest corner of the square, which has a small disco upstairs from a restaurant.

Shilmel Zoog
BAR

(Шилмэл Зоог; ⏰ noon-midnight) The Shilmel Zoog bar, with its white leather booths, attracts a slightly older drinking crowd.

Gun Bulag Zoog
PUB

(Гүн Булаг Зоог) Along the street that runs from the northwestern corner of the square, Gun Bulag Zoog offers a few Chinese dishes to go with your beer and karaoke.

🛈 Information

Government House (Main square) Ask for the latest info about permits to border areas here.
Internet Cafe (per hr T700; ⏰ 9am-9pm Mon-Fri, 10am-6pm Sat & Sun) Inside the Telecom office.
Khan Bank (Хаан Банк; ⏰ 9am-1pm & 2-5pm Mon-Fri) Just to the west of the main square.

Telecom Office (⏰ 24hr) The post office is also located here.

🛈 Getting There & Away

BUS

Buses and minivans depart from the bus station just to the northwest of the main square. Two daily buses (T26,500, 11 hours) depart for Ulaanbaatar at 8am and 5pm. The same buses can drop you in Chinggis Khot (229km) for T11,300. In Ulaanbaatar the bus leaves from the Bayanzürkh bus station (p94). Tickets are usually sold out one or two days before departure.

JEEP & MINIVAN

Shared jeeps and minivans leave Ulaanbaatar daily (560km) from the Naran Tuul jeep station (p87). From Baruun-Urt, vehicles wait at a jeep stand around 200m northeast of their old location behind the department store. Expect to pay around T16,000 for Chinggis Khot (229km) though drivers may want to charge the full fare all the way to UB; it's much cheaper to take the bus. The Chinggis Khot to Baruun-Urt road is well under way to being paved; at the time of research the tarmac extended for around 100km out of Chinggis Khot. Traffic is very light in the direction of Choibalsan (191km) and you may have to wait a day or two for a lift.

HITCHING

This is difficult because few vehicles come here. Still, if you have plenty of time on your hands, you can get a lift to Choibalsan, or Chinggis Khot; ask around at the jeep stand or the petrol station.

NATIONAL PARKS OF SÜKHBAATAR

Dornod Mongol Strictly Protected Area (570,374 hectares) Holds one of the last great plain ecosystems on earth, protecting seas of feather-grass steppe and 70% of Mongolia's white-tailed gazelle, whose large herds are under threat due to oil drilling and poaching.

Ganga Nuur Nature Reserve (28,000 hectares; p176) Protects dunes and the Ganga Nuur, an important habitat for migrating swans.

Lkhachinvandad Uul Nature Reserve (58,500 hectares) On the border with China, this steppe area has plenty of gazelle and elk.

Dariganga   Дарьганга

The vast grasslands of Dariganga are speckled with volcanic craters, small lakes and sand dunes, the sum of which makes the area one of the most scenic in eastern Mongolia. Before communism this area was a haven of aristocracy and its grasslands were the royal grazing grounds of horses belonging to the emperor in Běijīng. Silversmiths and blacksmiths made their homes here, providing local women with elaborate, fine jewellery that now features prominently in Ulaanbaatar's National Museum. These days, Dariganga is all about sacred mountains – one in town, and the other – Shiliin Bogd Uul – a shortish drive away. With a jeep and a good driver you can also explore the lakes, volcanoes, caves, sand dunes and ancient stones nearby.

◉ Sights

Altan Ovoo   MONUMENT
(Алтан Овоо, Golden Ovoo; GPS: N 45°18.690', E 113°50.180') The skyline of the neat little town of Dariganga – one of the few in Mongolia where the streets actually have names and numbers – is dominated by Altan Ovoo, a wide former crater topped with a **stupa**, which only men are allowed to visit. The stupa was built in 1990 on top of the ruins of the original Bat Tsagaan stupa, which was built

in 1820 and destroyed in 1937. At the base of the flat-topped hill there are a couple of stupas that women are allowed to visit, and they do so with gusto, making copious offerings.

Ovoon Khiid   BUDDHIST MONASTERY
(Овоон Хийд) In the village you can visit the small Ovoon Khiid, which was built in 1990 (and probably not repainted since) and is served by a handful of monks.

Balbals   MONUMENTS
In the steppe around the town there are dozens of broken *balbals* (stones carved into roughly human shape) – mostly dating back to the 13th- or 14th-century Mongol period. According to tradition, you should place an offering of food in the cup held in the statue's left hand. The three main *balbal* sights, on the north edge of town, consist of the the **King and Queen** (GPS: N 45°18.507', E 113°51.711'), the nearby **Son** (GPS: N 45°18.541', E 113°51.221') and, finally, a short walk away, the **Bride** (GPS: N 45°18.512', E 113°51.214') to whom women make offerings if they want to have healthy babies.

★ Ganga Nuur   LAKE
(Ганга Нуур; GPS: N45° 15.994', E113° 59.874'; per person/car T1500/500) Ganga Nuur is about 13km southeast of Dariganga. From the end of September until mid-October it is home to thousands of migrating swans. Along the

---

GAZELLE UNDER THREAT

A highlight of eastern Mongolia, as you bounce along in your jeep, is the sight of herds of up to 10,000 Mongolian gazelle darting across the steppe – among the very last of the great migratory herds. When pre-eminent biologist George Schaller first visited in 1989, he proclaimed the immense herds to be one of the world's greatest wildlife spectacles.

Sadly, indiscriminate poaching for subsistence and bush-meat sale has reduced their numbers by over 50% in the past 10 years, so you'll be lucky indeed to catch a glimpse of a great herd. There is an estimated one to two million Mongolian gazelle left in the wild, and it's believed that up to 200,000 of these creatures are illegally shot every year, about 20% of their entire population. Many are shot outside the legal hunting season, when females are lactating and make easier targets. An estimated 60% of herding households shoot about eight gazelle per year. Gazelle-leg horse-whips are brazenly sold even at Ulaanbaatar's Narun Tuul market – please do not purchase these.

Habitat loss to overgrazing, road construction and the erection of barriers further puts their numbers at risk. Mining is another threat: oil exploration in southeast Dornod has brought large-scale infrastructure and thousands of workers into a once-uninhabited region and the oil fields lie perilously close to the border of protected areas.

US-based international conservation NGOs such as the **Wildlife Conservation Society** (www.wcs.org) and **The Nature Conservancy** (www.tnc.org) now work to protect gazelle habitat on the eastern steppe. The BBC's *Planet Earth* featured the gazelles and the eastern steppe on their grassland series (go to YouTube and search for 'Mongolian gazelle').

shore, in a fenced compound, is delicious and safe spring water. If you don't fancy paying the car entry fee you can park by the gate and walk.

There are six lakes in the vicinity of Dariganga; all are part of the Ganga Nuur Nature Reserve, but apart from Ganga Nuur they are not really good for swimming, with boggy, muddy edges and plenty of reeds.

Moltsog Els   SAND DUNES

(Молцог Элс) The sand dunes in the region are known as Moltsog Els and stretch for 20km, coming to within walking distance of Dariganga village.

🛏 Sleeping & Eating

If you have a vehicle, you can camp on the shores of Ganga Nuur.

Dariganga has a few basic shops on the main street, alongside a couple of *tsainii gazar*.

Dagshin Bulag   TOURIST GER CAMP $

(Дагшин Булаг; ☑ 9626 0066, 9191 7257; ger T40,000) There is only really one working ger camp, Dagshin Bulag, that lies about 1.5km south of the village. It consists of four guest gers and an outdoor privy, though the owners have ambitious plans to redesign the camp, providing visitors with hot showers and beauty treatments that involve horse milk and mud from a nearby spring. Watch this space. If prodded, the owners may provide meals at extra cost.

ℹ Information

Permits are required for Dariganga and Shiliin Bogd and technically should be registered.

If you are coming from Dornod you shouldn't have any trouble getting to Shiliin Bogd and on to Dariganga; this allows you to travel directly from the Khalkhiin Gol area and Dornod Mongol Strictly Protected Area, bypassing Choibalsan and Baruun-Urt. This is the most scenic drive in eastern Mongolia and will be faster than heading back through Choibalsan. Make sure you have this route listed on your border permit.

ℹ Getting There & Away

Shared jeeps (T15,000, four hours) connect Dariganga with Baruun-Urt on Wednesday, Friday and Sunday (provided there's enough demand). A postal truck runs every Thursday from Baruun-Urt at 8am but you should reserve a ticket the day before.

One or two jeeps and even motorbikes may be available for charter.

Shiliin Bogd Uul
Шилийн Богд Уул

At 1778m, **Shiliin Bogd Uul** (GPS: N 45°28.509', E 114°35.909'), about 70km east of Dariganga, is the highest peak in Sükhbaatar aimag. The extinct volcano is sacred to many Mongolians, and it used to be the case of 'no girls allowed' when it came to climbing the mountain, but it seems that the local divine powers have a more egalitarian mindset these days; several local women climbed the mountain when we visited. A pungent odour surrounds the large main *ovoo* at the top, topped with a horsehair pennant and covered in offerings of food, milk and coins, and there's such a fantastic view over the green hills from the top that you can watch the rain sweep in from the nearby Chinese border, 3km to the south.

A jeep can drive about halfway up the mountain, and then it's a short, blustery walk to the top. After making your offerings, you can do a clockwise walk around the crater that leads you back to the car park. If you are camping, Shiliin Bogd offers one of the greatest sunrises in a country full of great sunrises.

On the road between Dariganga and Shiliin Bogd, 8km past Ganga Nuur, look out for the seated figure of **Toroi-Bandi** (GPS: N 45°17.305', E 114°04.465'), the Robin Hood of Mongolia, who stole horses from the local Manchurian rulers, then eluded them by hiding near Shiliin Bogd Uul. The statue, dedicated in 1999, pointedly faces China.

The only two roads to Shiliin Bogd start from Erdenetsagaan (70km) and Dariganga (70km). If you are coming from the Buir Nuur/Khalkh Gol area, once you've passed Tamsagbulag, a sometimes muddy shortcut road cuts across the countryside to the main road leading to the Chinese border near Erdenetsagaan. It runs close to the border of the Eastern Mongolia Nature Reserve, home of the endangered gazelle, and runs through the large oil field (also, alarmingly, located near said nature reserve).

Not far from the Chinese border, a minor road leads to the only accommodation option for miles around: **Wood House** (☑ +86 479 346 2000; GPS: N 45°56.177', E 115°46.511'; s/d/ ste T40,000/50,000/60,000), a hunting lodge with wood-panelled en-suite rooms; meals available only by advance booking. As it is frequented entirely by a Chinese clientele, the Mongolian staff may be flummoxed by your arrival.

EASTERN MONGOLIA SHILIIN BOGD UUL

Around Shiliin Bogd Uul

Assuming that you have a jeep to get to Shili-in Bogd Uul in the first place, you can make a good loop from Dariganga, to take in Ganga Nuur (p176) on the way to Shiliin Bogd Uul, and Taliin Agui and the valley Khurgiin Khundii on the way back to Dariganga.

Taliin Agui (Талын Агуй; GPS: N 45°35.417', E 114°30.044'), 15km northwest of the mountain, is one of the largest caves in Mongolia, but you have to descend into its subterranean gloom through a narrow crack to witness this – not an outing for the claustrophobic. Sometimes the entrance is covered in ice well into the warmer months, but if you see the cave's three chambers (the back wall looks like a dead end but you can squeeze under the overhang) in winter or spring, its walls, covered in ice crystals, emit an eerie glow. Even at the height of summer, the cave feels like a freezer and you'll need a torch for exploration. The cave is believed to project positive energy, and is visited by wrestlers seeking victory.

A **ger camp** (☑ 9926 1659, 9303 9050; GPS: N 45°35.376', E 114°29.869'; ger T40,000) is located right near the cave. Meals are available (T3500) or you can cook your own food in the lodge.

The Gobi

POP 310,300 / AREA 612,000 SQ KM

Best for Staying with Herdsmen

➡ Khongoryn Els (p195)
➡ Bayanzag (p197)
➡ Yolyn Am (p193)

Best Off-the-Beaten-Track

➡ Khermen Tsav (p201)
➡ Bayangiin Nuruu (p201)
➡ Road to Biger (p204)
➡ Eej Khairkhan Nature Reserve (p205)
➡ Khavtsgait Petroglyphs (p194)

Why Go?

The Gobi is a bleak place; vast, harsh and silent, and there are many who will question your sanity if you choose to travel here. But it is the profound emptiness and terrible isolation that draws adventurers to its fold. In a world of smartphones, social media and 24/7 cable news, there are few places on the planet where it is still possible to fall completely off the radar like you can do in the Gobi.

This is, nevertheless, one of Mongolia's top-draw regions. Colossal sand dunes, ice-filled canyons, dinosaur fossils and the promise of camel treks ensure that almost every tour company in the country runs trips out here. And a recent explosion of Gobi ger (traditional yurt) camps means you'll never have to rough it if you don't want to, although staying with a camel herdsman in a simple guest ger is half the fun.

When to Go
Dalanzadgad

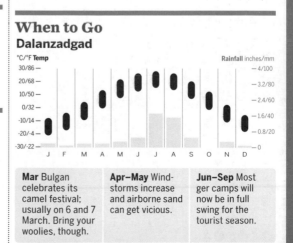

Mar Bulgan celebrates its camel festival; usually on 6 and 7 March. Bring your woolies, though.

Apr–May Windstorms increase and airborne sand can get vicious.

Jun–Sep Most ger camps will now be in full swing for the tourist season.

The Gobi Highlights

1 Take one step forward and slide three steps back on the awesome sand dunes of **Khongoryn Els** (p195).

2 Go fossil hunting at **Bayanzag** (p197), the beautiful 'flaming cliffs', rich in dinosaur bones and fossil eggs.

3 Look out for ibexes as you trek through the ice-filled canyon of **Yolyn Am** (p193), with vultures soaring above.

4 Camp by the river before picking your way through the monastery ruins of **Ongiin Khiid** (p185).

5 Shimmy up a granite face or just clamber over boulders in the eerie, moonscape-like **Ikh Gazryn Chuluu** (p186).

6 Search for the **Khavtsgait Petroglyphs** (p194); remote, prehistoric rock carvings that overlook the desert.

7 Get truly off the beaten track and venture south to **Khermen Tsav** (p201), a canyon some insist is more spectacular than Bayanzag.

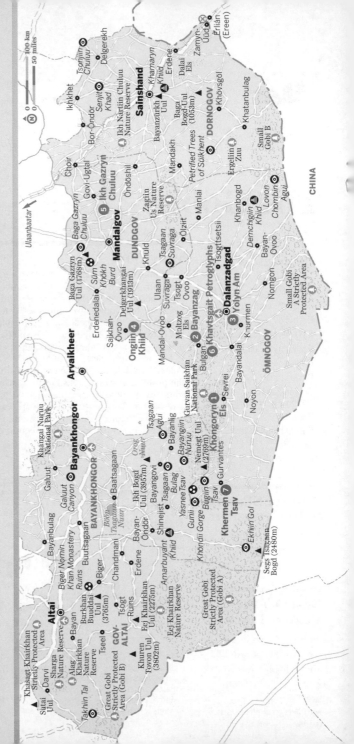

ⓘ Getting There & Away

There are plenty of shared minivans and jeeps, as well as the (normally) daily public buses, heading from Ulaanbaatar (UB) to all the Gobi aimag (province) capitals. Remember the travel times given are indicative only and don't take into account breakdowns and time spent in *guanz* (canteens) drinking *airag* (fermented mare milk) and watching sumo. Flying is also an option to Dalanzadgad, Altai and Bayankhongor. If you are travelling on local trains from China, it's possible to enter Mongolia at Zamyn-Üüd and continue on to Gobi towns such as Sainshand, although organising Gobi tours is best done in UB.

ⓘ Getting Around

Gobi infrastructure is almost nonexistent, but the lack of roads does not prevent vehicles from getting around. On the contrary, the rock-hard jeep trails are the best in the country and some times jeeps reach speeds of 100km/h, causing much excitement if an unexpected rise sends them airborne.

Breakdowns in the Gobi can be deadly and you shouldn't think of setting off without a reliable jeep and driver, a good sense of direction and plenty of water.

Annoyingly, public transport between aimag capitals is practically nil, and harder still out to national parks and other attractions. As it's easier to get off a bus heading back to Ulaanbaatar than trying to hop on an already full one on its way out, a good plan is to travel to your furthest destination first and work your way back to the capital.

If you are hitching, you will have the best chance of success if you ask around at markets, bus stations or any places selling petrol.

DUNDGOV ДУНДГОВЬ

POP 37,800 / AREA 78,000 SQ KM

Dundgov (middle Gobi) is something of a misnomer. The aimag would be best described 'North Gobi', as this area is the northernmost extent of the Gobi Desert. Lying just a few hours' drive south of Ulaanbaatar, it's also one of the most convenient Gobi regions to explore.

Dundgov's allure lies in its mysterious rock formations, which mainly appear at two locations: Baga Gazryn Chuluu and Ikh Gazryn Chuluu. At both you'll find large granite pinnacles and winding canyons that make for great hiking and climbing. The water that manages to collect in these areas supports wildlife such as argali sheep and ibexes.

Mandalgov   Мандалговь

☏ 01592, 7059 / POP 10,300 / ELEV 1427M

Mandalgov came into existence in 1942 and originally consisted of only 40 gers. Today it's a sleepy town that offers the usual amenities for an aimag capital: a hotel, a monastery, a museum and a few shops. A walk to the top of Mandalin Khar Ovoo, just north of the town centre, affords sweeping views of the bleak terrain. There is more to see in western Dundgov, but Mandalgov is a useful stop-off on the way to Dalanzadgad.

◉ Sights

Aimag Museum   MUSEUM

(☏ 01592-23690; Buyan Emekhiin Gudamj; admission T2000; ⊙9am-6pm) This Aimag Museum is divided into two main sections: a natural history section and a more interesting ethnography and historical section. There's also a collection of priceless *thangkas* (scroll paintings), old flintlock rifles, bronze arrowheads, silver snuffboxes, pipes, chess sets carved out of ivory, and an unnerving collection of castration knives.

Dashgimpeliin Khiid   BUDDHIST MONASTERY

(Дашгимпэлийн Хийд; ⊙closed Thu) In 1936 there were 53 temples in Dundgov; a year later the Mongolian KGB reduced nearly all to ashes and rubble. In 1991 Dashgimpeliin Khiid was opened for the people of Mandalgov. Around 20 monks now serve the monastery and services are held most days at around 10am and 2pm. It's 300m northeast of the Mandal Hotel.

Tree Nursery   PARK

(☏9959 8468; www.gobioasis.com) ✐ Retired forest engineer and local conservationist Byamba Tseyen helped establish, and now maintains this small tree-planting nursery on the edge of town in an attempt to fend off desertification from the Gobi's shifting sands. She and her family have planted more than 10,000 trees and shrubs here, and you can help their cause by planting one of your own. The equivalent of GBP£10 will get you lunch at their family home, and a sapling, which they will then help you plant. Contact Byamba, or her English-speaking daughter Goyo, through the nursery's website, or find her at Byamba's Family Homestay.

Mandalgov

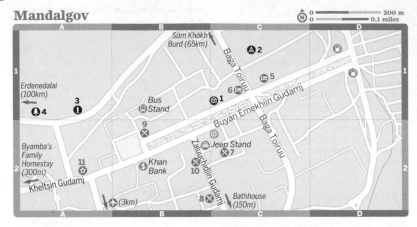

Mandalgov

🛏 Sleeping

Like other Gobi aimag capitals, Mandalgov has no great camping spots; the city has no river and it is flat and dusty. Perhaps walk north of town and find somewhere past Mandalin Khar Ovoo or the monastery.

Gobi Hotel HOTEL $
(☎01592-23690, 9115 2771; Buyan Emekhiin Gudamj; dm T10,000, tw T20,000-35,000) Even though all the rooms here share the hot showers and only the half-lux and lux rooms have their own toilets, this is one of the cleaner hotels in town and good value.

Byamba's Family Homestay GUEST GER $$
(☎9959 8468; www.gobioasis.com; A 6-13 Kheltsin Gudamj; per person with meals & tree GBP£50; @) 🛶 Byamba Tseyen, who manages the nearby tree nursery, also opens up her family home to guests. Accommodation is inside a guest ger, located in the compound of her home. It's clean, comfortable and comes with a warm welcome and tasty home-cooked meals. As part of the package, guests are given a tree sapling to plant in the nursery. The ger only sleeps three, but there is spillover accommodation in a wooden building in the yard. No shower, and the toilet is in an outhouse. No wi-fi, but you can get online using the family's computer. To get here, walk west along Kheltsin Gudamj, an extension of the town's main street, and look for the house number (A 6-13) on your right.

Mandal Hotel HOTEL $$$
(☎9813 7522; s/tw/q T40,000/60,000/110,000 lux tw T110,000; 🛜) The smartest hotel in town, rooms here are simple, but bright and clean and come with attached bathrooms, TV, wi-fi and complimentary breakfast. Has a decent restaurant-bar too.

🍴 Eating

Self-caterers can pick up food items at the **market** (⊙9am-5pm Tue-Sun). There's a **supermarket** nearby.

Gobi Anu MONGOLIAN $
(mains T4000-5000; ⊙9am-10pm) This clean and friendly *guanz* (canteen) knocks out all the usuals: *buuz* (dumplings), *khuushuur* (fried mutton pancakes), *tsuivan* (fried noodles). No English menu or signage – look for the pink and purple sign. Does beer.

Misheel Restaurant & Pub   MONGOLIAN $$
(mains T4000-7000; ⊘10am-10pm) The best restaurant in town. Misheel is bright and clean and has a photo menu with all your Mongolian favourites plus a back page of Korean dishes. It's on the 2nd floor.

☆ Entertainment

Central Mongolian Concert Theatre   MUSIC, DANCE
(Buyan Emekhiin Gudamj; ☑7059 2393; tickets T2500-5000; ⊘Sep-Jun, Jul during Naadam) Performances are sporadic but worth checking out while you're in town.

ⓘ Information

Internet Cafe (per hr T500; ⊘8am-10pm Mon-Fri, 9am-10pm Sat & Sun) Located in the Telecom office, along with the post office.
Khan Bank (⊘9am-6pm Mon-Fri, 10am-4pm Sat) Can change US dollars and has an ATM.
Bathhouse (shower T2000; ⊘9am-8pm Tue & Wed, 8am-9pm Fri-Sun) No sign. Look for the grey building next to a bright-green two-storey building on your right as you walk south along Zaluuchidiin Gudamj.

ⓘ Getting There & Away

BUS

A bus leaves every day at 8am and 2pm for Ulaanbaatar (T13,200, four to five hours, 260km) and another every Thursday at 8am for Choir (T11,700, five hours, 187km). Tickets for Choir must be bought the morning before the day of departure. The bus from Ulaanbaatar on its way to Dalanzadgad (nine hours, 293km) passes sometime between 2pm and 3pm. If there is room, tickets cost T14,000.

JEEP & MINIVAN

Daily shared jeeps to Ulaanbaatar (T16,000, four hours) leave when full from the jeep stand near the Telecom office. You're unlikely to find a shared jeep to Dalanzadgad (T16,000, seven hours), but Dalanzadgad-bound jeeps coming from Ulaanbaatar might be able to squeeze you

in. Wait for these at the petrol station in the south of town.

Baga Gazryn Chuluu   Бага Газрын Чулуу

This granite-rock **formation** (admission T3000) in the middle of the dusty plains sheltered Zanabazar during conflicts between the Khalkh and Oirat Mongols. Later it was home to two 19th-century monks who left **rock drawings** in the area. Locals who sometimes make pilgrimages here worship the rocks. Naturally, there is a legend that Chinggis Khaan grazed his horses here.

The **Delgeriin Choiriin Khiid** (GPS: N 46°08.691', E 106°09.142'), one of the many monasteries destroyed in the purges of the 1930s, is in the process of being rebuilt and sequestered. In a nearby ger is Luvsan Darjaa, a lama said to be the reincarnation of the famous Mongolian scholar Zava Damdin. Five hundred monks once called this monastery home. Now just 10 live here, including one young monk who speaks excellent English and who is always happy to show foreign visitors around. There are a few guest gers where pilgrims can stay for free, but there are no tourist facilities here.

Five kilometres away, the highest peak in the area, **Baga Gazryn Uul** (1768m), will take about an hour to climb. The fresh-water springs (if you can find them) and trees in the region make it a great spot to camp, and there are plenty of rocky hills topped by *ovoos* (shamanistic offerings to the gods) to explore. One unusual sight is the half-hidden stone ruins of the 200-year-old monastery, **Tsorjiin Khureenii Khiid** (GPS: N 46°12.064', E 106°02.103'). Concealed amongst the rocks, and shaded by trees, some of the rooms at the back of the now roofless complex still have traces of blue paint on their crumbling walls. Nearby, **Usan Bolortiin Agui** (GPS: N 46°12.686', E 106°01.717') is a cave which has

TIME TO COME CLEAN

After driving around the dusty Gobi for a few days, don't be surprised if you take on a reddish tinge under the accumulated layers of dirt and sweat. Most ger camps have hot showers but if you're camping, or staying in the guest gers of local herdsmen, then the easiest place to come clean is at a public bathhouse once you reach any small town.

Public bathhouses are far from luxurious – you'll need to bring your own towel and shampoo – flipflops aren't a bad idea either – but they tend to be more spacious than showers in cheap hotels, and, crucially, the hot water is reliable. The Mongolian for bathhouse is: *khaluun us* (literally 'hot water').

NATIONAL PARKS OF DUNDGOV

Ikh Gazryn Chuluu Nature Reserve
(60,000 hectares; p186) Extraordinary rock formations, argali sheep and ibexes.

Zagiin Us Nature Reserve (273,606 hectares) Protected mountain Gobi area, saxaul trees, salt marshes and black-tailed gazelle.

a funnel-like opening through which you can squeeze into a ger-sized cavern below. There's also a tiny **fresh-water spring** (GPS: N 46°12.249', E 106°01.135') near here, covered over with a stone. Lift the stone off the opening and use the long-handled spoon that locals have placed here to scoop up the spring water.

The **Bayan Bulag ger camp** (📞9825 0010; GPS: N 46°13.827', E 106°04.192'; with/without meals US$38/18) is a short walk from the ruins of Tsorjiin Khureenii Khiid and has good food and hot showers. Alternatively, herdsmen have family gers just a few hundred metres from here where you can grab a cheap lunch (T4000 to T5000) or stay in a simple guest ger (around T10,000 per person).

Baga Gazryn Chuluu is about 60km north by northwest of Mandalgov, and about 21km east of Süm Khökh Burd.

Süm Khökh Burd   Сум Хөх Бүрд

The dramatic ruined temple **Süm Khökh Burd** (GPS: N 46°09.621', E 105°45.590'), which sits on an island in the middle of a tiny, usually-dry lake, was built in the 10th century. Remarkably, the temple was built from rocks that can only be found more than 300km away. It was abandoned and left in ruins a few centuries after it was built.

Three hundred years ago a palace was built here, and 150 years later the writer Danzan Ravjaa built a stage on top of the ruins. Enough of the temple and palace remain to give you some idea of their previous magnificence. Even in ruins, it's an impressive sight, thanks largely to its remote location.

The lake itself, **Sangiin Dalai Nuur**, only encircles the palace after heavy rains; most of the time, you can walk or drive up to the ruins, but it's better to walk, given the ecological sensitivity of the area. There is good **birdwatching** here: various species of eagle, goose and swan come to this spring-fed lake in summer and autumn.

The **Süm Khökh Burd Ger Camp** (📞9906 4388; per person with meals T25,000) overlooks the ruins. It's an old socialist place that has a shower block with hot water and a generator, but little charm. It is, though, slated for renovation so could be a half-decent tourist camp by the time you get here.

The temple is located 72km northeast of Erdenedalai, 65km northwest of Mandalgov and 21km west of Baga Gazryn Chuluu.

Erdenedalai   Эрдэнэдалай

This sometime camel-herding community in the middle of nowhere (114km northwest of Mandalgov) is known for the **Gimpil Darjaalan Khiid** (admission T3000), an old monastery that survived Stalin's purges by becoming a warehouse and shop. The monastery was built in the late 18th century to commemorate the first ever visit to Mongolia by a Dalai Lama and was once used by about 500 monks. The monastery was reopened in 1990 and is now home to five monks.

The spacious temple has a central statue of Tsongkhapa (founder of the 'Yellow Hat' sect of Buddhism), some large parasols and huge drums. Seek permission if you want to take photographs inside the temple.

The small, dusty town here has a couple of very basic **guesthouses** (per person T10,000), a public **bathhouse** (shower T2500; 🕐8am-9pm) and an **internet cafe** (2nd fl; per hr T500; 🕐9am-7pm Mon-Fri, 10am-5pm Sat-Sun) next to a well-stocked supermarket.

About 25km north of Erdenedalai, the **Middle Gobi Camp** (📞11-367 316, 9912 8783; GPS: N 46°08.816', E 105°11.013'; with meals US$29-40, without meals US$15) is not a bad place to spend the night if you are headed in this direction.

Although Erdenedalai is small, it is on a major jeep trail so a few vehicles come through every day.

Ongiin Khiid   Онгийн Хийд

This small mountainous area along the river, Ongiin Gol, in the western *sum* (district) of Saikhan-Ovoo makes a pleasant place to break a trip en route to the southern Gobi.

⊙ Sights

★ **Ongiin Khiid**   BUDDHIST MONASTERIES
(GPS: N 45°20.367', E 104°00.306'; admission US$2)
The bend in the pretty river here marks the remains of two ruined monasteries: **Bari Lam Khiid** was built in 1810 on the north bank, the same side of the river as the tourist ger camps; **Khutagt Lam Khiid** was built in 1760 on the south, but can only be accessed when the water level of the river is low, or iced over in winter. Collectively they're known as Ongiin Khiid. Formerly one of the largest monasteries in Mongolia, and home to more than a thousand monks, the complex was destroyed in the 1937 communist purges when over 200 lamas were murdered. Since 1990 a small but growing contingent of monks has set up shop amid the ruins, completing a small temple in 2004, using some original beams from the old ruined monastery to build it. Two monks live here full time, in summer their numbers swell.

Locals claim that to reap the curative qualities of the **spring** (which apparently runs warm in winter and cool in summer), you must drink from it before sunrise. The ger beside the temple houses a small but interesting **museum** showcasing some artefacts found at the site, many of which were hidden by monks to save them from the purges. Look out for the only remaining drawing of the original monastery, plus the drinking cups made from the skulls of revered monks.

The **views** of the ruins, river, ger camps and the surrounding area are impressive from any of the nearby hills. A good way to start is with the one with the **ibex monument** on top.

Khoshuu Khuralin Khiid   BUDDHIST MONASTERY
(GPS: N 45°10.251', E 104°07.909') A third monastery is 21km south of the two at Ongiin Khiid, but very little remains of it, save a scattering of broken brickwork and Chinese pottery.

🛏 Sleeping & Eating

There are plenty of fine places to camp along the forested riverside and it's possible to stay in guest gers by the entrance to the ruins of Bari Lam Khiid; expect to pay T5000 to T7000 per person. There are also three ger camps by the river, all next to each other and within walking distance of Bari Lam Khiid.

Ongiin Khiid Guesthouse   TOURIST GER CAMP $
(☑9979 9721; ger per person T8000, brick hut T5000, meals T5000; Ⓟ) The smallest and best-value of the ger camps here, this place, which stays open year-round, has clean, comfortable gers overlooking the river and a new castle-lookalike restaurant made of stone. The beds in the brick huts are very cheap, but uncomfortably springy. There were no showers when we were here, and the toilets were out the back, but a new shower block was under construction. The

---

CAMELS

Known as ships of the desert, the Mongolian Bactrian camel is a two-humped ornery beast with a shaggy wool coat. They can still be seen today, hauling goods and people across the Gobi, as they have done for centuries.

Your first encounter with a camel may be a daunting experience: it will bark, spit and smell like a sweaty armpit. But, excusing its lack of graces, the camel is a versatile and low-maintenance creature: it can last a week without water and a month without food; it can carry a lot of gear (up to 250kg – equal to 10 full backpacks); it provides wool (on average 5kg per year) and milk (up to 600L a year); and is a good source of (somewhat gamey) meat. The camel also produces 250kg of dung a year; invaluable for fuel.

Monitoring the hump is an important part of camel maintenance. A firm and tall hump is a sign of good health, while a droopy hump means the camel is in need of food and water. If a thirsty camel hasn't had a drink for some time, it can suck up 200L of water in a single day. Most camels are tame, but male camels go crazy during the mating season in January and February – definitely a time to avoid approaching one.

Of the 260,000 camels in Mongolia, two-thirds can be found in the five aimags that stretch across the Gobi – 80,000 in Ömnögov alone. They are related to the rare wild camel known as the *khavtgai*, of which only around 800 remain in Mongolia. These are all found in the Great Gobi Stritctly Protected Area (Gobi A). For more information, see www.wildcamel.com.

owners don't speak English, but can arrange short treks on horses or camels. Located under the hill with the ibex statue on top.

Tsagaan Ovoo Ger Camp TOURIST GER CAMP **$$**
(☎ 9971 9392; with/without meals US$35/20) This camp features a small, green-painted restaurant with fine river views, and a games building with table tennis and a pool table. Has showers and decent gers, but closes earlier in the year than the other two nearby camps.

**Secret of Ongi
Tourist Camp** TOURIST GER CAMP **$$$**
(☎ 9888 6800; www.ongi.mongoliansecrethistory.mn; with/without meals US$89/40, mains T8000-11,000; P @) This is the most comfortable place to stay. The big draw is the log-and-stone restaurant-bar reminiscent of a Chinese-style temple, the smart gers with curved wooden doors and some of the cleanest toilets in the Gobi. There are guides (T3000 per person) available for hikes into the surrounding countryside, and nonguests can use the showers (T4000) and the massage services (T18,000 to T35,000), as well as the restaurant.

Ikh Gazryn Chuluu   Их Газрын Чулуу

Caves, canyons and some excellent **rock-climbing** routes are a few of the reasons travellers head out to this remote Gobi **nature reserve** (admission T3000), 70km east of Mandalgov in Gurvan Saikhan *sum*. The Ulaanbaatar-based tour company Wind of Mongolia (p37) can help with climbing. Non-climbers will enjoy simply wandering the moonscape-like, boulder-strewn scenery, with rocks to clamber over and caves to explore. One small **cave** (GPS: N 45°44.389', E 107°13.271') we found about 2.5km southwest of the ranger's camp has great views from its mouth, halfway up a rocky hillside, and a skylight, thanks to a collapsed roof. About 1.5km south of the ranger's camp is a rather surreal **open-air theatre** (GPS: N 45°43.913', E 107°15.005'). Concerts are occasionally held here in honour of two famous Mongolian long-song singers who used to live locally.

You can overnight at the comfortable **Töv Borjigan Ger Camp** (☎ 9976 9266; GPS: N 45°45.664', E 107°15.977'; with meals US$60). Two kilometres away, just over the rocks to the southwest, the park ranger, Munkh-Ochir,

THE LOST TREASURE OF DANZAN RAVJAA

Many tall tales exist about Noyon Khutagt Danzan Ravjaa (1803–56), a hot-headed rebellious monk, a writer and popular leader of Mongolia's Red Hat Buddhists. It is said that he could fly to Tibet in an instant, disappear into thin air and turn water into whisky. At age six he was proclaimed the Fifth Gobi Lord even though the Manchus had forbidden another after executing his predecessor.

Danzan Ravjaa would spend months in solitude writing, either in caves or in his ger, and his fame as a writer, artist and social critic spread far and wide. He was also an expert at martial arts, tantric studies, yoga and traditional medicine.

His mysterious death came either at the hands of the rival Yellow Hat Buddhist sect or a jealous queen who failed to gain his love. During his life, Danzan Ravjaa amassed a collection of statues, paintings, original manuscripts, opera costumes and ritual objects. It eventually fell to a man called Tuduv, the hereditary *takhilch* (caretaker) of Danzan Ravjaa's legacy, to protect these treasures during the 1937 communist purges. Every night, under the cover of darkness and in total secrecy, Tuduv buried a crate of treasure in the shifting sands of the Gobi. He only had time to bury 64 of the 1500 crates before they and the Khamaryn Khiid (monastery) were destroyed.

The only man alive today who knows their location is Zundoi Altangerel (Tuduv's grandson and the fifth *takhilch*), and in 1990 he retrieved all but 17 of them to found the Museum of Danzan Ravjaa in Sainshand (p187). Then in 2009, much to the delight of a worldwide audience courtesy of a live webcast (www.gobi-treasure.com), Altangerel dug up two more crates. In 2013, the ninth reincarnation of the Noyon Khutagt, a young man named Danzan Luvsan Tudev, was identified and installed as the head of the monastery in an elaborate ceremony that attracted more than 10,000 people.

For more information on Danzan Ravjaa, pick up a copy of his biography *Lama of the Gobi* (Blacksmith Books, 2010), by Michael Kohn.

has his family ger and a couple of basic **guest gers** (☑9589 4489; GPS: N 45°44.902', E 107°14.902'; per person T10,000, meals T4000). The view of the rocky landscape here is wonderful, but you'll need to bring your own sleeping bag.

DORNOGOV ДОРНОГОВЬ

POP 75,600 / AREA 111,000 SQ KM

Dornogov (east Gobi) is the first place visited by many overlanders, as the train line from Běijīng to Ulaanbaatar runs straight up its gut. The landscape seen from the train window is one of flat, arid emptiness and the occasional station where locals shuffle about on the platform. The railway supports local trade while the rest of the economy rides on the back of uranium development and small-scale oil extraction.

Sainshand   Сайншанд

☑01522, 7052 / POP 19,891 / ELEV 938M

This aimag capital is divided into two parts: a cluster of homes and businesses around the train station (though nowhere decent for tourists to stay), and the more developed centre, 2km south.

◉ Sights

Aimag Museum   MUSEUM
(☑01522-22657; admission T2000; ☺9am-1pm & 2-6pm) The well-appointed Aimag Museum houses plenty of stuffed Gobi animals, and a collection of seashells and marine fossils (Dornogov was once beneath the sea). There is also an impressive skeleton of a Protoceratops and a dinosaur egg. Upstairs, look out for the wooden breastplate used by a Mongol soldier of the imperial fighting days.

Museum of Danzan Ravjaa   MUSEUM
(☑01522-23221; www.danzanravjaa.org; admission T1000; ☺9am-1pm & 2-6pm) The life and achievements of Noyon Khutagt Danzan Ravjaa (1803–56), a well-known Mongolian writer, composer, painter and medic who was born about 100km southwest of Sainshand, are honoured in this small but well-put-together museum. Look out for the small glass jar which contains Danzan Ravjaa's bones; his mummified body was burned along with his monastery in the 1930s.

Sainshand

◉ Sights
1 Aimag Museum.............................A2
2 Museum of Danzan Ravjaa.............A2

🛏 Sleeping
3 Dornogobi Hotel..........................A1
4 Lux Hotel....................................B1
5 Shand Plaza.................................A1

✦ Eating
6 Altan Urag...................................B1
7 Best Restaurant...........................B1

✪ Entertainment
8 Saran Khöökhöö Drama
    Theatre....................................A2

🛏 Sleeping

Sainshand, like most aimag capitals in the Gobi, does not offer anywhere decent to pitch a tent. Try the hills between the train station and the town centre.

Lux Hotel   HOTEL $$
(☑9301 1278; tw T35,000-50,000; 🅿🛜) Simple, but neat-and-tidy rooms come with TV, wi-fi (when it works) and attached bathroom.

Shand Plaza   HOTEL $$
(☑7052 3509; tr/q T30,000/25,000; tw T40,000-65,000; 🅿🛜) Very popular so often full, this central hotel, with attached restaurant, disco and pool room has decent rooms, although the cheaper ones are pretty basic and have bathrooms without showers. Sometimes has wi-fi.

NATIONAL PARKS OF DORNOGOV

Ergeliin Zuu (90,910 hectares) A small protected area with interesting rock formations and palaeontology sites that include 30-million-year-old mammalian fossils.

Ikh Nartiin Chuluu Nature Reserve (67,000 hectares) Easily accessible from Ulaanbaatar and home to argali sheep, ibexes, black vultures and other wildlife.

Dornogobi Hotel HOTEL $$$
(☑ 7052 3657; tw T55,000-88,000; P 🛜) The newest and largest hotel in Sainshand, its five floors and circular design mean it dominates the northeast corner of the park. The rooms are clean and smart and have fine views over the surrounding town from private balconies. Showers are reliably hot, and there is a restaurant on the 2nd floor. Breakfast is included with the higher-category rooms, as is wi-fi, which also extends to the restaurant. Also has a very generous 6pm checkout!

✖ Eating

Altan Urag CHINESE $
(meals T4000-4500; ⊘ 9am-11pm) This unsigned restaurant can be found above a grocery store in a building that looks like an Arabian mini-castle. It has the usual range of Mongolian dishes, but the draw here is authentic, if somewhat oily, Chinese meals. Servings are large. No English menu.

Best Restaurant MONGOLIAN $$
(☑ 9925 5579; meals T5000-6500; ⊘ 10am-11pm; 🍴) Clean, friendly and fully licensed, this local favourite doles out excellent Mongolian dishes; we recommend the *bainshte shöl* (dumpling soup). Ask for the English menu – they only have one, and it sometimes takes a while to find. There's no sign but it's above a small supermarket.

☆ Entertainment

Saran Khöökhöö Drama Theatre THEATRE
(☑ 01522-22796) This theatre is named after the famous play by local hero Danzan Ravjaa, who would be proud that this Sainshand theatre group is considered the best outside of Ulaanbaatar. Check noticeboards by the entrance for scheduling.

ℹ Information

There's an ATM in the lobby of the Dornogobi Hotel and in the Telecom building.
Internet Cafe (per hr T600; ⊘ 9am-9pm Mon-Fri, 10am-6pm Sat & Sun) In the Telecom buliding, along with the post office.
Trade & Development Bank (⊘ 9am-5pm Mon-Fri) Changes US-dollar travellers cheques and gives cash advances on MasterCard and Visa.

ℹ Getting There & Around

Because at least two trains link Sainshand with Ulaanbaatar every day, there are no flights here. The new paved road linking UB and Zamyn-Üüd may make catching a shared taxi to either possible.

A shared taxi from the train station to the town centre costs T500/1000 per person during the day/night. You can walk the 2km in around 30 minutes. Walk away (south) from the station, turn right at the T-junction then take the next left and keep walking up and over the hill.

JEEP
Shared jeeps and taxis park themselves by the market. Ask here for a taxi to Khamaryn Khiid (T50,000 to T60,000 return).

TRAIN
Departure times here are based on the summer schedule (May to September), and are subject to slight variations each year.
UB to Sainshand Train 286; departs 9.35am daily; arrives 8.15pm
Sainshand to UB Train 285; departs 9pm daily; arrives 8.05am
UB to Zamyn-Üüd Train 276; departs UB 4.30pm daily; arrives in Sainshand 1.38am.
Zamyn-Üüd to UB Train 275; departs Sainshand 11pm daily; arrives in UB 9.25am

Tickets from Ulaanbaatar cost T7400/13,200/21,500 for hard seat/hard sleeper/soft sleeper. If you book your ticket more than a day ahead there is a T800 to T1200 fee, although we found it fairly easy to buy same-day tickets to Ulaanbaatar from here.

The Trans-Mongolian Railway and the trains between Ulaanbaatar and Èrlián (Ereen; just over the Chinese border) and Hohhot (in Inner Mongolia) stop at Sainshand, but you cannot use these services just to get to Sainshand unless you buy a ticket all the way to China.

Around Sainshand

Although the desert in this part of the Gobi is typically flat and featureless, it is worth hiring a vehicle for a day to explore the attractions outside of town. Negotiate a trip with the drivers at Sainshand's jeep stand.

◎ Sights

Khamaryn Khiid   BUDDHIST MONASTERY
(Хамарын Хийд; GPS: N 44°36.038', E 110°16.650')
This reconstructed monastery, an hour's drive south of Sainshand, has grown up around the cult of Danzan Ravjaa, whom many locals believe was a living god. His image is sewn into a **carpet** that hangs in the main hall. The original monastery and three-storey theatre, built by Danzan Ravjaa in 1821, was destroyed in the 1930s.

From the monastery (turn left as you exit it), a path, and more recently a paved road, leads for 2km to a **bell tower** which you must strike three times to announce your arrival at the 'energy centre', known as **Shambhala** (admission T500). In 1853, Danzan Ravjaa told the local people that he would die in three years but they could forever come to this place and speak to his spirit. Indeed, he died three years later and the site was marked by an *ovoo*. Shambhala is now surrounded by 108 new stupas ('108' being a sacred number in Buddhism) and festivities are held here on 10 September.

Bayanzürkh Uul   HISTORIC SITE
(GPS: N 44°41.644', E 110°02.707') Around 23km northwest of Khamaryn Khiid is the mountain home of the spirit of the third Noyon Khutagt (a predecessor of Danzan Ravjaa). The temple halfway up the mountain is as far

as local women are allowed to go (although no one seems to mind if foreign women go to the top). At the summit (1070m), reached by a newly built pathway, you are required to make three wishes at the so-called 'wishing *ovoo*', and circle the peak.

🛏 Sleeping & Eating

If you plan on making anything other than a day trip to Khamaryn Khiid, it is worth noting that the monastery has only very basic facilities. You'll probably need a tent.

Gobi Sunrise
Tavan Dohoi   TOURIST GER CAMP **$$**
(☑9908 0151; GPS: N 44°45.418', E 110°11.236'; with/without meals US$45/25; ℗) Set in the middle of a vast, deserted landscape, this comfortable ger camp has flush toilets and clean showers with hot water. To arrange transport to the camp, which is about 16km south of Sainshand, on the way to Khamaryn Khiid, ask **Altangerel** (☑9909 0151), the curator at the Museum of Danzan Ravjaa (p187). He speaks English. A taxi from town costs around T20,000 one way.

Ikh Nartiin Chuluu   Их Нартын Чулуу

The **Ikh Nartiin Chuluu Nature Reserve** (Ikh Nart; www.ikhnart.com) is seeing an increasing trickle of visitors thanks to its accessibility from Ulaanbaatar, improving tourist facilities and a healthy population of the globally threatened argali sheep. A team of international biologists have been conducting a long-term study that has partly habituated the sheep to the presence of humans, so you're almost guaranteed to see an argali

---

LOCAL KNOWLEDGE

RITUALS AT SHAMBHALA

There are several rituals to observe when you enter the Shambhala site. Try to do them in the following order.

➡ Write a bad thought on a piece of paper and burn it in the rocks to the left.

➡ Write down a wish, read it, throw some vodka in the air and drop some rice in the stone circles on the ground (representing the past, present and future).

➡ Take a white pebble from the ground, place it on the pile of other white pebbles and announce your family name.

➡ Take off your shoes and lie down on the ground, absorbing the energy of this sacred site.

➡ Circle the *ovoo* three times.

here. In recent years the Argali Project has expanded to include the ibex and been joined by the Carnivore Project and the Vulture Project.

Several ancient **burial mounds** (GPS: N 45°75.546', E 108°65.454') and **petroglyphs** (GPS: N 45°60.787', E 108°57.201'; N 45°60.237', E 108°55.959'; N 45°59.175', E 108°61.397') can also be found throughout the park. The petroglyphs are found on rocky outcrops and take the form of Buddhist prayers written in Tibetan script.

Some locals consider the **natural springs** near Khalzan Uul (Bald Mountain) a cure for everything from hangovers to HIV.

🛏 Sleeping

Red Rock Ger Camp   TOURIST GER CAMP **$$$**
(🖉11-328 737; www.nomadicjourneys.com; GPS: N 45°39.830', E 108°39.204'; per night US$95, 4 days & 3 nights with meals per person US$350; 🅿) 🖉 Nomadic Journeys (p36) operates this ger camp on the outskirts of the reserve, about 50km drive from Shiveegobi train station. Guided wildlife walks, camel rides and jeep drives are all usually available to guests. Advanced bookings are essential so that they can send a local driver (even with the GPS coordinates, local knowledge is invaluable when picking a route through the rocky formations) to collect you at either Shiveegobi, Tsomog or Choir train stations. Transport to and from the train stations is included in the package, as are guided tours of the reserve.

Zamyn-Üüd   Замын-Үүд
🖉 02524, 7052

The Trans-Mongolian Railway line serves as a life-sustaining artery for this small, otherwise insignificant village in the Gobi Desert. Most of the town's activity can be found around the square in front of the train station. The chief attractions here are the disused water fountain, some outdoor pool tables and grabbing a bite at one of the many eateries that cater to transit travellers killing time.

🛏 Sleeping

Zamyn Uud Hotel   HOTEL **$$**
(🖉7052 7032; tw T35,000) Located at the north end of the train-station platform, this half-decent hotel has smart rooms with kettle, wall-mounted TV and clean attached bathroom, and is the best choice in town. You'll find cheaper, grubbier options opposite the station.

ⓘ GETTING TO/FROM CHINA

Jeeps, trains and buses all trundle to and from the Chinese border town of Èrlián (Ereen). If you are on a Trans-Mongolian train, or the service between Ulaanbaatar and Hohhot or Èrlián (both in China), you will stop at Zamyn-Üüd for an hour or so while Mongolian customs and immigration officials do their stuff – usually in the middle of the night (see p281).

If you're on a train that only goes as far as the border, then you'll need to find a vehicle in which to cross the border (you can't walk or cycle across), before catching onward transport from the other side. It's best to catch the public bus (from Mongolia T8000 per person, from China ¥50 per person). This shuttles between the car park outside Zamyn-Üüd train station and the main bus station in Èrlián, via the border post. Shared jeeps/minivans offer the same service, usually for the same price, although you may need to negotiate.

Heading into Mongolia, the bus leaves Èrlián bus station at 1.30pm and 3pm. If you catch the 1.30pm bus across the border, you should have plenty of time to get a ticket for the 5.30pm train from Zamyn-Üüd to Ulaanbaatar (apart from around Nadaam season in July, when things get very busy). In Zamyn-Üüd, the public bus to Èrlián is usually there to meet passengers as they get off trains from Ulaanbaatar.

You'll need to pay a ¥5 departure tax in either direction, unless you're crossing the border on a train.

Once in Èrlián, it's almost always easiest to catch a long-distance bus to your next destination in China as trains are usually fully booked days in advance.

For details on your onward travel, head to shop.lonelyplanet.com to purchase a downloadable PDF of Lonely Planet's *China* guide.

✖ Eating

Outside the train station, you'll find a bunch of cheap restaurants and small supermarkets.

Khan Buuz　　　　　　　MONGOLIAN **$**
(mains T4500-5500; ⊘24hr) On the train station platform is this branch of the dependable canteen chain. No English menu, but some photos to point at. Does *buuz*, as well as *tsuivan*, various soups, *khuushuur* and warming mugs of *suutei tsai* (salty milk tea).

ℹ Information

The train station's new ticket office is on the platform and contains several ATMs that accept international cards. Moneychangers are on hand outside the station to change your tögrög or Chinese rénmìbì. Luggage storage is also available for T150 per item in the basement of the ticket office. Train tickets are bought on the 2nd floor.

ℹ Getting There & Away

Zamyn-Üüd to UB Train 275; departs 5.35pm daily; arrives 9.25am; seat/hard-sleeper/soft-sleeper seat to UB T9600/16,300/27,300; to Sainshand T4500/9300/14,300.

Èrlián to UB Train 21 departs Zamyn-Üüd 9.25pm Monday and Friday; arrives UB 10.35am; hard-/soft-sleeper to UB T22,100/39,200; to Sainshand T13,500/18,800.

For departures from Ulaanbaatar, see p95. There's also a Sunday 'express' train (No 43), which leaves Zamyn-Üüd for UB at 9.25pm, and a train (No 33) which originates in China's Hohhot and leaves Zamyn-Üüd for Ulaanbaatar at the same time on Tuesdays and Saturdays.

In short, there are trains from Zamyn-Üüd to Ulaanbaatar at 5.35pm daily, and at 9.25pm on Monday, Tuesday, Friday, Saturday and Sunday. Departure and arrival times are based on the summer schedule (May to September) and are subject to slight variations each year.

The new paved road connecting Zamyn-Üüd and Ulaanbaatar means catching a share taxi or ride with a trader may be possible.

ÖMNÖGOV　　ӨМНӨГОВЬ

POP 65,400 / AREA 165,000 SQ KM

Dalanzadgad　　Даланзадгад

☏ 01532, 7053 / POP 20,376 / ELEV 1465M

The capital of Ömnögov, Dalanzadgad is a speck of civilisation in the desert, sitting in the shadow of the mountainous Gurvan Saikhan National Park. You'll find decent

---

NATIONAL PARKS OF ÖMNÖGOV
••••••••••••••••••••••••••••••••••••

Gurvan Saikhan National Park
(2,000,000 hectares; p193) A wealth of sand dunes, canyons, dinosaur fossils and mountainous terrain. Desert wildlife includes argali sheep, ibexes and snow leopards.

Small Gobi A Strictly Protected Area
(1,839,176 hectares) On the border with China, this park includes dunes and saxaul forest. It is the last great bastion of the *khulan* (wild ass).

---

hotels here, with good restaurants and bars so it's not a bad place to recharge before you explore the region's big draws: the monstrous sand dunes known as Khongoryn Els and the 'Flaming Cliffs' of Bayanzag, both of which are within a day's drive from here.

⊙ Sights

South Gobi Museum　　　　　MUSEUM
(☏ 01532-23871; admission T2000; ⊘9am-6pm Mon-Fri) Surprisingly, this museum has little on dinosaurs – just a few legs, arms and eggs. (All of the best exhibits are in Ulaanbaatar or in other museums around the world.) There are a few nice paintings, a huge stuffed vulture and a display of scroll paintings and other Buddhist items. Look out for the unusual jade flute.

🛏 Sleeping

Like other Gobi aimag capitals, there is no river or any decent place to camp in Dalanzadgad. You will have to walk 1km or 2km in any direction from town, and pitch your tent somewhere secluded.

Bayan Govi Hotel　　　　　HOTEL **$$**
(☏ 8853 9211; s/d T20,000/25,000, tw T30,000, tr with/without bathroom T35,000/40,000) This friendly, motel-like place is the town's best budget choice. Rooms are simple, but clean and bright and management are welcoming to foreigners despite not speaking English. Most rooms have attached toilet, but only one has an attached shower. There is a common shower, though. The hotel is on your right as you walk towards the bus stand.

Mongol Baigali Hotel　　　　HOTEL **$$**
(☏ 5073 3038; tw T30,000-40,000, tr T30,000, q T40,000) A rather rundown Socialist-era

Dalanzadgad

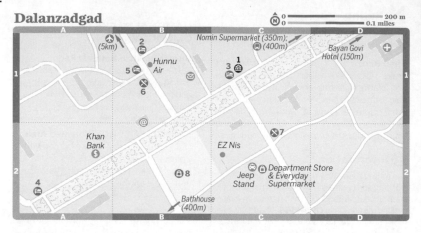

hotel, but rooms are large, making this OK for a night. Three of the four rooms have attached bathrooms (the quad doesn't), although hot showers are a trickle. There's a shared toilet and sink, but no common bathroom.

Gobi Sands Hotel   HOTEL $$$
(📞 7053 0024; s/d from T77,000/88,000; 📶) One of two new top-end hotels, Gobi Sands is smart, modern and immaculately clean throughout. Rooms are spacious and have plenty of natural light, and the 7th-floor bar-restaurant has great views of the distant mountains. Wi-fi throughout. Breakfast included. Note, there's no perceptible difference between standard and semi-deluxe rooms.

Khan Uul Hotel & Suite   HOTEL $$$
(📞 7053 4999; www.khanuul-hotel.mn; s/d from T70,000/120,000; 📶) More business-oriented than its top-end rival, Gobi Sands, but still a very slick option. Staff here seem to have better English-language skills, and are more professional, but the restaurant-bar doesn't have the same great views. Wi-fi throughout.

Dalanzadgad Hotel   HOTEL $$$
(📞 01532-24455; tw T60,000, d T80,000-100,000, tr/q T80,000/100,000; 📶) Recently usurped by the town's two new fancy-pants hotels, this one-time top choice is still clean and comfortable throughout. All rooms come with kettle, TV, wi-fi and attached bathroom. The restaurant and bar are also popular.

✖ Eating

Self-caterers should head to the open-air **market** (⊙9am-7pm) in the centre of town, or the large wholesale supermarket, **Nomin** (⊙8.30am-9.30pm), near the bus stand.

Khot Airl Cafe   MONGOLIAN $
(mains T4000-5000; ⊙8am-6.30pm) One of the more popular *guanz* (canteens) in town, this place has the added attraction of a photo menu.

**Dalanzadgad
Hotel Restaurant**   WESTERN, KOREAN $$
(mains T5000-9000; ⊙7am-10pm; 🍴) The picture menu, with English translations too, lays out all your options – salads, spaghetti, risotto, vegetable curry, Chinese hot pot and a bunch of Korean dishes. There are Mongolian options too. The attached bar (open

4pm to midnight) is a decent spot for a cold beer (from T2500).

Green Castle
Center Restaurant MONGOLIAN $$
(Luxury Restaurant; mains T8000-10,000; ☺10am-midnight; 📷) Overpriced, but clean and comfortable. The food here is tasty, and there's beer and fresh coffee (T5500). Has spaghetti bolognese and chicken dishes as well as Mongolian food. English menu.

Gobi Sands
Hotel Restaurant MULTICUISINE $$$
(mains T10,000-15,000; ☺8am-10pm, bar to midnight) With great views of the town and the distant mountains, this 7th-floor restaurant and bar is undeniably attractive. Portions are small for the price, but the food is tasty and well presented. There are plenty of Mongolian options, plus pizza and pasta, but there's no English menu, so you may have to mime your way through ordering. Beer from T2000.

ℹ Information

Bathhouse (shower T2000; ☺summer 8am-11pm, winter 9am-10pm) In a green building on your right as you walk away from the centre.
Internet Cafe (per hr T600; ☺8am-11pm) In the Telecom office.
Khan Bank (☺9am-6pm Mon-Fri, to 4pm Sat) Changes cash and has a foreign-friendly ATM. On the same side of the road as the Telecom office. Also has an ATM in the lobby of Dalanzadgad Hotel.

ℹ Getting There & Away

AIR
The airport is 5km north of town, along a paved road. Taxis cost about T10,000 one way.
EZ Nis (📞7005 2969; www.eznisairways.com; ☺9am-6pm) Daily flights to Ulaanbaatar (T180,000 to T250,000). English spoken. You can pay with a Visa card.
Hunnu Air (📞9400 0647; www.hunnuair.com; 3rd fl, above Golomt Bank; ☺9am-5pm) Flies to UB every day in summer, and Mondays, Wednesdays and Fridays in winter. One way from T135,000. Not much English spoken.

BUS
A twice-daily bus travels between Dalanzadgad and Ulaanbaatar (T28,000, 12 hours, 553km), departing at around 8am and 4pm via Mandalgov (T13,600, seven hours).

You can buy tickets up to two days in advance from the **ticket office** (☺7.30am-6pm) at the bus stand.

MINIVANS & TAXIS
Minivans leave when full for Ulaanbaatar (T30,000) via Mandalgov (usually same price). They gather outside the Department Store & Everyday Supermarket.

Hiring a taxi is fairly straightforward, even though no one here speaks English. Again, look for drivers outside the Department Store & Everyday Supermarket. A day trip to Yolyn Am with three hours of waiting time costs T60,000 to T70,000, although most foreigners end up paying around T100,000. An overnight return trip, taking in Yolyn Am, Khongoryn Els and the Flaming Cliffs will set you back between T250,000 and T300,000.

Readers have recommended **Tumee** (📞9953 8319) as a reliable local driver.

Gurvan Saikhan National Park
Гурван Сайхан

With its iconic sand dunes, ice canyon, striped badlands and stunning mountain vistas, this is understandably one of Mongolia's most popular national parks. Most travellers only see a fraction of it, sticking to the main sites – the standout one being the monstrous sand dunes known as Khongoryn Els. With more time, though, it's possible to drive to the remote western area – an eerie landscape so lacking in life that you may feel as if you've landed on Mars.

Gurvan Saikhan National Park (Three Beauties; entry fee T3000) is named after its three ridges (though there are four). Besides its spectacular natural beauty it contains more than 200 bird species, including the Mongolian desert finch, cinereous vulture, desert warbler and houbara bustard. Spring brings further waves of migratory birds.

The park also has maybe 600 or more types of plants, many of which only bloom after (very infrequent) heavy rain. The sparse vegetation does manage to support numerous types of animals, such as the black-tailed gazelle, Kozlov's pygmy jerboa, wild ass and endangered species of wild camel, snow leopard, ibex and argali sheep.

◉ Sights & Activities

★**Yolyn Am** VALLEY
(Ёлын Ам, Vulture's Mouth) Yolyn Am was originally established to conserve the birdlife in the region, but it's now more famous for its dramatic rocky cliffs and narrow, heavily shaded canyons that allow

sheets of blue-veined ice to survive well into the summer. Yolyn Am is in the Zuun Saikhan Nuruu, 46km west of Dalanzadgad (return taxi T100,000, one to two hours).

⇒ Nature Museum

(GPS: N 43°32.872', E 104°02.257'; admission T2000; ⊙8am-8pm 1 Jun-20 Oct) The small museum at the gate on the main road to Yolyn Am has a collection of dinosaur eggs and bones, stuffed birds and a snow leopard. Several souvenir shops and an 'information ger' can also be found here.

⇒ Gorge

From the museum, the dirt road continues for another 10km to a car park of sorts. From here, a pleasant 2km walk, following the Yol Stream, leads to the ice-filled gorge and one or two lonely souvenir salesmen. Locals at the car park also rent horses (T10,000, plus the same again for the compulsory horse guide) for the return trip to the gorge.

In winter, the ice is up to 10m high and continues down the gorge for another 10km, although it has largely disappeared by the end of July. It's possible to walk the length of

the gorge – an experienced driver could pick you up on the other side (GPS: N 43°30.537', E 104°06.616'), about 8km east of the car park.

The surrounding hills offer opportunities for some fine, if somewhat strenuous, day **hikes**. If you are lucky you might spot ibexes or argali sheep along the steep valley ridges.

⇒ Mukhar Shiveert

About 1km before the museum is a second ice valley called Mukhar Shiveert; visitors may be required to pay an additional T3000 to visit the site.

⇒ Dugany Am

If you are headed from Yolyn Am to Khongoryn Els, an adventurous and rough alternative route takes you through the Dugany Am, a spectacular and narrow gorge barely wide enough to allow a jeep to pass that eventually leads to some spectacular views and a **small stupa** (GPS: N 43°29.115', E 103°51.043') that has been built on the remains of a former temple. The gorge is blocked with ice until July and can be impassable even after the ice has melted, so check road conditions with the rangers at the park entrance.

OFF THE BEATEN TRACK

ANCIENT GOBI ROCK CARVINGS

If you take the long, sweeping, main route from Dalanzadgad to Khongoryn Els, keeping the Gurvan Saikhan National Park mountain range to your left as you go, you will have the chance to hunt in the hills for the **Khavtsgait Petroglyphs** (GPS: N 43°54.256', E 103°31.345', elev 1822m), an exceptional collection of rock carvings, dating from between 3000 BC and 8000 BC.

You'll pass a number of petroglyphs as you scale the rocky hill that leads up to your right from the **trailhead** (GPS: N 43°54.245', E 103°31.628', elev 1715m), where your jeep can park. Other, more impressive ones are located at the top of what is a 30-minute, 120m climb.

The **1st group** (GPS: N 43°54.207', E 103°31.514'; elev 1780m) you reach includes antelopes, ibexes and mountain sheep. Just beyond here, a **2nd group** (GPS: N 43°54.208', E 103°31.464'; elev 1808m) has a rare depiction of a camel. Once at the top of the hill, a **3rd group** (GPS: N 43°54.201', E 103°31.377'; elev 1836m) includes a large red deer, an ibex, hunters hunting other red deer and a cat-like animal, possibly a tiger. Nearby, a **4th group** (GPS: N 43°54.172', E 103°31.360'; elev 1831m) shows horses and hunters in a scene dominated by a mysterious spiral pattern. Further along the top of the hill, a **5th group** (GPS: N 43°54.256', E 103°31.345'; elev 1822m) is the highlight: on one 2m-wide rock face are a number of scenes of the era: galloping horses, hunters, camels with riders, wheeled carts beside a rudimentary ger and people offering gifts to their rulers. Not far away, towards the edge of the hill, overlooking the vast steppe, is a **6th group** (GPS: N 43°54.267', E 103°31.336'; elev 1819m), which offers one of the few clear depictions of a wolf, painted hunting a majestic red deer with huge antlers.

The trailhead is up to your left as you drive west from Three Camel Lodge (p196), 12km away, on the main route from Dalanzadgad (about 75km) to Khongoryn Els (about 100km). From the trailhead, climb the pathway leading up to your right. There are no facilities here.

★ **Khongoryn Els**   SAND DUNES

(Хонгорын Элс; camel rides per hr/day T5000/15,000) Khongoryn Els are some of the largest and most spectacular sand dunes in Mongolia. Also known as the Duut Mankhan (Singing Dunes – from the sound they make when the sand is moved by the wind or as it collapses in small avalanches), they are up to 300m high, 12km wide and about 100km long. The largest dunes are at the northwestern corner of the range. Getting to the top (45 minutes to one hour) is exhausting; every step forward is followed by a significant backslide, but the views of the desert from the sandy summit are wonderful.

The sand dunes are also a popular place for organising **camel rides**, (per hour/day T7000/25,000 plus the same again for the guide fee), and locals seem to appear from nowhere when a jeep full of tourists arrives. A **mini naadam** featuring horse racing and wrestling is held here on 15 August.

The dunes are about 180km from Dalanzadgad. There is no way to get here unless you charter a jeep or are part of a tour.

From Khongoryn Els it is possible to follow desert tracks 130km north to Bogd in Övörkhangai, or 215km northwest to Bayanlig in Bayankhongor. This is a remote and unforgiving area and you shouldn't undertake either trip without an experienced driver and full stocks of food, water and fuel.

🛏 Sleeping

🛏 Yolyn Am

There are two sets of guest gers, a couple of hundred metres from the Nature Museum. One is run by museum staff. The other by souvenir sellers. They had closed for the winter when we were here, but expect to pay around T10,000 per person per night. Meals will also be available.

Herdsmen
Household Cooperative   GUEST GER $

(Malchinii Khotkhon; ☎8853 5919; GPS: N 43°34.920', E 104°03.169'; per bed T10,000-15,000, breakfast/lunch/dinner T4000/6000/6000) A grand name for what is essentially a cluster of guest gers next to a herdsman's family ger, this welcoming place offers basic accommodation and a window into the life of a Gobi herder. Enkhtur and his wife Oyunsuren don't speak English but will do their best to introduce you to their daily routines; looking after the animals and making dairy products

PIKA-BOO

The small, mouse-like creatures, often seen darting between rock crevices at Yolyn Am, are called pikas and are actually members of the rabbit family. They're incredibly cute and frustratingly difficult to photograph.

Surprisingly, pikas don't hibernate, preferring to spend their summers making hay while the sun shines. You may witness them dragging grass into their burrows for winter consumption.

and felt souvenirs. And they'll pick you up from Dalanzadgad (30km, T50,000 one way) if you can get a Mongolian speaker to help with the phone call. Their place is about 4km before the Nature Museum, on the right.

🛏 Khongoryn Els

Within walking distance of the dunes, along their northern edge, you'll find two tourist ger camps and a number of guest gers run by nomadic families. Some remain open until mid-October.

Ganbold Delger   GUEST GER $

(☎9864 8184; GPS: N 43°46.297', E 102°21.289'; per person with/without meals T21,000/10,000; P) Ganbold, a local herdsman, runs one of the more popular guest ger outfits. You'll see his home to your left (east) as you approach the dunes from the north (which is the way most people come). Accommodation in the guest gers is basic, and Ganbold doesn't speak English, but this is a reliable place. Camel rides cost T30,000 per day, plus T20,000 for a guide and his camel. Only about 2km walk from the dunes, but at least a 12km-hike northeast of the tallest dunes.

Ulziibat's Family Ger   GUEST GER $

(☎9648 1214, 9701 1697; GPS: N 43°46.614', E 102°17.312'; per bed T7000, meals T5000) Run by local camel herder Ulziibat, guest gers here are basic but comfortable. Meals are available and camel riding is, of course, on offer (per hour T7000). About 2km from the dunes, not far from Gobi Discovery 2 ger camp, but around 8km northeast of the tallest dunes.

Nyamsuren's Family Ger   GUEST GER $

(☎5318 0356; GPS: N 43°47.631', E 102°12.141'; per bed T7000, meals T4000) One of the family gers closest to the tallest dunes (just 1km

THE GOBI GURVAN SAIKHAN NATIONAL PARK

LUXURY DESERT DIGS

An ever-growing number of high-end ger camps in this part of Mongolia, means you don't have to rough it if you want to stay in the Gobi Desert. There are dozens within shouting distance of Dalanzadgad and Bayanzag. A couple of them have taken things to a new level.

Three Camel Lodge (☑ 9888 0930, 11-313 396; www.threecamellodge.com; GPS: N 43°53.603', E 103°44.435'; ger per person with/without meals T431,000/315,000, lux T415,000/299,000; ☺ Apr-Nov; ℗) A veritable oasis in the desert 66km northwest of Dalanzadgad (on the route towards Khongoryn Els) and 28km south of Bayanzag, Three Camels sets the bar for the Mongolian ger camp experience. Visitors stay in luxurious gers, some of which step down into a side room with private toilet and sink (there's a modern shower block too). The restaurant-bar area is made from wood beams and local granite and is finished tastefully with Chinese-style upturned eaves. There's plenty of terraced seating with spectacular views over a great, grassy plain, and there's a bundle of activities on offer, including camel rides (per hour/day T28,000/86,000), mountain biking (T14,000/57,000), sand boarding (half/full day T14,000/28,000), Mongolian cooking classes (T28,000) and massage (T60,000 to T90,000).

Dream Gobi Camp (☑ 9890 5074, 11-315 379; dreamgobicamp@yahoo.com; GPS: N 43°54.458', E 103°51.999'; ger per person with breakfast/3 meals US$100/134) Has none of the class of Three Camel Lodge, but the facilities here are a notch above most other ger camps, not least because this is the only camp in the Gobi where every ger has an at-tached bathroom with hot shower. The large, raised, central wooden 'ger', which all the real gers fan out from, contains a bright and clean restaurant-bar area from where you can view the glass-walled kitchen as well as the surrounding desert. The camp is on the main route between Bayanzag (28km) and Dalanzadgad (60km).

Goviin Bayanburd 1 (☑ 9901 3017, 9595 3012; gobioasis_mn@yahoo.com; GPS: N 43°36.931', E 104°19.233'; ger with/without meals US$60/25, VIP r with meals US$250) The ger accommodation in this well-run camp, 10km north of Dalanzadgad (and only 5km from the airport), is smart but nothing special, but the 20 VIP rooms, which were in the process of being built when we were here, promise quality furnishings and en-suite bathrooms. Anna, the manager, speaks very good English. They have another camp, **Goviin Bayanburd 2** (☑ 9953 2020; GPS: N 44°09.754', E 103°40.634'; ger with/without meals US$50/20), 5km northwest of the 'Flaming Cliffs' at Bayanzag.

away), Nyamsuren and his family offer home cooking as well as a couple of basic guest gers.

Gobi Discovery 2   TOURIST GER CAMP $$
(☑ 9838 7299, 11-312 769; www.gobidiscovery. mn; GPS: N 43°46.495', E 102°20.307'; per person with/without meals US$60/30; ☺ May–mid-Oct; ℗) More modern than Juulchin Gobi 2, al-though offering much the same, Gobi Dis-covery 2 is a sound choice, 2km from the dunes (10km from the tallest section). Non-guests can use the showers (T9000) and the restaurant and bar (meals around US$15). Some staff speak English, and camel treks can be organised from here.

Juulchin Gobi 2   TOURIST GER CAMP $$
(☑ 8805 8559, 5053 5355; www.juulchingobi.com; GPS: N 43°47.845', E 102°16.402'; per person with/without meals T80,000/36,000; ℗) The closest camp to the tallest dunes (which are about 3km southwest of here), Juulchin has the ap-pearance of a ranch, with its stone-and-brick bungalow building, and is old-fashioned but tidy and welcoming. Showers and toilets are clean but cramped.

ℹ Information

You can pay the national park entry fee at the park office in Dalanzadgad or, more conven-iently, at the entrance to Yolyn Am or from the ranger at Khongoryn Els.

Keep your entry ticket as you may need to show it more than once.

Conservation Ink (www.conservationink.org) publishes the excellent *Gobi Gurvan Saikhan National Park Map and Guide,* a satellite map with informative articles.

Bayanzag   Баянзаг

★ **Bayanzag** (Flaming Cliffs; GPS: N 44°08.311', E 103°43.667'; admission T1000), which means 'rich in saxaul shrubs', is more commonly known as the 'Flaming Cliffs', a name penned by the palaeontologist Roy Chapman Andrews. First excavated in 1922, it is renowned worldwide for the number of **dinosaur bones and eggs** found in the area, which you can see in museums around the world.

Even if you are not a 'dinophile', the eerie beauty of the surrounding landscape is a good reason to visit. It's a classic desert of rock, red sands, scrub, sun and awesome emptiness. There's not much to do once you're here except explore the area, hire a **camel** (per hr/day T10,000/30,000) or grab a cold drink from the souvenir sellers who hang out on the edge of the cliff.

A further 22km northeast of Bayanzag is an area of sand dunes called **Moltzog Els**, which might be worth a visit if you're not planning to visit Khongoryn Els. Bayanzag is around 90km from Dalanzadgad.

🛏 Sleeping & Eating

Camping opportunities abound – the *zag* (scrub) forest, 5km from the cliffs, is one option – although water is scarce, so you may want to enlist the help of nomadic families come mealtime. Expect to pay them T5000 per meal. You can also camp for free at any of the tourist ger camps, then pay to use their facilities; showers, restaurant etc.

Sainzaya's Family Ger   GUEST GER $
(☎ 9822 0218; GPS: N 44°11.362', E 103°41.200'; per person T7000, meals T5000) There's a nice family atmosphere at the home of Sainzaya. She cooks tasty meals and the guest gers are basic but comfortable. No shower and only an outhouse toilet. No English spoken. Her gers are around 6km from the cliffs. Other members of her family, as well as other families, also have guest gers nearby.

Geleg-Araash's Family Ger   GUEST GER $
(☎ 9860 3335; GPS: N 44°10.806', E 103°41.478'; per person T7000, meals T5000) Geleg-Araash, the father of Sainzaya from Sainzaya's Family Ger, has his basic gers 1km closer to the cliffs. His wife cooks the meals.

Jamian Family Ger   GUEST GER $
(☎ 9822 0998; GPS: N 44°10.268', E 103°41.693'; per person T7000, meals T5000; P) Close to the cliffs (4km away) is the family ger of Jamian who can arrange camel rides (per hour/day T7000/25,000, plus the same again for the guide), including multiday treks such as the two-day round trip to Moltzog Els, or the five-day one-way trek to Khongoryn Els. You'll have to bring all your own supplies and camping equipment, though.

Bayanzag Tourist Camp   TOURIST GER CAMP $
(☎ 9953 8899; www.gobitour.mn; GPS: N 44°10.466', E 103°41.816'; ger bed T15,000; P) This old-fashioned, rather rundown camp offers a cheaper ger-camp option. Nonguests can use the showers (T3000) and eat in the undeniably tacky, giant tortoise-shaped restaurant (mains T4000 to T5000). It's by the scrub 'forest', a 4km-walk below the cliffs.

DON'T MISS

BULGAN CAMEL FESTIVAL

For 363 days of the year, the dusty, ramshackle village of Bulgan doesn't register on the tourist radar. But for two days in March (usually the 6th and 7th) visitors from around the country and beyond descend on the village for its annual **camel festival** (Temeeni Uraldaani Bayar). It's well worth making a detour to if you're around at the time. You'll see camel polo, camel shearing and camel races as well as demonstrations of how nomads look after their herds.

During the event, temporary ger camps pop up to house tourists. Year-round you can stay at **Ankhsan Cooperative Guesthouse** (☎ 9898 2829; treepool_06@yahoo.com; GPS: N 44°05.631', E 103°32.556'; per person T8000-10,000, meals T3500-5000), a simple family home that has a couple of guest gers, patchy internet access, a rudimentary sun-heated shower and a long-drop outhouse. Poli, the owner, doesn't speak English, but is used to hosting foreign guests.

Bulgan is around 95km northwest of Dalazadgad, and only a short drive from Bayanzag.

DINOSAURS

In the early 1920s, newspapers brought news of the world's first discovery of dinosaur eggs in the southern Gobi Desert by American adventurer Roy Chapman Andrews (1884–1960). Andrews, a real-life Indiana Jones, led expeditions worldwide, but became best-known for his expeditions based at Bayanzag, which he famously renamed the 'Flaming Cliffs'. Over a period of two years his team unearthed over 100 dinosaurs, including *Protoceratops andrewsi*, which was named after the explorer. The find included several Velociraptors (Swift Robbers), subsequently made famous by *Jurassic Park*. He also found a parrot-beaked Oviraptor, though his name for the creature (Egg Robber) was a misnomer as later discoveries proved that the Oviraptors were not stealing eggs, but incubating their own eggs.

Subsequent expeditions have added to the picture of life in the Gobi during the late Cretaceous period 70 million years ago. One of the most famous fossils unearthed so far is the 'Fighting Dinosaurs' fossil, discovered by a joint Polish–Mongolian team in 1971 and listed as a national treasure. The remarkable 80-million-year-old fossil is of a Protoceratops and Velociraptor locked in mortal combat. It is thought that this and other fossilised snapshots were entombed by a violent sandstorm or by collapsing sand dunes. One poignant fossil is of an Oviraptor protecting its nest of eggs from the impending sands.

A picture of prehistoric Gobi has emerged – a land of swamps, marshes and lakes, with areas of sand studded with oases. The land was inhabited by a colourful cast of characters: huge duck-billed hadrosaurs; Ankylosaurs, which were up to 7.6m tall, were armour-plated and had club-like tails that acted like a giant mace; long-necked, lizard-hipped sauropods such as Nemegtosaurus, which may have grown to a weight of 90 tonnes; and the mighty Tarbosaurus (alarming reptile), a carbon copy of a *Tyrannosaurus rex*, with a 1.2m-long skull packed with razor-sharp teeth up to 15cm long.

The Tarbosaurus hit the headlines in 2012 when a full skeleton that had sold for more than $US1 million was found to have been smuggled illegally from Mongolia by American paleontologist Eric Prokopi. The skeleton was seized, returned to Mongolia and put on temporary display until a permanent home can be found for it. Prokopi pleaded guilty, but was still awaiting sentencing at the time of writing. He was facing up to 17 years in prison.

Apart from the famous sites of Bayanzag and nearby Togrigiin Shiree, the richest sites of Bugiin Tsav, Ulaan Tsav, Nemegt Uul and Khermen Tsav are all in the remote west of Ömnögov aimag and impossible to reach without a jeep and dedicated driver (or a helicopter). Locals may approach you at Bayanzag, the ger camps and even Dalanzadgad to buy dinosaur bones and eggs. Remember that it is *highly* illegal to export fossils from Mongolia.

Today the finest collection of Gobi dinosaurs is housed in the **American Natural History Museum** (www.amnh.org) in New York City, which also has a fine website. At the time of research Mongolia was planning to build a new Museum of Dinosaurs to show off its collection, check with the Ulaanbaatar Information Centre (p92) for updates. As for books, check out *Dinosaurs of the Flaming Cliffs* by American palaeontologist Michael Novacek. For more information on Roy Chapman Andrews, read *Dragon Hunter*, by Charles Galenkamp.

Gobitour Camp TOURIST GER CAMP **$$**
(☑9909 1258; www.gobitourcamp.com; GPS: N 44°07.367', E 103°43.793'; with/without meals US$50/20) The closest camp to the cliffs, this friendly place is on the up side of the cliffs and you can see them clearly, 2km away. Good facilities. Good food (meals US$15). Camel rides available (per hour/day US$7/20).

Mongolia Gobi TOURIST GER CAMP **$$**
(☑9150 5550; GPS: N 44°07.818', E 103°42.101'; with/without meals US$45/25) Close to the cliffs (about 2.5km), and on the up-side this well-designed camp is run by Temuulen, who speaks English.

BAYANKHONGOR
БАЯНХОНГОР

POP 77,800 / AREA 116,000 SQ KM

One of the most diverse aimags in the Gobi, Bayankhongor has mountains in the north, deserts in the south, a handful of lakes and rivers, hot springs and a real oasis in the far south of the province.

Bayankhongor, which means 'rich chestnut' (named after the colour of horses), is home to wild camels and asses and the extremely rare Gobi bear.

Bayankhongor City
Баянхонгор

☎ 01442, 7044 / POP 26,250 / ELEV 1859M

Though short on sights, Bayankhongor is a relatively affluent aimag capital, making it a good place to rest up for a night and stock up on provisions before continuing on into more remote regions.

◉ Sights

Lamyn Gegeenii Gon Gandan Dedlin Khiid BUDDHIST MONASTERY
(Ламын Гэгээний Гон Гандан Дэдлин Хийд) The original monastery of this name was located 20km east of Bayankhongor City and was one of the biggest in the country. It was levelled by the communist government in 1937. The current monastery is home to only 15 monks. Daily services start at 10am in the main 'brick ger' temple which features a statue of Sakyamuni (the historical Buddha) flanked by a green-and-white Tara.

Aimag Museum MUSEUM
(☎ 01442-22339; admission T2500; ⊙ 9am-1pm & 2-6pm Mon-Fri, 10am-4pm Sat) The Aimag Museum, inside the sports stadium in the park, is well laid out and worth a quick look. There is a good display on Buddhist art, featuring two lovely statues of Tara, some fine old scroll paintings and *tsam* (lama dance) masks and costumes.

Natural History Museum MUSEUM
(admission T2000; ⊙ 9am-1pm & 2-6pm Mon-Fri) The Natural History Museum across the street from the Aimag Museum is filled with badly stuffed animals, a replica Tarbosaurus skeleton and some fossils, including a 130-million-year-old fossilised turtle.

☆ Activities

Bayankhongor is overlooked by a **stupa** (and the telecom tower beside it) on a hill to the west. Take a walk up here (20 minutes) for views of the town and surrounding countryside. For something more rewarding, head east to **Nomgon Mountain**, on the other side of the river, Tüin Gol. This small mountain takes one to two hours to climb. There's an *ovoo* at the top. From the town centre, cross the river then turn right and start climbing up to your left just before you reach the point where the river meets the main road.

⌷ Sleeping

The best place to camp is by the Tüin Gol, a few hundred metres east of the city. Head to the river, then start walking north (left).

Negdelchin Hotel HOTEL $
(☎ 7044 2278; dm T8000-10,000, d/tr T16,000/24,000, half-lux/lux T30,000/40,000) This long-standing Soviet-style cheapie is good value, but sometimes full. Only the half-lux and lux rooms have attached showers. Others have attached toilet and sink, but a common shower room. If this place is full, Soyombo restaurant has a few cheap rooms.

Seoul Hotel HOTEL $$$
(☎ 9944 4491, 9144 6677; tw/tr T55,000/68,000, lux tw T68,000; @🛜) Smart, friendly and well-equipped, this is probably the best choice in town. Some staff speak English, there's wi-fi and internet terminals, all rooms have attached bathrooms, and breakfast is included.

Bayankhongor Hotel HOTEL $$$
(☎ 7044 4000; s/tw/tr from T40,000/50,000/55,000; P🛜) The newest hotel in town, this place is smart throughout, though less welcoming than Seoul. The restaurant comes well recommended.

✕ Eating

Seoul Hotel and Bayankhongor Hotel both have good restaurants. As always, you'll find a number of *guanz* (canteens) selling *buuz* (mutton dumplings) and *khuushuur* (mutton pancakes) near both markets (*zakhs*). The smaller Central Market is behind Soyombo restaurant. The larger Black Market is just southwest of the bus stand. There's a trio of well-stocked supermarkets beside Seoul Hotel, and a big warehouse-like supermarket, called **Baruun Bus** (⊙ 10am-8pm), just south of the Black Market.

Uran Khairkhan · MONGOLIAN $
(meals T3500-5000; ⊘9am-10pm) With its cheery orange-and-yellow tablecloths and cosy booth dining, jovial Uran Khairkhan is an attractive choice. No English menu, but you'll find your usual favourites: *tsuivan*, goulash, *bif-shtek* (beef patty topped with a fried egg on rice), plus some vegetarian options, known collectively as *tsagaan khool* (white eats). The iced cakes in the cabinet cost T1000 a slice. Beers from T2500.

Mammoh · MONGOLIAN $$
(mains T6000-10,000; ⊘10am-midnight) Bayankhongor's most pleasant restaurant is clean and family-friendly, but doesn't have an English menu. They have two or three chicken dishes *(takhia ny makh)*, as well as the usual mutton offerings. Their *chinjutei makhan khuurag* (stir-fried meat, peppers and onions with rice) is tasty, as is their *on-dogtei bif-shtek* and *moogtei makhan huurag* (fried mutton with mushrooms). Walk down the left side of Khan Bank and it's on your left.

Soyombo · MONGOLIAN $$
(meals T5000-10,000; ⊘10am-11pm; 🛜📱) Extensive selection of Mongolian dishes, including vegetarian options. Reasonably smart place (if a little overpriced) with the added attraction of an English menu and free wi-fi. There are some hotel rooms (twins/triples T30,000/40,000) at the back of the restaurant.

ⓘ Information

Bathhouse (shower T2000, sauna T8000; ⊘10am-10pm) In a salmon-pink building.

Internet Cafe (per hr T600; ⊘9am-10pm) In the Telecom office, along with the post office.

Khan Bank (⊘9am-6pm Mon-Fri, to 4pm Sat) Changes US dollars and gives cash advances on Visa and MasterCard. There is an ATM next door.

ⓘ Getting There & Away

AIR

Hunnu Air (📞7044 2244; www.hunnuair.com/en; Bayankhongor Store, ground fl; ⊘9am-6pm Mon-Fri), formerly Mongolian Airlines, flies to Ulaanbaatar several times a week, check the

Bayankhongor City

Bayankhongor City map

EXPLORING THE GOBI

If you fancy yourself a bit of an Indiana Jones then you'll love the desert around Bayangovi. Few travellers make it this far and any DIY explorers need to carry plenty of water, fuel and spare parts for their 4WD vehicle. The area around Khermen Tsav is particularly barren and as water is extremely scarce, virtually no one lives here. A minimum of two vehicles and an experienced guide is recommended for this area.

From north to south, areas to explore in Bayankhongor include the following:

Galuut Canyon A 25m-deep canyon that narrows to around 1m wide in places. It is 20km southwest of Galuut *sum* centre, 85km northwest of Bayankhongor town.

Böön Tsagaan Nuur (GPS: N 45°37.114', E 99°15.350') A large, scenic saltwater lake at the end of Baidrag Gol with prolific birdlife, notably relic gulls, whooper swans and geese. The nearest *sum* centre is Baatsagaan. Locals from there sometimes come to swim in the lake. The east end of the lake is best for birdwatching. Camping is the only sleeping option.

Ikh Bogd Uul The highest mountain (3957m) in the Gobi Altai range. It's possible to part-jeep, part-hike your way to the top for stupendous views. On Ikh Bogd's southern flank you'll also find the beautiful **Bituut rock**, formed after an earthquake in 1957.

Tsagaan Agui (White Cave; GPS: N 44°42.604', E 101°10.187; admission T1000) This is a cave with a crystal-lined inner chamber that once housed Stone Age people. It is about 90km east of Bayangovi in a narrow gorge.

Tsagaan Bulag (GPS: N 44°35.156', E 100°20.733') Also near Bayangovi, this white rock outcrop has the faint imprint of a strange helmeted figure, which locals believe was created by aliens.

Gunii Khöndii Gorge A beautiful, 4km-long gorge with vertical walls. It is about 70km southwest of Bayangovi.

Bayangiin Nuruu (GPS: N 44°17.218', E 100°31.329') A canyon with well-preserved rock engravings and petroglyphs depicting hunting and agricultural scenes dating from 3000 BC.

Yasnee Tsav An eroded hilly region with some impressive buttes. Local guides claim they can point out authentic fossils at this site.

Bugiin Tsav (GPS: N 43°52.869', E 100°01.639') A large series of rift valleys running parallel to the Altan Uul mountain range and famous for its dinosaur fossils.

Khermen Tsav (GPS: N 43°28.006', E 99°49.976') The most spectacular canyons in the area – some say more impressive than Bayanzag. The closest town is Gurvantes (GPS: N 43°13.599', E 101°02.798') where you can buy fuel and basic supplies.

Severei Petroglyphs (GPS: N 43°33.678', E 102°01.052') These depict herds of animals including deer, ibexes and gazelles; 20km from the town of Sevrei.

website for details. Fares are T150,000 to T250,000 one way. The office is inside Golomt Bank on the ground floor of the large Bayankhongor Store. The airport is about 1km south of the city.

BUS
Buses leaves for Ulaanbaatar (T28,000, 15 hours, 630km) via Arvaikheer (same price, five hours, 200km) at 8am, 2pm and 6pm. Buy tickets the day before if you can.

JEEP & MINIVAN
Shared minivans leave from the bus stand for Ulaanbaatar (T32,000) throughout the day, but most commonly just after the evening bus has left. You should also be able to catch a shared minivan

to Altai (T36,000, 12 hours) most days, from where you can find onward transport to Khovd.

Shared vehicles also hang around outside the Black Market.

Bayangovi   Баянговь

The small town of Bayangovi is about 250km south of Bayankhongor (by road) in a beautiful valley dominated by Ikh Bogd Uul (3957m). While there is nothing of special interest in Bayangovi itself, the surrounding countryside offers some intriguing desert sites and ample opportunity for exploration.

Gobi Camels (☎9904 4108; GPS: N 44°45.750', E 100°20.585'; per person with meals US$48) is a ger camp in a beautifully remote location with a mountain backdrop, 6km northwest of town. The manager speaks English. The other alternative is the clean **Sumshig Hotel and Restaurant** (☎9915 2046; per person T10,000) within a compound on the western edge of the town 'square'. The restaurant has a photo menu (mains T4000–6000) and a bar. There's also a games room with pool and table tennis. No showers, but the tiny public **bathhouse** (shower T2000; ⊘9am-9pm) is opposite.

Shared minivans or jeeps occasionally run to Bayangovi from outside the central market at Bayankhongor. To get back to Bayankhongor (T17,000) ask at the post office, shops or petrol station, and wait. The road around Bogd can become an impassable quagmire after heavy rain.

Amarbuyant Khiid
Амарбуянт Хийд

Located 47km west of Shinejist, this ruined **monastery** (GPS: N 44°37.745', E 98°42.214') once housed around 1000 monks until its destruction in 1937 by Stalin's forces. Its claim to fame is that the 13th Dalai Lama, while travelling from Lhasa to Urga in 1904, stayed here for 10 days. The extensive ruins today include temples, buildings and walls, and the main temple has been partially restored. Locals can also show you a small *ovoo* built by the Dalai Lama; out of respect no rocks were ever added to the *ovoo*.

Ekhiin Gol   Эхийн Гол

This fertile **oasis** (GPS: N 43°14.898', E 90°00.295') located deep in the southern Gobi produces a tremendous amount of fruit and vegetables. This is probably the only place in Mongolia where, upon entering a ger, travellers are served tomato juice rather than tea. Until the 1920s, Chinese farmers tilled this soil and grew opium, an era that ended when a psychopathic lama-turned-bandit named Dambijantsan came by here and slaughtered them all. Ekhiin Gol is a good place to start or end a camel trek from Shinejist.

GOV-ALTAI   ГОВЬ-АЛТАЙ

POP 53,700 / AREA 142,000 SQ KM

Mongolia's second-largest aimag is named after the Gobi Desert and Mongol Altai Nuruu, a mountain range that virtually bisects the aimag to create a stark, rocky landscape. There is a certain beauty in this combination, but there is considerable heartbreak too. Gov-Altai is one of the least suitable areas for raising livestock, and therefore one of the most hostile to human habitation.

Somehow a few Gobi bears, wild camels, ibexes and even snow leopards survive, protected in several remote national parks. Most of the population live in the north-

---

NATIONAL PARKS OF GOV-ALTAI

The beauty of Gov-Altai's diverse and sparsely populated mountain and desert environment has led to the designation of large portions of the aimag as national parks.

Alag Khairkhan Nature Reserve (36,400 hectares) Protected Altai habitat with rare plants, snow leopards, argali and ibexes.

Eej Khairkhan Nature Reserve (22,475 hectares; p205) About 150km directly south of Altai, the reserve was created to protect the general environment.

Great Gobi Strictly Protected Area (p205) Divided into 'Gobi A' (Southern Altai Gobi, 4.4 million hectares) and 'Gobi B' (Dzungarian Gobi, 881,000 hectares), collectively this is the fourth-largest biosphere reserve in the world and protects a number of endangered animals. Takhiin Tal has been set up on the border of the northern section of Gobi B. *Takhi* (the Mongolian wild horse) have been reintroduced into the wild here since 1996 through the Research Station.

Khasagt Khairkhan Strictly Protected Area (27,448 hectares) The area protects endangered argali sheep and the Mongol Altai mountain environment.

Sharga Nature Reserve Like the Mankhan Nature Reserve in Khovd aimag, it helps to preserve highly endangered species of antelope.

eastern corner, where melting snow from Khangai Nuruu feeds small rivers, creating vital water supplies.

Mountaineers and adventurous hikers with a lot of time on their hands might want to bag an Altai peak. Opportunities include Khuren Tovon Uul (3802m) in Altai *sum*, Burkhan Buuddai Uul (3765m) in Biger *sum*, or the permanently snow-capped peak of Sutai Uul (4090m), the highest peak in Gov-Altai located right on the border with Khovd aimag. Most climbers approach Sutai Uul from the Khovd side.

Altai   Алтай

📞 01482, 7048 / POP 15,800 / ELEV 2181M

Nestled between the mountains of Khasagt Khairkhan Uul (3579m) and Jargalant Uul (3070m), the aimag capital has an attractive setting, but this is a remote, exposed town that's really only used by travellers as a place to refuel and plot the next move.

👁 Sights

Aimag Museum   MUSEUM
(📞 01482-24213; admission T2500; ⊙ 9am-1pm & 2-6pm Mon-Fri) The Aimag Museum includes some excellent bronze statues, scroll paintings, some genuine Mongol army chainmail, and an interesting shaman costume and drum. Look out for the 200kg statue of Buddha, which was hidden in a cave during the purges and recovered in 1965.

Shuteen Park   PARK
Climb the small hill for views of the town. There's a temple at the top (not to be confused with the drab monastery at its base).

🛌 Sleeping

Taigam Tal Hotel   HOTEL $$
(📞 9992 9003; tw T40,000-50,000) Housed in a reasonably new, green-and-white two-storey building by Shuteen Park, this place has neat and tidy modern rooms with TV and attached bathroom. No English sign (look simply for 'Hotel') or English spoken, but staff members are welcoming.

Zaiver Ger Camp   TOURIST GER CAMP $$
(📞 9948 4300; GPS: N 46°14.391', E 96°21.682'; per person with/without meals T60,000/20,000; 🅿) This pretty camp is nestled into the crook of a forested hillside, 16km south of Altai (west off the main road to Biger). Pick-up from, and drop-off back to town is included in the

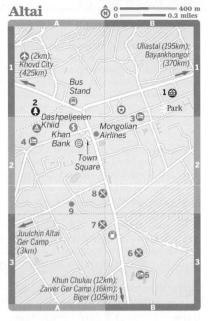

price. There is no shower. This spot is the nicest place for camping too.

Tulga Altai   HOTEL $$
(📞 01482-23747; tw T25,000-40,000, tr T40,000, lux T60,000-80,000) Although not so pretty from the outside, this large concrete block of a hotel, opposite the market, is pretty clean on the inside. All rooms apart from the T25,000 ones, have attached bathrooms, but with cold water only. The free-to-use common shower room has hot water, though.

OFF THE BEATEN TRACK

THE ROAD TO BIGER

A remote back route takes you from Altai southeast to Biger, from where you can continue to Chandmani, Bayangovi and Khongoryn Els in Ömnögov. The road cuts through the stark mountain-lined scenery of the Biger Depression, and passes a few rarely visited sights along the way. In Biger, a small town known for producing yak-milk vodka, there's a good-value guesthouse above a shop with two cosy triple rooms (per bed T10,000).

Khun Chuluu (GPS: N 46°15.830', E 96°16.484') About 8km west of the main road as you head south from Altai to Biger (and about 10km southwest of Altai itself), this *khun chuluu*, stone figures or *balbal*, is said to date back to the 13th century (possibly earlier).

Biger Red Yabar (GPS: N 45°51.306', E 96°52.677') About 28km before you reach Biger (74km from Altai), you'll see these striking, red-coloured cliffs off to your right (south). Their crenulated formation is accentuated in early-morning or late-afternoon light, and the snow-capped backdrop completes a dramatic scene.

Biger Nomin Khan Monastery Ruins (GPS: N 45°48.346', E 97°00.544') The official road-side sign for these monastery ruins states that they are around 750 years old. We doubt they are quite that old, but they are interesting nonetheless, and are fairly extensive, with a number of mudbrick walls still standing. Now desolate, save for scattered pieces of broken brickwork and pottery, the monastery once housed around 500 monks. The ruins are on your left, 16km before Biger (86km from Altai).

Altai Hotel HOTEL $$$
(☑ 01482-24134; r T60,000-150,000; ☏) Recently renovated, rooms in this green-and-white-painted hotel are smart and functional, with TV and bathroom, although the bathrooms in the cheaper rooms don't have showers. Has wi-fi and a decent restaurant.

✗ Eating

The restaurant at Altai Hotel was undergoing renovation at the time of research, but is generally well regarded.

Sutai MONGOLIAN $
(Zaluur Altai; ☑ 01482-23567; mains T4000-6000; ☺ 8am-8pm) The goulash- and mutton-based fare comes in full or half portions. The restaurant includes an attached billiards hall and karaoke bar.

Market MONGOLIAN $
(☺ 8am-8pm Sun-Fri) Reasonably well stocked with foodstuffs (and warm clothing). Cheap *guanz* (canteens) can also be found here.

Seoul Restaurant & Pub MONGOLIAN, KOREAN $$
(mains T5000-8000; ☺ 10am-10pm) The smartest restaurant in town has the usual range of Mongolian dishes plus some Korean hot-plate dishes (T15,000 to T18,000) that are big enough for two to share if bumped up with rice. No English on the menu, but some photos. Beer from T2000.

ℹ Information

Bathhouse (admission T2000; ☺ 9am-10pm) In the basement of a four-storey pink building.
Internet Cafe (per hr T500; ☺ 9am-10pm) Inside the Telecom office, with the post office.
Khan Bank (☺ 9am-6pm Mon-Fri) Currency exchange, an ATM (next door) and Western Union.

ℹ Getting There & Away

AIR

Mongolian Airlines (☑ 7048 4979, 9400 0715; ☺ 9am-6pm) flies to Ulaanbaatar (T240,000) via Bayankhongor (T110,000) at 10am on Tuesdays, Fridays and Sundays. Staff speak English. Cash only. The airport is 2km northwest of town (T4000 in a taxi). Note that Mongolian Airlines changed its name to Hunnu Air in 2013 but at the time of research had yet to change its branding in Altai so it still had the old Mongolian Airlines signage at the office here.

BUS

A bus leaves every Monday, Wednesday, Friday and Saturday at 11am for Ulaanbaatar (T45,000, 26 hours, 1000km) via Bayankhongor (T20,000, 371km), Arvaikheer (T20,000, 571km), several *guanz* stops, a couple of breakdowns and a small river crossing.

MINIVAN & JEEP

Minivans leave from the bus stand when full for Ulaanbaatar (T42,000, 20 hours) and will reluctantly take passengers for Bayankhongor (T25,000) and Arvaikheer (T30,000). Despite being on the main road to Khovd, it is quite difficult to find transport west as passing buses/minivans are invariably full. It is possible, though.

Great Gobi Strictly Protected Area
Говийн Их Дархан Газар

For both parts of the **park** (entry fee T3000) you will need a very reliable vehicle and an experienced driver, and you must be completely self-sufficient with supplies of food, water and camping gear. A ranger will probably track you down and collect park entry fees.

Gobi A (Southern Altai Gobi)   ГОВЬ 'А'

The majority of this 4.4-million-hectare national park lies in southern Gov-Altai. Established more than 25 years ago, the area has been nominated as an International Biosphere Reserve by the UN.

Gobi A is the last remaining area in Mongolia where you can find *khavtgai* (wild Bactrian camels), and the **Wild Camel Breeding Centre** (☑9915 6556; www.wildcamels.com) has been set up at Zakhyn-Us for their protection. The park is remote and very difficult to reach, which is bad news for visitors but excellent news for the fragile flora and fauna. To explore the park, start at Biger, turn southwest on the trail to Tsogt, and head south on any jeep trail you can find.

Gobi B (Dzungarian Gobi)   ГОВЬ 'В'

Although the majority of this 881,000-hectare park lies in neighbouring Khovd aimag, the Gov-Altai side contains the **Takhiin Tal Research Station** (☑9983 6979; GPS: N 45°32.197', E 93°39.055'; per person T10,000), which has been set up to protect the reintroduced *takhi* (Przewalski's horse). Most of the *takhi* now run free, although a few still live in enclosures near the research station, which is about 15km southwest of Bij village. However, it should be noted that casual tourists are not welcome to visit.

Eej Khairkhan Nature Reserve   Ээж Хайрхан Уул

Near the base of the Eej Khairkhan Uul (2275m), part of the **Eej Khairkhan Nature Reserve** just north of 'Gobi A' National Park, you can camp at some delightful **rock pools** and explore the nearby **caves**. You will need a guide to show you around. Almost no suitable drinking water is available in the area, so take your own.

About 30 minutes' walk west of the rock pools are some spectacular ancient **rock paintings** of ibexes, horsemen and archers. The mountain, which is a pilgrimage destination for some Mongolians, is about 150km south of Altai.

Western Mongolia

POP 307,200 / AREA 191,000 SQ KM

Best for Camping

➡ Khoton Nuur (p215)
➡ Uureg Nuur (p226)
➡ Chigistei Gol (p230)
➡ Around Tarialan (p226)
➡ Buyant Gol (p218)

Best for Trekking

➡ Altai Tavan Bogd National Park (p214)
➡ Kharkhiraa Uul & Türgen Uul (p226)
➡ Otgon Tenger Uul Strictly Protected Area (p231)
➡ Tsambagarav Uul National Park (p217)

Why Go?

Raw, rugged and remote, this off-the-beaten-track region has for centuries been isolated – both geographically and culturally – from the Mongol heartland. With its glacier-wrapped mountains, shimmering salt lakes and the hardy culture of nomads, falconry and cattle rustling, western Mongolia is, in many ways, a timeless slice of Central Asia.

Squeezed between Russia, Kazakhstan, China and the rest of Mongolia, this region has long been a patchwork of peoples including ethnic Kazakhs, Dörvöds, Khotons, Myangads and Khalkh Mongols. Traditional arts such as *khöömii* throat singing and eagle hunting are still practised here, as they have been for thousands of years.

The wild landscape creates fabulous opportunities for trekkers and climbers on peaks that rise to over 4000m. If that sounds too extreme for you, then just pick a lake, pitch a tent and have yourself a camping trip you'll never forget.

When to Go

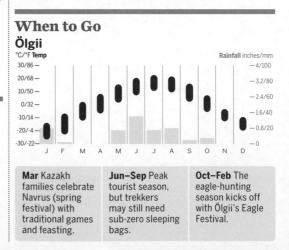

Ölgii

Mar Kazakh families celebrate Navrus (spring festival) with traditional games and feasting.

Jun–Sep Peak tourist season, but trekkers may still need sub-zero sleeping bags.

Oct–Feb The eagle-hunting season kicks off with Ölgii's Eagle Festival.

Western Mongolia Highlights

1 Hike to the base camp of snow-capped **Khuiten Uul** (p214), Mongolia's highest mountain, for stunning views of Altai Tavan Bogd National Park.

2 Walk around Tavan Bogd's **Khoton Nuur** (p215), a beautiful alpine lake dotted with Kazakh settlements around its shore.

3 Horse trek or hike around the lakes and valleys beneath the sacred mountain of **Otgon Tenger Uul** (p231).

4 Camp by the shores of **Üüreg Nuur** (p226), a lovely, accessible freshwater lake filled with fish (and devoid of mosquitoes).

5 Rub shoulders with Kazakh eagle hunters during Ölgii's **Eagle Festival** (p210).

6 Camp and trek in the mountains around **Tarialan** (p226), a rugged landscape of glaciers, green meadows and boulder fields.

ℹ️ ONE HOUR BEHIND

Note that the three westernmost aimags in Mongolia – Bayan-Ölgii, Khovd and Uvs – are in a different time zone from the rest of the country: they are one hour behind.

Zavkhan aimag, however, remains on Ulaanbaatar time.

History

The Mongol Altai Nuruu (commonly referred to as the Altai Mountains) was once the easternmost territory inhabited by the Scythians, a vast empire of nomadic pastoralists who dominated Central Asia from 700 BC to AD 300.

Prior to Mongol domination in the 13th century, western Mongolia was a stronghold of the Oirads, a warrior tribe that initially resisted the expansionary tactics of Chinggis Khaan, but later submitted. Following the collapse of the Mongol empire, the Oirads reasserted their domination over the area and expanded to the Volga. These pioneers became known as Kalmyks and still inhabit the Caspian shores of Russia.

Manchu military outposts were created in Khovd City and Uliastai during the Qing dynasty. Both capitulated soon after the fall of the Manchu empire in 1911. The fighting was particularly bloody in Khovd, where a mystic Kalmyk named Dambijantsan (also known as Ja Lama) gathered an army of 5000 Oirads and Mongols, razed the fortress to the ground and skinned the Chinese soldiers inside.

Under Ulaanbaatar rule, western Mongolia was called Chandmandi until it was broken up into three aimags (provinces) in 1931. One of the three, Bayan-Ölgii, was designated as a homeland for ethnic Kazakhs living in the region.

ℹ️ Getting There & Away

Transport between western Mongolia and Ulaanbaatar (UB) is mainly by plane and the cheaper seats on flights fill up fast in summer. Buy tickets a few weeks in advance if you can. Transport by land from Ulaanbaatar is a rough and tedious three-to-four days if you drive nonstop. The northern route via Arkhangai has several points of interest, but most share vehicles and public buses travel along the less-interesting southern route via Khovd, Altai and Bayankhongor.

Though not yet a main traveller route, it is possible to enter or leave Mongolia at the Tsagaannuur border crossing with Russia (best accessed from Ölgii) or the Bulgan border with China's Xinjiang province (best accessed from Khovd).

ℹ️ Getting Around

Hiring a jeep is relatively easy in Ölgii but can be more difficult elsewhere. All three westernmost aimag capitals are linked by decent jeep trails (Uliastai is much further east so less well connected to the west). You'll waste a lot of time if hitchhiking in the area; trucks will most likely be heading for the nearest border post and jeeps will be packed full of people. You are better off with the buses and the shared jeeps and minivans that congregate at the markets. As it is easier to get on a bus heading back to Ulaanbaatar than trying to hop on an already full one on its way out, a good plan is to fly out and overland it back to the capital.

BAYAN-ÖLGII
БАЯН-ОЛГИЙ

POP 90,500 / AREA 46,000 SQ KM

Travelling to Mongolia's westernmost aimag gives you the distinct feeling of reaching the end of the road, if not the end of the earth. High, dry, rugged and raw, the isolated, oddly shaped aimag follows the arc of the Mongol Altai Nuruu as it rolls out of Central Asia towards the barren wastes of the Dzungarian Basin.

Many peaks here are more than 4000m high and permanently covered with glaciers and snow, while the valleys have a few green pastures that support about two million head of livestock, as well as bears, foxes and wolves.

Ethnic groups who call Bayan-Ölgii home include the Kazakh, Khalkh, Dörvöd, Uriankhai, Tuva and Khoshuud. Unlike the rest of Mongolia, which is dominated by the Khalkh Mongols, about 90% of Bayan-Ölgii's population are Kazakh.

Ölgii   Өлгий

📲 01422, 7042 / POP 28,500 / ELEV 1710M

Ölgii city is a windblown frontier town that will appeal to anyone who dreams of the Wild West. It's a squat, concrete affair, straddling the banks of the Khovd Gol and surrounded by ger (traditional circular felt yurt) districts and rocky escarpments. Thunderclouds brew in the mountains above

Ölgii

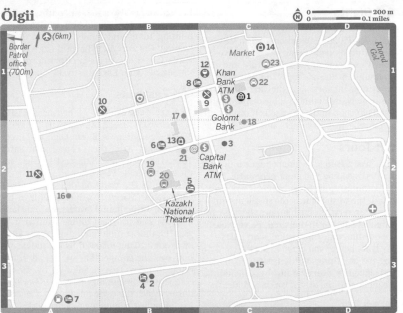

Ölgii

◎ Sights
1 Aimag Museum C1

◎ Activities, Courses & Tours
2 Blue Wolf Travel B3
3 Kazakh Tour C2

◎ Sleeping
4 Blue Wolf B3
5 Duman B2
6 Tavan Bogd Hotel B2
7 Traveller's Guest House A3
8 Tsambagarav Hotel B1

◎ Eating
9 Arvin Restaurant & Pub C1
10 Pamukkale B1
Tsambagarav Hotel .... (see 8)
11 Tsambagarav Supermarket A2

◎ Drinking & Nightlife
12 Aulum Sayajim Beer Garden C1

◎ Shopping
13 Altai Kerei B2
14 Market C1

◎ Information
15 Aumin Garage C3
16 Bathhouse A2
17 Immigration, Naturalisation &
Foreign Citizens Office B1
18 Mongol Altai Nuruu Protected
Areas Administration Office C2

◎ Transport
AeroMongolia .... (see 18)
19 Bus Stand B2
20 Bus Ticket Office B2
21 Ez Niz B2
22 Minivans C1
23 Shared Jeeps C1

town, making for some dramatic climatic changes throughout the day and brilliant light shows in the late afternoon.

The town is predominantly Kazakh, and you'll soon start feeling it has more in common with Muslim-influenced Central Asia than Buddhist Mongolia: there are signs in Arabic and Kazakh Cyrillic, and the market, which is called a bazaar rather than the Mongolian *zakh*, sells the odd shashlik (kebab) and is stocked with goods from Kazakhstan.

◉ Sights

Aimag Museum   MUSEUM
(admission T5000; ⊙9am-noon & 1-5pm Mon-Fri)
The old-fashioned Aimag Museum gives a
decent overview of Kazakh culture and the
geography of Bayan-Ölgii. The 2nd floor is
devoted to history, and the 3rd floor has
some interesting ethnographic displays. The
small gift shop in the foyer sells Kazakh wall
hangings, felt rugs, carpets and crafts.

☞ Tours

Ölgii has a clutch of independent tour operators, meaning you don't necessarily have
to fix things up in Ulaanbaatar if you want
to tour the west. Some of the smaller companies offer very reasonable rates, but can be
unreliable and/or ill-prepared. Be very clear
about what your tour includes on a day-to-
day basis before you agree to anything. Getting the key things written down on paper
and signed by everyone involved, including
the guide and the driver, isn't a bad idea.

Kazakh Tour   TOUR AGENCY
(☑9942 4505, 9942 2006; www.kazakhtour.com;
2nd fl NHU Bldg) Easily the most professional
and reliable of the Ölgii-based tour companies the excellent Kazakh Tour specialises
in tailor-made trips throughout Bayan-Ölgii
and consistently gets great reviews from
travellers. The Kazakh owner, Dosjan Khabyl,
has many contacts in the area and can organise trekking, horse treks and visits to
local eagle hunters, *khöömii* singers and the
local *böö* (shaman).

Blue Wolf Travel   TOUR AGENCY
(☑9910 0303, 01422-22772; www.bluewolftravel.
com) Blue Wolf is the original tour operator

in Ölgii and is also a well-run outfit. It offers
a variety of trips including winter eagle-
hunting tours and guided treks in Tsambagarav Uul and Altai Tavan Bogd National
Parks. It is also a good source of information
for Sagsai's Altai Eagle Festival.

✰ Festivals

★ Eagle Festival   TRADITIONAL CULTURE
(admission US$30; ⊙1st weekend Oct) There are
360 eagle hunters in Bayan-Ölgii and every
year around 70 of them converge at Sayat
Tube (Hunter's Hill), 8km east of Ölgii, for
the annual Eagle Festival.

Although the tradition dates back about
2000 years (Marco Polo mentions it in his
Travels), the inaugural festival was only held
in 1999. The program differs from year to
year but the opening ceremony usually kicks
off around 10am, followed by the judging of
how well the competitors are attired in traditional dress. This is followed by various
competitions, including one called *shakhyru*
during which the eagle must catch a piece of
fox fur pulled behind a galloping horse. The
festival culminates on Sunday, when a live
fox (and sometimes a wolf pup) is released as
bait for the top three eagles to hunt (animal
lovers may find this distressing as the fox is
killed).

The traditional horse games and camel
races that are staggered over the two-day
event are probably more thrilling than the
actual eagle-hunting competitions. The
most exciting are *kokbar* (a tug-of-war with
an animal skin between two riders) and
tenge ilu (a competition in which riders
must swoop down to pick up a scrap of material from the ground at full gallop).

NATIONAL PARKS OF BAYAN-ÖLGII

Most parks in Bayan-Ölgii come under the jurisdiction of the Mongol Altai Nuruu Protected Areas Administration office (p212).

Altai Tavan Bogd National Park (636,161 hectares; p214) Fauna includes argali sheep,
ibexes, *maral* (Asiatic red deer), stone martens, deer, elk, Altai snowcocks and eagles.

Develiin Aral Nature Reserve (10,300 hectares) A remarkable habitat around Develiin
Island in the Usan Khooloi and Khovd Rivers. It is home to pheasants, boars and beavers.

Khökh Serkh Strictly Protected Area (65,920 hectares) A mountainous area on the
border with Khovd, which protects argali sheep and ibexes.

Siilkhem Nuruu National Park (140,080 hectares) This park has two sections, one
around Ikh Türgen Uul, the other further west.

Tsambagarav Uul National Park (110,960 hectares; p217) Protects glaciers and the
snow-leopard habitat; borders on Khovd.

Be sure to hang onto your admission ticket as it will get you into the Saturday-night traditional music concert held in the Kazakh National Theatre.

The easiest way to get to the festival grounds is on the bus operated by Kazakh Tour (T5000 per person return, tickets available from its office) or by taxi (T10,000 one way).

Smaller eagle festivals are also held in Sagsai (p213) and Tolbo (p217).

Navrus   SPRING FEAST
(⊙22 Mar) The spring festival of Navrus is celebrated with family visits and feasting. You may see traditional games and contests at this time, including one in which men attempt to lift an ox off the ground.

🛌 Sleeping

To camp, walk east of the square to Khovd Gol and then head southeast, away from the market and ger suburbs.

⭐Traveller's Guest House   GUEST GER $
(☑9942 4505, 9942 9696; nazkana@fastmail.fm; per person T10,000; P 🛜) This small, no-frills, family-run operation is friendly and good value. The owner, Nazgul, who also works for Kazakh Tour, speaks good English and has extensive knowledge about the whole aimag. She'll rent you a mountain bike (T10,000 per day), put on a load of your laundry (T10,000) and pick you up or drop you off at the airport (T5000). Better yet, her gers, which are in the yard of her family home, and the shared shower are spotless, although the shared toilets are long-drop, pit-toilet jobs. Wi-fi extends to all the gers (when it's working). No restaurant.

Blue Wolf   GUEST GER $
(☑9910 0303, 01422-22772; www.bluewolftravel.com; per person T15,000; P @) Tour operator Blue Wolf offers three large Kazakh-style, and four smaller Mongolian-style gers, all with stoves. The toilet and shower block, at one end of the compound, is clean and comes with flush toilets and hot showers.

Tsambagarav Hotel   HOTEL $$
(Green Hotel; ☑9555 9365; s/tw T35,000/40,000, d lux T50,000; 🛜) Clean, comfy beds, reasonably modern bathrooms in working order and friendly staff. The reception is on the 3rd floor past the restaurant and karaoke bar (closed Fridays). Has wi-fi, although it's not always working.

Duman   HOTEL $$
(☑01422-21666, 9942 1515; tw T35,000-55,000; P 🛜) Well-appointed rooms with kettle, wall-mounted TV and hot showers in en-suite bathrooms. Wi-fi in the lobby. Breakfast included. Very little English spoken.

Tavan Bogd Hotel   HOTEL $$
(☑9908 8401; lenahidir@yahoo.com; s/d/tr/q T20,000/35,000/45,000/60,000; 🛜) This is the oldest hotel in town and has a slightly seedy feel to it, but rooms are neat and spacious so it's an OK choice if others are full.

🍴 Eating & Drinking

In respect for the large Muslim population, alcohol is seldom served on Fridays. Self-caterers should head to the market (p212), which has a decent selection of food supplies imported from Russia and China, or to one of the supermarkets dotted about town. We found Tsambagarav Supermarket (⊙9am-10pm) to be well stocked.

**⭐Arvin Restaurant
& Pub**   KAZAKH, MONGOLIAN $
(meals T3000-5000; ⊙10am-10pm) Smartly turned-out waiting staff, snappy service, an upmarket vibe and some tasty Kazakh favourites make this popular with locals and travellers alike. We recommend the *sirne* (a Kazakh dish of meat cooked in a pressure cooker). Beer from T2000. Photo menu.

Tsambagarav Hotel   WESTERN, MONGOLIAN $
(meals T4000-10,000; ⊙9am-10pm Mon-Sat) Smart hotel restaurant with a well-stocked bar and a decent choice of Mongolian fare.

Pamukkale   TURKISH $$
(meals T4000-8500; ⊙10am-11pm; 🛜 📶) A Turkish-run outfit that serves authentic kebabs, Turkish soups and tasty chicken dishes. The Turkish desserts are also excellent but portions are minuscule. Alcohol is not served here (apart from *koumiss*; fermented mare milk), but they do serve Turkish coffee. Has wi-fi and an English menu.

Aulum Sayajim Beer Garden   BEER GARDEN
(admission T300; ⊙noon-11pm Jun-Aug) Slightly shabby beer garden, but a novelty if the weather's nice. Beer from T2500.

🛍 Shopping

Altai Kerei   HANDICRAFTS
(⊙10am-6pm Tue-Sun) Small arts-and-crafts shop selling Kazakh felt handicrafts (bags,

purses, slippers, hats) as well as traditional clothing. Prices start at around T2000.

Market MARKET
(☉10am-5pm Tue-Sun) Traditional Kazakh skullcaps and jackets can be found amid the chaos here. Also good for fruit and veg. You can buy stoves and gas canisters too. Doesn't really get going until the afternoon.

ℹ Information

There's a Khan Bank ATM near the museum, and a Capital Bank ATM beside the Telecom Building. Both accept foreign cards. Golomt Bank, opposite the east side of the square, may be able to change money.

Aumin Garage (☏9942 2200, 01422-21660) Helps Mongol Rally drivers with mechanical repairs.

Bathhouse (shower T1500; ☉10am-10pm)

Immigration, Naturalisation & Foreign Citizens Office (INFC; ☏01422-22195, 9942 4338; Government House; ☉8am-noon & 1-5pm Mon-Sat) Can register your passport if you just arrived from Russia and issue an exit visa (US$43) if you are leaving and don't already have one. It cannot issue visa extensions. Minimal English-language skills make dealing with staff tricky.

Mongol Altai Nuruu Protected Areas Administration Office (Manspaa; ☏9942 9864, 01422-22111; manspaa@mongol.net; ☉9am-noon & 1.30-5pm Mon-Fri) The office doubles as an information centre, although local tour agencies are more informed.

Telecom Building (per hr T600; ☉9am-7pm) As with pretty much every town in Mongolia, the Telecom Building here is a post office, a telephone centre and an internet cafe.

ℹ Getting There & Away

AIR
The airport is 6km north of the centre, on the opposite side of the river. There is no bus but you can find cars for hire at the market (T500 per kilometre).

AeroMongolia (☏8808 0025; 2nd fl Manspaa Bldg) Flies Tuesday, Thursday and Saturday to UB. Prices similar to those at EZ Nis, but less English spoken. Cash only. The office is on the 2nd floor of Manspaa building.

Ez Nis Charges T280,000 to T360,000 one way to UB, and flies on Monday, Wednesday, Friday and Saturday. Staff speak some English, and you should be able to purchase flights with a Visa card. The office is next to the Telecom Building.

BUS
The nonstop, two- to three-day bus trip to Ulaanbaatar (T80,000, 1636km) leaves daily at around 2pm, and goes via Khovd (211km), Altai (635km), Bayankhongor (1006km) and Arvaikheer (1206km). Tickets for the latter destinations are only available if there are empty seats. The hard-to-find **ticket office** (☉8am-5pm) is in the basement of the Kazakh National Theatre, on the west side of the building. Duck in through a doorway beside a sign for 'Vision Centre' and you'll find the office down the corridor on the left.

MINIVAN & JEEP
Public shared jeeps to Khovd City (T20,000, six to seven hours) are far more frequent than those to Ulaangom (T40,000, 10 hours, 300km).

Like the bus, the shared minivans to Ulaanbaatar (T68,000, 60 hours) pass through Altai (T45,000), Bayankhongor (T68,000) and

---

ℹ ONWARDS TO RUSSIA & KAZAKHSTAN

Jeeps and/or minivans leave daily each morning at around 10am for the Russian border town of Kosh-Agach (T35,000 per person). From Kosh-Agach there should be a morning bus to Gorno Altaysk, the region's capital.

For Kazakhstan, there is a long-distance bus/minivan which leaves Ölgii every 10 days bound for Astana. It goes through Russia's Altai region so you'll need a Russian and a Kazakhstan visa to take it. It costs T130,000 per person. Kazakh Tour (p210) in Ölgii can help you buy the ticket for a T20,000 commission. They can also give you the latest on what date the bus leaves. The bus (usually just a minivan in fact) first heads to the Mongolian border at Tsagaannuur (three hours), where you stay the night (a guesthouse here charges T10,000 per bed including food). You then make the 36-hour trip to Astana from here on an actual bus. Shared minivans make the same trip more regularly from Ölgii, although not necessarily every day.

For further information, head to shop.lonelyplanet.com to purchase downloadable PDFs of chapters from Lonely Planet's *China* or *Russia* guides.

At the time of research, flights between Ölgii and Kazakhstan had been suspended indefinitely.

BAYTOLDA: EAGLE HUNTER

Eagle hunter Baytolda told us a little about the ancient practice.

Finding an Eagle

Eagles are like people; some are calm, some are lazy and some, like my eagle Sari Köz (Yellow Eye), become cantankerous in their old age.

I trapped Sari Köz 22 years ago in the Sairyn Mountains. Some people steal chicks from an eagle's nest but these birds lack killer instincts and never become good hunters. I think it is better to lure and trap a wild adult who has already learnt to hunt, using a previously caught eagle and some meat. Sari Köz, like all eagles used in hunting, is a *bürkit* (female). *Bürkits* are best as they are bigger, heavier and far more aggressive than the males *(sarsha)*.

Training an Eagle

To train a *bürkit* takes patience. At first she will flap wildly and try to bite whoever approaches. To 'break' her we rig a perch that spins and throws her off balance and causes her to fall. After two or three days she is hungry, exhausted and calm enough to take food from your hand. Eventually she will trust you and learn to come to you to be fed. This is the first step in training a *bürkit*.

When an eagle is first taken outside she is kept tethered to her *tugir* (pole) and taught to chase small animal skins or lures called *shirgas*, until the day comes when you must untie the tether and trust that she does not fly away.

The Hunt

After much practise, the *bürkit* is ready to go on a hunt. It is best to go with another, experienced eagle so that she can learn from it. When a fox or marmot is spotted, the *tomaga* (hood) is removed and, if trained correctly and of a strong spirit, she will chase and capture it. If she has been successful in her hunt, she is rewarded with fresh meat from the kill.

Arvaikheer (T68,000). They assemble at the road next to the museum.

Hiring a random driver at the Ölgii market is not a good idea – these drivers are not accountable to anyone and have a reputation for changing prices and itineraries mid-trip. The Manspaa office and local tour companies will have drivers more familiar with tourists' needs.

Sagsai   Сагсай

Most travellers pass through Sagsai on their way to the lakes in Altai Tavan Bogd National Park, with little reason to stop. That is until September when this tiny community hosts the **Altai Eagle Festival** (per person US$30; ◷3rd weekend Sep). The festival, held about 6km southwest of the town (GPS: N 48°52.250', E 89°37.170'), is smaller than the one in Ölgii, although it follows much the same program. One notable difference is that live animals are not used as bait. Blue Wolf Travel (p210) is a sponsor and a good source of information. It also operates a **ger camp** (☑9910 0303; with/without meals US$30/15) and arranges **homestays** (with

breakfast/3 meals US$10/15) and return transport from Ölgii (US$85 per eight-seat vehicle). A taxi from Ölgii should cost around T5000 per person one-way.

Tsengel   Цэнгэл

Of the 12 *sums* in Bayan-Ölgii, Tsengel is the largest. Although the town itself is bigger than most, it is still just a collection of gravel roads and wooden fences that surround compounds, each containing an earth and log home, possibly a ger or two and invariably a guard dog in a foul mood.

The principal reasons to stop here are to visit Tuvan *khöömii* throat singer **Bapizan** (☑9941 4816; 30min demonstration T10,000-20,000) and to grab a bite at the surprisingly excellent **Artysh Cafe & Hotel** (mains T1500-2000, sandwiches T500; ◷9am-10pm Mon-Sat). The menu will likely bamboozle your guide (if you have one) as it is written in Tuvan but the food is mostly Mongolian. If you are heading to the Altai Tavan Bogd National Park you can grab sandwiches and drinks from the chiller out back. The attached hotel (☎ 9542 8279; s/d T15,000/30,000) is also good value with clean and simple rooms.

Tsengel is 75km from Ölgii on the road to the twin lakes of Khoton Nuur and Khurgan Nuur. A share jeep leaves at 7am for Ölgii's market (T5000) and returns at around 5pm.

Altai Tavan Bogd National Park

Алтай Таван Богд

This stunning region stretches south from Tavan Bogd and includes the twin lakes of Khoton Nuur and Khurgan Nuur (and the less interesting Dayan Nuur), which are the source of the Khovd Gol that flows to Khar Us Nuur in Khovd aimag.

Despite its remote location, the **park** (admission T3000) and its beautiful scenery make it the premier attraction in western Mongolia. Divided from China by a high wall of snow-capped peaks, the area is a trekker's paradise.

The main entry to the park is by the bridge over the Khovd Gol, south of Tsengel. You can pay for entry there or at the Manspaa office in Ölgii (p212). Border permits are also required; see p216.

◉ Sights & Activities

◉ Tavan Bogd Region

Tavan Bogd (Five Saints) is a soaring cluster of mountains that straddles the border between Mongolia, Russia and China. The range includes Khuiten (Cold Peak), Naran (Sun), Ölgii (Land), Bürged (Eagle) and Nairamdal (Friendship) Uuls (mountains).

Tsagaan Sala   PETROGLYPHS

(Baga Oigor) The best petroglyphs in the area, if not all of Central Asia, can be found at Tsagaan Sala, on the route between Ulaankhus and Tavan Bogd. The drawings, more than 10,000 of them, are scattered over a 15km area; you'll need a guide to find the best ones.

Sheveed Uul (3350m) also contains some fascinating **petroglyphs** (GPS: N 49°06.238; E 88°14.918') depicting wild animals and hunting scenes.

★ Khuiten Uul   TREKKING

(Cold Peak) The highest peak in the Tavan Bogd range, Khuiten Uul (4374m), is the tallest mountain in Mongolia and is of interest to professional climbers who are properly equipped with ice axes, crampons and ropes. The best time to climb is August and September, after the worst of the summer rains. In 2006 the president of Mongolia climbed Khuiten and renamed it Ikh Mongol; however, no one seems to use this name.

Even if you are not a climber, it's worth trekking up to the Khuiten Uul **base camp** (GPS: N 49°09.036; E 87°56.528; 3092m), where you can get stunning views of all the peaks as well as the 12km-long **Potanii glacier**, which tumbles out of the range. It's possible to walk onto the glacier but be very careful of deep snow and crevasses. If you're not too exhausted already, head to the top of **Malchin Peak** (4050m). The three-hour walk is rewarded with views of Russia and the surrounding mountains.

Note that there are two trails to the base camp. One starts from the end of the road in Tsagaan Gol valley. From here it's a 14km trek to the base camp. The trailhead has a ranger station and a place to camp. Across the river are some gers occupied by an extended family of Tuvans. They rent horses (T10,000) and one of the younger family members can guide you up to the base camp (for around T15,000 with horse).

The other trail to the base camp begins in the Sogoog Gol valley (north of Tsagaan Gol); from here it's 13km to the base camp. This trailhead also has a ranger station.

◉ Khoton Nuur Region

This is one of the most beautiful regions in the park, with the scenery growing more spectacular the further west you travel. The area is best explored on foot or horseback. Kazakh families living around Khoton Nuur in summer can rent you horses.

★ Khoton Nuur   LAKE

The southern shore along Khoton Nuur has excellent camping spots, especially around **Ulaan Tolgoi**, the spit of land that juts majestically into the lake. The northern tip of the lake is marked by **Aral Tolgoi** (Island Head), a unique hill surrounded by verdant pastureland and rocky escarpments. A border station at the northern end of the lake will check to see if your border permit is in order.

Coming around the southern shore of Khoton Nuur, you can camp in secluded coves or explore the valleys that lead towards China. There are some difficult river crossings on your way back to Syrgal.

Khurgan Nuur
LAKE

The shoreline of Khurgan Nuur is dry and exposed. Few people travel along its southern shore, but if you are going this way there is a stupa-like construction and several burial sites. Nearby is a **balbal** (GPS: N 48°32.006, E 88°28.549').

Archaeological Sites
HISTORIC SITES

Numerous archaeological sites dot the region. Mogoit Valley contains a moustachioed **balbal** (GPS: N 48°44.099, E 88°38.930') and a Kazakh cemetery with an interesting beehive-shaped mausoleum about 2km to the north. Another **balbal** (GPS: N 48°39.506, E 88°37.863') can be found south of Mogoit Valley, on the way to Khurgan Nuur. More interesting Kazakh cemeteries and ancient burial mounds are easily spotted from the road.

Rashany Ikh Uul Hot Springs
HOT SPRINGS

(GPS: N48°55.655, E88°14.288'; admission US$10) About 25km northwest of Khoton Nuur you can visit Rashany Ikh Uul, an area of 35 hot springs. The springs are only just lukewarm.

Khoton Nuur to Tavan Bogd
TREKKING

Northwest of Khoton Nuur the mountains close in and there's some fine hiking possibilities. For experienced backcountry walkers, it is even possible to travel up river to Tavan Bogd (110km, seven days). You'll need local help from the Tuvan families to cross the powerful Tsagaan Gol (T2000).

☞ Tours

★ Eagle Hunting
TOUR

(⊙mid-Sep–Apr) Surprisingly, there are more Kazakh eagle hunters in Bayan-Ölgii than there are in Kazakhstan. Arguably, the areas in and around the Altai Tavan Bogd National Park (along with the mountain region of Tsast Uul between Khovd and Bayan-Ölgii, and the Deluun, Tsengel and Bayannuur regions of Bayan-Ölgii) are the best places in the world to experience eagle hunting first hand. It is only practised during winter once the birds have recovered from their summer moult.

All the tour companies in Ölgii arrange trips with eagle hunters on horseback, although to avoid disappointment be prepared for either an unsuccessful hunt or the possibility that the eagle catches its quarry (usually a fox, rabbit or marmot) behind a hill or out of sight.

✱ Festivals & Events

Altai Horse Games
HORSE GAMES

(admission US$30; ⊙ 3rd weekend Jul) Blue Wolf Travel (p210) sponsors a weekend of horse racing and horse games including *kokbar* and *kyz kul* (kiss the girl) between the two

---

KAZAKHS

Ask anyone in Kazakhstan for the best place to find genuine Kazakh culture and they will most likely point to a small plot of land, not in their own country, but in western Mongolia. Bayan-Ölgii, thanks to its isolation for most of the 20th century, is considered by many to be the last bastion of traditional Kazakh language, sport and culture.

Kazakhs first migrated to this side of the Altai in the 1840s to graze their sheep on the high mountain pastures during summer and returned to Kazakhstan or Xinjiang for the winter. After the Mongolian Revolution in 1921, a permanent border was drawn by agreement between China, the USSR and Mongolia.

The word 'Kazakh' is said to mean 'free warrior' or 'steppe roamer'. Kazakhs trace their roots to the 15th century, when rebellious kinsmen of an Uzbek khaan (king or chief) broke away, and settled in present-day Kazakhstan.

Kazakh gers are taller, wider and more richly decorated than the Mongolian version. *Tush* (wall hangings) and *koshma* (felt carpets), decorated with stylised animal motifs, are common. *Chiy* (traditional reed screens) are becoming less common.

Kazakhs adhere rather loosely to Sunni Islam, but religion is not a major force. This is because of their distance from the centre of Islam, their nomadic lifestyle and the suppression of Islam during the communist era. Islam is making a comeback in Bayan-Ölgii, thanks to the lifting of restrictions against religion, aid packages from other Muslim countries, the construction of mosques and the annual hajj (pilgrimage) to Mecca. The main Kazakh holiday is the pre-Islamic spring festival of Navrus, celebrated on 21 March.

Kazakhs speak a Turkic language with 42 Cyrillic letters, similar to Russian and a little different from Mongolian.

FAMILY PLANNING FOR GOATS

Depending on the time of year, you may notice many male goats wearing nifty, little leather aprons tied around their bellies in front of their hind legs. This age-old device, called a *khög*, is a trick employed by herdsmen to thwart the buck's attempts to successfully mount any does.

In Mongolia a kid born during the harsh winter months is not only likely to die itself, but also to imperil the life of its mother, who will struggle to find enough food to produce milk and maintain her own health. By selective employment of this device, herders are able to restrict kidding to the warmer months when grass is more readily available.

lakes in Altai Tavan Bogd National Park. A return trip from Ölgii in an eight-seater vehicle will cost US$280 per vehicle, if arranged through Blue Wolf.

🛏 Sleeping & Eating

There is no official accommodation in the park but during summer, **Tuvan and Kazakh families** (per person T10,000) will often host trekkers and may even supply a hot meal, although you will need to bring your own sleeping bag. Besides camping, the only other option is the small, unofficial and overpriced **Aksu Rashan Suvlal** (☑ 9942 2979; ger with/without meals US$25/20, tent site US$10), a ger camp set up by a local entrepreneur at the Rashany Ikh Uul Hot Springs, 25km northwest of Khoton Nuur.

The best camping spots are around the lakes. Dayan Nuur has some nasty mosquitoes but the other two lakes are largely bug-free. Be aware that unattended tents are sometimes robbed.

At **Syrgal** (GPS: N 48°36.004', E 88°26.672'), between the lakes, there are a couple of very basic shops selling sweets, vodka, water and little else.

ℹ Information

MAPS

Kazakh Tour (p210) sells the excellent satellite map *Altai Tavan Bogd National Park Map & Guide* published by **Conservation Ink** (www.conser-vationink.org) for T15,000 and topographic 1:500,000 maps for T18,000.

PERMITS

Border permits are required to enter the park and can be obtained in Ulaanbaatar (p92) or at the **Border Patrol office** (Khiliin Tserenk Alb; ☑ 01422-22341; ⊙ 8-11am & 2-5pm Mon-Fri) in Ölgii. The permit costs T5000 and is good for an entire group provided the group does not separate mid-trek. The border patrol office will only deal with Mongolians so you'll need a local, your guide or a tour agency in Ölgii to apply on your behalf.

Border guards at Dayan Nuur, Tavan Bogd base camp, Aral Tolgoi (western end of Khoton Nuur) and Syrgal (the point where Khoton Nuur meets Khurgan Nuur) will all ask to see your paperwork (photocopies are not accepted), and those without permits are fined US$150 and charged costs for the army to return them to Ölgii (around US$170).

If you approach the region from the north, you will have to purchase another military permit (T10,000) from the Tsagaannuur border patrol.

Fishing permits cost T500 per day, although in practise nobody seems to need them, or be able to get them.

ℹ Getting There & Away

The main road from Tsengel leads 45km south to the bridge over the Khovd Gol (there's a T2000 toll) and then continues 33km to the junction of Khoton and Khurgan Nuurs (lakes), where there is a bridge across the wide water channel between the two lakes.

A more scenic route takes you from Sagsai over a pass and up the beautiful Khargantin Gol valley, past Tsengel Khairkhan Uul and Khar Nuur, and then down to Dayan Nuur. A good option would be to enter the park this way and exit via the main road.

There are two main ways to access Tavan Bogd. One is via Tsengel and up the Tsagaan Gol (although fording the Khovd Gol after heavy rain can be tricky) to the south ranger station. The other is via Sogoog following the Sogoog Gol straight to Tavan Bogd via the north ranger station or alternatively by going over Hagiin Davaa (Hagiin Pass) that leads to Tsagaan Gol.

There is no public transport to the park, although Ölgii tour agencies can arrange a jeep to drop you off and collect you at the end of your trek. A jeep for one to five people typically costs around US$150 to either ranger station.

Tolbo Nuur Толбо Нуур

Tolbo Nuur (GPS: N 48°35.320', E 090°04.536') is a freshwater lake about 50km south of Ölgii, on the main road between Ölgii and Khovd City. It is high (2080m), expansive and eerie but the shoreline is treeless with few mosquitoes and a few families camp here every summer. A major battle was fought here in 1921 between the Bolsheviks and White Russians, with the local Mongolian general, Khasbaatar, siding with the Bolsheviks. The Bolsheviks won and there are a couple of memorial plaques by the lake.

A further 14km on from the eastern edge of the lake and 3km off the main jeep trail is the tiny settlement of Tolbo, which hosts a small Eagle Festival (☉ last Sun Sep) that includes horse games as well as eagle hunting. Tolbo *sum* (district), along with Deluun *sum* to the south are famed for their eagle hunters and this is a great place to meet them. In fact a local hunter often waits by the road around 95km from Ölgii where the road narrows (GPS: N 48°29.439', E 090°33.648') to show his eagle to passing travellers (T5000 to T10,000 for photos).

Kazakh Tour in Ölgii (p210) has contacts in this area and can arrange eagle-hunting trips, homestays, horse treks and transport to the eagle festival.

Tsambagarav Uul National Park
Цамбагарав Уул

The permanently snow-capped Tsambagarav Uul straddles the border between Khovd and Bayan-Ölgii aimags and the park (admission T3000) is accessible from either side. Despite its altitude of 4208m, the mountain's summit is relatively accessible and easy to climb compared with Tavan Bogd, but you'll need crampons and ropes. A neighbouring peak, Tsast Uul, is slightly lower at 4193m and is also good for climbing.

The southern side of the mountain (near the main Khovd–Ölgii road) contains the Namarjin valley, where there are outstanding views of Tsambagarav. From here you can head west and then south to rejoin the main Khovd–Ölgii road, via several Kazakh settlements and a beautiful turquoise lake.

An alternative route from the Khovd side leads from the town of Erdeneburen

(where you can see a deer stone dating back to the pre-Mongol era) and up the mountainside to the Bayangol Valley. The valley itself is nothing special but there are fine views southeast to Khar Us Nuur and you might be able to rent a horse for the hourlong ride to the Kazakh-populated Marra valley.

The Bayan-Ölgii (northern) side of the mountain is even more impressive. To reach the massif, a steep pass runs between Tavan Belchiriin Uul and Tsast Uul. Between the mountains is a 7m-high waterfall (GPS: N 48°44.741', E 090°42.378') that flows down a narrow gorge. A couple of kilometres to the east of the waterfall is a glacier and a small glacial lake.

From the glacier, the road dips through some spectacular rocky gorges before finally tumbling down to Bayan Nuur, a small, slightly salty lake.

The best time to visit the massif is late June to late August, when it's populated by Kazakh nomad camps. You can rent horses from the nomads to explore the area. Outside of these months it's a cold, empty and forbidding place.

From Bayan Nuur, a desert road travels east through a Martian landscape of red boulders and rocky mountains. Near the town of Bayannuur and close to the Khovd Gol is an interesting white-stone balbal (Turkic Stone Statue; GPS: N 48°50.533', E 091°16.525').

KHOVD ХОВД
POP 78,300 / AREA 76,000 SQ KM

Khovd aimag has long been a centre for trade, business and administration in western Mongolia, a status that began during the Qing dynasty when the Manchus built a military garrison here. The aimag still does robust trade with China through the border at Bulgan and its agricultural university is the largest of its kind outside Ulaanbaatar.

Besides its developing economy, Khovd is notable for being one of the most heterogeneous aimags in Mongolia, with a Khalkh majority and minorities of Khoton, Kazakh, Uriankhai, Zakhchin, Myangad, Oold and Torguud peoples. Its terrain is equally varied, with large salt lakes, fast-flowing rivers and the Mongol Altai Nuruu almost bisecting the aimag.

Khovd City   Ховд

☑ 01432, 7043 / POP 28,601 / ELEV 1406M

Khovd City is a pleasant tree-lined place developed by the Manchus during their 200-year rule in Outer Mongolia. Slightly more developed than other cities in western Mongolia (although still basically just a small town), it boasts an agricultural university, and some food processing and textile manufacturing.

The town offers a few sights to keep you busy for a day and some pleasant ger camps outside town. Shops are well stocked and there are plenty of jeeps, making this a reasonable place from which to launch a trip to the Altai Mountains or the lakes region. You can also cross into China from here (assuming you already have your China visa), using the little-used border at Bulgan.

◉ Sights

Aimag Museum   MUSEUM
(☑ 9943 4502; admission T2000; ⊙ 8am-noon & 1-5pm Mon-Fri) This regional museum has the usual collection of stuffed wildlife, plus some excellent ethnic costumes, Buddhist and Kazakh art and a snow-leopard pelt tacked up on the wall. One of the more interesting exhibits is the excellent re-creation of the cave paintings at Tsenkheriin Agui. There are also several examples of the many deer stones scattered around the aimag, plus a model of the original Manchurian fortress.

Sangiin Kherem   RUINS
At the northern end of the city are some crumbling walls built around 1762 by the Manchu (Qing dynasty) warlords who once brutally governed Mongolia. The 40,000 sq metre walled compound once contained several temples, a Chinese graveyard and the homes of the Manchu rulers, though there's little left to see. Three enormous gates provided access. At one time there was a moat (2m deep and 3m wide) around the 4m-high walls, but this has been completely filled in. The 1500-man Chinese garrison was destroyed after a 10-day siege and two-day battle in August 1912.

ℹ TO CHINA FROM KHOVD

It is possible to travel from Khovd to Ürümqi in China's Xinjiang province, via the Mongolian town of Bulgan. For further information, see p281.

Gandan Puntsag Choilon Khiid   BUDDHIST MONASTERY
Officially opened in 2010, this is the largest monastery in western Mongolia. The whole compound is surrounded by a wall (with a path on top) and 108 stupas. Morning prayers are held from 9am until 3pm inside the main temple, which features a statue of Buddha flanked by 10 divine protectors.

☞ Tours

Khovd Handicraft & Tours   TOURS
(☑ 9943 8849, 9907 9485; markasl2002@yahoo.com; ⊙ 8am-10pm in summer) Marima, the friendly owner here, is a great source of local information and can arrange tours to local attractions including Khar Us Nuur National Park, the caves of Tsenkheriin Agui and the *khöömii* singers in Chandmani. She can also arrange guides (T30,000 per day), jeeps (T70,000 per day plus fuel) and homestays (around T25,000 per person, including meals).

⊨ Sleeping

There are attractive (if buggy) camping spots along the Buyant Gol; head out of the town towards Ölgii, turn right (downstream) at the river, and pitch your tent anywhere.

★ Royal Hotel   HOTEL $$
(☑ 7043 3968; tw T40,000-60,000; P 🛜) Brand new at the time of research, this is easily the nicest hotel in town. Rooms are small, but smart and modern, and come with very clean bathrooms with reliable hot-water showers. They claim to have wi-fi, but it wasn't working when we were here.

Shuutiin Tokhoi   TOURIST GER CAMP $$
(☑ 9943 8200; gulchk_910@yahoo.com; GPS: N 48°02.960', E 091°40.253'; per person T40,000, meals T5000) About 6km to the northwest of town, this basic camp has a gorgeous, grassy location along the Buyant Gol, at the foot of a rocky escarpment. No toilets or showers, but they do have areas to play basketball and volleyball (it's all about priorities).

Tsambagarav Hotel   HOTEL $$
(☑ 01432-22260; tw T35,000-50,000; P 🛜) This large, rundown hotel remains one of the more popular in town (competition isn't great), thanks to helpful staff, large common areas, and wi-fi that extends from the lobby into the ground-floor restaurant. Rooms are a mixed bag, and plumbing is dodgy, but you should get your own bathroom with hot shower and

sit-down flush toilet. It's in a blue-painted building with a Cyrillic-only sign.

Buyant Hotel HOTEL $$
(☑7043 3807; buyanthotel@yahoo.com; dm T12,000-15,000, tr T36,000, half-lux tw T40,000, lux T60,000; @) Though slightly rough around the edges, the rooms here are bright and all have hot showers except the dorm whose bathroom is two floors below. The lux room is particularly spacious. Welcoming staff, though little English spoken. Brick building. No English sign.

🍴 Eating

Self-caterers should head to the daily market or to **Khovd Nomin** (⊘10am-7pm), a warehouse-like supermarket, which also stocks some basic camping equipment.

Tavan Erdene MONGOLIAN $
(snacks T500; ⊘8am-10pm) The best *khuushuur* (mutton pancakes) are currently being served in this no-frills single-storey, red-brick cafe behind the jeep stand. Four or five is enough grease for most people but a Mongolian with an appetite can easily finish 10. Look for the bright-red Cyrillic sign.

Altai MONGOLIAN, RUSSIAN $$
(meals T3500-9500; ⊘9am-midnight; 🍴) Justifiably popular, Altai's chef trained in Moscow and seems to care more about the quality of the food he serves than most. Some meals are served on a sizzling hotplate and salads are available. Also does hearty soups. English menu.

Winners MONGOLIAN, RUSSIAN $$
(meals T3500-8000; ⊘10am-midnight) A good choice, the two dining rooms are separated by a small and cosy bar. Goulash is the house speciality and desserts in the form of cream cakes are also available.

🛍 Shopping

Khovd Handicraft & Tours HANDICRAFTS
(⊘8am-10pm summer) This charming shop specialises in Kazakh embroidery, felt products and a few leather items. A 1.2m x 2m felt carpet costs around US$80 while a pair of felt slippers will set you back around US$10.

ℹ Information

Bathhouse (shower/sauna T1500/5000; ⊘9am-10pm)
Khar Us Nuur National Park Office (☑01432-22539; kharus2006@chinggis.com; ⊘8am-

5pm Mon-Fri) This office provides information on, and permits for, nearby Khar Us Nuur National Park.

Telecom Office (per hr T600; ⊘8am-10pm Mon-Fri, to 8pm Sat & Sun) Internet cafe, telephone services and post office rolled into one.

Khovd City

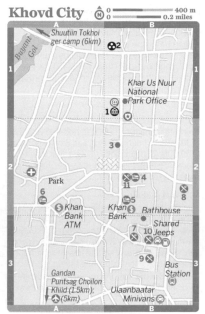

Khan Bank (☉8am-7pm Mon-Fri, 9am-3pm Sat) Changes money and has a 24-hour ATM. Opposite the park in the multicoloured building.

ℹ️ Getting There & Away

AIR

Mongolian Airlines (☎7043 8889; www.hun-nuair.com; Buyant Hotel; ☉9am-6pm Mon-Sat), now known as Hunnu Air but at the time of research still operating in Khovd under its old name, has a ticket office in the lobby of Buyant Hotel, and flies to UB (from T270,000 one way) on Monday, Wednesday and Friday. The airport is 5km south of the city.

BUS

Once a day a bus leaves for the two-day, nonstop trek to Ulaanbaatar (T65,000, 1425km) via Altai (T30,000, 15 hours, 424km) and Bayankhongor (T50,000, 28 hours, 795km). Buy your tickets in advance from the green railway carriage that serves as the **bus station**.

MINIVAN & JEEP

Minivans leave from the **shared-jeep stand** near the market for Ölgii (T15,000 to T20,000, six to seven hours, 238km) and Ulaangom (T18,000, seven to eight hours, 238km) if enough passengers show up (usually around four to eight hours after any suggested departure time).

Tickets for the daily Ulaanbaatar-bound minivan (T65,000, 45 hours) are sold in advance at the 'bus station'.

Jeeps cost around T500 per kilometre, including petrol, around town. Shared jeeps for local *sums* leave from the local jeep stand behind the market.

Marima, at Khovd Handicraft & Tours (p218), can also help travellers arrange local taxi rides.

If demand warrants it, there is usually a shared jeep or minivan that leaves from the south side of the market every afternoon for Bulgan (T30,000 per person, 10 to 12 hours), from where you cross the border into Xinjiang province in China. See p281 for more details.

Khar Us Nuur National Park Xap Yc Hyyp

About 40km to the east of Khovd City is **Khar Us Nuur** (Dark Water Lake), the second-largest freshwater lake (15,800 sq km) in Mongolia – but with an average depth of only 4m. Khovd Gol flows into this lake, creating a giant marsh delta. Khar Us Nuur is the perfect habitat for wild ducks, geese, wood grouse, partridges and seagulls, including rare relict gulls and herring gulls – and by late summer a billion or two of everyone's friend, the common mosquito.

Birdwatchers, however, may be a little disappointed: the lake is huge, difficult to reach because of the marshes and locals know very little, if anything, about the birdlife. The best idea would be to go with one of the national park workers and head for the delta where the Khovd Gol enters the lake in May or late August.

The easiest place to see the lake is from the main Khovd–Altai road at the southern tip of the lake, where a metal **watchtower** (GPS: N 47°50.541', E 092°01.541') has been set up to view the nearby reed islands.

The outflow from Khar Us Nuur goes into a short river called Chono Khairkhan, which flows into another freshwater lake, **Khar Nuur** (Black Lake), home to some migratory

---

THE GREEN TARA OF DÖRGÖN

In Dörgön *sum*, two hours' drive from Khovd City, an elderly woman is performing miracles. Megjin, who's in her sixties, has spent the past several years clearing out a demon-infested charnel ground near the shores of Dalay Nuur, a small saltwater lake beside the larger Khar Us Nuur. The once-barren ground has been planted with more than 3500 trees and shrubs; several Buddhist temples have also been erected here in what now acts as a small monastery.

In 2006, Megjin was officially recognised as a Green Tara (Buddha of enlightened activity) by the Mongolian Government and was given an enthronement ceremony in Ulaanbaatar.

The trees she has planted are suffering from the harsh climate and lack of fresh water, but Megjin's dedication is impressive nonetheless. You can take a tour of the **monastery grounds** (admission T5000), which includes five small temples, although this is best done with a guide, as Megjin speaks no English.

If you need to stay here, **Dörgön Zochid Budal** (beds T10,000, meals T3000) is five minutes' walk down the hill from the monastery, in the centre of the town, and has beds, but no shower.

> **LOCAL KNOWLEDGE**
>
> ## D TSERENDAVAA: KHÖÖMII SINGER
>
> D Tserendavaa took some time to tell us the secrets of *khöömii* (throat singing).
>
> ### Khöömii Training
> *Khöömii* has been part of my family for generations. I was six when my father first started teaching me and I continued to study *khöömii* when I moved away to start school.
>
> ### Khöömii Technique
> When foreigners first hear me sing they are amazed as they don't realise the human body is capable of producing such sounds. They are even more surprised to learn that I use seven different techniques to produce a whole harmonic range and that the 'song' is formed in the larynx, throat, stomach and palate. By singing this way I am able to produce two notes and melodies simultaneously: one a low growl, the other an ethereal whistle.
>
> ### Best Places to Hear Khöömii
> The best places to hear *khöömii* are in western Mongolia, particularly in Chandmani and Khovd or at a concert in Ulaanbaatar.

pelicans. The southern end of Khar Nuur flows into **Dörgön Nuur**, which is a large alkaline lake good for swimming. The eastern side of Dörgön Nuur is an area of bone-dry desert and extensive sand dunes.

Just to the south, and between the Khar and Khar Us lakes, are the twin peaks of **Jargalant Khairkhan Uul** (3796m) and **Yargaitin Ekh Uul** (3464m). You can see the massif as you drive to Ölgii from Altai in Gov-Altai aimag. With the help of a guide you'll find numerous springs in these mountains. The canyons also hide a 22m high **waterfall**.

In 2004, 22 *takhi* (Przewalski's horse) were introduced to the **Khomyn Tal** buffer zone and became the third herd of this critically endangered horse to be re-established in Mongolia.

Chandmani   Чандмань

Chandmani, on the southeastern side of Khar Us Nuur National Park, is a renowned centre for **khöömii** (www.khoomei.com), or throat singing, along with Khovd and, more famously, the republic of Tuva in Russia.

Thanks to some resident old masters, such as **Tserendavaa** (☑8840 6070) and Davaajav, it is sometimes possible to arrange some informal training or an impromptu demonstration (around T30,000 per group). Apparently *khöömii* isn't as difficult to learn as you might imagine, although to attain any degree of proficiency you will need at least a week. If you're lucky, your visit may coincide with one of the small concerts that are held in the purpose-built *khöömii ordon* (palace), although your best chance of this is during the third week of July when a **khöömii competition** is planned as part of a festival to celebrate traditional Mongolian arts (the inaugural festival was held in 2011).

Also in town you'll find the women's co-operative, **Bisness Enkhbator Töv**, which produces a small selection of garments and hats made from camel and yak wool.

Places to stay are thin on the ground. We found a room at **Zochid Buudal** (☑8918 9896; per person I10,000), which simply means 'hotel'. It has a clean-enough four-bed dorm with a shared outhouse and an attached restaurant which can rustle up a decent meal (T3000). You may be able to arrange a **homestay** for T5000 to T10,000 per night with one of the *khöömii* masters.

Numerous shared jeeps/taxis leave daily from Chandmani to Khovd (T10,000 per person, five hours, 150km).

Tsenkheriin Agui
Цэнхэрийн Агуй

Tsenkheriin Agui is famous for its cave paintings, and some of them depict long-extinct fauna including mammoths and ostrich-like birds. Today this area is known as a great place to spot saiga antelopes, especially on the road to Chandmani.

The surrounding valleys are excellent for camping (if you can bear the mosquitos) and short hikes.

⊙ Sights

★ Tsenkheriin Agui
CAVE PAINTINGS

(Khoid Tsenkher; GPS: N 47°20.828', E 091°57.225'; per person/vehicle T3000/10,000) This huge cave about 100km southeast of Khovd City looks deceptively small from the parking area but once you scramble up the loose rock path, you realise how big it is and how it must have afforded considerable shelter to the prehistoric humans who once lived here.

Unfortunately, this ancient art (c 13,000 BC) has inspired others and recent graffiti (c AD 2001) has seen much of it destroyed. In 2005 the area was incorporated into the Khar Us National Park and some of the paintings 'restored'.

To explore the cave you will need a strong torch (flashlight) and whatever kind of footwear you feel copes well with the dusty bird shit that blankets parts of the cave floor.

The paintings are very difficult to spot. There seem to be far fewer than the tourism spiel promotes – and we couldn't find the famed whooly mammoth paintings. The easiest to find are some antelope and bird paintings in the first cavern to your left as you descend the path into the main cave. Most of them are found within a small conical recess here. Beside this, through a hole in the wall which you can squeeze through, are more animal figures.

Exiting the main cave, you can turn left and climb slightly higher to find the entrance to another, deeper cave, although this does not contain paintings.

Burial Mounds
HISTORIC SITE

Only a few hundred metres further up the valley are some burial mounds that to the uninitiated would be just piles of rocks.

Petroglyphs
HISTORIC SITE

More interesting than the nearby burial mounds are these petroglyphs on the rise just behind the rock mounds. You'll find dozens of etched figures here, including antelopes and even tigers. Walk around the back of the stone hill that's just beyond the burial mound and you should be able to spot them.

⊨ Sleeping

The ranger has a handful of **gers** (☏9826 6607; per person with/without meals T55,000/25,000) set up for visiting travellers. There are hot showers (T2000), a bar-restaurant (meals around T5000) and you can camp for free and pay to use the facilities separately if you wish. Be warned, though, the mosquitos here are indescribably bad during summer.

The main cave is a 1.5km walk from the ger camp – keep the river to your right, and you'll soon see it up to your left. The valley and surrounding hills make for excellent camping and hiking.

Mönkh Khairkhan National Park
Мөнх Хайрхан Уул

At 4362m, **Mönkh Khairkhan Uul** (Tavan Khumit; park entrance T3000) is the second-highest mountain in Mongolia. You can walk up the peak if you approach from the

---

NATIONAL PARKS OF KHOVD

Bulgan Gol Nature Reserve (1840 hectares) On the southwestern border with China, this reserve was established to help preserve *minj* (beavers), sables and stone martens. A border permit is required.

Great Gobi Strictly Protected Area (Gobi B) Created to protect *khulan* (wild ass), gazelle, jerboas and *takhi* (wild horses).

Khar Us Nuur National Park (850,272 hectares; p220) Protects the breeding grounds of antelope and rare species of migratory pelican, falcon and bustard.

Khökh Serkh Strictly Protected Area (65,920 hectares) On the northwestern border with Bayan-Ölgii, it helps protect argali sheep, ibexes and snow leopards.

Mankhan Nature Reserve (30,000 hectares) Directly southeast of Khovd City, it preserves an endangered species of antelope.

Mönkh Khairkhan National Park Established in 2006, this protects an important habitat for ibexes and argali sheep.

northern side. There is plenty of snow and ice on top, so you'll need crampons, an ice axe and rope, but the climb is not technically difficult. A jeep trail runs to the base from Mankhan.

UVS УВС

POP 73,800 / AREA 69,000 SQ KM

After travelling around this aimag for a while you may start to wonder why they named it Uvs (Grass), as most of the region is classified as high desert. Really the main features of this diverse aimag are its lakes, which come in all shapes, sizes and levels of salinity. The biggest, Uvs Nuur, is more like an inland sea, while smaller lakes such as Khökh Nuur make excellent hiking destinations. Together, the lakes and the surrounding deserts make up the Ikh Nuuruudin Khotgor: the 39,000 sq km Great Lakes Depression that includes bits of neighbouring Khovd and Zavkhan aimags.

The main attraction of Uvs, though, has to be the twin peaks of Kharkhiraa Uul (4037m) and Türgen Uul (3965m). From these mountains spill permanent glaciers, fast-flowing rivers and verdant plateaus, and the hiking opportunites are excellent.

Ulaangom Улаангом

☎ 01452, 7045 / POP 22,300 / ELEV 939M

Ulaangom (Red Sand) has had a recent makeover and is now looking rather smart. Many of the roads have been sealed, including a 13km stretch that leads into the city following the pretty Kharkhiraa Gol, and a 37km stretch that leads out towards Uureg Nuur.

◉ Sights

Aimag Museum MUSEUM
(☎ 01452-24720; admission T3000; ⊙ 8am-noon & 1-5pm Mon-Fri, 8.30am-noon & 1pm-5.30pm Sat) This OK Aimag Museum has the usual stuff plus a section on the 16th-century Oirad leader Amarsanaa (the chainmail jacket is supposedly his). There's a wing dedicated solely to the reign of one-time dictator Yu Tsedenbal (who was born in Uvs), featuring photos of the man with other communist leaders like Fidel Castro and Ho Chi Minh.

Dechinravjaalin Khiid BUDDHIST MONASTERY
Dechinravjaalin Khiid was originally founded in 1738 and contained seven temples and 2000 monks. The place was pulverised in 1937 thanks to Stalin, and its current incarnation consists of a concrete ger and about 20 welcoming monks.

Ulaan Uulyn Rashaan SPRING
(GPS: N 49°57.427', E 092°03.142') Just outside of town on the south side of Ulaan Uul (Red Mountain), a small spring draws a steady crowd of picnicking locals who come here to drink the medicinal water and knock back vodka shots.

☞ Tours

Strictly Protected Areas Office GUIDES
(☎ 9145 6666; delhiinovuvsnuur_mn@yahoo.com; ⊙ 8am-5pm Mon-Fri) This government-run office may be able to help arrange guides (US$35 per day) and jeeps (US$60 per day plus petrol), but nobody here speaks English, making dealing with them difficult. Emailing may produce better results.

🛏 Sleeping

The best camping is along the Kharkhiraa Gol or anywhere south of the city on the road to Tarialan.

Bayalag Od Hotel HOTEL $
(☎ 01452-22445; dm/d with breakfast T10,000/18,000, lux tw with breakfast T40,000) Very run down, but an OK option as a last resort. All rooms have their own bathrooms, but they aren't the cleanest, and the hot water is sporadic.

Tavan Od HOTEL $$
(☎ 9945 2021, 01452-23409; tw T25,000, s/tw with bathroom T40,000/50,000; ℗) This mid-sized hotel on the north edge of town offers a variety of fairly clean and comfortable rooms. Only the lux rooms have their own bathrooms but the public bathhouse (T2000) is in the same compound. Also has a restaurant-cum-bar that gets favourable reviews from locals. Walking northwest from the market, take the second sealed road on your right (after about 500m) and the hotel, housed in a grey-and-red, three-storey brick building, will be on your left after about 200m. No English.

★ Achit Nuur Hotel HOTEL $$$
(☎ 9945 9019; tw standard/half-lux/lux T40,000/80,000/100,000; 🛜) New in 2012, this is the best hotel in town. Rooms are large, bright and modern and they come with spacious bathrooms with hot-water showers and

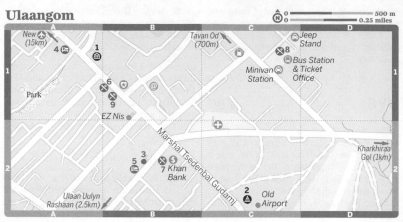

Ulaangom

Ulaangom

⊙ Sights
1 Aimag Museum.....................................A1
2 Dechinravjaalin Khiid...........................C2

⊙ Activities, Courses & Tours
3 Strictly Protected Areas Office...........B2

⊜ Sleeping
4 Achit Nuur Hotel A1
5 Bayalag Od Hotel B2

⊗ Eating
6 Ikh Mongol B1
7 Jangar Restaurant................................B2
8 Market...C1
9 Qinggis Pub & Restaurant B1

complimentary toiletries. Wi-fi in the lobby extends to some of the rooms and part of the restaurant. There's laundry available and breakfast is included. No English sign or English spoken, but welcoming staff.

🍴 Eating

For cheap *khuushuur* (mutton pancakes) or *buuz* (steamed dumplings), try the train-car *guanz* (canteen) outside the **market** (⊙Tue-Sun). There's an indoor supermarket here too.

Qinggis Pub & Restaurant   FUSION $
(📞9945 2688; Marshal Tsedenbal Gudamj 27; mains T3000-5000; ⊙9am-9pm; 📶) Probably the best Ulaangom has to offer; the stir-fried steak meals are called simply 'meat dishes'. Our favourite was the slightly spicy 'meat dish with pepper'. Also does dumplings, soup and the like. English menu. Has beer.

Ikh Mongol   MONGOLIAN, CHINESE $
(📞9983 9292; Marshal Tsedenbal Gudamj 29; mains T3000-5000; ⊙9am-9pm) Undergoing renovation at the time of research, but always used to be one of the better places in town for a meal and a drink.

Jangar Restaurant   MONGOLIAN $$
(mains T3000-6000; ⊙9am-9pm) Housed in a concrete ger, the animal pelts hanging from the beams might put some off, but this is a comfortable place to sample decent Mongolian dishes. Has some Western-style dishes too. No English menu. Dishes on offer include *jimsnii salat* (fruit salad), *öndögnii salat* (egg salad), *suutei tsagaan budaa* (rice-milk porridge), *tsuivan* (fried noodles), *grildej sharsan takhiany makh* (grilled chicken leg), *jignsen guriltai shöl* (pasta and mutton soup) and goulash.

ⓘ Information

Bathhouse (shower T2000, sauna per hr T5000; ⊙8am-8pm) In the Tavan Od Hotel compound.

Internet Cafe (per hr T600; ⊙8am-8pm Mon-Sat) At the Telecom office. The post office is also here.

Khan Bank (⊙8am-5.30pm Mon-Fri) Will exchange US dollars. Has an ATM.

ⓘ Getting There & Away

AIR
Ulaangom's new airport is 15km northwest of town. A taxi will cost T10,000-15,000 one way.

EZ Nis (📞9904 9939, 7045 5252; ⊙9am-6pm Mon-Fri, 10am-6pm Sat) Flies to UB (from

T240,000) on Monday, Wednesday, Friday and Sunday. English spoken. Cards accepted.

BUS

The **bus ticket office** (☉10am-4pm), which is a kiosk inside the white building at the bus stand, sells tickets for the bus to UB (daily except Tuesday; T63,000; two days), via Tosontsengel, which tend to leave mid-afternoon.

JEEP & MINIVAN

If you are heading to Ölgii it is generally easier to catch a share jeep or minivan to Khovd (T30,000, seven to eight hours, 238km) and make your way from there, as vehicles heading directly to Ölgii are few and far between. Even rarer are vans heading to Mörön (about 25 hours, 680km); if there is nothing available, consider riding a UB-bound minivan as far as Tariat (T30,000, 26 hours, 700km) and then attempting to bum a lift to Mörön from other backpackers at Terkhiin Tsagaan Nuur.

Share minivans to Ulaanbaatar (T65,000, about 48 hours), via Tosontsengel, Tariat and Tsetserleg, leave daily. If you want to get off at Tsetserleg or Tariat you may have to pay the full UB fare.

Uvs Nuur   Увс Нуур

Uvs Nuur is a gigantic inland sea in the middle of the desert. The lake's surface occupies 3423 sq km, making it Mongolia's largest lake, though it's very shallow at an average depth of 12m. (Still, legend has it that the lake is bottomless.)

Uvs Nuur is five times saltier than the ocean and devoid of edible fish. It has no outlet, so a lot of the shoreline is quasi-wetland. This environment, plus the clouds of mosquitoes, make it tourist unfriendly.

Ornithologists have documented more than 200 bird species around **Uvs Nuur Strictly Protected Area** (permit T3000), including cranes, spoonbills, geese and eagles, as well as gulls that fly thousands of kilometres from the southern coast of China to spend a brief summer in Mongolia.

The small **Argai Az Ger Camp** (GPS: N 50°04.156; E 092°22.329'; with meals US$30) on the southwestern side of the lake is rather neglected and sees few guests.

OFF THE BEATEN TRACK

ULAANGOM TO ÖLGII: THE ROUGH ROUTE

This two-day jeep journey begins with a 40km tarmac road heading northwest out of Ulaangom before turning left onto a jeep trail just past Turgen village. The jeep trail heads up to **Ulaan Davaa** (Red Pass; elevation 1972m), notable for its enormous *ovoo* (shamanistic offering).

From the pass there are two routes. One heads due south and then southeast to Khökh Nuur. The other leads west to lovely Üüreg Nuur.

From Üüreg Nuur, cargo trucks take a less-rugged (but longer) route (301km) via **Bohmörön village** (where you can check out the 8th-century Turkic *balbal*, or anthropomorphic statue). Light vehicles (jeeps and vans) bypass Bohmörön and take the short cut (254km) over the steep **Bairam Davaa**. Look out for several **ancient graves and balbals** (GPS: N 50°00.484; E 091°02.932') on this route a few kilometres south of Üüreg Nuur. The 8th-century *balbals* represent either local heroes or, possibly, enemies killed in battle. Another set of **graves and balbals** (GPS: N 50°00.220; E 091°02.713') is a further 550m south. The circular piles of stones in the area are *kurgans* (burial mounds).

On the south side of Bairam Davaa, the road passes more *kurgans* and standing stones (thin, stone pillars used as grave markers). The most impressive, 7km north of Khotgor, include two **mounds** (GPS: N 49°54.910; E 090°54.527') surrounded by concentric circles and radiating spokes.

Khotgor is a desolate coal-mining village but long-distance cyclists take note: this is the only place to pick up supplies between Ulaangom and Ölgii. Most maps show no road via Bairam Davaa but, rest assured, you can make it with a halfway decent vehicle or bike (and the lungs of a yeti).

From Khotgor you could opt for a detour into the **Yamaat Valley**, which leads to Türgen Uul. Otherwise, continue south for 60km to the **Achit Nuur** bridge. From here it's another 75km to Ölgii. The road passes the surprisingly lush riverside forests of the **Develiin Aral Nature Reserve**, a 16km stretch along the fast-flowing Khovd Gol.

Üüreg Nuur Үүрэг Нуур

Large and beautiful **Üüreg Nuur** (GPS: N 50°05.236; E 091°04.587'), at an elevation of 1425m, is surrounded by stunning 3000m-plus peaks, including **Tsagaan Shuvuut Uul** (3496m), which are part of the Uvs Nuur Strictly Protected Area (p225). The freshwater lake has some unidentified minerals and is designated as 'saltwater' on some maps, so it's best to boil or purify all water from the lake. There is a freshwater well on the southeastern edge of the lake near some deserted buildings.

The lake is great for swimming (albeit a little chilly) and locals say there are plenty of fish. One added attraction is that it's one of the few mosquito-free lakes in the region.

You should buy your T3000-permit at the Strictly Protected Areas Office in Ulaangom (p223), although there is no one here to check whether or not you have one.

Camping spots abound by the lake shore. The only tourist facilities are about 25km southeast of the lake, at the beautifully situated, but rather overpriced **OT Tour Camp** (☑ 8684 0561; GPS: N 49°56.724; E 91°16.348'; with/without meals T99,000/42,000, tent pitch T15,000). The gers here are spotlessly clean, spacious and come with fabulous meadow views. Showers are also clean and have sit-down toilets. There's good hiking to be done in the surrounding hills, and the lake is within striking distance. The camp can arrange horse treks if given a few days notice.

Kharkhiraa Uul & Türgen Uul
Хархираа Уул & Түргэн Уул

The twin peaks of Kharkhiraa Uul (4037m) and Türgen Uul (3965m), which dominate the western part of the aimag, are vital sources of the Uvs Nuur and the mountains are also part of the Uvs Nuur Strictly Protected Area (p225).

In summer, the area has some excellent hiking opportunities and the chance to meet Khoton nomads who graze their flocks in here. Khoton people are unusual in being the only ethnic Mongols to practice Islam.

The village of **Tarialan** (Тариалан; GPS: N 49°46.614; E 91°54.525') makes a good base for exploration. It is 11km off the main Ulaangom–Khovd road, about 25km out of Ulaangom (watch for the blue sign). The Strictly Protected Areas office in Ulaangom (p223) sells permits for the protected area.

🏃 Activities

The wonderfully scenic mountains here can be approached on hikes from different directions. Locals say the most scenic hike is the two-week, one-way hike from Tarialan to Telmen Mod. You can also hike to Goojuur Waterfall (eight days). More common, though, is the shorter five- to six-day hike from Tarialan to Khotgor.

If you're short on time, consider the 15km hike to the pretty lake, Khökh Nuur.

NATIONAL PARKS OF UVS

The Great Lakes Depression in Uvs aimag is a globally important wetland area for migratory birds and is a Unesco World Biosphere Reserve. Many other parks have been established in Uvs and, together with parks in Russia, Tuva, China and Kazakhstan, form a Central Asian arc of protected areas.

Altan Els Strictly Protected Area (148,246 hectares) Contains the world's northernmost sand dunes and protects threatened desert plants.

Khan Khökhii National Park (220,550 hectares) An important ecological indicator and home to musk deer, elk, red deer and wolves.

Khyargas Nuur National Park (332,800 hectares; p228) An area of springs and rocky outcrops that harbours abundant waterfowl.

Tes River Reserve (712,545 hectares) The newest conservation area in Uvs protects waterfowl, beaver and fish.

Uvs Nuur Strictly Protected Area (712,545 hectares; p225) Consists of four separate areas: Uvs Nuur, Türgen Uul, Tsagaan Shuvuut Uul and Altan Els. Contains everything from desert sand dunes to snowfields, marsh to mountain forest. Snow leopards, wolves, foxes, deer and ibexes are among the animals protected.

Tarialan to Khotgor Hike TREKKING

From Tarialan follow the **Kharkhiraa Gol**, past the local bathhouse, and up into the mountains; you'll need to cross the river up to nine times as you go up the valley. Three days and 50km later you'll cross over the **Kharkhiraa Davaa** (2974m), which is accessible on foot but difficult going for pack camels.

From the pass you descend into the pretty **Olon Nuur Valley**, a marshy area of lakes and meadows. Turn north to walk over **Yamaat Davaa** (2947m) into Yamaat Valley, an area inhabited by snow leopards. In summer a **ger camp** is sometimes open in this valley. At the end of the valley you can easily reach the town of Khotgor, where, with a bit of luck, you might be able to arrange a taxi to drive you back to Ulaangom (five to six hours).

☞ Tours

UB-based tour companies such as Tseren Tours (p37), Mongolia Expeditions (p36) and Off the Map Tours (p39) run walking trips through this area.

Alternatively, try to hunt down **Dash** (☑9421 1004; guide services per day T30,000), a local guide who lives in his family ger at the mouth of the valley which leads from Tarialan up into the hills. To find him, head to the local **bathhouse** (shower T1000), which is in a small white concrete building, beyond the far western edge of the village, and keep walking for a couple of hundred metres up the valley.

Dash can take you on some fabulous multiday treks; anything ranging from a few days to two weeks. He can arrange horse or camel rides for around T20,000 per person per day, plus the same again for an animal guide. It's an extra T30,000 per day if you want a cook to come along too. You'll have to bring your own food and camping equipment, although water is plentiful here. Dash can also help arrange a car transfer, to or from Ulaangom, for example, for around T50,000 to T60,000 per day plus petrol.

Dash doesn't speak English, but is very experienced. His son, **Shinee** (☑9949 3110), a university student in Khovd, does speak English, though, and is usually around to help out during the summer holidays. He also works as a guide.

ⓘ Getting There & Away

Shared minivans between Ulaangom and Tarialan cost around T4000 per person, although if you've come here for hiking it wouldn't be out of the question to walk to Tarialan from Ulaangom.

Khökh Nuur   Хөх Нууp

This pretty alpine **lake** (Blue Lake; GPS: N 49°50.413′, E 91°41.141′) is surrounded by mountains and makes a great destination on foot or horse from Tarialan; the trip is about 15km up Davaan Uliastai (one valley north of the Kharkhiraa Gol).

It's possible for a car to reach the lake in a very roundabout manner (120km), although only an experienced driver could do it. The road route involves driving up Ulaan Davaa (from Ulaangom), sweeping around the mountains close to Üüreg Nuur, and then heading southeast.

Trekkers can continue from the lake for 25km to the glacier-wrapped Türgen Uul. The walk takes about two days through a harsh landscape of prairie, mountains, glaciers and rivers, but the topography is wide open so it's fairly easy to navigate. There are good **camping spots** (GPS: N 49°42.485′, E 91°29.525′) along the Türgen Gol, near the northern base of Türgen Uul.

Uvsiin Khar Us Nuur
Увс Аймгийн Хар Ус Нууp

Another freshwater lake in the region is Uvsiin Khar Us Nuur (literally 'Khar Us Nuur of Uvs Aimag' to distinguish it from the more famous lake of the same name in Khovd). You can swim and fish here, and it makes a logical camping spot if travelling between Ulaangom and Khovd City. The lake is 102km south of Ulaangom.

Achit Nuur   Ачит Нууp

The largest freshwater lake in Uvs, Achit Nuur is on the border of Uvs and Bayan-Ölgii aimags, and is an easy detour between Ulaangom and Ölgii. It offers stunning sunsets and sunrises and good fishing.

The lake is home to flocks of geese, eagles and other **birdlife**. One drawback is the absolute plethora of mosquitoes during the summer. Some camping spots are better than others for mozzies, so look around. Locals claim they are almost bearable by October.

The small Kazakh encampment on the southeastern edge has a *guanz*.

A **bridge** (GPS: N 49°25.446′, E 90°39.677′) just south of the lake allows for relatively steady traffic between Ulaangom and Ölgii.

Khyargas Nuur National Park

Хяргас Нуур

Khyargas Nuur National Park (park fee T3000), based on a salt lake amid desert and scrub grass, provides an attractive summer home for birds but sees little tourist traffic.

On the northwestern side of Khyargas Nuur there is a **cold spring** (GPS: N 49°18.952; E 093°13.257') that dribbles out of the mountain – locals say drinking from it has health benefits. Five kilometres further on is **Khar Temis** (☑ 9307 2513; GPS: N 49°18.954; E 093°09.625'; per person with meals T30,000, 4-bed r without meals T30,000, meals T4000-5000), an old Soviet holiday camp that is falling into disrepair, but popular with holidaying Mongolians. It has a number of spartan four-bed rooms, half of which have balconies facing the lake. The sandy beach by the main road here is a surreal sight, given that it's about 2000km from the nearest coastline.

The main attraction of the lake is over the other side, though. **Khetsuu Khad** is an enormous rock sticking out of the water that attracts migratory cormorant birds. The birds arrive in April and hatch their young in large nests built on the rock. When the chicks hatch, their squawking is constant and deafening. The aura created by the white cliffs, shrill birds and the prevailing smell of guano makes you feel as if you've arrived at the ocean. By mid-September the cormorants are off, migrating back to their wintering grounds in southern China.

The well-equipped **Khetsuu Khad Ger Camp** (☑ 9945 6796, 9911 7524; GPS: N 49°01.968; E 093°28.783'; per person with/without meals US$48/12) is set down here, seemingly in the middle of nowhere. It has hot showers, flush toilets, a restaurant (breakfast/lunch/dinner US$9/14/10) and clean, comfortable gers as well as rooms in a small guesthouse building. The rocks between the camp and the lake are fun to clamber over, and the lake views from the top of them are superb.

The turn-off from the main road towards the camp is signposted, just east of Khar Temis holiday camp, but it's still quite a long drive from here. The last 15km are very sandy and it's easy to get stuck, so don't attempt it without a reliable 4WD.

The national park fee applies around the lake, though you'd be lucky (or unlucky) to find a ranger to pay it to.

ZAVKHAN ЗАВХАН

POP 79,000 / AREA 82,000 SQ KM

Zavkhan aimag occupies a transitional zone between the well-watered Khangai mountain range of central Mongolia and the harsh Great Lakes Depression of western Mongolia. In between the two regions, Zavkhan has its own microclimates and varied terrain that ranges from snowy peaks to steppe to lakes surrounded by sand dunes.

The aimag is in an awkward location and very few travellers are likely to pass through much or any of Zavkhan. This is a pity because the scenery is some of the most dramatic and varied in the country; one minute you are travelling through lush valleys and hills, and then a few kilometres further you are in a desert reminiscent of *Lawrence of Arabia*.

Uliastai Улиастай

☑ 01462, 7046 / POP 64,600 / ELEV 1760M

Along with Khovd, Uliastai is one of Mongolia's oldest cities, founded by the Manchus during their reign in Mongolia. Sadly, the old garrison is long gone, save for some ruins on the outskirts of town. Rivers flowing nearby and a lush valley surrounded by mountains complete the picture and make it a great place to camp.

Note, if you've travelled from other western aimags, you're back into Ulaanbaatar time here, one hour ahead of Ölgii.

History

Manchurian generals established a military garrison here in 1733 to keep one eye on the Khalkh Mongols to the east and the other on the unruly Oirad Mongols who lived west of the Khangai mountains. The fortress once housed 3500 soldiers and was surrounded by an inevitable Chinese trading quarter called Maimaicheng.

The fort was emptied in 1911 with the disintegration of the Manchu dynasty, but Chinese troops made an attempt to retake the fort four years later, only to be booted out once and for all in March 1921, following the taking of Urga (Ulaanbaatar) by White Russian forces.

◉ Sights

History Museum MUSEUM
(☑01462-23097; admission T4000; ◎9am-6pm Mon-Fri) This decent History Museum contains a mammoth bone, some fine religious

Uliastai

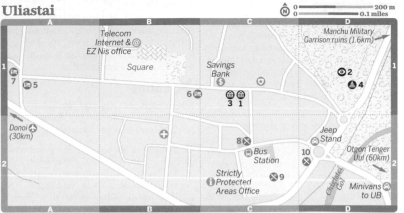

art and a *tsam* mask, worn during lama dances, made from coral. There is also a good collection of photographs of Uliastai taken in the early 20th century and a few grisly reminders of the Manchu era in the form of shackles and torture devices. The map on the wall depicting Uliastai's layout when it was still a garrison is also interesting.

Museum of Famous People MUSEUM
(⊙9am-6pm Mon-Fri) Next door to the History Museum, the Museum of Famous People features well-known Zavkhanites (including Mongolia's first two democratically elected presidents, P Ochirbat and N Bagabandi), and is included in the admission price.

Javkhlant Tolgoi VIEWPOINT
(Жавхлант Толгой) This hilltop near the river and just to the north of the main street features a pavilion, nine stupas and the concrete likenesses of an elk, ibex and argali sheep. The views from the top are good. To the northeast, 1.6km away, you can just make out the ruined remains of the once-walled **Manchu military garrison** (GPS: N 47°44.922', E 96°52.198') between the river and the distant hills. You can walk to the ruins across the grassy meadow in about 20 minutes. There's little to see, but it's a pleasant stroll.

Tögs Buyant
Javkhlant Khiid BUDDHIST MONASTERY
(Төрс Буянт Жавхлант Хийд) The small monastery towards the base of the hill has around 20 monks, and daily ceremonies at 10am.

Uliastai

☞ Tours

Chigistei Restaurant HORSE TREKS
(☑9811 2507, 9946 0506; enkh_tuya5@yahoo.com) Tuya, who owns the Chigistei Restaurant and speaks some English, can also help organise tours, including hiking and horse treking in the Otgon Tenger Uul Strictly Protected Area. She can arrange transport (US$80 per day per jeep), guides (US$40 to US$50 per day) and horses (US$20 per day, plus the same again for a horse guide). She particularly recommends the seven-day hike or horse trek from Uliastai to Dayan Mountain and back.

🛏 Sleeping

The grassy meadow leading towards the ruined Manchu military garrison is great for camping. For some truly gorgeous camping spots, though, follow Chigistei Gol out of town for around 5km to 10km along the lush valley that eventually leads to Otgon Tenger Uul Strictly Protected area.

Jim Hotel   HOTEL $
(☑9998 0300; tw/tr T20,000/30,000 tw with bathroom T25,000) This small guesthouse has basic but tidy rooms. All have bathrooms with toilets, but only some have showers. Uugaa, the owner, speaks some English.

Uliastai Hotel   HOTEL $$
(☑8993 4004, 7046 2414; s/tw/half-lux/lux with breakfast T20,000/20,000/30,000/40,000, half-lux tw with breakfast T60,000, lux with breakfast T100,000) A polished marble foyer, glass chandeliers and a swanky restaurant create a fine first impression at the Uliastai Hotel. A trifle disappointingly this standard isn't maintained but, when all is said and done, these digs are the cleanest in town. Not all rooms have their own showers, although there is a common shower (T3500), and hot water is only available from 7am to 10am and 7pm to 10pm.

OFF THE BEATEN TRACK

WESTERN ZAVKHAN

If you are travelling overland from Uliastai to western Mongolia (or vice versa) there are a few places of interest to stop on the way.

Khar Nuur (Хар Нуур) Located in the *sum* of Erdenekhairkhan, this is a pretty freshwater lake bordering on alpine and desert zones. Most of the lake is ringed by sand dunes, making vehicle access difficult.

Ikh Khairkhan Nuruu (Их Хайрхан) An area of cliffs that provides shelter for ibexes and wolves. There are caves in the area, including **Ikh Agui** (Big Cave; GPS: N 47°57.080', E 94°59.854'), one of the largest caves in Mongolia.

Ereen Nuur (Эрээн Нуур) A beautiful lake surrounded by rolling sand dunes, some of them high enough to resemble small mountains. It's technically in Gov-Altai aimag but most travellers reach the lake via Uliastai.

Örgöö Hotel   HOTEL $$
(☑9546 9642; tw/d T30,000/40,000) Bright, spacious rooms come with small attached bathrooms with hot showers. It's clean and friendly, although no English is spoken and there's a karaoke bar next door.

🍴 Eating

Self-caterers can try the **market** (◷11am-6pm Mon-Sat) or **Tesiin Gol Supermarket** (◷10am-6pm) near the roundabout.

Chigistei Restaurant   MONGOLIAN $
(☑9946 0506; mains T4000-7000; ◷9am-10pm; ✎) A large restaurant with retro-Soviet decor and mostly Mongolian dishes. No English menu, although if the English-speaking owner, Tuya, is around she'll talk you through it. Dishes include *sharsan zagas* (fried fish from Khar Nuur), *sharsan makhtei moog* (fried meat with mushroom), *bif-stek* (meat patty served with mashed potato and salad) and *tsuiven* (fried noodles).

★ Uliastai Hotel
Restaurant   MONGOLIAN, INTERNATIONAL $$
(mains T4000-8000; ◷7am-9pm; 📵) The cleanest, smartest restaurant in town, and the only one with an English menu, Uliastai Hotel serves up BBQ chicken, beef stew and fried fish to go along with a range of traditional Mongolian dishes. Has a bar, although it is reluctant to keep serving either food or drinks after around 9pm.

ℹ Information

Savings Bank (◷9am-6pm Mon-Fri) Has an ATM and changes dollars.

Strictly Protected Areas Office (☑9809 9466, 01462-22361; ◷9am-1pm & 2-5pm Mon-Fri) This office contains a small information room with brochures and pictures, though no English is spoken. The staff can also sell you entry tickets to Otgon Tenger Uul Strictly Protected Area.

Telecom Internet Cafe (per hr T600; ◷9am-10pm Mon-Fri, 11am-5pm Sat & Sun) One of two internet cafes in the Telecom Building. The other is open 7am to 9pm daily.

Telecom Building Catch-all location with two internet cafes, a post office and a branch of EZ Nis airlines.

ℹ Getting There & Away

AIR
EZ Nis (☑9990 3959, 7046 3033; ◷9am-5pm) flies daily to UB (around T225,000 one way) at 10.25am. A free shuttle bus to Uliastai's Donoi

Airport (30km west of town) leaves from the square outside the office at 7.40am. The office is inside the Telecom Building. Staff speak English.

BUS

Buses leave five days a week for Ulaanbaatar (T48,000, 30 hours) from near the Chigistei Restaurant at 9am.

MINIVAN & JEEP

Several minivans and jeeps leave each day for Ulaanbaatar (T40,000 to T50,000 per person, 26 hours, 984km) via Tosontsengel (T20,000 to T30,000, five to six hours, 181km). If you want to get off at Tariat (for Terkhiin Tsagaan Nuur; 10 to 11 hours, 399km) or Tsetserleg (15 hours, 531km), you may have to pay the full Ulaanbaatar fare.

It is virtually impossible to find a vehicle heading north to Mörön, south to Altai or even west to Ulaangom, although that doesn't stop people trying. You may be forced to hire a jeep privately at the jeep station to head in these directions (around T70,000 per day plus fuel).

In the last week of August it is easy to get a ride to Khovd City (around T40,000, 18 hours, 480km) when vans fill up with students headed back to university.

The road between Uliastai and Tosontsengel is unpaved, but pretty reasonable and easy to follow. The turn-off to Tosontsengel is 148km north of Uliastai and 33km west of Tosontsengel.

Zagastain Davaa
Загастайн Даваа

Forty-eight kilometres northeast of Uliastai on the Uliastai–Tosontsengel road is a spectacular mountain pass with the unusual name of Zagastain Davaa (Fish Pass; GPS: N 48°04.157', E 097°09.900'). At the top, there are fine views, a large *ovoo* and infamously changeable weather. Look out for the two balbals and burial mounds (GPS: N 47°56.396', E 097°00.824'), located 20km south of the pass.

Otgon Tenger Uul Strictly Protected Area
Отгон Тэнгэр Уул

One of Mongolia's most sacred mountains, Otgon Tenger Uul (3905m), 60km east of Uliastai, is the spiritual abode of the gods and an important place of pilgrimage for many Mongolians. The mountain is the highest peak in the Khangai Nuruu and part of the Otgon Tenger Strictly Protected

Area (95,510 hectares; admission T3000). The mountain's sanctity means that climbing is prohibited, and attempting to do so will incur the wrath of park rangers and the authorities in Uliastai.

You'll need to be content with viewing Otgon Tenger from the smaller Dayan Uul, a 60- to 90-minute drive past the children's camp, passing pretty Tsagaan Nuur (GPS: N 47°39.937', E 97°15.804') en route, and where you'll also get views of lovely Khökh Nuur (GPS: N 47°37.447', E 97°20.546'). The children's camp is just past the ranger's station (GPS: N 47°41.394' E 97°15.263'), where you can buy your park permit. A second route into the area is via the town of Otgon, 138km southeast of Uliastai, where a decent road heads up the Buyant Gol towards the southeastern flank of the mountain. This route is littered with impressive pre-Mongol-era burial mounds.

Otgon Tenger is a great area for hiking and horse trekking (guide/horse per day T15,000/20,000). The scenery is lush and beautiful. It takes three to four days to hike here from Uliastai. Camping opportunities abound the whole way. Tuya at the Chigistei Restaurant (p229) and the rangers at the ranger station in Dayan Uul can put you in touch with horse wranglers. You'll find herdsmen with guest gers en route to Tsagaan Nuur, from where it's another hour's drive up to Dayan Uul.

Tosontsengel   Тосонцэнгэл
📞 01462, 7046 / ELEV 1716M

Occupying a pretty valley along the Ider Gol, with forested mountains on all sides, Tosontsengel is Zavkhan's second-biggest city and a transit hub for west-bound traffic. Tosontsengel once supported a booming timber trade and its many wood-fronted buildings, coupled with unpaved lanes and wandering horsemen, give it a Wild West atmosphere.

If you need to stop for the night, or just for lunch, the newly-opened Skyline Hotel & Restaurant (📞9908 4393; skyline.hotel@yahoo.com; tw US$25-40) is your best bet. Rooms are smart and clean and come with sinks and toilets, although showers are shared. The bright and cheery restaurant (mains T3500-5000; ⏰8am-11pm; 📶📱) has chicken dishes and some vegetarian options, plus beer. The hotel overlooks the grassy, main square.

As a transit hub between eastern and western Mongolia there is plenty of traffic, including a daily minivan to Ulaanbaatar (T45,000) and Tariat (T15,000, five hours, 190km). Occasionally you may find one heading to Uliastai (T15,000, five hours, 181km) and Mörön (seven hours, 273km) but this is by no means guaranteed. The Uliastai–Ulaanbaatar bus calls into a canteen (called simply **Buudal Guanz**) on the main road through town at around 2pm and, if there is room, will take you to Ulaanbaatar for T39,500.

If you are heading to Mörön from Uliastai or Ulaangom, you don't need to come to Tosontsengel at all; the turn-off to Mörön is 33km to the west of the city.

Understand Mongolia

Mongolia Today

Mongolia may be a little fish in the big pond of globalisation but its importance on the world stage has only just started to grow. Pundits have dubbed the country 'Mingolia', a nod to its enormous mineral wealth. Mongolians are stepping cautiously ahead, wary of the fact that other natural-resource-rich countries have been ruined by corruption and mismanagement. The government has set up checks to ensure transparent accounting of mining revenue but whether or not the bonanza is spent wisely is something only time will tell.

Best on Film

The Weeping Camel (2005) Docu-drama that follows a camel-herder family in the Gobi.
Mongol (2007) Dramatic depiction of the rise of Chinggis Khaan.
Tracking the White Reindeer (2009) Docu-drama on reindeer herders, available online.

Best in Print

Ghenghis Khan and the Making of the Modern World (Jack Weatherford; 2005) Groundbreaking book and a bestseller on the Mongol empire.
When Things Get Dark (Matthew Davis; 2010) Raw examination of life in Tsetserleg from an American teacher.
Hearing Birds Fly (Louisa Waugh; 2003) Recollections of a year spent in remote Bayan-Ölgii by a British teacher.
Wild East (Jill Lawless; 2000) Slices of Mongolian life written by a Canadian expat editor of the *UB Post*.
Mörön to Mörön (Tom Doig; 2013) Wacky adventures of two Aussies making their way across Mongolia on pushbikes.

The Great Leap Forward

The hot topic of conversation in Mongolia is the US$6.6 billion Oyu Tolgoi copper and gold mine, developed by the Anglo-Australian company Rio Tinto, but 34% owned by the Mongolian government. Copper concentrate exports began in 2013 and the company says that by 2018 the mine will account for one-third of the country's total GDP. The hope is that this single world-class deposit will lift the whole country up by the bootstraps.

China is a ready market for Mongolia's raw materials and the government is rapidly trying to build up its infrastructure to deliver the goods. New rail and road links to China are being built, and in a bid to diversify its markets, Mongolia is also planning a 1000km railway from Ömnögov all the way to Russia (via Choibalsan).

Mongolia's political leaders seem keenly aware of the need to invest their newfound wealth back into the country. A copper smelter, oil refinery and coal washing plants are a few of the planned factories. A new international airport is expected to open in 2016 and the government is also planning to build a new university and IT campus outside Ulaanbaatar.

Democrats Sweep to Power

Mongolians went to the polls in June 2012 and gave the Democratic Party (DP) a narrow victory over the rival Mongolian People's Party (MPP). A year later President Elbegdorj was re-elected, giving the DP control of all top political positions until 2016.

Calling itself the 'Reform Government', the DP made some surprisingly radical (and progressive) political decisions soon after taking office.

Ulaanbaatar Mayor E Bat-Uul kicked things off with a new traffic system in the capital (banning cars from driving on certain days based on their licence-plate number). Another popular move was a strict ban on smoking in all public areas. A provision in the law forced vendors to stop selling cigarettes if they are located 500m from a school.

The DP has made sweeping promises to modernise Ulaanbaatar, including the redevelopment of ger areas and the construction of highways. Rural areas are also tapped for development and billions in debt have been raised to pay for it all. The DP is attempting to make these changes at the grassroots level, by putting funds in the hands of local government to spend money on projects as they see fit.

More controversially, the president put his foot down on corruption, resulting in the jailing of dozens of officials, from MIAT employees right up to former president N Enkhbayar. Critics pointed out that none of the convicted felons came from the president's own party, the DP.

The Future

For Mongolia, the challenge lies largely in the task of nation building. From a cultural point of view, Mongolia has moved on from the Soviet period and has established a new path of strong nationalism fused with Western influences. One only needs to look at urban youth culture in Ulaanbaatar – tattooed with *soyombo* (the national symbol) and rapping about the blue skies – to realise that the country is forging a unique new identity.

But on the ground, life is still hard. Poverty, especially in rural areas, has forced thousands to the city in search of work. Many end up jobless in the sprawling ger districts. Work, housing, education and good healthcare remain elusive for many, while a small segment of the population is widening the wealth gap, largely through shady business deals and political connections.

There has been some trickle-down effect and the beginnings of a middle class but this development still depends on Mongolia's economic growth prospects, which itself largely hangs on external factors such as the price of minerals and China's continued growth.

Despite the challenges ahead, surveys show widespread support for the economic reforms. There is strong optimism among most of the population, but the country still has a long way to go before it can claim success.

POPULATION: **2.9 MILLION (2013)**

GDP: **US$4745 PER CAPITA (2012)**

GDP GROWTH: **12.4% (2012)**

LITERACY RATE: **98%**

NUMBER OF LIVESTOCK: **41 MILLION**

INFLATION: **12.5%**

if Mongolia were 100 people

95 would be Mongol (mostly Khalkh)
5 would be Turkic (mostly Kazakh)

belief systems
(% of population)

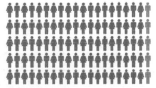

80 Mahayana Buddhism
5 Islam
5 Christianity
10 Atheism

population per sq km

MONGOLIA RUSSIA USA

🚹 ≈ 2 people

History Jack Weatherford & Dulmaa Enkhchuluun

Dulmaa Enkhchuluun graduated from Augsburg College in Minnesota and now works to promote culturally and environmentally responsible tourism and commercial development in Mongolia.

Over the past 2000 years, there is possibly no other place on the planet that has exported as much history as Mongolia. Hordes of warriors rode their small but powerful horses down from the Mongolian Plateau in three dramatic waves – Hun, Turk and, finally, Mongol – to challenge and transform the world. The steppe warriors not only conquered nations, they swept up whole civilisations and reassembled them into intercontinental empires of a scale never before reached by any other people.

Although each of the three waves produced its distinctive influence, the name of Chinggis Khaan has achieved a unique spot in the world's imagination. He created the nation in 1206 and named it after his Mongol lineage. Mongols still maintain an intimate tie to him, but beyond the use of his iconic image and name, there seems to be surprisingly little to show of him in the nation. Chinggis Khaan did not leave a monument to himself, a temple, pyramid, palace, castle or canal, and even his grave was left unmarked in the remote area where he grew up and hunted as a boy. As he himself wished, his body could wither away so long as his great Mongol nation lived – it is that nation today that is his monument.

Anthropologist Jack Weatherford wrote *Genghis Khan and the Making of the Modern World*, for which he received the Order of the Polar Star, Mongolia's highest state honour.

The lack of tangible ties to Chinggis Khaan presents both a challenge and an opportunity to visitors; Mongolia does not yield its history promiscuously to every passer-by. Its story is not told in great books, large stone monuments or bronze statues. A hiker crossing a hilltop can easily find etchings of deer with baroque configurations of antlers, soaring falcons or shamans without faces, but how would they know if the image was etched last year by a bored herder, a century ago by a pious lama or 25,000 years ago by a passing hunter? A small stone implement could have been abandoned on that same site centuries ago by a Hun mother preparing a family meal or by a Turk warrior on a raid; the modern visitor might easily be the first human to clutch it in 3000 years. These artefacts don't come labelled, classified and explained – the stories of the steppe are incomplete – but you'll find that Mongolia's history emerges slowly, from the objects, the soil and the landscape around you.

People of the Sun

The first of the steppe nomads to make an impact beyond Mongolia were the Hunnu, whom the Mongols now call the 'People of the Sun', better known as the Huns. They created the first steppe empire in 209 BC under Modun, a charismatic leader who took the title *shanyu* (king) and ruled until his death in 174 BC. Modun created a disciplined and strong cavalry corps personally devoted to him, and used the corps to overthrow and kill his father, the tribal chief.

Between the creation of the Qin dynasty in China in 221 BC and the collapse of the Han dynasty in AD 220, the Chinese became the dominant economic power in East Asia. Even still, under the Huns the steppe tribes grew into a great military power. During this period, the Chinese and the Huns vied for dominance through protracted wars with intermittent truces, during which the Chinese lavished the steppe warriors with tributes of goods and women, including imperial princesses (in exchange the Huns agreed not to slaughter them all). Using the merchandise extracted from the Chinese, the Huns extended their trade routes, connecting the civilisations around them.

Following the collapse of the Hun empire in the 4th century AD, various newly independent tribes left the Mongolian homeland, wandering from India to Europe in search of new pastures and new conquests. By the 5th century, one of these branches reached Europe and created a new Hun empire that stretched from the Ural Mountains to Germany. Under their most famous leader, Attila the Hun, they threatened Rome and ravaged much of Western Europe. For the first time in history, mounted archers from the Mongolian steppe created an intercontinental reputation for their fierceness and tenacity in battle.

Descendents of the Wolf

In the 6th century, a new sense of order returned to the Mongolian Plateau with the rise of a series of tribes speaking Turkic languages. These tribes claimed descent from a boy who was left for dead but was saved and adopted by a mother wolf who raised him and then mated with him, creating from their offspring the ancestors of the various steppe clans. Compared with both the Huns before them and the Mongols after them, the literate Turks sought to blend traditional nomadic herding with a life of agriculture, urbanisation and commerce; consequently, they left more physical remains than the others in the ruins of Turkic cities and

> *Khan* means chief or king; *khaan* means emperor or great khan.

> At Noyon Uul in Selenge aimag, archaeologists have made curious finds inside Hunnu-era tombs. Unearthed objects include Hellenistic mirrors and jewellery from Afghanistan. Historians believe these were brought from Persia or Central Asia and traded by steppe nomads until they reached the Siberian border.

1162	1204
Birth of Temujin, the child destined to become Chinggis Khaan, near the Onon River. According to legend, Temujin emerges with a blood clot clutched in his fist.	Chinggis Khaan establishes the Mongolian state script based on the Uighur alphabet; it has Semitic origins but is written vertically from top to bottom.

DAVOR LOVINCIC/GETTY IMAGES ©

→ Chinggis Khaan statue, Ulaanbaatar (p56)

CHINGGIS KHAAN

Known to the world as a conqueror, Mongolians remember Chinggis Khaan as the great lawgiver and proudly refer to him as the Man of the Millennium (a title bestowed on him by the *Washington Post* in 1995). His laws derived from practical considerations more than from ideology or religion.

After the abduction of his wife Borte, Chinggis recognised the role of kidnapping in perpetuating feuds among clans and outlawed it. Similarly, he perceived religious intolerance as being a source of violence in society, and so decreed religious freedom for everyone and exempted religious scholars and priests from taxes.

To promote trade and communications, Chinggis built an international network of postal stations that also served as hostels for merchants. He decreased and standardised the taxes on goods so that they would not be repeatedly taxed. Under these laws, the Mongol empire formed the first intercontinental free-trade zone.

In an era when ambassadors served as hostages to be publicly tortured or killed during times of hostilities, Chinggis Khaan ordered that every ambassador be considered an envoy of peace. This law marked the beginning of diplomatic immunity and international law. Today nearly every country accepts and promotes, at least in theory, the ideas and policies behind the 'Great Law of Chinggis Khaan'.

ceremonial centres. Along the Orkhon Gol in central Mongolia, they built their small cities of mud, the most famous of which were erected during the time of the Uighurs, the last of the great Turkic empires of Mongolia. The Turkic era reached its zenith in the early 8th century under Bilge Khan and his brother Kultegen, the military general. Their monuments near the Orkhon Gol are probably the oldest known examples of writing in a Turkic language.

Like the Huns before them, the Turks moved down off the Mongolian Plateau, spreading from what is today China to the shores of the Mediterranean. Another invading Turkic tribe, the Kyrgyz, overthrew the Uighur empire in AD 840, destroying its cities and driving the Uighur people south into the oases of western China. But the Kyrgyz showed no inclination to maintain the cities or the empire they had conquered. With the expulsion of the Uighurs came another period of decentralised feuding and strife, before the greatest of all Mongolian empires arose at the beginning of the 13th century: the rise to power of Chinggis Khaan.

Turkic-Era Sites

Uushigiin Uver

Stele of Tonyukok

Kul-Tegenii Monument

Tavan Bogd balbals (stone figures)

Children of the Golden Light

The decline of the Turkic tribes gave the opening for a new tribe to emerge. Scholars offer varying explanations for when and where these new people arrived, but the Mongols ascribe their origins to the mating

1206	1235	1258	1260
Chinggis Khaan calls a massive conclave at Kherlen Gol and creates his empire – he calls it the Great Mongol Nation.	Ögedei Khaan completes the imperial capital at Karakorum. In addition to a great palace, the city has Muslim mosques, Christian churches and Buddhist temples.	Mongolian soldiers destroy Baghdad and kill some 100,000 people. The siege marks the end of the 500-year-old Abbasid Caliphate.	The end of Mongol expansion with their defeat by the Mamluk army of Egypt at the Battle of Ayn Al-Jalut near the Sea of Galilee.

of a blue wolf and a tawny doe beside a great sea, often identified as Lake Baikal (in Russia). They further credit the origin of Chinggis Khaan's own clan to a mysterious and sacred woman called Alan Goa, who gave birth to two sons during her marriage, and had an additional three sons after her husband died. The elder sons suspected that their younger brothers had been fathered by an adopted boy (now a man) whom their mother had also raised and who lived with her.

Upon hearing of their suspicions and complaints, Alan Goa sat her five sons around the hearth in her ger and told them that the three younger sons were fathered by a 'Golden Light'. She then handed each an arrow with the command to break it. When they had done this, she handed each a bundle of five arrows with the command to break them all together. When the boys could not do so, she told them that it mattered not where the brothers came from so long as they remained united.

No matter what the Mongol origin, the story of Alan Goa has had a persistent and profound influence on the development of Mongolian culture, on everything from the role of women and attitudes towards sexuality to the political quest for unity and the herder's value of practical action over ideology or religion.

A Mongol is a member of the Mongol ethnic group; a Mongolian is a citizen of Mongolia. Kazakhs of Bayan-Ölgii are Mongolians but not Mongols; the Kalmyks of New Jersey are Mongols but not Mongolians.

The Mongol Empire

The Mongols were little more than a loose confederation of rival clans until the birth of Temujin in 1162. Overcoming conditions that would have crushed lesser men, Temujin rose to become the strongest ruler on the steppe, and in 1206 founded the Mongol empire and took the title 'Chinggis Khaan'. He was already 44 years old at this stage, but since the age of 16, when his bride was kidnapped, he had been fighting one clan feud and tribal war after another. Frustrated with the incessant chaos, he began killing off the leaders of each clan as he defeated them and incorporating the survivors into his own following. Through this harsh but effective way, Chinggis Khaan forced peace onto the clans around him.

He named his new state Yeke Mongol Ulus (Great Mongol Nation). His followers totalled probably less than a million people, and from this he created an army of nine units of 10,000 and a personal guard of another 10,000. With a nation smaller than the workforce of a large, modern multinational corporation, and an army that could fit inside a modern sports stadium, the Mongols conquered the greatest armies of the era and subdued hundreds of millions of people.

In battle, Chinggis Khaan was merciless, but to those who surrendered without fighting, he promised protection, religious freedom, lower taxes and a heightened level of commerce and prosperity. His law did more to attract people into his empire than his military power.

Chinggis Khaan never erected any statues or grand monuments to himself, but recent years have seen modern Mongolians trying to rectify this. Statues of Chinggis can be seen at Chinggis Khaan (Sükhbaatar) Sq in UB, on the Ulaanbaatar–Khentii road, in Chinggis Khot (Öndörkhaan) and in Dadal.

1271	1368	1395	1448
Kublai Khaan claims the office of great khan and also makes himself Emperor of China by founding the Yuan dynasty.	Yuan dynasty collapses in China but the Mongol government returns to Mongolia refusing to submit to the newly created Ming dynasty. They continue ruling as the 'Northern Yuan'.	Geoffrey Chaucer's *The Canterbury Tales*, recognised as the first book of poetry written in English, includes an early account of Chinggis Khaan in the 'Squire's Tale'.	Birth of Mongolia's greatest queen, Manduhai the Wise Queen, who reunites Mongolia by the end of the century.

Based on military success and good laws, his empire continued to expand after his death until it stretched from Korea to Hungary and from India to Russia.

The Decline

The English word 'horde' derives from the Mongol *ordu*, meaning 'royal court'.

After Chinggis Khaan's death, his second son Ögedei ruled from 1229 to 1241, followed by Ögedei's widow Töregene Khatun and the brief 18-month reign of Ögedei's son Guyuk from 1246 through 1248. Tensions began to develop among the branches of his descendants, and broke into open civil war in 1259 when Arik Boke and Kublai each claimed the office of great khan after the death of their brother Möngke. Arik Boke controlled all of Mongolia, including the capital Karakorum, and enjoyed widespread support from the ruling Borjin clan. Yet Kublai controlled the vast riches of northern China, and these proved far more powerful. Kublai defeated his brother, who then perished under suspicious circumstances in captivity.

THE LOST LEGION OF SAXON MINERS

Twenty thousand mounted Mongols crossed Poland toward Western Europe in 1241. Urged by the pope to defend the Christian world, Henry II of Silesia conscripted thousands of Saxon miners to make their mining tools into weapons to fight the Mongols. In April at the Battle of Liegnitz and a nearly simultaneous one in Hungary, the Mongols permanently crushed European knighthood and killed Henry, but they transported the captive miners and their tools to work the mines in greater Mongolia.

Shortly thereafter in 1245, fearing growth of the mining and arms industry in Asia, Pope Innocent IV sent Giovanni of Plano Carpini, a surviving companion of Francis of Assisi, in search of the lost legion of Saxon miners. He returned with little news of the miners but with Guyuk Khaan's stern command for the pope's submission. Another expedition sent by French King Louis IX under William of Rubruck in 1253 produced little information about the lost miners other than a tantalising encounter with a captured Parisian goldsmith whom the Mongols commissioned to build a silver tree fountain in Karakorum.

After the Mongol decline, commercial development, including mining, was forbidden until the end of the 19th century when mining engineer (and future US president) Herbert Hoover arrived on horseback to meet the Bogd Khan and open Mongolia to the world. Despite an American trading-post compound at American Denj, the European firm Mongol Ore secured the main mining concessions. Following heavy investment in German equipment transported via railroad and ox cart, the company failed to persuade Mongolians to work as miners and had to rely on thousands of coolies from China. In WWI and the ensuing financial chaos, Mongol Ore disappeared into the Mongolian dust like the Lost Legion of Saxon Miners.

1449

Esen Taishi defeats the Chinese and captures the Ming emperor. His reign marks the rise of western Mongolia and the Oirat people as major powers of inner Asia.

1586

Founding of Erdene Zuu Khiid, the first Buddhist monastery in Mongolia, at the site of the Mongol capital, Karakorum (modern Kharkhorin).

TIM MAKINS/GETTY IMAGES ©

➡ Stupas at Erdene Zuu Khiid (p114), Kharkhorin

Kublai had won the civil war and solidified his hold over China, but it had cost him his empire. Although still claiming to be a single empire, the nation of Chinggis Khaan had been reduced to a set of oft-warring sub-empires. The Mongols of Russia became in effect independent, known later as the Golden Horde, under the lineage of Chinggis Khaan's eldest son Jochi. Persia and Mesopotamia drifted off to become the Ilkhanate, under descendants of Kublai's only surviving brother Hulegu, the conqueror of Baghdad.

Kublai went on to create a Chinese dynasty named Yuan, took Chinese titles and, while still claiming to be the great khan of the Mongols, looked southward to the lands of the Sung dynasty, which he soon conquered.

Much of Central Asia, including Mongolia, pursued an independent course and acknowledged the Yuan dynasty only when forced to by military invasion or when enticed with extravagant bribes of silk, silver and other luxuries. By 1368, the subjects had mostly overthrown their Mongol overlords, and the empire withdrew back to the Mongolian steppe where it began. Although most Mongols melted into the societies that they conquered, in some distant corners of the empire, from Afghanistan to Poland, small vestiges of the Mongolian empire still survive.

In 1368, the Ming army captured Běijīng, but the Mongol royal family refused to surrender and fled back to Mongolia with the imperial seals and their bodyguards. Much to the frustration of the Ming emperors in China, the Mongols continued to claim to be the legitimate rulers of China and still styled themselves as the Yuan dynasty, also known as the Northern Yuan. However, even within Mongolia, the imperial court exerted little power. Unaccustomed to the hardships of the herding life, and demanding vast amounts of food, fuel and other precious resources for their large court and retainers, the Mongol rulers devastated their own country, alienated the increasingly impoverished herders and eventually became the captive pawns of the imperial guards.

In the 15th century, the Mongols united with the Manchus, a Tungusic people related to Siberian tribes, for a new conquest of China and the creation of the Qing dynasty (1644–1911). Initially, the ruling Manchus treated the Mongols with favour, gave them an exalted place in their empire and intermarried with them. Gradually, however, the Manchus became ever more Sinicised by their Chinese subjects and less like their Mongol cousins. The Mongols were reduced to little more than a colonised people under the increasingly oppressive and exploitative rule of the Manchus.

CHINGGIS KHAAN

The best source for information on the life of Chinggis Khaan can be found in *The Secret History of the Mongols*, which was written in the 13th or 14th century and not made public until the 20th century.

Revolutions

In 1911 the Qing dynasty crumbled. The Mongols broke away and created their own independent country under their highest Buddhist leader, the Jebtzun Damba (Living Buddha), who became both spiritual and temporal

1603	1634	1639	1644
A descendant of Chinggis Khaan and great-great grandson of Queen Manduhai is enthroned in Lhasa, Tibet, as the fourth Dalai Lama, the only Mongolian Dalai Lama.	Death of Ligden Khaan, the last of Chinggis Khaan's descendants to rule as great khan. Eastern Mongolia becomes part of the Manchu empire, but western Mongolia holds out.	Zanabazar, a direct descendent of Chinggis Khaan and the greatest artist in Mongolian history, is recognised as the first Jebtzun Damba, the supreme religious leader of Mongolia.	The Manchus expel the Ming dynasty and with the support of their Mongolian allies create the Qing dynasty in China.

head of the nation as the Bogd Khan (Holy King). When the Chinese also broke free of the Manchus and created the Republic of China, the new nation did not recognise Mongolia's independence, claiming portions of

WARRIOR QUEENS OF MONGOLIA

Chinggis Khaan's greatest disappointment in life was the quality of his sons, but his greatest pride was in his daughters. He left large sections of his empire under the control of his daughters, although they did gradually lose power to his sons.

Mongol women presented a strange sight to the civilisations they helped conquer – they rode horses, shot arrows from their bows and commanded the men and women around them. In China, the Mongol women rejected foot-binding; in the Muslim world, they refused to wear the veil.

At the death of Ögedei (Chinggis Khaan's second son) in 1241, probably in an alcoholic stupor, his widow Töregene assumed complete power. She replaced his ministers with her own, the most important of whom was another woman, Fatima, a Tajik or Persian captive from the Middle Eastern campaign. In addition to the rule of Töregene and Fatima from Karakorum in Mongolia, two of the other three divisions of the empire also had female governors – only the Golden Horde of Russia remained under male rule. Never before had such a large empire been ruled by women.

Töregene passed power on to her inept son Guyuk in 1246, but he died mysteriously within 18 months and was replaced by his widow Oghul Ghamish, who had to face Sorkhokhtani, the most capable woman in the empire. With the full support of her four sons, whom she trained for this moment, Sorkhokhtani organised the election of her eldest son Möngke on 1 July 1251. So great was her achievement that a Persian chronicler wrote that if history produced only one more woman equal to Sorkhokhtani, then surely women would have to be judged the superior sex.

While Kublai Khaan ruled China, his cousin Khaidu continued to fight against him from Central Asia and, true to the Mongol tradition, Khaidu's daughter Khutlun fought with him. According to Marco Polo, who called her Aiyaruk, she was both beautiful and powerful. She defeated so many men in wrestling that today, Mongolian wrestlers wear an open vest in order to visibly distinguish the male from the female wrestlers.

After the fall of the Mongol empire in 1368, the men returned to squabbling over sheep and stealing horses, but the women kept the imperial spirit alive. In the late 15th century a new conqueror arose, determined to restore the empire. Known to the grateful Mongols as Manduhai the Wise Queen, she took to the battlefield and united the scattered tribes into a single nation. She fought even while pregnant and was once injured while carrying twins; she and the twins survived, and her army won the battle.

Faced with Manduhai's tenacity and skill, the Chinese frantically expanded the Great Wall. Although she left seven sons and three daughters, the era of the great warrior queens of Mongolia had passed with her death. Even so, Mongolians still watch and wait for a new Manduhai.

1696	1911	1915	1921
The Manchus defeat Galdan Khan of Zungaria and claim western Mongolia for the Qing dynasty, but some western Mongolians continue to resist foreign rule for several generations.	Mongolia declares independence from the dying Manchu empire and sets up religious leader the Bogd Khan as the head of state.	The Treaty of Khyakhta is signed by Mongolia, China and Russia, granting Mongolia limited autonomy.	The mad Russian baron, von Ungern-Sternberg, briefly conquers Mongolia but the Red Army and Mongolian forces under D Sükhbaatar defeat him.

the Manchu empire, including Tibet and Mongolia. In May 1915 the Treaty of Khyakhta, which granted Mongolia limited autonomy, was signed by Mongolia, China and Russia.

The Russian Revolution of October 1917 came as a great shock to Mongolia's aristocracy. Taking advantage of Russia's weakness, a Chinese warlord sent his troops into Mongolia in 1919 and occupied the capital. In February 1921, retreating White Russian (anti-communist) troops entered Mongolia and expelled the Chinese. At first the Bogd Khan seemed to welcome the White Russians as saviours of his regime, but it soon became apparent that they were just another ruthless army of occupiers.

Mongolian nationalists believed their best hope for military assistance was to ask the Bolsheviks for help. The White Russians disappeared from the scene when their leader, Baron von Ungern-Sternberg, was captured, tried and shot. In July 1921, Damdin Sükhbaatar, the leader of the Mongolian army, marched uncontested into Urga (modern-day Ulaanbaatar) alongside Bolshevik supporters. The People's Government of Mongolia was declared and the Bogd Khan was retained as a ceremonial figurehead with no real power. Led by a diverse coalition of seven revolutionaries, including Sükhbaatar, the newly formed Mongolian People's Party (MPP), the first political party in the country's history (and the only one for the next 69 years), took the reins of power. Soon after its birth the MPP adopted a new name, the Mongolian People's Revolutionary Party (MPRP). The party reinstated the original name in 2010.

> Russian Cossacks adopted the Mongol battle cry of 'hurray!' and spread it to the rest of the world.

Soviet Control

After Lenin's death in Russia in 1924, Mongolian communism remained independent of Moscow until Stalin gained absolute power in the late 1920s. Then the purges began in Mongolia – MPRP leaders were disposed of until Stalin finally found his henchman in one Khorloogiin Choibalsan.

Following Stalin's lead, Choibalsan seized land and herds from the aristocrats, which was then redistributed to nomads. Herders were forced to join cooperatives and private business was banned. The destruction of private enterprise without time to build up a working state sector had the same result in Mongolia as in the Soviet Union: famine. Choibalsan's policy against religion was just as ruthless – in 1937 some 27,000 people were executed or never seen again (3% of Mongolia's population at that time), 17,000 of whom were monks.

> Rivers in Mongolia are female and may be called *eej* (mother). A river, spring or lake that never runs dry is called a *khatun* (queen).

Choibalsan died in January 1952 and was replaced by Yumjaagiin Tsedenbal – no liberal, but not a mass murderer – and Mongolia enjoyed a period of relative peace. With the Sino-Soviet split in the early 1960s, the Mongolians sided with the Soviet Union. The Mongolian government expelled thousands of ethnic Chinese and all trade with China came to a halt.

1924	1937	1937	1939
The Bogd Khan, the eighth reincarnation of the Jebtzun Damba, dies. The People's Republic of Mongolia is created on 26 November.	Choibalsan's Buddhist purge leaves 700 monasteries destroyed and 27,000 monks and civilians dead.	Former Mongolian prime minister Genden is tried in Moscow on trumped-up espionage charges, found guilty and executed by firing squad on 26 November.	Japan invades Mongolia from Manchuria in May. With help from the Soviet Union, and after heavy fighting along the Khalkh Gol, the Mongols defeat Japan by September.

THE MAD BARON

Baron Roman Nikolaus Fyodirovich von Ungern-Sternberg, an unusual character in Mongolia's history, was a renegade officer of a group of White Russians (anti-communists), who believed he was the reincarnation of Chinggis Khaan, destined to restore the Mongol warlord's previous empire. Contemporaries paint a fine picture of Baron von Ungern-Sternberg, later known as the Mad Baron, describing him as haunted-looking, with a psychotic stare that fixed on people 'like those of an animal in a cave'. He spoke with a high-pitched voice and his bulging forehead bore a huge sword scar, which pulsed with red veins whenever he grew agitated. As a finishing touch, one of his eyes was slightly higher than the other.

The Bolshevik victory in Russia forced the baron east, and he slowly accumulated a desperate army of renegade mercenaries. He enforced discipline with a reign of terror, roasting deserters alive, baking defiant prisoners in ovens and throwing his rivals in locomotive boilers. He was also a fervent Buddhist, convinced that he was doing his victims a favour by packing them off to the next life sooner rather than later.

With an army of 6000 troops (and tacit backing of the Japanese), the baron crossed the Mongolian border in the summer of 1920 with the aim of establishing a Pan-Mongol empire. By October, his forces attacked Urga, but were driven back four times before finally taking the city. He freed the Bogd Khan (who had been imprisoned by the Chinese) but Mongol joy turned to horror as the next three days saw an orgy of looting, burning and killing. In May 1921 the baron declared himself the emperor of Russia.

After only a few months, the Bolshevik advance forced the baron to abandon Urga. Out on the steppes, his own followers tried to kill him, shooting him in his tent, but he managed to escape. A group of Mongolian herders later found him wounded in the grass, tortured by biting ants. He was eventually taken by the Bolsheviks, deported to Novosibirsk and shot on 15 September 1921, presumed mad.

Dr Ferdinand Ossendowski, a Polish refugee living in Mongolia in the early 1920s, offers an excellent account of the Mad Baron in his book *Beasts, Men and Gods*. For a more recent account, read James Palmer's *The Bloody White Baron,* published in 2009.

Throughout the 1970s, Soviet influence gathered strength. Young Mongolians were sent to the USSR for technical training, and Tsedenbal's wife, a Russian woman of modest background named Filatova, attempted to impose Russian culture – including food, music, dance, fashion and even language – on the Mongolians.

The Great Transition

The unravelling of the Soviet Union resulted in decolonisation by default. In March 1990, in sub-zero temperatures, large pro-democracy protests erupted in the square in front of the parliament building in Ulaanbaatar.

1945	1956	1961
In a UN-sponsored plebiscite, Mongolians vote overwhelmingly to confirm their independence but the USA and China refuse to admit Mongolia to the UN.	The Trans-Siberian Railway through Mongolia is completed, connecting Běijīng with Moscow. The Chinese and Russian trains still operate on different gauges, requiring the bogies to be swapped at the border.	Mongolia is admitted to the UN as an independent country, but the Soviet Union continues to occupy Mongolia with troops and run the country as a satellite state.

TIM MAKINS/GETTY IMAGES ©

➡ Zamyn-Üüd (p190) train

Hunger strikes were held and in May 1990 the constitution was amended to permit multiparty elections in July of the same year.

The political liberation of Mongolia from the Soviets came as an economic disaster for Mongolia because of the heavy subsidies that the Soviets had paid to keep Mongolia as a buffer state between itself and China. The Mongols lost much of their food supply and, unable to pay their electrical bills to the Russian suppliers, the western districts were plunged into a blackout that lasted for several years. The economy of Mongolia withered and collapsed.

The harsh conditions called for stringent measures and Mongolians created a unique approach to the new challenges. They began a radical privatisation of animals and large state-owned corporations. Unlike the other Soviet satellites in Eastern Europe and Central Asia that expelled the communist party, the Mongolians created a new democratic synthesis that included both the old communists of the MPRP and a coalition that became known as the Democrats. Freedom of speech, religion and assembly were all granted – the era of totalitarianism had ended.

The Mongolians gradually found their way towards the modern global economy and embraced their own brand of capitalism and democracy that drew heavily on their ancient history while adjusting to the modern realities of the world around them. Despite difficult episodes, such as the unsolved murder of the Democratic leader S Zorig in 1998 and some

During WWII, Mongolia donated 300kg of gold and more than six million animals to Soviet and Allied forces. More than 2000 Mongolians died fighting Japan.

HISTORY THE GREAT TRANSITION

THE MONGOL WHO SLAPPED STALIN

In 1932 P Genden became the ninth prime minister of Mongolia, using the slogan 'Let's Get Rich!' to inspire Mongolians to overcome the troubled fighting since the breakup of the Manchu empire and the establishment of an independent country. Mongolia was the second communist state, after the Soviet Union, but at this time Genden was trying to establish Mongolia as an ally of the Soviets rather than a colony or satellite.

Genden, standing up to Stalin, resisted demands that Mongolia purge the Buddhist monks and charged the Russians with 'red imperialism' for seeking to send Soviet troops into Mongolia. Amid much drinking at a reception in the Mongolian embassy in Moscow in 1935, the two men clashed, literally. Stalin kicked Genden's walking stick and Genden slapped Stalin and broke Stalin's trademark pipe, which always accompanied him.

Stalin held Genden under house arrest until he was convicted as a Japanese spy and executed by firing squad on 26 November 1937 – a day of great symbolic importance to the Mongols because it was the date of their declaration of independence and the creation of the Mongolian People's Republic.

In 1996 Genden's daughter, G Tserendulam, opened the Victims of Political Persecution Memorial Museum in Ulaanbaatar in memory of her father and all those who died in defence of Mongolian independence.

1990	1981	1996	1998
Democracy demonstrations break out in Ulaanbaatar. In June the first free, multiparty elections are held, with the Mongolian People's Revolutionary Party (MPRP) winning 85% of the vote.	On 22 March, J Gurragchaa, a pilot in the Mongolian air force, becomes the first Mongolian in space. The cosmonaut spends seven days and 20 hours in orbit.	The Democratic Coalition becomes the first noncommunist government to win an election (although a series of scandals causes the fall of four successive governments).	On 2 October the 'Golden Magpie of Democracy' S Zorig, credited with leading the 1990 democratic revolution, is assassinated in his home by masked assailants. To this day the murder remains unsolved.

heated clashes between government and citizens, Mongolia managed to move forward with tremendous cultural vigour. While maintaining staunch friendships with old allies such as North Korea, Cuba and India, Mongolia reached out to Europe, South Korea, Japan and, most particularly, to the USA, which they dubbed their 'Third Neighbour' in an effort to create a counterpoint to China and Russia.

2008	2008	2012	2013
In hotly contested parliamentary elections the MPRP narrowly defeats the Democratic Coalition. Protestors allege vote rigging and subsequent riots end with four people shot dead and hundreds arrested.	Naidan Tuvshibayar wins Mongolia's first ever Olympic gold medal while competing in judo at the Běijīng summer games. Enkhbat Badar-Uugan, a boxer, also wins gold in Běijīng.	The Democratic Party narrowly wins parliamentary elections and joins smaller parties to form a Coalition government. Former president N Enkhbayar is sentenced to 2½ years in prison for corruption.	The first stage of the US$6.6 billion Oyu Tolgoi mine is completed and copper concentrate shipments begin to China. One month later the company fires 1700 workers amid a dispute over funding the mine's underground phase.

The Mongolian Way of Life

Every Mongolian, no matter how long he or she has lived in a city, is a nomad at heart. The nomadic way of life was born out of necessity as herders were forced to range their animals over vast distances in search of grass. Even in the modern age the country remained a nomadic one, in large part because the nomadic way of life became more than a necessity – it became an unbreakable lifestyle. While today, more than ever, Mongolians are lured to the city in search of work, some are choosing to stay on the land with their animals, unable to give up the freedom and independence afforded to them by their traditional lifestyle.

Ingredients for Life

The nomadic way of life is defined largely by the ger and a family's livestock. The ger is a portable shelter that allows the family to move with the seasons while the animals provide all of life's necessities, including food (mutton and beef), milk, fuel (in the form of dung) and transport.

Mongolians are attached to their animals in the same way that Westerners feel a certain affinity for their cars. The horse in particular is a much-beloved animal, forming an intimate part of the Mongolian lifestyle. It was the horse that allowed ancient tribes to spread across the steppes and cover their great distances. Later, it was the horse that carried the Mongol tribes across Asia as they built their empire. An old Mongolian proverb says: 'A man without a horse is like a bird without wings'.

Today you'll see symbolic images of horses everywhere, from the tops of fiddles to the tail of MIAT aeroplanes. It is frequently stated that Mongolian children start riding a horse at the age of two; in fact the horse riding begins earlier, essentially from birth, as parents will carry babies in their *dels* (traditional coat or dress) when they need to travel by horse.

> The device used in ceremonial milk rituals is a *tsatsal*, a wooden spoon decorated with carved symbols such as Tibetan Buddhist, mythical, animistic or zodiacal. The spoon is used to flick milk into the air as a spiritual offering. Such offerings are nearly always made by women.

The Forces of Nature

Nomadic peoples are, for all intents and purposes, on a lifelong camping trip. As such, they are greatly affected by the climate and other natural forces around them. Reverence towards the land, a product of their

FUNERARY RITES

Up until the early 20th century, Mongolians typically disposed of their dead by leaving them out in the elements, where dogs, birds and wild animals would devour the body. The practice followed the tradition of sky burial, common in Tibet. This act was seen to be the best way to return a body to the natural world, while the soul could safely be reincarnated into another body (either human or animal). When the Russians forbade the practice, Mongolians began following the Russian tradition of burying their dead. In the post-communist era, some families are reverting to the old method of sky burial, although this is still quite rare. The more popular option now is cremation and several crematoriums have been built around Ulaanbaatar in recent years.

shamanic beliefs, has attuned them to nature; the thought of degrading the land or altering nature strikes many Mongols as profane. Nature is not something that must be tamed or dominated, but something that thrives on balance and harmony.

Mongolia's reverence towards nature can still be seen in modern daily ritual. For example, the act of flicking milk into the sky is seen as an offering to the sky spirits. Tossing a rock on an *ovoo* (a shamanistic collection of stones) and walking around it three times is a way to bless earthly spirits. In the modern world some compromises do need to be made – for example, pits need to be dug for buildings and mines. In such cases lamas are often summoned to not only bless the project but also to pray for the damaged earth.

Reverence of nature is seen in all aspects of Mongolian culture, especially song, dance and art. Ride in a van full of Mongolians and you'll soon hear them break into song, crooning about the clear rivers and high mountains. These influences seem to have also affected the very nature of the Mongolian character. A Mongolian is typically humble, stoic and reserved; it is unusual to see a Mongolian express emotions vocally or in public. These personality traits must certainly be rooted in the quiet, motionless steppes that remain unchanged through the aeons of time.

Seasons also shape Mongolian life. Spring in particular is a crucial time for Mongolians. Spring is usually dry, dusty, windy and unforgiving. This is the time when the weaker animals die and, it is said, when people die. Despite the severe temperatures, it is during winter that Mongolians feel most comfortable. After a difficult summer filled with chores and tending to livestock, winter is generally a time of relaxation.

Steppe Rules

Mongolia's vast, open steppes and great distances have made hospitality a matter of sheer necessity rather than a social obligation. It would be difficult for anyone to travel across the country without this hospitality, as each ger is able to serve as a guesthouse, restaurant, pub and repair shop. As a result, Mongolians are able to travel rapidly over long distances without the weight of provisions. This hospitality is readily extended to strangers and usually given without fanfare or expectation of payment.

Nomads tend to move two to four times a year, although in areas where grass is thin they move more often. One nuclear family may live alone or with an extended-family camp of three or four gers (known as an *ail*); any more than that would be a burden on the grassland. A livestock herd should contain around 300 animals per family to be self-sustaining, although some wealthy herders may have 1000 head of livestock.

Mongolia's nomads are surprisingly well informed. Nearly all families have a short-wave radio to get national and world news. Many can receive satellite TV and certainly everyone reads newspapers when they

MONGOL GAMES

Day-to-day life may be a struggle on the steppes but families will still find time for games and leisure activities. In the evenings, children (and sometimes adults) play with *shagai* (ankle bones), which have four distinct sides representing horse, sheep, goat and camel. There are numerous *shagai* games but the most common is *moir uraldulakh* (horse race), which entails rolling four *shagai* (like dice) and then moving your 'horse *shagai*' a certain number of moves depending on the roll (roll four camels, move four spaces). The first person to reach the end of their ger wins the race. Other indoor games include ankle-bone shooting (like darts but with *shagai*), *shatar* (chess), *hözör* (cards) and *duu dulakh* (singing songs).

A WOMAN'S WORLD

Women enjoy a great amount of freedom in Mongolian society. They always have, dating back to a time when Mongol queens helped rule the great Mongolian empire.

In the countryside Mongolian women are often in charge of managing household activities, such as selling sheep, bartering for flour and rice, or managing the family cash reserves. These responsibilities usually fall upon the woman of the house because the men are often busy herding livestock, making repairs around the home or travelling to market.

Women also tend to achieve higher levels of education because, on average, they go to school longer than men (80% of higher-education students are women). Men often need to stay behind in the countryside to take care of ageing parents and their livestock. As a result of this lopsided male-female ratio, it's estimated that women hold some 70% to 80% of skilled jobs in Ulaanbaatar.

are available (literacy is 98%). In winter, children go to school in the nearest town (where they live in dorms), visiting their parents during holidays and summer. These days, mobile phones are ubiquitous at nomad camps, allowing herders to stay in touch with friends, family and business associates.

Life on the steppes is by no means easy or idyllic. Constant work is required to care for the animals, cook food and collect dung and water. It is also a precarious life – one bad winter can kill an entire herd, instantly wiping out a family's fortune. Life is even harder in the Gobi Desert, where grass is sparse and just one dry summer can threaten livestock.

City Slickers

Mongolians have carried their rural traditions with them into the city. The unplanned ger districts around the capital seem just a step away from the countryside. Wags also note that driving habits in UB tend to mirror the way Mongols ride their horses. Mongolia's strong democratic values are another reflection of nomadic traditions and their basic tenets: freedom, independence and pluralism.

Life in the city is changing as more Mongolians become accustomed to an urban lifestyle. Ger districts in Ulaanbaatar, once considered a regular part of the fabric, are on their way out as developers transform these areas into modern apartment complexes.

Youth culture is highly influenced by Western TV, music and movies. A thriving culture of rap music exists in Ulaanbaatar. You'll also spot skaters, Harley Davidson biker gangs, girl bands, punks and a handful of neo-Nazis. But the traditional Mongolian way of life is far from dead. In fact, its restoration is a unique blend of foreign trends and Mongolian culture. There may be plenty of tattoos now, but many are traditional Mongolian designs and symbols.

In Ulaanbaatar many locals look like they've just stepped off the streets of New York or London, so convincing is their Western fashion sense. But talk to them and you'll soon realise that their hopes and dreams lie not only in the West but also in the future of Mongolia, its success, prosperity and the continuation of its unique culture.

The 'haircut ceremony' (usnii nair) is a traditional rite of passage for Mongolian children. Their heads are shaved (girls at the age of two and boys at the age of three) and a special party is held in their honour. The person who cuts the hair must have been born in a year that corresponds to the child's year, and lamas sometimes come to the ceremony and read prayers. Afterwards, the hair is usually burnt.

Traditional Gers

Of all the different types of domiciles ever conceived, the Mongolian ger has to be one of the most useful, versatile and perfectly adapted for the user. Here is a home that one can take apart in less than an hour, move to a different location (with the help of a camel or two) and set up again, all on the same day. Gers are not unique to Mongolia; versions can be found across Central Asia, from Xinjiang to Turkmenistan. But while other traditions are fading, use of the ger is still common. For travellers, a visit inside a ger is central to the Mongolian experience.

Structural Integrity

An average ger weighs about 250kg and can be carried by two camels. These days most families tend to hire a truck to transport their ger to a new location.

The outermost and innermost material of the ger is usually canvas, with an insulating layer of felt sandwiched in between (more layers in winter and fewer in summer), supported by a collapsible wooden frame. Ropes made from horsehair are cinched around the perimeter to hold the ger together. The roof tends to be low, which helps in deflecting wind. During hot weather the sides can be rolled up and mosquito netting added. Anchoring ropes held down with rocks are set in strong wind.

The felt *(esgi)* is made in the autumn by stretching out several layers of sheep's wool on the ground, sprinkling it with water, adding grass and rolling it up tight, wetting it again and then rolling the whole thing back and forth over the steppe. As the wool dries the threads tighten up and harden into a stiff (yet still flexible) mat. The poles traditionally come from Mongolia's forests but recent limits on wood use have forced ger makers to acquire timber from Russia.

Inside a Ger

The internal layout of the ger is universal throughout Mongolia. Anywhere from Khovd to Dornod you will see the same set up and go through the same motions. The door always faces south, primarily because the wind comes from the north and a south-facing door will catch the most sunlight. Visitors should not step on the threshold as they enter, as this is symbolic of stepping on the neck of the ger patriarch.

GER CARTS

It is said that the great Mongol khaans (emperors) had enormous gers that they placed on ox carts to be pulled around their empire, like some sort of ancient Winnebago. This is depicted on some Mongolian banknotes. Some modern scholars, however, dispute this story. Whatever the case, the Mongols certainly did use their gers everywhere they went, only rarely adopting the life of the settled peoples they conquered. It is even said that the Mongols never lived in their own capital, Karakorum. Instead they parked their gers on the grasslands outside the city walls, used to the freedom they provided. The city itself was inhabited by foreign artisans, traders, labourers and priests, accustomed to the stone houses and to life within the city walls.

DOS & DON'TS IN THE GER

Do

➡ Sleep with your feet pointing towards the door.

➡ Say hello *(sain bain uu)* when you first arrive, but don't repeat it when you see the same person again.

➡ Try to converse in Mongolian as much as possible (have a phrasebook handy) and avoid long conversations in your own language.

➡ Bring a gift (even if it's just small) for the family or children. Your host will likely accept it humbly, so don't feel bad if they don't look too thrilled.

Don't

➡ Touch another person's hat (even to move it out of the way).

➡ Whistle.

➡ Lean against the support column.

➡ Touch a child's (or anyone else's) head.

➡ Open drawers (or look at personal items).

➡ Serve yourself (wait for the host to serve you).

Once inside, men move to the left (to the west, under the protection of the great sky god, Tengger), women to the right (east, under the protection of the sun). Towards the back, and a little to the west, is the place of honour set aside for guests. After two or three ger visits, this routine becomes like clockwork and you'll be amazed how everyone in your group easily falls into the same place during each ger visit.

The back of the ger is the *khoimor*, the place for the elders, where the most honoured people are seated and treasured possessions are kept. On the back wall is the family altar, decorated with Buddhist images and family photos (mostly taken during trips to Ulaanbaatar). Near the door, on the male side are saddles, ropes and a big leather milk bag and churn, used to stir *airag* (fermented mare's milk). On the female side of the door are the cooking implements and water buckets. Around the walls there are two or three low beds and cabinets. In the centre sits a small table with several tiny chairs. Hanging in any vacant spot, or wedged between the latticed walls, are toothbrushes, clothes, children's toys and plenty of slabs of uncooked mutton.

Building Your Ger

The small cartwheel-shaped opening at the top, called a *toon*, allows smoke to exit and sunlight to enter. It is covered with an *örkh*, which can be adjusted from the ground using ropes. The wooden roof poles *(uni)* are orange (the colour of the sun); the concertina-like latticed walls are called *khan*.

Most gers have five *khan*, although they can be bigger or smaller depending on the preference (and sometimes wealth) of the family. Each wall has about 10 to 15 roof poles. Depending on the mobility and wealth of the family, the ger is placed on a wooden platform or bare earth floor.

The first part of the ger to be assembled is the floor (if there is one). Next, the stove is placed in the centre. It is symbolic of the ritual fire worship practised by Central Asian nomads for centuries, and is therefore considered holy. The walls and the brightly painted door *(khaalga)* are erected along with the two central columns that support the roof. Once the frame is put together the felt coverings are wrapped around the ger.

GER SET-UP

Timothy Allen of BBC Earth filmed the set-up of a ger using time-lapse photography. Check out the 80-second clip on YouTube, called 'No Place Like Home' – search 'Timothy Allen BBC Earth'.

TWENTY-FIRST-CENTURY GERS

Some gers today sport many of the mod cons found in apartments. Most have a TV, radios are common and some have DVD players. Many families also own a generator (sometimes small solar panels or mini windmills), which allows them to watch TV and DVDs, charge their mobile phones and use electric lights. At a ger we stopped by in Dornogov, 100km from any town, the owners said they use their phones to keep in touch with relatives in Los Angeles and Chicago.

The ger itself has not changed much, although at some tourist camps (fancy ones), you may see gers built with windows cut in the sides. Handcrafted gers with the delicate wood carvings made for celebrations and naadams are also growing in popularity. These can be seen in Ulaanbaatar pitched on Chinggis Khaan (Sükhbaatar) Sq in summer or set up at the horse-race area during Naadam.

Everyone in the family is expected to contribute to this process in some way. However, once the ger is set up it's the sole responsibility of the woman of the home to hang the curtain (*khushig*) that covers the lattice frame.

The ger plays a vital role in shaping both the Mongolian character and family life. The small confines compel family members to interact with one another, to share everything and work together, tightening relationships between relatives. It prevents privacy but promotes patience and reduces inhibitions. It also creates self-sufficiency; ger dwellers must fetch their own water and fuel, and subsist on the food they themselves produce.

Nomads tend to move two to four times a year, although in areas where grass is thin they move more often. One nuclear family may live alone or with an extended-family camp of three or four gers (known as an *ail*); any more than that would be a burden on the grassland.

Staying Overnight

If you are particularly fortunate you may be invited to spend a night or two out on the steppes in a genuine ger, rather than a tourist ger camp. This is a wonderful chance to experience the 'real' Mongolia.

Gers are growing in popularity in the US and Europe, where they often serve as accommodation at national parks. In the US, they are produced by Oregon-based Pacific Yurts (www.pacific yurts.com).

If you are invited to stay in a family ger, only in very rare cases will you be expected to pay for this accommodation. Leaving a gift is strongly recommended. While cash payment is usually OK as a gift, it's far better to provide worthwhile gifts for the whole family, including the women (who look after the guests). Cigarettes, vodka and candy are customary gifts, but with some creativity you can offer more useful items. Welcome gifts include sewing kits, multi-tools, fleece sweaters, T-shirts, toothbrushes/toothpaste, Mongolian-language books and newspapers, and hand-powered torches and radios. Children will enjoy colouring books, pens, paper, puzzles and postcards from your home country.

Your host may offer to cook for you; it is polite for you to offer to supply some food, such as biscuits, bread, fruit, salt, rice and pasta. Pack out any garbage or packaging left over from these items. Mongolians love being photographed. If you take pictures of your host family, remember to take down their name and mail them a copy. For address purposes, you'll need their name, *sum* (district) and aimag.

The easiest way to organise such a visit is through a tour company, which can find you a homestay (for a fee). If travelling independently, don't take advantage of nomad hospitality by expecting a free night in a ger. Always have a tent handy in order to sleep separately from families you encounter.

Spiritualism in Mongolia

Mongolians are a deeply spiritual people. This, however, is not always apparent, as organised religion is but one small part of the spiritual matrix. Spirituality comes in many other forms, much of it day-to-day rituals rooted in Mongolia's shamanic past. The ancient animist beliefs of the Siberian and steppe tribes who worshipped the sun, earth and sky are still very much alive, woven intimately into the fabric of modern Mongolia.

Shamanism

Mongol tribes have long believed in the spirit world as their shamans described it to them. Their cosmic view of the universe did not differentiate between the worlds of the living and dead nor did they consider themselves any greater than other creatures in this or other worlds. Any imbalance between the human and natural world could cause calamity.

Shamanism is based around the shaman – called a *bo* if a man or *udgan* if a woman – who has special medical and religious powers (known as

THE NINTH JEBTZUN DAMBA

In 1924 the eighth Jebtzun Damba ('Bogd Khan' in Mongolian) passed away, marking the end of two centuries of Buddhist rule in Mongolia. Soon after his death Mongolia was declared a republic and the then-communist government forbade the recognition of a ninth Jebtzun Damba.

But the great lamas of Tibet had other plans. Tradition held that new incarnations of the Jebtzun Damba would be found in Tibet, so when the time was right, the regent of Lhasa recognised a ninth incarnation. His identity was kept secret to protect him from Russian secret agents, who were busy ridding Mongolia of its Buddhist clergy. The young Jebtzun Damba, named Jampal Namdrol Chokye Gyaltsen, was born in 1932 and undertook Buddhist studies at Drepung Monastery for 14 years.

At the age of 21 he left the monastery to live as a hermit, practising meditation at sacred caves throughout central Tibet. When he was 29 he fled Tibet for India, following the Dalai Lama and thousands of other Tibetans escaping Chinese persecution. The Jebtzun Damba lived in obscurity for decades until being re-recognised by the Dalai Lama in 1991.

In 1999, at the age of 67, he turned up unannounced in Ulaanbaatar, having received a tourist visa in Moscow. (One can only imagine the customs form: 'Occupation: Reincarnation of Tibetan deity Vajrapani'!)

He stayed in Mongolia for 60 days, visiting monasteries in Ulaanbaatar and the countryside. Although mobbed by adoring fans wherever he went, he was deemed persona non grata by the Mongolian government, which at the time was unsure of his motives. He was finally pressured to leave after overstaying his visa.

In 2010 he was allowed to return to Mongolia, where a more confident government welcomed him and even granted him Mongolian citizenship. The Jebtzun Damba spent his remaining days at Gandan Monastery, where he died in March 2012. Speculation persists that the 10th incarnation will eventually be found in Mongolia.

For more information on Mongolia's spiritual leader, see www.jetsundhampa.com.

udmyn if inherited; *zlain* if the powers become apparent after a sudden period of sickness and apparitions).

Two of a shaman's main functions are to cure sickness caused by the soul straying, and to accompany souls of the dead to the other world. As intermediaries between the human and spirit worlds, they communicate with spirits during trances, which can last up to six hours.

Shamanist beliefs have done much to shape Mongolian culture and social practices. For example, nomads today still fill in the holes left by their horse posts when they move camp, inherited from an old shamanic custom of returning the land to its natural state. The fact that Mongolia's landscape is being torn up in search of minerals is inexcusable according to shamans, and may lead to retribution from the *tengers* (sky gods).

Sky worship is another integral part of shamanism; you'll see Mongolians leaving blue scarves (representing the sky) on *ovoos*. Sky gods are honoured by flicking droplets of vodka in the air before drinking.

Shamanism has seen an explosion in popularity in recent years and hundreds of shamans now offer their healing and consultation services in Ulaanbaatar and other cities. On weekends, shamans gather south of the Tuul River, about 2km east of Zaisan Hill.

> *Ovoos,* the large piles of rocks found on mountain passes, are repositories of offerings for local spirits. Upon arriving at an *ovoo*, walk around it clockwise three times, toss an offering onto the pile (another rock should suffice) and make a wish.

Buddhism

The Mongols had limited contact with organised religion before their great empire of the 13th century. It was Kublai Khaan who first found himself with a court in which all philosophies of his empire were represented, but it was a Tibetan Buddhist, Phagpa, who wielded the greatest influence on the khaan (emperor).

In 1578 Altan Khaan, a descendant of Chinggis Khaan, met the Tibetan leader Sonam Gyatso, was converted, and subsequently bestowed on Sonam Gyatso the title Dalai Lama (*dalai* means 'ocean' in Mongolian). Sonam Gyatso was named as the third Dalai Lama and his two predecessors were named posthumously.

Mass conversions occurred under Altan Khaan. As Mongolian males were conscripted to monasteries, rather than the army, the centuries of constant fighting seemed to wane (much to the relief of China, which subsequently funded more monasteries in Mongolia). This shift from a warring country to a peaceful one persists in contemporary society – Mongolia is the world's only UN-sanctioned 'nuclear-weapons-free nation'. Buddhist opposition to needless killing reinforced hunting laws already set in place by shamanism. Today Buddhist monks are still influential in convincing local populations to protect their environment and wildlife.

Buddhism in Mongolia was nearly wiped out in 1937 when the young communist government, at the urging of Stalin, launched a purge that wiped out nearly all of the country's 700 monasteries. Up to 30,000 monks were massacred and thousands more sent to Siberian labour camps. Freedom of religion was only restored in 1990 shortly after the democratic revolution.

Restoring Buddhism has been no easy task, as two generations had been essentially raised as atheists. Most people no longer understand the Buddhist rituals or their meanings but a few still make the effort to visit the monasteries during prayer sessions. Numbers swell when well-known Buddhist monks from Tibet or India (or even Western countries) visit Mongolia.

> The word 'shaman' derives from the word 'saman' in the Evenk language, later passed on to the Western world in the late 1600s by Dutch traveller Nicolaes Witsen, who came into contact with Tungistic-speaking tribes of Siberia.

> In 1903, when the British invaded Tibet, the 13th Dalai Lama fled to Mongolia and spent three years living in Gandan Khiid in Urga (modern-day Ulaanbaatar).

Islam

In Mongolia today, there is a significant minority of Sunni Muslims, most of them ethnic Kazakhs, who live primarily in Bayan-Ölgii. Because of its great isolation and distance from the major Islamic centres of the Middle

IMPORTANT FIGURES & SYMBOLS OF TIBETAN BUDDHISM

This brief guide to some of the deities of the Tibetan Buddhist pantheon will allow you to recognise a few of the statues you'll encounter in Mongolia, usually on temple altars. Sanskrit names are provided as these are most recognisable in the West; Mongolian names are in brackets.

Sakyamuni The Historical Buddha was born in Lumbini in the 5th century BC in what is now southern Nepal. He attained enlightenment under a bo (peepul) tree and his teachings set in motion the Buddhist faith. Statues of the Buddha include 32 distinctive body marks, including a dot between the eyes and a bump on the top of his blue hair. His right hand touches the earth in the *bhumisparsa mudra* hand gesture, and his left hand holds a begging bowl.

Maitreya (Maidar) The Future Buddha, Maitreya is passing the life of a bodhisattva (a divine being worthy of nirvana who remains on the human plane to help others achieve enlightenment) and will return to earth in human form 4000 years after the disappearance of Sakyamuni to take his place as the next earthly buddha. He is normally seated with his hands by his chest in the *mudra* of turning the 'wheel of law'.

Avalokitesvara (Janraisig) The Bodhisattva of Compassion is either pictured with 11 heads and 1000 pairs of arms (Chogdanjandan Janraisig), or in a white, four-armed manifestation (Chagsh Janraisig). The Dalai Lama is considered an incarnation of Avalokitesvara.

Tara The Saviour, Tara has 21 different manifestations. She symbolises purity and fertility and is believed to be able to fulfil wishes. Statues of Tara usually represent Green Tara (Nogoon Dar Ekh), who is associated with night, or White Tara (Tsagaan Dar Ekh), who is associated with day. White Tara is the female companion of Avalokitesvara.

Four Guardian Kings Comprising Virupaksa (red; holding a snake), Dhitarastra (white; holding a lute), Virudhaka (blue; holding a sword) and Vaishrovana (yellow; sitting on a snow lion), the kings are mostly seen guarding monastery entrances.

The Symbols & Objects

Prayer Wheel These are filled with up to a mile of prayers and are turned manually by pilgrims to gain merit.

Wheel of Life Drawings of the wheel symbolise the cycle of death and rebirth, held by Yama, the god of the dead.

Stupas (Suvrag) Originally built to house the cremated relics of Sakyamuni, they have become a powerful symbol of Buddhism. Later stupas became reliquaries for lamas and holy men.

East, Islam has never been a major force in Bayan-Ölgii. However, most villages have a mosque and contacts have been established with Islamic groups in Turkey. Several prominent figures in the community have been on a hajj to Mecca. Besides the Kazakhs, the only ethnic Mongols to practice Islam are the Khoton tribe, who live primarily in Uvs aimag.

Christianity

Nestorian Christianity was part of the Mongol empire long before the Western missionaries arrived. The Nestorians followed the doctrine of Nestorious (AD 358–451), patriarch of Constantinople (428–31), who proclaimed that Jesus exists as two separate persons: the man Jesus and the divine son of God. Historically the religion never caught hold in the Mongol heartland, but that has changed in recent years with an influx of Christian missionaries, often from obscure fundamentalist sects. In Mongolia, there are an estimated 65,000 Christians and more than 150 churches.

Religions of Mongolia, by Walther Heissig, provides a look at Buddhist and shamanist faiths as they developed in Mongolia.

Mongolian Cuisine

The nomadic Mongols have lived off their herds for centuries. Meat and milk are the staples while (traditionally, at least) vegetables were written off as feed for animals. Seasoning is not used in traditional cooking, although Mongolians have long added salt to their foods (including tea). Mongolians typically cook with a wok, so most foods are stir-fried or boiled. A steamer is usually available for cooking dumplings. In contrast, in Ulaanbaatar there's a surprisingly cosmopolitan restaurant scene.

Staples & Specialties

Because of his failing health, the advisors of Ögedei Khaan (a son of Chinggis) suggested that he halve the number of cups of alcohol he drank per day. Ögedei readily agreed, then promptly ordered that his cups be doubled in size.

Almost any Mongolian dish can be created with meat, rice, flour and potatoes. Most meals consist of *talkh* (bread) in the towns and cities and *bortzig* (fried unleavened bread) in the gers, and the uncomplicated *shölte khool* (literally, soup with food) – a meal involving hot broth, pasta slivers, boiled mutton and a few potato chunks. Two of the most popular menu options you'll find in restaurants are *buuz* (steamed dumplings filled with mutton and sometimes slivers of onion or garlic) and *khuushuur* (fried mutton pancakes). Miniature *buuz*, known as *bansh*, are usually dunked in milk tea. *Tsuivan* is a Mongolian version of pasta made from steamed flour noodles, carrots, potato and mutton chunks.

The classic Mongolian dinner staple, especially in the countryside, is referred to simply as *makh* (meat) and consists of boiled sheep bits (bones, fat, various organs and the head) with some sliced potato for variety. The other highlight of Mongolian cuisine is *khorkhog*, made by placing hot stones from an open fire into an urn with chopped mutton, some water and sometimes vodka. The container is then sealed and left on the fire. While eating this, it's customary to pass the hot, greasy rocks from hand to hand, as this is thought to be good for your health.

WHAT'S YOUR DRINK?

Mongolians are big tea drinkers and will almost never start a meal until they've had a cup of tea first, as it is said to aid digestion.

Süütei tsai, a classic Mongolian drink, is milk tea with salt. The taste varies by region; in Bayan-Ölgii it may even include a dollop of butter. *Khar tsai* (black tea), is often available, served with sugar but no milk.

Alcoholic drinks are never far away and Mongolians can drink you under the table if challenged. There is much social pressure to drink, especially on males – those who refuse to drink *arkhi* (vodka) are considered wimps. Chinggis black-label vodka, just US$8 a bottle, is popular. Jalam Khar (Dark Horse), GEM, Altan Gobi, Chinggis, Borgio and Senguur are popular local beers.

While it may not be immediately apparent, every countryside ger doubles as a tiny brewery or distillery. One corner of the ger usually contains a tall, thin jug with a plunger that is used for fermenting mare's milk. The drink, known as *airag*, has an alcohol content of about 3%. Go easy on it at the start or your guts will pay for it later.

MONGOLIAN CUISINE CELEBRAT ONS

DOS & DON'TS AT THE TABLE

Do

➡ Cut food towards your body, not away; pass knives by offering the handle.

➡ Accept food and drink with your right hand; use the left *only* to support your right elbow if the food is heavy.

➡ Drink tea immediately; don't put it on the table until you have tried some.

➡ Take at least a sip, or a nibble, of the delicacies offered, even if they don't please you.

➡ Hold a cup by the bottom, not by the top rim.

Don't

➡ Get up in the middle of a meal and walk outside; wait until everyone has finished.

➡ Cross your legs or stick your feet out in front of you when eating – keep your legs together if seated, or folded under you if on the floor.

In summer, Mongols snack on *tsagaan idee* (dairy products; literally 'white foods'): yogurt, milk, delicious fresh cream, cheese and fermented milk drinks. When you visit a ger, you will be offered dairy snacks such as *aaruul* (dried milk curds). Finally, if you get a chance, don't miss the opportunity to try blow-torched marmot (prairie dog), a delicacy of the steppes.

Celebrations

Tsagaan Sar, the Mongolian New Year, is a festival for a new beginning. A full belly during Tsagaan Sar is said to represent prosperity in the year ahead; *buuz* in their thousands are prepared and consumed during the holiday. The central meal of the holiday must be the biggest sheep a family can afford; pride is at stake over how much fat appears on the table. During Tsagaan Sar, food is even part of the decoration: the centrepiece is made from layers of large biscuits called *ul boov*. Young people stack three layers of biscuits, middle-aged couples five layers and grandparents seven layers.

At Mongolia's other big holiday, Naadam, the customary food is *khuushuur*. Food stands all around the Naadam stadium and the horse race fields sell stacks of the meat pancakes.

Habits & Customs

While traditions and customs do surround the dinner table, Mongolian meals are generally casual affairs and there is no need to be overly concerned about offending your hosts.

In a ger in the countryside, traditional meals such as boiled mutton do not require silverware or even plates; just trawl around the bucket until a slab catches your fancy. Eat with your fingers and try to nibble off as much meat and fat as possible; Mongolians can pick a bone clean and consider leftovers to be wasteful. There should be a buck knife to slice off larger chunks. Most other meals in the rest of Mongolia are eaten with bowls, knives, forks and spoons.

It is always polite to bring something to contribute to the meal; drinks are easiest, or in the countryside you could offer rice, bread or fruit. 'Bon appétit' in Mongolian is *saikhan khool loorai*.

Meals are occasionally interrupted by a round of vodka. Before taking a swig, there's a short ritual to honour the sky gods and the four cardinal directions. There is no one way of doing this, but it usually involves dipping your left ring finger into the vodka and flicking into the air four times before wiping your finger across your forehead.

The well-researched www.mongolfood.info includes notes on Mongolian cuisine, plus cooking techniques and recipes to dispel the myth that Mongolian menus stop at boiled mutton.

It is customary to flick spoonfuls of milk in the direction of departing travellers, whether they are going by horse, car, train or plane.

Tribal Mongolia

Mongolia is an ancient tribal society that can be broken down into more than a dozen ethnic subgroups. To this day, Mongolia still counts around 20 different *undesten* (nations), with numerous subclans. Most of these tribes are located along the borders of modern Mongolia and in some cases they spill over the borders into Russia and China. Inner Mongolia (in China) also has a tribal order that persists today.

Tribal Groups

A thousand years ago tribes regularly squared off against each other in seasonal warfare and bouts of bride theft. They went by the names of Kerait, Tatar, Merkit and Naiman, to name a few; linked by culture, they were divided by old feuds and rivalries. The tribes were united during the great Mongol empire (1206 to 1368) but after its demise they went back to their periodic squabbles.

The tribes of modern Mongolia lack the political, economic or social independence that one might encounter in tribal areas of Pakistan, southern Africa, India or the Americas. However, many Mongols still associate closely with their tribal roots. The Buriats, for example, sponsor the biannual Altargana Festival, which draws Buriats from all over the country as well as Buriats from Russia and China.

While it can be difficult to differentiate between some of these tribes, a few are starkly unique. The Tsaatan, who live in *orts* (tepees), speak a distinct Turkic language and herd reindeer, are one of the most identifiable ethnic groups. The Khoton people in western Mongolia are also easily distinguished as the only Mongols to practice Islam.

THE MONGOLIAN NAME GAME

In the 1920s Mongolia's communist government forbade the use of clan names, a dedicated effort to stamp out loyalties that might supersede the state.

In the 1990s, after the fall of communism, few families were able to recall their own clan name. The first phone books featured pages listing just one name. Elections also proved confusing when six or seven candidates with the same name would appear on one ballot.

A more serious problem was inbreeding, the result of cousins inadvertently marrying each other. Historians pointed out that this problem could be avoided by employing an old tradition, which stated that seven generations must pass before a family member could again marry within their clan.

In order to reverse this trend, the government ordered all citizens to start using their clan names again. The identity crisis that ensued sparked a boom in amateur genealogy, with families contacting relatives to uncover possible clan names. Authorities have encouraged creativity and people who could not retrace their name simply made one up – usually after a hobby, a profession, favourite mountain or nickname. Mongolia's lone spaceman, Gurragchaa, named his family 'Cosmos'. Another clan name currently up for grabs is 'Family of Seven Drunks', which hasn't had many takers.

When meeting minority groups, ask about their traditional clothing, which can be quite distinctive, as is the case with the Dariganga peoples of Sükhbaatar aimag. The Kazakhs, who live primarily in Bayan-Ölgii aimag, are a Turkic tribe with cultural roots in Islamic Central Asia.

Tribes in Modern Mongolia

The following is a list of some of the main ethnic groups you may encounter:

Barga Originally from the Lake Baikal region of Siberia, the Barga number about 2000 and live in remote border areas of Dornod aimag. Many Barga also live in Inner Mongolia (China) around Dalai Nuur and Hailar. Barga consider themselves descended from Alan Goa, a mythical figure described in *The Secret History of the Mongols*.

Bayad Descendants of Oirat Mongols; about 50,000 live in the Malchin, Khyargas and Züüngov *sums* of Uvs aimag. The most famous Bayad was the 13th-century princess Kököchin (Blue Dame), whom Kublai Khaan betrothed to the Il-Khanate khan Argun. It was Marco Polo who was selected to escort Kököchin on her journey to Persia.

Buriat There are around a half million Buriats in North Asia (around 50,000 live in Mongolia with others in Russia and China), making them the largest ethnic minority in Siberia. Buriats are known for their strong associations with shamanism. Among Mongols, they are also unique in their lifestyle; most live in log cabins instead of gers. You'll meet many Buriats in northern Khentii and Dornod aimags.

Dariganga During the Qing dynasty era, this ethnic group received special recognition from the emperor. They were responsible for supplying horses to the emperor in Běijīng and today they are still regarded as excellent horse breeders. During the Qing era, the Dariganga also gained skills as blacksmiths and silversmiths. Their traditional headdress, chock-full of silver, is considered the most elegant and valuable of its kind.

Darkhad This 20,000-member tribe can be found in the Darkhad valley in northern Khövsgöl aimag. During the Qing era, they served as ecclesiastical serfs to the Bogd Gegeens and were required to perform services such as pasturing animals. Darkhads are known as powerful shamans but are also beloved for their great sense of humour. A pastime is to sing humorous songs about each other; ask politely and they may make one up about you!

Dörvöd There are around 66,000 Dörvöds in western Mongolia. In the 17th century, a group of Dörvöds split from the main clan and trekked west to settle in the Volga region of Russia. Historically, the Dörvöd have sometimes clashed with Khalkh Mongols (during the communist era some proposed ceding their territory to the Soviet Union). Yu Tsedenbal (r 1954–84) and J Batmönkh (r 1984–90) were both Dörvöd.

Khalkh The majority (about 86%) of Mongolians are Khalkh Mongolians. The origin of the word Khalkh is a topic of great debate: some believe it means shield, while others suggest it's derived from the Turkic word Halk, which means people.

Torguud About 7000 live in Khovd aimag. Originally from northern Xinjiang, a large group of them moved to the Volga to become the core Kalmyks. Today most Torguuds in Mongolia live in Bulgan *sum*.

Tsaatan About 500 of these reindeer herders live in northern Khövsgöl.

Uriankhai (Tuvans) About 21,000 Uriankhai live in western Mongolia – you'll meet some if you visit Tsengel Sum, near Altai Tavan Bogd National Park. The Uriankhai are renowned for their throat-singing abilities. Today, most Uriankhai live in the Tuva Region of Russia.

Uzemchin Most Uzemchin live in Inner Mongolia. In 1945, about 2000 of them migrated to Outer Mongolia and they can still be found in some remote corners of Dornod aimag. Uzemchin are well known for their elegant embroidered *dels* (traditional coat dresses). During Naadam, Uzemchin wrestlers wear bad-ass leather jackets with brass studs.

CLAN NAMES

In the 1990s, when the government of Mongolia asked its citizens to choose a clan name, 20% of the population adopted the name 'Borjigan', the clan of Chinggis Khaan.

Wild Lands & Wildlife

Mongolia is the sort of country that naturalists dream about. With the world's lowest population density, huge tracts of virgin landscape, minimal infrastructure, varied eco-systems and abundant wildlife, Mongolia is rightfully considered to be the last bastion of unspoilt land in Asia. Mongolia's lack of urban development, along with shamanic prohibitions against defiling the earth, have for centuries protected the country from degradation. Traditional beliefs, however, are always at odds with modern economics.

The Wildlife Conservation Society's Mongolia program strives to address wildlife conservation issues through various approaches that reach local communities, wildlife biologists, provincial governments and national ministries. Read more at www.wcs.org/mongolia.

The Land

Mongolia is a huge landlocked country. At 1,566,500 sq km in area, it's about three times the size of France. The southern third of Mongolia is dominated by the Gobi Desert, which stretches into China. Only the southern sliver of the Gobi is 'Lawrence of Arabia'–type desert with cliffs and sand dunes. The rest is desert steppe and has sufficient grass to support scattered herds of sheep, goats and camels. There are also areas of desert steppe in low-lying parts of western Mongolia.

Much of the rest of Mongolia is covered by grasslands (or mountain forest steppe). Stretching over about 35% of the country, these steppes are home to vast numbers of gazelle, birdlife and livestock. The far northern areas of Khövsgöl and Khentii aimags are essentially the southern reaches of Siberia and are covered by larch and pine forests known by the Russian word 'taiga'.

Near the centre of Mongolia is the Khangai Nuruu range, with its highest peak, Otgon Tenger Uul, reaching 3905m. On the northern slope of these mountains is the source of the Selenge Gol, Mongolia's largest river, which flows northward into Lake Baikal in Siberia. Just to the northeast of Ulaanbaatar is the Khentii Nuruu, the highest mountain range in eastern Mongolia and by far the most accessible to hikers. It's a heavily forested region with meandering rivers and impressive peaks, the highest being Asralt Khairkhan Uul (2800m). The range provides a major watershed between the Arctic and Pacific oceans.

Mongolia has numerous saltwater and freshwater lakes, which are great for camping, birdwatching, hiking, swimming and fishing. The

ECO-WARRIOR

Tsetsegee Munkhbayar, a herder from central Mongolia, is Mongolia's most famous eco-warrior. In 2007 Munkhbayar won the prestigious Goldman Environmental Prize for his efforts to block aggressive mining on the Ongii River.

He has since turned increasingly radical, leading a group called Gal Undesten (Fire Nation) on periodic stunts that some have called 'eco-terrorism'. Several times the group has shot up equipment at mining sites, and in 2011 members shot arrows at the parliament building in UB, in protest of government mining policies.

In 2013 Munkhbayar and four others were arrested after brandishing rifles and hand grenades at a mining protest in the capital. In January 2014, a court found Munkhbayar and his friends guilty of 'domestic terrorism' and sentenced them to 21½ years in jail.

PROTECTED AREAS

The Ministry of Nature and Green Development and its Department of Special Protected Areas Management control the national park system with an annual budget of around US$4 million. The 76 protected areas in Mongolia now constitute an impressive 17.4% of the country (223,000 sq km). The strictly protected areas of Bogdkhan Uul, Great Gobi, Uvs Nuur Basin, Dornod Mongol and Khustain are biosphere reserves included in Unesco's Man and Biosphere Network.

The government has a goal of protecting 30% of Mongolia (potentially creating the world's largest park system). This goal, however, has stalled in recent years as the government has favoured expanding mining operations and the sale of mining rights.

The Ministry of Nature classifies protected areas into four categories (from most protected to least):

Strictly Protected Areas Very fragile areas of great importance; hunting, logging and development are strictly prohibited and there is no established human influence.

National Parks Places of historical and educational interest; fishing and grazing by nomadic people is allowed and parts of the park are developed for ecotourism.

Natural & Historical Monuments Important places of historical and cultural interest; development is allowed within guidelines.

Nature Reserves Less-important regions protecting rare species of flora and fauna, and archaeological sites; some development is allowed within certain guidelines.

largest is the low-lying, saltwater Uvs Nuur, but the most popular is the magnificent Khövsgöl Nuur, the second-oldest lake in the world, which contains 65% of Mongolia's (and 2% of the world's) fresh water.

Wildlife

In Mongolia, the distinction between domestic and wild (or untamed) animals is often blurry. Wild and domesticated horses and camels mingle on the steppes with wild asses and herds of wild gazelles. In the mountains there are enormous (and horned) wild argali sheep and domesticated yaks along with wild moose, musk deer and roe deer.

Reindeer herds are basically untamed, but strangely enough they can be ridden and are known to return to the same tent each night for a salt-lick.

Animals

Despite the lack of water in the Gobi, numerous species (many of which are endangered) somehow survive. These include the Gobi argali sheep *(argal)*, wild camel *(khavtgai)*, Asiatic wild ass *(khulan)*, Gobi bear *(mazaalai)*, ibex *(yangir)* and black-tailed gazelle *(khar suult zeer)*.

In the wide open steppe you may see the rare saiga antelope, Mongolian gazelle *(tsagaan zeer)*, several species of jerboa *(alag daaga)*, which is a rodent endemic to Central Asia, and thousands of furry marmots *(tarvaga)*, waking up after their last hibernation or preparing for the next. Further north in the forests live the wild boars *(zerleg gakhai)*, brown bears *(khuren baavgai)*, roe deer *(bor görös)*, wolves *(chono)*, reindeers *(tsaa buga)*, elks *(khaliun buga)*, musk deer *(khuder)* and moose *(khandgai)*, as well as plenty of sables *(bulga)* and lynx *(shiluus)*, whose fur, unfortunately, is in high demand.

Most of the mountains are extremely remote, thus providing an ideal habitat for argali sheep, ibexes, the very rare snow leopard *(irbis)*, and smaller mammals such as foxes, ermines and hares.

A *zud* (extremely harsh winter) is a natural phenomenon that occurs in Mongolia every five to 10 years. *Zud* typically means extreme cold for extended periods, or heavy snows. A particularly bad *zud* in 2000 and 2001 killed more than 10 million animals.

The *takhi* horse also goes by the name Przewalski's horse. It was named after Colonel Nikolai Przewalski, an officer in the Russian Imperial Army who made the horse's existence known to Europe after an exploratory expedition to Central Asia in 1878.

Birds

Mongolia is home to 469 recorded species of bird. In the desert you may see desert warblers, saxaul sparrows *(boljmor)*, McQueen's bustards *(too-dog)*, sandgrouse, finches *(byalzuuhai)* and the cinereous vultures *(tas)*.

On the steppes, you will certainly see the most charismatic bird in Mongolia – the demoiselle crane *(övögt togoruu)* – as well as the hoopoe *(övöölj) and* the odd falcon *(shonkhor)*, vulture *(yol)*, and golden and steppe eagle *(bürged)*. Other steppe species include upland buzzards *(sar)*, black kites *(sokhor elee)* and some varieties of owl *(shar shuvuu)* and hawk *(khartsaga)*. Some black kites will even swoop down and catch pieces of bread in mid-air if you throw the pieces high enough. These magnificent raptors, perched majestically on a rock by the side of the road, will rarely be disturbed by your jeep or the screams of your guide ('Look. Eagle!! Bird!! We stop?') but following the almost inaudible click of your lens cap, these birds will move and almost be in China before you have even thought about apertures.

In the mountains, you may be lucky to spot species of ptarmigan *(tsagaan yatuu)*, bunting *(khömrög byalzuuhai)*, woodpecker *(tonshuul)*, owl and endemic Altai snowcock *(khoilog)*. The lakes of the west and north are visited by Dalmatian pelicans *(khoton)*, hooded cranes *(khar togoruu)*, relict gulls *(tsakhlai)* and bar-headed geese. Eastern Mongolia has several species of crane, including the hooded and Siberian varieties and critically endangered white-naped cranes *(tsen togoruu)*, of which only 5000 remain in the wild.

> Mongolians consider wolf parts and organs to have curative properties. The meat and lungs are good for respiratory ailments, the intestines aid in digestion, powdered wolf rectum can soothe the pain of haemorrhoids and hanging a wolf tongue around ones neck will cure gland and thyroid ailments.

Fish

Rivers such as the Selenge, Orkhon, Zavkhan, Balj, Onon and Egiin, as well as dozens of lakes, including Khövsgöl Nuur, hold 76 species of fish. They include trout, grayling *(khadran)*, roach, lenok *(zebge)*, Siberian

---

ENDANGERED SPECIES

According to conservationists, 28 species of mammal are endangered in Mongolia. The more commonly known species are wild asses, wild camels, argali sheep and ibexes; others include otters, wolves, saiga antelopes and some species of jerboa. The red deer is also in dire straits; over the past two decades its numbers have plunged from 130,000 to around 20,000. Poachers also prize brown bears for their gall bladders, which are used in traditional medicine. The mammal closest to extinction is the Gobi bear, the world's only desert-dwelling bear. With just 22 *mazaalai* (eight male, 14 female) left in the wild, they are in a precarious state. Mongolia's government declared 2013 the 'Year of Saving the Mazaalai' and established special reserves for the bears.

There are 22 species of endangered birds, including many species of hawk, falcon, buzzard, crane and owl. Every year the government exports around 150 falcons; the major buyers are the royal families of Kuwait and the United Arab Emirates. A licence for each bird costs around US$12,000. In the late 1990s the press frequently reported stories of smugglers caught at the airport with falcons stuffed in their overcoats (presumably many made it out without detection). The illegal export of these birds still occurs albeit on a much smaller scale. There are an estimated 6800 breeding pairs left in Mongolia.

One positive news story is the resurrection of the *takhi* wild horse. The *takhi* was actually extinct in the wild in the 1960s. It has been successfully reintroduced into three special protected areas after an extensive breeding program overseas. In preserved areas of the mountains, about 1000 snow leopards remain. They are hunted for their pelts (which are also part of some shamanist and Buddhist traditional practices), as are the leopards' major source of food, marmots.

Each year the government sells licences to hunt ibexes, argali, red deer, gazelles, roe deer, wolves and other creatures. In 2012 the hunting permits netted the government T3.5 billion.

NATIONAL PARKS & PROTECTED AREAS

NATIONAL PARKS	FEATURES	ACTIVITIES	TIME TO VISIT
Altai Tavan Bogd National Park	mountains, glaciers, lakes; argali sheep, ibexes, snow leopards, eagles, falcons	mountaineering, horse trekking, backpacking, fishing, eagle hunting (winter)	Jun–Sep
Gorkhi-Terelj National Park	rugged hills, boulders, streams	river rafting, hiking, mountain biking, rock climbing, camping, cross-country skiing, horse riding	year-round
Gurvan Saikhan National Park	desert mountains, canyons, sand dunes; Gobi argali sheep, ibexes, black-tailed gazelles	hiking, sand-dune sliding, camel trekking, birdwatching	May–Oct
Khorgo-Terkhiin Tsagaan Nuur National Park	lake and mountains; wolves, deer, foxes	fishing, hiking, horse trekking, birdwatching	May–Sep
Khövsgöl Nuur National Park	lake, mountains, rivers; fish, moose, wolverines, bears, sables, elk, roe deer	mountain biking, kayaking, fishing, hiking, horse trekking, birdwatching	Jun–Sep
Khustain National Park	rugged hills, Tuul River; *takhi* horses, gazelles, deer, wolves, lynx, manul wild cats	trekking, wildlife spotting	Apr–Oct
Otgon Tenger Uul Strictly Protected Area	mountains, rivers, lakes; argali sheep, roe deer, wolves	horse trekking, hiking, swimming	May–Sep

sturgeon *(khilem)*, pike *(tsurkhai)*, perch *(algana)*, the endemic Altai osman and the enormous taimen, a Siberian relative of the salmon, which can grow up to 1.5m in length and weigh up to 50kg.

Plants

Mongolia can be roughly divided into three zones: grassland and shrub land (55% of the country); forests, which only cover parts of the mountain steppe (8%); and desert (36%). Less than 1% of the country is used for human settlement and crop cultivation.

Forests of Siberian larch (sometimes up to 45m in height), Siberian and Scotch pine, and white and ground birch cover parts of northern Mongolia. In the Gobi, saxaul shrub covers millions of hectares and is essential in anchoring the desert sands and preventing degradation and erosion. Saxaul takes a century to grow to around 4m in height, creating wood so dense that it sinks in water.

Khentii aimag and some other parts of central Mongolia are famous for the effusion of red, yellow and purple wildflowers, mainly rhododendrons and edelweiss. Extensive grazing is the major threat to Mongolia's flowers, trees and shrubs; more than 200 species are endangered.

Environmental Issues

Due to its sparse population and vast territory, there are huge tracts of untouched landscape in Mongolia. However, some pockets of the country are on the verge of an eco-disaster. A rising threat on the steppes is overgrazing by livestock, especially sheep and goats. A 2013 environmental report said that 70% of the grassland has been degraded and 12% of Mongolia's biomass has disappeared over the past two decades. Forest fires, nearly all of which are caused by careless human activity, are common

PLANTS

Mongolians collect various wild herbs and flowers for their medicinal properties: yellow poppies to heal wounds, edelweiss to add vitamins to the blood, and feather grass to cure an upset stomach.

WILD LANDS & WILDLIFE ENVIRONMENTAL ISSUES

GREEN ENERGY

For centuries Mongolians have been fighting against the elements, now they are trying to harness nature's power to develop a giant renewable-energy infrastructure. The country's first foray into renewables is a 50 megawatt wind farm, opened in 2013 at Salkhit, 75km southwest of Ulaanbaatar. The farm is expected to save 122,000 tons of coal, 1.6 million tons of water and eliminate 180,000 tons of carbon-dioxide emissions a year. It generates around 5% of the energy needed by the central grid. Mongolia has set a goal to get 20% to 25% of its energy from renewables by 2020. Currently, coal supplies about 80% of Mongolia's energy.

More wind farms are planned for the Gobi Desert. Experts say wind in the Gobi could generate 300,000 megawatts of wind power and the sun could yield 11 gigawatts, and Mongolia could one day export power to an 'Asia Super Grid' that might share energy from Japan to India.

during the windy spring season. The fires destroy huge tracts of forest and grassland, mainly in Khentii and Dornod aimags.

Perhaps the biggest concern is mining, which has polluted 28 river basins in eight aimags. As one mining executive told us, parts of the Tuul River near the village of Zaamar look like a WWI battlefield. Water usage by mines in the Gobi has prompted a backlash by local communities. The huge Oyu Tolgoi mine in Ömnögov requires the use of 360L of water *per second*; a group of citizens representatives in Ömnögov approved of a ban on using underground water after 2016 (a decision the central government will surely fight).

In 2012 President Elbegdorj was awarded the 'Champion of the Earth' award by the United Nations Environmental Programme for his efforts to fight climate change.

China's appetite for minerals is opening up new mines but another threat lies in China's hunt for the furs, meat and body parts of endangered animals. Chinese demand has resulted in an 80% decline in the number of marmots and an 85% drop in the number of saiga antelope.

Urban sprawl, coupled with a demand for wood to build homes and for heating and cooking, is slowly reducing the forests. This destruction of the forests has also lowered river levels, especially the Tuul Gol near Ulaanbaatar. Large-scale infrastructure projects are further cause for concern. The 18m-tall Dörgön hydropower station, built on the Chon Khairkh Gol in Khovd, has submerged canyons and pastures. The dam threatens fish and will only operate in summer when electricity is in lower demand compared with winter.

Conservationists are also concerned about the expansion of paved roads and railways, which are cutting across important animal migration routes in eastern Mongolia and the Gobi Desert. These new routes increase mining and commerce inside fragile ecosystems.

The International Crane Foundation (www.savingcranes.org) works to preserve important crane habitats and wetland areas in Mongolia.

Ulaanbaatar is an environmental catastrophe in its own right. The air pollution is ranked among the worst in the world (particularly in winter) and toxic chemicals and coal dust have polluted the soil and water. The sudden rise of consumerism has also resulted in mountains of garbage and construction waste. Efforts to enforce waste management have so far failed and large piles of trash are commonly found in playgrounds and parking lots. On the city outskirts, garbage dumps are inhabited by gangs of human scavengers who pick through the piles in search of scrap metal.

Survival Guide

Directory A–Z

Accommodation

Seasons

Rates listed in reviews are generally for the high season. High season is May to September. Some places may keep the same rates year-round, while others will offer a discount in the low season.

Bookings

It's a good idea to book ahead for any accommodation.

Countryside In rural areas, accommodation is limited, so if you turn up at the same time as a big tour group or if a government conference is underway, you may find every bed already booked out.

Ulaanbaatar You also need to book ahead for accommodation in Ulaanbaatar (UB), especially the guesthouses, which get packed in summer.

Gers Booking ahead at a ger (traditional yurt) camp allows your hosts to have enough food available for your party. Your tour operator can help make bookings.

Ger Buudals

Ger *buudals* (ger hotels) are found in popular tourist destinations, including Khövsgöl Nuur National Park, Terkhiin Tsagaan Nuur and Terelj. These are family-run operations and usually consist of an extra ger next to the family's ger. Basically, these are homestays with local families. They are very basic: no toilets, no showers and thin bedding.

Expect to pay T7000 to T10,000 per night. Lunch or dinner costs around T5000 while breakfast is around T2500.

Be aware that some families running ger *buudals* might not be able to cope with the trash you produce and may dispose of it improperly. For this reason, the rangers at Khövsgöl Nuur National Park and Gorkhi-Terelj will hand you a plastic bag when you enter the park (you're expected to carry your own rubbish out of the park). Bags are not handed out at other national parks, so bring a few of your own if you plan to camp or stay at a ger *buudal*.

Ger Camps

One unique option, particularly popular with organised tours, is to stay in tourist gers, which are like those used by nomads – except for the hot water, toilets, sheets and karaoke bars.

The camps are found all over Mongolia. They may seem touristy and are often surprisingly expensive, but if you are going into the countryside, a night at one is a great way to experience a Western-oriented, 'traditional Mongolian nomadic lifestyle' without the discomforts or awkwardness of staying in a private ger. For information on staying in a family ger, see p252.

A tourist ger camp is a patch of ground consisting of several (or sometimes dozens of) traditional gers, with separate buildings for toilets, hot showers and a ger-shaped restaurant-bar. Inside each ger, there are usually two to four beds, a table, tiny chairs and a wood stove that can be used for heating during the night – ask the staff to make it up for you.

Toilets Usually the sit-down types, though they may be (clean) pit toilets.

Prices Often depends on the location. Where there is lots of competition, ie Khövsgöl Nuur, Kharkhorin and Terkhiin Tsagaan Nuur, you can find basic camps for around T10,000 per night. Better camps or camps in remote areas may charge

US$40 to US$50 per person per night, including three meals. The cheapest camps charge US$20 to US$25 per person without meals. Activities such as horse or camel riding will cost extra. As meals add so much to the bill, you can save considerable cash by bringing your own food.

Meals Taken in a separate restaurant ger. With only a few exceptions, expect the usual Mongolian fare of meat, rice and potatoes. Most camps have a bar (and sometimes satellite TV). There's often little to differentiate between ger camps; it's normally the location that adds the charm and makes your stay special.

Bring If you plan to stay in a ger camp, you may want to bring a torch for nocturnal visits to the toilets, candles to create more ambience than stark electric lights (though not all have electricity), towels (the ones provided are invariably smaller than a handkerchief), and toilet paper (it may run out).

Seasons Except for a handful of ger camps in Terelj, most ger camps are only open from June to August, although in the Gobi they open a month earlier and close a little later.

Guesthouses

Ulaanbaatar now has around 15 guesthouses firmly aimed at foreign backpackers. Most are in apartment blocks and have dorm beds for around US$6 to US$8, cheap meals, a laundry service, internet connection and travel services. They are a great place to meet other travellers to share transport costs, but can get pretty crowded before and during Naadam (11 and 12 July).

Outside Ulaanbaatar only a handful of places, including Kharkorin and Khatgal, have accommodation aimed at backpackers.

Hotels

For cheap digs in Ulaanbaatar, try the guesthouses. If you plan to stay in budget hotels in the countryside, you should bring a sleeping bag.

SLEEPING PRICE RANGES

Prices in reviews are for a standard double room in the summer high season (May to September). Tax (10%) is almost always built into the price.

Outside Ulaanbaatar, accommodation price ranges are defined as follows:

$	less than T30,000
$$	T30,000–T60,000
$$$	more than T60,000

In Ulaanbaatar, accommodation price ranges are defined as follows:

$	less than US$70 (T112,000)
$$	US$70–US$120 (T112,000–T192,000)
$$$	more than US$120 (T192,000)

An inner sheet (the sort used inside sleeping bags) is also handy if the sheets are dirty. Blankets are always available, but are generally dirty or musty.

Midrange places are generally good but rather overpriced, charging US$70 to US$120 for a double in Ulaanbaatar. These rooms will be comfortable and clean and probably have satellite TV. Hot water and heating is standard for most buildings and hotels in Ulaanbaatar, and air-con is rarely needed. A private room or apartment, available through guesthouses, may be a better idea.

Prices May be quoted in either dollars or tögrög. Either way, you should pay in tögrög because it is now the law, though some hotels will act as moneychangers. Payment for accommodation is usually made upon checkout, but some receptionists will ask for money upfront.

Facilities In the countryside, most hotels are generally empty and falling apart, though facilities continue to improve and almost every aimag capital will have one decent new place. Even at the best places you can expect dodgy plumbing, broken locks, rock-hard beds and electrical outages. Service can be pretty lacklustre. The quality

of hotels in the countryside is reason enough to take a tent and go camping.

Bathing If the hotel has no hot water (most likely outside UB) or no water at all, it's worth knowing that most aimag capitals have a public bathhouse.

Security Always keep your windows and door locked (where possible). Be aware that staff may enter your room while you're not around. Err on the side of caution by keeping your valuables with you, or at the very least lock up valuables inside your luggage. Most hotels have a safe where valuables can be kept.

HOTEL CLASSES

Most *zochid buudals* (hotels) in the countryside (and budget hotels in Ulaanbaatar) have three types of rooms:

Lux (deluxe) rooms Include a separate sitting room, usually with TV and private bathroom.

Khagas lux (half-deluxe, or half-lux) Only a little smaller but often much cheaper.

Engiin (simple) room Usually with a shared bathroom.

Sometimes *niitiin bair* (dorm-style) rooms are available, but are rarely offered to foreigners. Invariably, hotel staff will initially show you their deluxe room, so ask to see the standard rooms if you're on a budget. Simple rooms cost around T25,000 per person per night. In *sum* (district) centres, expect to pay around T10,000 per person.

Rental Accommodation

Apartment rental is really only an option in Ulaanbaatar.

Children

Children can be a great icebreaker and are a good avenue for cultural exchange with the local people; however, travelling in Mongolia is difficult even for a healthy adult. Long jeep rides over nonexistent roads are a sure route to motion sickness and the endless steppe landscape may leave your children comatose with boredom. That said, children often like the thrill of camping, for a night or two at least. There are also lots of opportunities to sit on yaks, horses and camels, and plenty of opportunities to meet playmates when visiting gers. Check out LP's *Travel with Children* for more general tips.

Practicalities

➜ Items such as formula, baby food, nappies (diapers) and wipes are sold in nearly every supermarket in Ulaanbaatar and many of these items are now available in other cities too. In the countryside, the best place to get milk is directly from a herder, but make sure it has been boiled.

➜ It's unlikely that your tour company will have a child seat for the vehicle. This is something to clarify when booking your tour. Chinese-made safety seats are sold in some Ulaanbaatar shops. Another option is to bring your own car seat. Note that Air China and MIAT will weigh the car seat and count it as part of your luggage (some other airlines won't count it against your luggage allotment).

➜ When travelling in the countryside, deluxe hotel rooms normally come with an extra connecting room, which can be ideal for children.

➜ Many restaurants in Ulaanbaatar have a high chair available. This will be rare in the countryside.

➜ Nappy-changing facilities are rare.

➜ Breastfeeding in public is common in the countryside but is slightly rarer in the city.

Customs Regulations

If you are legally exporting any antiques, you must have a receipt and a customs certificate from the place you bought them. Most reliable shops in Ulaanbaatar can provide this. If the shop cannot produce a receipt or if you buy the item from a roadside stall, assume that you will not be able to export the item; it will be confiscated upon departure.

At some sites (especially Kharkhorin and Bayanzag) you'll be offered furs of rare animals and even fossilised dinosaur bones and eggs. Please do not take up these offers. There are stiff penalties for illegally exporting fossils, including jail time.

Travellers entering at the airport with extra baggage can expect to have their luggage opened and inspected. You can bring the following into Mongolia duty-free:

➜ 1L of spirits

➜ 2L of wine

➜ 3L of beer

➜ three bottles of perfume

➜ 200 cigarettes

Discount Cards

An ISIC student card will get you a 25% discount on train

PRACTICALITIES

➜ **English-language newspapers** *Mongol Messenger* (www.mongolmessenger.mn) and the *UB Post* (ubpost. mongolnews.mn) both have good articles, events listings and classified sections.

➜ **Floors** As in the USA, the ground floor is called the 1st floor, as opposed to the UK style, where the next floor above ground level is the 1st floor.

➜ **Mongolian-language newspapers** *Ardiin Erkh* (People's Right), *Zunny Medee* (Century News), *Odriin Sonin* (Daily News) and *Önöödör* (Today).

➜ **Radio** BBC World Service has a nonstop service at 103.1FM. Local stations worth trying include Jag (107FM), Blue Sky (100.9FM) and Radio Ulaanbaatar (102.5FM). Voice of America news programs are occasionally broadcast on 106.6FM.

➜ **Smoking** All public places in Mongolia are no-smoking zones, including hotel lobbies, cafes, restaurants, public transport and even stairwells of apartment blocks. Cigarette sales are banned within 500m of a school.

➜ **TV & Video** TV and video are both PAL.

➜ **Weights & Measures** Mongolia follows the metric system.

tickets plus discounts with some tour operators. Check the **ISIC website** (www.isic card.com) for updates.

A student price might not always be listed but may be available; it's a good idea to inquire if you've got a student card on you.

Electricity

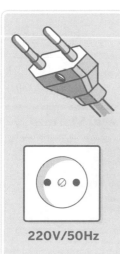

220V/50Hz

220V/50Hz

EATING PRICE RANGES

The following price ranges refer to a standard main course.

$	less than T7000
$$	T7000–T14,000
$$$	more than T14,000

Embassies & Consulates

Mongolian Embassies & Consulates

You'll find a full listing of Mongolia's embassies and consulates at www.mongo lianconsulate.com.au/mon golia/embassies.shtml.

Embassies & Consulates in Mongolia

A few countries operate embassies in Ulaanbaatar, though for most nationalities the nearest embassy is in Běijīng. If your country has an embassy in Ulaanbaatar, it's a good idea to register with it if you're travelling into the remote countryside, or in case you lose your passport.

Note that the German embassy also looks after the interests of Dutch, Belgian, Greek and Portuguese citizens. The British embassy can handle normal consular duties for Commonwealth countries that do not already have an embassy or consulate.

Australian Consulate (Map p60; ☑7013 3001; www. austrade.gov.au; Seoul St 21, 4F, Naiman Zovkhis Bldg)

Canadian Embassy (Map p60; ☑011-332 500; www. mongolia.gc.ca; Central Tower 6th fl, Peace Ave)

Chinese Embassy (Map p60; ☑011-323 940; http:// mn.china-embassy.org; Zalu-uchuudyn Örgön Chölöö 5) The consular section is actually on Baga Toiruu.

French Embassy (Map p60; ☑011-324 519; www. ambafrance-mn.org; Peace Ave 3)

German Embassy (Map p60; ☑011-323 325; www. ulan-bator.diplo.de; Negdsen Undestnii Gudamj 7)

Japanese Embassy (Map p60; ☑011-320 777; www. mn.emb-japan.go.jp; Elchingiin Gudamj)

Kazakhstan Embassy (☑011-345 408; kzemby@ mbox.mn; Zaisan Gudamj, Khan Uul District) The embassy is located on the way to Zaisan; take the last right turn before the bridge, into an alley with hideous-looking villas. Look for the Kazakh flag on the right.

Russian Embassy (Map p60; ☑011-327 191, 011-312 851; www.mongolia.mid.ru/en; Peace Ave A6)

South Korean Embassy (Map p70; ☑011-321 548; www. mofat.go.kr; Elchingiin Gudamj)

Swiss Consulate (Map p60; ☑011-331 422; www.swisscon-sulate.mn; Olympiin Gudamj 12)

UK Embassy (Map p70; ☑011-458 133; www.british -embassy.net/mongolia.html; Peace Ave 30)

US Embassy (Map p70; ☑011-329 095; http://ulaan baatar.usembassy.gov; Ikh Toiruu 59/1)

Gay & Lesbian Travellers

While homosexuality re-mains a fairly taboo topic in Mongolia, attitudes towards the LGBT community are changing, especially in Ulaan-baatar. Homosexuality was

GOVERNMENT TRAVEL ADVICE

The following government websites offer travel advisories and information on current hot spots.

Australian Department of Foreign Affairs (☎1300 139 281; www.smarttraveller.gov.au)

British Foreign Office (☎020 7008 1500; www.fco.gov.uk/travel-and-living-abroad)

Canadian Department of Foreign Affairs (☎800-267 8376; www.dfait-maeci.gc.ca)

US State Department (☎888-407 4747; www.travel.state.gov)

decriminalised in 2002 and in 2013 the LGBT community hosted its first **Pride Week** (⏲Sep), with a film festival, workshops and a parade (all in a private venue). Harassment by police is becoming less of a problem and the gay community has become better organised; an **LGBT centre** (☎7011-0323) opened in 2007.

'Given the youthful, tolerant and adaptable nature dominating the society, more and more people get to understand the realities of the community and to promote non-discrimination,' D Otgoo, the head of the LGBT centre, told us.

Meeting places come and go quickly, so you'll need to tap into the scene and ask. At the time of writing the best gathering spot was **Hanzo Lounge & Night Club** in UB (Map p60; ☎11-310 019; Sambuugiin Örogon Chölöö; Fri & Sat from T5000; ⏲6pm-midnight Sun-Wed, 6pm-3am Thu-Sat; 📶). As you never know what sort of reaction you'll get from a Mongolian in person, try making contacts through the web. Insight can be found at www.globalgayz.com/asia/mongolia.

Insurance

A policy covering loss, theft and medical expenses, plus compensation for delays in your travel arrangements, is essential for Mongolia. If items are lost or stolen you'll need to show your insurance company a police report. You may also need to prove damage or injury, so make sure to take photos. All policies vary, so check the fine print.

Worldwide travel insurance is available at www.lonelyplanet.com/travel_services. You can buy, extend and claim online anytime – even if you're already on the road. For information on health insurance, see p292.

Internet Access

A handful of internet cafes can be found in Ulaanbaatar and other cities. Signs are often in English or Mongolian (Интэрнэт Кафэ). Most hotels, guesthouses, cafes and restaurants in Ulaanbaatar have wi-fi, although this is less common outside the capital.

Internet cafes Every aimag capital has an internet cafe at the central Telecom office. Some *sum* centres also have internet access. Expect to pay around T800 per hour at internet cafes, double or triple that for hotel business centres.

Wi-fi and cable Places in reviews with free wi-fi, or internet-connected computers, are indicated with an icon (📶). Some hotels will just have an internet cable sticking out of the wall but require you to have your own laptop; if this is the case, it is described in the hotel listing.

ISPs Internet service providers include **Magicnet** (Map p60), Citinet, Skytel and Mobicom. **Citinet** (Map p60; ☎11-7011 1010; www.citinet.mn; Ikh Toiruu) is one of the most popular. Rates are reasonable, costing around T20,000 per month for a 1mbs (megabyte per second) connection.

Mobile broadband For expats living in Mongolia, especially in rural areas where internet is limited, mobile broadband is available. Mobile-phone companies in Ulaanbaatar sell the USB stick (T100,000 to T200,000) and monthly plans (unlimited data usage costs around T50,000).

Legal Matters

Foreigners' rights are generally respected in Mongolia.

Drugs If caught, drug use will give you a peek into Mongolia's grim penitentiary system.

Borders The most common offence committed by foreigners is straying too close to a border without a permit. Violators end up paying a fine and a few unlucky souls have been imprisoned for a few days. If you run into serious trouble, ask to contact your embassy.

Police The police get mixed reviews. Some travellers have reported fast response and results while others have been let down with lacklustre work. Overall, police are harmless, but can be unreliable when you really need them. In Mongolia, it is often the victim who is blamed (because of 'carelessness'), so never expect much sympathy from the police in any given circumstance.

Maps

Among the maps produced outside Mongolia, the best is the 1:200,000 *Mongolia* map published by **Gizi Maps** (www.gizimap.hu). The map is in both Latin and Cyrillic letters, handy for both you and your driver. It's available at **Seven Summits** (Map p60; 🕿11-329 456; www.active-mongolia.com/seven_summits; btwn Peace Ave & Seoul St) in Ulaanbaatar for T20,200.

While shopping for maps in Ulaanbaatar, look out for the 1:1,500,000 *Road Network Atlas* (T14,990) produced by MPM Agency. Another handy map is the 1:2,000,000 *Road Map of Mongolia* (T10,800). It has the most accurate road layout and town names and usefully marks the kilometres between all towns. Also useful is the *Tourist Map of Mongolia* (T8100), which marks a host of obscure historical, archaeological and natural sights, as well as ger camps. Most maps are updated every couple of years.

Explorers will want to check out the 1:500,000 series of topographic maps, which covers Mongolia in 37 maps. Each sheet costs around T5500 to T7000, but don't count on all being available. The topographic maps are particularly useful if travelling by horse or foot or using a GPS, but they can get expensive. A cheaper alternative is a series of all 21 aimag maps (T25,000, or T1500 per sheet).

You will also spot handy regional maps (T4000 each) to the most popular tourist areas, including Khövsgöl Nuur (1:200,000), Gobi Gurvan Saikhan (1:200,000) and Terelj (1:100,000).

Conservation Ink (www.conservationink.org) produces maps (US$8) using satellite images combined with useful information on culture, wildlife and tourist facilities. The national park series includes Altai Tavan Bogd, Khövsgöl Nuur, Gobi Gurvan Saikhan, Gorkhi-Terelj and Khustain.

Chinggis Khaan junkies will want to check out the *Chinggis Khaan Atlas*, available around Ulaanbaatar for about T8000, which maps his every presumed movement in obsessive detail.

Money

Currency The Mongolian unit of currency is the tögrög (T), often spelled tugrik because it reflects the more accurate pronunciation. It comes in notes of T5, T10, T20, T50, T100, T500, T1000, T5000, T10,000 and T20,000. (T1 notes are basically souvenirs.) The highest-value note is worth around US$12.

Moneychangers Banks and exchange offices in Ulaanbaatar will change money with relative efficiency. Banks in provincial centres are also fine; they change dollars and give cash advances against debit and credit cards.

Payments When paying out large sums of money (to hotels, tour operators and sometimes airlines), it's fine to use either US dollars or tögrög; the merchant will act as a moneychanger, though the rate will not generally be very good. Other forms of currency aren't usually accepted, although the euro is probably the next best. Cash offers the best exchange rates and you won't be paying any commission charge, but for security purposes you can also use debit cards.

Travellers cheques It's possible to cash travellers cheques in Mongolia, usually for a 2% fee. American Express travellers cheques can be cashed at the **Trade & Development Banks** (T&D Bank; Map p60; 🕿11-327 095; ⏱9am-4pm Mon-Fri) and Golomt Banks in Ulaanbaatar but getting cheques

cashed outside Ulaanbaatar is more difficult.

Leaving Mongolia Remember to change all your tögrög when leaving the country, as it's worthless elsewhere.

Depreciation Bear in mind that the tögrög depreciates around 10% to 15% per year, so prices in this book are likely to adjust upwards to compensate for the falling value of the currency.

ATMs

➡ Golomt, Trade & Development Bank, Khan Bank and XacBank all have ATMs in their Ulaanbaatar and countryside branches. These ATMs accept Visa and MasterCard and work most of the time, allowing you to withdraw up to T600,000 per day.

➡ Ordinary ATM cards issued from your bank at home probably won't work; try to get a 'debit' card linked to your bank account. It should be associated with a credit-card company.

➡ Before leaving home check with your bank about fees for making ATM transactions overseas. A 3% charge is standard nowadays but some banks will only charge 1%. If you plan to use your debit card a lot, it may be worth opening an account at a bank that has the lowest ATM fees.

Credit Cards

➡ You can't rely on plastic for everything, but credit

FLUCTUATING TÖGRÖG

Mongolia's central bank policy of non-intervention leaves its currency highly susceptible to fluctuation. In 2010 the currency was the world's best, gaining 15% against the US dollar. Then in 2013 it was among the world's worst, sliding 25% against the dollar. Tied to this is an inflation rate that climbs around 10% to 15% per year. Local businesses frequently jack up prices when the currency depreciates, thus listings in this book should be used as a general guide and a point of comparison between the various options offered – not the exact price point of the item in question.

cards are becoming more widely accepted in upmarket hotels, travel agencies and antique shops. Most of these, however, charge an additional 3% if you use a credit card.

➡ Banks can give cash advances on credit cards, often for no charge if you have Visa, but for as much as 4% with MasterCard.

Tipping

Traditionally, Mongolians don't tip. However, Mongolians working in tourism-related fields (guides, drivers, bellhops and waitresses at restaurants frequented by foreigners) are now accustomed to tips. If you do feel service was good, a 10% tip is appreciated.

Opening Hours

Lunch break In the countryside, banks, museums and other facilities may close for an hour at lunch, sometime between noon and 2pm.

Markets Outdoor markets are usually open from 9am to 7pm daily (or sunset in winter), while indoor markets open from 10am to 8pm.

Museums Open reduced hours in winter and normally closed an extra couple of days a week.

Opening hours in Ulaanbaatar:

Banks 9am to 6pm Monday to Friday, 10am to 3pm Saturday

Government offices 9am to 5pm Monday to Friday

Restaurants 10am to 10pm

Shops 9am to 10pm

PHOTOGRAPHY CHARGES IN MUSEUMS

In most museums throughout the country you need to pay an extra fee (often outrageously high) to use your still or video camera. The fees tend to vary, between T12,000 to T25,000 for photos and T25,000 to T50,000 for videos. It is best to have a look around first before you decide whether to fork out the extra tögrög.

Photography

Mongolia's remote and beautiful landscapes make for some incredible photography, but it's this same remoteness that requires extra planning when taking pictures. For professional tips on how to take better photos, check out LP's *Travel Photography*, by Richard I'Anson.

Digital photography As you may go several days in a row without seeing a shop, internet cafe or electrical outlet, you'll need extra batteries and memory cards for your digital camera. These are best bought at home or in Ulaanbaatar as electronic goods in aimag centres can be hard to find. Once you reach an aimag capital you can go to an internet cafe and upload your pictures to the cloud or save them on a CD or USB stick.

Light In summer, days are long, so the best time to take photos is before 10am and between 6pm and 8pm, when Mongolia basks in gorgeous light. As bright, glaring sunshine is the norm, a polarising filter is essential.

Dust If you do a jeep trip on an unsurfaced road, you can expect plenty of dust, so keep the camera well sealed in a plastic bag.

Photographing People

Always ask before taking a photograph. Keep in mind that monks and nomads are not photographic models, so if they do not want to be photographed, their wishes should be respected. Point a camera at an urban Mongol on the street and chances are they will cover their face. Don't try sneaking around for a different angle as this may lead to an argument. Markets are also places where snap-happy foreigners are often not welcome.

On the other hand, people in the countryside can be happy to pose for photographs if you ask first. If you have promised to send them a copy, please do it. One way to do this is to print out the photos at an aimag centre or in Ulaanbaatar. To simplify matters, bring blank envelopes and ask them to write their address on the outside. On the inside, make a note to yourself about who they were in case you forget.

When Mongolians pose for a portrait they instantly put on a face that looks like they are in mourning at Brezhnev's funeral. You may need to take this Soviet-style portrait in order to get a more natural shot later. 'Can I take your photograph?' in Mongolian is *Bi tany zurgiig avch bolokh uu?*

Restrictions

➡ Photography is prohibited inside monasteries and temples, although you may photograph building exteriors and monastery grounds. You can sometimes obtain special permission to take photographs for an extra fee.

➡ Don't photograph potentially sensitive areas, especially border crossings and military establishments.

Post

Service The postal service is generally reliable. Allow at least a couple of weeks for letters and postcards to arrive home from Mongolia.

Stamps You can buy stamps in post offices (and top-end hotels) in Ulaanbaatar and aimag capitals.

Poste restante The poste restante at the **Central Post Office** (CPO, Töv Shuudangiin Salbar; Map p60; ☎11-313 421;

cnr Peace Ave & Sükhbaataryn Gudamj; ⊘7.30am-9pm Mon-Fri, 9am-8pm Sat & Sun) in Ulaanbaatar seems to work quite well; bring along your passport as proof of identification. Don't even think about using poste restante anywhere else in the country.

Couriers The more reliable courier services include DHL and FedEx.

Postal rates Normal-sized letters cost T1320 and postcards cost T1100 to all countries. A 1kg airmail parcel to the UK will cost T45,670, or T50,500 to the USA.

Public Holidays

Mongolians do not get many holidays. Naadam and Tsagaan Sar each warrant three days off, plus there's a day off for New Year's and Chinggis Khaan's birthday. Most tourist facilities remain open during holidays, but shops and offices will close down. The following holidays are observed:

Shin Jil (New Year's Day) 1 January

Constitution Day 13 January; to celebrate the adoption of the 1992 constitution (generally a normal working day)

Tsagaan Sar (Lunar New Year) January/February; a three-day holiday celebrating the Mongolian New Year

Women's Day 8 March (generally a normal working day)

Mothers' & Children's Day 1 June; a great time to visit parks

Naadam Festival 11 and 12 July; also known as National Day celebrations

Chinggis Khaan's Birthday Early November; the date is the first day of the first winter month, based on the lunar calendar. Most government offices and banks are closed

Safe Travel

Mongolia is a reasonably safe country in which to travel,

but given the infrastructure of the country, state of the economy and other development problems, you are bound to run into bumps along the way. With a bit of patience, care and planning, you should be able to handle just about anything.

Alcoholism

Alcoholism is a problem in Mongolia and you are bound to encounter drunks in both the city and countryside. Drunks (*sogtuu khun*) are more annoying than dangerous, except when they are driving your vehicle. Drivers who work for tour companies have been disciplined to hold their alcohol on trips, but hitchhikers may encounter drunk drivers.

Trains Drinking is pretty common on the trains, which is another reason to travel in coupe class or 'soft seat' (you can close your cabin door). If the offending drunk happens to be in *your* cabin, ask the attendant to move you to another cabin.

Camping If camping, always make sure that you pitch your tent somewhere secluded, and that no drunks see you set up camp; otherwise, they will invariably visit you during the night.

Dogs

Stray dogs in the cities and domestic dogs around gers in the countryside can be vicious and possibly rabid. In the countryside, some dogs are so damn lazy that you wouldn't get a whimper if 100 lame cats hobbled past; others will almost head-butt your vehicle and chase it for a kilometre or two.

Before approaching any ger, especially in the countryside, make sure the dogs are friendly or under control and shout the phrase *Nokhoi khor*, which roughly translates as 'Can I come in?' but literally means 'Hold the dog!'. Getting rabies shots is no fun; it's easier to just stay away from dogs, even if they appear friendly.

If you need to walk in the dark in the countryside, perhaps for a midnight trip to the toilet, locals have suggested that if you swing a torch in front of you it will stop any possible dog attacks.

Scams

Professional scamming is not common; the main thing to be aware of is dodgy tour companies that don't deliver on their promises. We've had letters from readers who booked tours where the promised accommodation, food and service standards fell short of expectations. It might be good to get in writing exactly what is offered, and ask about compensation if things don't work out as planned. The riskiest tour companies are the ones operated by guesthouses and the ones that specialise in onward trips to Russia.

Theft

Ulaanbaatar Petty theft is a fact of life in Ulaanbaatar and you need to stay vigilant of bag-slashers and pickpockets, especially around Naadam time when muggers do a brisk trade on all the starry-eyed tourists wandering about.

Countryside In the countryside, keep an eye on your gear and don't leave valuables lying around your campsite if you wander off. Lock your kit inside your jeep or hotel whenever possible (drivers do a good job of watching your stuff).

Horse trekking When horse trekking, be wary of Mongolians who seem to be following you; they may be after your valuables or even your horses, which are easily stolen while you sleep.

Other Annoyances

Heat Heating and hot-water shortages and electricity blackouts are common in aimag capitals. Some villages go for days (or weeks) without any utility services at all.

Quarantine This sometimes affects travel in Mongolia. Foot-and-mouth disease, malignant anthrax and the plague pop up all the time and may prevent you from travelling to certain areas. Some regions that have been hit by foot-and-mouth disease require drivers to decontaminate their cars when they enter and leave cities. This requires the spraying of tyres (or the whole car) and can cost a few thousand tögrög.

Telephone

It's easy to make international or domestic calls in Ulaanbaatar and the aimag capitals. Technology is still lagging in many *sum* centres; however, it's now possible to use mobile (cell) phones in most of the country.

Phonecards Prepaid, international phonecards are available at the Central Post Office in UB, starting from T2000. You can use these when calling from a landline or from the 'taxophones' located on the wall in the lobby of the post office.

Online services These days, most travellers make international calls with **Skype** (www. skype.com) or a similar service. Calls to landlines are cheap, only around US$0.02 a minute to most Western countries (or free for computer-to-computer calls). You can do this on your own device at a wi-fi hotspot or use an internet cafe.

Calling Mongolia To make a call *to* Mongolia, dial the international access code in your country (normally 00) and then the Mongolian country code (976). Then, for a landline number, dial the local code (minus the '0' for Ulaanbaatar, but include the '0' for all other areas) and then the number. If you are calling a mobile phone, dial the country code (976) without the area code. Be aware, though, that there are different requirements for area codes if you're using a mobile phone.

Calling out of Mongolia If you are calling *out of* Mongolia and using an IDD phone, dial 00 and then your international country code.

Operator In Ulaanbaatar, the domestic operator's number is 109. Outside normal working hours, call 1109.

Phone Codes

➠ Numbers starting with 99, 96, 95, 91, 88, 77, 94 or 81 are mobile numbers and therefore don't require an area code.

➠ Every aimag has its own area codes; we have listed them in this book under the aimag capital headings (but we also include the full number in listings).

➠ Ulaanbaatar has several area codes: 11 is the most widely used. If a phone number begins with a 23, 24 or 25, then the area code is 21. If the phone number begins with a 26, the code is 51.

➠ If calling from a landline to a number in Ulaanbaatar, add a '0' before the phone code.

➠ If you are calling from a mobile phone, just dial the number in the listing.

Note that Mongolia has two types of phone codes.

New codes Have four digits (which always start with 70) followed by another four digits.

Old codes Those in Ulaanbaatar have two digits (followed by six-digit phone numbers) while in the countryside the codes have five digits (followed by five-digit phone numbers numbers).

Mobile Phones (Cell Phones)

The main companies are Mobicom, Skytel, Unitel and G-Mobile. Mobicom and Unitel operate on GSM (Global System for Mobile communication) 900/1800. G-Mobile and Skytel are both on the CDMA network. (Make sure you buy a SIM card appropriate for your phone.)

➠ Buying a SIM card in Mongolia will probably work out cheaper than paying roaming charges on your home-country network.

➠ Mobicom booths can be found in the Central Post Office (p272) and on the 5th floor of the **State Department Store** (Их Дэлгүүр; Map p60; 11-313 232; Peace Ave 44) in UB. Buy a SIM card (around T7000), and top up with units as needed. It is free to receive calls and text-messaging charges are almost negligible.

➠ Every aimag capital (and many *sum* centres) has mobile-phone service, and calls are fairly cheap, making this a good way to keep in touch with home. If a *sum* centre is not covered by Mobicom, it probably will be covered by an alternative network, such as G-Mobile.

➠ It's a good idea to have a phone while travelling in the countryside, as it allows you to communicate with your tour operator should problems arise on your trip. You can also use it to call ger camps or hotels to make a reservation.

➠ If you have a smartphone (Edge, 3G or 4G), you should be able to access the internet with a local SIM card.

BUYING A MOBILE PHONE

New and used mobile-phone shops are everywhere in UB and also in some rural cities. The cheapest phones will cost around US$35. In UB, try the Tedy Centre on Baruun Selbe Gudamj.

Satellite Phones

If you're planning a serious mountaineering or horse-trekking expedition, considering bringing or renting a satellite phone, which isn't too bulky and can be used anywhere. If you haven't already purchased one in your home country, these are available for sale at the **Mobicom office** (Map p70; cnr Beijing Gudamj & Tokyogiin Gudamj) in UB.

Time

Time zones Mongolia is divided into two time zones: the three western aimags of Bayan-Ölgii, Uvs and Khovd are one hour behind Ulaanbaatar and the rest of the country.

Daylight saving Mongolia does not observe daylight-saving time, which means that the sun can rise at very early hours in summer.

Standard time The standard time in Ulaanbaatar is UTC/GMT plus eight hours. This puts Ulaanbaatar in the same time zone as Beijing, Hong Kong, Singapore and Perth.

24-hour clock The 24-hour clock is used for plane and train schedules.

Toilets

Pit toilets In most hotels in UB, aimag capitals and most ger camps, toilets are the sit-down European variety. In other hotels and some more-remote ger camps, you will have to use pit toilets and hold your breath.

Outdoors In the countryside, where there may not be a bush or tree for hundreds of kilometres, modesty is not something to worry about – just do it where you want to, but away from gers. Also, try to avoid such places as *ovoos* (sacred cairns of stones), rivers and lakes (water sources for nomads) and marmot holes.

Toilet paper The plumbing is decrepit in many of the older hotels, and toilet paper can easily jam up the works. If there is a rubbish basket next to the toilet, this is where the waste paper should go. Toilet paper in the basic hotels resembles industrial-strength cardboard, or may be scraps of newspaper or old books. To avoid paper cuts, stock up on softer brand toilet paper, available in the larger cities.

Tourist Information

There are two tourist information desks in Ulaanbaatar: at the **Ulaanbaatar Bank building** (Map p60; ☑7010 8687; www.tourism.ub.gov.mn; Baga Toiruu 15; ⊗9am-6pm) and inside the **Erel Bank** (Map p60; ☑7010-1011; cnr Baga Toiruu West & Peace Ave; ⊗9am-9pm May-Sep, 10am-7pm Oct-Apr). Each is run by a separate entity. Outside UB, the only similar tourist desk is in Mörön.

Travellers with Disabilities

Mongolia is a difficult place for wheelchair travellers. Pavements are rough and buildings and buses are generally not wheelchair accessible. Still, travel to Ulaanbaatar and jeep trips to places such as Khustain National Park shouldn't cause too many insurmountable problems.

If any specialised travel agency might be interested in arranging trips to Mongolia, the best bet is the US company **Accessible Journeys** (☑800-846-4537; www.disability travel.com) in Pennsylvania. At the very least, hire your own transport and guide through one of the Ulaanbaatar agencies. If you explain your disability, these agencies may be able to assist you.

Visas

Tourist visas Currently, a 30-day tourist visa is easily obtained at any Mongolian embassy, consulate, consulate-general or honorary consul.

Visa on arrival If you are travelling to Mongolia from a country that has no Mongolian consulate, you can pick up a 30-day tourist visa on arrival at the airport in Ulaanbaatar. You'll need T108,000 (or dollar equivalent) and two passport photos – you should also have an invitation from an organisation or company in Mongolia.

US citizens US citizens can stay in Mongolia for up to 90 days without a visa. If you stay less than 30 days, nothing needs to be done, other than having your passport stamped when you enter and leave the country. If you stay more than 30 days, you need to register.

Other visa-free nationalities Citizens of Canada, Germany, Israel, Japan, Malaysia and Turkey can stay visa-free for up to 30 days and Hong Kong and Singaporean citizens can stay visa-free for up to 14 days.

Registration All visitors who plan to stay more than 30 days must be registered within seven days of their arrival.

Regulations To check current regulations, try the website of the Mongolian embassy in Washington DC (www.mongolian embassy.us). Another website to check is www.immigration.gov.mn.

Tourist Visas

Cost Standard tourist visas generally last 30 days from the date of entry and you must enter Mongolia within three months of issue. Each embassy or consulate sets its own price. For single-entry/exit visas you can expect to pay: A$100 in Canberra, UK£40 in London, C$90 in Ottawa and Y250 in Beijing.

Issuing time Visas normally take several days, or even up to two weeks, to issue. If you want your visa quicker, possibly within 24 hours, you will have to pay an

VISAS FOR ONWARD TRAVEL

China

The best place to get a visa for China is in your home country. Applying at home will require less paperwork and you'll have a better shot at getting a multiple-entry visa. If you cannot get one in your home country, the Chinese embassy (p269) in Ulaanbaatar is another option. Drop off passports between 9.30am and noon Monday, Wednesday and Friday (pickup is 4pm to 5pm). Transit visas (single or double entry) last up to seven days from each date of entry, and single- and double-entry tourist visas are valid for 30 days from the date of each entry – you must enter China within 90 days of being issued the visa. Single-/double-entry tourist visas cost US$30/60 and take four days to issue. For two-day or same-day service, you'll have to fork out an extra US$20 or US$30. You must pay in US dollars. Visas for US citizens are US$140, regardless of type.

When you apply for the visa you must provide one passport photo, proof of departure from China (eg, an air or train ticket), proof of a booked hotel stay of three nights, and a bank statement. This is not as difficult as it sounds. For the proof of departure, you can go to any travel agent in Ulaanbaatar, make a booking for a flight and get a print-out (you don't need to actually buy the ticket). As for the hotel bookings, the best way to do this is to book three nights at a hostel in Běijīng using your credit card. These bookings are usually 90% refundable so even if you never stay at the hostel this exercise should only cost a few dollars. Payment for the visa is made at the Golomt Bank across the street from the embassy front gate.

In August and early September, lines are long due to students lining up for visas. At this time the line starts to form at 6am (or earlier). Before the embassy opens, the guard will give out a limited number of tickets. If you don't get a ticket, it's highly unlikely you'll get inside that day. For updated information, see http://mn.china-embassy.org.

Kazakhstan

The consular section at the Kazakhstan embassy (p269) is open from 10am to noon Monday, Tuesday, Thursday and Friday. Single-entry, one-month visas cost US$160 for Americans and $30 for most other nationalities and take four to five days to process. Double-entry and multiple-entry visas are not usually available. Before trekking down here, call the embassy to make sure the consul is in town and the hours are still the same (and to check that they are even issuing visas as this service periodically stops).

Russia

Getting a visa is by no means a straightforward process, but it's getting easier. The consular section of the Russian embassy (p269) is open for visas from 2pm to 3pm daily. Almost everyone ends up paying a different price for their visa; costs vary between US$25 and US$200, depending on your itinerary and nationality. You will need one photo. Some (not all) nationalities can get a visa for one month. On our last visit to the Russian embassy we were told that the old requirement of having a sponsor and hotel vouchers has ended. However, tour agents that specialise in tours to Russia told us the requirement still exists, so beware of tour companies trying to sell you something you may not need.

Americans, Australians, French, Dutch and Italians are a few of the nationalities that can get a tourist visa here. Processing time is 14 business days (so about three weeks total). Prices change all the time: Americans pay US$131, while Australians pay US$55.

Citizens of Germany, UK and New Zealand are a few of the nationalities that cannot get a tourist visa here (unless the applicant has been living in Mongolia more than 90 days). However, you can get a transit visa. You must bring all your tickets into and out of Russia to get the visa. The length of the transit visa depends on your travel route but you are usually given a maximum of seven days (enough to take the Trans-Siberian to Europe). Regular processing time for a transit visa is four days, although rush visas can be done the following day. Prices are different for each nationality. UK citizens pay US$59 while a rush visa is US$116.

The consul will hand you business cards for local tour operators that can organise your trip. For additional information, contact http://waytorussia.net.

'express fee', which is double the normal cost.

Multiple-entry visas Multiple-entry/exit tourist visas are usually only issued to foreign residents who do a lot of travel.

Transit Visas

These visas last 72 hours from the date of entry. This period will only allow you to get off the Trans-Mongolian train for a very short time before catching another train to Russia or China. A single-entry/exit transit visa costs between US$25 and US$60, depending on where you apply for it, but cannot be extended. You will need to show the train or plane ticket and a visa for the next country (Russia or China).

Visa Extensions

If you have a 30-day tourist visa, you can extend it by another 30 days. For extensions, go to the **Office of Immigration, Naturalisation & Foreign Citizens** (INFC; ☑11-1882; ◷9am-1pm & 2-6pm Mon-Fri) in UB. The only catch is that if you stay longer than 30 days you have to be registered at this office (which you should have done within seven days after arrival).

The office is located about 1.8km east of the airport (next to the large sports arena), an inconvenient 15km trek from the city centre. The office is usually quite busy, so you should expect to spend an hour or two here getting your stuff done. There is a small cafe here that serves lunch if you get stuck during the lunch hour. An information desk with English-speaking staff can help answer your questions and point you to the correct line.

The INFC office is a branch of the main visa office of the **Ministry of External Relations** (Map p60; cnr Peace Ave & Olympiin Gudamj; ◷9.30am-noon Mon-Fri). You may be sent to the ministry if your visa situation is complicated (ie you require a work per-

mit). The entrance is around the back. In Mongolian it's known as: Gadaadiin Irgen Haryatiin Asuudal Erhleh Gazar (Гадаадын Иргэн Харьяатын Асуудал Эрхлэх Газар).

If you have already registered, you should apply for an extension about a week before your visa expires. It costs T3600 per day but the minimum extension is seven days. You will need a passport-sized photo and must pay a T5000 processing fee. The extension will be issued on the same day. Credit cards may be accepted, but it's best to bring cash in case the machine isn't working.

Several guesthouses in Ulaanbaatar will take care of visa extensions (and registration) for a small fee. If you don't have a letter of support, you can write your own (handwritten is OK); the letter should state the date of your arrival, the date of extension and the reason for travel.

Getting a visa extension outside Ulaanbaatar is difficult, as officials would need to send your passport back to Ulaanbaatar. In an extreme situation this might be possible at the **INFC office in Ölgii** (NFC; Map p209; ☑01422-22195, 9942 4338; Government House; ◷8am-noon & 1-5pm Mon-Sat).

Exit Visas

Transit and tourist visas are good for one entry and one exit (unless you have a double or multiple-entry/exit visa). If you are working in Mongolia, or if you obtained your visa at an honorary consul, you are usually issued a single-entry visa (valid for entry only). In this case, another visa is required to *leave* the country. These visas are available from the **INFC office** (INFC; ☑11-1882; ◷9am-1pm & 2-6pm Mon-Fri) in UB.

The exit visa situation in particular applies to Israeli and US passport holders (who usually enter without

visas). Israelis need an exit visa if they stay more than 30 days and Americans need one if they stay more than 90 days.

Cost For most nationalities the exit visa costs around US$15, plus an additional US$2 per day that you stay beyond the expiry of your entry visa.

Duration It is valid for 10 days, which means that you can stay 10 days after your normal visa has expired.

Registration

If you intend to stay in Mongolia for more than 30 days you must register before the end of your first seven days of being in the country (although this rule is sometimes overlooked and you might be able to register in the first 30 days). Note that you can only register twice per calendar year at the INFC office.

Requirements Registration takes place at the **INFC office** (INFC; ☑11-1882; ◷9am-1pm & 2-6pm Mon-Fri) in UB. The process is free, but you have to pay T1000 for the one-page application. You'll need one passport-sized photo. Most guesthouses can rustle up an invitation to Mongolia for you if you require one.

Signing out As a formality, the registration also needs to be 'signed out'; however, the official you are dealing with will usually do this when you register so you won't have to come back. A specific date is not needed, just set the exit date as far out as possible and you can leave any time before that date.

Ölgii office If you've arrived in western Mongolia from Russia, the INFC office in Ölgii can get you registered.

Fine If you don't register, you are liable for a fine (theoretically from US$100 to US$300) when you leave the country.

Long-Term Stays

The only way to remain in Mongolia on a long-term basis (ie more than three months) is to get a work or study permit. The company or organisation you are working for should handle this for you, but if you are working independently you need to go it alone. You will almost certainly need a letter from an employer providing a legitimate reason for your stay. Registration typically takes place at the **INFC office** (INFC; ☎11-1882; ☉9am-1pm & 2-6pm Mon-Fri) in UB.

Volunteering

Some organisations are anxious to receive help from qualified people, particularly in education, health and IT development. Agencies are more interested in committed people who are willing to stay two years or more, although short-term projects are available. In most instances, you will be paid in local wages (or possibly a little more). Besides the following, a good starting reference is **Golden Gate Friends of Mongolia** (www.ggfom.org).

Asral (☎9595 2272, 011-304 838; www.asralmongolia.org; PO Box 467, Ulaanbaatar-23) Travellers can volunteer as English teachers at this Buddhist social centre or work on the project farm in Gachuurt.

Australian Youth Ambassadors for Development (AYAD; ☎1800 995 536; www.ayad.com.au) AYAD has a handful of Australian volunteers in Mongolia.

Khustain National Park (☎21-245 08; www.hustai.mn) The park runs a three-week ecovolunteer program where you can help with research.

Meg's Adventure Tours (☎9964 3242; www.megsadventuretours.com) Small tour operator that organises volunteer projects for short-term travellers. The work usually involves assisting at an orphanage.

Peace Corps (Enkh Tavnii Korpus; ☎011-311 518) The organisation is well represented throughout the country. Alterna-

tively, contact your local Peace Corps office (☎1-800-424 8580; www.peacecorps.gov) in the USA.

UN Development Programme (UNDP; ☎011-327 585; www.undp.mn; PO Box 46/1009, Ulaanbaatar, Negdsen Undestnii Gudamj 12) The UNDP is always on the lookout for committed and hard-working volunteers but normally recruits abroad.

Voluntary Service Overseas (VSO; ☎011-313 514; www.vso.org.uk; PO Box 678, Ulaanbaatar) This British-run organisation is set up mainly for Brits. It prefers you to contact the organisation through its UK head office (☎020-8780 7500).

Women Travellers

Mongolia doesn't present too many problems for foreign women travelling independently. The majority of Mongolian men behave in a friendly and respectful manner, without ulterior motives. However, you may come across an annoying drunk or the occasional macho idiot. The phrase for 'Go away!' is *Sasha be!*

Travelling solo There are occasional incidents of solo female travellers being harassed by their male guide. If your guide is male, it is best to keep in touch with your tour agency in Ulaanbaatar (having a mobile phone with a local SIM card makes it easier to contact them). Better yet, take a female guide whenever possible.

Practicalities Tampons and pads are available in Ulaanbaatar and most other main aimag capitals, though these will be very hard to find the deeper you go into the countryside. Many women also find it useful to wear long skirts while in the countryside, so that they can relieve themselves in some semblance of privacy on the open steppes.

Clothing Although attitudes towards women are more conservative in the mostly Muslim

Bayan-Ölgii aimag, you don't need to cover up as you would in other areas of Central Asia.

Work

Work options for foreigners in Mongolia typically include teaching English or working for a development organisation or NGO. The pay for teaching can be decent (compared with typical local salaries). If you have specialised skills the best money is paid by mining companies.

Contacts If you are keen to work in Mongolia and are qualified in teaching or health, contact volunteer organisations, network through the internet or check the English-language newspapers in Ulaanbaatar.

Permits Permission to work is fairly easy to obtain if you have been hired locally. In most cases, your employer will take care of this for you.

Language Teaching

Many Mongolians are hungry to learn a second language, particularly English, so there is a demand for teachers. Colleges and volunteer agencies are ever on the lookout for qualified teachers who are willing to stay for a few terms (if not a few years), not just for a week or two.

In Ulaanbaatar try the following options:

American School of Ulaanbaatar (☎011-348 888; www.asu.edu.mn)

International School (☎7016 0010; www.isumongolia.edu.mn)

National University of Mongolia (NUM; Map p60; ☎7730 7730; www.num.edu.mn; Ikh Surguuliin Gudamj 1, PO Box 46a/523, 210646)

Orchlon School (☎011-353 519; www.orchlon.mn)

TalkTalk English (Map p60; ☎7013 5135; www.talktalkenglish.mn)

Turkish School (☎011-462 020; www.monturk.edu.mn)

Transport

GETTING THERE & AWAY

Entering the Country

When entering Mongolia, by land or air, fill out the straightforward entry form. You'll have to register if you plan to be in Mongolia for more than 30 days. Registering in Ulaanbaatar (UB) is fairly straightforward, and it's also possible in Ölgii if you arrive in western Mongolia; see p277 for details.

Passport

Make sure that your passport is valid for at least six months from your date of arrival. If you lose your passport, your embassy in Ulaanbaatar can replace it, usually in one day.

Air

Airports & Airlines

Ulaanbaatar's **Chinggis Khaan airport** (✐11-983 005, 198; www.airport.mn; ☎) is Mongolia's major international airport; the code is ULN. At the time of writing a new airport was under construction 52km southwest of Ulaanbaatar. It is expected to be complete by December 2016.

FLIGHTS TO ULAANBAATAR

FROM	AIRLINE	FREQUENCY	ONE-WAY/RETURN FARE*
Bangkok	Hunnu	2 weekly	US$460/741
Běijīng	Air China	6 weekly	US$193/332
Běijīng	MIAT	daily	US$173/348
Berlin	MIAT	2 weekly (via Moscow)	US$590/1024
Bishkek	Turkish Airlines	2 weekly	US$478/796
Hohhot	AeroMongolia	5 weekly	US$208/360
Hong Kong	Hunuu	3 weekly	US$336/454
Hong Kong	MIAT	4 weekly	US$456/778
Irkutsk	AeroMongolia	3 weekly	US$141/248
Istanbul	Turkish Airlines	2 weekly (via Bishkek)	US$681/842
Moscow	Aeroflot	daily (summer), 3 weekly (winter)	US$586/871
Moscow	MIAT	2 weekly	US$533/787
Seoul	Korean Air	4 weekly	US$325/510
Seoul	MIAT	6 weekly	US$339/478
Shànghǎi	Hunnu	2 weekly (summer only)	US$336/454
Tokyo	MIAT	1 weekly	US$454/666

*Fares change markedly based on exchange rate and availability.

Flights to/from Ulaan-baatar can be pricey, as there is a limited number of carriers. The main carriers are MIAT, Air China, Korean Air, Turkish Airlines and Aeroflot. Apart from major cities like Běijīng, Seoul and Moscow, there are flights to smaller destinations in China, Russia and Kyr-gyzstan. These include an AeroMongolia flight to/from Hohhot five times a week for US$208 one way. Other regional flights to places like Mănzhōulǐ, Ulan-Ude and Èrliàn, however, change with the seasons.

In the high-season (June to August), prices are cheaper for midweek travel (Monday and Tuesday flights are gener-ally cheaper than Friday and Saturday flights). In July and August most flights are full, so book well in advance.

Airlines flying to and from Mongolia:

Aeroflot (⌂in UB 011-320 720; www.aeroflot.ru)

AeroMongolia (⌂in UB 011-330 373; www.aeromongolia.mn) Mongolia-based airline that uses Fokker 50 propeller aircraft and Fokker 100 jets.

Air China (⌂in UB 7575 6600; www.airchina.cn)

EZ Nis (⌂in UB 7575 3232; www.eznisairways.com) Mongolia-based airline with a handful of Saab 340B aeroplanes.

Hunnu Airlines (⌂in UB 7000 1111; www.hunnuair.com)

Korean Air (⌂in UB 011-317 100; www.koreanair.com)

MIAT (⌂in UB 011-333 999; www.miat.com) Mongolia's national airline has brought its safety practices for international flights to near-Western stand-ards. Online booking is available through its website. On interna-tional flights, MIAT allows 30kg of baggage for business travellers and 20kg for economy travellers.

Turkish Airlines (⌂in UB 7585 9999; www.turkish airlines.com)

Tickets

Airfares to Mongolia peak between June and August. Overlanders should con-sider purchasing an open-jaw ticket. This option could involve, for example, flying into Běijīng and then flying out of Moscow. This allows you to travel slowly along the Trans-Siberia Railway.

Flights, tours and rail tick-ets can be booked online at lonelyplanet.com/bookings.

Land

For info on visas, see p275.

China

There are two border points open to foreigners, the main one being between Zamyn-Üüd and Èrliàn (Ereen).

EN ROUTE TO MONGOLIA

Flying to Mongolia usually requires one or two stops en route and you are likely to spend some time in either Běijīng International Airport (PEK) or South Korea's Incheon Interna-tional Airport (ICN). Moscow's Sheremetyevo International Airport (SVO) and Istanbul's Ataturk Airport (IST) are possible stops if you are coming from Europe. Here is what you need to know while in transit:

➡ Your luggage weight is determined by the airline with which you begin your journey, not any middle segment or final segment. So if you are flying from overseas it doesn't matter that MIAT's baggage allowance is only 20kg; you can bring as much as your original flight allows. This applies only if you check your baggage *all the way through* to Ulaanbaatar. If you pick up your luggage midway through the journey you will be subject to luggage restrictions when you check in with MIAT or Air China.

➡ If you have an onward ticket, most nationalities can now stay in China for 72 hours without a visa. Luggage storage is available at the airport in Běijīng for about Y30 per bag. Terminal 3 also has a tiny hotel on the arrivals level where you can stay in between flights (rooms start from Y100 per hour). The airport is open all night. A free shuttle bus connects Terminal 3 and Terminal 2. Free internet is available but to get a password you need to scan your passport at one of the machines on the departure level.

➡ If you want to pop into Běijīng for a few hours, take the Airport Line light rail (Y25), which runs every 15 minutes to Dongzhimen subway station.

➡ Incheon airport is amazingly transit-friendly. It has a comfortable lounge with big sofas where you can sleep, free internet, free showers and even free city tours that can last from two to six hours! The airport also has a hotel, see www.airport.kr for details.

➡ When leaving Mongolia, if you are catching a connecting flight, you must be able to show proof of your onward ticket at the counter in Ulaanbaatar and in Běijīng (so have a print-out handy). If you cannot show an onward ticket and you have no visa for China, you won't be allowed on the flight.

CLIMATE CHANGE & TRAVEL

Every form of transport that relies on carbon-based fuel generates CO_2, the main cause of human-induced climate change. Modern travel is dependent on aeroplanes, which might use less fuel per kilometre per person than most cars but travel much greater distances. The altitude at which aircraft emit gases (including CO_2) and particles also contributes to their climate change impact. Many websites offer 'carbon calculators' that allow people to estimate the carbon emissions generated by their journey and, for those who wish to do so, to offset the impact of the greenhouse gases emitted with contributions to portfolios of climate-friendly initiatives throughout the world. Lonely Planet offsets the carbon footprint of all staff and author travel.

ZAMYN-ÜÜD–ÈRLIÁN (EREEN) BORDER CROSSING

Most travellers end up in Èrlián in the middle of the night on the international through train. Zamyn-Üüd, on the Mongolian side, is not an interesting place, so you aren't missing anything if you are on the overnight train. For more info see p190.

Opening hours The Zamyn-Üüd–Èrlián crossing is open daily but note that on holidays only the train (not the road) crossing will operate. For vehicles the border is open 8am to 6pm.

Processing Mongolian customs and immigration officials take about two hours to do their stuff.

Walking It's not possible to walk across the border.

Change money If you have just come from Mongolia, change any remaining tögrög here or you'll be keeping it as a souvenir.

Onward travel Remember that if you are carrying on to the Chinese interior there is no need to go to Bëijing first. From Èrlián you can travel to the rail junction at Dàtóng and then catch trains or buses to Píngyáo, Xī'ān and points south. For western China and Tibet, get off at Jining where you can change to Hohhot, Lánzhōu and beyond. Read Lonely Planet's *China* guide for details on connections from these cities.

BULGAN–TAKASHIKEN BORDING CROSSING

After Zamyn-Üüd–Èrlián, the other main border crossing with China is in a remote corner of western Mongolia

where Bulgan (Khovd aimag) meets Takashiken (Xīnjiāng).

Opening hours This border is open year-round (except Mongolian and Chinese holidays) Monday to Friday from 9am to 6pm. The border can close for lunch so arrive as early as possible.

Processing Expect multiple passport checks on both sides of the border. On the Chinese side there are extensive bag searches and they will probably also want to inspect photos on your camera.

Walking Travellers are allowed to cross by foot and bicycle.

Bulgan The village of Bulgan is a 12-hour drive from Khovd so you need a full day just to get there from Khovd, plus another half-day to cross the border. The jeep to Bulgan (T30,000) departs in the afternoon from the jeep stand in Khovd. You can save time by flying directly to Bulgan (one way/return US$252/443) from Ulaanbaatar on Hunnu Airlines. However, the flight is on Friday afternoon so there isn't much time to get over the border before it shuts for the weekend. Bulgan has no hotel so you just need to ask your driver for a homestay, or camp. A taxi ride to the border from Bulgan should cost T5000 per person. The 30-minute ride is on a paved road.

Time difference Khovd is one hour behind Xīnjiāng.

Onward travel Once across the border into China, there are share taxis to Ürümqi (seven hours, Y250). Buses are also available for Y250, but these are slower and require at least one change.

Entering Mongolia If you are heading in the other direction (from China to Mongolia), there are two buses per day from Ürümqi to Qinghe (清河; 10 hours, Y140). From Qinghe, there are minivans and taxis to Takeshiken (塔克什肯; two hours, Y60), from where you can take a taxi to the border (20 minutes, Y20 per person). Once in Mongolia, find a shared vehicle to Bulgan and wait around for any vehicle continuing to Khovd.

CAR & MOTORCYCLE

As long as your papers are in order there is no trouble crossing the China–Mongolia border in your own car. Driving around Mongolia is a lot easier than China, where drivers require a guide and Chinese driving permit. For more details on driving in Mongolia, see p40.

JEEP

➡ Minivans shuttle between the train stations of Zamyn-Üüd and Èrlián. Either way the trip is Y50 for a seat in a jeep.

➡ When the train arrives in Zamyn-Üüd there is a frantic rush for minivans and then a jockeying for position at the border as Mongolian traders race to be the first into China for a full day of shopping. Note that the first jeeps charge about Y30 more than the ones in the back of the line.

➡ In Èrlián, jeeps assemble at the bus station and the market; ask the Mongolian drivers. There is a Y5 tax that you need to pay going either way (you can pay the driver in tögrög or yuan and they will pay the tax for you).

TRAIN

Mongolia has trains to both Russia and China. Getting a ticket in Ulaanbaatar can be very difficult during the summer tourist season, so you need to plan ahead.

Ticket office The yellow **International Railway Ticketing Office** (Narny Gudamj) is about 200m northwest of the train station. Inside the office, specific rooms sell tickets to Běijīng, Irkutsk (Russia), Moscow, and Èrlián and Hohhot (both in China), but as a foreigner you'll

be directed to a **foreigners' booking office** (☎21-24133, enquiries 21-243 848; room 212; ⊕8am-8pm Mon-Fri). It's upstairs and staff here speak some English. On weekends you can use the downstairs booking desk.

Buying tickets You'll need your passport to buy a ticket. You can book the ticket by phone for a T4500 booking fee. If you cancel a ticket there is a T1000 charge. There is no departure tax if travelling on the train.

Advance bookings You can book a ticket for international trains out of Ulaanbaatar up to one month in advance, but for

the Moscow–Běijīng or Běijīng–Moscow trains you will have to scramble for a ticket on the day before departure (although you could try asking two days in advance). If you have trouble booking a berth, ask your guesthouse manager or hotel reception desk for assistance.

Getting there In UB, a taxi between Chinggis Khaan (Sükhbaatar) Sq and the train station costs about T5000.

DIRECT TRAIN

Most travellers catch the direct train between Běijīng and Ulaanbaatar.

ÈRLIÁN (EREEN) MINI GUIDE

Overlanders heading to/from Mongolia may need to spend some time in Èrlián (二连; in Mongolian called Ereen or Ereen Khot), a small city (by Chinese standards) just over the border from Zamyn-Üüd.

You can kill some time by visiting the **Geological Museum** (地质博物馆, Dizhi Bowuguan), which contains a scattered collection of dinosaur bones. A taxi here costs Y30. Otherwise, there are some bustling markets around town built entirely for Mongolian traders.

If you are heading for Mongolia and need a visa, there is a **Mongolian consulate** (Menggu Lingshiguan; 蒙古领事馆; ☎+86-151-6497-1992; 1206 Youyi Beilu; ⊕8.30am-4.30pm Mon-Fri) in Èrlián. To find the consulate from the bus station, walk east half a block to the T-junction and make a left. Walk north along this road (Youyi Beilu) for 10 minutes until you see the Mongolian flags on your left. From the train station, walk west one block and at the first intersection turn right. Walk north on this road (Youyi Beilu) for 1.2km (15 to 20 minutes) until you see the Mongolian flag. A 30-day rush tourist visa (Y495) can be issued on the same day you apply; you'll need one passport-sized photo. A taxi can take you there for Y4.

The **Haifeng Hotel** (海丰大酒店; Haifeng Dajiudian; ☎0479 7515555; 2 Xinhua Jie; tw from Y378) is a reliable midrange hotel; you'll see it to the left as you walk out of the train station. There are some cheapies opposite the train station with rooms for about Y100.

The airport is 25km south of the city. Air China has a daily flight to/from Běijīng (Y540). MIAT and Air China have offered flights between Èrlián and Ulaanbaatar but schedules tend to be seasonal.

Getting same-day train tickets out of Èrlián is darn near impossible for Běijīng, so most people opt for the bus. The long-distance bus station is halfway between the consulate and the train station. From Èrlián there are buses to Běijīng (Y180 to Y220, 12 hours, five daily between 2.30pm and 4.30pm), Hohhot (Y95, six hours, seven daily between 8am and 1.30pm) and Dàtóng (Y120, six hours, one daily at 8.40am).

In Běijīng, buses depart/arrive at the Mùxīyuán bus station (木樨园汽车站; Mùxīyuán Qìchēzhàn). All buses to Èrlián leave around 4pm to 5pm so turn up by 3pm for a ticket. To reach Mùxīyuán bus station by subway take line five to Liujiayuan station, take Exit D, and walk straight for 1km. Just before the road goes under Mùxīyuán bridge bear left and then left again down Dahongmen Lu (大红门路); the bus station will be on your right after 500m. A taxi to/from the Drum Tower should cost around Y40; make sure to use genuine blue-and-yellow painted cabs that have a meter, and avoid the dodgy black cabs that won't use a meter.

TRAIN SCHEDULES TO/FROM MONGOLIA

Schedules change from one summer to another, and services reduce in winter, and can increase in summer. For fares see the tables on p284 and p285. K23 departures vary, see p284.

TRAIN	TRAIN NUMBER	DAY OF DEPARTURE	DEPARTURE TIME	DURATION FROM UB (HR)
China–Mongolia				
Běijīng-Ulaanbaatar	K23	Tue or Sat	8.03am	30
Běijīng-Ulaanbaatar	K23 (summer-only extra train)	Mon or Sat	8.03am	30
Běijīng-Ulaanbaatar-(Moscow)	K3	Wed	7.47am (varies)	30
Èrlián-Ulaanbaatar	21	Mon, Fri	5.10pm	14
Hohhot-Ulaanbaatar	33	Mon, Fri	9.31pm	37
Mongolia–China				
Ulaanbaatar-Běijīng	24 (year-round)	Thu or Mon	1.50pm	30
(Moscow)-Ulaanbaatar-Běijīng	4	Sun	7.15am	30
Ulaanbaatar-Èrlián	22	Thu, Sun	8pm	14
Ulaanbaatar-Hohhot	34	Mon, Fri	8pm	25
Mongolia–Russia				
Ulaanbaatar-Irkutsk	263	daily	9.10pm	36
Ulaanbaatar-Moscow	5	Tue, Fri	1.50pm	70
(Běijīng)-Ulaanbaatar-Moscow	K3	Thu	1.50pm	100
Russia–Mongolia				
Irkutsk-Ulaanbaatar	264	daily	7.10pm	36
Moscow-Ulaanbaatar	6	Wed, Thu	9pm	70
Moscow-Ulaanbaatar-(Běijīng)	4	Sun	7.55pm	100

→ There are two direct trains a week each way between Běijīng and Ulaanbaatar. One of these (K3 and 4) is the Trans-Mongolian Railway (see p46), which runs between Běijīng and Moscow. It's easier to get a ticket for the other train (K23 and 24).

→ The K23 changes its departure day each year (depending on whether it's run by China or Mongolia railways). The Chinese train typically departs Běijīng on Tuesday, while the Mongolian train typically departs Běijīng on Saturday. Note that the Chinese and Mongolians switch operating duties in May.

→ The K23 summer train is an extra train put on for the summer holiday season (it usually runs mid-June to early October). When operated by Mongolia it will most likely depart Běijīng on a Monday, when run by China it will most likely depart Běijīng on Saturday.

→ Train K23 passes through Dàtóng at approximately 2.15pm, Jíníng at 4.15pm, Èrlián at 8.45pm and Zamyn-Üüd at 11.45pm.

→ It is also possible to travel directly between Ulaanbaatar and Hohhot twice a week, allowing you to either bypass Běijīng completely or catch a train or flight (Y630) on to Běijīng from there.

→ Trains leave from **Běijīng Train Station** (📞 8610-5101 9999). If your luggage weighs more than 35kg, on the day before departure you'll have to take it to the Luggage Shipment Office, which is on the right-hand side of the station. The excess is charged at about US$11 per 10kg, with a maximum excess of 40kg allowed.

→ Tickets are sold at the **China International Travel Service** (CITS, Zhōngguó Guójì Lǚxíngshè; 📞 8610-6512 0507; 9 Jianguomennei Dajie, Běijīng International Hotel, Dōngchéng; 🕐 9am-noon & 1.30pm-5pm Mon-Fri, 9am-noon Sat-Sun). Tickets are also available at **BTG Travel & Tours** (📞 8610-6515 8010; Beijing Tourism

Bldg, 28 Jianguomenwai Dajie, btwn New Otani & Gloria Plaza hotels).

➡ With CITS it is possible to book one month in advance for trains originating in Běijīng, and you can collect your ticket from one week to one day before departure. A booking fee applies.

➡ CITS only sells tickets from Běijīng to Moscow or Ulaanbaatar – no stopovers are allowed. Tickets to Ulaanbaatar cost Y1067/1969 in hard/soft sleeper. Prices can change slightly depending on which country is operating the train.

➡ You can also buy train tickets privately; they will be more expensive than from CITS, but you may also be able to arrange a stopover and visas. In Běijīng, **Monkey Business Shrine** (☑8610-6591 6519; www.monkeyshrine.com; 27 Beisanlitun, bldg 2, room 202) can put together all kinds of stopovers and homestay programs. The company has a lot of experience in booking international trains for independent travellers. In Hong Kong, it goes under the name **Moonsky Star Ltd** (☑852-2723 1376; www. monkeyshrine.com; Flat D, 11th fl, Liberty Mansion, 26E Jordan Rd, Yau Ma Tei, Kowloon).

➡ Note that the Russian embassies in most countries only accept visa applications from official residents. So it's best to apply for your Russian visa in your home country (or country where

you have a residency card). Visa rules at the Russian embassy in Ulaanbaatar are relaxing a little for some nationalities but it's often the case that applications are handled on a case-by-case basis.

LOCAL TRAIN

If you're on a tight budget it's possible to take local trains between UB and Běijīng. This will save some money but involves more hassle and time. Unless you have booked your seats weeks in advance, the local train may be your only option during the peak summer travel period.

➡ The first option is train 21 or 22, which runs between Ulaanbaatar and Èrlián just inside China. Mongolian train 22 leaves Ulaanbaatar at 8pm on Thursday and Sunday and arrives in Èrlián at about 10.25am the next morning, after completing immigration and customs formalities. In reverse, train 21 leaves Èrlián on Monday and Friday evenings and arrives the next day. The schedules for this train change regularly.

➡ The second option is to take local trains to Zamyn-Üüd in Mongolia and then cross the border by minivan or jeep. From Èrlián you can go deeper into China by either train, bus or plane.

➡ From Běijīng, the local train for Jíníng departs at 11.42am and takes about nine hours. A second train departs at 9.20pm and continues to Hohhot. The train from Jíníng

to Èrlián departs around noon and takes six hours. (Alternatively, a 7am bus takes just four hours.) If you have to stay the night in Jíníng, there's a budget hotel on the right (south) side of the plaza as you walk out of the train station.

➡ If you need help with the logistics of train travel, a good contact is freelance guide **Daka Nyamdorj** (☑9984 4844; www. happymongolia.net), who specialises in tours by train.

Kazakhstan

At the time of writing a bus travelled between Bayan-Ölgii and Astana in Kazakhstan. See p212 for details.

Russia
BORDER CROSSINGS

Most travellers go in and out of Russia at the Naushki–Sükhbaatar train border crossing.

Naushki You can have a look around Naushki, but there is little to see and the train border crossing usually takes place in the middle of the night. Surprisingly, you may have difficulty finding anyone at the Naushki station to change money, so wait until Sükhbaatar or Ulaanbaatar, or somewhere else in Russia. (Get rid of your tögrög before you leave Mongolia, as almost no one will want to touch them once you are inside Russia.)

Sükhbaatar The train may stop for one or two hours at, or near, the pleasant Mongolian border town of Sükhbaatar. You may be able to buy some Russian roubles or Mongolian tögrög from

ULAANBAATAR–CHINA TRAIN FARES

Prices are for Chinese trains. Deluxe cars are not available on Mongolian trains. Mongolian trains are about 5% to 10% cheaper for 1st class. For schedules, see the table on p283.

DESTINATION	2ND CLASS HARD SLEEPER (T)	1ST CLASS SOFT SLEEPER (T)	DELUXE COUPE (T)
Běijīng	130,050	217,750	184,550
Dàtóng	113,250	188,450	160,250
Èrlián (Ereen)	80,050	131,350	111,650
Hohhot	118,150	166,650	

ULAANBAATAR–RUSSIA TRAIN FARES

Exact costs depend on whether the train is Russian, Chinese or Mongolian; we have listed the most expensive. For schedules, see the table on p283.

DESTINATION	2ND CLASS (T)	1ST CLASS (T)
Irkutsk	97,850	146,950
Krasnoyarsk	142,750	220,350
Moscow	266,250	445,050
Naushki	42,250	66,750
Novosibirsk	164,450	268,950
Omsk	183,450	301,650
Perm	226,350	373,950
Ulan Ude	64,150	99,050
Yekaterinburg	216,350	359,950

a moneychanger at the train station, but the rate will be poor. If there aren't any moneychangers, you can use US dollars cash to get by until you change money elsewhere.

Road crossings There are two road crossings: Tsagaannuur–Tashanta in Bayan-Ölgii aimag and Altanbulag–Kyakhta (near Sükhbaatar) in Selenge. The crossings are open from 9am to noon and 2pm to 6pm daily except holidays. The Khankh Mondy border in northern Khövsgöl and the Ereentsav–Solovyevsk crossing in Dornod are not open to third-country nationals.

Processing Both the road and rail crossings are slow but at least on the road journey you can get out and stretch your legs. Train travellers have been stranded for up to 10 hours on the Russian side, spending much of this time locked inside the train wagons. Procedures on the Ulaanbaatar–Moscow train are faster than on the local trains. Heading out of Russia, you will be asked to fill out a customs declaration form. You should note on the form how much currency you are taking out of the country.

BUS

Bus is probably the fastest form of public transport between Mongolia and Russia.

From Mongolia A daily bus operated by **Vostok Trans** (☎7011 0696) departs Ulaanbaatar

bound for Ulan Ude. It departs at 7.30am, and the journey takes 12 hours and costs T47,000. Buses leave from the parking lot in front of the train station. Tickets are sold inside the domestic railway ticket office on the 2nd floor. You can buy a ticket one week in advance.

To Mongolia An Ulan Ude bus (R1300) departs at the same time for Ulaanbaatar, leaving from the fountain/Opera House in Ulan Ude. In Ulan Ude contact **Trio-Impex** (☎3012-217 277; trio-tour@mail.ru) or **Buryat-Intour** (☎3012-216 954; www.buryatintour.ru; ul Kirova 28a).

CAR & MOTORCYCLE

It's possible to drive between Russia and Mongolia at Tsagaannuur (Bayan-Ölgii) and Altanbulag (Selenge). For more details on the classic Mongolian road trip, see p40.

Processing These road crossings can be difficult and time consuming – up to six hours if traffic is backed up or if you have visa problems.

Paperwork In order to speed things up, it may help to have a letter written by the Mongolian consular (or Russian consular if you are headed that way) when you get your visa. The letter should state that you are authorised to take a car or motorcycle across the border. A carnet (passport for your car) may be useful but is not necessary.

Walking Foreigners are currently not allowed to 'walk' across the Kyakhta–Altanbulag border, but they are allowed to pass through in a car or even on a motorcycle, so you may have to pay someone to drive you across.

TRAIN

Besides the Trans-Mongolian Railway (see p46) connecting Moscow and Běijīng, there is a direct train twice a week connecting Ulaanbaatar and Moscow, which is easier to book from Ulaanbaatar. The epic trip takes four days.

Lake Baikal If you are headed to Lake Baikal, there is a daily train between Ulaanbaatar and Irkutsk, which stops in Darkhan. These trains stop at every village, however, and train 263 travels past Lake Baikal at night, so if you are in a hurry or want to see the lake, take the Ulaanbaatar–Moscow train (5) as far as Irkutsk. Note that departure and arrival times at Irkutsk are given in Moscow time, although Irkutsk is actually five hours ahead of Moscow.

Staged travel This trip can be done more cheaply by travelling in stages on local trains (eg from Ulan Ude to Naushki, Naushki to Sükhbaatar, and Sükhbaatar to Ulaanbaatar). However, this route is covered much more quickly by shared taxi.

Tickets In Moscow you can buy tickets at the building on ulitsa Krasnoprudnaya 1, next door to the Yaroslavl train station, from where the trains to Ulaanbaatar and Bëijīng leave. **Unifest Travel** (☑495-234 6555; http://unifest.ru/en.html; Komsomolsky prospekt 16/2) in Moscow is a reliable travel agent that can sell train tickets on the Trans-Siberian Railway. A reliable agency in Ulan Ude is **Buryat-Intour** (☑3012-216 954; www. buryatintour.ru; ul Kirova 28a). In Irkutsk, you can try **Irkutsk Baikal Travel Inc** (☑3952-200 134; www.irkutsk-baikal. com; 1a Cheremhovsky Ln).

GETTING AROUND

Travelling around the countryside independently is the best way to see Mongolia and meet the people. Note that annual outbreaks of forest fires, the plague, foot-and-mouth disease and even cholera may affect your travel plans if there are quarantine restrictions.

Air

Mongolia, a vast, sparsely populated country with very little infrastructure, relies heavily on air transport. It has 44 functioning airports, although only 15 of these have paved airstrips.

Almost all of the destinations are served directly from Ulaanbaatar, so flying from, say, Dalanzadgad to Bayan-Ölgii is impossible without first returning to UB.

Airlines in Mongolia

AeroMongolia (☑in UB 011-330 373; www.aeromon-golia.mn) Operates two Fokker aircraft. Routes change but at last check it flew domestic services to Ölgii, Dalanzadgad, Mörön, Ulaangom, Gov-Altai and Khovd. It is really stingy on baggage allowance, allowing only 15kg (including hand luggage); any kilogram over the limit costs around T3000. Credit card and cash payments are accepted. AeroMongolia also serves Hohhot in China, and Irkutsk in Russia.

EZ Nis (☑in UB 7575 3232; www.eznisairways.com) Operates Swedish-built Saab 340B propeller aeroplanes. Has domestic flights to/from UB and Choibalsan, Mörön, Donoi (Uliastai), Ulaangom, Tosontsengel, Bayan-Ölgii, Dalanzadgad and Oyu Tolgoi. Schedules change frequently so check the website for the latest information. It's a slick and reliable operation, but more expensive than AeroMongolia.

Hunnu Airlines (☑in UB 7000 1111; www.hunnuair.com) Operates Fokker 50 and Airbus 319 aircraft. Domestic destinations include Donoi (Uliastai), Dalanzadgad, Khovd, Mörön, Choibalsan, Bayankhongor and Altai. It also flies to Bulgan *sum* in southern Khovd aimag.

MIAT (☑in UB 011-333 999; www.miat.com) The state-owned airline that once flew to every corner of the country. It no longer operates any domestic routes.

Checking In

Get to the airport at least one hour before your flight. Even if you have a ticket, flight number and an allocated seat number, don't assume the plane won't be over-booked. Try to make certain your luggage has gone on the plane. Gas canisters are not allowed on any flight.

Costs

➡ AeroMongolia seems to have the best deals on domestic flights; a one-way fare to Dalanzadgad costs US$112 while a flight to Bayan-Ölgii goes for about US$185. This is good value, considering the overland alternative to Ölgii is a 50-hour trip in an overstuffed van.

➡ Children aged between five and 16 years pay half; under fives fly free. If you've come on a student visa you can get 25% to 50% off the cost of the ticket. Ticket fares may increase during the summer holiday season.

➡ Ask about baggage allowances when you buy your aeroplane ticket. EZ Nis allows you to carry 20kg without extra charges.

Reservations & Tickets

E-tickets It's now possible to buy a domestic airline e-ticket with Mongolia's domestic carriers (EZ Nis, Hunnu, and AeroMongolia). Airlines can usually hold a reservation for two or three days.

One-way tickets If you wish to fly in one direction and return by road in the other (for example to Mörön), it's best to fly from Ulaanbaatar, where you are more likely to get a ticket and a seat, and then return overland – otherwise you may wait days or more for a flight and ticket in Mörön.

Peak seasons Seats can be difficult to get in summer, especially in the July tourist peak and in late August as students return to college. Book flights as soon as you can.

Bicycle

For keen cyclists with a sense of adventure, Mongolia offers an unparalleled cycling experience. The vast, open steppes make for rough travel but if properly equipped there is nothing stopping you from travelling pretty much anywhere (although a trip to the Gobi could only be done with vehicle support). For more information on cycle touring, see p32.

Boat

Although there are 397km of navigable waterways in Mongolia, rivers aren't used for transporting people or cargo. The biggest boat in the country is the *Sükhbaatar*, which occasionally travels around Khövsgöl Nuur. Some ger camps at Khövsgöl Nuur also own small boats that can be chartered.

Bus

Private bus companies connect Ulaanbaatar to the other aimag capitals. Large buses that can accommodate 40-plus passengers make a daily run to most cities. However, cities in the far west such Bayan-Ölgii and Uvs are served by minivans less frequently.

The benefit of the regularly scheduled buses and vans is that they leave on time and drive straight to their destination, as opposed to private vans, which run on 'Mongolian time' (ie whenever they have crammed in enough passengers). With the government buses you also get an assigned seat.

However, the private buses have their share of discomforts. One problem is that there seems to be no restriction on luggage, so boxes and bags tend to pile up in the aisles, which makes getting on and off the bus at breaks a real chore. Try getting a seat closer to the front of the bus to avoid the pile. Note that in winter, the heater will be turned to maximum, which is fine if you're up front or in the back (the heater is in the middle). However, if you are unfortunate enough to get the seat over the heater it will feel like you are hovering over a blast furnace. No matter what time of year it is, the driver will probably crank up the music. This is bearable for an hour or two but if you want to get some sleep (or maintain sanity) consider bringing noise-cancelling headphones.

Camel & Yak

➡ Intractable yaks and confrontational camels are recognised forms of transport in Mongolia. Camels can carry the weight of an average-sized sumo wrestler. Yaks are also a useful and environmentally

friendly way of hauling heavy cargo.

➡ At Ongiin Khiid and Khongoryn Els you can arrange camel treks. A few travel agencies include a ride on a camel or yak in their program. Otherwise, you can always ask at a ger.

Hitching

Hitching is never entirely safe, and we don't recommend it. Travellers who hitch should understand that they are taking a small but potentially serious risk. Hitchers will be safer if they travel in pairs and let someone know where they are planning to go.

Hitching in Mongolia Because public transport is so limited, hitching (usually on trucks) is a recognised – and, often, the only – form of transport in the

Mongolian countryside. Hitching is seldom free and often no different from just waiting for public transport to turn up. It is *always* slow; after stopping at gers to drink, fixing flat tyres, breaking down, running out of petrol and getting stuck in mud and rivers, a truck can take 48 hours to cover 200km.

Hazards Hitching is not generally dangerous personally, but it is still hazardous (because getting stranded in remote areas is a real possibility) and often extremely uncomfortable. Don't expect much traffic in remote rural areas; you might see one or two vehicles a day and sometimes nobody at all for several days. In the towns, ask at the market, where trucks invariably hang around, or at the bus/truck/jeep station. The best place to wait is the petrol station on the outskirts of town, where most vehicles stop before any journey.

TAKING A GPS

When travelling around the featureless plains, a global positioning system (GPS) can be very useful in determining where exactly you are, as long as you have a reliable map on which to pinpoint your coordinates. We have given GPS coordinates for many hard-to-find places in reviews, plus coordinates for *sum* (district) and aimag centres.

A GPS won't help you every time, as you'll still need to know which road to take, even if you know the rough direction. Every few kilometres the track you're on will veer off in the wrong direction, requiring constant corrections and zigzagging.

Most smartphones also have GPS capability (and you can download GPS navigation apps). But be aware that the coordinates displayed on a mobile phone (which uses mobile-phone towers to determine a location) are less accurate than those given by a dedicated GPS unit (which uses satellites).

It is always a good idea to ask about road conditions at gers along the way. Often a good-looking road will become impassable, running into a river, swamp or wall of mountains; herders can offer good info on the best route to take.

If all else fails, you can always rely on Mongolian GPS (ger positioning system), which requires following the vague sweep of the ger-owner's hand over the horizon, until you reach the next ger.

The table shows latitude and longitude coordinates for various locations in Mongolia, in degrees, minutes and decimal minutes (DMM). To convert to degrees, minutes and seconds (DMS) format, multiply the number after the decimal point (including the decimal point) by 60. The result is your seconds, which can be rounded to the nearest whole number. The minutes is the number between the degree symbol and the decimal point. For example: 43°52.598' DMM is equal to 43°52'36" DMS.

CENTRAL MONGOLIA	Latitude (N)	Longitude (E)
Arvaikheer	46°15.941	102°46.724
Bat-Ölzii	46°49.028	102°13.989
Battsengel	47°48.157	101°59.040
Bayan-Öndör	46°30.018	104°05.996
Bayan Önjuul	46°52.859	105°56.571
Bayangol	45°48.505	103°26.811
Bayantsagaan	46°45.806	107°08.709
Bogd	44°39.971	102°08.777
Burenbayan Ulaan	45°10.276	101°25.989
Chuluut	47°32.830	100°13.166
Delgerkhan	46°37.097	104°33.051
Eej Khad (Mother Rock)	47°18.699	106°58.583
Erdenemandal	48°31.445	101°22.265
Erdenesant	47°19.071	104°28.937
Guchin Us	45°27.866	102°23.726
Gunjiin Süm	48°11.010	107°33.377
Ikh Tamir	47°35.221	101°12.413
Jargalant	48°43.716	100°45.120
Khandgait	48°07.066	106°54.296
Khangai	47°51.553	99°26.126
Kharkhorin	47°11.981	102°50.527
Khashant	47°27.034	103°09.708
Khotont	47°22.196	102°28.746
Khujirt	46°54.225	102°46.545
Khustain National Park	47°45.459	105°52.418
Mandshir Khiid	47°45.520	106°59.675
Möngönmorit	48°12.192	108°28.291
Naiman Nuur	46°31.232	101°50.705
Ögii Nuur (Lake)	47°47.344	102°45.828
Ögii Nuur	47°40.319	102°33.051
Ölziit	48°05.573	102°32.640
Ondor Ulaan	48°02.700	100°30.446
Orkhon Khürkhree	46°47.234	101°57.694
Övgön Khiid	47°25.561	103°41.686
Stele of Tonyukuk	47°41.661	107°28.586
Tariat	48°09.574	99°52.982
Terelj	47°59.193	107°27.834
Tögrög	45°32.482	102°59.657
Tövkhön Khiid	47°00.772	102°15.362
Tsakhir	49°06.426	99°08.574
Tsenkher	47°26.909	101°45.648
Tsetseguun Uul	47°48.506	107°00.165
Tsetserleg City	47°28.561	101°27.282
Tsetserleg Soum	48°53.095	101°14.305
Ulaanbaatar	47°55.056	106°55.007
Uyanga	46°27.431	102°16.731
Zaamar	48°11.843	104°46.629
Züünbayan-Ulaan	46°31.176	102°34.971
Zuunmod	47°42.357	106°56.861

EASTERN MONGOLIA	Latitude (N)	Longitude (E)
Asgat	46°21.724	113°34.536
Baldan Baraivun Khiid	48°11.910	109°25.840
Baruun-Urt	46°40.884	113°16.825
Batnorov	47°56.952	111°30.103
Batshireet	48°41.405	110°11.062
Bayan Tumen	48°03.076	114°22.252
Bayan Uul	49°07.550	112°42.809
Bayandun	49°15.276	113°21.565
Binder	48°36.967	110°36.400
Chinggis Statue	47°06.157	109°09.356
Choibalsan	48°04.147	114°31.404
Chuluunkhoroot	49°52.163	115°43.406
Dadal	49°01.291	111°37.598
Dashbalbar	49°32.794	114°24.720
Delgerkhaan	47°10.735	109°11.423
Erdenetsagaan	45°54.165	115°22.149
Galshar	46°13.324	110°50.606
Khalkhgol	47°59.565	118°05.760
Khalzan	46°10.019	112°57.119
Kherlen Bar Khot	48°03.287	113°21.865
Khökh Nuur (Blue Lake)	48°01.150	108°56.450
Matad	46°57.007	115°16.008
Mönkh Khaan	46°58.163	112°03.418
Norovlin	48°41.449	111°59.596
Öglöchiin Kherem	48°24.443	110°11.812
Ömnödelger	47°53.469	109°49.166
Chinggis Khot (Öndörkhaan)	47°19.416	110°39.775
Ongon	45°21.509	113°08.297
Shiliin Bogd	45°28.350	114°35.349
Sükhbaatar	46°46.285	113°52.646
Sümber	47°38.174	118°36.421
Tsagaan Ovoo	48°33.864	113°14.380
Tsenkhermandal	47°44.673	109°03.909
Uul Bayan	46°30.036	112°20.769

NORTHERN MONGOLIA	Latitude (N)	Longitude (E)
Altanbulag	50°19.225	106°29.392
Amarbayasgalant Khiid	49°28.672	105°05.121
Arbulag	49°54.949	99°26.537
Baruunburen	49°09.753	104°48.686
Bayangol	48°55.472	106°05.486
Borsog	50°59.677	100°42.983
Bugat	49°02.874	103°40.389
Bulgan City	48°48.722	103°32.213
Chandman-Öndör	50°28.436	100°56.378
Chuluut and Ider	49°10.415	100°40.335
Darkhan	49°29.232	105°56.480
Dashchoinkhorlon Khiid	48°47.821	103°30.687
Dashinchilen	47°51.179	104°02.281
Dulaankhaan	49°55.103	106°11.302
Erdenebulgan	50°06.880	101°35.589
Erdenet	49°01.855	104°03.316
Five Rivers	49°15.475	100°40.385
Gurvanbulag	47°44.499	103°30.103

	Latitude (N)	Longitude (E)
Jiglegiin Am	51°00.406	100°16.003
Khangal	49°18.810	104°22.629
Khankh	51°30.070	100°41.382
Khar Bukh Balgas	47°53.198	103°53.513
Khatgal	50°26.517	100°09.599
Khishig-Öndör	48°17.678	103°27.086
Khötöl	49°05.486	105°34.903
Khutag-Öndör	49°22.990	102°41.417
Mogod	48°16.372	102°59.520
Mörön	49°38.143	100°09.321
Orkhon	49°08.621	105°24.891
Orkhontuul	48°49.202	104°49.920
Renchinlkhumbe	51°06.504	99°40.234
Saikhan	48°39.448	102°37.851
Selenge	49°26.647	103°58.903
Shine-Ider	48°57.213	99°32.297
Sükhbaatar	50°14.196	106°11.911
Teshig	49°57.649	102°35.657
Toilogt	50°39.266	100°14.961
Tosontsengel	49°28.650	100°53.074
Tsagaan Uur	50°32.391	101°31.806
Tsagaannuur (Khövsgöl)	51°21.778	99°21.082
Isagaannuur (Selenge)	50°05.835	105°25.989
Tsetserleg	49°31.959	97°46.011
Ulaan Uul	50°40.668	99°13.920
Uran Uul	48°59.855	102°44.003
Züünkharaa	48°51.466	106°27.154

THE GOBI	Latitude (N)	Longitude (E)
Altai City	46°22.388	96°15.164
Altai Soum	44°37.010	94°55.131
Altanshiree	45°32.046	110°27.017
Baatsagaan	45°33.266	99°26.188
Baga Gazryn Chuluu	46°13.827	106°04.192
Bayan Dalai	43°27.898	103°30.763
Bayan-Ovoo	42°58.607	106°06.994
Bayan-Uul	46°59.129	95°11.863
Bayanbulag	46°48.223	98°06.189
Bayangovi	44°44.017	100°23.476
Bayankhongor	46°11.637	100°43.115
Bayanlig	44°32.555	100°49.809
Bayanzag	44°08.311	103°43.667
Biger	45°42.583	97°10.354
Bömbogor	46°12.279	99°37.234
Böön Tsagaan Nuur	45°37.114	99°15.350
Bugat	45°33.440	94°20.571
Bulgan	44°05.312	103°32.297
Buutsagaan	46°10.411	98°41.637
Choir	45°47.994	109°18.462
Dalanzadgad	43°34.355	104°25.673
Delger	46°21.074	97°22.011
Delgerekh	45°48.157	111°12.823
Erdenedalai	46°00.418	104°56.996
Erdentsogt	46°25.080	100°49.234
Galuut	46°42.061	100°07.131
Govi-Ugtal	46°01.916	107°30.377
Gurj Lamiin Khiid	43°29.030	103°50.930
Gurvantes	43°13.759	101°03.360
Jargalant	47°01.480	99°30.103
Khamaryn Khiid	44°36.038	110°16.650
Khanbogd	43°12.000	107°11.862
Khatanbulag	43°08.882	109°08.709
Khökhmorit	47°21.248	94°30.446
Khövsgöl	43°36.314	109°39.017
Khüreemaral	46°24.523	98°17.037
Mandakh	44°24.122	108°13.851

	Latitude (N)	Longitude (E)
Mandal-Ovoo	44°39.100	104°02.880
Mandalgov	45°46.042	106°16.380
Manlai	44°04.441	106°51.703
Nomgon	42°50.160	105°08.983
Ondorshil	45°13.585	108°15.223
Ongiin Khiid	45°20.367	104°00.306
Orog Nuur	45°02.692	100°36.314
Saikhan-Ovoo	45°27.459	103°54.110
Sainshand	44°53.576	110°08.351
Sevrei	43°35.617	102°09.737
Shinejist	44°32.917	99°17.349
Süm Khökh Burd	46°09.621	105°45.590
Taihshir	46°42.671	96°29.623
Takhi Research Station	45°32.197	93°39.055
Tsagaan Agui	44°42.604	101°10.187
Tseel	45°33.266	95°51.223
Tsogt	45°20.813	96°37.166
Tsogt-Ovoo	44°24.906	105°19.406
Tsogttsetsii	43°43.541	105°35.040
Ulaanbadrakh	43°52.598	110°24.686
Yolyn Am	43°29.332	104°04.000
Zag	46°56.168	99°09.806
Zamyn-Üüd	43°42.967	111°54.651

WESTERN MONGOLIA	Latitude (N)	Longitude (E)
Altai	45°49.115	92°15.497
Altantsögts	49°02.700	100°26.057
Batuunturuun	49°38.578	94°23.177
Bulgan (Bayan-Ölgii)	46°55.559	91°04.594
Bulgan (Khovd)	46°05.486	91°32.571
Chandmani	47°40.100	92°48.411
Darvi	46°56.181	93°37.158
Deluun	47°51.553	90°44.160
Dörgön	48°19.768	92°37.303
Erdeneburen	48°30.131	91°26.811
Erdenkhairkhan	48°07.228	95°44.229
Khökh Nuur	47°37.207	97°20.546
Khovd (Uvs)	49°16.720	90°54.720
Khovd City	48°00.430	91°38.474
Mankhan	47°24.557	92°12.617
Möst	46°41.626	92°48.000
Naranbulag	49°23.164	92°34.286
Nogoonuur	49°36.923	90°13.577
Ölgii (Uvs)	49°01.306	92°00.411
Ölgii City	48°58.070	89°58.028
Öndörkhangai	49°15.849	94°51.154
Otgon	47°12.488	97°36.391
Sagsai	48°54.688	89°39.429
Telmen	48°38.197	97°09.900
Tes	49°39.013	95°49.029
Tolbo	48°24.557	90°16.457
Tolbo Nuur	48°35.320	90°04.536
Tosontsengel	48°45.286	98°05.992
Tsagaanchuluut	47°06.531	96°39.497
Tsagaankhairkhan	49°24.209	94°13.440
Tsagaannuur	49°31.437	89°46.697
Tsengel	48°57.213	89°09.257
Tsenkheriin Agui	47°20.828	91°57.225
Tüdevtei	48°59.390	96°32.229
Ulaangom	49°58.764	92°04.028
Ulaankhus	49°02.525	89°26.929
Uliastai	47°44.591	96°50.582
Urgamal	48°30.653	94°16.046
Üüreg Nuur	50°05.236	91°04.587
Zavkhan (Uvs)	48°49.463	93°06.103
Zavkhanmandal	48°19.071	95°06.789

Limitations If you rely on hitching entirely, you will just travel from one dreary aimag town to another. You still need to hire a jeep to see, for example, the Gobi Desert, the mountains in Khentii or some of the lakes in the far west.

Payment Truck drivers will normally expect some negotiable payment, which won't be much cheaper than a long-distance bus or shared jeep; figure on around T5000 per hour travelled.

Bring Take a water- and dust-proof bag to put your backpack in. The most important things to bring, though, are an extremely large amount of patience and time, and a high threshold for discomfort. Carry camping gear for the inevitable breakdowns, or suffer along with your travel mates.

Local Transport

Bus, Minibus & Trolleybus

In Ulaanbaatar, crowded trolleybuses and buses ply the main roads for T200 to T400 a ride. Cities such as Darkhan and Erdenet have minibuses that shuttle from one end of town to the other, but you are unlikely to need them because most facilities are located centrally.

Minivan & Jeep

Both minivans and jeeps are used for long- and short-distance travel in the countryside. They can be shared among strangers, which is good for a group of people headed from one aimag centre to another (or usually to/from Ulaanbaatar). Alternatively, they can be hired privately.

Furgon minivans In most cases, the grey 11-seat Furgon minivans are used for longer cross-country trips that see a lot of traffic. Jeeps, khaki-coloured or green, are found in more-remote areas such as *sum* (district) centres. They are nicknamed *jaran yös* (shortened to *jaris*), which means '69' – the number of the original model.

Toyota Land Cruisers The large and comfortable Toyota Land Cruiser–style jeeps are owned by wealthy Mongolians and never used for share purposes (though some travel agencies might have them for hire, but expect to pay at least 30% more than for a good Russian jeep).

Travelling speed Jeeps and minivans are an important form of local transport, and them because most facilities are located centrally.

are mandatory when visiting more-remote attractions. They can typically only travel between 30km/h and 50km/h. The Gobi region generally has the best roads and here you can average 60km/h.

Share Minivan & Jeep

Share jeeps and minivans are the most common form of public transport in Mongolia.

Destinations Private vehicles go from Ulaanbaatar to all aimag capitals, major cities and tourist destinations. Less frequent and reliable services operate between most aimag capitals, but very few jeeps go to the *sums*.

Bring For a long-distance trip bring snacks and water; stops at a roadside *guanz* (canteen or cheap restaurant) can be few and far between.

Breakdowns You can expect at least one breakdown and it would be a good idea to bring a sleeping bag and warm clothes just in case you have to spend the night somewhere.

Discomfort Long-distance travel of over 10 hours is fiendishly uncomfortable. Most people who take a long-distance minivan to Mörön or Dalanzadgad end up flying back.

Cost Minivan or jeep fares are usually about 10% more than a bus fare, largely because they can drive faster than a bus.

Postal vans In the countryside, the post office operates postal vans, which accept passengers. They have fixed departure times, normally running once a week between an aimag capital and a *sum* capital. The local post office should have a list of departure times and fares.

HIRING A MINIVAN OR JEEP

The best way to see the countryside of Mongolia independently is to hire your own minivan or jeep, which will come with a driver and, for a little extra, a guide. If you share the costs with others it doesn't work out to be too expensive. For details on hiring your own vehicle, see the Organised Tours

---

THE MINIVAN WAITING GAME

A real problem with share vehicles is that they are privately operated and won't leave until they are packed tighter than a sardine tin. The waiting game sometimes has the effect of turning your hair grey.

In the countryside, most vans just park at the local market and wait for passengers to turn up, which means that if the van isn't already mostly full you'll be waiting around all day for the seats to fill up, if they ever do.

Typically, even after the 11-seat van has 20 or so passengers, the driver will vanish for an hour or two for lunch, or to find more cargo, spare parts and petrol.

One solution is to ask the driver to pick you up at your hotel or the local internet cafe when they are ready to go, which they usually agree to. If you have a mobile phone, give the driver your number and they will call you when they are ready to go.

The waiting time from Ulaanbaatar isn't as bad, but you can still count on two hours or more.

chapter on p35, and for planning your trip see our Road Trip chapter on p40.

Taxi

Mongolia claims to have about 49,250km of highway – of which only around 5000km is actually paved. Taxis are only useful along these paved roads, eg from Ulaanbaatar north to Darkhan, Erdenet and Bulgan; west to Kharkhorin, Tsetserleg and Bayankhongor; south to Mandalgov, Sainshand and Zamyn-Üüd; and east to Chinggis Khot (Öndörkhaan). However, most sights worth seeing lie a considerable distance from the main roads, so even short trips require some off-roading. It should raise a red flag in your mind if a freelance guide tells you it's OK to tour the countryside in his brother's Toyota Prius taxi.

Train

Lines The 1810km of railway line is primarily made up of the Trans-Mongolian Railway, connecting China with Russia. In addition, there are two spur lines: to the copper-mining centre of Erdenet (from Darkhan) and the coal-mining city of Baganuur (from Ulaanbaatar). Another train runs weekly from Choibalsan, the capital of Dornod aimag, to the Russian border.

Services From Ulaanbaatar, daily express trains travel north to Darkhan, and on to Sükhbaatar or Erdenet. To the south, there are daily direct trains from Ulaanbaatar to Zamyn-Üüd, via Choir and Sainshand. You can't use the Trans-Mongolian Railway for domestic transport.

Food The food available on the local trains is usually of poor quality so it's best to bring snacks, fruit and instant noodles.

Booking If you're travelling from Ulaanbaatar, it is important to book a soft seat in advance – this can be done 60 days before departure. There is a small booking fee of T1000. In general, booking ahead is a good idea for any class, though there will almost always be hard-seat tickets available. In summer, just getting a ticket on your own is difficult and will require standing in long lines. Your guesthouse or hotel can usually purchase the ticket for you, saving lots of headaches. For inquiries call the train station on ☎21-24137 (Mongolian only).

Getting a seat When travelling in hard-seat class, you will almost certainly have to fight to get a seat. If you're not travelling alone, one of you can scramble on board and find seats and the other can bring the luggage on board.

CLASSES

There are usually three classes on domestic passenger trains: hard seat, hard sleeper and soft seat.

Hard seat In hard-seat class, the seats are actually padded bunks but there are no assigned bunks or any limit to the amount of tickets sold, so the carriages are always crowded and dirty.

Hard sleeper Called *platzkartnuu*, this looks just like the hard seat but everyone gets their own bunk and there is the option of getting a set of sheets and a blanket (T1000). Upgrades are available to soft seat if you decide you can't stand the hard seats.

Soft seat These are only a little bit softer, but the conditions are much better: the price difference (usually at least double the price of the hard seat) is prohibitive for most Mongolians. The soft-seat carriages are divided into compartments with four beds in each. You are given an assigned bed, and will be able to sleep, assuming, of course, that your compartment mates aren't riproaring drunk and noisy. If you travel at night, clean sheets are provided for about T1100, which is a wise investment since some of the quilts smell like mutton. Compared with hard-seat class, it's the lap of luxury, and worth paying extra.

Health

Mongolia's dry, cold climate and sparse human habitation means there are few of the infectious diseases that plague tropical countries in Asia. The rough-and-tumble landscape and lifestyle, however, presents challenges of its own. Injuries sustained from falling off a horse are common in the summer season. In winter, the biggest threats are the flu and pneumonia, which spread like wildfire in November. If you do become seriously ill in Mongolia, your local embassy can provide details of Western doctors. Serious emergencies may require evacuation to Seoul or Běijīng. If in the countryside, make a beeline for Ulaanbaatar to have your ailment diagnosed. The advice here is a general guide only; be sure to seek the advice of a doctor trained in travel medicine.

BEFORE YOU GO

Prevention is the key to staying healthy while abroad. A little planning before departure, particularly for pre-existing illnesses, will save trouble later. See your dentist before going on a long trip, carry a spare pair of contact lenses and glasses, and take your optical prescription with you. Bring medications in their original, clearly labelled containers. A signed and dated letter from your physician describing your medical conditions and medications, including generic names, is also a good idea. Western medicine can be in short supply in Mongolia. Most medicine comes from China and Russia, and the labels won't be in English, so bring whatever you think you might need from home. Take extra supplies of prescribed medicine and divide it into separate pieces of luggage; that way if one piece goes astray, you'll still have a back-up supply.

Insurance

Adequate cover If your health insurance does not cover you for medical expenses abroad, consider supplemental insurance. Check the Lonely Planet (www.lonelyplanet.com/travel-insurance) site for more information.

Payment policy While you may prefer a policy that pays hospital bills on the spot, rather than paying first and sending in documents later, the only place in Mongolia that might accept this is the SOS Medica clinic (p91).

Pre-existing conditions Declare any existing medical conditions to the insurance company; if your problem is pre-existing, the company will not cover you if it is not declared.

Adventurous activities You may require extra cover for adventurous activities – make sure you are covered for a fall if you plan on riding a horse or a motorbike. If you are uninsured, emergency evacuation is expensive, with bills over US$100,000 not uncommon.

Medical Checklist

Following is a list of items you should consider including in your medical kit – consult your pharmacist for brands available in your country.

➡ Antibacterial cream (eg Muciprocin)

➡ Antibiotics (prescription only) – for travel well off the beaten track; carry the prescription with you in case you need it refilled

➡ Antifungal cream or powder (eg Clotrimazole) – for fungal skin infections and thrush

➡ Antinausea medication (eg Prochlorperazine)

➡ Antiseptic (such as povidone-iodine) – for cuts and grazes

➡ Aspirin or paracetamol (acetaminophen in the USA) – for pain or fever

➡ Bandages, Band-Aids (plasters) and other wound dressings

➡ Calamine lotion, sting-relief spray or aloe vera – to ease irritation from sunburn and insect bites or stings

➡ Cold and flu tablets, throat lozenges and nasal decongestant

➡ Insect repellent (DEET-based)

➡ Loperamide or diphenoxylate – 'blockers' for diarrhoea

➡ Multivitamins – consider them for long trips, when

REQUIRED & RECOMMENDED VACCINATIONS

Ask your doctor for an International Certificate of Vaccination (otherwise known as the yellow booklet), which will list all of the vaccinations you have received, and take it with you. The World Health Organization (WHO) recommends the following vaccinations for travel to Mongolia:

Adult Diphtheria & Tetanus Single booster recommended if none in the previous 10 years. Side effects include sore arm and fever.

Hepatitis A Provides almost 100% protection for up to a year; a booster after 12 months provides at least another 20 years' protection. Mild side effects such as headache and a sore arm occur with some people.

Hepatitis B Now considered routine for most travellers, it provides lifetime protection for 95% of people. Immunisation is given as three doses over six months, though a rapid schedule is also available, as is a combined vaccination for Hepatitis A. Side effects are mild and uncommon, usually headache and a sore arm.

Measles, Mumps & Rubella (MMR) Two doses of MMR are recommended unless you have had the diseases. Occasionally a rash and flu-like illness can develop a week after receiving the vaccine. Many young adults need a booster.

Typhoid Recommended unless your trip is less than a week. The vaccine offers around 70% protection, lasts for two to three years and comes as a single dose. Tablets are also available, although the injection is usually recommended, as it has fewer side effects. A sore arm and fever may occur.

Varicella If you haven't had chickenpox discuss this vaccination with your doctor.

The following are recommended for long-term travellers (more than one month) or those at special risk:

Influenza A single jab lasts one year and is recommended for those over 65 years of age or with underlying medical conditions such as heart or lung disease.

Pneumonia A single injection with a booster after five years is recommended for all travellers over 65 years of age or with underlying medical conditions that compromise immunity, such as heart or lung disease, cancer or HIV.

Rabies Three injections are required. A booster after one year will then provide 10 years' protection. Side effects are rare – occasionally headache and a sore arm.

Tuberculosis (TB) A complex issue. High-risk, adult, long-term travellers are usually recommended to have a TB skin test before and after travel, rather than a vaccination. Only one vaccine is given in a lifetime. Children under five spending more than three months in China and/or Mongolia should be vaccinated.

---

dietary vitamin intake may be inadequate

➡ Rehydration mixture (eg Gastrolyte) – to prevent dehydration, which may occur during bouts of diarrhoea (particularly important when travelling with children)

➡ Scissors, tweezers and a thermometer – note that mercury thermometers are prohibited by airlines

➡ Sunscreen, lip balm and eye drops

➡ Water purification tablets or iodine (iodine is not to be used by pregnant women or people with thyroid problems)

Websites

Lonely Planet (www.lonely-planet.com) For further information this is a good place to start.

World Health Organization (www.who.int/ith) The WHO publishes a superb book called *International Travel &*

Health, which is revised annually and is available online at no cost.

MD Travel Health (www.mdtravelhealth.com) Another website of general interest which provides complete travel health recommendations for every country and is updated daily.

Further Reading

Healthy Travel Asia & India Lonely Planet's handy pocket-sized health guide.

Traveller's Health by Dr Richard Dawood.

Travelling Well by Dr Deborah Mills (www.travellingwell.com.au).

Travel with Children Lonely Planet guide useful for families.

IN MONGOLIA

Availability & Cost of Health Care

Advice Health care is readily available in Ulaanbaatar, but choose your hospital and doctor carefully. Ordinary Mongolians won't know the best place to go, but a reputable travel agency or top-end hotel might. The best advice will come from your embassy.

Cost Consultations cost around US$5, although SOS Medica (p91), a reliable clinic in Ulaanbaatar with Western doctors, charges around US$195.

Medication Most basic drugs are available without a prescription.

Regional areas Health services in the countryside are generally poor but improving in some aimag capitals. Taking very small children to the countryside is therefore risky.

Women's health Female travellers will need to take pads and tampons with them, as these won't be available outside the main cities.

Infectious Diseases

Brucellosis

➡ The most likely way for humans to contract this disease is by drinking unboiled milk or eating homemade cheese. People with open cuts on their hands who handle freshly killed meat can also be infected.

➡ In humans, brucellosis causes severe headaches, joint and muscle pains, fever and fatigue. There may be diarrhoea and, later, constipation.

➡ The onset of the symptoms can occur from five days to several months after exposure, with the average time being two weeks.

➡ Most patients recover in two or three weeks, but people can get chronic brucellosis, which recurs sporadically for months or years and can cause long-term health problems. Fatalities are rare but possible.

➡ Brucellosis is a serious disease and requires blood tests to make the diagnosis. If you think you may have contracted the disease, seek medical attention, preferably outside Mongolia.

Bubonic Plague

➡ This disease (which wiped out one-third of Europe during the Middle Ages) makes an appearance in remote parts of Mongolia in late summer. Almost 90% of reported cases occur in August and September.

➡ The disease (also known as the Black Plague) is normally carried by rodents and can be transmitted to humans by bites from fleas that make their home on the infected animals. It can also be passed from human to human by coughing.

➡ The symptoms are fever and enlarged lymph nodes. The untreated disease has a 60% death rate, but if you get to a doctor it can be quickly treated.

➡ The best (but not only) drug is the antibiotic Gentamicin, which is available in Mongolia.

➡ During an outbreak, travel to infected areas is prohibited, which can greatly affect overland travel. All trains, buses and cars travelling into Ulaanbaatar from infected areas are also thoroughly checked when an outbreak of the plague has been reported, and vehicles are sprayed with disinfectant.

Hepatitis

➡ This is a general term for inflammation of the liver.

➡ The symptoms are similar in all forms of the illness, and include fever, chills, headache, fatigue and aches, followed by loss of appetite, nausea, vomiting, abdominal pain, dark urine, light-coloured faeces, jaundiced (yellow) skin and yellowing of the whites of the eyes.

➡ People who have hepatitis should avoid alcohol for some time after the illness, as the liver needs time to recover.

➡ Hepatitis A is transmitted by contaminated food and drinking water. You should seek medical advice, but there is not much you can do apart from resting, drinking lots of fluids, eating lightly and avoiding fatty foods.

➡ Hepatitis E is transmitted in the same way as hepatitis A; it can be particularly serious in pregnant women.

➡ Hepatitis B is endemic in Mongolia. It is spread through contact with infected blood, blood products or body fluids. The symptoms of hepatitis B may be more severe than type A and the disease can lead to long-term problems such as chronic liver damage, liver cancer or long-term carrier status.

➡ Hepatitis C and D are spread in the same way as hepatitis B and can also lead to long-term complications.

➡ There are vaccines against hepatitis A and B, but there are currently no vaccines against the other types of hepatitis.

Rabies

➡ In the Mongolian countryside, family dogs are often vicious and can be rabid; it is their saliva that is infectious.

➡ Any bite, scratch or even a lick from an animal should be cleaned immediately and thoroughly. Scrub with soap and running water, and then apply alcohol or iodine solution.

➡ Seek medical help promptly to receive a course of injections to prevent the onset of symptoms and death.

➡ The incubation period for rabies depends on where you're bitten. On the head, face or neck it's as little as 10 days, whereas on the legs it's 60 days.

Tuberculosis (TB)

➡ TB is a bacterial infection usually transmitted from person to person by coughing, but which may be transmitted through consumption of unpasteurised milk.

➡ Milk that has been boiled is safe to drink, and the souring of milk to make yoghurt or cheese also kills the bacilli.

➡ Travellers are usually not at great risk as close household contact with an infected person is usually required before the disease is passed on. You may need to have a TB test before you travel, as this can help diagnose the disease later if you become ill.

Environmental Hazards

Heatstroke

➡ This serious, occasionally fatal, condition can occur if the body's heat-regulating mechanism breaks down and the body temperature rises to dangerous levels.

➡ Long, continuous exposure to high temperatures and insufficient fluids can leave you vulnerable to heatstroke.

➡ The symptoms are feeling unwell, not sweating very much (or at all) and a high body temperature. Where sweating has ceased, the skin becomes flushed and red.

➡ Victims can become confused, aggressive or delirious.

➡ Get victims out of the sun, remove their clothing and cover them with a wet sheet or towel and fan continually. Give fluids if they are conscious.

Hypothermia

➡ In a country where temperatures can plummet to -40°C, cold is something you should take seriously.

➡ Hypothermia occurs when the body loses heat faster than it can produce it and the core temperature of the body falls.

➡ If you are trekking at high altitudes or simply taking a long bus trip across the country, particularly at night, be especially prepared. Even in the lowlands, sudden winds from the north can send the temperature plummeting.

➡ It is best to dress in layers; silk, wool and some of the new artificial fibres are all good insulating materials. A hat is important, as a lot of heat is lost though the head. A strong, waterproof outer layer is essential (and a 'space' blanket for emergencies if trekking).

➡ Carry basic supplies, including fluid to drink and food containing simple sugars to generate heat quickly.

Bites & Stings

Bees and wasps Stings are usually painful rather than dangerous. Calamine lotion or sting-relief spray will give relief and ice packs will reduce the pain and swelling. However, people who are allergic to bees and wasps may require urgent medical care.

Snakes Mongolia has four species of venomous snakes: the Halys viper (agkistrodon halys), the common European viper or adder (vipera berus), Orsini's viper (vipera ursine) and the small taphrometaphon lineolatum. To minimise your chances of being bitten, always wear boots, socks and long trousers where snakes may be present. Don't put your hands into holes and crevices, and be careful when collecting firewood.

Bedbugs These live in various places, but particularly in dirty mattresses and bedding, evidenced by spots of blood on bedclothes or on the wall. Bedbugs leave itchy bites in neat rows. Calamine lotion or a sting-relief spray may help.

Lice All lice cause itching and discomfort. They make themselves at home in your hair, your clothing, or in your pubic hair. You catch lice through direct contact with infected people or by sharing combs, clothing and the like. Powder or shampoo treatment will kill the lice and infected clothing should then be washed in very hot, soapy water and left in the sun to dry.

DRINKING WATER

➡ Bottled water is generally safe – check that the seal is intact at purchase.

➡ Tap water in Ulaanbaatar and other cities is considered bacteria-free, however antiquated plumbing means the water may contain traces of metals that won't be good for your long-term health.

➡ Be cautious about drinking from streams and lakes, as they are easily polluted by livestock. Water is usually OK if you can get it high up in the mountains, near the source. If in doubt, boil your water.

➡ The best chemical purifier is iodine, although it should not be used by pregnant women or those with thyroid problems.

➡ Water filters should filter out viruses. Ensure your filter has a chemical barrier such as iodine and a small pore size (eg less than four microns).

Language

Mongolian is a member of the Ural-Altaic family of languages, and as such it is distantly related to Turkish, Kazakh, Uzbek and Korean. It has around 10 million speakers worldwide. The traditional Mongolian script (cursive, vertical and read from left to right) is still used by the Mongolians living in the Inner Mongolia Autonomous Region of China. In 1944 the Cyrillic alphabet was adopted and it remains in use today in Mongolia and two autonomous regions of Russia (Buryatia and Kalmykia).

Mongolian also has a Romanised form, though the 35 Cyrillic characters give a better representation of Mongolian sounds than the 26 of the Roman alphabet. Different Romanisation systems have been used, and a loose standard was adopted in 1987 – so the capital city, previously written as Ulan Bator, is now Ulaanbaatar.

It's well worth the effort to familiarise yourself with the Cyrillic alphabet so that you can read maps and street signs. Otherwise, just read the coloured pronunciation guides given next to each word in this chapter as if they were English, and you'll be understood.

Mongolian pronunciation is explained in the alphabet table on the next page. It's important to pronounce double vowel letters as long sounds, because vowel length can affect meaning. In our pronunciation guides the stressed syllables are in italics.

Hello.	Сайн байна уу?	sain *bai*·na uu
Yes./No.	Тийм./ Үгүй.	tiim/*ü*·*güi*

WANT MORE?

For in-depth language information and handy phrases, check out Lonely Planet's *Mongolian Phrasebook*. You'll find it at **shop.lonelyplanet.com**, or you can buy Lonely Planet's iPhone phrasebooks at the Apple App Store.

Thank you.	Баярлалаа.	ba·yar·la·*laa*
You're welcome.	Зүгээр.	zü·*geer*
Excuse me.	Уучлаарай.	uuch·*laa*·rai
Sorry.	Уучлаарай.	uuch·*laa*·rai
Goodbye.	Баяртай.	ba·yar·*tai*

What's your name?
Таны нэрийг хэн гэдэг вэ? — ta·*ny* ne·*riig* khen ge·deg ve

My name is ...
Миний нэрийг ... гэдэг. — mi·*nii* ne·*riig* ... ge·deg

Do you speak English?
Та англиар ярьдаг уу? — ta an·*gliar* yair·dag uu

I don't understand.
Би ойлгохгүй байна. — bi *oil*·gokh·güi *bai*·na

ACCOMMODATION

Do you have any rooms available?
Танайд сул өрөө байна уу? — ta·*naid* sul ö·*röö* *bai*·na uu

How much is it per night/week?
Энэ өрөө хоногт/ долоо хоногт ямар үнэтэй вэ? — e·ne ö·*röö* kho·nogt/ do·*loo* kho·nogt ya·mar ün·*tei* ve

I'd like a single/double room.
Би нэг/хоёр хүний өрөө авмаар байна. — bi neg/*kho*·yor khü·*nii* ö·*röö* av·*maar* *bai*·na

air-con	агааржуулалт	a·gaar·*juul*·alt
bathroom	угаалгын өрөө	u·*gaal*·gyn ö·*röö*
cot	хүүхдийн ор	khüükh·*diin* or
dormitory	нийтийн байр	*nii*·tiin bair
hotel	зочид буудал	zo·chid *buu*·dal
window	цонх	tsonkh
youth hostel	залуучуудын байр	za·*luu*·chuu·dyn bair

DIRECTIONS

Where's ...?
... хаана байна вэ?   ... khaan *bai*·na ve

How can I get to ...?
... руу би яаж очих вэ?   ... ruu bi yaj o·chikh ve

Can you show me on the map?
Та газрын зураг   ta gaz·*ryn* zu·rag
дээр зааж өгнө үү?   deer zaaj ög·*nö üü*

address	хаяг	kha·yag
behind	хойно	khoi·no
in front of	өмнө	öm·nö
straight ahead	чигээрээ урагшаа	chi·*gee*·ree u·rag·*shaa*
to the left	зүүн тийш	züün tiish
to the right	баруун тийш	ba·*ruun* tiish

EATING & DRINKING

Can I have a menu, please?
Би хоолны цэс авч   bi *khool*·nii tses avch
болох уу?   bo·lokh uu

What food do you have today?
Өнөөдөр ямар хоол   ö·*nöö*·dör ya·mar khool
байна вэ?   *bai*·na ve

I'd like to have this.
Би энэ хоолыг авья.   bi en *khoo*·lyg a·vi

I don't eat (meat).
Би (мах) иддэггүй.   bi (makh) id·deg·gui

Cheers!
Эрүүл мэндийн төлөө!   e·*rüül* men·*diin* tö·*löö*

The bill, please.
Тооцоогоо бодуулья.   too·*tsoo*·goo bo·*duu*·li

Key Words

appetisers	хүйтэн зууш	*khüi*·ten zuush
bottle	шил	shil
breakfast	өглөөний хоол	ög·*löö*·nii khool
canteen	гуанз	guanz
cold	хүйтэн	*khüi*·ten
cup	аяга	a·yag
dessert	амтат зууш	*am*·tat zuush
dinner	оройн хоол	o·*roin* khool
dining room	зоогийн газар	*zoo*·giin *ga*·zar
dumplings	банштай	*ban*·shtai
food	хоол	khool
fork	сэрээ	se·*ree*
fried	шарсан	*shar*·san
fried food	хуураг	*khuu*·rag
glass	шилэн аяга	*shi*·len a·*yag*
hot	халуун	kha·*luun*
knife	хутга	*khu*·tag
lunch	үдийн хоол	ü·*diin* khool
market	зах	zakh
menu	хоолны цэс	khool·*ny* tses
plate	таваг	*ta*·vag
restaurant	ресторан	res·to·*ran*
set dish	бэлэн хоол	be·*len* khool
spoon	халбага	*khal*·bag
tea shop	цайны газар	*tsai*·ny *ga*·zar
vegetarian	ногоон хоолтон	no·*goon* *khool*·ton

CYRILLIC ALPHABET

Cyrillic		Sound	
А а	a		as the 'u' in 'but'
Г г	g		as in 'get'
Ё ё	yo		as in 'yonder'
И и	i		as in 'tin'
Л л	l		as in 'lamp'
О о	o		as in 'hot'
Р р	r		as in 'rub'
У у	u		as in 'rude'
Х х	kh		as the 'ch' in Scottish *loch*
Ш ш	sh		as in 'shoe'
Ы ы	y		as the 'i' in 'ill'
Ю ю	yu		as the 'yo' in 'yoyo'
	yü		long, as the word 'you'
Б б	b		as in 'but'
Д д	d		as in 'dog'
Ж ж	j		as in 'jewel'
Й й	i		as in 'tin'
М м	m		as in 'mat'
Ө ө	ö		long, as the 'u' in 'fur'
С с	s		as in 'sun'
Ү ү	ü		long, as the 'o' in 'who'
Ц ц	ts		as in 'cats'
Щ щ	shch		as in 'fresh chips'
Ь ь			'soft sign' (see below)
Я я	ya		as in 'yard'
В в	v		as in 'van'
Е е	ye		as in 'yes'
	yö		as the 'yea' in 'yearn'
З з	z		as the 'ds' in 'suds'
К к	k		as in 'kit'
Н н	n		as in 'neat'
П п	p		as in 'pat'
Т т	t		as in 'tin'
Ф ф	f		as in 'five'
Ч ч	ch		as in 'chat'
Ъ ъ			'hard sign' (see below)
Э э	e		as in 'den'

The letters ь and ъ never occur alone, but simply affect the pronunciation of the previous letter – ь makes the preceding consonant soft (pronounced with a faint 'y' after it), while ъ makes the previous consonant hard (ie not pronounced with a faint 'y' after it).

Meat & Fish

antelope	цагаан зээр	tsa·*gaan* zeer
beef	үхрийн мах	ü·*khriin* makh
carp	булуу цагаан	bu·*luu* tsa·*gaan*
chicken	тахианы мах	ta·khia·*ny* makh
duck	нугас	nu·gas
fillet	гол мах	gol makh
fish	загас	za·gas
goat	ямаа	ya·*maa*
kebab	шорлог	shor·log
marmot	тарвага	tar·vag
meat	мах	makh
(fried) meat pancake	хуушуур	khuu·shuur
meat with rice	будаатай хуураг	bu·*daa*·tai khuu·rag
mutton	хонины мах	kho·ni·*ny* makh
mutton dumplings (steamed)	бууз	buuz
patty	бифштекс	*bif*·shteks
perch	алгана	*al*·gan
pike	цурхай	tsurh·*kai*
pork	гахайн мах	ga·*khain* makh
salmon	омуль	o·*mul*
sausage	хиам/зайдас/сосик	khiam/*zai*·das/so·sisk
sturgeon	хилэм	*khi*·lem
antevenison	бугын мах	bu·*gyn* makh
wild boar	бодон гахай	bo·don ga·*khai*

Fruit & Vegetables

apple	алим	a·lim
banana	гадил	ga·dil
cabbage	байцаа	bai·tsaa
carrot	шар лууван	shar *luu*·van
cucumber	өргөст хэмэх	ör·göst khe·mekh
fruit	жимс	jims
onion	сонгино	son·gin
potato	төмс	töms
radish	улаан лууван	u·*laan luu*·van
salad	салат	sa·lad
tomato	улаан лооль	u·*laan loo*·il
turnip	манжин	man·jin
vegetable	ногоо	no·goo

Other

bread	талх	talkh
butter	цөгийн тос	tsöts·*giin* tos
cake	бялуу	bya·*luu*
camel yogurt	хоормог	khoor·mog
cheese	бяслаг	byas·lag
cream	өрөм	ö·röm
dairy	цагаан-идээ	tsa·*gaan* i·dee
(dried) curds	ааруул	aa·ruul
egg	өндөг	ön·dög
honey	зөгийн бал	zö·*giin* bal
ice cream	зайрмаг	zair·mag
jam	жимсний чанамал	jims·*nii* cha·na·mal
noodle soup	гоймонтой шөл	goi·mon·toi shöl
pasta	хөндий гоймон	khön·*diin* goi·mon
pepper	поваарь	po·*vaair*
rice	цагаан будаа	tsa·*gaan* bu·daa
salad	ногоон зууш	no·*goon* zuush
salt	давс	davs
soup	шөл	shöl
sour cream	тараг/цөцгий	ta·rag/tsöts·*gii*
stewed fruit	компот	kom·pot
sugar	чихэр	chi·kher
sweets	цаастай чихэр	tsaas·tai chi·kher
with rice	будаатай	bu·daa·tai

Drinks

beer	пиво	piv
coffee	кофе	ko·fi
(buckthorn) juice	(чацарганы) шүүс	(cha·tsar·ga·*ny*) shüüs
koumiss (fermented mare milk)	айраг	ai·rag
lemonade	нимбэгний ундаа	nim·beg·*nii* un·*daa*
milk	сүү	süü
milk tea	сүүтэй цай	süü·tei tsai
milk with rice	сүүтэй будаа	süü·tei bu·daa
mineral water	рашаан ус	ra·shaan us
tea	цай	tsai
vodka	архи	a·rikh
wine	дарс	dars

Signs	
ГАРЦ	Exit
ЛАВЛАГАА	Information
ОРЦ	Entrance
ХААСАН	Closed
ХАДГАЛСАН	Reserved/Engaged
ЭРЭГТЭЙН	Men
ЭМЭГТЭЙН	Women

EMERGENCIES

Help!	Туслаарай!	tus·*laa*·rai
Go away!	Зайл!	zail
I'm lost.	Би төөрчихлөө.	bi töör·chikh·*löö*

There's been an accident.
Осол гарчээ.   o·sol gar·*chee*

Call a doctor/the police!
Эмч/Цагдаа   emch/tsag·*daa*
дуудаарай!   duu·*daa*·rai

I'm ill.
Би өвчтэй байна.   bi övch·*tei* bai·na

I'm allergic to (antibiotics).
Миний биед (анти-   mi·*nii* bi·ed (an·ti·
биотик) харшдаг.   bi·o·tik) harsh·dag

SHOPPING & SERVICES

I'd like to buy ...
Би ... авмаар байна.   bi ... av·*maar* bai·na

I'm just looking.
Би юм үзэж байна.   bi yum *ü*·zej bai·na

Can you show me that?
Та үүнийг надад   ta *üü*·niig na·dad
үзүүлнэ үү?   *ü*·zü*ü*·len üü

I don't like it.
Би үүнд дур、үй байна.   bi üünd dur·*gü*i bai·na

How much is it?
Энэ ямар үнэтэй вэ?   en ya·mar ün·*tei* ve

That's very expensive.
Яасан үнэтэй юм бэ.   yaa·san ün·*tei* yum be

Can you reduce the price?
Та үнэ буулгах уу?   ta ün *buul*·gakh uu

exchange rate	мөнгөний ханш	möng·*nii* khansh
post office	шуудан	*shuu*·dan
public phone	нийтийн утас	*nii*·tiin u·tas
signature	гарын үсэг	ga·*ryn ü*·seg
travellers check	жуулчны чек	*juulch*·ny chek

TIME & DATES

What time is it?
Хэдэн цаг болж   *khe*·den tsag bolj
байна?   *bai*·na

Question Words		
What?	Юу?	yuu
When?	Хэзээ?	khe·*zee*
Where?	Хаана?	khaan
Which?	Ямар?	ya·mar
Who?	Хэн?	khen

It's (nine) o'clock.
(Есөн) цаг болж байна.   (*yö*·sön) tsag bolj *bai*·na

It's half past (four).
(Дөрөв) хагас болж   (dö·röv) *kha*·gas bolj
байна.   *bai*·na

morning	өглөө	ög·*löö*
afternoon	өдөр	ö·dör
evening	орой	o·*roi*
yesterday	өчигдөр	ö·*chig*·dör
today	өнөөдөр	ö·*nöö*·dör
tomorrow	маргааш	mar·*gaash*
Monday	даваа	da·*vaa*
Tuesday	мягмар	*myag*·mar
Wednesday	лхагва	*lkha*·vag
Thursday	пүрэв	*pü*·rev
Friday	баасан	*baa*·sang
Saturday	бямба	byamb
Sunday	ням	nyam

Remember to add the word car sar (literally 'month', 'moon') after each of the following words:

January	нэгдүгээр	neg·dü·*geer*
February	хоёрдугаар	kho·yor·du·*gaar*
March	гуравдугаар	gu·rav·du·*gaar*
April	дөрөвдүгээр	dö·röv·dü·*geer*
May	тавдугаар	tav·du·*gaar*
June	зургадугаар	zur·ga·du·*gaar*
July	долдугаар	dol·du·*gaar*
August	наймдугаар	naim·du·*gaar*
September	есдүгээр	yes·dü·*geer*
October	аравдугаар	a·rav·du·*gaar*
November	арваннэг- дүгээр	ar·van·neg· dü·*geer*
December	арванхоёр- дугаар	ar·van·kho·yor· du·*gaar*

TRANSPORT

Public Transport

What times does the ... leave/arrive?
... хэдэн цагт   ... *khe*·den tsagt
явдаг/ирдэг   *yav*·dag/ir·deg
вэ?   ve

bus	Автобус	av·*to*·bus
plane	Нисэх онгоц	ni·seh on·gots
train	Галт тэрэг	galt *te*·reg
trolleybus	Троллейбус	trol·*lei*·bus

Numbers

1	нэг	neg
2	хоёр	kho·yor
3	гурав	gu·rav
4	дөрөв	dö·röv
5	тав	tav
6	зургаа	zur·gaa
7	долоо	do·loo
8	найм	naim
9	ес	yös
10	арав	ar·av
20	хорь	kho·ri
30	гуч	guch
40	дөч	döch
50	тавч	taiv
60	жар	jar
70	дал	dal
80	ная	na·ya
90	ер	yör
100	зуу	zuu
1000	мянга	myang·ga

I want to go to ...
Би ... руу явмаар байна. bi ... ruu yav·maar bai·na

Can you tell me when we get to ...?
Бид хэзээ ... хүрэхийг bid khe·zee ... khu·re·hiig
хэлж өгнө үү? helj ög·nö uu

I want to get off!
Би буумаар байна! bi buu·maar bai·na

1st class	нэгдүгээр зэрэг	neg·dü·geer ze·reg
2nd class	хоёрдугаар зэрэг	kho·yor·du·gaar ze·reg
one-way ticket	нэг талын билет	neg ta·lyn bi·let
return ticket	хоёр талын билет	kho·yor ta·lyn bi·let
first	анхны	ankh·ny
next	дараа	da·raa
last	сүүлийн	süü·liin
airport	нисэх онгоцны буудал	ni·sekh on·gots·ny buu·dal
bus stop	автобусны зогсоол	av·to·bus·ny zog·sool
platform	давцан	dav·tsan
ticket office	билетийн касс	bi·le·tiin kass
timetable	цагийн хуваарь	tsa·giin khu·vaair
train station	галт тэрэгний буудал	galt te·re·ge·nii buu·dal

Driving & Cycling

Excuse me, am I going in the right direction for ...?
Уучлаарай, би ... руу uuch·laa·rai bi ... ruu
зөв явж байна уу? zöv yavj bai·na uu

How many kilometres is it?
Замын урт хэдэн za·myn urt khe·den
километр вэ? ki·lo·metr ve

bicycle	унадаг дугуй	u·na·dag du·gui
map	газрын зураг	gaz·ryn zu·rag
mechanic	механик	me·kha·nik
motorcycle	мотоцикл	mo·to·tsikl
petrol	бензин	ben·zin

Visiting the Locals

We'd like to see inside a herder's yurt.
Бид малчны гэрт bid malch·ny gert
орж үзэх гэсэн юм. orj ü·zekh ge·sen yum

We'd like to drink some koumiss.
Бид айраг уух bid ai·rag uukh
гэсэн юм. ge·sen yum

I hope your animals are fattening up nicely.
Мал сүрэг тарган mal sü·reg tar·gan
тавтай юу? tav·tai yü

Please hold the dogs!
Нохой хогио! nok·hoi kho·ri·o

I'd like to ride a ...	Би ... явах гэсэн юм.	bi ... ya·vakh ge·sen yum
camel	тэмээгээр	te·mee·geer
horse	мориор	mo·rior
yak	сарлагаар	sar·la·gaar
camel	тэмээ	te·mee
chicken	тахиа	ta·khia
cooking pot	тогоо	to·goo
cow	үнээ	ü·nee
cowdung box	араг	a·rag
donkey	илжиг	il·jig
felt material	эсгий	es·gii
goat	ямаа	ya·maa
herding	мал аж ахуй	mal aj ak·hui
horse	морь	mo·ri
koumiss bag	хөхүүр	khö·khüür
pig	гахай	ga·khai
saddle	эмээл	e·meel
sheep	хонь	kho·ni
summer camp	зуслан	zus·lan
yak	сарлаг	sar·lag
yurt	гэр	ger

GLOSSARY

agui – cave or grotto

aimag – a province/state within Mongolia

airag – fermented mare's milk

am – mouth, but often used as a term for canyon

aral – island

baatar – hero

baga – little

balbal – stone figures believed to be Turkic grave markers; known as *khun chuluu* (man stones) in Mongolian

baruun – west

bayan – rich

bodhisattva – Tibetan Buddhist term; applies to a being that has voluntarily chosen not to take the step to nirvana in order to save the souls of those on earth

Bogd Gegeen – the hereditary line of reincarnated Buddhist leaders of Mongolia, which started with Zanabazar; the third-holiest leader in the Tibetan Buddhist hierarchy; also known as *Jebtzun Damba*

bulag – natural spring

Buriat – ethnic minority living along the northern frontier of Mongolia, mostly in Khentii and Dornod

chuluu – rock; rock formation

davaa – mountain pass

deer stones – upright grave markers from the Bronze and Iron Ages, on which are carved stylised images of deer

del – the all-purpose, traditional coat or dress worn by men and women

els – sand; sand dunes

erdene – precious

gegeen – saint; saintlike person

ger – traditional circular felt dwelling

gol – river

gov – desert

guanz – canteen or cheap restaurant

gudamj – street

ikh – big

Inner Mongolia – a separate province within China

Jebtzun Damba – see *Bogd Gegeen*

Kazakh – ethnic minority, mostly living in western Mongolia

khaan – emperor; great *khan*

khad – rock

Khalkh – the major ethnic group living in Mongolia

khan – king or chief

khar – black

kherem – wall

khiid – Buddhist monastery

khoid – north

khöömii – throat singing

khoroo – district or subdistrict

khot – city

khulan – wild ass

khuree – originally used to describe a 'camp'; it is now also in usage as 'monastery'

lama – Tibetan Buddhist monk or priest

Living Buddha – common term for reincarnations of Buddha; Buddhist spiritual leader in Mongolia (see *Bogd Gegeen*)

man stones – see *balbal*

morin khuur – horse-head fiddle

MPRP – Mongolian People's Revolutionary Party

naadam – games; traditional festival with archery, horse racing and wrestling

nuruu – mountain range

nuur – lake

ömnö – south

örgön chölöö – avenue

Outer Mongolia – northern Mongolia during Manchurian rule (the term is not currently used to describe Mongolia)

ovoo – a shamanistic collection of stones, wood or other offerings to the gods, usually found in high places

rashaan – mineral springs

soyombo – the national symbol of Mongolia, signifying freedom and independence; its components represent natural elements and virtues; legend has it that Zanabazar created the Soyombo in 1686

stupa – a Buddhist religious monument composed of a solid hemisphere topped by a spire, containing relics of the Buddha; also known as a pagoda, or *suvrag* in Mongolian

sum – a district; the administrative unit below an *aimag*

süm – Buddhist temple

suvrag – see *stupa*

taiga – subarctic coniferous evergreen forests (Russian)

takhi – the Mongolian wild horse; also known as Przewalski's horse

tal – steppe

talbai – square

thangka – scroll painting; a rectangular Tibetan Buddhist painting on cloth, often seen in monasteries

tögrög – the unit of currency in Mongolia

töv – central

Tsagaan Sar – 'white moon' or 'white month'; a festival to celebrate the Mongolian New Year (start of the lunar year)

tsainii gazar – teahouse/cafe

tsam – lama dances; performed by monks wearing masks during religious ceremonies

tsuivan gazar – noodle stall

tugrik – another spelling of tögrög

ulaan – red

us – water

uul – mountain

yurt – the Russian word for *ger*

zakh – market

Zanabazar – see *Bogd Gegeen*

zochid buudal – hotel

züün – east

Behind the Scenes

SEND US YOUR FEEDBACK

We love to hear from travellers – your comments keep us on our toes and help make our books better. Our well-travelled team reads every word on what you loved or loathed about this book. Although we cannot reply individually to postal submissions, we always guarantee that your feedback goes straight to the appropriate authors, in time for the next edition. Each person who sends us information is thanked in the next edition – the most useful submissions are rewarded with a selection of digital PDF chapters.

Visit **lonelyplanet.com/contact** to submit your updates and suggestions or to ask for help. Our award-winning website also features inspirational travel stories, news and discussions.

Note: We may edit, reproduce and incorporate your comments in Lonely Planet products such as guidebooks, websites and digital products, so let us know if you don't want your comments reproduced or your name acknowledged. For a copy of our privacy policy visit lonelyplanet.com/privacy.

OUR READERS

Many thanks to the travellers who used the last edition and wrote to us with helpful hints, useful advice and interesting anecdotes:
Rachael Clapson, Sarah Desabrais, Kieran Drake, Alexandru Dumitru, Nelli Engel, Noreen Francis, Jana Frolen, Rachel Godley, Ask Gudmundsen, Mark Hohenberg, David Hunt, Clive Johnson, Cale Lawlor, Paul Liu, Wojciech Maciolek, Alexandre Muller, Patrick Phillips, Alexandra Röllin Odermatt, Gayle Singh, Tony James Slater, Kate Williams, Han Wong, Hong Youngjoo, Cindy Zhi

AUTHOR THANKS

Michael Kohn
Many thanks to my coauthors Anna and Daniel, editors Angela, Suzannah and Brigitte, and cartographer David. In Ulaanbaatar, special thanks to Toroo, Daniel, Cliffe, Lhagva, Khongorzul, Nomin, Marc, Jan, Goyo, Olly and Mogi, plus all the taxi drivers and bus drivers who got me around the city. Mostly, thanks to Lallie for all her support and companionship during the project.

Anna Kaminski
A huge thank you to Suzannah for entrusting me with this project, to fellow authors Michael Kohn and Daniel McCrohan for all the advice and encouragement, and to the rest of the Lonely Planet team for all the hard work. 'Boss Lady' would also like to thank Khongor Guesthouse and Boojum for sorting out the logistics, Pikhekh and Mishig the drivers, Mandakh the tireless interpreter, Kurt for the cheerful company, Zaya for the Tsaatan knowledge, as well as Jonathan, Michelle, Tobias and Honza, Ganbaa, Amar and everyone else who helped me.

Daniel McCrohan
My biggest thanks this time goes to my Uncle David, who travelled with me for almost half of this research trip. I couldn't have wished for a better companion. Special thanks to Michael Kohn for all his help and support, to map maestro David Kemp, and to stellar editing duo Brigitte Ellemor and Suzannah Shwer (you guys will be missed!). Thanks too to Murray (Tsetserleg); Tunga (Tariat); Nazka, Dosjan and Canat (Ölgii); Marima (Khovd); Tuya (Uliastai); and Goyo Travel (the Gobi). Love, as always, to my family in the UK. And to Taotao and the kids: *wo ai nimen*.

ACKNOWLEDGMENTS

Climate map data adapted from Peel MC, Finlayson BL & McMahon TA (2007) 'Updated World Map of the Köppen-Geiger Climate Classification', *Hydrology and Earth System Sciences*, 11, 1633-44.

Cover photograph: A ger in northern Mongolia, Gavriel Jecan/Getty.

THIS BOOK

This 7th edition of Lonely Planet's *Mongolia* guidebook was researched and written by Michael Kohn, Anna Karninski and Daniel McCrohan. The History chapter was written by Jack Weatherford and Dulmaa Enkhchuluun. The 6th edition was written by Michael Kohn and Dean Starnes; Michael Kohn wrote the 4th and 5th editions. This guidebook was commissioned in Lonely Planet's Melbourne office, and produced by the following:

Commissioning Editor Suzannah Shwer

Coordinating Editors Carolyn Boicos, Monique Perrin

Senior Cartographer David Kemp

Senior Editors Catherine Naghten, Karyn Noble

Managing Editors Brigitte Ellemor, Angela Tinson

Assisting Editors Carolyn Bain, Ross Taylor

Book Designer Katherine Marsh

Cover Research Naomi Parker

Language Content Branislava Vladisavljevic

Thanks to Ryan Evans, Larissa Frost, Anna Harris, Genesys India, Jouve India, Indra Kilfoyle, Baigalmaa Kohn, Wayne Murphy, Chad Parkhill, Trent Paton, Martine Power, Dianne Schallmeiner, John Taufa, Juan Winata

Index

Map Legend

Sights

- Beach
- Bird Sanctuary
- Buddhist
- Castle/Palace
- Christian
- Confucian
- Hindu
- Islamic
- Jain
- Jewish
- Monument
- Museum/Gallery/Historic Building
- Ruin
- Sento Hot Baths/Onsen
- Shinto
- Sikh
- Taoist
- Winery/Vineyard
- Zoo/Wildlife Sanctuary
- Other Sight

Activities, Courses & Tours

- Bodysurfing
- Diving/Snorkelling
- Canoeing/Kayaking
- Course/Tour
- Skiing
- Snorkelling
- Surfing
- Swimming/Pool
- Walking
- Windsurfing
- Other Activity

Sleeping

- Sleeping
- Camping

Eating

- Eating

Drinking & Nightlife

- Drinking & Nightlife
- Cafe

Entertainment

- Entertainment

Shopping

- Shopping

Information

- Bank
- Embassy/Consulate
- Hospital/Medical
- Internet
- Police
- Post Office
- Telephone
- Toilet
- Tourist Information
- Other Information

Geographic

- Beach
- Hut/Shelter
- Lighthouse
- Lookout
- Mountain/Volcano
- Oasis
- Park
- Pass
- Picnic Area
- Waterfall

Population

- Capital (National)
- Capital (State/Province)
- City/Large Town
- Town/Village

Transport

- Airport
- Border crossing
- Bus
- Cable car/Funicular
- Cycling
- Ferry
- Metro station
- Monorail
- Parking
- Petrol station
- Subway station
- Taxi
- Train station/Railway
- Tram
- Underground station
- Other Transport

Note: Not all symbols displayed above appear on the maps in this book

Routes

- Tollway
- Freeway
- Primary
- Secondary
- Tertiary
- Lane
- Unsealed road
- Road under construction
- Plaza/Mall
- Steps
- Tunnel
- Pedestrian overpass
- Walking Tour
- Walking Tour detour
- Path/Walking Trail

Boundaries

- International
- State/Province
- Disputed
- Regional/Suburb
- Marine Park
- Cliff
- Wall

Hydrography

- River, Creek
- Intermittent River
- Canal
- Water
- Dry/Salt/Intermittent Lake
- Reef

Areas

- Airport/Runway
- Beach/Desert
- Cemetery (Christian)
- Cemetery (Other)
- Glacier
- Mudflat
- Park/Forest
- Sight (Building)
- Sportsground
- Swamp/Mangrove

OUR STORY

A beat-up old car, a few dollars in the pocket and a sense of adventure. In 1972 that's all Tony and Maureen Wheeler needed for the trip of a lifetime – across Europe and Asia overland to Australia. It took several months, and at the end – broke but inspired – they sat at their kitchen table writing and stapling together their first travel guide, *Across Asia on the Cheap*. Within a week they'd sold 1500 copies. Lonely Planet was born.

Today, Lonely Planet has offices in Melbourne, London and Oakland, with more than 600 staff and writers. We share Tony's belief that 'a great guidebook should do three things: inform, educate and amuse'.

OUR WRITERS

Michael Kohn

Coordinating Author, Ulaanbaatar Michael first arrived in Mongolia from his native California in 1997 to edit the *Mongol Messenger* newspaper. Three years at the state news agency gave him enough fodder for his first book, *Dateline Mongolia*. A second book soon followed, *Lama of the Gobi*, a biography of the poet-monk Danzan Ravjaa. Michael has since written about Mongolia for the Associated Press, the *New York Times* and other news outlets. Lonely Planet has dispatched him across Mongolia and into neighbouring countries to research Siberia, the Silk Route and Central Asia. He lives in Ulaanbaatar. Michael also wrote the Plan Your Trip, Understand Mongolia and Survival Guide sections.

Anna Kaminski

Northern Mongolia, Eastern Mongolia Having travelled widely in Mongolia and parts of Central and Northern Asia in past years for both research and pleasure, Anna was particularly pleased to sate her love of wide-open spaces by heading to parts of the country she hadn't previously explored. This trip involved days in the saddle, in jeeps and long-distance minivans, pursuing the trail of Chinggis Khaan – a possible ancestor of hers. Major research highlights included getting to know the Tsaatan reindeer herders, as she has a particular interest in other reindeer-herding cultures – Sámi, Even, Evenk – and attending more than one naadam. In her spare time, she contributes to BBC Travel and other online publications, and roams as widely as possible; catch up with her adventures at http://cheeseofvictory.wordpress.com.

Daniel McCrohan

Central Mongolia, The Gobi, Western Mongolia Daniel's first adventure in Mongolia was the result of a harebrained idea of his to cycle solo across the Gobi Desert. On a road bike. Unsurprisingly, he walked most of it. But he survived, so we sent him back to the Gobi, this time with a jeep. Originally from the UK, these days Daniel lives in Beijing and has become a bit of an expert on the Trans-Mongolian, thanks to multiple train trips between China and Mongolia. This is Daniel's 19th Lonely Planet book. He is also the creator of the smartphone app *Beijing on a Budget*. You can get hold of him on Twitter (@danielmccrohan) or through his website (www.danielmccrohan.com).

Read more about Daniel at:
lonelyplanet.com/members/danielmccrohan

Contributing Authors

Dulmaa Enkhchuluun Dulmaa graduated from Augsburg College in Minnesota and now works to promote culturally and environmentally responsible tourism and commercial development in Mongolia.
Jack Weatherford Anthropologist Jack Weatherford wrote *Genghis Khan and the Making of the Modern World*, for which he received the Order of the Polar Star, Mongolia's highest state honour.

Published by Lonely Planet Publications Pty Ltd
ABN 36 005 607 983
7th edition – July 2014
ISBN 978 1 74220 299 0
© Lonely Planet 2014 Photographs © as indicated 2014
10 9 8 7 6 5 4 3 2 1
Printed in China